Refusing to Kiss the Slipper

OXFORD STUDIES IN HISTORICAL THEOLOGY

MORALITY AFTER CALVIN
Theodore Beza's Christian Censor and Reformed Ethics
Kirk M. Summers

THE PAPACY AND THE ORTHODOX
A History of Reception and Rejection
Edward Siecienski

DEBATING PERSEVERANCE
The Augustinian Heritage in Post-Reformation England
Jay T. Collier

THE REFORMATION OF PROPHECY
Early Modern Interpretations of the Prophet & Old Testament Prophecy
G. Sujin Pak

ANTOINE DE CHANDIEU
The Silver Horn of Geneva's Reformed Triumvirate
Theodore G. Van Raalte

ORTHODOX RADICALS
Baptist Identity in the English Revolution
Matthew C. Bingham

DIVINE PERFECTION AND HUMAN POTENTIALITY
The Trinitarian Anthropology of Hilary of Poitiers
Jarred A. Mercer

THE GERMAN AWAKENING
Protestant Renewal after the Enlightenment, 1815–1848
Andrew Kloes

THE REGENSBURG ARTICLE 5 ON JUSTIFICATION
Inconsistent Patchwork or Substance of True Doctrine?
Anthony N. S. Lane

AUGUSTINE ON THE WILL
A Theological Account
Han-luen Kantzer Komline

THE SYNOD OF PISTORIA AND VATICAN II
Jansenism and the Struggle for Catholic Reform
Shaun Blanchard

CATHOLICITY AND THE COVENANT OF WORKS
James Ussher and the Reformed Tradition
Harrison Perkins

THE COVENANT OF WORKS
The Origins, Development, and Reception of the Doctrine J. V. Fesko

RINGLEADERS OF REDEMPTION
How Medieval Dance Became Sacred
Kathryn Dickason

Refusing to Kiss the Slipper

Opposition to Calvinism in the Francophone Reformation

MICHAEL W. BRUENING

OXFORD
UNIVERSITY PRESS

OXFORD
UNIVERSITY PRESS

Oxford University Press is a department of the University of Oxford. It furthers
the University's objective of excellence in research, scholarship, and education
by publishing worldwide. Oxford is a registered trade mark of Oxford University
Press in the UK and certain other countries.

Published in the United States of America by Oxford University Press
198 Madison Avenue, New York, NY 10016, United States of America.

Library of Congress Cataloging-in-Publication Data
Names: Bruening, Michael W. (Michael Wilson), author.
Title: Refusing to kiss the slipper : opposition to Calvinism in the
francophone Reformation / Michael W. Bruening.
Description: New York, NY, United States of America : Oxford University Press, 2021. |
Series: Oxford studies in historical theology series |
Includes bibliographical references and index.
Identifiers: LCCN 2020051797 | ISBN 9780197566954 (hardback) |
ISBN 9780197566978 (epub) | ISBN 9780197566985 (oso) | ISBN 9780197566961 (updf)
Subjects: LCSH: Reformation—France. |
Calvin, Jean, 1509–1564. | Calvinism.
Classification: LCC BR370 .B78 2021 | DDC 274.4/06—dc23
LC record available at https://lccn.loc.gov/2020051797

DOI: 10.1093/oso/9780197566954.001.0001

1 3 5 7 9 8 6 4 2

Printed by Integrated Books International, United States of America

For my parents, Philip and Alice Bruening

Contents

Acknowledgments   xiii
Abbreviations   xv

Introduction   1

1. Reforming the French National Church: Marguerite
   of Navarre's Network   9
   1.1. Introduction   9
   1.2. The Duchess, the Bishop, and the Scholar   10
        1.2.1. The Duchess, Marguerite of Navarre   11
        1.2.2. The Bishop, Guillaume Briçonnet   13
        1.2.3. The Scholar, Jacques Lefèvre d'Étaples   15
   1.3. The Meaux Experiment, 1521–1525   17
   1.4. Gérard Roussel and the Choice between National Reform and
        International Protestantism, 1526–1534   21
        1.4.1. Gérard Roussel and the Strasbourg Exile   22
        1.4.2. Marguerite as Evangelical Patron   25
        1.4.3. Expansion of the Evangelical Movement, 1530–1533   26
        1.4.4. The Evangelical Movement Stalls, 1533–1534   28
   1.5. Gérard Roussel in Oloron: Diocesan Reform Revisited,
        1536–1555   29
        1.5.1. Roussel's *Forme de visite de diocese*   31
        1.5.2. Roussel's *Familiere exposition*   33
   1.6. Reconsidering Roussel and Early French Reform   34

2. The Formation of the Farellian and Calvinist Networks   36
   2.1. Introduction   36
   2.2. Guillaume Farel Makes French Reform "Reformed," 1521–1530   37
        2.2.1. Farel with Lefèvre and the Meaux Group, 1509–1523   38
        2.2.2. Farel, the Reformed Theologians, and the Eucharist,
               1523–1529   40
        2.2.3. Farel's Break from His French Colleagues, 1526   44
   2.3. Farel's Network in the Suisse Romande, 1526–1536   46
        2.3.1. Farel, the Bernese, and the French Exiles   47
        2.3.2. The Propaganda Campaign   48
        2.3.3. Early Anti-Nicodemism   50
        2.3.4. Evangelical Success and Failure in Romandie   53

2.4. The Calvinist Network   54
    2.4.1. Calvin's Shifting Position on Nicodemism, 1530–1536   55
    2.4.2. Calvin's Introduction of Ecclesiastical Discipline,
        1536–1538   58
    2.4.3. The Formation of the Calvinist Network   61
    2.4.4. The Calvinist Doctrinal Trinity: Excommunication,
        the Eucharist, and Predestination   63

3. Anti-Calvinists of Francophone Switzerland   65
3.1. Introduction   65
3.2. Pierre Caroli and the Origins of the Opposition   67
    3.2.1. Caroli's Early Career in France, 1520–1534   68
    3.2.2. Caroli in Geneva, Basel, and Neuchâtel, 1535–1536   69
    3.2.3. Caroli versus the Calvinists, 1536–1537   72
3.3. Antoine Marcourt and the Supporters of Close
    Church–State Relations   75
    3.3.1. Marcourt in Neuchâtel, 1531–1538   75
    3.3.2. Marcourt and Jean Morand Replace Calvin and Farel in
        Geneva, 1538   77
    3.3.3. Conflict over the Christmas Eucharist in Geneva, 1538   79
    3.3.4. Political and Theological Factionalism in Geneva and
        the Vaud, 1538–1540   81
    3.3.5. The Lausanne Quarrel over Ecclesiastical Goods, 1542–1543 86
    3.3.6. Swiss and French Precedents for Church–State Relations   87
3.4. The Formation of Anti-Calvinist Outposts in the Pays de Vaud   89
    3.4.1. The Failure of Calvinist Reform Efforts, 1541–1542   89
    3.4.2. Farel's Failure in Neuchâtel   91
    3.4.3. Viret's Failures in Lausanne   93
    3.4.4. Yverdon   94
    3.4.5. Pays de Gex   95
    3.4.6. Morges   96
    3.4.7. A Test Case: Jean Chaponneau's Critique of Fraternal
        Corrections, 1544   97

4. The Consolidation of Anti-Calvinism in Francophone
   Switzerland   101
4.1. Introduction   101
4.2. André Zébédée's Early Career: From Friend to Foe of the
    Calvinists, 1534–1547   102
    4.2.1. Zébédée at the Collège de Guyenne, 1533/34–1538   104
    4.2.2. Zébédée as a "Zwinglian Calvinist" While Pastor of Orbe
        and Yverdon, 1538–1547   106
    4.2.3. Zébédée's Appointment to the Lausanne Academy, 1547   112
4.3. Zébédée and the Fight for the Future of the Lausanne Academy   114
    4.3.1. Disputes on the Ministry at the Lausanne Colloquies,
        Autumn 1547   114

4.3.2. Disputes on the Eucharist at the Houbraque Examination,
December 1547   118
4.3.3. Zébédée's Denunciation of Viret to the Bernese,
Spring–Summer 1548   119
4.3.4. Supporters of Both Zébédée and Viret, and Bern's
Final Decision   120
4.4. Jerome Bolsec, the Seigneur de Falais, Zébédée, and
the Consolidation of the Anti-Calvinist Party in
the Suisse Romande   122
4.4.1. The Bolsec Affair in Geneva, 1551   124
4.4.2. Falais's Break from Calvin, 1551–1552   126
4.4.3. Falais's Estate as Center of Opposition to Calvin, 1551–1554   127
4.4.4. Philippe de Ecclesia and Jean Trolliet against Calvin,
1552–1553   128
4.4.5. François de Saint-Paul against the Calvinists on
Predestination, 1552–1553   129
4.4.6. Zébédée Enters the Fray, 1553–1554   130
4.4.7. Calvin, "Heretic," 1554–1555   132
4.4.8. The Condemnation of Calvinism in Bern, 1555   133
4.5. The Critical Year of 1555: Calvinist Victory or Defeat?   136
4.6. Epilogue: The Collapse of Calvinism in the Vaud   137

5. Sebastian Castellio's Liberal Challenge   139
5.1. Introduction   139
5.2. Castellio's Early Life, Schooling in Lyon, and Move to
Geneva, 1515–1543   141
5.3. Castellio's Break with Calvin, 1543–1544   143
5.4. Castellio's Early Publications in Basel, 1545–1551   145
5.5. The Servetus Affair and Concerning Heretics   148
5.5.1. Opposition to Servetus's Execution   149
5.5.2. Castellio's First Criticism of the Execution, December 1553   151
5.5.3. Concerning Heretics, 1554   153
5.6. The Castellian Theological Program   156
5.6.1. "To kill a man is not to defend a doctrine, but to kill a
man": Castellio on Religious Toleration   156
5.6.2. "Reason, I say, is a sort of eternal word of God": Doubt,
Belief, and Exegesis   161
5.6.3. "God wants all to be saved through Christ": Predestination   168
5.6.4. "The way to salvation is to obey God's will": Faith, Works,
and Justification   173
5.7. Castellio and the Liberal Protestant Tradition   178

6. Castellio's Long Shadow   180
6.1. Introduction   180
6.2. Castellionists in the Suisse Romande and Montbéliard   180
6.2.1. The Suisse Romande   181
6.2.2. Montbéliard   184

6.3. Persecution, Predestination, and Piety: The Ties That Bound
    International Networks of Castellionists   186
    6.3.1. Persecution and Toleration   187
    6.3.2. Predestination and Free Will   193
    6.3.3. Piety and Discipline   198
6.4. The Pivotal Case of a Castellionist in France: Jean
    Saint-Vertunien de Lavau   204
    6.4.1. The Charges against Lavau   204
    6.4.2. Impact of the Lavau Affair on French Church Organization
    and Geneva's Missionary Program   208

7. The Gallican Evangelicals: State-Sponsored French Religious
Reform Revisited   211
7.1. Introduction   211
7.2. Jean de Monluc, François Bauduin, and the Colloquy of Poissy   213
    7.2.1. Jean de Monluc in Roussel's Footsteps, 1554–1560   214
    7.2.2. François Bauduin's Path from Calvinism to Religious
    Concord, 1545–1558   219
    7.2.3. Bauduin and Antoine of Navarre's Plan for Reform, 1558   223
    7.2.4. The Colloquy of Poissy, 1561   225
7.3. Bauduin versus The "Lemannic Lord," 1561–1565   227
    7.3.1. Calvin's Argument   228
    7.3.2. Bauduin's Response   229
    7.3.3. Bauduin's Postwar Efforts at Religious Concord   233
7.4. Charles Du Moulin: Idiosyncratic Prophet for a Syncretistic
    Religion in France   237
    7.4.1. Du Moulin among the Reformed, 1552–1556   239
    7.4.2. Du Moulin's Continued Evangelicalism in France,
    1557–1565   243
    7.4.3. Du Moulin's Assault on the Calvinists   247
7.5. The External Attack on the French Evangelical Movement   252

8. Jean Morély's Assault on Calvinist Ecclesiology   256
8.1. Introduction   256
8.2. Morély's Controversial Book: The Treatise on Christian
    Discipline and Polity   258
    8.2.1. The Calvinist Status Quo   258
    8.2.2. Morély's Program   260
    8.2.3. Reassessing Morély's Model   268
8.3. Morély's Path to Fame (or Infamy)   270
    8.3.1. Morély among Calvinists and Anti-Calvinists, 1545–1560   271
    8.3.2. Possible Influences on Morély's Ecclesiology   273
    8.3.3. Publication and Condemnation of Morély's Treatise   274
8.4. Morély's Network   278
    8.4.1. Morély's Supporters among the Reformed Pastors   280

8.4.2. Morély and the Huguenot Nobility	285
8.4.3. Morély and Jeanne d'Albret	287
8.4.4. French Churches with Morellian Ecclesiology	289
8.4.5. Petrus Ramus, Nicolas Bergeron, and the 1572 Synod of Nîmes	290
8.5. Epilogue: Pierre Charpentier's "God-Fearing Ministers Who Detest 'The Cause'"	294
Conclusion	299
C.1. Overlapping Networks of Opposition	300
C.2. Why Did the Calvinists Win?	304
C.3. The Anti-Calvinists and the Protestant Principle	309
Glossary of Key Individuals	311
Bibliography	321
Index	345

Acknowledgments

I am greatly indebted to the many individuals and institutions that have helped to make this book possible. Several years of research went into this book, much of it in Europe, with funding from various agencies. I am indebted, first, to the University of Missouri Research Board for funding trips to both Switzerland and France, and to the Fulbright U.S. Scholar program for funding a semester in Paris. In addition, an NEH summer seminar in Rome introduced me to the network theory that has helped to inform this book. Finally a Harris-Manchester Summer Research Institute grant allowed me to track down some rare editions at the University of Oxford. For all this financial and institutional support, I am deeply grateful.

In France, I was hosted at the Sorbonne's Centre Roland Mousnier by Denis Crouzet. My sincere thanks to him for his sponsorship, conversation, and invitation to present my early research on Charles Du Moulin to his seminar that semester. Many thanks are due also to Yves Krumenacker who invited me to Lyon to present on Jean Morély. These presentations in France, as well as others at the Sixteenth Century Society and Conference garnered valuable feedback. I offer thanks as well to the staff at the many archives and libraries where I conducted research for this book, in particular the French national library and archives, the Protestant library in Paris, the libraries and cantonal archives in Geneva, Lausanne, Neuchâtel, Bern, Basel, and Zurich, the Rotterdam library, and the Meeter Center for Calvin Studies at Calvin University. Special thanks, too, to the library staff at the Missouri University of Science and Technology. Working at a STEM-focused university, I am dependent on interlibrary lending for almost all my research materials, so the assistance of the campus library team is essential and much appreciated.

In many ways, the most valuable help I have received has been from other scholars who have engaged in discussions of the topics presented or read parts of the manuscript. I thank especially Karine Crousaz, who read and commented on most of the manuscript; Bernard Roussel, who read parts of the manuscript and pointed me to several useful sources; and the anonymous reviewers for Oxford University Press. I am also grateful to Philip Benedict, who read and discussed my book prospectus at length, and to John Frymire, who helped with some German texts. The comments and suggestions of these scholars have made this a better book than it otherwise would have been. Whatever faults remain are, of course, entirely my own.

I owe many thanks to Cynthia Read, Drew Anderla, Brent Matheny, Haripriya Ravichandran, and the rest of the team at Oxford University Press for their assistance from manuscript submission to publication. I am particularly thankful to Richard Muller for agreeing to publish this book in the Oxford Studies in Historical Theology series. As always, my wife Jeanine has been tremendously supportive throughout the research and writing process, and she has read and corrected multiple drafts of the manuscript. If the book reads well (and I hope it does), it is because of her superlative editing abilities.

Finally, I owe an indescribable debt to my parents, Phil and Alice Bruening. Their example showed clearly that one can be a serious person of faith and a critical thinker at the same time, much like the individuals featured in this book. Their love and support saw me through childhood and college, and continues to sustain me through adulthood. With much love, I dedicate this book to them.

Abbreviations

Amerbachkorrespondenz	Amerbach, *Die Amerbachkorrespondenz*
ARG	*Archiv für Reformationsgeschichte*
BDS	Bucer, *Bucers Deutsche Schriften*
Bèze Cor.	Bèze, *Correspondance de Théodore de Bèze*
BHR	*Bibliothèque d'Humanisme et Renaissance*
BSHPF	*Bulletin de la société de l'histoire du Protestantisme français*
Buisson	Buisson, *Sébastien Castellion*
Calv. Ep.	Calvin, *Epistolae*
CO	Calvin, *Ioannis Calvini Opera quae supersunt omnia*
COR	Calvin, *Ioannis Calvini Opera denuo recognita*
D'Argentré	D'Argentré, *Collectio Judiciorum de novis erroribus*
Du Moulin, *Opera*	Du Moulin, *Caroli Molinaei . . . omnia quae extant opera* (1681)
Epistolae Vireti	Viret, *Epistolae Petri Vireti*
Guillaume Farel	Comité Farel, *Guillaume Farel 1489–1565*
Haag	Haag, *La France Protestante*, 1st edition
Haag[2]	Haag, *La France Protestante*, 2nd edition
HBBW	Bullinger, *Heinrich Bullinger Briefwechsel*
Herminjard	Herminjard, *Correspondance des Réformateurs*
Hist. eccl.	Bèze, *Histoire ecclésiastique des Églises Réformées*
LW	Luther, *Luther's Works* (American Edition)
Mémoires de Condé	Condé, *Mémoires de Condé*
OS	Calvin, *Opera selecta*
RC	Hochuli Dubui, *Registres du Conseil de Genève à l'époque de Calvin*
RCP	Fatio, ed., *Registres de la Compagnie des Pasteurs de Genève*
Roget	Roget, *Histoire du peuple de Genève*
Ruchat	Ruchat, *Histoire de la Réformation de la Suisse*, Vulliemin edition
SCJ	*Sixteenth Century Journal*
SMRT	Studies in Medieval and Reformation Thought
THR	Travaux d'Humanisme et Renaissance
Viénot	Viénot, *Histoire de la Réforme dans le Pays de Montbéliard*
Vuilleumier	Vuilleumier, *Histoire de l'Église Réformée du Pays de Vaud*

Introduction

At the edge of this carpet they go down on both knees. There the ambassador, who was presenting them, knelt on one knee and pulled back the Pope's robe from his right foot, on which there is a red slipper with a white cross on it. Those who are on their knees drag themselves in this position up to his foot and lean down to the ground to kiss it.

—Michel de Montaigne, *Travel Journal*

There is no more ceaseless or tormenting care for man, as long as he remains free, than to find someone to bow down to as soon as possible.

—The Grand Inquisitor, Dostoevsky, *The Brothers Karamazov*

The Reformation was a struggle over authority. As much as sixteenth-century Europeans fought over individual religious doctrines and practices such as justification, indulgences, the Eucharist, and purgatory, the outcome of these quarrels ultimately depended on one larger question, namely, "Who defines orthodoxy?" Martin Luther offered a radically new position on the question of authority, stating that Scripture alone (*sola scriptura*), not popes, councils, or unwritten traditions, should determine religious truth and practice. But the Protestant doctrine of *sola scriptura* simply modified the question; it became "Who gets to interpret Scripture?" The theologically correct answer, namely, "those enlightened by the Holy Spirit," further begged the question. Anyone could claim inspiration of the Holy Spirit and, thus, the right to interpret Scripture. Thus, the Protestant Reformation was almost by definition a movement without a master.

The principal reformers, initially Luther and Ulrich Zwingli, sought to contain the chaos that they had unleashed by issuing catechisms, confessions of faith, biblical commentaries, and postils (model sermons) in an attempt

Refusing to Kiss the Slipper. Michael W. Bruening, Oxford University Press (2021). © Oxford University Press.
DOI: 10.1093/oso/9780197566954.003.0001

to teach their particular version of Christianity and convince the people that it was the correct one. In the francophone world, John Calvin assumed the role of self-appointed religious authority. Initially just another humanist associated with the French evangelical network around Marguerite of Navarre, Calvin soon became convinced of his own prophetic calling and believed that a divine seal of approval marked his own teaching.[1] From his base in Geneva, Calvin tried to bring the evangelical churches, especially the French-speaking ones, to follow his prescriptions—which he firmly believed were God's as well—for Christian doctrine and practice. In the long run, he was remarkably successful. His theology strongly influenced most of the churches that called—and still call—themselves "Reformed." For centuries, almost any theology that was mainline Protestant but not Lutheran was routinely labeled "Calvinist." This characterization was due in part to the dominance of Calvin's admirers among the theologians and historians who have examined the Reformation in French-speaking Europe. In addition, opponents of Reformed Christianity found in the severe, puritanical, Servetus-burning Calvin a suitable figurehead on whom to focus their animosity.

Recent historiography has begun to challenge this dominant image of Calvin. On the theological side, we have become aware of a larger cast of characters who played significant roles in the history of theology. Any full examination of Reformed theology must now consider the influence of Johannes Oecolampadius, Martin Bucer, Heinrich Bullinger, Peter Martyr Vermigli, and Theodore Beza, among others.[2] On the historical side, scholars have paid closer attention to the political and diplomatic contexts in which Reformed Christianity developed.[3] Meanwhile, social historians have mined archival records, especially consistory registers, for evidence about the identities, roles, and cultural practices of early francophone Protestants.[4]

---

[1] See Jon Balserak, *John Calvin as Sixteenth-Century Prophet* (Oxford: Oxford University Press, 2014); Bruce Gordon, *Calvin* (New Haven, CT: Yale University Press, 2009), 145–46, 291–95. See also 205.

[2] See, for example, Richard Muller, *Calvin and the Reformed Tradition: On the Work of Christ and the Order of Salvation* (Grand Rapids, MI: Baker Academic, 2012); Emidio Campi, *Shifting Patterns of Reformed Tradition*, Reformed Historical Theology 27 (Göttingen: Vandenhoeck & Ruprecht, 2014).

[3] See, for example, E. William Monter, *Calvin's Geneva*, New Dimensions in History: Historical Cities (New York: John Wiley and Sons, 1967); William Naphy, *Calvin and the Consolidation of the Genevan Reformation, 1541–1557* (Manchester, UK: Manchester University Press, 1994); Hughes Daussy, *Le Parti Huguenot: Chronique d'une désillusion (1557–1572)*, 2nd ed., Titre courant 54 (Geneva: Droz, 2015).

[4] See, for example, Raymond Mentzer, ed., *Sin and the Calvinists: Morals Control and the Consistory in the Reformed Tradition*, Sixteenth Century Essays and Studies 32 (Kirksville, MO: Sixteenth Century Journal Publishers, 1994); Robert Kingdon and John Witte, Jr., *Sex, Marriage, and Family in John Calvin's Geneva* (Grand Rapids, MI: Eerdmans, 2005); Karen Spierling, *Infant Baptism in Reformation Geneva: The Shaping of a Community, 1536–1564* (Louisville, KY: Westminster John

There remain significant blind spots in the literature, however. First, in an age of allegedly transnational historiography, scholarship remains stubbornly stuck in the old national paradigms. The vast majority of work related to francophone Protestantism deals specifically with the kingdom of France or the republic of Geneva. A few studies have focused on other individual regions, such as Montbéliard, the Pays de Vaud, or the refugee churches in the Rhineland,[5] but rarely does one encounter studies that treat all francophone regions together (see Map I.1 of Francophone Europe).[6] This circumstance is particularly surprising, and unfortunate, since there was so much movement across these borders in the sixteenth century.

The second major blind spot stems from the first, for the story of the francophone Reformation is still essentially the story of the steady construction of a single, unified, Calvinian, French Reformed Church. This narrative began to emerge already in the sixteenth century from two works by Theodore Beza, his *Life of Calvin* and his *Ecclesiastical History of the French Reformed Churches*.[7] It starts with the reform circle of Meaux, moves with the persecuted religious exiles to Geneva, and re-enters France with the Genevan missionaries, the synods of the French Reformed Churches, and the Wars of Religion. Stemming from two works penned by Calvin's successor in Geneva, the story of the francophone Reformation as it has been told thus far is a classic case of history written by the winners.

The present book seeks to introduce, by contrast, a history of the losers. A great many people living in francophone Europe sought religious reform

---

Knox, 2005); Raymond Mentzer et al., eds., *Dire l'interdit: The Vocabulary of Censure and Exclusion in the Early Modern Reformed Tradition*, Brill's Series in Church History 40 (Leiden: Brill, 2010); Robert Kingdon and Thomas Lambert, *Reforming Geneva: Discipline, Faith, and Anger in Calvin's Geneva*, Cahiers d'Humanisme et Renaissance 103 (Geneva: Droz, 2012); Suzannah Lipscomb, *The Voices of Nîmes: Women, Sex, and Marriage in Reformation Languedoc* (New York: Oxford University Press, 2019).

[5] See, for example, John Viénot, *Histoire de la Réforme dans le Pays de Montbéliard depuis les origines jusqu'à la mort de P. Toussain, 1524–1573*, 2 vols. (Paris: Fischbacher, 1900); Henri Vuilleumier, *Histoire de l'Eglise Réformée du Pays de Vaud sous le régime bernois*, 4 vols. (Lausanne: La Concorde, 1927–1933); Michael Bruening, *Calvinism's First Battleground: Conflict and Reform in the Pays de Vaud, 1528–1559*, Studies in Early Modern Religious Reforms 4 (Dordrecht: Springer, 2005); Philippe Denis, *Les églises d'étrangers en pays rhénans, 1538–64*, Bibliothèque de la Faculté de Philosophie et Lettres de l'Université de Liège 242 (Paris: Les Belles Lettres, 1984).

[6] See Philip Benedict, "Global? Has Reformation History Even Gotten Transnational Yet?" *ARG* 108 (2017): 52–62; Philip Benedict, "The Spread of Protestantism in Francophone Europe in the First Century of the Reformation," *ARG* 109 (2018): 7–52.

[7] Théodore de Bèze, *Vie de J. Calvin, CO* 21:1–50; Théodore de Bèze, ed., *Histoire ecclésiastique des Églises Réformées au royaume de France*, 3 vols., new edition, edited by G. Baum and E. Cunitz (Paris: Fischbacher, 1883–1889).

Map I.1 Francophone Europe

but did not agree with Calvin's vision for it. Indeed, many of them truly detested Calvin. The principal criticism leveled at him was that he would brook no opposition and was instead setting himself up as a new pope with his seat in Geneva. The pope in Rome, everyone knew, required those seeking an audience to kiss the papal slipper; Calvin's opponents appropriated the ritual to criticize the Genevan reformer, charging that Calvin required the Protestant faithful to kiss his slipper. Those who refused to do so have been marginalized in the history of Reformed Protestantism. Certainly, a number of Calvin's key opponents are well known, but scholars have almost always treated them as idiosyncratic voices whose chief interest lies in what they can tell us about Calvin himself.[8]

This study, by contrast, treats Calvin's evangelical opponents together, not as a collection of distinct voices but as networks of opposition to Calvin, Beza, the Genevan Reformation, and the French Reformed churches. It shows that these opponents were more numerous, better organized, and

---

[8] See, for example, Gary Jenkins, *Calvin's Tormentors: Understanding the Conflicts That Shaped the Reformer* (Grand Rapids, MI: Baker, 2018).

more interconnected across national borders than has been recognized. In the process, it demonstrates that the early francophone religious reform movement was more diverse than scholars have acknowledged. In short, it demands that we abandon altogether the common identification of French Protestantism with Calvinism.

Here, we may take a cue from historians of early Christianity. Recent work in that field has highlighted the diversity of the early Christian movements and relabeled what would become the dominant strand as "proto-orthodox."[9] Just as Eusebius in the *Ecclesiastical History* rewrote the history of the early church to highlight the orthodoxy of his own party,[10] Beza in his *Ecclesiastical History* rewrote the history of French Protestantism to highlight the orthodoxy of the Calvinists. In both cases, the competing strands of belief that formed the early histories of these movements were lost. Consequently, the rich tapestry of competing ideas and networks fell away to expose the single thread of "orthodox belief" that Eusebius and Beza wanted us to see. Future scholarly efforts must seek to reconstruct the old tapestry. This book is an initial effort to do so.

Calvin's opponents disagreed with him on a range of issues from overall reform strategy to biblical hermeneutics, to specific points of doctrine and ecclesiology. This book will explore four main networks of opposition. Chapter 1 will introduce the early reformers in France who sought to reform the church from within. These figures had no love for Rome and believed the medieval church required significant alteration, but they also believed that the fundamental structures of church and state remained sound. Chapter 2 will provide context for what follows, explaining the construction of the Calvinist network itself, showing how it broke from the early reform movement in France and established unique positions on moral discipline, church–state relations, predestination, and the Eucharist. Chapters 3 and 4 present a second network, namely, Calvin's earliest opponents in francophone Switzerland. Their opposition emerged initially from their adherence to Zwingli's thought and their rejection of Calvin's innovations in doctrine and practice. Eventually, their criticisms extended to Calvin's doctrine of double predestination, his support for the execution of Michael Servetus, and much else that made Calvin distinctive. A third network is the focus

---

[9] See, for example, Bart Ehrman, *Lost Christianities: The Battle for Scripture and the Faiths We Never Knew* (New York: Oxford University Press, 2003).

[10] Bart Ehrman, *The Orthodox Corruption of Scripture: The Effect of Early Christological Controversies on the Text of the New Testament* (New York: Oxford University Press, 1993), 4–6.

of Chapters 5 and 6, which examine Sebastian Castellio and his admirers. Castellio harshly criticized Calvin for Servetus's execution, and he departed from the Calvinists on a range of theological issues, including justification, exegesis, predestination, and universal election. Castellio gained followers throughout francophone Europe and exerted significant influence on international communities of religious refugees and humanists. Chapter 7 looks again at those in France who sought to reform the church from within, focusing on those who took the baton from the early reformers treated in Chapter 1. Finally, Chapter 8 explores the challenge to French Reformed ecclesiology presented by Jean Morély and his allies, with their proposals to give religious authority to local churches rather than to Reformed synods and consistories.

Throughout the book, we will see that opposition to Calvin was not based solely on doctrinal disagreement. Networks of opposition often formed out of existing friendships and alliances. Personal animosity toward Calvin or his disciples likewise aided the formation of anti-Calvinist groups. Several of the individuals treated in this book were at one time friends of Calvin until a bitter personal fight broke out between them. When such conflicts arose, Calvin's enemies sought solace and acceptance among others who had fallen out with the Genevan reformer. Too often, the Reformation is treated exclusively as a history of doctrines, and although doctrine was, of course, important, emotional responses driven by personal friendships and animosities often accompanied—and in some cases drove—the doctrinal differences.[11]

Many in the sixteenth century had an aversion to absolute claims of religious authority. Late medieval anticlericalism drove an antipathy toward the pope, as evidenced in the virulently antipapal woodcuts of the German

---

[11] Recent discoveries in the fields of social science and neurobiology have shown that humans are not the rational actors we like to think we are. Jonathan Haidt, for example, notes that we make moral judgements based principally on our emotions and use reason to support our gut reactions. "Moral reasoning," he explains, "when it occurs, is usually a post-hoc process in which we search for evidence to support our initial intuitive reaction." Moreover, this process appears to apply to reasoning in general: "Furthermore, studies of everyday reasoning demonstrate that people generally begin reasoning by setting out to confirm their initial hypothesis. They rarely seek disconfirming evidence, and are quite good at finding support for whatever they want to believe." Jonathan Haidt, "The New Synthesis in Moral Psychology," *Science* 316 (2007): 998–1002; here, 998. See also Jonathan Haidt, *The Righteous Mind: Why Good People Are Divided by Politics and Religion* (New York: Pantheon, 2012); Antonio Damasio, *Descartes' Error: Emotion, Reason, and the Human Brain* (New York: Putnam, 1994); Jaak Panksepp, *Affective Neuroscience: The Foundations of Human and Animal Emotions* (New York: Oxford University Press, 1998); Jaak Panksepp and Kenneth L. Davis, *The Emotional Foundations of Personality: A Neurobiological and Evolutionary Approach* (New York: W. W. Norton, 2018). Reformation historian Alec Ryrie uses these findings as the basis of his examination of the role of emotion in the development of doubt in early modern England. Alec Ryrie, *Unbelievers: An Emotional History of Doubt* (Cambridge, MA: Harvard University Press, 2019).

Reformation.[12] In the francophone Reformation, this antiauthoritarian streak affected views toward Calvin as well. In 1997, Thierry Wanegffelen captured those often described as "moderate Catholics" in *Ni Rome, ni Genève (Neither Rome nor Geneva)*.[13] As the title indicates, the individuals he discusses had no great love of Rome but did not want to go so far as to separate fully from the French church and follow the Geneva Reformation. Wanegffelen's book led scholars to recognize the variety of belief within Catholicism in sixteenth-century France. This book argues that a similar shift is required with regard to francophone Protestantism and that *ni Rome, ni Genève* also aptly describes many individuals who broke fully, in fact, from the Catholic Church and identified clearly as Protestants but still refused to take orders from Geneva.

This narrative problematizes the terminology we use for the period. The more complex the picture we draw of sixteenth-century religious belief, the more apparent becomes the inability of our vocabulary to describe it accurately. The terms *evangelical, biblicist, humanist, Gallican, Reformed,* and even *Protestant* and *Catholic* all contain nuances of meaning that do not always apply when looking beyond the traditional groups of hardline Catholics and convinced Calvinists. Few today, for example, would call Sebastian Castellio a Catholic, but his semi-Pelagian views on justification seem to render the label *evangelical* inaccurate. By contrast, Charles Du Moulin, whom many have labeled a moderate Catholic or a Gallican, had a Reformed understanding of the Eucharist, an evangelical understanding of justification, and a Protestant notion of *sola scriptura*. One strategy to overcome this terminological obstacle is to use contemporary polemical labels, such as *papist, heretic, Nicodemite,* or *moyenneur*. This is, I suggest, an acceptable approach when trying to convey accurately a particular sectarian perspective from the period. Too much use of this approach, however, runs the risk of privileging the view of one side or the other. Repeated use of Calvin's derogatory label *moyenneur*, for example, leads us again into the trap of telling the story of the francophone Reformation from the Genevan perspective.

To avoid these pitfalls, I have chosen to use the term *evangelical* in the broadest sense possible. *Evangelicals*, as I use the term, were individuals who believed that the existing church had to be reformed in a way that went

---

[12] See Robert W. Scribner, *For the Sake of Simple Folk: Popular Propaganda for the German Reformation* (New York: Oxford University Press, 1994).

[13] Thierry Wanegffelen, *Ni Rome ni Genève: Des fidèles entre deux chaires en France au XVIe siècle*, Bibliothèque littéraire de la Renaissance, ser. 3, 36 (Paris: Honoré Champion, 1997).

well beyond correcting clerical abuses, and they insisted that the Gospel be preached to the people (although what exactly was meant by "preaching the Gospel" varied from person to person). In other words, they all believed that major changes in doctrine and/or practice were required, and this conviction sets them apart from those whom we might label traditional Catholic reformers. I use the term *Calvinist* with some frequency, but I apply it specifically to those who identified as Calvin's supporters and allies. The term is, therefore, a factional designation, not a theological one. Similarly, I often use *anti-Calvinist* to designate those who opposed the Calvinist faction. I use *Calvinian* on the rare occasions when I want to convey a general theological affinity with Calvin.

As traditional terminology has skewed the story of the francophone Reformation in the Calvinists' favor, so also have the surviving sources. Once again, the history of the early Christian church offers a suitable comparison. The proto-orthodox sources from that period survived and were read and reread throughout history, while those of the competing sects either disappeared or lay abandoned for centuries. Similarly, the sources from the Calvinists have survived in much greater abundance than those of their opponents. Thus, we have hundreds of letters written by Calvin and Pierre Viret, for example, but just over two dozen written by Castellio and far fewer than that by most of the other individuals highlighted here.

To overcome this inherent source bias, wherever possible, I have tried to use sources written by the anti-Calvinists themselves. Fortunately, recent book digitization projects have made published sources written by Calvin's opponents more easily available than they were just a few years ago. When forced to rely on hostile sources from the Calvinists, I have tried to present them in a way that would be fair to the anti-Calvinists' position. For this reason, the book may seem more hostile to the Calvinists than to their opponents. That is by design. I am trying to tell the story of the francophone Reformation for the first time from the perspective of Calvin's opponents, rather than from that of his friends. In this way, we might begin to redress the overwhelming bias in favor of the Calvinists that has prevailed for over four hundred years. The Calvinists have had their say. It is time to listen to the other side.

1

Reforming the French National Church

Marguerite of Navarre's Network

1.1. Introduction

The Calvinists came late to the game of French reform. The strategy they developed reflected neither the initial nor the default inclinations of church reformers in francophone Europe. The key feature that distinguished early French reform from its Calvinist offshoot was that its first proponents envisioned a state-sponsored, national reform that would take place within the existing French church.[1] The movement coalesced in Meaux around the reform-minded bishop Guillaume Briçonnet, the humanist scholar Jacques Lefèvre d'Etaples, and the king's sister, Marguerite of Navarre. They sought to "bring the Gospel to the people," testing on a diocesan scale an approach that, with the king's support, could later be applied nationally. Despite opposition from the Sorbonne and hardline Catholics across the country, the original group never lost sight of this goal to reform the national church from within.

As we will see in Chapter 7, this push for national religious reform continued well into the 1560s and the period of the Wars of Religion. Historians often lose sight of this continuity and generally treat the period of the 1520s to the 1540s, and that of the 1550s and 1560s, as almost entirely different phases of French reform. This is a false dichotomy; the Gallican evangelicals (or *moyenneurs*) of the 1550s and 1560s were simply continuing the push for national, evangelical reform that had begun in Meaux in the 1520s.

---

[1] Older narratives of the early French reform movement, starting with Beza's *Histoire ecclésiastique*, tended to portray it as a tentative, mystical, individualistic, humanist movement. In this view, the early reformers challenged the dominance of the traditionalist hardliners in the Sorbonne but failed to embrace fully the ideas of the Reformation or to work together to propagate the new faith in the kingdom. By contrast, more recent scholars, such as Henry Heller and Jonathan Reid, have revealed a far more dedicated and organized movement to reform the French church along evangelical lines. Reid's argument is convincing, and I rely extensively on his work in this chapter. Jonathan Reid, *King's Sister—Queen of Dissent: Marguerite of Navarre (1492–1549) and Her Evangelical Network*, SMRT 139 (Leiden: Brill, 2009); see also Henry Heller, "The Evangelicalism of Lefèvre d'Étaples: 1525," *Studies in the Renaissance* 19 (1972): 42–77.

Refusing to Kiss the Slipper. Michael W. Bruening, Oxford University Press (2021). © Oxford University Press.
DOI: 10.1093/oso/9780197566954.003.0002

Calvinist reformers would oppose both the early "Nicodemites" and the later *moyenneurs*, and John Calvin himself saw them as the same wolf in the clothing of two different sheep. This reflects the Calvinists' core belief that reform from within was impossible. In their eyes, the only option was a complete break from the "church of Antichrist."

We can date the divergence of these two reform paths to 1525. That year saw most of the principal francophone reformers together in Strasbourg, and it was the last time they would be so unified. At the end of that year, Guillaume Farel moved on, literally toward the Swiss Confederation and figuratively away from the compromise necessary to continue the work of reforming the existing church. Lefèvre and Gérard Roussel, on the other hand, maintained their old route, returning from Strasbourg to France in order to continue to push for reform from within. Their efforts made significant headway into the early 1530s, but international diplomacy and the confrontational tactics of Farel's followers hindered their progress after the 1534 Affair of the Placards. Even after 1534, however, Marguerite of Navarre's network continued to promote evangelical reform across the kingdom. Roussel, in particular, used his position as bishop of Oloron to return to the principles established in Meaux and encourage evangelical reform on a diocesan basis into the 1550s. Thus, these "Nicodemites" whom Calvin excoriated for weakness and fear were neither feeble nor afraid. They simply continued to believe that reforming the church from within was the best strategy to introduce the Gospel throughout the kingdom.

1.2. The Duchess, the Bishop, and the Scholar

Early French reform efforts revolved around three key players: Marguerite of Navarre, duchess of Alençon and sister to King Francis I; Guillaume Briçonnet, bishop of Meaux; and Jacques Lefèvre d'Étaples, a former professor at the University of Paris with strong humanist leanings. Not only were these among the main proponents of early church reform in France, but their positions also represent in microcosm the main thrusts of that reform: from the duchess, a push for reform sponsored by the king and his court; from the bishop, an effort at local, diocesan reform; and from the scholar, a movement characterized not by radical theological reform but by humanist biblical study and encouragement of Christ-like piety. Calvin would later depart from each of these emphases, giving up on state reform in France, abolishing the episcopacy, and insisting on comprehensive and precise theological definitions.

1.2.1. The Duchess, Marguerite of Navarre

Marguerite of Navarre was the linchpin that held early French reform together. Earlier generations of scholars saw her as a significant early supporter of reform, but also as fickle, lacking conviction, and perhaps most damning of all in their eyes, not a "true Protestant." This perception stemmed from studying her from a decidedly Calvinist perspective—and most early scholars of the French Reformation were Calvinists themselves. Recent historiography has refuted these early characterizations. Most notably, Jonathan Reid's important work has revealed the depth of Marguerite's commitment to evangelical reform throughout her life.[2] Additionally, she was at the center of an evangelical network that spread throughout France. Marguerite also gave the early evangelical movement its royal flavor. As the king's sister and later Queen of Navarre in her own right, she can hardly have been expected to do otherwise. Indeed, why would she have wanted to? In the sixteenth century, everyone understood that the best way to effect change was to gain the ear of the king. She had it.

Marguerite was born in 1492, two years before her brother, Francis.[3] She was, thus, a mature but still youthful twenty-eight years old when French reform got into full swing in Meaux. Marguerite was a paragon of that important new Renaissance figure, the well-educated noblewoman. Her parents were Louise of Savoy, who gave birth to Marguerite at age sixteen, and Charles, Count of Angoulême. Charles was a descendant of King Charles V (r. 1338–1380), but it was by no means obvious at the birth of Marguerite's brother, Francis, that he would later become king. Francis and Marguerite's father died when Marguerite was just three years old. Their nineteen-year-old widowed mother did her best to ensure that her children's prospects remained undiminished. She arranged for each to receive a sound education and moved them to the court of King Louis XII (r. 1498–1515), a cousin of her deceased husband.[4] Thus, Marguerite and her younger brother

---

[2] Reid, *King's Sister*.

[3] For Marguerite's biography, see Pierre Jourda, *Marguerite d'Angoulême, Duchesse d'Alençon, Reine de Navarre (1492–1549): Étude biographique et littéraire*, 2 vols., Bibliothèque littéraire de la Renaissance (Paris: Honoré Champion, 1930).

[4] On Marguerite's childhood and education, see Jourda, *Marguerite*, 1:2–30.

grew up without a father, but with a strong female role model, an excellent Renaissance education, and long experience at court. King Louis, who had no male heirs, espoused his daughter Claude to Francis, whom he named as his successor. Francis I assumed the throne on January 1, 1515, and ruled until his death in 1547.

Marguerite married, but it was not a happy union. Her husband, Charles, Duke of Alençon, was Marguerite's intellectual inferior and shared none of her passion for literature and learning.[5] A man of arms, he was often at war, which seems to have suited Marguerite. She and her mother played prominent roles at her brother's court, to the point where some began to refer to Francis I, Louise of Savoy, and Marguerite as the "royal trinity."[6] Louise, one should note, tended to see the reign as a power *duo*. Largely ignoring Marguerite's role, Louise reveled in the power she shared with "her Caesar," as she frequently refers to Francis in her journal.[7] Nevertheless, Francis bestowed important powers and revenues on his sister, most notably the duchy of Berry and an annual pension of 24,000 *livres tournois*.[8] Marguerite also played a role in assisting her brother with church reform, and particularly in reforming women's monastic houses. She had a hand in reforms at the women's houses at Yerres, at Almenêches in Alençon, and at Saint-Andoche and Saint-Jean in Autun.[9] In 1520, she founded a woman's house at Essai.[10] Although little is known of her personal religious views before 1521, Marguerite's early life had made her a fixture at the royal court, first in that of Louis XII and then as part of the "royal trinity" in her brother's. She was a royalist through and through, and any reform program she would embark on would almost necessarily involve the king. After 1521, we gain a better understanding of Marguerite's religious views, for at that time, she began to correspond with the bishop of Meaux, Guillaume Briçonnet.[11]

---

[5] They were married on December 2, 1509. On the marriage, see Jourda, *Marguerite*, 1:31–40.

[6] Reid, *King's Sister*, 85.

[7] Reid, *King's Sister*, 88.

[8] Reid, *King's Sister*, 89.

[9] Reid, *King's Sister*, 107–8.

[10] Jourda notes that she did this "'pour le salut' de son âme, en 'recognoissance des grands biens' reçus de Dieu et pour obtenir 'de sa miséricorde infinie pardon et rémission' de ses péchés. L'énumération de ces motifs témoigne de sa parfaite orthodoxie." Jourda, *Marguerite*, 1:57.

[11] Marguerite's first letter to Briçonnet was written sometime before June 12, 1521. Their correspondence is published in Guillaume Briçonnet and Marguerite d'Angoulême, *Correspondance (1521–1524)*, 2 vols., edited by Christine Martineau and Michel Veissière, THR 141, 173 (Geneva: Droz, 1975, 1979).

1.2.2. The Bishop, Guillaume Briçonnet

Briçonnet's early life and career would seem to make him the poster child for clerical abuses, rather than a reformer of such abuses. He was the son— albeit legitimate—of a cardinal-bishop. He profited from nepotism and held several benefices simultaneously, including the bishoprics of Lodève and Meaux. Frequently absent from both dioceses, he was perceived as a lackey of the king. His path was hardly typical of the sixteenth-century reformers, but he had received a humanist-influenced education, and his association with the king brought him into contact with Marguerite and a monarch intent on reforming the church.[12]

Briçonnet came from a line of royal advisors. His grandfather, Jean Briçonnet, was secretary to King Charles VII and collector-general of customs. His father, also named Guillaume, had a distinguished secular career at court before being widowed and taking holy orders, becoming bishop of St.-Malo and later a cardinal.[13] Cardinal Briçonnet led the effort to hold a reform council at Pisa in opposition to Pope Julius II, and for his efforts Louis XII rewarded him with an appointment as commendatory abbot of St.-Germain-des-Prés in Paris.[14]

The father's career set the stage for that of the son. Both Briçonnets, father and son, were first and foremost servants of the king, who sought to reform the church along royal lines. Their goals fit well with those of Francis I, who made church reform a central thrust of his early reign. According to Denis Crouzet, Francis had an almost messianic view of himself as the monarch who would reform France politically, educationally, and religiously.[15] The monarch's first step toward religious reform was to gain greater control over the French church. To that end, Francis sought agreement on the Concordat

---

[12] On Briçonnet, see Michel Veissière, *L'évêque Guillaume Briçonnet (1470–1534): Contribution à la connaissance de la Réforme catholique à la veille du Concile de Trente* (Provins: Société d'histoire et d'archéologie, 1986).

[13] On Guillaume Briçonnet the elder, see Bernard Chevalier, *Guillaume Briçonnet (v. 1445–1514), un cardinal-ministre au début de la Renaissance: Marchand, financier, homme d'État et prince de l'Église*, Collection 'Histoire' (Rennes: Presses universitaires de Rennes, 2005).

[14] A commendatory abbot was someone not of the abbey's religious order, usually a bishop, who was given certain rights over the abbey *in commendam*. Initially, the commendatory abbot was a temporary position until a member of the order could be named abbot *in titulum*. By the sixteenth century, however, the provisional character of many commendatory abbacies had been lost. See Michael Ott, "Commendatory Abbot," *The Catholic Encyclopedia*, vol. 4 (New York: Robert Appleton Company, 1908), online at http://www.newadvent.org/cathen/04155b.htm.

[15] Denis Crouzet, *La Genèse de la Réforme française*, Regards sur l'histoire 109 (Paris: Sedes, 1996), 115–17.

of Bologna, and it was at this point that the younger Briçonnet, bishop of Meaux, became involved with Francis's religious initiatives. The Concordat would rescind the Pragmatic Sanction of Bourges and give the king greater control over nominations to the chief bishoprics in France.[16] Francis appointed Briçonnet as one of his representatives to Rome, where the bishop would spend ten months, from May 1516 to March 1517, negotiating the Concordat of Bologna with the pope.[17] Briçonnet conducted himself well, and during his time in Rome, Pope Leo X signed the Concordat. Agreement in France took longer; ultimately, Francis had to force the Paris parlement and the University of Paris to accept the Concordat.[18]

From early in his career, Briçonnet was interested in institutional church reform in addition to his royal roles. In 1507, he replaced his father as abbot of St.-Germain-des-Prés and immediately demanded the monks' strict adherence to the monastic rule.[19] In his diocese of Meaux, Briçonnet wanted to ensure that church affairs were running smoothly and that suitable preaching was taking place. His long sojourn in Italy made him keen to learn, on his return to France, what had been happening in his diocese while he was gone. In 1518, therefore, he undertook a visitation of the diocese over several months. He concluded that the state of preaching in the diocese was poor and had been so for at least fifteen years.[20] His predecessors had largely transferred the task of preaching from the parish priests to the Franciscans, who, Briçonnet believed, had not acquitted themselves well of their task.[21] The bishop was particularly troubled by the state of the small, rural parishes, which had remained "several years, as many as ten, 'without receiving the nourishment of the Word of God.' No sermons, no Christian instruction, together with the

---

[16] In essence, the Pragmatic Sanction gave most ecclesiastical appointments in France to local ecclesiastical officials, such as cathedral chapters and abbeys. The University of Paris also benefitted by having a third of all vacancies reserved for its graduates. While the Pragmatic Sanction was the cornerstone of Gallican liberties and had been chiefly intended to free the French church from papal oversight, it also marginalized the role of the king in nominating candidates. Francis wanted those rights of nomination to be restored to the crown. In addition, reversing the Pragmatic Sanction would help him gain papal support for his territorial claims in Italy. R. J. Knecht, *Renaissance Warrior and Patron: The Reign of Francis I* (Cambridge: Cambridge University Press, 1996), 94.

[17] On this period, see Veissière, *L'évêque Guillaume Briçonnet*, 107–13.

[18] See Knecht, *Renaissance Warrior and Patron*, 94–103.

[19] St.-Germain-des-Prés was a Merovingian foundation that had joined the Cluniac network of monasteries in the eleventh century. A new effort at restoring Cluniac discipline started in the late fifteenth century, and Briçonnet's efforts sought to bring the monks closer in line with that reform and ensure strict adherence to the Rule of St. Benedict. In 1514, he further subjected the monks of St.-Germain to the discipline practiced by the reformed Cluniac monastery of Chezal-Benoît. See Veissière, *L'évêque Guillaume Briçonnet*, 76–85.

[20] Veissière, *L'évêque Guillaume Briçonnet*, 129–30.

[21] Veissière, *L'évêque Guillaume Briçonnet*, 130.

consequences for everyday moral life."[22] To ameliorate the poor preaching in Meaux, Briçonnet divided his diocese of two hundred thirty parishes into twenty-six (later thirty-two) "preaching stations," with one preacher devoted to ensuring that preaching was being conducted competently throughout his station.[23] To improve preaching further, he insisted at the diocesan synod of 1519 that priests reside in their parishes and preach to the people, especially during Advent and Lent.[24] Thus, from the beginning of his tenure in Meaux, Briçonnet's strong interest in reforming the preaching in his diocese was clear. Initially, his efforts were entirely traditional; there was nothing unusual about a bishop using diocesan synods to improve the quality of preaching and religious life in his diocese. In 1521, however, Briçonnet's efforts took a novel turn as the "Meaux group" began to focus on bringing the Word of God directly to the people, with or without a beneficed priest. Central to that effort was Jacques Lefèvre d'Etaples.

1.2.3. The Scholar, Jacques Lefèvre d'Étaples

While Marguerite provided the early French evangelicals with royal patronage and Briçonnet gave them an institutional, ecclesiastical base from which to work, Jacques Lefèvre d'Etaples provided the intellectual foundation on which they built their reform program. Lefèvre was born sometime around 1460, making him by far the oldest of the trio and indeed the oldest of most who would be associated with the reform efforts that took hold in Meaux.[25] He spent the majority of his career at the Collège du Cardinal Lemoine in Paris and as an editor and commentator on Aristotle, although from a humanist rather than scholastic perspective. Lefèvre made three trips to Italy, where he came under the influence of several humanist scholars. In France, his studies of Aristotle aimed "to purge the study of logic of the noxious sophistry" of the late Middle Ages.[26]

---

[22] Veissière, L'évêque Guillaume Briçonnet, 130.

[23] Veissière, L'évêque Guillaume Briçonnet, 132–34.

[24] Veissière, L'évêque Guillaume Briçonnet, 162–63.

[25] On Lefèvre, see Eugene F. Rice, Jr., ed., The Prefatory Epistles of Jacques Lefèvre d'Etaples and Related Texts (New York: Columbia University Press, 1972); Guy Bedouelle, Lefèvre d'Etaples et l'intelligence des Ecritures, THR 152 (Geneva: Droz, 1976); Philip Edgcumbe Hughes, Lefèvre: Pioneer of Ecclesiastical Renewal in France (Grand Rapids, MI: Eerdmans, 1984).

[26] Rice, ed., The Prefatory Epistles of Jacques Lefèvre d'Etaples, xiii.

Lefèvre met Briçonnet by 1504 at the latest, most likely through Lefèvre's student Josse Clichtove, who was teaching Briçonnet at that time. When Briçonnet took over as abbot of St.-Germain, Lefèvre quit teaching at the university to pursue his studies at the abbey. During this stage of his career, Lefèvre turned his interests to the study of the Bible. One of his first publications from the St.-Germain period was one of his most successful. In the 1509 *Quincuplex Psalterium*, or *Fivefold Psalter*, Lefèvre, in good northern-humanist fashion, presented the Psalms in five translations, including his own revision of the Vulgate.[27] Three years later, he published an influential commentary on St. Paul's letters.[28] The two works earned Lefèvre a reputation as a theologian despite his lack of formal theological training (an absence wryly noted later by Noël Beda, syndic of the Paris faculty of theology, who described Lefèvre as a *humanista theologizans*, a humanist dabbling in theology). Lefèvre's dedicatory epistle in the Paul volume was addressed to Briçonnet, and it is the very first letter in A.-L. Herminjard's nine-volume *Correspondance des Réformateurs*.[29]

To this point, there was nothing unusual or threatening in Lefèvre's work, or indeed in the careers of Marguerite or Briçonnet. Together, the three represent typical models of late medieval reform. Marguerite's role reflected a belief that the Most Christian King of France had a duty to live up to his title by reforming and leading the church in the realm. Briçonnet adopted the attitude of a diligent bishop and loyal servant of the king who sought to reform his diocese by fixing the clerical abuses therein. And Lefèvre was a northern humanist who conducted careful philological study of the Bible in an effort to correct the misinterpretations of late medieval scholasticism. None of this was novel or revolutionary—but the times were.

Most importantly, the Paris Faculty of Theology was taking an increasingly hardline conservative stance to combat religious heterodoxy. This shift stemmed at least in part from lingering resentment over the Concordat of

---

[27] Jacques Lefèvre d'Etaples, *Quincuplex Psalterium*, THR 170 (Geneva: Droz, [1513] 1979). The five translations were (1) the Old Latin Bible; (2) the Roman version, that is, Jerome's first revision of the Psalter that saw continued use at St. Peter's in Rome; (3) the Gallic version, that is, Jerome's second revision, so named because the bishops in Gaul were the first to adopt it; (4) the Hebraic version, that is, Jerome's third revision, in Latin, based on the Hebrew text; and (5) Lefèvre's revision of the Vulgate, corrected by comparison with the Hebrew text. Hughes, *Lefèvre*, 53. See also the extensive study by Guy Bedouelle, *Le Quincuplex Psalterium de Lefèvre d'Etaples: Un guide de lecture*, THR 171 (Geneva: Droz, 1979).

[28] Jacques Lefèvre d'Etaples, *S. Pauli Epistolae XIV. ex Vulgata editione, adiecta intelligentia ex Graeco, cum commentariis Jacobi Fabri, Stapulensis* (Paris: Henri Estienne, 1512).

[29] Herminjard 1:3–9, no. 1, Paris, December 15, 1512.

Bologna, which the Faculty had strongly opposed because of its elimination of preferential treatment for the university's graduates. This political resentment probably exacerbated the Faculty's ideological opposition to the king and to his efforts at religious and humanist reform.

But of course, the most striking religious event of the late 1510s was the dramatic entrance onto the European stage of Martin Luther. The Luther affair changed everything. Almost overnight, "moderate reform" disappeared; there no longer seemed to be any middle ground. Once the Paris Faculty of Theology condemned Luther's doctrines in April 1521,[30] one was either with Luther or against him. Such, at least, was the perception of Luther's opponents. The Meaux group came together just after the Faculty's condemnation of Luther. Thus, the duchess, the bishop, and the scholar were about to initiate a reform program that the theologians and *parlementaires* in Paris increasingly viewed as dangerous and heretical.

1.3. The Meaux Experiment, 1521–1525

In 1521, Marguerite, Briçonnet, and Lefèvre launched the French evangelical movement. First, Marguerite and Briçonnet began their lengthy correspondence. Second, Briçonnet invited Lefèvre to join him in his diocese of Meaux, with the specific goal of instituting a reform program that would go further than all earlier efforts. They were soon joined by other key individuals, such as Guillaume Farel, Gérard Roussel, Michel d'Arande, and Pierre Caroli. Known as the Meaux group, together they would become the first evangelical French reformers.[31]

Two key features characterized the Meaux group's teachings and lent them a resemblance to those of Luther: a Christocentric theology and an emphasis on making the Bible available to the laity. Before Lefèvre's arrival in Meaux, Briçonnet had focused on reforming the clergy. Lefèvre influenced the group to expand its mission to bring the Scriptures directly to the laity, making the Bible available in the vernacular and providing the tools to interpret it. The overriding goal was the "restoration of Christ and his Gospel," an

---

[30] D'Argentré 1:357–74.

[31] The early group also included François Vatable, Martial Masurier, and Jean Lecomte (whom we will meet again in Chapter 3). Caroli came a little later, in 1523, to form the "second group of Meaux," which also included Lefèvre, Roussel, Vatable, Masurier, Jean Lange, Jean Canaye, Jacques Pauvan, and Mathieu Saunier, among others. See Veissière, *L'évêque Guillaume Briçonnet*, 201–10, 233–37.

effort described by Marguerite in her correspondence with Briçonnet as *le seul nécessaire*, sole imperative.[32] This important phrase reveals that the goals of the French evangelicals were at once limited and lofty, narrowly focused but constituting a movement far more ambitious than a typical late medieval program intended to correct abuses. Marguerite's words also become a touchstone of sorts in later clashes with Calvin, who would insist on a long list of requirements for a truly reformed church. For Calvin, there was no *seul necessaire*; instead, a great many things were required to reform the church properly. The Meaux group set out to achieve their goals nationally through a two-step process. First, at the diocesan level, they would translate the Bible into the vernacular. Next, they would convince Francis I and Louise of Savoy to adopt their model on the national level. Meaux was thus to be the testing ground for a kingdom-wide Gallican, evangelical reform. Initially, hopes were high; Marguerite reported in 1521 that "Madame [Louise] and the king are more inclined to a reform of the church than ever."[33]

Meanwhile, in Meaux itself, Lefèvre was hard at work on the centerpiece of their reform, translating the Bible into French. The excitement that this project generated among the Meaux reformers is almost palpable in the opening lines of the dedicatory epistle, addressed significantly not to a single patron or notable person, but "to all Christian men and women":

When St. Paul was on the earth, preaching and announcing the word of God with the other apostles and disciples, he said, "Behold, now is the acceptable time; behold, now is the day of salvation" (2 Cor. 6[:2]). So also now in our day the time has come when our Lord Jesus Christ—sole salvation, truth, and life—wants his Gospel to be purely announced through all the world, so that people no longer wander off by other doctrines of men who think they are something but (as St. Paul says) are really nothing, since they deceive themselves (Gal. 6[:3]). Therefore, now we can say, as he said: "Behold, now is the acceptable time; behold, now is the day of salvation."[34]

---

[32] Reid, *King's Sister*, 187.

[33] "de la reformacion de l'Eglise, où plus que jamais le Roy et Madame sont affectionnéz." Briçonnet and Marguerite, *Correspondance* 1:75–76, Marguerite to Briçonnet, Compiègne, December 1521. Translation from Reid, *King's Sister*, 191.

[34] "Quant sainct Pol estoit sur terre preschant et annonceant la parolle de dieu avec les autres apostres et disciples il disoit: Ecce nunc tempus acceptibile, ecce nunc dies salutis: Voicy maintenant le temps acceptable, voicy maintenant le jour de salut. Aussi maintenant le temps est venu que nostre seigneur Jesuchrist, seul salut, verité et vie, veult que son Evangile soit purement annoncée par tout le monde, affin que on ne se desvoye plus par autres doctrines des hommes qui cuydent estre

Lefèvre and his companions believed they were living in an extraordinary time and that they were called to play a principal role in it. Gérard Roussel referred to this age as an "Evangelical Enlightenment."[35] In a breathless flurry of activity from June 1523 to February 1524, Lefèvre and his colleagues produced a translation of the entire New Testament. In 1525, they published the *Letters and Gospels for the Fifty-two Sundays of the Year*, a preaching handbook for the entire church year.[36] All the energy and activity of the Meaux group was in service of its goal to bring the Bible to the people.

Even as the Meaux group strove to make the Scriptures accessible, there emerged among its members theological positions similar to those of Luther and at odds with those of the conservatives at the Sorbonne. Already in the summer of 1521, before the Meaux experiment began, Marguerite and Briçonnet were drawing the suspicion of the Faculty.[37] Events in the subsequent years only deepened those suspicions. In November 1522, Marguerite's personal preacher Michel d'Arande was denounced for attacking the veneration of the saints, ridiculing the Faculty of Theology, and defending Luther. Troublingly for Marguerite, this denunciation came not from the Faculty itself but from the king's own confessor, Guillaume Petit, who had formerly supported Lefèvre.[38] It quashed the plans Marguerite and Briçonnet had made for a national reform proposal and fueled a growing perception that the Meaux group was associated with Luther. In October 1523, Briçonnet attempted to counter this perception by issuing a synodal letter condemning Luther, a move that ironically coincided with the publication of the French New Testament. Briçonnet's letter attacks Luther for undermining the ecclesiastical hierarchy, interpreting Scripture erroneously, and promoting individual, libidinous freedom.[39] The letter does not, however, condemn any of Luther's doctrines specifically, possibly because Briçonnet himself may have

---

quelque chose et (comme dict sainct Pol) ilz ne sont riens, mais se decoyvent eulx mesmes. Parquoy maintenant povons dire comme il disoit: Ecce nunc tempus acceptibile, ecce nunc dies salutis: Voicy maintenant le temps acceptable, voicy maintenant le jour de salut." Rice, ed., *The Prefatory Epistles of Jacques Lefèvre d'Etaples*, 449–50, no. 137, [Meaux], [ca. June 8, 1523]. Translation from Michael Bruening, ed., *A Reformation Sourcebook: Documents from an Age of Debate* (Toronto: University of Toronto Press, 2017), 112.

[35] Reid, *King's Sister*, 250.
[36] Guy Bedouelle and Franco Giacone, eds., *Epistres et Evangiles pour les cinquante et deux dimanches de l'an: Texte de l'édition de Pierre de Vingle, édition critique avec introduction et notes* (Leiden: Brill, 1979).
[37] Reid, *King's Sister*, 189.
[38] Reid, *King's Sister*, 199.
[39] Reid, *King's Sister*, 203–204; the text of Briçonnet's letter is in Herminjard 1:153–55, Briçonnet to the faithful in his diocese, Meaux, October 15, 1523.

shared many of them. He and Lefèvre were both coming closer to adopting Luther's position on justification. Indeed, Philip Edgcumbe Hughes argues that Lefèvre adopted the doctrine of *sola fide* well before Luther did.[40]

In the summer of 1523, when the king was away from Paris on campaign against the emperor, condemnations from the Sorbonne came flying. In the Faculty's sights were heretical books seized from Louis de Berquin, the sermons of Pierre Caroli, Lefèvre's *Commentary on the Gospels*, and the doctrines of the Meaux preachers generally.[41] The Faculty met 104 times that year, five times more often than usual. Most of their meetings were called to prosecute heresy.[42] Condemnations were issued and "errors" noted, but the Faculty were unable to convince the king to take rigorous punitive action against the evangelicals.

Significantly, the actions of the Paris Faculty seem to have produced an effect contrary to the one intended. Rather than drive the group underground or force them back to Catholic orthodoxy, the condemnations seem only to have strengthened the reformers' resolve, expanded their geographical reach, and pushed them closer to Luther. From Meaux, Lefèvre reported to Farel, who had since left France:

> After the publication of the French New Testament, you would hardly believe how eager God has made the minds of the simple folk in some places for embracing his Word. . . . Some, on the authority of the parlement, have tried to prohibit it, but the king has been a most generous defender of Christ in this, wishing that his kingdom freely hear the Word of God without any obstacle in language. Now, throughout the diocese, on feast days and especially on Sundays, the epistle and the Gospel are read to the people in the vernacular, and the preacher sometimes adds a word of exhortation to one or the other, or to both.[43]

---

[40] Hughes, *Lefèvre*, 96–99.

[41] Portions of the condemnations are printed in D'Argentré 2:x–xi (Lefèvre's *Commentary*), xi–xiii (Berquin), xiv–xx (Meaux doctrines in general), 21–30 (Caroli), 35–40 (*Epistres et Evangiles*).

[42] Reid, *King's Sister*, 118.

[43] "Vix crederes, posteaquam libri gallici Novi Organi emissi sunt, quanto Deus ardore simplicium mentes, aliquot in locis, moveat ad amplexandum verbum suum. . . . Nonnulli, authoritate Senatus interveniente, prohibere conati sunt: sed rex generosissimus in hoc Christo patrocinatus adfuit, volens regnum suum libere, ea lingua qua poterit, audire absque ullo impedimento Dei verbum. Nunc in tota dioecesi nostra, festibus diebus, et maxime die dominica, legitur populo et epistola et evangelium lingua vernacula; et si paroecus aliquid exhortationis habet, ad epistolam aut evangelium, aut ad utrumque adiicit." Herminjard 1:220–21, no. 103, Lefèvre to Farel, Meaux, July 6, 1524.

Despite the efforts of the Sorbonne and the Paris parlement, the Meaux group remained almost giddily optimistic. Their enthusiasm stemmed both from their success at the diocesan level and from the support of the king. In short, their program was working. And it was expanding. Beyond Meaux, French reformers François Lambert, Anémond de Coct, and Pierre de Sébiville were traveling throughout Germany and Switzerland and discussing religious reform directly with Luther, Zwingli, and Oecolampadius, among others, while staying in touch with the Meaux group. Increasingly, reformers elsewhere in France attached themselves to the Meaux group.[44] Reid summarizes their enterprise:

> Sources reveal that, circa 1524, a far-flung group knit together around Lefèvre and Marguerite. Its members did not merely admire Luther; they actively collaborated with German reformers in order to bring a shared vision of religious renewal to France. From that time forward, French evangelicals were, as they saw it, "bearing their crosses" in an effort to propagate evangelical views within the Most Christian Realm. Calling it "Christ's cause," "the Gospel," and like terms, they tried to advance their program through six interrelated projects: 1) preaching; 2) printing religious books; 3) nourishing evangelical conventicles; 4) protecting their brethren from prosecution; 5) promoting members to positions of influence; and 6) advocating "evangelical politics" at the French court.[45]

What had been a local Meaux group had grown to become a national evangelical network. State-sponsored reform was not yet a reality, but hopes remained high as the movement spread across the kingdom.

1.4. Gérard Roussel and the Choice between National Reform and International Protestantism, 1526–1534

Gérard Roussel was one of Lefèvre's early followers and later one of the principal leaders of the evangelicals in France. His birthdate is unknown, but we know that he hailed from Vaquerie, near Amiens in northern France.[46] He

---

[44] See Reid, *King's Sister*, 260–68.

[45] Reid, *King's Sister*, 252.

[46] The standard biography of Roussel remains C. Schmidt, *Gérard Roussel, Prédicateur de la Reine Marguerite de Navarre: Mémoire servant à l'histoire des premières tentatives faites pour introduire la Réformation en France* (Strasbourg: Schmidt & Grucker, 1845).

took holy orders and became a curate in the diocese of Reims. At some point (the date is unclear), he moved to Paris and became part of Lefèvre's circle at Saint-Germain. When Briçonnet called Lefèvre to Meaux, Roussel joined them, becoming curate of the parish of Saint-Saintin and later a canon and treasurer of the Meaux cathedral. Briçonnet authorized him, along with Farel and Michel d'Arande, to preach throughout the diocese. In 1525, under pressure from the Paris Faculty and parlement, he and Lefèvre fled the kingdom for Strasbourg. This was a defining moment for French evangelicalism. At that point, Roussel and Lefèvre could have broken with Marguerite and joined Farel in exile by embracing the international Reformed community. They chose not to. Instead, their continued embrace of national French reform forever set them at odds with colleagues who would flee the kingdom, and it created a lasting division between the Calvinists abroad and the evangelicals who remained in France.

1.4.1. Gérard Roussel and the Strasbourg Exile

For the Reformation generally, as well as for the francophone reformers, 1525 was a watershed year. In Germany, it marked the year of the Peasants' War and the start of Protestant discord over the Eucharist, which threatened and ultimately broke apart Protestant unity. In France, the capture of King Francis I at Pavia emboldened religious conservatives, whose hostility toward the Meaux reformers forced Lefèvre and Roussel to flee the country.

While the fighting in the German Peasants' War barely spilled over the French border, the conflict came as a shock to all of Europe. The Reformation, already viewed by many as a heretical assault on the doctrine and practice of the church, now appeared to be a revolutionary social movement as well. Lutherans, it seemed, wanted not merely to mock the pope and the Catholic hierarchy, but to overturn society. Despite Luther's disavowal of the peasants, Catholics everywhere saw the uprising as a consequence of Luther's movement. In France, the peasants' move into the Lorraine was described as a "Lutheran invasion" of France; many were thankful when it was brutally put down by Claude de Lorraine, duke of Guise.[47]

For French evangelicals, the war could not have come at a worse time. When Francis I was captured at the Battle of Pavia in February 1525, nearly

---

[47] Reid, King's Sister, 300.

every major French nobleman who fought for the king was likewise captured or killed in the battle,[48] excepting only Marguerite's husband, Charles, Duke of Alençon; he, too, died shortly after returning to France. Francis was subsequently held as a prisoner of Emperor Charles V for over a year. During his imprisonment, Francis's mother, Louise of Savoy, acted as regent. The hardline Catholics in the Sorbonne and the Paris parlement saw the king's absence as their opportunity to launch a full-scale assault on heresy in the kingdom. Less than a month after the king's capture, the parlement instructed the bishop of Paris to establish a commission to try cases of heresy. The *juges délégués*, as the commissioners became known, soon had power to investigate heresy throughout the jurisdiction of the Paris parlement, which included the diocese of Meaux.[49] Squarely in the sights of the *juges délégués* were the Meaux reformers. The parlement ordered the prosecution of Lefèvre and Roussel, along with Pierre Caroli, Martial Mazurier, and others. Upon hearing of the accusations, Francis I wrote the parlement from captivity and ordered it to suspend the proceedings, but the parlement ignored him.[50] Caroli and Mazurier remained in France and were prosecuted. Briçonnet, too, remained in France, but finding his episcopal status threatened, he renounced his evangelical leanings and cooperated fully with the conservatives in Paris. With Briçonnet's leadership gone, the Meaux group effectively disbanded.

Lefèvre and Roussel fled to Strasbourg, where they stayed at the home of Wolfgang Capito and collaborated on a French translation of the Old Testament. To Roussel, Strasbourg was an evangelical's paradise:

Here Christ alone is worshipped through his Word and is alone held up as the head and foundation. . . . Almost everything that seemed harmful to piety has been removed, such as the images affixed to the churches, which fabricated the cult of the saints, masses, and other prayers for the dead. . . . In the church services, nothing is said or sung that is not understood by all. . . . Scripture is explained most simply, not with insipid allegories, and has generally been freed of human inventions.[51]

---

[48] On the battle, see Knecht, *Renaissance Warrior and Patron*, 216–27.

[49] Knecht, *Renaissance Warrior and Patron*, 236–37.

[50] Knecht, *Renaissance Warrior and Patron*, 238; letter printed in Herminjard 1:401–403, no. 165, Madrid, November 12 [1525].

[51] "Hic solus Christus colitur per suum Verbum, solusque pro capite suscipitur et fundamento. . . . Ablegata sunt pene omnia quae pietati incommodare videbantur, cuius generis erant imagines templis affixae, quae cultum Sanctorum ementiebantur, missae et alia pro defunctis suffragia. . . . In conventu populi nihil dicitur aut canitur quod non intelligatur ab omnibus. . . . Scriptura simplicissime tractatur, reiectis frigidissimis allegoriis, ac in totum libera est ab humanis inventionibus." Herminjard 1:411,

Strasbourg presented to Roussel a clear vision of what French evangelical reform could ultimately become.

Roussel and Lefèvre's sojourn in Strasbourg briefly brought all the branches of early French reform together in one place. The two were joined by Michel d'Arande, Guillaume Farel, François Lambert, Nicolas d'Esch of Metz, Jean Védaste, and Simon Robert. Collectively, they represented Marguerite's network in microcosm, and their community in Strasbourg was an extraordinary confluence of the principal players in the early French reform movement.[52] But they differed on several points of doctrine and strategy,[53] and the very freedom they enjoyed ensured that they would never again be so united. Their stay prefigures, in a way, Calvin's Strasbourg period thirteen years later. At liberty to pursue their work there, as Calvin would later be, they were hesitant to return from exile, as he would be as well.

Thus, when Francis I returned to France from captivity,[54] Roussel and Lefèvre must have had mixed feelings about returning to their native land. The fertile fields of Meaux had been slashed and burned. Briçonnet had abandoned their cause, and they were left without the patronage and financial support they had once enjoyed. Meanwhile, in Strasbourg, their ties to Reformed theologians, such as Martin Bucer and Wolfgang Capito, had become stronger. They were no doubt tempted to abandon the idea of diocesan, state-sponsored reform and instead to join Farel in exile and throw in their lot with the international Reformed community. But the king's return to France and Marguerite's unflagging support restored their optimism for a French solution. Moreover, the confessional clashes that had begun to divide the German evangelicals and the increasingly vitriolic propaganda that Protestants were publishing likely struck them as poison pills which would

---

412, no. 168, [Roussel to Nicolas Le Sueur], [Strasbourg], [December 1525]. Roussel sent a similar letter around the same time to Briçonnet, which suggests that the bishop had not yet broken from his former allies. Ibid., 404–408, no. 167. A French translation of most of the letter to Briçonnet is available in Schmidt, *Gérard Roussel*, 55–58.

[52] On their stay there, see Rodolphe Peter, "Strasbourg et la Réforme française vers 1525," in *Strasbourg au coeur religieux du XVIe siècle, Hommage à Lucien Febvre, Actes du Colloque international de Strasbourg (25–29 mai 1975)*, edited by Georges Livet and Francis Rapp, 269–83, Société savante d'Alsace et des régions de l'Est, Collection "Grandes publications," 12 (Strasbourg: Librairie Istra, 1977).

[53] Peter, "Strasbourg et la Réforme française," 273.

[54] Francis was released on March 17, 1526, following the Peace of Madrid, in which the French king agreed, first, to surrender the duchy of Burgundy and his claims in Italy to Charles V; second, to force Henri d'Albret, king of Navarre and soon-to-be husband of Marguerite, to give up his possessions on the Spanish side of the Pyrenees; and third, to surrender his two eldest sons, Henri (II) and François (d. 1536), as hostages. Knecht, *Renaissance Warrior and Patron*, 246–48.

only hinder the cause of the Gospel in France.[55] Thus, they returned to the kingdom, firm in their belief that the best way to spread the Gospel was to continue working within the existing system.

1.4.2. Marguerite as Evangelical Patron

At this uncertain time, Marguerite stepped in and effectively replaced Briçonnet as the group's patron and leader. Throughout the group's time in Meaux, Marguerite had been supportive of their efforts but remained on the sidelines. After their exile, she assumed leadership of the network of French evangelicals. Upon leaving Strasbourg, Roussel, Lefèvre, and Arande headed for Marguerite's court. There, Arande was restored to his role as Marguerite's almoner, and Lefèvre became librarian of the royal château at Blois, as well as tutor to the king's third son, Charles, and his daughter Madeleine.[56] Roussel seems, in fact, to have considered returning to Strasbourg or going to Venice,[57] but Marguerite named him her court preacher. Thus, Marguerite ensured the former exiles' continued support and well-being. Their status in France restored, the evangelicals could once again hope for religious reform on a national scale. In July 1526, Pierre Toussain, who had been imprisoned and tortured during the king's imprisonment, wrote, "Certainly I would return to Germany if I did not hope that the Gospel of Christ would soon reign throughout France."[58] The evangelicals' hopes would have been raised further by the news, in January 1527, of Marguerite's second marriage, which elevated the Duchess of Alençon to the position of Queen of Navarre. Henri d'Albret, King of Navarre, was a much better match for Marguerite than Charles d'Alençon had been.[59] Most importantly for our story, he was sympathetic to her religious views and did nothing to stop her from leading her network of evangelicals.

---

[55] On the confessional clashes among Protestants, especially over the interpretation of the Eucharist, see Amy Nelson Burnett, *Karlstadt and the Origins of the Eucharistic Controversy: A Study in the Circulation of Ideas*, Oxford Studies in Historical Theology (New York: Oxford University Press, 2011). In addition to this controversy, in late 1525 Luther further distanced himself from those who sought moderate reform with the publication of a vicious attack on Erasmus in *On the Bondage of the Will* (LW 33).

[56] Bedouelle, *Lefèvre d'Etaples et l'intelligence des Ecritures*, 110.

[57] "Si res non cesserit prout sub Deo speramus, mox ad vos convolabo, vel petam Venetias." Herminjard, 1:440, no. 178, Roussel to Farel, Blois, June 17, 1526.

[58] "Et certe Germaniam repeterem, nisi sperarem brevi regnaturum Christi Evangelium per Galliam." Herminjard 1:445, no. 181, Toussain to Oecolampdius, Malesherbes, July 26 [1526].

[59] On the marriage and its arrangement, see Jourda, *Marguerite*, 143–47.

Between 1526 and 1530, however, the evangelical movement made little progress in France, and there is scant evidence of public evangelical preaching.[60] Indeed, two events threatened the movement once again. First, on May 31, 1528, a statue of the Madonna and Child was mutilated in Paris. Forced to act, Francis I replaced the statue and held a solemn procession to the scene of the desecration.[61] More importantly, he allowed the Paris Faculty of Theology to reopen the case against Louis de Berquin, who was found guilty of heresy and sentenced to life in prison. Berquin appealed the sentence to the Paris parlement, a decision he would live—briefly—to regret. With the king out of town, the parlement not only rejected Berquin's appeal but also changed the sentence to death. On April 17, 1529, Berquin was burned at the stake.[62] These actions typify Francis I's attitude toward religious heterodoxy: he would defend the right of scholars to pursue their academic interests, to translate the Bible, and to question existing practice and doctrine, but he could not tolerate violent, public actions that threatened to disturb the peace.[63] Francis was not about to let the Sorbonne burn Lefèvre over erudite doctrinal disagreements, but iconoclasm and deliberate public provocation would bring harsh punishment.[64]

1.4.3. Expansion of the Evangelical Movement, 1530–1533

The persecutions of 1528 and 1529 proved to be a setback for the reform movement rather than its death knell. Otherwise, French reform was

---

[60] Reid, *King's Sister*, 361.

[61] Knecht, *Renaissance Warrior and Patron*, 282.

[62] Knecht, *Renaissance Warrior and Patron*, 282–83.

[63] Roussel's biographer, Charles Schmidt, wonders what would have happened to the French evangelical movement if Farel had accepted a call to return to France after 1525 to preach for the seigneurs de la Marck: "Toutefois n'est-il pas permis de regretter qu'il [Farel] ait cru devoir obéir plutôt à une autre vocation qu'à celle qui le rappelait en France? Qui peut dire quelle voie se fût ouverte à la réformation, si au lieu de la foi mystique et accommodante de Roussel, de Michel d'Arande, de Marguerite, la foi énergique et dévouée de Farel eût dirigé le mouvement et eût décidé les princes de la Marche à se placer courageusement à la tête des protestants français? . . . A l'époque surtout dont nous parlons, la présence d'un homme comme Farel eût été un immense bienfait pour les réformés de France." Schmidt, *Gérard Roussel*, 71–72. Based on everything we know about Francis, however, it seems that Farel's presence in France would not have been "of immense benefit" to the evangelicals; on the contrary, his aggressive tactics would likely have harmed the movement irreparably, and he himself would probably have been executed.

[64] To clarify: there is no evidence that Berquin was guilty of the iconoclasm. He was simply in the wrong place at the wrong time. The Faculty of Theology had tried him twice already and used the act of anonymous iconoclasm as an excuse to reopen his trial.

proceeding apace, and by the early 1530s, hopes were once again high. In her duchy of Berry, Marguerite had been quietly staffing the University of Bourges with known evangelicals, chief among them Melchior Wolmar.[65] Calvin and Theodore Beza both studied at Bourges. Jean Chaponneau and Augustin Marlorat preached there at the time. Even in Paris, the evangelicals once again had reason for optimism. Francis continued to support humanist learning, a pursuit which by this point in the Reformation was usually accompanied by evangelical sympathies. Johannes Sturm, Guillaume Budé, and Günther von Andernach all taught in Paris at this time. The bishop of Paris himself, Jean du Bellay, was closely associated with Marguerite's network. Arande, meanwhile, had been made bishop of Saint-Paul-Trois-Châteaux.

Thus, by 1533, the optimism of the French evangelicals was probably at its highest point since the early successes in Meaux. Their program seemed slowly but surely to be working. A few individuals had secured bishoprics or had assumed positions at key educational institutions. The time seemed ripe for bolder action. To that end, Marguerite had Roussel deliver public sermons at the Louvre during Lent 1533.[66] He drew huge crowds, with some contemporaries' estimates reaching as high as ten thousand people.[67] All accounts agree that his sermons supported the doctrines of justification by faith alone and the primacy of Scripture, and that he rejected as unscriptural fasting, the veneration of the saints, and the penitential cycle.[68] The Faculty of Theology complained bitterly but to no avail. In the absence of official action, they started a pulpit war, with individuals preaching against Roussel, Marguerite, the bishop of Paris, and even the king himself.[69] Francis, needless to say, was not pleased. He banished from Paris Noël Beda, the syndic of the Faculty of Theology, along with three other conservatives. Evangelical preaching in the city intensified. Finally, on All Saints' Day 1533, the new rector of the University of Paris, Nicolas Cop, gave his famous address supporting the doctrine of *sola fide*. The university was perhaps not the best choice of venue for such an address. Cop fled the city along with John Calvin, who may have coauthored the address.[70] Their flight, however, is far more indicative of the mood within the university than at the royal court or perhaps

[65] On this and the rest of the paragraph, see Schmidt, *Gérard Roussel*, 81–84.
[66] See Reid, *King's Sister*, 419–26; Schmidt, *Gérard Roussel*, 85–87.
[67] Read, *King's Sister*, 420.
[68] Reid, *King's Sister*, 423.
[69] Reid, *King's Sister*, 424–25.
[70] On Calvin's possible authorship of the address, see Chapter 2, n. 59.

even in the streets of Paris. At the time of Cop's address, the evangelicals were riding a triumphal wave.

1.4.4. The Evangelical Movement Stalls, 1533–1534

And then the wave broke. A series of major setbacks scuttled hopes, at least temporarily, for French evangelical reform on a national level. First, in October 1533, Francis I met with Pope Clement VII to celebrate the marriage of the pope's niece, Catherine de Medici, to Francis's eldest son and heir, Henri.[71] Additionally, although Francis still refused to act against the German Protestants, with whom he hoped to form an alliance against the emperor, diplomacy demanded that he promise to combat heresy in France. In support of this effort, Pope Clement issued a bull against French "Lutherans."[72] In December 1533, Francis sent the papal decrees to the Paris parlement, directing it "to inquire diligently about all those who are or are suspected to be part of the Lutheran sect, so that you may proceed against them, excepting no one, by seizing them wherever they may be found."[73] Dozens were imprisoned, including Roussel.

The second event that quashed French evangelicals' hopes was the famous Affair of the Placards. On Sunday, October 18, 1534, people in Paris, Orléans, Amboise, Blois, Tours, and Rouen awoke to find broadsheets in the street decrying the abominations of the Catholic Mass.[74] Having pledged less than a year before to eradicate heresy, the king could not ignore the placards or tolerate this public act of aggression against the chief sacrament of the church. To make matters worse for the French evangelicals, in January 1535,

---

[71] They were married on October 27, 1534. See Knecht, *Renaissance Warrior and Patron*, 300.

[72] Knecht, *Renaissance Warrior and Patron*, 301. A taste of Francis's newfound desire to act against heresy is found in his letter to the Bern City Council, which had written to the king to seek clemency for Farel's family in Gap. Francis replied, "Nous avons trouvé vostre requeste si très-estrange, qu'il n'est possible de plus, et ne vous povons respondre sinon que Nous, desirans la conservacion du nom qui Nous a esté acquiz par Noz prédécesseurs de Roy très-chrestien, n'avons en ce monde chose plus à cueur que l'extirpacion et entière abolicion des hérésies." Herminjard 3:96, no. 433, Francis I to the Bern City Council, Marseille, October 20, 1533.

[73] "Nous vous mandons et très-expressément enjoignons, que vous commetez aulcuns d'entre vous, pour, toutes choses laissées, curieusement et diligemment eulx enquerir de tous ceulx qui tiennent icelle secte Lutherienne, et qui en sont suspects et vehementement suspectionnéz, et qui y adherent et les suivent, afin que vous procedez contre eulx, sans nul excepter, par prise de corps, en quelque lieu qu'ils soyent trouvéz." Herminjard 3:115, no. 440, Francis I to the Paris Parlement, Lyon, December 10, 1533.

[74] On the Affair of the Placards, see Knecht, *Renaissance Warrior and Patron*, 313–16; Gabrielle Berthoud, *Antoine Marcourt: Réformateur et pamphlétaire du 'Livre des Marchans' aux Placards de 1534*, THR 129 (Geneva: Droz, 1973), 157–222.

a second literary assault on the Mass followed the placards; copies of the *Petit traicté tres utile et salutaire de la saincte eucharistie*, written by Antoine Marcourt, who had also written the text of the placards, appeared around Paris.[75] These two attacks on the Mass in no way reflect the *modus operandi* of Marguerite's network in France. Rather, they bear the hallmark of Farel's operations in Switzerland. Not only did the aggressive, public confrontation echo the tactics of Farel's network, the subject matter reflected their ideology as well. Marguerite's circle did not focus on the "evils of the Mass"; Farel and his followers did, and this difference of opinion would lead to the split between the two groups on the question of Nicodemism. We will return to both of the polemic against the Mass and the question of Nicodemism in the next chapter. Starting in January 1535, in reaction to these public assaults on the Mass, Francis took increasingly punitive action against heresy in his realm. Several members of Marguerite's network found themselves on a list of those to be summoned by the Paris parlement for heresy. At the very top of this list was Pierre Caroli; also included were the evangelical poet Clément Marot and Calvin's teacher Mathurin Cordier.[76] Many evangelicals, on the list or not, took the opportunity to flee to Switzerland or Germany. Any hopes that Marguerite and Roussel had nurtured for an imminent national evangelical reform in France died with the martyrs burned in the Affair of the Placards' wake.

1.5. Gérard Roussel in Oloron: Diocesan Reform Revisited, 1536–1555

For Marguerite's circle in France, there remained one option that had been part of the original program in Meaux: diocesan reform. Having made substantial progress in Meaux over just a few years, Roussel still saw a path for significant reform at the local level. The network already had two bishops in place, Jean Du Bellay in Paris and Michel d'Arande in Saint-Paul-Trois-Châteaux. In 1536, Roussel himself became the third such bishop when Marguerite named him bishop of Oloron in her sovereign state of Béarn. As bishop, Roussel continued

---

[75] See Berthoud, *Antoine Marcourt*, 189–99.

[76] In addition to those three, Reid has identified Jehan Retif, Jean Couraud, François Bertaud, Simon Du Bois, Lyon Jamet, and François Ledevyn as suspects who were part of Marguerite's network. Reid, *King's Sister*, 432–33. See also the list published in Anonymous, "Pierre Caroli, Clément Marot, Mathurin Cordier, et quarante-six autres, ajournés par les gens du Roi comme suspects d'hérésie," *BSHPF* 10 (1861): 34–39.

to preach the fundamental doctrines of the Protestant Reformation, preparing his diocese for the full break from Catholicism that Marguerite's daughter Jeanne d'Albret would later institute.

After the Affair of the Placards, Roussel accompanied Marguerite when she left Paris for her estates in the south. He would never again preach in Paris. In Béarn, however, he had ample opportunity both to preach and to influence the preaching and teaching of others. Roussel's acceptance of the episcopal miter infuriated Calvin and prompted him to write one of the letters in his first anti-Nicodemite treatise, the *Duae epistolae*. Calvin's views on Nicodemism are well known.[77] Not as commonly understood are Roussel's views on his role as bishop. Fortunately, two texts written by Roussel during this period, the *Familiere exposition*[78] and the *Forme de visite de diocese*,[79] shed light on the question posed by Calvin and so many other Calvinists since: "What was he thinking?"

In fact, the question is not difficult to answer. In every respect, Roussel's acceptance of the bishopric of Oloron fit exactly with the French evangelical reform program since its inception. After the Affair of the Placards, Roussel had three options (apart from returning, like Briçonnet, fully and faithfully to the Catholic Church): First, he could flee France altogether, thereby abandoning his patron Marguerite, who had supported him for so many years. This was the option Calvin would have encouraged. Second, he could remain quietly in France as Marguerite's personal preacher and confessor without accepting the bishopric. Or, third, he could accept the position and continue to work for meaningful change from within the French church. Roussel chose the third option, and it should not be the least bit surprising that he did so. Here was his chance to institute reform throughout an entire diocese, much as he had helped Briçonnet to do earlier in Meaux.

---

[77] See, for example, Carlos Eire, *War against the Idols: The Reformation of Worship from Erasmus to Calvin* (New York: Cambridge University Press, 1986), ch. 7; David F. Wright, "Why Was Calvin So Severe a Critic of Nicodemism?" in *Calvinus Evangelii Propugnator: Calvin, Champion of the Gospel*, edited by David F. Wright et al., 66–90 (Grand Rapids, MI: Calvin Studies Society, 2006).

[78] Gérard Roussel, *Familiere exposition du simbole, de la loy et oraison dominicale en forme de colloque*, transcription in Paul J. Landa, "The Reformed Theology of Gérard Roussel, Bishop of Oloron (1536–1555)" (PhD diss., Vanderbilt University, 1976), 269–599; original manuscript, BNF, ms. fr. 419, available online at https://gallica.bnf.fr/ark:/12148/btv1b90581045.

[79] Gérard Roussel, *Forme de visite de diocese*, transcription in Schmidt, *Gérard Roussel*, 226–39, also in Landa, "The Reformed Theology of Gérard Roussel," 600–610.

1.5.1. Roussel's *Forme de visite de diocese*

Roussel did, in fact, seek to revive the Meaux experiment.[80] Since creating vernacular biblical translations was no longer necessary at this point, Roussel focused on preaching the Word of God to the common people. Consequently, preaching formed the principal focus of his *Forme de visite de diocese*. During this period, episcopal visitations were common, but few late medieval episcopal visitations focused on preaching, making Roussel's approach distinctive.[81] Moreover, Roussel wanted not only to ensure that his priests were preaching to the people but also to inform what they were preaching. He insisted that "no other word should be preached and announced than the pure word of God, the Gospel which Jesus Christ commanded to be preached to every creature."[82] He explains that the creeds and the Ten Commandments serve as a summary of what should be preached; together, these texts show what the Christian should believe and do (*croire et faire*—a refrain throughout the *Forme de visite*). Roussel emphasizes, however, that "belief must effect deed, faith effect work, such that work cannot be good if it is not done in faith."[83] Here he clearly echoes Luther in *The Freedom of a Christian*.[84] Roussel continues in very Lutheran terms:

---

[80] In this Reid and I disagree with Wanegffelen's assessment that "L'évêque Roussel n'a jamais trahi l'idéal de Réforme episcopale qui animait le group de Meaux auquel il avait appartenu." Wanegffelen, *Ni Rome ni Genève*, 94. Wanegffelen does not use Roussel's *Forme de visite*, which is crucial for such an assessment, and as Reid points out, Wanegffelen misinterprets Roussel's understanding of the Eucharist as traditionally Catholic, when in fact, it was quite close to that of Calvin. On Roussel's diocesan reform program and view of the Eucharist, see Reid, *King's Sister*, 525–45.

[81] See, for example, the two published fifteenth-century episcopal visitations for the diocese of Lausanne. They focused on the moral character of the priests and the physical condition of the churches and books, but hardly anything was said about the preaching being done in the parishes. Anonymous, *La visite des églises du diocèse de Lausanne en 1416–1417*, Mémoires et documents publiés par la société d'histoire de la Suisse romande ser. 2, 11 (Lausanne: Georges Bridel & Cⁱᵉ, 1921); Ansgar Wildermann, ed., *La visite des églises du diocèse de Lausanne en 1453*, 2 vols., Mémoires et documents publiés par la société d'histoire de la Suisse romande ser. 3, 19–20 (Lausanne: Société d'histoire de la Suisse romande, 1993).

[82] "Quant à la doctrine et parolle qui doibt estre annuncée au peuple assemblé, nous doibt estre persuadé et du tout notoire, que aultre parolle ne doibt estre preschée et annuncée que la pure parolle de Dieu, l'evangile que Jesuchrist a commandé estre presché à toute creature." Schmidt, *Gérard Roussel*, 227.

[83] "Croire doibt proceder faire, la foy proceder l'oeuvre, de sorte que l'oeuvre ne peult estre bon s'il n'est faict en foy." Schmidt, *Gérard Roussel*, 227.

[84] For example, "As the man is, whether believer or unbeliever, so also is his work—good if it was done in faith, wicked if it was done in unbelief. . . . As works do not make a man a believer, so also they do not make him righteous. But as faith makes a man a believer and righteous, so faith does good works." *LW* 31:361.

The justice of faith is called the justice of God, not, as Augustine says, that it is the justice by which God himself is just, but in which God freely clothes the sinner, when he pardons his sins and receives him in his grace, which properly can be called the justice of Jesus Christ. He is the author of it, and it is his, but it is attributed and imputed [*approprier*] to us by the faith which receives it from him and grants it to us. . . . We must say that the obedience of Jesus Christ, who is true and perfect justice . . . is communicated, attributed, and imputed to us and made ours by grace, in such a way that by grace we are made participants and beneficiaries of the fruit and merits.[85]

Roussel continues by discussing the justice of the law, and once again the Lutheran teaching on Law and Gospel is apparent:

The one who recognizes the powerlessness of the law to justify and save and who sees that he cannot fulfill and satisfy the law by his works and in this way gives up on himself and leaves this path aside, seeks his justification in Jesus Christ and by Jesus Christ who is the end, perfection, and accomplishment of the law. Trusting in him by means of faith, he embraces and receives him . . . , for man has no other means of fulfilling the law than by faith.[86]

Roussel concludes the *Forme de visite* with a discussion of prayer in a scarcely disguised attack on the cult of the saints:

Therefore, those who individualize the saints think wrongly and abuse them, tying them to times, places, and persons, as if they were not united perfectly to Jesus Christ and as if they had a will separate from that of Christ, and it would be good to reform such abuses and superstitions. . . . To

---

[85] "La justice de foy est appellée la justice de Dieu; non point, dict sainct Augustin, que soit la justice de laquelle Dieu est juste en soy, mais de laquelle Dieu vest gratuitement le pecheur, quant il luy pardonne ses pechez et le recoipt en sa grace, laquelle proprement peult estre appellée la justice de Jesuchrist, pource qu'il est l'autheur d'icelle, et est la sienne, mais nous est attribuée et appropriée par la foy qui nous l'impetre et la recoipt de luy. . . . ainsi debvons nous dire que l'obeissance de Jesuchrist qui est vraye et parfaicte justice . . . nous est communiquée, attribuée, imputée, et faicte nostre par grace, de sorte que par grace sommes faictz participans et joyssans du fruict et merite." Schmidt, *Gérard Roussel*, 227, 229.

[86] "Mais celluy qui recongnoist la loy impuissante à justifier et saulver, et qui se voit ne pouvoir par oeuvre et effect accomplir et satisfaire à la loy, et par ainsi se defiant de soy et laissant ceste voye, cherche sa justification en Jesuchrist et par Jesuchrist, qui est la fin, perfection et accomplissement de la loy, et se fiant en luy par le moyen de foy, l'embrasse et recoipt. . . . Car aultre moyen l'homme n'a d'accomplir la loy que par foy." Schmidt, *Gérard Roussel*, 230.

conclude, it is in Jesus Christ and by Jesus Christ that we have access to the Father and to the saints; therefore, it is in him and by him that we ought to pray to the Father and to the saints and be associated with all their prayers and benefits.[87]

Roussel thus inverts the traditional role of the saints and of Christ: the saints are not mediators between humans and Christ; rather, Christ is the mediator between humans, on the one hand, and God and the saints, on the other. Roussel's *Forme de visite*, therefore, is nothing other than a program for instilling evangelical doctrine in his diocese, thus following perfectly the Meaux program of diocesan evangelical reform.

1.5.2. Roussel's *Familiere exposition*

To further explain his religious views, Roussel wrote a much longer treatise entitled *Familiere exposition du simbole, de la loy, et oraison dominicale*.[88] As Schmidt describes it, "Apart from some slight concessions made to the exterior forms of Catholicism—for example, what he says about ceremonies—it is a book that could have come from the pen of a reformer."[89] Roussel argues that the foundation of Christian doctrine is justification by faith alone, that Scripture is the only valid Christian authority, that Christ is the sole head of the church, that Peter has no superior authority, that the church properly defined is not the ecclesiastical hierarchy but the invisible communion of the saints, and that the marks of the visible church are the preaching of the Gospel and the proper administration of the *two* sacraments, baptism and the Eucharist.[90] Roussel's doctrine of the Eucharist was decidedly influenced by Calvin's thought.[91] Thus, the text reveals Roussel to be anything but weak

---

[87] "Parquoy sentent mal et abusent des sainctz, ceulx qui les particularisent, les allient aux temps, lieux et personnes, comme si parfaictement n'estoient unyz avec Jesuchrist et avoient aultre voulloir que Jesuchrist; et seroit bon refformer telz abuz et superstitions. . . . Pour conclusion donc, c'est en Jesuchrist et par Jesuchrist qu'avons acces au pere et aux sainctz, parquoy c'est en luy et par luy que debvons prier le pere et que pouvons prier les sainctz et estre associez à toutes leurs prieres et biens." Schmidt, *Gérard Roussel*, 236–37.

[88] Schmidt provides a lengthy summary of the text in *Gérard Roussel*, 129–55, and Paul Landa based much of his dissertation, "The Reformed Theology of Gerard Roussel," especially pages 63–261, on the text.

[89] Schmidt, *Gérard Roussel*, 153.

[90] Schmidt, *Gérard Roussel*, 153.

[91] Schmidt, *Gérard Roussel*, 160; Reid, *King's Sister*, 536–45.

or indecisive, as many have characterized him.[92] He was unequivocally an evangelical reformer—if not necessarily one who adhered to a single official confession. Throughout his career he believed that the best way to spread the Gospel was not through contentious debate or rash abandonment of France, but through continuous striving within the existing system.

1.6. Reconsidering Roussel and Early French Reform

The tendency of both modern scholars and Roussel's critical contemporaries to paint him as indecisive has been driven by Protestant polemic, which lumps Roussel and the early French reformers together with the papacy. This treatment is misguided. Nothing in the careers of Roussel, Lefèvre, or Maguerite hints at the slightest attachment to Rome or the papacy. Indeed, as Schmidt points out, the word *Rome* appears nowhere in Roussel's writings.[93] The overall success of the reforms of Trent and the international reach of Rome in the modern Catholic Church blind us to the fact that in the first half of the sixteenth century, one could be a bishop in France without displaying any regard for the affairs or concerns of Rome. Roussel's identity was wrapped up first in his diocese and second in France; nothing in his writings or career suggests any affinity for Rome. Thus, to describe Roussel as a "papist" or "Roman Catholic" is profoundly misleading. He was committed to the doctrines of the Protestant Reformation and used his influence as bishop to try to spread those teachings in his diocese.

Jonathan Reid's work has revealed dozens of individuals like Roussel who saw themselves as part of Marguerite's evangelical network. While some may not have had the same level of evangelical commitment as Roussel or Farel, all supported what Briçonnet and Marguerite had described as *le seul nécessaire*, the preaching of the Gospel. Likewise, as Reid states, "they did articulate, publish, preach, teach, and attempt to transform the church according to a

---

[92] Despite Roussel's important role in the early French reform movement, Beza barely mentions him in the *Histoire ecclésiastique*. When he does, he highlights Roussel's "self-bastardization": "Ruffi [i.e., Roussel] donc fut retiré par la Royne de Navarre, et s'abatardit peu à peu, ne faisant conscience d'accepter l'Abbaie de Clerac et finalement l'Evecsché d'Oleron." *Hist. eccl.* 1:27. For centuries, other Protestant historians followed Beza's lead: for example, "ses tendances réformatrices n'allèrent jamais jusqu'à admettre la possibilité d'une séparation complète d'avec Rome, et, son caractère doux et timide y aidant, il s'arrêta à moitié chemin, satisfait de quelques essais infructueux de réforme" (Haag, 9:53).

[93] Schmidt, *Gérard Roussel*, 153.

recognizable and commensurate set of doctrines."[94] Collectively, theirs was a limited understanding of reform, more measured than the program favored by Calvin and Farel. They were not preoccupied with the ceremonies of the church or the alleged "evils" of the Catholic Mass. They did not argue over the fine points of theology, such as predestination or the proper understanding of the Eucharist. And they did not seek fundamental change in the structure of the church. Instead, they believed that the best hope for reform was to be found by working within the system, at the French royal court and on the diocesan level within the church. It is important to note that their strategy often worked well. The Meaux experiment made real progress in the early 1520s. Hopes were high after Francis I's return from captivity in 1526. Perhaps the apogee of their efforts came in 1533, when Roussel preached to huge crowds in Paris and Noël Beda was in exile. Although hope for a truly national reform may have faded after the Affair of the Placards, Roussel and other bishops continued a program of diocesan reform for decades to come. As we will see in Chapter 7, these hopes would be revived once again in the late 1550s.

The leading characteristics and strategies of Marguerite's network, however, would soon come under withering attack from Protestant reformers who saw their approach as inadequate. These opponents did, in fact, focus on ceremonies and targeted the Mass in particular. They believed that a right understanding of the Eucharist and predestination was essential, and they lambasted the church hierarchy and its officials as evil by association. Guillaume Farel would lead this group initially, superseded eventually by John Calvin. Both men had been friends of Roussel in France, but by 1536, when Roussel accepted the bishopic of Oloron, Calvin had turned so decisively against him that he famously concluded his letter to him in the *Epistolae Duae*, "Think what you like about yourself, but to me, you certainly are neither a Christian nor a good man."[95]

---

[94] Reid, *King's Sister*, 64.
[95] "de te, ut voles, aestimabis: mihi certe nec vir bonus eris, nec Christianus." Calvin, *Epistolae Duae, OS* 1:362.

2

The Formation of the Farellian and Calvinist Networks

2.1. Introduction

Guillaume Farel and John Calvin were both initially connected to Marguerite of Navarre's network. Both men, however, eventually pursued a more radical approach to church reform. First, Farel became convinced that hope for true reform lay not in France but in the international Reformed community. In particular, his connections with the reformers in Strasbourg and Basel led him to become the father of francophone Reformed Protestantism, a role too commonly attributed to Calvin. Like his colleagues in France, Farel initially believed that the political authorities could be useful in establishing meaningful reform, and that their involvement might even be necessary. Unlike his friends in France, however, he believed one had to leave the kingdom to find them. Farel found sympathetic magistrates first in the Swiss canton of Bern, and then on the city council of Geneva. For a crucial decade, he worked to spread the message of Protestant reform to the French-speaking towns under Bern's influence. He soon found help from former colleagues who had been exiled from France and from one notable native son of Romandie, Pierre Viret. Farel and his allies also tried to hasten reform in France itself, albeit with little success. Despite their failures in France, Farel and his colleagues were able to build in the Suisse romande a Reformed network committed to bringing Protestantism to individual towns through the abolition of the Mass.

After successfully pushing the magistrates in Geneva to abolish the Mass, Farel persuaded Calvin to join him in his efforts. Calvin's sharper theological mind transformed Farel's campaign to abolish the Mass into a broader effort to establish an entirely new theological system. As we shall see in the following chapters, not everyone welcomed Calvin's innovations. His reforms were what might be called in today's business lingo "creative disruption." Calvin broadened Reformed Protestantism beyond the urban program

Refusing to Kiss the Slipper. Michael W. Bruening, Oxford University Press (2021). © Oxford University Press.
DOI: 10.1093/oso/9780197566954.003.0003

launched by Ulrich Zwingli but in the process alienated many members of Farel's core network. Further, by excluding the magistrate from his concept of "the church," Calvin weakened the link between religious reform and the secular authorities. Cooperation with the magistrate was to be hoped for, certainly, but in contrast to both Marguerite of Navarre and Zwingli, Calvin believed that a Reformed church could theoretically exist independent of the secular magistrate. When Calvin and Farel tested this position in 1538, the Geneva council banished them from the city, but Calvin would return three years later unchanged in his convictions.

During his exile in Strasbourg (1538–1541), Calvin developed a set of core doctrines that departed from earlier Reformed thought. These included a new interpretation of the Eucharist, the belief in double predestination, and the need for a consistory to exercise moral discipline and wield the power of excommunication. These theological innovations won over several of the reformers in Switzerland, most notably Farel and Viret. Calvin's influence on Viret was particularly important, for Viret would seek to ensure that the faculty at the Lausanne Academy were allied to the Calvinists. With some significant exceptions whom we shall encounter in later chapters, he was successful, and these professors' instruction was a key factor in the creation of a Calvinist network of francophone clergy. Later, Theodore Beza and the Geneva Academy would take the baton and perpetuate Calvin's legacy for decades—and arguably centuries—to come.

2.2. Guillaume Farel Makes French Reform "Reformed," 1521–1530

Explanations for the French adoption of Reformed Protestantism rather than Lutheranism often refer in some way to John Calvin. In fact, Calvin had nothing to do with it. It was Guillaume Farel who played the decisive role.

That French reform would become Reformed was by no means a foregone conclusion. The Meaux group read Luther more than Zwingli, and the peripatetic early reformers François Lambert, Anémond de Coct, and Pierre de Sébiville spent more time in Wittenberg than in Zurich. French Protestants could easily have taken a Lutheran path rather than following the Reformed route.

The reason they did not can largely be ascribed to Farel. In the 1520s, in the midst of the first Eucharistic controversy, Farel became associated with the leading German-speaking Reformed theologians and adopted their views rather than those of Luther on the Eucharist. Subsequently, nearly all early French Protestant publications propagated a Reformed understanding of the doctrines that divided Protestants. Thus, for a decade before Calvin arrived on the scene, Farel's Reformed vision paved the way for French Protestants.

2.2.1. Farel with Lefèvre and the Meaux Group, 1509–1523

Guillaume Farel's early departure from Meaux and his later, well-known career in Switzerland make it easy to forget that he spent thirteen years at the feet of Jacques Lefèvre d'Étaples in Paris and Meaux. Farel was a native of the town of Gap in the French Alps of the Dauphiné.[1] His parents wanted him to become a soldier—a common profession for those who lived so close to the ceaseless wars in Italy—or at least a churchman. Farel insisted instead on pursuing a scholarly career. In 1509, he arrived in Paris and studied at the Collège du Cardinal Lemoine, where Lefèvre was teaching. He also found his way into Lefèvre's circle at Saint-Germain. In 1517, Farel received a master of arts degree and remained at Cardinal Lemoine as a lecturer (*régent*). In 1521, he joined Lefèvre and Gérard Roussel in Meaux. As a layman, Farel could not be assigned a parish, but Bishop Guillaume Briçonnet nevertheless gave him permission to preach throughout the diocese. We have no direct evidence of Farel's beliefs or doctrine at this stage of his career, but it is reasonable to assume that he was a devoted disciple of Lefèvre and likely shared his teacher's Christocentric and biblical emphases. Farel did not remain in Meaux for long. The circumstances surrounding his departure are obscure, but his decision to leave may be the first hint that he thought evangelical reform effort required more dramatic action than Briçonnet and Lefèvre were prepared to undertake.

Briçonnet seems to have revoked Farel's preaching permission in April 1523, prompting Farel to leave Meaux for Basel.[2] We find perhaps the best

---

[1] The standard biography of Farel is Comité Farel, *Guillaume Farel 1489–1565: Biographie nouvelle écrite d'après les documents originaux par un groupe d'historiens, professeurs et pasteurs de Suisse, de France et d'Italie* (Neuchâtel: Delauchaux & Niestlé S.A., 1930).

[2] Most biographies explain Farel's departure from Meaux as the result of a quarrel that started with Jean de Roma, later the Inquisitor of the Waldensians. Roma and his fellow Jacobins, the story goes, complained to Briçonnet, and Briçonnet withdrew his preaching permission. All of

evidence of Farel's early views in theses he published in Basel in 1524. These texts indicate that Farel broadly supported the principles of the Meaux program and that he had not yet adopted his later, more aggressive stance against the Catholic Mass and the doctrine of transubstantiation. The first few Basel theses indicate simply that nothing should be added to what Christ taught.[3] The fifth perfectly represents the biblicism of the Meaux group: "The truest duty of priests is to insist upon the Word of God and attach themselves to it to the point where they think nothing above it."[4] Farel expresses the doctrine of *sola fide* in thesis eight: "Those who hope to save themselves and be justified by their own strength and power, rather than by faith, raising themselves up and making themselves God by their free choice, are blinded by impiety."[5] In striking contrast to his later works, Farel's Basel theses make no mention of the Mass or the Eucharist.[6] These were the targets of neither the Meaux group nor Farel during his early career.

this, however, is based on a good deal of conjecture. Briçonnet's order indicates that he indeed withdrew preaching permissions from some of the preachers in the diocese, but it provides no names. The text of Briçonnet's order is in Toussaints Du Plessis, *Histoire de l'Église de Meaux, avec des notes ou dissertations, et les pièces justificatives*, 2 vols. (Paris: Julien-Michel Gandouin and Pierre François Giffart, 1731), 2: 557–58, no. 10 (also cited in Reid, *King's Sister*, 204–5, n. 72). Much later, a letter from Farel to the Duke of Lorraine alludes to Farel's alleged quarrel with De Roma; it reads: "Et non seulement le Pape ose ainsi parler et faire, comme il a faict; mais je l'ay ouy d'un Jacobin nommé de Roma. Auquel, quand propos estoit tenu de l'Évangile, et ce, quand premièrement le nouveau Testament fut imprimé en françoys, où Monsieur Fabry [Lefèvre] avoit besongné, et (où il) estoit dict, que l'Évangile auroit lieu au Royaume de France, et qu'on ne prescheroit plus les songes des hommes, de Roma respondit: 'Moy et autres comme moy, lèverons une cruciade de gens, et ferons chasser le Roy de son Royaume par ses subjectz propres, s'il permet que l'Évangile soit presché.' " Herminjard 8:275, no. 1203, Farel to the Duke of Lorraine, Gorze, February 11, 1543.

[3] "1. Christ nous a prescrit une règle de vie définitive à laquelle il n'est permis de rien ajouter ou enlever. 2. Seules les choses à nous ordonnées par Dieu peuvent être mises en pratique par la foi, de sorte qu'il est impie de se joindre à un parti ou de vivre sous d'autres préceptes que ceux de Christ . . . 3. Il est contraire à la lumière de l'Evangile d'observer la coutume judaïque de la diversité des vêtements, des aliments et des cérémonies. 4. Les prières composées de beaucoup de paroles et qui ne sont pas conformes à la règle établie par Christ sont contraires à ce qu'il a prescrit et ne peuvent être instituées et récitées sans péril." The entire French translation of Farel's theses is printed in *Guillaume Farel*, 122–23; here, 122. The original Latin text is in Herminjard 1:193–95, no. 91, Farel to Christian Readers, Basel, ca. February 20, 1524.

[4] "5. Presbyterorum verissimum officium verbo Dei instare, cui ita addictos oportet, ut nihil ducant augustius." Herminjard 1:194, no. 91.

[5] "8. Qui suis viribus et potentia se salvari sperat ac iustificari, et non potius fide: sese erigens, et deum per liberum arbitrium faciens, impietate excaecatur." Herminjard 1:195, no. 91.

[6] For more on the development of Farel's Eucharistic theology, see Michael Bruening, "Guillaume Farel et les réformateurs de langue allemande: Les origines de la doctrine réformée dans l'espace romand," in *La construction internationale de la Réforme et l'espace romand à l'époque de Luther*, edited by Daniela Solfaroli Camillocci et al. (Paris: Classiques Garnier, forthcoming).

2.2.2. Farel, the Reformed Theologians, and the Eucharist, 1523–1529

Farel's stay in Basel forever changed the face of francophone reform, for it brought him—and consequently most of the major francophone reformers after him—fully under the influence of Reformed rather than Lutheran Protestantism. In Basel, Farel stayed with Johannes Oecolampadius who, together with Zwingli, led the early Reformed movement. Farel began to ship books written by Oecolampadius and other Reformed theologians back to his friends in Meaux.[7] He also happened to be in Basel at the same time as Hinne Rode. Rode was instrumental in forging the symbolic understanding of the Eucharist among the Reformed by introducing them to the works of Wessel Gansfort and Cornelis Hoen.[8] It is possible that Farel made the first French translation of Hoen's treatise.[9] For the next couple of years, Farel's contacts with the Reformed grew even stronger. In May 1524, he left Basel intending to visit both Zwingli and Luther, but he traveled only as far as Zurich. In 1525, after a missionary trip to Montbéliard,[10] he went to Strasbourg, where he became close to Martin Bucer and Wolfgang Capito, with whom he lived for nineteen months.

The timing of Farel's Strasbourg visit placed him at the center of the growing dispute between the Lutherans and the Reformed over the Eucharist. The Strasbourg pastors had fallen under the influence of Zwingli, Rode, and Andreas Bodenstein von Karlstadt and, consequently, had adopted a symbolic understanding of the Eucharist.[11] Bucer spent his later career trying to mediate between the Lutheran and Reformed positions, but in 1525, he was a staunch Zwinglian. Farel, having recently come under the influence

---

[7] Lefèvre thanked him for the books he had sent with the comment, "Omnia quae a te veniunt et Germania mihi maxime placent," and he asked Farel to send Zwingli his greetings should he write to the Zurich reformer ("Si aliquando scribes ad egregium virum Zynglium, memineris salutationis meae"). Herminjard 1:208–9, no. 98, Lefèvre to Farel, Paris, April 20 [1524].

[8] On Hoen's letter, see Bart Jan Spruyt, *Cornelis Henrici Hoen (Honius) and His Epistle on the Eucharist (1525): Medieval Heresy, Erasmian Humanism, and Reform in the Early Sixteenth-Century Low Countries*, SMRT 119 (Leiden: Brill 2006). The Latin text of the letter is printed in ibid., 226–35. On Rode's travels through Germany and the Swiss Confederation, see ibid., 187–218.

[9] *Guillaume Farel*, 118. Jean-François Gilmont does not, however, include this translation in his bibliography of Farel's works, "L'Oeuvre imprimé de Guillaume Farel," in *Actes du Colloque Guillaume Farel, Neuchâtel, 29 septembre–1er octobre 1980*, 2 vols., edited by Pierre Barthel et al., Cahiers de la Revue de Théologie et de Philosophie 9 (Geneva: Revue de théologie et de philosophie, 1983), 2:105–45.

[10] See *Guillaume Farel*, 131–49.

[11] On the development of the Strasbourg pastors' positions at this time, see Burnett, *Karlstadt and the Origins of the Eucharistic Controversy*, 101–12.

of Oecolampadius in Basel, found himself squarely in the midst of the Reformed opposition to Luther on the sacrament. He was not shy about joining the fray. In August 1525, the Lutheran Johann Bugenhagen published an *Open Letter against the New Error on the Sacrament*, in which he attacked Zwingli's and Karlstadt's symbolic positions on the Eucharist.[12] The treatise inflamed passions on both sides of the debate. In October, the Strasbourg pastors sent Gregor Caselius, a Hebrew instructor, to Wittenberg to defend their position before Luther.[13] Farel sent with Caselius a letter addressed to Bugenhagen. This letter contains Farel's first extended treatment of the Eucharist and reveals him to be, like his friends in Strasbourg and Basel, a convinced Zwinglian:

> If we are justified and blessed by faith alone in the incarnate Christ who suffered and died for us, why force him into the bread? . . . It is the view of all that the bread is an external matter, which neither saves if it is present nor condemns if it is absent. . . . Let all preach with one voice: When this bread is eaten, our mind should be occupied with this alone, namely that we give thanks to God and recognize that the Father so loved the world that he gave his only Son, by whose death we have been saved and by whose blood we have been cleansed.[14]

Farel stresses the commemorative function of the Eucharist, insisting that if faith alone justifies, externals such as the bread do not matter. From this point on, Farel, who had not even mentioned the Lord's Supper in the 1524 Basel Theses, would make adherence to the Reformed position on the Eucharist a central focus of his ministry.

As Farel's thought developed through the 1520s, even more important than the symbolic understanding of the elements in the Eucharist was the vigorous denunciation of the Catholic Mass. To Farel, the Catholic doctrine of transubstantiation raised the sacrament to dangerously superstitious heights, reinforced by the focus of the Mass on the corporeal presence of

---

[12] See Burnett, *Karlstadt and the Origins of the Eucharistic Controversy*, 99–101.

[13] See their instructions to Caselius in *BDS* 3:421ff.; see also Jean Rott, "Bucer et les débuts de la querelle sacramentaire," *Revue d'histoire et de philosophie religieuses* 34 (1954): 234–54.

[14] "Si sola fides in Christum incarnatum, passum et mortuum pro nobis, salvet et beet, quid iterum ad panem cogimur? . . . Ea est omnium sententia, panem rem esse externam, qui si adsit non servat, nec absens perdit. . . . Dum panis hic editur, mentem in hoc solum occupandam, ut gratias agat Deo, recogitetque Patrem sic dilexisse mundum, ut Filium suum unigenitum dederit, cuius morte salvati sumus, sanguine repurgati." Herminjard 1:394–95, no. 163, Farel to Bugenhagen (Pomeranus), Strasbourg, [ca. October 8, 1525].

Christ. By contrast, when the sacrament is stripped of the notion of the presence of Christ, Farel believed, it can more soberly serve to focus the thoughts of the communicant on Christ's original sacrifice on the cross. In his 1529 *Summaire*, Farel more fully developed his ideas on the sacrament and the Catholic Mass. On the Eucharist, he again takes a decidedly Zwinglian position:

> Sacraments are signs and public attestations of that which ought to be in the faithful. They serve to maintain and increase love among them. For the Christian is pushed more to love those who confess and believe truly and publicly that in the death and passion of Jesus and the blood that he shed, they have the remission of their sins and are transplanted from the old Adam into Jesus Christ. . . . We must not believe that we have forgiveness of sins and eternal life simply because we come to the holy table of our Lord, nor that we have the assurance and guarantee of divine grace by the sacraments. For our sins are only forgiven if we believe that our Lord Jesus Christ died for them. We have life only by believing in him.[15]

Once again, Farel highlights the commemorative significance of the sacrament and adds to it a communal element that was important to the Zwinglians. Rather than feeding the individual communicant with the true body of Christ, for Farel, the Eucharist brought the Christian community together more closely and led the individuals within it to remember Christ's death.

The section on the Mass in Farel's *Summaire* is double the length of the section on the Sacraments. In the latter, he lays out a simple, positive explanation of the sacraments, but in his treatment of the Mass, he takes the gloves off and goes on the attack. First, he complains of the financial abuses surrounding the Mass:

---

[15] "Les sacrementz sont signes et protestations des choses qui doivent estre ès fideles, servantz et proffitans à conserver, croistre, et augmenter la charité, l'ung avec l'autre. Car le chrestien est plus esmeu de charité envers ceulx qui confessent croyre vrayement devant tous, que par la mort et passion de Jesus et le sang qu'il a espandu, ilz ont remission de leurs pechez: et sont transplantez du vieil homme Adam en Jesuchrist. . . . Semblablement ne fault croyre que pour venir à la table de nostre Seigneur on ayt remission des pechez et vie eternelle: et que par les sacramentz soyons asseurez et confirmez que Dieu nous faict grace. Car noz pechez nous sont remis en ce seulement que croyons que nostre Seigneur est mort pour iceulx. Et avons vie croyans en luy." Guillaume Farel, *Le Sommaire de Guillaume Farel, réimprimé d'après l'édition de l'an 1534*, edited by J.-G. Baum (Geneva: Jules-Guillaume Fick, 1867), 34, 36. English translation modified from Jason Zuidema and Theodore Van Raalte, *Early French Reform: The Theology and Spirituality of Guillaume Farel*, St. Andrews Studies in Reformation History (Burlington, VT: Ashgate, 2011), 134–35.

It is clear that the Mass was introduced to overturn the holy table of the Lord. . . . By the Mass, the poor, the widows, and orphans are destroyed. For by it the church of the pope gains all the goods of the world. And that which should come to the poor members of Jesus is offered and employed in rich clothing and diverse methods of vestments taken both from the infidels or pagans and from Jewish ceremony. . . . All of these abuses were introduced by the greed of Satan. God will not let these abuses go unpunished.[16]

He then criticizes the use of Latin in the Mass and lambasts the associated doctrine of purgatory:

In the Mass all is said in a language that people do not understand, in singing and in laughing. . . . In the Mass we are urged to give to those who are outside of this world, to get them, as the priests say, out of purgatory, which is an invention of Satan and his helpers against holy scripture. By this invention innumerable souls go to eternal perdition.[17]

Finally, Farel goes to the very heart of the matter with the critique that the Protestant reformers would level time and again against the Mass, namely that by understanding it as a repeated sacrifice of Christ, Catholics denied the efficacy of Christ's original sacrifice on the cross:

At the table of our Lord, the faithful give thanks to God for giving us a perfect and accomplished sacrifice which need not be repeated. . . . In the Mass, instead of giving thanks to God for our redemption, the priest, with his assistants, offers bread and wine for their redemption and salvation. And this day after day, as if the sacrifice of Jesus was insufficient, without full

---

[16] "Il est tout cler qu'elle [la Messe] a esté controuvée au lieu de la saincte table de nostre Seigneur, et ne fault grand esperit pour congnoistre si elle est de Dieu ou non . . . Par la messe les paovres sont destruictz, les vefves aussi et orphelins; car par elle l'eglise du pape attire tous les biens du monde. Et ce qui devoit venir aux paovres membres de Jesus, est exposé et employé en riches habitz et diverses manieres d'abillemens, prins tant des infideles et payens, que des ceremonies des Juifz." Farel, *Sommaire*, 36–37. Translation from Zuidema and Van Raalte, *Early French Reform*, 135–36.

[17] "En la messe tout est dict en langage que le peuple n'entend pas en chantant et riant. . . . [M]ais en la messe on incite à donner à ceulx qui sont hors de ce monde pour les tirer (comme disent les prebstres) hors de purgatoire, qui est une invention de Satan et de ses ministres, contre la saincte escripture. Par laquelle innumerables vont en perdition eternelle." Farel, *Sommaire*, 38–39; translation from Zuidema and Van Raalte, *Early French Reform*, 136.

efficacy, like those offered by Moses. The bread is not taken or eaten by all, but elevated and worshipped as if it were God.[18]

Farel concludes by indicating that he has left out a large number of abuses surrounding the Mass, "for to show the iniquity and abominations which are in the Mass would take a very long book. There is no one who could sufficiently show how much it is against our Lord."[19] This polemic against the Mass would dominate the early publications—almost all coming out of Pierre de Vingle's press in Neuchâtel—from Farel and his network in the Suisse romande. Indeed, opposition to the Catholic Mass was arguably the single most important issue binding Farel's network together.

2.2.3. Farel's Break from His French Colleagues, 1526

Farel's former colleagues in Marguerite's network, by contrast, remained largely noncommittal on the subject of the Eucharist,[20] an attitude that may well have accelerated his breach with them. One sees in Farel's early correspondence a good deal of continued contact with Roussel and Lefèvre. Late 1526, however, marked a major turning point. As we saw in the last chapter, following their exile in Strasbourg, Lefèvre and Roussel chose to pursue a version of reform that led them back to France. Initially, it seems that Farel indicated a desire to follow, and his friends were eager to help.[21] In December 1526, Roussel wrote to offer Farel a plum position as preacher for the sons

---

[18] "En la table de nostre Seigneur les fideles rendent graces à Dieu, que pour tous les sacrifices qu'il avoit commandé par Moyse, pour avoir la sanctification selon la chair (lesquelz imparfaictz estoient reiterez: pour tant qu'ilz ne pouvoient pleinement sanctifier) il nous en a donné ung parfaict et consommé.... En la messe au lieu de rendre graces à Dieu pour nostre redemption, le prebstre avec les assistens offrent pain et vin pour leur redemption et leur salut. Et ce de jour en jour, comme si le sacrifice de Jesus estoit insuffisant sans pleine efficace, semblable à ceulx de Moyse. Le pain n'est point prins ne mangé de tous, mais eslevé et adoré comme Dieu." Farel, *Sommaire*, 39–40; translation from Zuidema and Van Raalte, *Early French Reform*, 137.

[19] "Je laisse toutes les singeries, invocations pour les trespassez, et semblables choses qui sont droictment contre la saincte escripture. Car declairer l'iniquité et abomination de la messe requerroit ung livre fort grand, voire s'il y a aucun qui suffisamment puisse montrer combien elle est contre nostre Seigneur." Farel, *Sommaire*, 40; translation from Zuidema and Van Raalte, *Early French Reform*, 137.

[20] On the early French reformers' views of the Eucharist, see Marcel Royannez, "L'eucharistie chez les évangéliques et les premiers réformés français (1522–1546)," *BSHPF* 125 (1979): 548–76.

[21] See, for example, Roussel's letter to him of August 17, 1526: "Egi pluribus literis cum magistro Petro [probably Pierre Vitier, professor at the Collège de Navarre in Paris] de tuis rebus; pollicitus est omnem operam." Herminjard 1:449, no. 182, Amboise.

of Robert de la Marck, prince of Sédan and duke of Bouillon.[22] Finally, no doubt after much effort on Roussel's part, here was an opportunity to return to France. As preacher to a noble family, Farel would have protection from the ebb and flow of the Sorbonne's wrath, much as Roussel and Lefèvre did as members of Marguerite's court. But the job came with one critical condition: Farel would have to tone down his polemic on the Eucharist and "be content to teach Christ and the true benefit of his works."[23] The demand was too much; Farel rejected the position and chose instead the path of continued exile.

Roussel's job offer appears in the last extant letter between him and Farel. In all likelihood, Farel wrote back, but his response is lost; hence, we cannot be sure of his reasons for rejecting the offer. At this point, he was already preaching in Bern's town of Aigle in the Pays de Vaud, but whatever rewards that position offered, they would not likely have been sufficient to tempt him from such an attractive offer back in France.[24] After all, there was reason for optimism among French reformers at that time. It was in July 1526 that Pierre Toussain expressed his "hope that the Gospel of Christ would soon reign throughout France."[25] Moreover, since Farel had recently expressed a desire for a position in the kingdom, his rejection of the offer cannot reflect a total loss of hope for the Gospel in France. Instead, Farel's refusal seems to have stemmed from an evolution in his reform ideology. In fall 1525, he had been in the thick of the dispute over the Eucharist. His involvement, together with the break in communications with Roussel following the job offer, suggests that he had come to believe that a Reformed understanding of the Eucharist and rejection of the Catholic Mass were sine qua non conditions for true evangelical reform. In France, his old friends did not see things the same way. Marguerite's network continued to work within the system, which included continuing to say and attend Mass. For Farel, the Mass made working within

[22] "Cum iissem in curiam . . . , incidi in generosos principes, filios Roberti a Marcia principis. . . . Audiunt, assentiuntur; tum subiicio, te unum ei negocio fore non parum idoneum, coepi talenta tibi credita in Christi gloriam praedicare, et demum ita direxit sermonem Christus, ut plus quam ego te cupiant, te perinde ac filium et fratrem, imo si vis patrem, habituri." Herminjard 1:459, no. 184, Roussel to Farel, [St.-Germain-en-Laye], December 7 [1526].

[23] "Sed quid optemus probe nosti, ne scilicet spargatur per quod demum suboriatur dissidium. Quantum mihi displiceat dissentio nuper orta, vix effari possum. Abstine, oro, ab ea, sed contentus esto docere Christum et verum usum operum illius." Herminjard 1:460, no. 184.

[24] On Farel's significant difficulties in Aigle and its environs, see Bruening, *Calvinism's First Battleground*, 106–11.

[25] See 25.

the system unacceptable and demanded a full break. Farel made one: from the Mass, from the old church, and from his old friends.

A network analysis of Farel's extant letters shows that after 1526, his correspondence with his former colleagues in France broke down completely.[26] Central among his new associates were the German-speaking leaders of the Reformed movement: Zwingli, Oecolampadius, Bucer, and Capito. Pierre Toussain, an old friend from France, remained an important colleague, and he, too, broke with Marguerite's network relatively early. Although Toussain would separate from the Calvinists after the Servetus affair, for more than twenty-five years, he would be among Farel's closest allies.[27] Thus, in 1526, Farel's vision for the future of evangelical reform shifted, and his path to leadership of that movement now led through the international Reformed community rather than Marguerite's network in France.

More than anyone, Farel himself turned French reform Reformed. Farel's influence was particularly profound through two of his early books. His *Summaire* (1529) provided the first French Protestant summary of faith, and his *Manière et fasson* (1533) presented the first French Protestant liturgy.[28] These texts became crucial as French refugees, often former members of Marguerite's circle, fled to Switzerland and began to lead the congregations there. They may have had reservations about Farel's assaults on the Mass while they remained in France, but once they arrived in the Suisse romande, almost all seem to have embraced Farel's views and used his order of worship. Hence, well before Calvin's arrival in Geneva, the francophone pastorate was united behind the Reformed cause.

2.3. Farel's Network in the Suisse Romande, 1526–1536

By the time Farel rejected the position with the De la Marck family, he was already working new ground; he had found the Suisse romande. Most of the region was off-limits to him, for most of the Pays de Vaud lay under the control of either the duke of Savoy or the bishop of Lausanne. The treaties concluded

---

[26] Bruening, "Guillaume Farel et les réformateurs de langue allemande."

[27] On Toussain's break from Farel and Calvin, see 184–86.

[28] Guillaume Farel, *La maniere et fasson qu'on tient en baillant le sainct baptesme* . . . (Neuchâtel: Pierre de Vingle, 1533). English translation in Zuidema and Van Raalte, *Early French Reform*, 195–223. Although 1533 is the earliest publication date for this work, Farel likely composed parts of this book as early as 1528 or 1529. See Zuidema and Van Raalte, *Early French Reform*, 191.

after the Burgundian Wars (1474–1477), however, gave the canton of Bern control over several key outposts in the region.[29] In 1526, the Bernese had not yet officially adopted the Reformation (they would do so in 1528), but substantial factions both in the city council and among the ministers identified as Protestants. Some seem to have exerted their influence to support Farel on a mission to Aigle, one of Bern's territories in the Four Mandated Territories (*Quatre Mandements*) southeast of Lake Geneva. Farel's ministry in Aigle was the start of a ten-year phase of his career in Romandie that ended only in 1536 with Bern's conquest of the Pays de Vaud and Calvin's arrival in Geneva. Farel led the francophone reformers who trickled into the region from France, either escaping persecution or simply finding better religious and financial support from the Bernese. Farel's *Summaire* gave them a confession of faith, his *Maniere et fasson* gave them a liturgy, and his opposition to the Mass gave them a focal point for their assaults on the Catholic Church.

2.3.1. Farel, the Bernese, and the French Exiles

The surviving evidence indicates little dissension within the ranks of the pastors who joined Farel in the Suisse romande, several of whom had moved there at his encouragement. As early as 1528, Farel was pleading with his friends to send more French-speaking ministers his way.[30] He realized that there were several francophone areas either under Bern's control or allied to the city that could be evangelized with sufficient missionary effort. In 1528, Bern itself adopted Protestantism and wanted to see it spread throughout its francophone territories. These included the Four Mandated Territories and the Common Lordships (*bailliages communs/gemeine Herrschaften*), namely Orbe-Echallens, Murten, and Grandson, which were under the joint control of Bern and Catholic Fribourg. Moreover, although Neuchâtel was technically under the authority of Countess Jeanne de Hochberg, she had only recently regained possession of the *comté* from the Swiss.[31] In addition, Bern

---

[29] See Bruening, *Calvinism's First Battleground*, 26–29. For a much fuller treatment of Swiss politics on the eve of the Reformation, see Tom Scott, *The Swiss and Their Neighbors, 1450–1560: Between Accommodation and Aggression* (Oxford: Oxford University Press, 2017).

[30] For example, "Aliis opus esset ministris, sed extrudet eos Dominus; in qua re si nos iuvare potes, labora, quaeso." Herminjard 2:150, no. 244, Farel to Zwingli, Aigle, July 23, 1528.

[31] In 1512, the Swiss had annexed Neuchâtel in response to Count Louis d'Orléans-Longueville's decision to side with King Louis XII against the Swiss in the Italian Wars. In 1529, jurisdiction was restored to Countess Jeanne, but the Swiss, and particularly the Bernese, maintained a strong influence over the area in the following years. See *Guillaume Farel*, 209–14.

had signed treaties of *combourgeoisie*—effectively a military alliance with other reciprocal rights attached to it—with several city councils in the region, namely those of Payerne, Lausanne, and eventually Geneva. In most of these areas—Lausanne was an exception—the Bernese were able to exert political pressure on the local magistrates to allow Protestant preaching, and Farel himself spent time in each.

Farel could not do it alone, however, so he recruited help wherever he could find it. Most of his collaborators came from France, including a few of his former associates in Lefèvre's circle, such as Jean Lecomte, who had been in Meaux, and Thomas Malingre, who had preached at Blois in 1527. These two would later break from Farel, but in the early 1530s there is no sign of discord. Many others also found their way to Switzerland from France, including Antoine Marcourt and Jean Morand, who would later replace Calvin and Farel in Geneva; Mathurin Cordier, Calvin's teacher at the Collège de la Marche in Paris; Antoine Saunier, who would join Cordier in opposition to Marcourt and Morand; Antoine Froment, another early ally in Geneva; and André Zébédée, who would emerge in the late 1540s as the Calvinists' chief opponent. Zébédée would clash in Lausanne with one of Farel's few local recruits, Pierre Viret. A native of Orbe in the Pays de Vaud, Viret would lead the church in Lausanne and help make the city's Academy a bastion of Calvinism. All these individuals (except Zébédée) were active in the Suisse romande before Calvin's arrival and constituted the first network of francophone Reformed pastors with an official calling.

2.3.2. The Propaganda Campaign

The network's chief goal in the Suisse romande was the abolition of the Mass. Due to a provision in the peace treaty ending the First Kappel War, a parish in a Common Lordship could abolish the Mass with a simple majority of the heads-of-household in a vote called the *plus* (or *Mehr*).[32] The process, which required voting for either "the Mass" or "the Sermon," created an incentive among the reformers not just to disseminate positive Protestant teachings but also to develop incendiary propaganda against the Mass.[33] Several of the texts produced in the early 1530s by Pierre de Vingle's press specifically

---

[32] See Bruening, *Calvinism's First Battleground*, 33–36.
[33] See Bruening, *Calvinism's First Battleground*, 113–17.

targeted the Mass, including most famously the text involved in the 1534 Affair of the Placards, Marcourt's *True Articles on the Huge, Horrible, and Unbearable Abuses of the Papal Mass*.[34]

As the Affair of the Placards and Marcourt's *Petit traicté tres utile et salutaire de la saincte eucharistie* demonstrate, the treatises produced by Farel's network in Switzerland were intended not only, and perhaps not even primarily, for a local audience. They were targeting France and aimed to provoke rupture with the Catholic Church.[35] Another classic example of a text addressing an international audience is the pseudonymous *Confession et raison de la foy de maistre Noel Beda*, which certainly was not written by the famous conservative syndic of the Paris Faculty of Theology, nor published in Paris, as the title page indicates, but in Neuchâtel, having been written by one of Farel's associates. None of these works which circulated in France were produced in consultation with the central figures of Marguerite's network. Indeed, appearing as they did just when Marguerite's network was beginning to make real inroads in Paris, these polemical works likely irritated or even alarmed Marguerite and her associates. From Farel's perspective, however, his former colleagues in France needed prodding to embrace the Gospel openly. In 1531, he complained to Zwingli, "We have called with numerous letters those pious and suitable for the work of God. But the delights of France have so held them captive that they prefer to perish without fruit and to be silent under tyranny than to profess Christ openly."[36] Farel goes on to cite the example of Pierre Toussain, whom Oecolampadius and Farel had tried to call to Switzerland several times, noting that "he could never be drawn, until he

---

[34] [Antoine Marcourt], *Articles veritables sur les horribles, grandz et importables abuz de la Messe papalle* ([Neuchâtel]: [Pierre de Vingle], 1534). Other polemical works against the Mass included [Marcourt], *Petit traicté tres utile et salutaire de la saincte eucharistie de nostre Seigneur Jesuchrist* ([Neuchâtel]: [Pierre de Vingle], 1534); [Marcourt] and "Cephas Geranius," *Declaration de la Messe, le fruict d'icelle, la cause et moyen pourquoy et comment on la doibt maintenir* ([Neuchâtel]: [Pierre de Vingle], [1534]). The identity of the pseudonymous author Cephas Geranius has been much disputed, with Viret and Peter Cyro of Bern the most commonly cited candidates. See references in Bruening, *Calvinism's First Battleground*, 115n74; Hans Rudolf Lavater, "Kurzbiographien, II. Peter Cyro," in *Der Berner Synodus von 1532: Edition und Abhandlungen zum Jubiläumsjahr 1982*, edited by Gottfried Locher, 2 vols., 2:370–74 (Neukirchen-Vluyn: Neukirchener Verlag, 1984).

[35] On the aims and strategies of the Neuchâtel group, and how they differed from those of the early Calvin, see Nathalie Szczech, *Calvin en polémique: Une maïeutique du verbe*, Bibliothèque d'histoire de la Renaissance 10 (Paris: Classiques Garnier, 2016), 293–328.

[36] "Vocavimus crebris literis pios et ad opus Dei non ineptos. Verum delitiae Gallicae ita detinent captivos, ut malint sine fructu perire, et mussitabundi latere sub tyrannis, quam palam Christum profiteri." Herminjard 2:356, no. 351, Farel to Zwingli, Orbe, [July or August] 1531. This quotation suggests that despite the absence of extant letters, Farel was still in contact with his former colleagues in France, but the nature of their correspondence appears to have changed dramatically from the early 1520s.

went to you after having been expelled from France."[37] These statements reveal two important facts: First, Farel is highly critical of his former colleagues in France for refusing to "profess Christ openly." Second, he saw from the example of his friend Toussain that potentially the best way to draw ministers to Switzerland was to get them expelled from France.

Thus, the publishing program by Farel and his colleagues must be seen, at least in part, as a way to confront Lefèvre, Roussel, and the other members of Marguerite's network in France. Farel and his new network were convinced that vigorous confrontation over the Mass would either "provoke them to piety" or lead to more expulsions like that of Toussain, which would inevitably swell the ranks of Farel's allies in Switzerland. They were right. The royal crackdown following the Affair of the Placards did indeed lead several prominent French evangelicals to seek refuge in Switzerland, and many became ministers there. Thus, while the Placards were a catastrophe from the perspective of the national, royal reform pursued by Marguerite's network, they had exactly the effect Farel and his network sought. Previously covert evangelicals were exposed and came to the Suisse romande to profess the Gospel openly.

2.3.3. Early Anti-Nicodemism

The singular focus on the Mass in the Suisse romande also supported the evolution of a strong anti-Nicodemite position among Farel and his associates. While this position, too, is usually associated with Calvin, Farel and his colleagues clearly laid the groundwork for Calvin's arguments well before the latter's arrival in Geneva. In part, their anti-Nicodemite rhetoric may have been an effort to shame sympathetic local clergy in Romandie, impelling them to join the Reformed cause. It also became a means, however, to confront once again the members of Marguerite's network.

One of the first "anti-Nicodemite" passages was printed in 1534 by the pseudonymous Cephas Geranius[38] in the appendix to Marcourt's *Declaration de la Messe*:

---

[37] "Quod expertus est frater pius qui isthic nunc agit, Petrus Toussanus, per Oecolampadium saepe huc vocatus literis, quibus nostras frequentes addidimus. Verum adduci nunquam potuit, donec e Galliis pulsus ad te se contulit." Herminjard 2:356, no. 351.
[38] On the identity of "Cephas Geranius," see n. 34.

And above all, you scoundrel who completely understands the truth, how dare you procure, hold, and retain benefices [*benefices*] that should rightly be called venomous potions [*venefices*] proceeding from this filthy, vile, and abominable source of Rome? You know that these are the goods of anathema, more horrible than those of conquered Jericho. You know very well that in accepting bishoprics, abbeys, parishes, and canonries, you consent to all the abominations against God's honor that take place daily in those places. What excuse can you make before God and men, seeing as you know by the Word of God that these are nothing but abuses?[39]

In 1536, around the time of Lefevre's death, Farel sent a letter expressing similar sentiments to his former Meaux colleague Michel d'Arande. In 1526, Arande had become bishop of Saint-Paul-Trois-Châteaux.[40] Although Farel's letter is lost, Arande's response indicates that Farel had scolded him for accepting and retaining his episcopal position: "I ask and beg you through our Lord Jesus Christ to assist me with your continuous prayers and never to cease from your exhortations until I can finally be freed from this deep mire in which there is no substance."[41] Whether or not Arande was serious about his desire either to "leave the mire" or to be continuously harassed by Farel, the point is that Farel, together with "Geranius" before him, believed that continued employment in the Catholic Church was utterly unacceptable. Finally, Farel alluded to his former friend Roussel in his concluding arguments at the Lausanne Disputation in October 1536. Here, his argument is based on the poor example that continued attendance at the Mass sets for the common people:

We must consider what edifies and can serve our neighbor. . . . And so those people greatly sin who know well the abuse and abomination of the things established and ordained by the popes and all their estate. . . . They

---

[39] "Et encore sur tout, toy miserable qui as entiere intelligence de verité, comme ose tu procurer, prendre, et retenir les benefices que justement on debvroit nommer venefices procedans de ceste orde, villaine, et abominable source de Romme? Tu scais que ce sont biens de anathema plus horrible que celuy de Hierico conquis. Tu ne ignore point en recevant Evesché, Abbaye, Cure, Chanoinerie, que tu consens à toutes les abominations qui se sont journellement èsdictz lieux contre l'honneur de Dieu. Quelle excusation peulx tu pretendre devant dieu, et devant les hommes, veu que tu scais par la parolle de dieu que ce ne sont que abuz?" Marcourt and Geranius, *Declaration de la Messe*, F3r°–F3v°.

[40] Veissière, *L'évêque Guillaume Briçonnet*, 370.

[41] "Quare, ne te diutius impediam, rogo te atque obtestor per eundem Dominum nostrum Iesum, ut me continuis vestris precibus adiuvetis, atque interim vestris exhortationibus semper sollicitare non desistatis, quo tandem ex hoc profundo limo, in quo non est substantia, eripi queam." Herminjard 3:401, no. 544, Arande to Farel, [Saint-Paul-Trois-Châteaux?], [mid-March 1536].

are found in their idolatries with head uncovered and knees bent before images at the masses and offices that the priests perform, and they say that they do not hold the image of any more account than a dead dog, nor the host of the priest more than a turnip . . . and do not think of anything but of God, whom they revere from the heart, as He knows. . . . Even in their heart they detest and hold in abomination the estate and all that is of the papal church, and in brief, all that is not from the pure word of God as contrary to God. . . . But others who began a bit to understand and detest the papal abominations and to leave the huge shadows, seeing such persons do these things, are ruined and return to idolatry, believing that it does not displease God . . . since one such preacher, who defended himself against the entire Sorbonne, chants the Mass and knows what he is doing.[42]

From a general denunciation of anyone who knows the truth but refuses to act accordingly, Farel turns to castigating a single person, and he seems to be referring specifically to Roussel, who had defended himself against the Sorbonne but accepted the bishopric of Oloron in February 1536.[43] Farel continues to lambast Roussel in his speech at the disputation:

Thus, the poor brother and the poor people perish because of you, in what you do, and God will demand their soul and their blood of your hand. . . . Demolisher and destroyer of people, you serve the devil! You dishonor God, neither loving nor serving him, since you do not love your neighbor, whom you abandon and destroy, confounded and given to perdition.[44]

[42] "fault que nous regardions ce que edifie et peult servir à nostre prochain. . . . En quoy grandement pechent et faillent ceux qui bien sçavent l'abus et l'abomination des choses constituées et ordonnées par les papes et tout son estat . . . ilz se trouvent en leurs idolatries la teste descouverte et les genoux ployez devant les imaiges, aux messes et offices que les prestres font, et disent qu'ilz ne tiennent compte de l'imaige non plus que d'un chien mort, ne de l'oblie du prestre non plus que d'une piecce de rave . . . et qu'ilz ne font aucune reverence à rien, et ne pensent à rien que à Dieu, auquel de cueur font reverence, comme il sçait . . . mais, mesme en leur cueur, ilz detestent et ont en abomination l'estat et tout ce qui est de l'eglise papale, et, en somme, de tout ce qui n'est par la pure parolle comme chose contraire à Dieu . . . Et ceux qui commençoient aucunement à entendre et detester les abominations papales et sortir de grosses tenebres, voians telz personnaiges ainsi faire, sont ruinez et retournent à l'idolatrie, en croiant qu'elle ne desplaist à Dieu . . . puis que ung tel prescheur, qui a maintenu son dire contre toute la Sorbonne, chante messe, il sçait bien qu'il faict." Arthur Piaget, ed., *Les actes de la Dispute de Lausanne 1536, publiés intégralement d'après le manuscrit de Berne*, Mémoires de l'Université de Neuchâtel 6 (Neuchâtel: Secrétariat de l'Université, 1928), 396–97.

[43] Frans Pieter Van Stam, "The Group of Meaux as the First Target of Farel and Calvin's Anti-Nicodemism, *BHR* 68 (2006): 253–75, here, 257–62.

[44] "Ainsy le povre frere et le povre peuple perit à cause de toy, en ce que tu fays, et Dieu demandera son ame et son sang de ta main . . . Ruyneur et destructeur de peuple, tu sers au diable. Tu deshonorez Dieu, ne l'aymant et ne luy servant, puis que tu n'aymes ton prochain, lequel tu perdz et destruictz, confondz et meines à perdition." Piaget, ed., *Les actes de la Dispute de Lausanne*, 397.

Roussel's acceptance of the bishopric of Oloron made the split between Marguerite's and Farel's networks complete. Calvin would soon attack Roussel as well, but he did not invent the anti-Nicodemite argument; he appropriated it from Farel and his colleagues.

2.3.4. Evangelical Success and Failure in Romandie

While Farel's network was actively expostulating in print against the Mass and closet evangelicals in France, they were also preaching to the people of the Suisse romande. Their efforts met with varied success. The people of Aigle vigorously resisted Farel for two years, but the Bernese held sole jurisdiction over that city. Once the Bernese adopted the Reformation in 1528, it was a matter of time before they imposed it on the people of Aigle and the Four Mandated Territories.[45] Farel's first major success was in Neuchâtel in November 1530, when he was able to engineer a victory in the *plus*.[46] Murten and a few small parishes in the Common Lordships likewise voted to abolish the Mass, but the vast majority, including the main towns of Orbe, Echallens, and Grandson, did not. Bern exerted some pressure on Lausanne, but the presence of the bishop, over whom they had no official diplomatic leverage, hindered their ability to proselytize there; Farel met with a chilly reception in Lausanne and was run out of town.[47] His greatest victory before 1536 was in Geneva. Although Geneva's adoption of Protestantism was enormously important to the early francophone Reformed community, one must not lose sight of the fact that the vast majority of towns in the Suisse romande remained Catholic until 1536.

The situation changed entirely when Bern conquered the Pays de Vaud in 1536, bringing the entire region under its jurisdiction.[48] In October of that year, Farel and Viret dominated the Lausanne Disputation against an almost entirely silent Catholic opposition.[49] Bern's two Edicts of Reformation

---

[45] See *Guillaume Farel*, 173–86; Bruening, *Calvinism's First Battleground*, 106–10.

[46] See *Guillaume Farel*, 224–30.

[47] *Guillaume Farel*, 188–89.

[48] For the details on the conquest, see Charles Gilliard, *La conquête du Pays de Vaud par les Bernois*, Histoire Helvétique (Lausanne: L'Aire, 1985 [Lausanne, 1935]).

[49] On the Lausanne Disputation, see the published acts in Piaget, ed., *Les Actes de la Dispute de Lausanne*; see also the collected articles in Eric Junod, ed., *La Dispute de Lausanne (1536): La théologie Réformée après Zwingli et avant Calvin*, Bibliothèque historique vaudoise 90 (Lausanne: Bibliothèque historique vaudoise, 1988).

followed, officially making the Pays de Vaud a Protestant territory.[50] The preachers, whose former role had them fighting Catholicism vigorously in the towns, now encountered no official opposition and found themselves at the head of an established church. Their preaching no longer focused on condemning the Mass; rather, they now had to defend Protestantism to people who had been forced to convert. It was not an easy task. Some preachers faced physical violence, others empty churches, others clandestine masses.[51] Many of the former Catholic clergy remained, for the Bernese allowed them to do so and to keep their benefices if they agreed to accept the Reformation. In these new circumstances, opposition to the Mass could no longer unify the members of Farel's network; they needed a new, positive doctrine to rally behind. Some—but by no means all—found it in the work of a French newcomer to the area: John Calvin.

2.4. The Calvinist Network

By the time John Calvin arrived in Geneva in 1536, the Reformed network constructed by Farel over the previous decade was well established. It consisted largely of French refugees and, following Farel, it had adopted Reformed doctrines and practice. Its members focused heavily on opposition to the Mass and had already adopted an anti-Nicodemite position aimed in part at Marguerite's French network. Farel had written a summary of faith and had produced a French liturgy for use in the churches. Thus, the francophone evangelicals active in Switzerland before Calvin's arrival were hardly the ragtag group of leaderless agitators that they are sometimes made out to be.[52] Circumstances changed dramatically, however, with Bern's 1536 conquest. Among the francophone reformers, no one could match the theological dexterity of Zwingli, Bullinger, Oecolampadius, or Bucer—until Calvin entered Romandie. In Calvin, francophone evangelicals found a theologian of the first rank. Farel himself soon adapted his theology to align with

---

[50] The edicts are published in *Sources du Droit Suisse* 19.C.1, 13–20, no. 2d–e, online at https://www.ssrq-sds-fds.ch/online/VD_C_1/index.html#p_13.

[51] On opposition to the new religion, see Bruening, *Calvinism's First Battleground*, 123–31; 147–60; 222–37; Sylvie Moret Petrin, "Ces Lausannois qui 'pappistent': Ce que nous apprennent les registres consistoriaux lausannois (1538–1540)," *Revue historique vaudoise* 119 (2011): 139–51.

[52] This caricature likely started with Calvin himself, who claimed on his deathbed, "Quand je vins premierement en ceste Eglise il n'y avoit quasi comme rien. On preschoit et puis c'est tout. On cerchoit bien les idoles et les brusloit-on, mais il n'y avoit aucune reformation." *CO* 9:891–92, *Discours d'adieu aux ministres*.

Calvin's thought. Later, following Calvin's return from exile in Strasbourg, Viret became one of Calvin's closest friends and brought Calvinian theology to the Lausanne Academy. These three men formed the core of the Calvinist network, prompting contemporaries to label them a "holy triumvirate."[53]

The triumvirate's central beliefs challenged the Reformed status quo. Between 1536 and 1541, Calvin's doctrine and sense of his own vocation shifted.[54] By 1541, with his return to Geneva from Strasbourg, Calvin's theology of the Eucharist departed significantly from Zwingli's by insisting on the real, spiritual presence of Christ in the Eucharist. Calvin also departed from Zwingli's political and ecclesiological thought, for he divorced the church from the secular magistrate, while Zwingli had united church and state. This theoretical division had two practical consequences. First, Calvin insisted that the church, through the body of elders usually called the consistory, should have the right of excommunication. Second, as we will see in the next chapter, Calvin and his followers believed that ecclesiastical goods, including those of the medieval Church, still belonged to the church. Consequently, the magistrate had no right to sell them and keep the profits for the state. A third central teaching (to be explored more fully in Chapter 4) was Calvin's controversial doctrine of double predestination, by which he claimed that God predestined both the elect for salvation and the reprobate for damnation. Thus, while Calvin provided evangelicals of the Suisse romande with a skilled theologian, he was far from a unifying figure. On the contrary, the unified group of Farel's early followers splintered in the face of Calvin's theological innovations.

2.4.1. Calvin's Shifting Position on Nicodemism, 1530–1536

Calvin's conversion to the evangelical faith is famously difficult to date.[55] He was, however, closely connected to members of Marguerite's network

[53] See Jean-François Gilmont, "La très sainte triade," chapter 1 of idem, *Insupportable mais fascinant: Jean Calvin, ses amis, ses ennemis, et les autres*, Nugae humanisticae sub signo Erasmi (Turnhout: Brepols, Musée de la Maison d'Érasme, 2012), 13–30; Michael Bruening, "Triumvirs, Patriarchs, or Friends? Evaluating the Relationship between Calvin, Viret, and Farel," *Reformation & Renaissance Review* 10 (2008): 125–36;

[54] Szczech, in particular, demonstrates how in the late 1530 and early 1540s Calvin largely abandoned his earlier aspirations as a French humanist in order to take up the polemical and theological combat of a Reformed pastor and theologian. Szczech, *Calvin en polémique*, 537–605.

[55] As François Wendel pithily sums up, "Calvin's conversion has been the topic of innumerable and not very interesting controversies." *Calvin: Origins and Development of His Religious Thought*,

from around 1530, when he briefly studied at the University of Bourges—in Marguerite's domains—under Melchior Wolmar.[56] The next few years, between about 1530 and 1534, have tied historians in knots, as they have tried to determine the exact nature of Calvin's religious beliefs at the time. In fact, he seems to have fit very well into Marguerite's network. The principal reason for the endless controversies has been an unrealistic expectation that Calvin was one day a Catholic and the next a fully Reformed Protestant.[57] As we saw in Chapter 1, the chief aim of Marguerite's network was to reform the church from within. Thus, for several years, Calvin quite likely saw himself as a humanist reformer much like Jacques Lefèvre d'Etaples and Gérard Roussel.[58] Calvin was, in short, a Nicodemite.

In 1533, Calvin was implicated in the controversial speech delivered by the new rector of the University of Paris, Nicolas Cop.[59] In the wake of this affair, he fled Paris, seeking refuge in Marguerite's Angoulême. After further wandering, first to Marguerite's Nérac, then to Noyon, where he resigned the benefices he had held since adolescence, Calvin made brief and poorly documented stays in Paris and Orléans. Finally, the harsh royal reaction to

---

translated by Philip Mairet (Grand Rapids. MI: Baker Books, 1963 [Paris, 1950]), 37. Wilhelm Neuser, following Paul Sprenger (*Das Rätsel um die Bekehrung Calvins*, Beiträge zur Geschichte und Lehre der Reformierten Kirche 11 (Neukirchen: Kreis-Moers, 1960)), persuasively suggests that a double conversion must be understood, first the *subita conversio ad docilitatem* mentioned by Calvin himself in his 1557 commentary on the Psalms and second, the *conversio ad fidem*, which came later. Neuser dates the "sudden conversion to teachableness" to 1528–1529 during Calvin's time in Orléans, with a more gradual "conversion to the faith" afterward, until his public proclamation of his new faith in the preface to the first edition of the *Institutes*. Wilhelm Neuser, "Stations: France and Basel," in *The Calvin Handbook*, edited by Herman J. Selderhuis, 23–30 (Grand Rapids, MI: Eerdmans, 2009), 25. Bruce Gordon likewise downplays the "sudden conversion" described in the Psalms commentary and points instead to Calvin's account in his 1539 letter to Sadoleto, where "he speaks of it in terms of gradual transition." Gordon, *Calvin*, 33.

[56] On Calvin's time in Orléans and Bourges, see Alexandre Ganoczy, *The Young Calvin*, translated by David Foxgrover and Wade Provo (Edinburgh: T&T Clark, 1987 [Wiesbaden, 1966]), 63–71.

[57] A good example is Wendel's discussion of Calvin's conversion. He describes a session of the Noyon chapter in August 1533, at which Calvin was present and at which it was decided to organize a procession against the plague. Wendel insists that Calvin's later anti-Nicodemism "render[s] it unthinkable that he already considered himself one of the reformed at that time." Wendel, *Calvin*, 39. On the contrary, as part of Marguerite's network, he quite likely considered himself an evangelical at the time (if not a full-blown—and anachronistic—"confessional Reformed Christian") and had not yet developed his anti-Nicodemite attitude toward those who participated in Catholic worship. After all, everyone around him still did.

[58] See Szczech, *Calvin en polémique*, 163–97; Neuser, "Stations: France and Basel," 25–26.

[59] On the speech and the reaction, see 27–28. Scholars debate whether Calvin had a hand in writing it. Ganoczy follows Karl Müller in believing that "the best solution is to acknowledge that the speech of Cop is simply that, a speech by Cop!" (*The Young Calvin*, 80). Neuser, however, states that "most researchers attribute the speech to Calvin" ("Stations: France and Basel," 26).

the Affair of the Placards seems to have prompted Calvin to leave France for good, and in January 1535, he arrived in Basel.[60]

Calvin's flight from France marks his initial break from Marguerite's network. At the time, however, he would not likely have characterized his departure this way. Indeed, in one of the most recent and interesting reappraisals of Calvin during this time, Natalie Szczech has argued that between 1535 and 1537, Calvin still thought of himself as a humanist intellectual between the two confessional camps.[61] Increasingly, however, he adopted Farel's view that hope for a reform-from-within was doomed in France and that a clean break from the Catholic Church was necessary. His definitive split from his former friends came with his brutal assault on Roussel and Nicolas Duchemin in the *Epistolae Duae*. This is his first attack on what would become known as "Nicodemism." Despite having been a Nicodemite himself for several years, Calvin instructed Duchemin to avoid polluting himself with "superstitious idolatry" and denied the possibility of dissimulation:

> There is no room, therefore, for anyone to indulge in crafty dissimulation, or to flatter himself with a false idea of piety, pretending that he cherishes it in his heart, though he completely overturns it by his outward behavior. Genuine piety begets genuine confession.[62]

Moreover, it was by no means acceptable, Calvin now believed, to hold a position within the Catholic hierarchy, as Roussel did.[63] In the following years, Calvin intensified his attack on Marguerite's network, publishing several further works against Nicodemism, attacking Antoine Poquet and Quintin of Hainaut in *Contra la secte des Libertins* (1545), and Heinrich Cornelius Agrippa, Étienne Dolet, and Rabelais in *De scandalis* (1550).[64] Once part of Marguerite's network, Calvin now sought actively to wrest influence over the French Reformation from the group's original members.

---

[60] Ganoczy labels 1534 Calvin's "Year of Wandering." *The Young Calvin*, 83–91.

[61] Nathalie Szczech, *Calvin en polémique*, 199–358.

[62] "Quare non est quod callida dissimulatione iam hic sibi quisquam placeat, aut falsa pietatis opinione blandiatur, eam se fovere in corde fingens, quam externis testificationibus prorsus evertat. Vera enim pietas veram confessionem parit." OS 1:294; translation from John Calvin, *Tracts Relating to the Reformation*, 4 vols., translated by Henry Beveridge (Edinburgh: Calvin Translation Society, 1844–1851), 3:366.

[63] See 35.

[64] Reid, *King's Sister*, 557–60.

2.4.2. Calvin's Introduction of Ecclesiastical
Discipline, 1536–1538

With the publication of the first edition of the *Institutes of the Christian Religion* (1536), Calvin launched himself suddenly onto the stage of international Reformed Protestantism.[65] More complete and better argued than Farel's *Summaire*, Calvin's *Institutes* was arguably the first major theological writing by a French Protestant. Farel and others recognized Calvin's talent, and Farel was eager to keep him in Geneva when he arrived there in 1536. He succeeded, and the two worked together to further reform Geneva, which had abolished the Mass before Calvin's arrival.

It did not take long, however, for the inhabitants of Geneva to learn that Calvin's arrival brought new demands from the city's ministers. In particular, the pastors demanded unprecedented conformity to their doctrine and sought to regulate the moral behavior of the citizens.[66] This was Calvin's doctrine of ecclesiastical discipline in action. In particular, he believed that the church needed to have the power of excommunication.[67] In his *Instruction et confession* of 1536, Calvin explained:

> Excommunication is the means by which open lechers, adulterers, thieves, murderers, etc., if they do not mend their ways after being warned, are according to the commandment of God rejected from the company of the faithful. . . . Now, this discipline is necessary among the faithful, since the

[65] See, for example, Leo Jud's letter to him full of praise for the work: "Quum enim nuper tua legerem, vir eruditissime, cerneremque omnia tam esse docta, elegantia insuper et fortia, quae tu pro Christo in adversarios veritatis torques et eiacularis, quibus eos tenes et stringis, ut elabendi nulla eis via pateat, quum rursum expenderem fidei dogmata tam esse solida tamque firma taliqe arte tradita ut vel nolentem vincere possent ac persuadere, ingenti quadam laetitia cor meum perfusum est, ita ut in me subsiliret, quin et os meum coram throno coelestis Regis in laudem et gratiarum actionem erupit." *Calv. Ep.* 1:125, no. 24, Jud to Calvin, Zurich [after March 1536].

[66] On Calvin and Farel's efforts to require obedience to a new confession of faith, see Robert Kingdon, "Confessionalism in Calvin's Geneva," *ARG* 96 (2005): 109–16. In essence, they sought to require an oath of allegiance to a new confession of faith, Farel's *Confession de la foy, laquelle tous bourgeois et habitans de Genève et subjets du pays doivent jurer de garder et tenir*, printed in CO 22:77–96. This was a distillation of Calvin's own *Instruction et confession de foy dont on use en l'église de Genève* (CO 22: 25–74). In Kingdon's words, "There was massive popular resistance to it" ("Confessionalism in Geneva," 112).

[67] On Calvin's ideas about ecclesiastical discipline, see Christian Grosse, *L'excommunication de Philibert Berthelier: Histoire d'un conflit d'identité aux premiers temps de la Réforme genevoise, 1547–1555* (Geneva: Société d'histoire et d'archéologie de Genève, 1995), 13–50; Harro Höpfl, *The Christian Polity of John Calvin* (New York: Cambridge University Press, 1982), 58–70, 115–21; Robert M. Kingdon, "La discipline ecclésiastique vue de Zurich et Genève au temps de la Réformation: L'usage de Matthieu 18, 15–17 par les réformateurs," *Revue de théologie et de philosophie* 133 (2001): 343–55.

church is the body of Christ, and it should not be polluted and contaminated by such depraved members who bring dishonor to the head.[68]

Calvin's position was not entirely new to the Reformed faith. Oecolampadius had supported the use of excommunication in Basel several years before Calvin.[69] Perhaps under Oecolampadius's influence, Farel had also supported the continued use of excommunication. In his *Summaire*, Farel writes, "Excommunication is barring from the table of our Lord him who is in sin and who has not pulled back from it after the admonition of one, two, or three, and after that of the whole congregation of our Lord. . . . It is a loving correction and full of charity, to pull the poor sinners out of their sins."[70] Here, too, therefore, Calvin was perhaps not as original as scholars have claimed. Calvin's rationale, however, differed markedly from that of Farel, who discusses excommunication almost entirely in terms of correcting those who have gone astray. Calvin, by contrast, emphasizes the pollution of the body of Christ caused by unworthy communicants. Moreover, he insists that excommunication derives from the power of the keys given to the apostles by Christ. Farel and the other Geneva ministers quickly lined up behind Calvin, and in January 1537, they presented to the Geneva council a list of requirements they believed should be imposed on the church. The "principal order required," they argued, was that the Lord's Supper "not be polluted and contaminated" by those whose wicked lives show that they do not belong to Jesus, "for in this profanation of the sacrament, our Lord is greatly dishonored."[71] They went on to request that the council

[68] "Excommunication est par laquelle les manifestes paillars, adulteres, larrons, homicides . . . , s'ilz ne se amendent apres avoir esté admonestez, sont selon le commandement de Dieu rejectez de la compagnie des fideles. . . . Or, ceste discipline est necessaire entre les fideles, pourtant que, veu que l'Eglise est le corps de Christ, elle ne doibt pas estre pollué et contaminée par telz membres punais et pourriz, lesquelz tournent à deshonneur au chef." *CO* 22:72; translation from Bruening, *A Reformation Sourcebook*, 121–22.

[69] See Olaf Kuhr, *"Die Macht des Bannes und der Buße": Kirchenzucht und Erneuerung der Kirche bei Johann Oekolampad (1482–1531)*, Basler und Berner Studien zur historischen und systematischen Theologie 68 (Bern: Peter Lang, 1999); also, Kuhr's distillation of his arguments in English: "Calvin and Basel: The Significance of Oecolampadius and the Basel Discipline Ordinance for the Institution of Ecclesiastical Discipline in Geneva," *Scottish Bulletin of Theology* 16 (1998): 19–33.

[70] "Excommuniement, ou excommunication est rejection de la table de nostre Seigneur d'iceluy qui est en peché duquel il a esté admonesté de ung, de deux, ou de troys, puis de toute la congregation de nostre Seigneur (c'est de ceulx de sa parroisse) de soy retirer, lequel n'en a rien faict. . . . C'est une correction amyable et pleine de charité pour tirer les paovres pecheurs de leurs pechez." Farel, *Sommaire*, 78; translation from Zuidema and Van Raalte, *Early French Reform*, 156.

[71] "Mays le principal ordre qui est requis et duquel il convient avoyr la plus grande sollicitude, c'est que ceste saincte cene—ordonnée et instituée pour conjoindre les membres de nostre Seigneur Jesuchrist avecq leur chefz et entre eux mesmes en ung corps et ung esprit—ne soyt souillé et contaminée, si ceux qui se declairent et manifestent par leur meschante et inique vie n'appertenir

elect certain persons of good life and reputation . . . to keep an eye on the life and conduct of each person. And if they see some notable vice to correct in some person, they should talk to the pastors in order to admonish and fraternally encourage him to correct himself. And if one sees that such warnings do no good, they should warn him that his obstinacy will be reported to the church. . . . And if he perseveres in his hardness of heart, then it will be time to excommunicate him.[72]

The Geneva magistrates shuddered at this project. Some saw it as a heavy-handed attempt by the pastors both to restrict the freedom of Geneva's citizens and to take for themselves power that should belong to the council. Opposition to Calvin and Farel increased among members of the council after the presentation of these articles and centered on two elements in particular: first, their attempt to require that all Genevan citizens swear an oath accepting their confession of faith and, second, the pastors' insistence on the right of excommunication. In early 1538, Calvin and Farel announced that they would refuse to give communion to anyone who sowed discord in the city. The council responded by ordering that no one be denied communion. On Easter 1538, Calvin and Farel ignored the council's demands and refused to administer the sacrament. The council banished them from the city.[73]

Calvin's first phase in Geneva was brief, just the year and a half from autumn 1536 to spring 1538, but it was instrumental in forging some of the foundational doctrines of his network, namely the independence of the church from secular authority and the necessity of moral discipline and excommunication under the jurisdiction of the church. These teachings challenged the Zwinglian position held by most francophone pastors in the region and by the politically powerful Bernese. For them, church and

nullement à Jesus, viennent à y communiquer. Car en ceste profanation de son sacrement nostre Seigneur est grandement deshonoré." *Calv. Ep.* 1:162–63, no. 31, [Geneva Ministers] to the Geneva Council, [Geneva], [shortly before January 14, 1537].

[72] "Et pour ce faire nous avons desliberé requerir de vous, que vostre playsir soy ordonner et eslire certaynes personnes de bonne vie et de bon tesmoignage entre tous les fideles . . . ayant l'oil sus la vie et gouvernement d'ung chascun; et s'il voyent quelque notable vice à reprendre en quelque personne, qu'il en communiquent avecq quelcung des ministres pour admonester—quicunque sera celluy lequel sera en faulte—et l'exorter fraternellement de se corriger. Et si on veoyt, que telles remonstrances ne profitent rien, le advertir que on signiffiera à l'esglise son obstination. . . . Adoncques on cognoestra s'il veult perseverer en la dureté de son cueur, et lors sera temps de l'excommunier." *Calv. Ep.* 1:165, no. 31.
[73] The events leading to the banishment of Calvin and Farel in 1538 are well known and rehearsed in almost every Calvin biography. See, for example, Gordon, *Calvin*, 78–81.

state were distinct, but not separate in the sense that Calvin desired. Thus, there was only one proper authority with coercive power, the city council. Likewise, the Zwinglians embraced essentially only one kind of excommunication, namely political banishment. The banishment of Calvin and Farel themselves illustrates both sides of the argument perfectly. When they refused to administer communion, in effect excommunicating the town, the town responded by banishing them from the city.

2.4.3. The Formation of the Calvinist Network

By the time of their exile, Calvin and Farel had already begun to construct a new Calvinist network that was slowly replacing the old Farellian group. Their most important ally, and increasingly their most frequent correspondent, was Pierre Viret in Lausanne. A network analysis of their surviving correspondence between 1536 and 1544 clearly demonstrates that they were more closely bound to one another than to anyone else (see Figure 2.1).

It shows too that their connections to the leading reformers of German-speaking Switzerland were still strong. Likewise, Pierre Toussain in Montbéliard remained an important figure for them. One sees, in particular, a lively correspondence developing between Calvin and Simon Sulzer in Bern, Simon Grynaeus and Oswald Myconius in Basel, and Heinrich Bullinger in Zurich. Thus, the connections with the German-speaking Reformed leaders that Farel had initially forged remained strong. Similarly, Farel's earlier break from Marguerite's network persisted; very few letters survive between the Calvinist triumvirate and evangelicals who chose to remain in France.[74] Moreover, as we will see in the next chapter, the connections with the other francophone pastors in Romandie were also starting to fray.

Viret's support for Calvin was especially important because Lausanne was the chief city in the Pays de Vaud and the site of the first Protestant Academy in French-speaking Europe, predating the Geneva Academy by twenty years.[75] While the Lausanne Academy was not a seminary dedicated only to

---

[74] Of course, the absence of surviving letters does not mean that no correspondence was exchanged. The evidence suggests that there was still some contact, but it also indicates that the relationship between the Calvinists and Marguerite's network was fraying badly in the 1540s and 1550s. See Reid, *King's Sister*, 550–63.

[75] On the Lausanne Academy, see Karine Crousaz, *L'Académie de Lausanne entre Humanisme et Réforme (ca. 1537-1560)*, Education and Society in the Middle Ages and Renaissance 41 (Leiden: Brill, 2012).

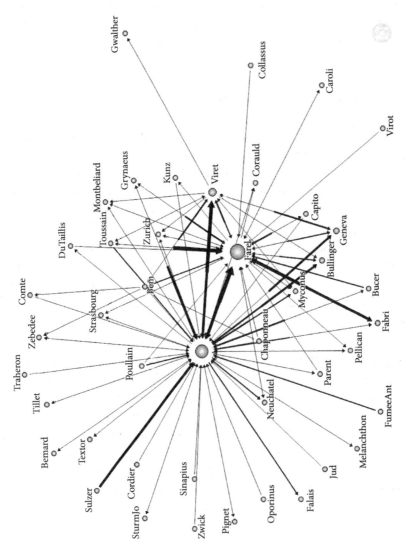

Figure 2.1 Network analysis of Calvin, Farel, and Viret's correspondence, 1536–1544

training future ministers, pastoral formation was part of its purpose from the beginning. From 1537, Viret lectured on the Bible in Lausanne and played an important role in recruiting professors; in this way, he tried to ensure that those who came to Lausanne were allies. He did not always succeed— notably, for example, he failed to get Farel an appointment at the Academy— but during most of Viret's career in Lausanne, most of the professors could be counted on as reliable members of the Calvinist network. Calvin's former teacher Mathurin Cordier taught there after 1545. Later, Huguenot political thinker François Hotman briefly held a low-level teaching position. Perhaps most importantly, Theodore Beza arrived in Lausanne in 1549 as a professor of Greek. Along with their allies, these individuals, particularly Viret and Beza, ensured that, until 1559, the Lausanne Academy remained the strongest bastion of Calvinism in the Pays de Vaud.

2.4.4. The Calvinist Doctrinal Trinity: Excommunication, the Eucharist, and Predestination

After Calvin's return from exile to Geneva in 1541, new disputes arose in the Suisse romande that continued both to bind Calvin's network together and drive others away. The most important new controversies concerned the interpretation of the Eucharist and the doctrine of predestination. On the Eucharist, Calvin believed that Zwingli's symbolic doctrine, which was widely supported by the francophone pastors in the region, left the sacrament an empty shell. Calvin taught instead that "the signs are the bread and the wine, under which the Lord presents to us the true, spiritual communication of his body and blood. . . . Christ with all his riches is presented to us there no less than if he were placed in the presence of our eyes and was touched by our hands."[76] This doctrine of the real, spiritual presence of Christ in the sacrament departed significantly from Farel's commemorative interpretation in the *Summaire*.[77]

---

[76] "Les signes sont le pain et le vin, soubz lesquelz le Seigneur nous presente la vraye communication de son corps et de son sang, mais spirituelle. . . . Christ avec toutes ses richesses nous y est presenté non pas moins que s'il estoit mis en la presence de noz yeulz et estoit touché de noz mains." Calvin, *Instruction et confession*, CO 22:69–70. Richard Muller describes Calvin's early Eucharistic thought as primarily "Melanchthonian." See also his bibliographic references to other scholarship on the same subject in "De Zurich ou Bâle à Strasbourg? Étude sur les prémices de la pensée eucharistique de Calvin," *BSHPF* 155 (2009): 41–53.

[77] See 40–42.

Likewise, on the subject of predestination, Farel's *Summaire* says almost nothing, while Calvin's discussion of faith in his *Instruction and Confession* places it front and center:

> The seed of the word of God takes root and bears fruit only in those whom the Lord by his eternal election has predestined as his children and heirs of the heavenly kingdom. To all others, who by the same counsel of God before the creation of the world are rejected, the clear and evident preaching of the truth cannot be anything but the stench of death in death.[78]

From the beginning of his career, then, Calvin expressed this doctrine of double predestination by which God, before the creation of the world, both elected those who would be saved and condemned those who would be damned. Although it would be several years before resistance to Calvin developed around this issue, opposition would burst forth in the 1550s and shake not just the Suisse romande but much of Protestant Europe.

These three doctrines—excommunication, the Eucharist, and predestination—and their corollaries would become the doctrinal nodes that linked Calvin's network together. By contrast, opposition to Calvin's position on any of these issues put one outside Calvin's circle of trusted allies. Later, as the French Reformed churches began to organize, two additional teachings became central, namely the primacy of the consistories in the appointment of pastors and the acknowledgment of the French synods as the proper arbiter in matters of doctrine and practice. Networks of francophone evangelicals emerged in opposition to each of these issues and to Calvin's— and later Beza's—leadership in general. Calvin's circle would not always prevail, and the Calvinists' victory was never a foregone conclusion. Nor was it as complete as Calvin's followers would have us believe. His opponents were fierce, frequently united, and occasionally successful. It is to them that we must now turn our attention.

---

[78] "car la semence de la parolle de Dieu prent racine et fructifie en ceux-là seulement lesquelz le Seigneur par son election eternelle a predestiné pour ses enfans et heretiers du royaulme celeste. A tous les autres, qui par mesme conseil de Dieu devant la constitution du monde sont reprouvez, la claire et evidente predication de verité ne peult estre aultre chose sinon odeur de mort en mort." Calvin, *Instruction et confession, CO* 22:46; translation from Bruening, *A Reformation Sourcebook*, 120.

3

Anti-Calvinists
of Francophone Switzerland

3.1. Introduction

For ten years after Guillaume Farel's arrival in the Suisse romande in 1526, there was little conflict among the evangelical reformers. Farel and his associates united against the Mass, "papist superstition," and anything that smacked of "popery." After Bern's 1536 imposition of Protestantism in the Pays de Vaud, however, the reformers discovered that it was easier to unite against a common enemy than to agree on a common alternative. As long as the Farellists were criticizing Catholic priests and attacking the Mass, they had little trouble finding common cause. When they had to create a positive program for change, however, their alliance began to crack, and the fissures widened with time.

The first major challenge came from Pierre Caroli (1480–1550), a former member of the Meaux group and a doctor of the Sorbonne. Almost immediately upon his arrival in Geneva in 1535, Caroli came into conflict with Farel. The reasons for their mutual hostility are not entirely clear, but a clash of egos was at least partly to blame; the Sorbonne doctor did not want to play second fiddle to a firebrand who could barely write Latin, while the indefatigable missionary refused to yield leadership over the movement he had created and on which he had expended so much time and energy. Later, Caroli sought to bring with him to Romandie a variation of the French model of reform, a quasi-diocesan program like that of Briçonnet and Roussel which would have made Caroli himself effectively bishop of Lausanne. Better known are the struggles that pitted the Calvinists against Caroli over his prayer for the dead and his accusations of Arianism against Calvin and Farel, but these disputes merely exacerbated tensions that had been roiling the Swiss evangelical community for some time.

Caroli had allies in his disputes with Farel, probably more than have hitherto been acknowledged. Among his strong supporters was a friend from

Refusing to Kiss the Slipper. Michael W. Bruening, Oxford University Press (2021). © Oxford University Press.
DOI: 10.1093/oso/9780197566954.003.0004

Meaux, Jean Lecomte,[1] and Lecomte's friend Thomas Malingre.[2] Antoine Marcourt, who probably called Caroli to the Reformed ministry, supported him as well.

When Calvin and Farel were exiled from Geneva in 1538, Marcourt replaced them, alongside Jean Morand, another refugee doctor of theology from Paris. The Calvinists in Geneva and elsewhere bitterly opposed these new pastors because their call came directly from the Geneva magistrates, without consultation of the other pastors. By accepting the positions, Marcourt and Morand implicitly rejected the developing Calvinist

[1] Jean Lecomte (or Le Comte, sometimes with "de la Croix" added—in Latin *Cruciatus*) was born in Picardy around 1500. Like Calvin, he studied with Mathurin Cordier at the Collège de la Marche in Paris, and later also with Jacques Lefèvre d'Etaples. He joined Briçonnet, Lefèvre, and Roussel in Meaux, where he met Pierre Caroli. Although the details are scant, he seems to have been in Marguerite of Navarre's circle throughout the 1520s, possibly working in Béarn. Probably in 1532, he arrived in Switzerland, where he joined Farel's missionary efforts. He traveled around in the early years, but then became pastor of Grandson, where he remained most of his life. Details of Lecomte's biography are difficult to discern; as both Reinhard Bodenmann and Geneviève Gross have noted—independently and almost simultaneously—the chief source on Lecomte's life, his alleged *Journal*, was, in fact, a later compilation heavily edited by a descendant. Excerpts of this text were published by Henri Vuilleumier, "Quelques pages inédites d'un réformateur trop peu connu," *Revue de théologie et de philosophie* 19 (1886): 313–39; on this text, see Geneviève Gross, "Pratique du ministère et terrains d'activité de deux acteurs de la Réforme: Jean Reymond Merlin (1510–1578) et Jean Lecomte de la Croix (1500–1572)" (PhD diss., University of Geneva, 2012), esp. ch. 5; Reinhard Bodenmann, "Le réformateur Jean Le Comte (1500–1572): De l'oubli à une mémoire remodelée," *Zwingliana* 42 (2015): 177–93; Reinhard Bodenmann, *Les Perdants: Pierre Caroli et les débuts de la Réforme en Romandie*, Nugae humanisticae (Turnhout: Brepols, 2016), 175–86, 381–415. The other primary works on Lecomte, but which must now be read in the light of Gross's and Bodenmann's findings, are Edouard Besson, "Jean Le Comte de la Croix: Un réformateur peu connu," *Berner Taschenbuch* 26 (1876): 139–68; and Edouard Bähler, *Jean Le Comte de la Croix: Ein Beitrag zur Reformationsgeschichte der Westschweiz* (Biel: Ernst Kuhn, 1895).

[2] Thomas (*alias* Mathieu) Malingre was a former Dominican from a noble family in Normandy. He claims to have preached evangelical sermons in Blois in 1527. It is possible that he was in Switzerland as early as 1531, but his presence there cannot be confirmed until 1533, when he started publishing texts with the Neuchâtel printer, Pierre de Vingle. Malingre was a poet and used his nom de plume Mathieu for almost all his publications. These included *Moralité de la maladie de Chrestienté, à xiii personnages: en laquelle sont monstrez plusieurs abuz, advenuz au monde, par la poison de peché et l'hypocrisie des hereticques* ([Neuchâtel]: [Pierre de Vingle], 1533); *S'ensuivent plusieurs belles et bonnes chansons, que les chrestiens peuvent chanter en grande affection de cueur* ([Neuchâtel]: [Pierre de Vingle], 1533); *Noelz nouveaulx* ([Neuchâtel]: [Pierre de Vingle], [1533?]); *Chansons nouvelles demonstrantz plusieurs erreurs et faulsetez, desquelles le paovre monde est remply par les ministres de Satan* ([Neuchâtel]: [Pierre de Vingle], [1534?]); *L'Epistre de M. Malingre envoyée à Clement Marot, en laquelle est demandée la cause de son departement de France* (Basel: Jacques Estauge, 1546); and *Indice des principales matieres contenues en la Bible* (Geneva: Jean Girard, 1543), the text of which first appeared in Olivétan's 1535 Bible. Malingre became pastor in Yverdon in 1536, where he stayed most of his life, except for a ten-year period from 1546 to 1556 when he was pastor in Aubonne. He died in 1572 in Vuarrens. On Malingre, see Théophile Dufour, *Notice bibliographique sur le Catéchisme et la Confession de foi de Calvin (1537) et sur les autres livres imprimés à Genève et à Neuchâtel dans les premiers temps de la Réforme (1533-1540)* (Geneva: Jules-Guillaume Fick, 1878), 48–52; Vuilleumier, 1:385–86. A list of Malingre's publications may be found in Francis M. Himan, *Piety and the People: Religious Printing in French, 1511-1551*, St. Andrews Studies in Reformation History (Aldershot, UK: Ashgate, 1996), 301–3.

ecclesiology that called for pastoral elections to be performed by their future colleagues, embracing instead the Bernese Zwinglian model, in which the pastors are effectively civil servants who serve at the pleasure of the Christian magistrate. Marcourt's support for this model became still clearer in his conflict with Pierre Viret over Bern's sale of church goods in the Pays de Vaud. Unlike Viret, Marcourt accepted the Bern council's assertion of its right to sell goods confiscated from the Catholic Church and to do as it pleased with the revenues.

Marcourt's opposition to Viret on this account was one prong of the developing resistance to Calvinist ideas that Farel and Viret sought to implement after Calvin's return to Geneva in 1541. Both of Calvin's friends failed in their initial efforts to influence official policy. They did, however, bring most of the pastors in Geneva, Neuchâtel, and Lausanne under the Calvinist banner. By contrast, their opponents created anti-Calvinist bastions in their own regions: Lecomte and Malingre in Yverdon, Morand and Jacques Le Coq in Morges, and Marcourt in the Pays de Gex. By 1545, therefore, the Suisse romande was fairly evenly distributed in geographic terms between Calvin's opponents and his followers.

3.2. Pierre Caroli and the Origins of the Opposition

Pierre Caroli's contemporaries attacked him viciously, calling him a "wicked apostate" (Beza)[3] and "a hydra with seven heads . . . [although] the hydra never had as many heads as he holds contradictory opinions" (Viret);[4] they described him as one "abandoned by God . . . not only deprived of reason and judgment but also obsessed with cruelty, who asks only to drink blood like a wild beast" (Calvin and Viret).[5] Even modern scholars speak of him with scarcely disguised contempt, describing him as a "sometime Reformer

---

[3] Théodore de Bèze, *Vie de Calvin* (1565), *CO* 21:59.

[4] "Il troubloit chacun par ses sophisteries, et estoit comme le serpent nommé Hydra, qui avoit sept testes . . . Hydra n'eut jamais tant de testes, qu'il a d'opinions contraires les unes aux autres." Pierre Viret, *Disputations chrestiennes, touchant l'estat des trepassez, faite par dialogues* ([Geneva]: [Jean Girard], 1552), 259–60. Viret discusses Caroli at some length in this text; see also pp. 252–62; 281–84.

[5] "Ce qui nous a meuz de faire imprimer l'un et l'autre [textes] a esté premierement pour representer, comme en un miroir, que c'est d'un homme abandonné de Dieu comme Caroly. Car il se monstre en ceste Epistre estre du tout hors du sens, et non seulement desprouveu de jugement et raison, mais forcené en cruauté, qui ne demande que boir le sang comme une beste enraigée." *CO* 9:840 (*Préface des lettres de Farel à Caroli*).

and apostate,"[6] whose "natural instability did not allow him to follow consistently a single and clearly defined line."[7] It is not difficult to understand the basis for this almost universal contempt for Caroli, for he switched camps during the Reformation—officially anyway—at least four times, from Catholic to Protestant to Catholic to Protestant and finally back to Catholic. If one counts his various recantations before the Paris Faculty of Theology, the number of such reversals increases significantly. In the days before strict confessional adherence was the Reformation norm, however, it is better to think of Caroli not as a serial apostate but as someone who never fit comfortably in either the Protestant or Catholic camp. In *Ni Rome ni Genève*,[8] Thierry Wanegffelen points to Caroli as his first example of the "faithful between two pulpits," and James Farge notes, "Caroli could never be a martyr, since he could never agree fully enough with any established religion of his time to die for it. He could neither live nor die happily in the camp of a [Noël] Beda or of a Calvin."[9] Caroli certainly never fit in well with either Farel's or Calvin's network, and his opposition to Calvin, Farel, and Viret was the first major challenge to the trio in the Suisse romande.

3.2.1. Caroli's Early Career in France, 1520–1534

We first met Caroli in Chapter 1, for he was an important member of Marguerite of Navarre's network. A native of the diocese of Meaux (from Rozay-en-Brie), he returned there to join Briçonnet's circle after earning his doctorate in theology at the University of Paris. Nothing in his early career indicates the slightest hint of heterodoxy, and his doctoral examiner was the Sorbonne hardliner Guillaume Duchesne.[10] Upon entering the Meaux group, however, he began to fall under the constant scrutiny of the Sorbonne. In the decade starting in 1523, the Faculty of Theology discussed Caroli's case

---

[6] Richard Muller, *The Unaccommodated Calvin: Studies in the Foundation of a Theological Tradition*, Oxford Studies in Historical Theology (New York: Oxford University Press, 2000), 52.

[7] Ganoczy, *The Young Calvin*, 115. For a classic character assassination of Caroli by an eighteenth-century Reformed minister, but also a detailed account of the whole Caroli affair, see Abraham Ruchat, *Histoire de la Réformation de la Suisse, Edition avec appendices*, edited by Louis Vulliemin, 7 vols. (Nyon: M. Giral-Prelaz, 1835–1838), 5:17–42.

[8] Wanegffelen, *Ni Rome ni Genève*, 38–47.

[9] James K. Farge, *Biographical Register of Paris Doctors of Theology 1500–1536*, Subsidia Mediaevalia 10 (Toronto: Pontifical Institute of Mediaeval Studies, 1980), 71. More recently, Reinhard Bodenmann has published the most detailed and evenhanded account of Caroli to date in *Les Perdants*.

[10] Farge, *Biographical Register*, 66.

more than a hundred times.[11] They issued the first censure on September 26, 1523, and Caroli made his first retraction on January 16, 1524.[12] Six months later, Lefèvre reported to Farel that Caroli was preaching again in Meaux, and the Faculty of Theology reopened the case against him in August 1524; this time he refused to recant and was removed from the Faculty.[13] Marguerite then interceded, helping him find a benefice in or near Alençon and charging him to reform the hospital in Almenêches, north of Alençon.[14] After the Affair of the Placards, however, Caroli found his name at the top of the list of those accused of heresy. He fled the kingdom and found his way to Geneva.[15]

3.2.2. Caroli in Geneva, Basel, and Neuchâtel, 1535–1536

Caroli arrived in Geneva by May 1535 and soon had his first public confrontation with Farel. It is unclear how well the two men knew each other in France, for Caroli most likely arrived in Meaux after Farel had left the diocese. In Geneva, the two may have started out briefly as allies. Together with Viret, they visited the Dominican Guy Furbity in prison. Furbity, one of Caroli's former students, had debated Farel and Viret in Geneva in January 1534.[16] According to Jeanne de Jussie, a Catholic nun who chronicled the Reformation in Geneva,

> When [Furbity] saw his theology teacher and realized he was perverted, he fainted and fell to the floor. But they revived him, and Caroli said to him, "What, Friar Guy, do you want to die in your stubbornness and heresy? Up until now, we were in error, and at present we have seen the truth of the Gospel. Do you not wish to recognize your error and turn back to God?"[17]

---

[11] Farge, *Biographical Register*, 66.

[12] Farge, *Biographical Register*, 66.

[13] Farge, *Biographical Register*, 67.

[14] Bodenmann, *Les Perdants*, 13–14. Bodenmann casts doubt on the oft-repeated claim that Caroli assisted the printer Simon du Bois in Alençon. Ibid., 20.

[15] Bodenmann, *Les Perdants*, 49–50; Farge, *Biographical Register*, 68–69.

[16] "Ce dict londy de pentecoste, apres digner, environ unze heure, les quatres eschevins menerent le Satan Guilliaume Faret, Pierre Viret d'Orbe, avecq ung grand docteur de Paris, nommée maistre Pierre Caroly, lequel avoit estée maistre dudict pere Reverend." Jeanne de Jussie, *Petite chronique: Einleitung, Edition, Kommentar*, edited by Helmut Feld, Veröffentlichungen des Instituts für europäische Geschichte Mainz, Abteilung abendländische Religionsgeschichte 167 (Mainz: Philipp von Zabern, 1996), 125(B).

[17] "Mais quand il vit son maistre en theologie et qu'il estoit pervertir, il tomba pausmée à terre. Il fut revenus: et se Caroly luy vat dire, 'Et comme frere Guys, veulx tu moryr en ton obstination

At this point, therefore, Caroli seems to have been working alongside Farel and Viret. Just a few weeks later, however, Caroli participated in the Rive Disputation in Geneva and argued the "Catholic side" against Farel.[18] Caroli was no hardline Catholic apologist, however. He later described his participation as follows:

> The day of the disputation approached, but none of those who had been summoned were present, except by chance a certain Dominican (who has now cast off his habit) whom the syndics had forced by threat to come to the disputation. . . . Lest the disputation turn into a laughing-stock, the syndics called on me, whom Farel did not find a worthy presider and judge in that place, to take on the role of the Papist (as they say). . . . On every argument, Farel thundered forth a long speech, almost *ad nauseam* in his usual way. Several times, his supporters asked that I not be too forceful and harsh in debating, since not a few (as they say) were confirmed in the papal faith by my reasoning.[19]

By the time Caroli wrote this account, he had moved back into the Catholic fold, so he wanted to emphasize his Catholic apologetic skills. In fact, on many of the topics debated, Caroli seems not to have put up a fight. Nonetheless, he

---

et heresie? Jusques à maintenant avons estée en herreur, et à present sommes venuz à la verité de l'evangille. Ne veulx tu point recognoistre ton herreur, et te retorner à dieu?" Jeanne de Jussie, *Petite chronique*, 125–26; translation from Jeanne de Jussie, *The Short Chronicle: A Poor Clare's Account of the Reformation of Geneva*, edited and translated by Carrie F. Klaus, The Other Voice in Early Modern Europe (Chicago: University of Chicago Press, 2006), 96.

[18] Farel's account of the debate is published in Guillaume Farel, *Un opuscule inédit de Farel: Le résumé des actes de la Dispute de Rive (1535)*, edited by Théophile Dufour (Geneva: Charles Schuchardt, 1885).

[19] "Dies itaque certaminis advenit, quo vocatorum nullus adfuit, nisi forte dominicanus quidam [Jean Chapuys] (is nunc cucullam exuit) minis ad disputandum per syndicos urbis adactus. . . . Ne tamen suscepta disputatio abiret in ludibrium, rogant, ut ego, quem nec praesidis nec iudicis loco Farellus dignabatur, opponentis (ut loquuntur) papistae personam induerem. . . . Quum . . . Farellus ad singula quaeque argumenta prolixum ad nauseam usque suo more sermonem detonaret, rogarunt me sectatores eius aliquoties, ne tam vehemens et acris essem in disputando, cum (ut dicebant) non pauci, meis rationibus adducti, in papismi fide confirmarentur." Pierre Caroli, *Refutatio blasphemiae Farellistarum in sacrosanctam Trinitatem*, edited by Olivier Labarthe and Reinhard Bodenmann, COR, ser. IV, vol. 6, 145–242 (Geneva: Droz, 2016), 177–78. As recently as 1994, this text was believed to be lost. Frans Pieter van Stam discovered a copy in the Bibliothèque Municipale de Troyes and first discussed his findings in 1995; F. P. van Stam, "Le livre de Pierre Caroli de 1545 et son conflit avec Calvin," in *Calvin et ses contemporains, Actes du colloque de Paris 1995*, edited by Olivier Millet, Cahiers d'Humanisme et Renaissance 53, 21–41 (Geneva: Droz, 1998). Today, in addition to the critical edition cited above, the full text of Caroli's original book (Metz: Jean Palier, 1545) is freely available online via Google Books. Bodenmann also published the autobiographical excerpts from the *Refutatio* in an appendix to *Les Perdants*, 347–79.

martialed the testimony of the Church fathers in a genuine effort to defend the Mass, the invocation of the saints, and the existence of purgatory.[20] After the Rive Disputation, Caroli's relationship with Farel deteriorated further. Caroli explains:

> Farel . . . pursued me with such impotent hatred that he sent slanderous letters, as he is accustomed to do, to all of his followers throughout France and Germany. . . . A certain Frenchman . . . in order to strike terror into me, announced to me that some assassins [*sicarii*] who were Farel's associates were conspiring to enter my room one night and kill me with ten strikes of the dagger.[21]

Caroli then moved to Basel, where, he says, he worked on learning Hebrew with Sebastian Münster and frequently visited his neighbor Erasmus.[22]

Caroli was then called to preach in Neuchâtel.[23] This period in his life is somewhat obscure, but it had a significant impact on his later conflicts with the Calvinists. He was reunited there with Jean Lecomte, his old friend from Meaux, and it was Lecomte who officiated at his wedding. Also among Caroli's fellow preachers in Neuchâtel was Antoine Marcourt. Reinhard Bodenmann suggests that Marcourt, in fact, ordained Caroli as a Reformed pastor and that it was this action that initially rendered Marcourt suspicious in the eyes of the Calvinists.[24] Caroli, Lecomte, Marcourt, and their friend

---

[20] See, for example, Wolfgang Capito's response to a lost letter from Farel: "Quod ad nos Disputationem perscripseris, habeo gratiam. . . . Ecquid pro missa ex Patribus Carolus?" Herminjard 3:337 and n. 10, no. 523, Capito to Farel, Basel, [August 23, 1535].

[21] "Hinc Farellus . . . tam impotenti odio me persecutus est, ut suis (quod solet) maledicis literis apud suos omneis per Gallias et Germanas traduxerit. . . . Gallus quidam . . ., ut terrorem incuteret, mihi denunciavit nonnullos sicarios, Farelli satellites, conjurasse una sub noctem cubiculum meum ingressuros ac decem me pugionis ictibus confossum interfecturos." Caroli, *Refutatio blasphemiae Farellistarum*, 179–80. Calvin provides a much different reason for the breakdown in relations between Caroli and Farel. Like Caroli, he dates it to their time together in Geneva in 1535, but he blames the rift on Caroli's scandalous behavior with a young girl. Jean Calvin, *Pro G. Farello et collegis ejus, adversus Petri Caroli theologastri calumnias, defensio Nicolai Gallasii*, edited by Olivier Labarthe, COR ser. IV, vol. 6, 1–143 (Geneva: Droz, 2016), 48–49; see also the French translation, Jean Calvin, *Défense de Guillaume Farel et de ses collègues contre les calomnies du théologastre Pierre Caroli par Nicolas Des Gallars*, translated by Jean-François Gounelle, Etudes d'histoire et de philosophie religieuses 73 (Paris: Presses universitaires de France, 1994), 45–46.

[22] "Fugiens itaque Farellistarum minas et odia e Geneva . . . Basileam tandem me recepi, ubi Sebastiano Munstero in Hebraicis octo menses indefessas dabam operas, Erasmum Roterodamum (cum Frobenianis aedibus, in quibus hospitabatur, vicinus essem) ad familiare colloquium saepe visitans." Caroli, *Refutatio blasphemiae Farellistarum*, 180–81. On Caroli's stay in Basel, from September 1535 to May 1536, see Bodenmann, *Les Perdants*, 70–96.

[23] On Caroli's stay in Neuchâtel, see Bodenmann, *Les Perdants*, 120–30; Berthoud, *Antoine Marcourt*, 23–24.

[24] Bodenmann, *Les Perdants*, 126–27.

Thomas Malingre, pastor in Yverdon, would form the nexus of the earliest Protestant opposition to the Calvinists.

3.2.3. Caroli versus the Calvinists, 1536–1537

The definitive break between Caroli and the Calvinists, however, occurred soon after the Bernese named Caroli chief pastor of the church of Lausanne. The Calvinists believed that the post should have gone to Viret, who had already been preaching in Lausanne for several months. They also complained that Caroli was setting himself up as the de facto head of the Reformed Church in the Pays de Vaud, thus reviving a quasi-episcopal hierarchy.[25] These accusations initiated what came to be known as the Caroli Affair.[26] With the notable exception of Bodenmann, the authors who have described the affair have generally portrayed Caroli as utterly alone, and they have characterized his behavior as positively malicious.[27]

In reality, however, Caroli enjoyed significant support from his colleagues at the time, particularly from Lecomte and Malingre. The Caroli Affair began when Viret complained that Caroli had initiated a liturgical prayer for the dead in Lausanne.[28] Caroli quickly countered with the accusation that Calvin, Farel, and Viret were guilty of Arianism since they did not acknowledge the Athanasian Creed as canonical. Although Calvin's view of the

---

[25] "Vidimus literas quas Carolus scribit 'ad fratres qui agunt in ecclesiis sibi creditis.' Nisi me fallit sensus, omnes videtur suae curae creditas innuere; quid hoc siet tandem, novit Dominus. . . . Praeterea, non satis capio qui magis negligant Viretum nostrum, Bernatesne an Lausanenses, ut fratris nullam rationem habeant, sed eorum tantum qui vix inspiciunt opus Domini." Herminjard 4:108–109, no. 582, Farel to Christophe Fabri, Geneva, November 21, 1536. See also, ibid., 104–7, no. 581, Pastors of Geneva to the Synod of Lausanne, Geneva, November 21, 1536.

[26] On the Caroli affair, see, for example, Bodenmann, *Les Perdants*, 143–75; the "Introduction" to Calvin, *Défense de Guillaume Farel*; Eduard Bähler, "Petrus Caroli und Johannes Calvin: Ein Beitrag zur Geschichte und Kultur der Reformationszeit," *Jahrbuch für schweizerische Geschichte* 29 (1904): 39–168.

[27] See, for example, Ruchat's introduction to the conflict: "Pierre Caroli, docteur de Sorbonne, mais plus chargé de vices que de science, parut avoir quelque penchant pour la doctrine des réformés: et soit pour cette raison, ou parce qu'il n'était pas aimé de ses confrères à cause de sa vanité, il fut chassé de cette maison vers l'an 1525. Farel, qui l'avait connu à Paris, et qui était instruit de sa mauvaise conduite et de ses débauches, l'exhorta sérieusement à penser à sa conscience. . . . Farel . . . lui avait adressé d'abord des avertissemens salutaires, sans ménager sa délicatesse et sa vanité, qui dans la suite le censura vivement de ses débauches, et qui enfin découvrit la turpitude de son avarice, à l'occasion d'un sacrilège qu'il avait commis en gardant pour lui une collecte qu'il avait fait pour les pauvres!" Ruchat 5:17–18.

[28] On this quarrel, see Olivier Labarthe, "Faut-il prier pour les morts? Un débat de pastorale entre Viret et Caroli," in *Pierre Viret et la diffusion de la Réforme: Pensée, action, contextes religieux*, edited by Karine Crousaz and Daniela Solfaroli Camillocci (Lausanne: Antipodes, 2014), 289–309.

controversy has dominated scholarship since then, in Lecomte's eyes, Caroli was simply playing the part of the orthodox Athanasius to Calvin's heretical Arius.[29] Moreover, the episode raised doubts that lingered for years about the orthodoxy of Calvin's trinitarian beliefs. According to Edouard Bähler, this disagreement over Caroli was the basis for Lecomte's persistently frosty relationship with Calvin, Farel, and Viret.[30] A few years later, when Caroli returned to Switzerland, Lecomte and Malingre met with Caroli privately and appealed to the other ministers for his restoration to the ministry.[31]

Thus, Caroli had supporters. Some of the initial reports of the accusations against Calvin use the plural to indicate that Caroli was not the only one bringing the charges. Calvin and his colleagues in Geneva certainly did not believe that the opposition came from Caroli alone. In calling for a synod to address the controversy, they claimed, "That dogma of Caroli's is stirring up great turmoil everywhere. Many pastors have not shown themselves sufficiently proper; others, unless they are prodded to do their duty, will grow inactive."[32] Just before the Synod of Lausanne in May 1537, where the Caroli affair would be discussed, Calvin advised Viret to "see to it that all of our men [*omnes nostri*] come prepared to the synod."[33] His use of the phrase *omnes nostri* suggests that Calvin was starting to conceive of himself and his associates as one faction of francophone pastors among others in the region.

The Synod of Lausanne deposed Caroli, an action confirmed at a synod in Bern in June 1537.[34] Not everyone rejoiced at the decision. Even the leading pastors in Basel and Zurich were equivocal. Heinrich Bullinger wrote, "I can neither absolve nor condemn Caroli."[35] Moreover, even after

---

[29] See n. 31.

[30] Bähler, *Jean Le Comte de la Croix*, 58. As we have seen, however, one must date Farel's break from Caroli back to May 1535. And the Calvinists undoubtedly were aware of Lecomte's friendship with Caroli well before the dispute over Arianism in 1537.

[31] "Fratres aliquot, cum intelligerent quae Capunculo dixerat, et rursus quae Grandissonensis [i.e., Lecomte], dum Carolum Athanasium, nos Arrium faceret, hortantur ut aliter pergat. . . . Recepit se acturum cum Comite qui agit Grandissoni, super iis quae in nos est locutus. . . . Abiens secessit [Carolus] in locum in quem convenerunt Malingrius, Io. Comes, an alii non satis teneo. Quid egerint, ipsi norunt. Hoc scimus nos nihil sensisse actum fuisse de iis quae promiserat." Herminjard 6:92–93, no. 830, Farel to Calvin, Neuchâtel, October 21, 1539.

[32] "Graves turbas passim excitavit Carolinum illud dogma. Plerique ministri non admodum probe se gerunt; alii, nisi ad officium stimulentur, torpescunt." *Calv. Ep.* 1:176, no. 32, [Geneva Minsters to the Bern Ministers], [Geneva], [ca. February 20, 1537].

[33] "Tu insta quantum poteris, quo diem conventus antevertamus, ad quem ut omnes nostri optime comparati accedant, interim effice." *Calv. Ep.* 1:198, no. 37, Calvin to Viret, Geneva, April 23, [1537].

[34] See Bodenmann, *Les Perdants*, 163–73.

[35] "Quod Carolum attinet, hominem neque absolvere neque damnare possum. . . . Nihil ergo de his iudicare possum, nec, si possem, debeo. Debeo autem curare, ut omnis inter fratres dissentio sopiatur." *HBBW* 7:204, no. 1025, Bullinger to Oswald Myconius, [Zurich], July 23, 1537. See also the letter from Myconius to which Bullinger is responding here: "Equidem Carolum non defendo, quamvis olim, id

Caroli's exile, pastors in the Pays de Gex and elsewhere complained that Calvin and his party were trying to do away with the words *trinity* and *person*.[36]

The accusations persisted for several years. In 1543, Jean Chaponneau (Farel's colleague in Neuchâtel) and Chaponneau's son-in-law Jean Courtois drafted a series of articles denouncing Calvin's "heresies." Unfortunately, the original articles seem to be lost, but Calvin's reply survives and indicates that the articles chiefly concerned the nature of Christ and the trinity.[37] Chaponneau was another member of Caroli's network in the Suisse romande.[38] Like Caroli, he was close to Malingre and Lecomte, and he was Marcourt's colleague in Neuchâtel from 1536 until Marcourt's departure for Geneva in 1538. As we will see later, when Farel eventually came to preach in Neuchâtel, Chaponneau clashed with him repeatedly.[39]

Thus, the Caroli affair was hardly as one-sided as Calvin and others have made it out to be. By the end of the affair, the Calvinists conceived of themselves as one faction opposed by a competing faction that included Lecomte, Malingre, Marcourt, Chaponneau, and some of the pastors of Gex. An anti-Calvinist network was forming in francophone Switzerland.

---

est, ante annos duos, ipse se apud me coram defenderit, postquam a Farello turpissimis literis huc scriptis esset accusatus de iisdem criminibus. Non tamen probare possum, taliter eum tractari apud bonos et pios viros." Herminjard 4:255, no. 640, Myconius to Bullinger, Basel, July 9, 1537. Moreover, the Bernese pastor Peter Kunz seems to have been a supporter of Caroli: "Quae pridie D. Carolus de sacerdotio Christi, eiusque gloria diseruit, de triumpho item resurrectionis . . . de iugi spe, ardentique desyderio quo electi omnes, tam superstites quam vita functi, flagrant, nihil dubito. . . . Et cur haec, propter bonum Carolum, displicerent, cum istaec doctrina non quidem Caroli sed Spiritus Sancti sit in divinis Scripturis luculenter prodita?" Herminjard 4:242, n. 14, Kunz to Eberhard von Rümlang, [Bern], ca. June 3, 1537.

[36] "Nous somes esté advertis par aulcungs de nous predicants tant de la terre de Gex que aultres, que cherchés tousjours de leurs inculquer vostre intention et opinion de la nullité des moctz trinité et personne, pour yceulx jadicts predicants devier de la costume et maniere de parle(r) de la trinité recephue de l'esglise catholique." *Calv. Ep.* 1:243–44, no. 46, Bern city council to Farel and Calvin, Bern, August 13, 1537.

[37] "Quantum ad locum illum, ubi, quasi ex tripode haereticos pronunciat, qui dicunt Christum, in quantum Deus est, a seipso esse, facilis est responsio. . . . De essentia Dei non visa patribus ante Christi adventum, quam pueriles ineptiae!" Herminjard 8:381–82, no. 1236, Calvin to the Pastors of Neuchâtel, May 28, [1543].

[38] Jean Chaponneau earned his doctorate in theology at the University of Louvain and became an Augustinian monk in Bourges—Marguerite of Navarre's territory—where he met Calvin, and where he began to preach evangelical sermons by 1533. He arrived in Neuchâtel around mid-December 1536. See *Guillaume Farel*, 411, and n. 1.

[39] See 97–100. At one point, however, Farel reports a falling out between Chaponneau and Lecomte. *Guillaume Farel*, 541.

3.3. Antoine Marcourt and the Supporters
of Close Church–State Relations

Antoine Marcourt, the pastor who probably called Caroli to the Reformed ministry,[40] is best known as the author of the 1534 Paris placards. He also wrote three other early polemical treatises that proved significant in the formative years of francophone Swiss Protestantism: the *Livre des Marchans*, the *Petit traicté de la saincte eucharistie*, and the *Declaration de la Messe*.[41] Marcourt's career as an author was decidedly short; these three works and the placards constitute the entirety of his published œuvre, and all appeared in 1533 and 1534. But Marcourt had a much longer career as a pastor in the Suisse romande. Through most of his career, he opposed the Calvinists, particularly on issues of ecclesiology. In his appointment as Calvin's successor in Geneva, and in his support of the Bern council's right to dispose of the goods seized from the Catholic Church, Marcourt showed himself a supporter of the magistrate's authority over ecclesiastical affairs. As such, he stood opposed to Calvin's insistence on the independent jurisdiction of the Church.

3.3.1. Marcourt in Neuchâtel, 1531–1538

Almost nothing is known of Marcourt's life before his arrival in Neuchâtel in 1531. One of the few clues we have is that he seems to have known Jean Lecomte in France.[42] Marcourt replaced Farel as pastor in Neuchâtel in 1531, and for several years there was no sign of trouble between him and Farel or the other pastors in the region. In 1534, a disagreement seems to have arisen in Neuchâtel, when François Marthoret warned Farel of possible trouble at an upcoming synod from a group of "rabbis."[43] It

---

[40] See 71–72.

[41] (1) *Le livre des marchans, fort utile à toutes gens* ([Neuchâtel]: [Pierre de Vingle], 1533); (2) *Petit traicté tres utile et salutaire de la saincte eucharistie*; (3) *Declaration de la Messe*. Geneviève Gross has recently published a critical edition of the first: *Le Livre des marchans d'Antoine Marcourt: Une satire anticléricale au service de la Réforme*, Textes littéraires de la Renaissance 17 (Paris: Honoré Champion, 2016).

[42] Lecomte wrote the following verse mentioning him: "Hinc Neocumum eo, veteres nactus amicos,/ Marcurtus multo tempore sedit ibi,/ Parisiis scriptis sunt laeti, is atque Farellus/ Qui me postridie suscipit urbe Morat." Cited in Berthoud, *Antoine Marcourt*, 5. Berthoud's biography is the standard source on Marcourt's life and works. She points out that he was probably a Picard and came to Neuchâtel from Lyon. Ibid., 3–6.

[43] "Sumus tamen eo animo nostris rabinis resistere in faciem et non amplius dissimulare, ut nos saepe monuisti; sed quid inde, nisi clamores et vociferationes et tandem magnum scandalum?" Herminjard 3:217 (no. 482), François Marthoret du Rivier to Farel, Murten, October 8, [1534].

is impossible to determine the exact nature of this problem or to know whether Marcourt was even involved. In January 1537, however, Christophe Fabri reported to Farel that "our rabbis" objected to Jacques Le Coq's appointment to the church in Morges and wanted that important position to go to Marcourt.[44] There may also have been other causes for the growing division among the pastors, for around the same time, the Bern city council warned its French-speaking pastors not to introduce "ceremonies and sacraments different from those we have prescribed, which conform to the reformation of our church."[45] Given the role that the dispute over Bernese ceremonies would play in the 1538 crisis with Calvin and Farel, it is possible that this disagreement was already fermenting among the pastoral factions in the Pays de Vaud. The precise reasons for the early alienation between Marcourt and the Calvinists are not entirely clear, but as Gabrielle Berthoud notes, "In the years following Calvin's arrival in Geneva, we find Marcourt attached to a group that remained faithful to the old school, to the Zwinglian doctrine, and to the regime of the state Church."[46]

[44] "Jacobum fratrem Morgiis quandiu licuit de omnibus compellavimus, qui Rabinorum nostrorum conatus et studia mihi aperuit: 'Quod junior et imberbis talem locum occupare non debeat, ideoque necessarium ut Marcurt(ius) illic praeficiatur, etc.'" Herminjard 4:153, no. 601, Fabri to Farel, Thonon, January 11, 1537. Herminjard suggests that the term "rabbi" is used to designate "les ministres qui voulaient dominer leurs collègues." Ibid., 153n9. Bodenmann suggests that the "rabbis" were "Marcourt, Le Comte, Malingre, tous des hommes instruits, auteurs d'ouvrages imprimés: ce qui explique parfaitement le qualificatif de 'rabbins' dont Farel les affublait en janvier 1537, en incluant évidemment dans ce groupe Caroli." Les Perdants, 142. It is possible that the terms could also denote ministers who were perceived as too legalistic or tied too closely to the government.

[45] "En après vous avertissant estre venuz à nostre notice, comme aulcuns entre vous soyent d'opinion d'ensuivre leur fasson de faire, touchant les cérémonies et sacraments, en aultre sourte que nous l'avons advisés conformez à nostre réformation de nostre église. Sur quoy vous admonestons et aussy commandons que, en tous endroits, vous ensuivés et observés la réformation et mandement que sur ce avons faict, lesquels nous commis vous communiqueront." Herminjard 4:151, no. 600, Bern council to its francophone pastors, Bern, January 5, 1537. At just this moment, Bern was introducing a new liturgy to its French-speaking lands, La Maniere, Ordre et Fasson, rediscovered by Marianne Carbonnier-Burkard. This was intended to replace Farel's Maniere et Fasson in Bern's francophone territories, while Geneva continued to use Farel's liturgy. Marianne Carbonnier-Burkard, "Une cène inconnue: Morceau choisi de la liturgie bernoise en version française (1537)," in Bible, Histoire et Société: Mélanges offerts à Bernard Roussel, edited by R. Gerald Hobbs and Annie Noblesse-Rocher, Bibliothèque de l'École des Hautes Études, Sciences Religieuses 163 (Turnhout: Brepols, 2013), 323–44. The full reference to the liturgy: [Johannes Rhellican and Antoine Morelet du Museau, trans.], La maniere, ordre et fasson d'espouser et confirmer les mariages devant la compaignie et assemblee des fideles . . . (Geneva: Wigant Köln, 1537), available online at www.bvh.univ-tours.fr/Consult/index.asp?numfiche=626.

[46] Berthoud, Antoine Marcourt, 28.

3.3.2. Marcourt and Jean Morand Replace
Calvin and Farel in Geneva, 1538

The bombshell dropped in 1538, when the Geneva city council called
Marcourt and Jean Morand to replace the exiled Calvin and Farel as leaders
of the Genevan church. Morand, like Caroli, had a doctorate in theology from
Paris.[47] He had arrived in Switzerland only months before, in late 1537, and
he took a position as pastor of Cully, near Lausanne. At first, Farel was supportive and tried to find him a position in Geneva,[48] but he later complained
that Lecomte had turned Morand away from the Calvinists.[49] Initially, the
Geneva council called him to administer, a week late, the Easter Eucharist
that Calvin and Farel had refused to distribute.[50] Marcourt accepted the call
to Geneva in June. Neither he nor Morand received a warm welcome from
the Calvinists in the region; not only were they proverbial scabs crossing the
picket line, but they had been simply appointed by the Geneva city council,
rather than elected by their fellow pastors. The Calvinists believed that the
right of election belonged to the pastors and elders. They saw Marcourt and
Morand's acceptance of a call directly from the Geneva city council, therefore, as a betrayal of the rights of the church.[51] Marcourt and Morand, on

[47] On Morand, see Farge, *Biographical Register*, 337–39. Farge notes that he did not attend the
Sorbonne, but probably Cholets or Cardinal Lemoine.

[48] "Item demande que l'on veuille provoitre au docteur Morand.... Sus le propos de Farel pour
soubstenir Morand, est arresté faire du meilleur." *RC* 3:5–6, January 3, 1538. Morand was from
Vervins in Picardy and received his doctorate in 1530. In December 1533, while a canon and vicar-
general of the bishop of Amiens, the Paris Parlement ordered his arrest for heresy. The Paris Faculty
of Theology condemned ninety-nine propositions from his sermons and manuscript writings
(D'Argentré 2, pt. 1:101–19). Morand apparently recanted but was ordered to stay in a monastic
prison for another year. Nothing is known of the two years between his scheduled release from prison
and his arrival in Geneva. Farge, *Biographical Register*, 337–39.

[49] "Furit Morandus, qui a nobis Comitem abalienavit, unde apud Conzenum incendia, ut iam
intelligo. Sed audi quam sint nobis fatales et ecclesiae Dei Sorbonici!" Herminjard 5:115–16, no. 745,
Farel to Calvin, Neuchâtel, September 18, [1538]. Of course, Farel has actually written that it was
Morand who turned Lecomte against them, but since Farel was aware that Lecomte had been against
them for a long time before Morand's arrival in Switzerland, it seems much more likely that he intended to say that Lecomte turned Morand against them. Because *Comes* can refer to several people,
however, there are other possible interpretations. For example, Farel could mean that Morand has
turned Béat Comte, at this time pastor in Lausanne, but B. Comte seems at this point still to have
been in the Calvinists' good graces. Less likely still is that *Comitem* could refer to an unnamed noble
"count." Thus, I believe Farel simply meant to write "Morandus, quem a nobis Comes abalienavit..."

[50] "vous priant qu'il soyt de vostre bon playsir de vous transporter de par deçà dans nostre ville,
pour nous preschés le Sainct Evangièle et donner laz Cenne dymenche prochaine, cart nous prédicans
n'ont voulsu nullement optempérer az ce que dernièrement az esté résoluz az Lausanne touchant les
cérémonies." Herminjard 4:420–21, no. 703, Geneva council to Jean Morand, Geneva, April 24, 1538.

[51] "Neque maiore dexteritate administrant officium, quam usurparunt. Eo enim se ingesserunt,
fratribus totius provinciae partim inconsultis, partim reclamantibus." Herminjard 5:29, no. 717, Farel
and Calvin to Bullinger, [Basel], [between June 6 and 10, 1538].

the other hand, saw it as a legitimate call made by the duly elected Christian magistrate.[52]

The Calvinists' campaign against Marcourt and his colleagues continued for months. In August 1538, Farel complained to Calvin, "In the congregations, they are striving to overturn everything we built."[53] On October 1 of that year, Calvin addressed a letter "to the remnant of the dissipation of the church of Geneva,"[54] implying that the official church of Geneva was no true church at all. Indeed, Calvin suggests that the new church order in Geneva is nothing short of diabolical:

> Since . . . by the Lord's just permission, the devil strives incessantly to disperse the church which was started among you, it is my job to remind you of your duty. You need to recognize and understand that whatever perversity there is in the men who vex and trouble you, nevertheless, the assaults on you are not so much their work as that of Satan, who uses their malice as an instrument to wage war against you.[55]

Although Calvin does not name the "men who vex and trouble you," there is little doubt they included the new pastors, who by implication are the "instruments of Satan." Moreover, in assigning blame for the troubles in Geneva, Calvin explicitly identifies his opponents not individually, but as a coalition: "Those who separated from us in order to create and lead their separate faction, have introduced division in both your church and your town."[56] Thus, Calvin paints a clear picture of a cosmic struggle in Geneva pitting the "remants of the true Church"—that is, his followers—against the

---

[52] See, for example, Marcourt's initial response to Geneva's call, in which he defers to the permission of the Neuchâtel political authorities for permission to leave but says not a word about the pastors of either Geneva or Neuchâtel: "Quant à moy je desireroye fort, selon la Parolle de Dieu, vous faire service, si le povoir et suffisance y estoit; mais . . . mon très-honoré seigneur Monsieur le gouverneur général du pays et conté de Neufchastel n'est pas au lieu pour ceste heure, auquel toutesfoys il se fauldroit premièrement adresser, et au Conseil de la ville de Neufchastel pareillement." Herminjard 5:10–11, no. 711, Marcourt to the Geneva Council, Neuchâtel, May 12, 1538.

[53] "In concionibus omnia quae conati sumus erigere evertere student." Herminjard 5:81, no. 733bis, Farel to Calvin, [Neuchâtel], [beginning of August 1538].

[54] "A mes bien-ayméz frères en Nostre Seigneur qui sont les reliques de la dissipation de l'Église de Genefve." Herminjard 5:126, no. 748, Strasbourg, October 1, 1538.

[55] "Or . . . pource que . . . par sa [le Seigneur] juste permission le diable s'efforce incessamment de dissiper l'église qui estoit commencée entre vous, il est mestier de vous admonester de vostre office. C'est que vous recongnoissiez et méditiez, quelque perversité qu'il y aict aux hommes qui vous troublent et griefvent, toutesfois que les assaultz ne vous sont pas tant donnéz d'eux comme de Sathan, lequel use de leur malice comme d'instrument pour vous guerroier." Herminjard 5:122, no. 748.

[56] "Ceux qui se sont séparéz de nous pour faire et mener leur faction à part, ont introduit division tant en vostre église comme en vostre ville." Herminjard 5:122, no. 748.

"instruments of Satan" who represent "a separate faction" and are responsible for division in the Genevan church.

Others in Geneva drew a similar picture. Notable among them were Calvin's former teacher in Paris, Mathurin Cordier, and the lecturer at the Collège de Rive, Antoine Saunier, along with his assistants. In September 1538, the Geneva council expelled Saunier's assistants, Gaspard Carmel and Eynard Pichon, for casting insults (*grosses paroles*) at the new pastors and inciting tumult.[57] When asked in Bern about this expulsion, Marcourt and Morand blamed it on "a type of people who try only to stir up trouble and who do not want to obey the magistrate."[58] Their view, in stark contrast to Calvin's, attributed the divisions in the city to a seditious Calvinist faction intent on stirring up trouble in a rejection of secular authority.

3.3.3. Conflict over the Christmas Eucharist in Geneva, 1538

The story of Calvin and Farel's exile from Geneva, which started in April 1538, does not culminate until the following Christmas. Between their initial expulsion and the Christmas Eucharist, they and their supporters waged a continuous war of propaganda and insults against the city council that had expelled them and the ministers who had replaced them. At Christmas, however, the final act played out. Saunier, Cordier, and many Guillermins[59] on the city council and in the city at large refused to receive the Christmas Eucharist from the hands of the new pastors. Already in October 1538, Saunier had written to Calvin for his advice on the matter.[60] Calvin suggested

[57] "Heynard et Gaspard demorant aut colliege; Ordonance—Les^dtz Heynard et Gaspardar, lesqueulx demorent az Rivaz, lesquieulx ne font que contrerolé nous predicans, usans de grosses parolles contre icyeulx, les voulliant resprendre publiquement affin de fere tymulte. . . . Pour ce que il ne veullent pas vivre selon l'ordonnance de Messrs, quel il ce doygent retyré dans troys jours prochaien." *RC* 3:400, September 10, 1538.

[58] "Auspurguez (Michael Augsburger) les interroga pourquoy est-ce que l'on avoy ausy dechassé Heynard et son compagnyon dernierement, lesquieulx respondirent que c'estoy pour ce que il son[t] une seste [read: secte] de gens que ne cherchent que de mecstres noyses les ungs avecque les aultres, et que il ne vollyent point obeyr aut magistral." *RC* 3:432, October 7, 1538.

[59] I have been using the term "Calvinists" to refer to all those who identified as Calvin's supporters. The term "Guillermins," by contrast, refers to a specific political faction in Geneva, based among the followers of Guillaume Farel. See Naphy, *Geneva and the Consolidation of the Genevan Reformation*, 34–41.

[60] "Sonerius alteram a nobis quaestionem discuti voluit: an liceat sibi ac similibus Coenam Domini cum ex eorum manibus accipere, tum etiam cum tanta hominum colluvie participare." Herminjard 5:168, no. 755, Calvin to Farel, Strasbourg, October 24, [1538].

that he should take the Lord's Supper, indicating that "there ought to be so great a dislike of schism that they may always avoid it so far as lies in their power. There ought to prevail among them such a reverence for the ministry of the Word and of the Sacraments, that wherever they perceive these things to be, there they may consider the church to exist."[61] In the same breath, however, Calvin implied that Marcourt and his colleagues were not legitimate pastors but instead had fraudulently, indeed nefariously, usurped the office of the true pastors.[62] Had the question regarded solely the reception of Lord's Supper from the new pastors, Saunier might have heeded Calvin's advice to take the sacrament. The Geneva council complicated the matter, however, when it insisted that Saunier and his assistants aid Marcourt and the other pastors with the actual distribution of the Christmas Eucharist as well. For Saunier, this demand went too far, for it required active cooperation with the "illegitimate" pastors. He and his assistants refused both to serve and to receive the Christmas Eucharist, and the Geneva council banished them all, together with Cordier, from the city.[63] Moreover, the council required those who had refused the Lord's Supper to promise not stir up additional trouble.[64]

The bitterness surrounding the 1538 Christmas Eucharist reveals the depth of the enmity between the Calvinists and the new pastors. Marcourt and his colleagues, despite the support of the city council, felt strongly the sting of the Calvinists' wrath and wrote a letter to the Geneva council offering their resignations. They claimed that their opponents constantly accused

---

[61] "Tantum debere inter Christianos esse odium schismatis, ut semper quoad licet refugiant; tantam ministerii ac sacramentorum reverentiam esse oportere, ut ubicunque extare haec cernunt, ecclesiam esse censeant." Herminjard 5:169, no. 755. Translation from Jules Bonnet, ed., *The Letters of John Calvin: Compiled from the Original Manuscripts and Edited with Historical Notes*, 4 vols., translated by David Constable et al. (Edinburgh, 1855–1858), 1:77.

[62] "Nec illud nos remoratur, quod legitimus haberi pastor non debet qui in locum veri ministri non tantum irrepserit fraudulenter, sed nefarie irruperit." Herminjard, 5:169, no. 755.

[63] "Pour ce que led.[tz] maystre Antoienne [Saunier] ne ces gens n'ont poient voulsu obayr aut magistral az servy az ministrer laz Cennaz, arresté qu'il doygent vuyder laz ville dans troys jour prochaien." *RC* 3:534, December 26, 1538. The two assistants who replaced Pichon and Carmel were Jérôme Vindocin and Claude Vautier; for the command to them and to Cordier to distribute communion, see *RC* 3:530, December 23, 1538; and for the aftermath, *RC* 3:536–38, December 27, 1538. On the whole affair, see Berthoud, *Antoine Marcourt*, 45–47.

[64] "Et quant az cieulx de laz ville, que l'on les fasse venyr ceans et scavoyr d'eulx voyr si ne veulent pas vivre selon les arrest et resolucion du Grand Conseyl, et puys, selon leur responce, l'on adviseraz de mecstre le cas en Grand Conseyl." *RC* 3:534, December 26, 1538. See also *RC* 3:538–39, December 27, 1538. Between December 27, 1538, and January 8, 1539, thirty-six citizens and foreigners were summoned to appear before the council to explain why they had not received the Christmas Eucharist. *RC* 3:534n59.

them of being "infidels, papists, and corrupters of Scripture"[65] and that the troubles were so great that they feared for their own safety.[66] Significantly, they defended themselves on the basis of having simply preached the Reformation as it had been adopted in Bern and the other German-speaking Protestant cantons.[67] They were, in essence, appealing to the unity of the Swiss Protestant churches. By implication, therefore, they saw the Calvinists as threatening that unity and introducing a new religion in the Suisse romande.

3.3.4. Political and Theological Factionalism in Geneva and the Vaud, 1538–1540

William Naphy reminds us of the significance of the factional political struggles between the Articulants and the Guillermins in Geneva during Calvin's exile.[68] The conflict between the Calvinists, on the one hand, and Marcourt and his colleagues, on the other, was an integral part of those struggles. On one side, the political Guillermins favored greater independence from Bern, and the Calvinist pastors sought to make the church more independent of state control. On the other side, the political Articulants supported closer ties to Bern, and Marcourt and his colleagues supported both religious conformity with Bern and the rights of the magistrate in church affairs. The two conflicts—Guillermins versus Articulants and Calvinists versus Marcourt and his allies—went hand in hand. As long as the Articulants had political power in Geneva, Marcourt and a Zwinglian, pro-Bern theology held sway. When the Guillermins took political power in 1540, the Calvinists saw an opportunity to gain the upper hand.

---

[65] "Ains avons esté et sommes journellement réputéz pour infidèles, papistes et corrupteurs de l'Escripture et pour telz qui vouldrions décepvoir vostre peuple, qui nous est chose trop dure à porter." Herminjard 5:209, no. 763, Geneva Pastors to the Geneva Council, [Geneva], December 31, 1538.

[66] "Et, davantage, que vostre ville et républicque, à raison de telles partialités, tourneroit en danger trop apparent; et que nos personnes aussy ne seroient en seureté au millieu de tant de malveuillans." Herminjard 5:210, no. 763.

[67] "Ces choses considérées et que l'injure ne tourne point sur nous tant seulement, mais aussy et plustost sur vous et vos ordonnances et mesme de toute la réformation des églises de la Germanie, et signantement de l'église de Berne, à laquelle conformément avez faict ordonnance pour la vostre; et (que) nous, conformément à leur doctrine, qui est purement évangélicque, avons presché et preschons à vostre peuple, estans certains par la Parolle de Dieu que ce que nous enseignons est très-véritable, et néantmoins que nostre ministère n'est point seulement inutile, mais aussy tourne en contemnement et mocquerie." Herminjard 5:209, no. 763.

[68] Naphy, *Calvin and the Consolidation of the Genevan Reformation*, esp. ch. 1.

For two years, from 1538 to 1540, Marcourt, Morand, and the Articulants were in power. The Geneva council rejected the resignations offered by Marcourt and Morand, and the pastors remained in the city. Nevertheless, the upheaval between Calvin's exile in April 1538 and that of Saunier after Christmas was so disruptive that pastors on both sides recognized the need to heal the schism. In March 1539, they held a meeting in Morges to try to reconcile the two sides.[69] This location, twelve kilometers west of Lausanne and forty-eight kilometers from Geneva, reveals that the divisions extended far beyond Geneva itself. Indeed, it was likely the Bernese, and in particular their pastor Peter Kunz, who initiated the meeting.[70] It seems that all of the chapters of the Pays de Vaud were involved and sought Geneva's agreement to the meeting.[71] Unfortunately, we do not know who attended the conference or what exactly they discussed, but the pastors agreed to a set of articles that have survived. Marcourt and his colleagues acknowledged that they should have consulted other pastors, including Calvin and Farel, before accepting their positions in Geneva and that they should not have spoken so harshly against their predecessors from the pulpit.[72] Their opponents, described as the "ministers in Bernese territory," agreed in turn to accept the Geneva pastors as faithful ministers of the Word.[73] The meeting seems to have been successful in patching things up for a time, but tensions between the two factions remained.

Pierre Caroli's return to Switzerland in June 1539 did nothing to relieve those tensions. As we saw earlier, Marcourt had known Caroli earlier in Neuchâtel. Farel claimed that Marcourt and Caroli's relationship continued

---

[69] On the meeting, see Berthoud, *Antoine Marcourt*, 51–55.

[70] Berthoud, *Antoine Marcourt*, 52.

[71] In Bern's French-speaking territories, the pastors were divided into six regional *classes*, or chapters (*Kapitel* in German) based in Lausanne, Payerne, Yverdon, Morges, Gex, and Thonon. Each chapter was headed by a dean (*doyen*), who was assisted by four jurors (*jurés*). The chapters met a few times a year to address questions, problems, and other matters of importance to the pastors in the region. See Bruening, *Calvinism's First Battleground*, 169–71; Vuilleumier, 1:267–305.

[72] "Primo fatentur fratres Genevenses charissimi satius et consultius, ante ingressum suum ad Ecclesiam Genevensem, plures doctos viros consuluisse, inprimis vero Farellum, Iohannem Calvinum et Coraldum, charissimos fratres, qui fidi pastores eius loci erant et statum eius ecclesiae melius noverant. [Secundo,] Quia non paucas occasiones e concionibus nostris intelligimus, quas nollemus, minime eo tendente instituto menteque nostra, ad calumniandum ministerium et doctrinam charissimorum fratrum, antecessorum nostrorum, Farelli dicimus, Calvini et Coraldi—pollicemur summo studio et quoad fieri potest advigilaturos, ne quemquam incautiore dicto offendamus aut ab illis alienemus." Herminjard 5:244–45, no. 771, Reconciliation of the Geneva pastors with Farel, Calvin, and their Supporters, [Morges], [March 12, 1539].

[73] "Nos vicissim, in agro Bernensi Ministri, recipimus et amplectimur dictos Ministros Genevenses tanquam fratres charissimos et verbi Iesu Christi fidos Ministros, et admittimus mutuas liberasque admonitiones et Colloquia." Herminjard 5: 245–46, no. 771.

after the latter's expulsion and that Caroli wrote to congratulate Marcourt on obtaining his position in Geneva.[74] Caroli's return brought Marcourt, Lecomte, and Malingre together again in support of their friend's efforts at reinstatement. As Bodenmann rightly points out, contrary to the claims of earlier scholarship, Caroli was not being unrealistic in trying to return to Switzerland, for Calvinist control there was far from complete. Instead, Caroli was returning to a "heterogeneous and divided Romandie."[75]

Thus, even after the Morges conference, religious divisions persisted in Geneva and throughout the Suisse romande. Although Calvin now more clearly encouraged the Genevans to accept his replacements as true pastors,[76] he indicated at the same time that his exile was caused by the devil,[77] and in a letter to Farel he referred to Lecomte and Malingre as "little beasts."[78] The distrust ran both ways. In January 1540, the Geneva printer Michel du Bois sought permission to print Calvin's famous reply to Jacopo Sadoleto. In March 1539, Sadoleto, the bishop of Carpentras, had written to the Genevans to encourage them to rejoin the Catholic Church. In September, at the request of the Geneva council, Calvin wrote his reply. The council initially withheld permission, however, to print it.[79] Instead, the council members asked their own pastor, Jean Morand, to draft a reply.[80] Morand does not seem to have done so, and Du Bois eventually published Calvin's response.[81] This episode

[74] "Non levem facit me habere coniecturam gratulatio ad Antonium quod aërem Genevensem viderit, ut optabat, tandem." Herminjard 6:85–86, no. 830, Farel to Calvin, Neuchâtel, October 21, 1539.

[75] Bodenmann, Les Perdants, 254.

[76] "Quia vero mihi constat de fratribus nostris qui apud vos hodie ministerii locum tenent, doceri vos Evangelium per illos, non video quid excusare liceat coram Domino dum illos negligetis aut rejicietis." Herminjard 5:340, no. 798, Calvin to the Geneva Church, Strasbourg, June 25, 1539.

[77] "Quanvis enim mutatio illa quae nostro discessu facta est, Diaboli artificio deputanda sit, ut quidquid eam est consequutum vobis merito suspectum esse possit, in ea tamen singularis Domini gratia agnoscenda vobis est, qui destitui vos plane non sustinuit, neque vos relabi sub Antichristi iugum, a quo vos semel asseruit." Herminjard 5:338, no. 798.

[78] "Bestiolas illas Malingrium et Cruciatum non melius conterere possis quam contemptu." Herminjard 6:114, no. 832, Calvin to Farel, Strasbourg, October 27, 1539.

[79] "Le sr Estienne Chappeau Rouge; P. Ameaux; Michiel Du Boes, imprimeur—Lesquieulx ont proposer coment il avyent desliberé fere imprimer aulchongs lyvres, mesmement l'espitre du cardinal Sadolet et laz responce d'icelle faycte par Johan Caulvin, predicant, dactee Estrasbourg le premier de septembre 1539, priant leur donné licence de imprimer en appourtant le premier lyvre ceans, coment az esté ordonné . . . quant à ladte epistre et responce de Sadolet et Caulvin, que l'on il adviseraz et que, d'icelles, l'on aye conferance avecque les predicans." RC 5:14, January 6, 1540.

[80] "Cardinal de Carpentras, Jaques Sadolet—Lequelt, l'annee passé nous rescripvyt une espitre exortative à laz loy papistique estant en latin et luy fust rescript de luy fere responce en brief, parquoy az esté arresté, sus icelle, luy fere responce et que l'on ballie ladte espitre az maystre Morand, predicant, pour fere icelle responce." RC 5:31, January 12, 1540. The decision was repeated four days later, RC 5:50, January 16, 1540.

[81] "Et luy [Michel Du Bois] az esté donné licence d'ymprimer laz responce faycte par Caulvin aut cardinal Sadolet." RC 5:79, January 30, 1540. Calvin and Sadolet's texts in OS 1:437–89. See

illustrates, however, just how unpopular Calvin remained with the Geneva council and pastors at this point.

In the spring of 1540, however, Marcourt's and Morand's positions in Geneva became more precarious. In April, a Bernese delegation arrived in Geneva to conclude the terms of the Articles (whence the Articulant faction got its name) of the treaty that concluded the 1536 war against Savoy. When the terms of the Articles became public, the Genevan people believed the Articulants had failed in the negotiations and conceded too much to the Bernese.[82] Soon after the Geneva council drew up its list of complaints against the treaty,[83] the pastors appeared before the council to complain of new criticisms against them.[84] It had been over a year since the pastors had complained of such things, so it seems likely that the new accusations against them were tied closely to the political shift against the Articulants in the city. In June 1540, the Articulant leaders were tried and sentenced to death in absentia, for they had already fled the city. The next month, Jean Morand left Geneva, explaining,

[S]uch calumnies were hurled against the truth and against our true preaching that I never thought could be suffered, much less spoken or thought among people who bear the name *Christian*. Considering this and that plainly idle people, saying they were "of the Gospel," withdrew more and more every day from our preaching . . . , I withdrew towards my magnificent lords of Bern.[85]

also John C. Olin, ed., *A Reformation Debate: Sadoleto's Letter to the Genevans and Calvin's Reply* (New York: Fordham University Press, 2000 [New York, 1966]).

[82] The terms of the Articles essentially ceded to Bern control over the contested former lands of the Geneva cathedral chapter and priory of St.-Victor. The texts of the Articles are in *RC* 4:623–30 (German), 630–37 (French). See also Monter, *Calvin's Geneva*, 66–70.

[83] Printed in *RC* 4:747–51, [April 20, 1540].

[84] "Les quattres s^rs predicans ont exposer coment il ont entendus que pluseurs leur blasment et que, si ne sont suffisant, que l'on leur notiffie affin qu'il ayent advys. Resoluz qu'il nous notiffient cieulx que les ont blasmé, affin en fere justice." *RC* 5:270, April 30, 1540.

[85] "calumnies se sont démenées en telle sorte contre vérité et contre nostre prédication véritable, que je n'eusse jamais pensé estre souffert, beaucoup moins dict ne pensé, entre gens qui auroient nom de chrestiens. Ce donc considéré, et que gens plainement oysifz, soy disans de l'Évangile, se sont retiré et retirent chascun jour de nostre prédication . . . , je me suis retiré vers mes magnifiques Seigneurs de Berne." Herminjard 6:264, no. 877, Jean Morand to the Geneva council, [Pays de Vaud], August 9, 1540. Morand says that he received payment from the treasurer through July 22, "après lequel jour, je me suis parti de vostre ville" (ibid., 265). He was appointed pastor of Nyon on August 5, 1540.

The same day that Morand's letter was read to the city council, Marcourt appeared in chambers, saying that "if one continues to permit the insolence that takes place every day, he would prefer to leave Geneva."[86] By September 21, 1540, he had done just that, without taking leave of the council.[87] Marcourt, too, found new employment in Bern's Pays de Vaud.[88]

Just before he left Geneva, Marcourt had suggested that the Geneva council call Pierre Viret to come to Geneva. It seems an odd choice, given Viret's close relationship with Calvin and Farel.[89] Perhaps it is an indication of Viret's moderate temperament; he was often called upon to mediate disputes within the church. One must also bear in mind, however, that Viret became much closer to Calvin after Marcourt left Geneva. Initially, Viret declined the call to Geneva, claiming, significantly, that it had been made without the requisite "order in ecclesiastical elections."[90] He was not going to make the same mistake as Marcourt and Morand. Nevertheless, the pastors eventually approved the call, and Viret was in Geneva during the months leading up to Calvin's return in September 1541, as well as for several months afterward.[91] The nine months when Calvin and Viret were together in Geneva were crucial for their relationship; after this period, Viret effectively replaced Farel as Calvin's closest friend and colleague.[92] This period also turned Viret into a devoted disciple of Calvin.

---

[86] "Maystre Anthoienne Marcour, predicant—Lequelt ausy az exposé coment, si l'on veult permecstre les insolences que journellement ce font, qu'il ayme mieulx absenter Geneve." RC 5:451, August 10, 1540.

[87] "Maystre Anthoienne Marcour, predicant—Lequelt s'en est allez, delayssant son ministere sans prendre congé de laz Seygneurie, synon par une lectre qu'il az envoyé." RC 5:542, September 21, 1540.

[88] First at Orzens and Essertines, then in 1541 in Curtilles. Berthoud, *Antoine Marcourt*, 85–86.

[89] "[Marcourt, Bernard, and De la Mare] ont mys en avant qu'il seroy bien propice, si l'on le povoyt avoyer, maystre Pierre Vyret, predicant à Lausanne. Parquoy az esté resoluz luy envoyé led[tz] maystre Anthoienne, avecque lectre de requeste qu'il viengne." RC 5:451, August 10, 1540.

[90] "Mais d'acquiescer à vostre demande je ne puys, … pour ce que je suy lié à ceste église en laquelle le Seigneur m'a appellé et constitué, laquelle je ne puys facilement abandonner sans scandale et sans offenser mes princes et mes frères ministres, si ainsin la délaissoye sans garder l'ordre qui est requis aux élections ecclésiastiques, ce que vous ne ignorés pas." Herminjard 6:271–72, no. 880, Viret to the Geneva Council, Lausanne, August 14, 1540.

[91] Viret was in Geneva from January 10, 1541, to July 1542. See Michael Bruening, "Pierre Viret and Geneva," ARG 99 (2008): 175–97.

[92] Bruening, *Calvinism's First Battleground*, 177–78.

3.3.5. The Lausanne Quarrel over Ecclesiastical Goods, 1542–1543

Shortly after his return to Lausanne in 1542, Viret's devotion to Calvin brought him into conflict with Marcourt. The issue in question was the sale of ecclesiastical goods. When the Bernese conquered the Vaud in 1536, they seized a substantial quantity of such goods, both moveable (e.g., church ornaments and vestments) and immoveable (e.g., land and tithe revenues). In autumn 1542, the Bern council sent its representatives to the Vaud to begin selling a large number of these goods.[93] Once again, as with Marcourt's appointment to Geneva, the Calvinists saw this move as an infringement of the rights of the church. Once again, their opponents believed that the Christian magistrates were well within their rights to sell the goods as they saw fit.

Calvin counseled Viret on the matter, "What has once been consecrated to Christ and the church does not belong to the magistrate."[94] Viret took this advice to the next meeting of the Lausanne chapter, which subsequently sent a letter of protest to the Bern council.[95] In essence, their argument was that the revenues from the sale of the goods of the Catholic Church had to remain within the new Protestant Church, and they should fund only three things: pastors, schools, and the poor.[96] Marcourt was at the meeting of the chapter and spoke against Viret.[97] Newly uncovered evidence from a largely unknown manuscript by Beza also reveals that Marcourt was not the only one who opposed Viret's position.[98] Beza refers to the opposition in the plural, calling them "backbiters" and "false brothers," and indicates that after the Lausanne pastors' first appearance in Bern in early February 1543, these "false brothers" sent a document to the Bernese, accusing Viret of "certain very serious crimes."[99] Viret and his colleagues were summoned

---

[93] On this conflict, see Crousaz, *L'Académie de Lausanne*, 209–16; Berthoud, *Antoine Marcourt*, 86–88; Vuilleumier, 1:656–59.

[94] "Non esse magistratus quod Christo et Ecclesiae semel fuerit consecratum." Herminjard 8:167, no. 1171, Calvin to Viret, Geneva, [between October 25 and 28, 1542].

[95] Herminjard 8:171–76, no. 1174, Lausanne Chapter to the Bern Council, Vevey, November 1, 1542.

[96] Crousaz, *L'Académie de Lausanne*, 211.

[97] Berthoud, *Antoine Marcourt*, 86.

[98] This unpublished and largely unknown apology for the Lausanne pastors and professors was written shortly after their expulsion from the city in 1559. See my forthcoming article about this manuscript, "Before the *Histoire Ecclésiastique*: Theodore Beza's Unknown Apologetic History of the Lausanne Pastors and Professors," in *Theodore Beza at 500: New Perspectives on an Old Reformer*, edited by Kirk Summers and Scott Manetsch (Göttingen: Vandenhoek & Ruprecht, 2020), 57–77.

[99] "Postea vero consul ad Petrum Viretum se convertens, denuntiavit ut ad gravissima quaedam crimina responderet quorum accusatus esset, coram Senatu. Erat autem ista accusatio a malevolis quibusdam et falsis fratribus profecta, qui quicquid Viretus in fratrum coetu saepe dixerat quum

to Bern, where Viret had to answer their accusations. In the end, the Bern council sided with Marcourt and his allies and indicated that "the preachers of the Lausanne chapter . . . should not get so agitated nor rush to judgment, without better weighing the circumstances and my lords' [of Bern] reasoning. . . . And in the future, my lords wish to put away this matter and will not suffer such reproaches and unmerited calumnies."[100] Viret was acquitted of criminal action, but Bern's decision was an early blow to Calvinist ecclesiology in the Vaud. Moreover, Beza commented that Bern's inaction against the "sycophants" emboldened them afterward to "be more audacious in their calumnies and to disturb the peace of the churches."[101]

3.3.6. Swiss and French Precedents for Church–State Relations

The divisions between the Calvinists and their opponents that had begun with the Caroli affair widened with the exile of Calvin and Farel from Geneva. During the Caroli affair, what started as two factions based on personal friendships and animosities expanded into a theological quarrel over the trinity. Marcourt and Morand's replacement of Calvin and Farel in Geneva sharpened the focus to the very practical matter of the magistrate's power in church affairs. This issue had the potential to rally supporters to the anti-Calvinist cause, as it seems to have done. The conflict over the magistrate's authority with regard to the church has often been portrayed as a

---

de Ecclesiarum misero statu et bonorum Ecclesiasticorum dissipatione ageretur, malignissime detorserant, et clam conscripta certa capita ad senatum miserant, adeo quidem, ut hominem sicut postea constitit innocentem laesae maiestatis causam dicere oportuerit. Acta fuit igitur haec causa per aliquot dies, quibus quum nunquam potuisset Viretus obtinere ut ederentur eorum nomina qui nomen ipsius detulerant, et ita tamen obiecta crimina diluisset ut de ipsius innocentia constaret, absolutus est, ac demum dimissus." BGE, ms. Archives Tronchin 64, 52ᵛ.

[100] "Et, pour les raisons susdictes, disent mes Seigneurs et entendent que les prédicans du dict Chapitre de Lausanne, auteurs du traicté composé contre la distraction des biens ecclésiasticques, ne se debvroyent tellement eschauffer, ni faire si soudain jugement, sans mieulx peser les circonstances de la matière et les raisons mouvantes mes Seigneurs à suyvre ce conseil, ce qui les eust gardez de composer tel traicté. De quoy, pour l'advenir, mes Seigneurs veulent estre desportez et non souffrir telles reproches et calomnies imméritées." Herminjard 8:283, no. 1204, Bern council to its Deputies in Lausanne, Bern, February 12, 1543.

[101] "In sycophantas vero quos tamen satis liquebat ex numero ministrorum esse, nihil penitus est constitutum, qua impunitas effecit ut eo audacius postea quidvis calumniari et pacem Ecclesiarum perturbare sint ausi." BGE, ms. Archives Tronchin 64, 52ᵛ.

Calvinist/Zwinglian debate,[102] and in many ways, of course, it was. One must remember that in Switzerland in the 1530s and 1540s, Zwingli's theology was the default Protestant position, and Zwingli had given the Christian magistrate a great deal of power over church affairs.[103]

One must also remember that Zwingli's motive for conceding such power to the magistrate was, in part, to avoid any appearance of reinstating the Catholic ecclesiastical hierarchy. From the beginning of the Reformation, Protestants continually castigated the Catholic Church for usurping the rights of the secular authorities and for creating an untouchable separate jurisdiction, impervious to reform. From Erasmus's belief that only the Christian magistrate could effectively reform the church,[104] to Luther's call on the German nobility to seize the reins of church reform,[105] to the Zurich and Bern city councils' introduction of Protestantism through civic religious disputations and government fiat; in all cases, evangelical reformers were wary of ecclesiastical independence from secular authority. The Calvinists seemed to be reintroducing it.

Finally, one must bear in mind the French precedents. As we saw in Chapter 1, early French reform was characterized, at least in part, by episcopal reform and a desire for national, royal reform. The Reformed doctrine of the "equality of ministers" was not yet fully formed.[106] In Switzerland, most cities still had a head pastor called the *Antistes*. Zwingli himself is frequently addressed in correspondence as the *episcopus* (bishop) of Zurich. Thus, when Pierre Caroli was named first pastor of Lausanne and wanted to call together the ministers "in his jurisdiction," few Protestants would necessarily have shared the Calvinist conviction that such language was arrogant and self-serving. Caroli was simply the new *Antistes/episcopus* of Lausanne who

---

[102] See, for example, Karl Bernard Hundeshagen, *Die Conflikte des Zwinglianismus, des Luthertums und des Calvinismus in der Bernischen Landeskirche, 1532–1558* (Bern: C. A. Jenni, 1842); Bruening, *Calvinism's First Battleground.*

[103] See, for example, Robert C. Walton, *Zwingli's Theocracy* (Toronto: University of Toronto Press, 1967).

[104] See James Estes, "*Officium principis christiani*: Erasmus and the Origins of the Protestant State Church," *ARG* 83 (1992): 49–72.

[105] Luther, *To the Christian Nobility of the German Nation, LW* 44:115–217.

[106] On the equality of ministers, see, for example, the Confession of Faith of the French Reformed Churches (1559): "Nous croyons tous vrais pasteurs, en quelque lieu qu'ilz soyent, avoir mesme authorité et esgale puissance soubs un seul chef, seul souverain et seul universel Evesque, Jésus Christ. Et pour ceste cause, nulle église ne doit prétendre aucune Domination ou Seigneurie sur l'autre." Heiner Faulenbach et al., eds., *Reformierte Bekenntnisschriften* (Neukirchen-Vluyn: Neukirchener Verlag, 2002–), 2/1:26 (art. 30). See also the Second Helvetic Confession (1566): "Una et aequalis potestas ministrorum. Data est autem omnibus in ecclesia ministris una et aequalis potestas sive functio (ch. 18)." Ibid., 2/1:321.

would lead the reform efforts in a chaotic area where there were not enough pastors and where most of the people had recently been forced to convert. Moreover, the early French reformers' ultimate goal of state-sponsored church reform had, in essence, been realized in Switzerland. The Swiss cantons were not monarchies, and they were a fraction of the size of the France. But city councils that had embraced Protestant reform were doing exactly what the French reformers of the 1520s had hoped the Most Christian King of France would do.

Thus, Zwinglian ecclesiology, Protestant anticlericalism, and the French reform model all cast suspicion on Calvinist claims for ecclesiastical independence from the magistrate. Marcourt and Morand exemplified the defense of the old model during their Genevan ministry and in the quarrel over church goods. Together with their old friends, they would continue to fight the Calvinists on this issue, as on many others, in the years to come.

3.4. The Formation of Anti-Calvinist Outposts in the Pays de Vaud

Thus far in this chapter, we have focused on individuals who were opposed to the Calvinists. The sames names have recurred: Caroli, Lecomte, Malingre, Marcourt, and Morand. Starting in 1541, the Calvinists made concerted efforts in Geneva, Neuchâtel, and Lausanne to advance their new agenda. Most of the pastors near those cities were behind Calvin, Farel, and Viret in that effort. The Calvinists faced much opposition from the city councils, however, and from other pastors of the Suisse romande. Most of these pastors were based in a few geographical locations in Romandie, and their leaders were the same individuals we have already examined in this chapter. Thus, by 1545, there were discernible centers of anti-Calvinism behind Malingre and Lecomte in Yverdon, Morand in Morges, and Marcourt in the Pays de Gex (see Map 3.1).

3.4.1. The Failure of Calvinist Reform Efforts, 1541–1542

Just after Calvin and Farel were expelled from Geneva in 1538, they drafted a response to the decisions of the Synod of Lausanne, which had established

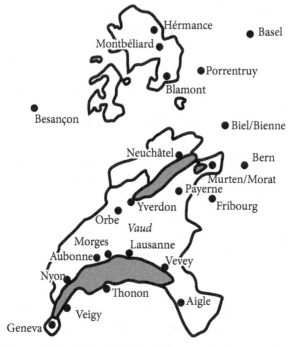

Map 3.1 The Pays de Vaud, Neuchâtel, and the Comté of Montbéliard

the ceremonies to be used throughout Bern's lands. The Bern-approved ceremonies included the use of baptismal fonts, unleavened bread, and the celebration of the Lord's Supper only three times a year.[107] In their response, Calvin and Farel laid out in fourteen articles the core principles of Calvinist praxis, including the use of leavened bread, the need to establish effective moral discipline, the use of excommunication by the consistory, the establishment of the legitimate calling of ministers, frequent celebration of the Lord's Supper, and the singing of Psalms in worship.[108] With Calvin and

---

[107] See Vuilleumier, 1:305–309.

[108] "2. In mutando pane paulo maiori difficultate constringimur . . . 6. Erit deinde studium adhibendum disciplinae stabiliendae, alioqui mox collabetur quidquid in praesens instauratum fuerit . . . 9. Ut germanus excommunicationis usus restituatur eo quem praescripsimus modo, nempe ut a senatu eligantur ex singulis urbis regionibus probi et cordati viri, quibus in commune nobiscum ea cura incumbat. 10. Ut in ministrorum vocatione legitimus ordo servetur: ne manuum impositio, quae penes ministros esse debet, magistratus potentia tollatur e medio, quod non semel nostri conati sunt . . . 12. Prius est, ut frequentior coenae usus instituatur, si non secundum veteris ecclesiae consuetudinem, at saltem singulis quibusque mensibus semel. 13. Alterum, ut ad publicas orationes psalmorum cantio adhibeatur." *Calv. Ep.* 1:470–72, Appx. no. 3, [Farel and Calvin to the Zurich Synod], [Zurich], [between May 2 and June 10, 1538].

Farel's exile, these principles lay in abeyance for over three years. This was an important yet underappreciated interlude, for it allowed Bern's rites to become entrenched throughout Romandie. The longer one form of church practice continues, the more difficult it is to replace it with another. In this way, Bern's liturgy and ceremonies, not those of the Calvinists, became the status quo throughout the region.

Calvin's return to Geneva in September 1541, however, emboldened his followers to seek to overturn the Bern model. In Geneva, Viret and Calvin worked together to implement the Calvinist vision of reform. Although they were initially unsuccessful at winning the right of excommunication, many of their other ideas were put into practice in the Geneva's well-known church ordinances.[109] This early victory was confined to Geneva, however. In Neuchâtel and the Pays de Vaud, the Bernese system remained in force, despite Farel's and Viret's best efforts.

3.4.2. Farel's Failure in Neuchâtel

In Neuchâtel, Farel modeled his first reform proposal, the *Articles Concerning the Reformation of the Church of Neuchâtel*, on the Geneva ecclesiastical ordinances that Calvin had sent him.[110] The *Articles* called for the same four ecclesiastical offices (pastors, doctors, elders, and deacons) as the Geneva ordinances, the election of pastors by the rest of the chapter, the monthly celebration of the Lord's Supper, and the establishment of a consistory with the power of excommunication.[111] More controversially, they also called for quarterly "fraternal censures," which were occasions for the pastors to

---

[109] Text in *CO* 10:15–30.

[110] The text of and background to the *Articles concernans la réformation de l'église de Neufchastel* are in J. Pétremand, "Etudes sur les origines de l'Église Réformée neuchâteloise: Les premiers essais d'organisation de la Classe, serment et discipline du clergé, les Articles calvinistes de 1541 et les Ordonnances de 1542," *Revue d'histoire suisse* 8 (1928): 321–70; text of articles, 356–70. See also on this period *Guillaume Farel*, 457–66.

[111] The Articles do not use the terms *excommunication* or *consistory*, but they do call for weekly meetings of the pastors and elders together "pour voir et entendre s'il n'y a nul désordre en l'Eglise de nostre Seigneur, et traicter ensemble secrettement les moiens et remèdes pour gagner en nostre Seigneur nostre frère chrestien quand il en sera besoin." Pétremand, "Etudes sur les origines de l'Eglise Réformée neuchâteloise," 368–69. The Articles also stipulate that "ceux qui se seront mocquez des admonitions particulières de leur prochain soyent admonestés derechef par l'Eglise, et s'ilz ne vouloyent nullement venir à raison ni recognoistre leur faulte, quand ilz en seront convaincus, qu'on leur dénonce qu'ilz ayent à s'abstenir de la Cène jusqu'à ce qu'ilz viennent à meilleure disposition de vie et d'esprit." Ibid., 369.

critique each other's doctrine and morals.[112] Farel's *Articles* went nowhere. Soon after the pastors drafted them, the Neuchâtel council passed instead the *Constitutions and Ordinances* of 1542,[113] which detailed a series of moral offenses. All of the accused, however, were to be judged and punished by the secular magistrate. There is no mention of a role for pastors, elders, or a consistory.

Unwilling to give up, Farel called a synod, which was held on May 9, 1542, and produced a new set of articles, the *Articles Drafted by the Ministers of Neuchâtel*,[114] which demanded the chapter's right to examine potential pastors, the appointment of "good men" to watch over the moral lives of the parishioners, and the establishment of a consistory with coercive power (although the pastors stopped short this time of requesting the right of excommunication). The Neuchâtel council ignored nearly all their demands, agreeing only to provide an additional deacon. Instead, on July 1, 1542, the council issued the *Ordonnances pour la ville*, which required the pastors to preach only things that can be easily proved by Scripture, prohibited excommunication or witholding communion, and indicated clearly that coercive power in punishing immoral behavior lay exclusively with the secular authorities.[115] Thus, Farel's first efforts to bring Calvinism to Neuchâtel failed utterly. The city council stood firmly in the Zwinglian, Bernese tradition.

[112] "Et entendons que pour maintenir ceste correction et discipline en son estat, de trois en trois mois les pasteurs et ministres, ensemble les anciens auront specialement regard s'il y a rien à redire entre eux pour y remedier comme de raison." Pétremand, "Etudes sur les origines de l'Eglise Réformée neuchâteloise," 360. We will return to the controversy over fraternal censures, 97–100.

[113] *Constitutions et Ordonnances*, text in Jonas Boyve, *Annales historiques du Comté de Neuchâtel et Valangin depuis Jules-César jusqu'en 1722*, 5 vols. (Bern: Edouard Mathey, 1854–1861), 2:423–28.

[114] *Articles dressez par les ministres de Neufchastel*, text in Pétreman, "Etudes sur les origines de l'Eglise Réformée neuchâteloise," 348–50.

[115] "Voulons et statuons par ces présentes que désormais nul de nos ministres n'ait à tenir, dans ses sermons et prêches, paroles, dits et propos, termes, comparaisons, similitudes ou autres cas semblables que facilement il ne puisse montrer pas la Parole de Dieu. . . . Item, ordonnons et statuons que pour le présent, nos dits ministres et pasteurs ne s'entremettent à nous introduire la pratique et usage d'excommunication, qu'ils appellent autrement la correction ou discipline de l'Eglise, puisque sur les vices et péchés avons ordonnances et statuts portant punition corporelle et pécuniaire, passée par la seigneurie et conseigneurie. . . . Ordonnans en outre et statuons que nos pasteurs dorénavant n'aient à refuser la sainte cène à personne de suffisant âge, et qui de sa foi rende bonne confession." Ruchat 2:520–21. Ruchat entitles this text "Premières ordonnances ecclésiastiques à Neuchâtel," likely following Olivier Perrot, who dated them to 1534. *Guillaume Farel* 464n2.

3.4.3. Viret's Failures in Lausanne

Later in 1542, Viret likewise tried and failed to introduce Calvinist innovations in Lausanne. Viret's conflict with Marcourt over ecclesiastical goods was one element of this larger debate. In Lausanne, disputes over ecclesiology were compounded by a Eucharistic controversy that began to boil over in Bern.[116] In August 1542, the Bern council summoned the francophone chapters to hear its decision on the matter. Calvin was displeased both with the decision itself and with what he saw as the secular magistrate's interference on a theological issue. He counseled Viret to resist.[117]

Thus, in the letter in which the pastors of the Lausanne chapter registered their discontent about the profits from the sale of ecclesiastical goods, they also—indeed chiefly—complained about the magistrate's involvement in theological affairs.[118] Moreover, in the course of the debates that followed this letter, it is clear that Viret and the Lausanne pastors began to push for independent ecclesiastical discipline and the right of excommunication. The Bern council's decision, like that of Neuchâtel, was an unequivocal rejection:

> First of all, with regard to ecclesiastical discipline, also called excommunication, many discussions and meetings have been held about the subject by my lords and their adherents who follow the Gospel, but they have never found it useful to establish such a discipline in the form requested by the ministers of Lausanne for several reasons.[119]

---

[116] On this debate, see Hundeshagen, *Die Conflikte des Zwinglianismus, des Luthertums und des Calvinismus.*

[117] See Bruening, *Calvinism's First Battleground*, 179–82.

[118] "Ni nobis iam satis persuasum esset, quam benevolo animo et quanto zelo accensi sitis erga ecclesiam Dei, ut eam in sua libertate conservetis, et ministros Christi in ea dignitate qua Pastorum et Ministrorum Evangelicorum Princeps eos constituit, ut et vestris postremis literis amplius testificati estis, potius quam eam dura tyrannide opprimere, ansam ac occasionem haberemus vos admonendi, non esse Principum qui in hoc saeculo agunt, quamlibet potentium aut cuiuscunque conditionis, praescribere sola sua auctoritate Ministris, quae docere debeant, neque Ecclesiae quae credere debeat et sequi, sed soli Deo per suam Ecclesiam iuxta verbum eius convocatam, atque ordinem ab eodem constitutum." Herminjard 8:172, no. 1174.

[119] "Premièrement: quant à la Discipline ecclésiastique, autrement nommée excommunication, que plusieurs pourparlemens et journées en ont esté tenues par mes Seigneurs et leurs adhérans qui tiennent le parti de l'Évangile, sans avoir jamais trouvé commodité de dresser telle discipline à la forme requise par les ministres de Lausanne, pour plusieurs raisons." Herminjard 8:280–81, no. 1204, Bern council to its Deputies in Lausanne, Bern, February 12, 1543. Translation from Bruening, *Calvinism's First Battleground*, 181.

Although the Bernese granted the chapters the right to examine new pastors, they refused to permit the rite of the laying-on-of-hands at ordinations, and they required the pastors to allow Bern's bailiffs to attend their meetings, which they indicated should no longer be secret, at least not from the Bernese authorities.[120] Despite Farel's and Viret's best efforts, therefore, the Calvinist program was going nowhere outside of Geneva.

Apart from Farel in Neuchâtel and Viret in Lausanne (and to a lesser extent their ally Christophe Fabri in Thonon),[121] none of the other francophone clergy had any desire to introduce Calvinism. Instead, the other chapters of the Suisse romande were perfectly content with the status quo. Not surprisingly, the leading pastors in those areas were the traditional adversaries of the Calvinists.

3.4.4. Yverdon

In Yverdon, Caroli's allies Malingre and Lecomte ensured perhaps the strongest continuous resistance to the Calvinists.[122] In addition to Malingre and Lecomte, the Yverdon chapter included Claude de Glant, one of the first pastors to have suffered at the hands of the Calvinists. De Glant was a former Catholic priest and native of Yverdon who had joined Farel's evangelical mission by 1530.[123] The 1536 Synod of Yverdon, however (which preceded

---

[120] "Touchant la vocation des ministres, sont mes Seigneurs délibérez de n'accepter ministre nouveau quelconque qu'il ne soit premièrement examiné par les ministres du lieu et Classe en laquelle il doibt exercer son office . . ., sans aultres cérémonies ni imposition des mains, qui n'est chose fort nécessaire, la reste estant bien constituée et gardée. . . . Et, pour conclusion, se sont mes Seigneurs résoluz que le serment par lequel les prédicans s'obligent de tenir secretz les actes de leurs congrégations, ne doibge aulcunement déroger ni estre préféré au serment et debvoir qu'ilz ont à mes dictz Seigneurs en choses concernant leur bien et honneur. Item, que les Baillifz ne soyent excluz des congrégations et colloques, afin qu'ilz oyent et congnoissent si en aulcuns lieux l'on cesse ou deffault d'exécuter les mandemens et ordonnances de mes Seigneurs." Herminjard 281–83, no. 1204.

[121] Christophe Fabri (ca. 1509–1588) had been a close ally of Farel since 1531, and he remained an ally of the Calvinists as pastor of Thonon, on the south shore of Lake Geneva. Thonon would later preach in Neuchâtel and was in Lyon at the same time as Viret in the 1560s. On him, see Gabriel Mützenberg, "Christophe Fabri et les débuts de la Réforme dans le Chablais," in *La Dispute de Lausanne (1536): La théologie Réformée après Zwingli et avant Calvin*, edited by Eric Junod, Bibliothèque historique vaudoise 90 (Lausanne: Bibliothèque historique vaudoise, 1988), 189–99.

[122] In *Calvinism's First Battleground*, I noted Calvin's snide remark about Yverdon, when his enemy André Zébédée was sent there: "De Zebedaeo nihil habeo consilii nisi ut ecclesiae Iverdunensi reddatur siquidem impetram hoc poterit. Ipse tali populo dignissimus, nec iniuria populo fiet qui talem pastorem meretur." CO 13:300, no. 1205, Calvin to Viret, Geneva, June 15, 1549. I commented, "I do not know the origin of Calvin's negative opinion of the people of Yverdon." Bruening, *Calvinism's First Battleground*, 193 and n. 92. It now seems clear that Calvin was expressing his disdain not so much toward the common people as toward the anti-Calvinist chapter of Yverdon.

[123] See Herminjard 2:252n4.

the Lausanne Disputation later that year), was presided over by Viret, and it declared De Glant unworthy of the ministry on account of his moral character and dereliction of duty.[124] In 1539, De Glant reconciled with the ministers of Yverdon and became rector of the town's school. In Yverdon, he would have found a sympathetic audience for his grievances against the Calvinists. In 1550, Viret remarked to Farel, "I am not at all surprised by what you write concerning what is being done in the Yverdon chapter. . . . You know what kind of character certain individuals there have and in what way they have set themselves up since the beginning. Just as the first origin of all of our troubles was from there, so kindling for fire there will never be absent."[125]

3.4.5. Pays de Gex

In the Pays de Gex, we have already seen that some of the pastors sided with Caroli in his conflicts with Calvin, Farel, and Viret.[126] In early 1543, the Gex chapter appears to have opposed Calvin on the subject of the Eucharist as well. Simon Sulzer wrote Calvin from Bern, "I am sorry that you were recently so poorly received by the brothers in Gex, especially since I would guess that even more sinister suspicion will follow."[127] Anti-Calvinist sentiment in the Pays de Gex was no doubt elevated further when Marcourt was reassigned to the chapter, as pastor of Versoix, following his fight with Viret over ecclesiastical goods. In 1547, the Geneva ministers drew up a list of complaints about the failures of the pastors there. Some, they complained, spent too much time in the tavern or at games and dances, "resembling soldiers more than

---

[124] "Item omnes fratres uno consensu censuerunt Claudium Glandinaeum, qui nunc praefectus est Couldrefin, ministerio Verbi indignum, ob multas et graves caussas, praesertim: I. Quia multa loca, ut fertur, muneribus ambivit, et absque facultate Ecclesiae. II. Proprias oves reliquit absque pastore. . . . III. Item, quia contempsit, ab hinc quinquennium, congregationes fratrum, colloquia, admonitiones et censuras. . . . IV. Item, notatur ab eisdem fratribus avaritia, inhospitalitate et maxime erga fratres. V. Item, cauponarium exercet, quod maxime Verbi ministrum dedecet, ubi fovet blasphemos, ebriosos, etc. VI. Item, litigiosus est et percussor, qui publice, cum magno scandalo populi, alium fratrem Verbi ministrum invasit. VII. Item, maledicus est et compertus ordinarius mendax, tam in accusando quam in excusando." Herminjard 4:64, no. 562, [Synod of Yverdon] to the Bern Council, [Yverdon], [June 8, 1536].
[125] "Nihil miror ista quae scribis in classe Iverdunensi tractari. . . . Nosti qualia illic sint quorundam ingenia et quales se iam inde ab initio praestiterunt quidam. Ut prima inde nostrarum turbarum omnium origo fuit, ita illic nunquam fomes defuit." *Epistolae Vireti*, 206, no. 54, Viret to Farel, Lausanne, May 21, 1550.
[126] See 73–74.
[127] "A Gaiensibus fratribus parum te amice nuper acceptum doleo, tum maxime quod plusculum sinistrae suspicionis subesse conjiciam." Herminjard 8:256, no. 1200, Sulzer to Calvin, Bern, January 31, 1543.

ministers."[128] The Genevans accused other pastors of beating and mistreating their wives and of committing fornication.[129] Some, they said, "have hardly any heart or zeal for upholding the reformation of the Gospel, for restraining and correcting superstitions repugnant to it, and even have more contact with the papists than with those who walk the straight path according to the Gospel."[130] The Pays de Gex bordered Geneva, and some of its pastors were in the contested lands of "St. Victor et chapitre," which were under the shared jurisdiction of Geneva and Bern. Thus, the Genevan pastors claimed that "there is no good or evil on the one side that is not felt by the other."[131] Nevertheless, the pastors of Gex likely believed that the Genevan pastors had little right to correct them.

3.4.6. Morges

The Morges chapter became another outpost of opposition to Calvinism. In 1540, after the Guillermins returned to power in Geneva, Jean Morand moved to Nyon and likely became a leading voice of the chapter. The pastor of Morges itself, Jacques Le Coq, had been an early ally of the Calvinists,[132] but in 1542, he quarreled with Farel over preaching in Metz. The people of Metz had called Le Coq to be their pastor, and he became annoyed when Farel decided to preach in the city on his own initiative, without a proper call.[133]

---

[128] "Item sur ceulx qui au lieu d'estre vigilantz sur le troppeau en la paroisse où ilz sont commis ne font que trotter çà et là à leurs esbats, et au lieu de vivre paisiblement en leur mesnage seront tousjours en la taverne, depensantz plus pour leur personne qu'ilz n'ont pour nourrir toute leur famille, mesmes qui y font beaucoup d'insolences. Item à ceulx qui se desbordent en dissolutions, tant de jeux que de dances, et au lieu de se maintenir en honnesteté convenable en l'estat de ministres, tant en gestes que en habitz et en toutes contenances, ressemblent plus souldartz que ministres." CO 12:533–34, no. 914, Geneva Ministers, Memoir for the envoys to the Pays de Gex, June 3, 1547.

[129] "Item à ceulx qui battent et traictent mal leurs femmes et mesmes qui ne sont point sans grand suspicion de paillardise, pour le moins en ont mauvais bruict au grand prejudice de la parolle de Dieu." CO 12:534, no. 914.

[130] "Item qui n'ont gueres de cueur ne de zele à maintenir la reformation de l'evangille, à reprendre et corriger les superstitions repugnantes à icelle, et mesmes ont plus d'accointance aux papistes qu'à ceulx qui cheminent droictement selon l'evangille." CO 12:545, no. 914.

[131] "Item que le voisinage porte cela qu'il n'y peut avoir ne bien ne mal d'un costé que l'autre ne s'en sente." CO 12:543–44, no. 914.

[132] See 75–76.

[133] Guillaume Farel, 488–89. See also Herminjard 8:116, no. 1153, Calvin to Farel, Geneva, August 30, 1542: "Interea mirum quas querelas spargat hic passim Jacobus Morgiensis: te currere, cum ipse vocatus esset: sibi gravem iniuriam factam esse. Te invitis piis omnibus qui istic sunt, advolasse." And Herminjard 8:215–16, no. 1187, Calvin to Viret, Geneva, [ca. December 8, 1542]: "De Jacobo mihi non placet quod tam molliter acceptum dimiseris. . . . Ego vero statueram, nisi memoria excidisset, literis adscribere: 'Legas, Jacobe, et si quem habes humanitatis sensum, fleas.' Si causam ex me quaesiisset, multo asperius exposuissem quam Farellus. Sic tractandi sunt isti ἀλάζονες."

Thus, Le Coq became another friend-turned-enemy of the Calvinists, and together with Morand, he led the Morges chapter to resist their innovations. There are few references to overt opposition from the Morges chapter at this time, but one episode hints at tensions. Viret once attended a meeting of the Morges chapter and presented to the attendees Calvin's advice on a defrocked Carmelite from Lyon. Rather than attribute these recommendations to Calvin, however, Viret first presented Calvin's advice as his own. He explains to Calvin that he had done this to avoid alienating those in attendance who were not favorable to Calvin.[134]

3.4.7. A Test Case: Jean Chaponneau's Critique of Fraternal Corrections, 1544

A conflict between Farel and his colleague in Neuchâtel, Jean Chaponneau, reveals clearly the geographical fault lines that divided the Calvinist and anti-Calvinist factions in the Suisse romande during the mid-1540s. Chaponneau was a doctor of theology who had studied in Louvain. He had also been an Augustinian monk in the abbey of Saint-Ambroise in Bourges, where he met Calvin and began delivering evangelical sermons.[135] He and Farel seem to have tolerated each other well enough during most of their time together in Neuchâtel. Chaponneau viewed Farel as his intellectual inferior, however, and Farel thought Chaponneau was not fully committed to Protestant doctrine; he believed Chaponneau was too attached to the opinions of the Church fathers and thus not completely dedicated to the doctrine of *sola scriptura*.[136]

In 1544, the two men quarreled over fraternal censures, the quarterly meetings where pastors in the Neuchâtel region would critique one another's life and doctrine.[137] The quarrel soon spilled over into Chaponneau and

---

[134] "Quod ad negocium Carmelitae attinet, placuit sententia quam mihi tuis literis significabas. Eam primum proposui quasi meam, priusquam tui interiecta esset mentio. Cum autem quidam ex iis quos tibi putabam minus favere, audirem tuam quoque requirere, tum palam indicavi eandem esse cum ea quam a me audierant." Herminjard 9:363, no. 1409, Viret to Calvin, Lausanne, November 9, 1544.

[135] On Chaponneau, see Emile Picot, *Notice sur Jehan Chaponneau, Docteur de l'Eglise réformée, metteur en scène du Mistère des Actes des Apostres, joué à Bourges en 1536* (Paris: Damascene Morgand and Charles Fatout, 1879); *Guillaume Farel*, 541–50.

[136] For example, "Offendi collegam [Chaponneau] tantum non conculcantem Scripturas, intelligentiam solis attribuentem veteribus." Herminjard 5:154, no. 752, Farel to Calvin, Neuchâtel, October 14, 1538.

[137] See 91–92.

Courtois's criticism of Calvin's doctrine of the trinity.[138] On the fraternal censures, Chaponneau's position was that pastors guilty of sin should be treated as prescribed in Matthew 18:15–17: first, admonished privately, then with one or two others, and finally denounced to the church.[139] He also argued that the censures need not take place at prescribed times, as was the practice in Neuchâtel.[140] Farel presented Chaponneau's very words to Bullinger, but concluded disingenuously, "The adversary says that the censure is completely contrary to the Word of the Lord."[141] The other pastors of the Neuchâtel chapter seem to have supported Farel, but they wrote to the other chapters in Romandie, as well as to some of the German-speaking churches to seek their advice on the matter.

The responses reflect in part the factional divisions among the chapters. Unsurprisingly, Calvin wrote in the name of the Geneva pastors to offer his strong support of Farel.[142] The Morges chapter, however, issued a brief statement showing only tepid support for Farel.[143] The Gex chapter came to Chaponneau's defense, stating that his articles were "good and true."[144] Unfortunately, the response from Yverdon, if there was one, no longer exists.

Most striking, perhaps, is the universal support among the German-speaking churches for Farel's position, at least among those whose responses survive.[145] The Zwinglians' unanimous support for Farel highlights the fact that opposition to the Calvinists in Romandie was not simply a Zwinglian/

---

[138] See 74.

[139] "Adversarius Classis:. . . 'Quisquis Christiana charitate erga fratrem afficitur, vel notorio peccato laborantem, sancte fecerit, si eum primo clam monuerit, deinde non audientem, praesente uno atque altero teste iuxta ordinem a Christo praescriptum, iterum admonuerit, ac tandem iteratis monitionibus non cedentem ecclesiae denunciaverit.'" Herminjard 9:349–50, no. 1403, Farel to Bullinger, Neuchâtel, [ca. October 28, 1544].

[140] "Praeceptum fraternae correctionis, cum sit affirmativum, non pro quolibet tempore obligat. Licebit igitur correctionem, cuius finis est fratris delinquentis emendatio, non solum differre, sed et nonnunquam prorsus ab ea abstinere." Herminjard 9:349–50, no. 1403.

[141] "Adversarius ait omnino contrariam esse censuram verbo Domini." Herminjard 9:350, no. 1403.

[142] Herminjard 9:353–58, no. 1407, Geneva Pastors to the Classe of Neuchâtel, Geneva, November 7, 1544.

[143] Herminjard 9:350–51, no. 1404, [Classe of Morges] to the Neuchâtel Pastors, Bursins, November 4, 1544.

[144] "les frères ont advisé que les lettres ne informent point suffisamment des différens esmeuz entre les frères de Neufchastel et celuy qui leur est répugnant, veu que les articles d'icelluy, bons et veritables, ne contrarient point à la correction fraternelle et chrestienne." Herminjard 9:352, no. 1406, Gex chapter to [the Neuchâtel pastors], Saconnex-le-Grand, November 6, 1544.

[145] See the responses from Basel (Herminjard 9:429–34, no. 1427, Oswald Myconius to Farel, Basel, December 23 and 26, 1544), Strasbourg (ibid., 436–43, Strasbourg Pastors to the Neuchâtel Pastors, Strasbourg, December 29, 1544), and Zurich (CO 12:45–46, Bullinger to the Neuchâtel Pastors, Zurich, March 12, 1545). Unfortunately, no response from Bern exists.

Calvinist theological conflict; the German-speaking Zwinglians supported the Calvinists on this issue. Their position reflected, at least in part, the fact that Bullinger had been administering fraternal corrections in Zurich by means of the synod since 1532.[146] More important in the early years of the Reformation was the development of personal hostilities, which later evolved into geographical factional divisions. Lecomte and Malingre broke from the Calvinists over the Caroli affair and led the Yverdon chapter in opposition; Claude de Glant added to the anti-Calvinist hostility there. Morand and Marcourt alienated the Calvinists by replacing Calvin and Farel in Geneva without a call from the pastors. Jacques Le Coq broke with Farel over a similar issue, although, ironically, on that occasion it was Farel who preached in Metz without a proper call. Morand and Le Coq would lead the Morges chapter, and Marcourt would join a pastorate in the Pays de Gex that was already hostile to Calvin in the wake of the Caroli affair.

Chaponneau's rejection of fraternal censures also points to another strand of opposition to Calvinism, one that would later emerge more strongly when Jean Morély attempted to elevate the lay church members at least to the level of the pastors themselves. Despite Farel's misleading characterization of his position, Chaponneau was by no means opposed to correcting vice among the pastors; he simply believed that such correction should be done in strict accord with Matthew 18:17, so that the final adjudication would be by "the church." The Calvinists, of course, would also point repeatedly to the same biblical passage, but for them "the church" meant not the local congregation but its officers and representatives: the pastors and the consistory.

The Chaponneau affair ended abruptly on October 22, 1545, when Chaponneau died. Nonetheless, by this time, the battle lines had been drawn in the Suisse romande. Calvin, Farel, and Viret led the Calvinist faction in Geneva, Neuchâtel, and Lausanne. Malingre, Lecomte, Marcourt, and Morand led the opposition in Yverdon, Morges, and Gex. One of the keys to the Calvinists' eventual success lies simply in the nature of these locations: the Calvinists held the largest and most important cities in the region. This advantage, however, did not make victory inevitable. As we have

---

[146] See Bruce Gordon, *Clerical Discipline and the Rural Reformation: The Synod in Zürich, 1532–1580*, Zürcher Beiträge zur Reformationsgeschichte 16 (Bern: Peter Lang, 1992); Bruce Gordon, *The Swiss Reformation*, New Frontiers in History (Manchester, UK: Manchester University Press, 2002), 251–53.

seen, Farel's and Viret's initial efforts to introduce Calvinism to their cities failed. Moreover, the following years brought no dramatic reversal of fortune. Instead, a series of conflicts over the Eucharist, predestination, and ecclesiastical discipline sharpened the divisions between the two sides and introduced a new cast of anti-Calvinist leaders.

4

The Consolidation of Anti-Calvinism in Francophone Switzerland

4.1. Introduction

The Calvinists were on the defensive in the 1550s. Typically, historians have portrayed these years, and in particular 1555, as the time of John Calvin's triumph over resistence in Geneva. Beyond Geneva's city walls, however, this period was a high point for Calvin's opponents and a disaster for the Calvinists themselves. A series of quarrels over the Eucharist, pastoral power, predestination, and excommunication put Calvin and his supporters at odds with other pastors in francophone Switzerland, with the political authorities in Bern, and with the reformers in Zurich, Bern, and Basel. Calvin's rivals in the region, by contrast, grew stronger as anti-Calvinist sentiment spread more broadly and coalesced in Romandie around André Zébédée, Jerome Bolsec, and Jacques de Bourgogne, Seigneur de Falais.

Zébédée, one of the least studied but most important opponents of the Calvinists, started his career in the Suisse romande as an ally of Calvin and his supporters, but he turned against them in the late 1540s. The precipitating event was a bitter quarrel in Lausanne over the Eucharist and the power of the ministry. Zébédée's challenge to the Calvinist position, championed by Pierre Viret, nearly resulted in the expulsion of Viret and his allies from the Lausanne Academy. Afterward, in the early 1550s, Zébédée assumed leadership of the anti-Calvinist faction in the Pays de Vaud when he supported Bolsec's criticisms of Calvin's doctrine of double predestination. Bolsec's patron, Falais, likewise broke with Calvin and made his estate at Veigy a center for anti-Calvinist activity in the region. Zébédée's leadership, Bolsec's denunciations, and Falais's patronage united the previously scattered centers of anti-Calvinism in francophone Switzerland.

For the most part, this coalition succeeded. In 1555, Zébédée convinced the Bernese to ban Calvin's catechism and to prohibit the use of his *Institutes* at the Lausanne Academy. They also forebade their subjects to

Refusing to Kiss the Slipper. Michael W. Bruening, Oxford University Press (2021). © Oxford University Press.
DOI: 10.1093/oso/9780197566954.003.0005

take communion in Geneva, prohibited their pastors to preach on predestination, and ordered their bailiffs to burn any books, by Calvin or others, found in their lands that were judged contrary to Bern's reformation. It was a humiliating defeat for Calvin and his allies and a stunning victory for the anti-Calvinists.

The coalition's success is perhaps the clearest evidence that Calvinism's ultimate dominance of francophone Protestantism was far from inevitable. In 1555, Calvin led reform efforts only within Geneva itself. Although he would soon find a new mission field in France, his network in the Suisse romande weakened quickly in the face of increasingly coordinated opposition, nearly collapsing altogether in 1559 with the expulsion of Viret and his associates from Lausanne. Neuchâtel alone remained a regional ally. Meanwhile, the influence of the anti-Calvinists grew throughout the region. Bern, the Vaud, and Montbéliard all stoutly resisted Calvin's pretensions to leadership over the movement. In short, even in the late 1550s, there was no clear indication that francophone Protestantism would ever become synonymous with Calvinism.

4.2. André Zébédée's Early Career: From Friend to Foe of the Calvinists, 1534–1547

Perhaps no evangelical opponent of the Calvinists is as underappreciated as André Zébédée. No biography or even encyclopedia entry on him exists.[1] Like Pierre Caroli, Zébédée has been much maligned by Calvinist-dominated historiography, which commonly calls him "ambitious" or "quarrelsome"[2]—terms that could as easily describe Calvin

---

[1] For example, there is no entry for Zébédée in Hans Hillerbrand, ed., *Oxford Encyclopedia of the Reformation*, 4 vols. (New York: Oxford University Press, 1996), Haag's *La France Protestante*, or the online *Dictionnaire historique de la Suisse* (https://hls-dhs-dss.ch/fr/). There is likewise no mention of him in any of the following major works (a representative but not exhaustive list): Wendel, *Calvin: Origins and Development of His Religious Thought*; William Bouwsma, *John Calvin: A Sixteenth Century Portrait* (New York: Oxford University Press, 1988); Herman J. Selderhuis, *John Calvin: A Pilgrim's Life*, translated by Albert Gootjes (Downers Grove, IL: Intervarsity Press, 2009); there is only one mention of him in Hermann J. Selderhuis, ed., *The Calvin Handbook* (Grand Rapids, MI: Eerdmans, 2009).

[2] For example, (1) "Il était en effet très infatué de sa personne et passablement ambitieux." (2) "Ce que l'on connait du caractère entier et ambitieux de cet homme . . ." (3) "Entraîné par son caractère querelleur" (4) "Très zélé, mais présomptueux, tracassier et parfois violent" (5) "a quarrelsome character, rash, vain, unmanageable, wholly without tact" (6) "cet enfant terrible . . . il était ambitieux et intéressé." Citations: (1) Ernest Gaullieur, *Histoire du Collège de Guyenne, d'après un grand nombre*

himself.[3] Zébédée's career began brilliantly in Bordeaux, France, where he was a notable and well-paid young teacher at the Collège de Guyenne. His move to Switzerland initially required him to serve as pastor in Viret's hometown of Orbe, a significant step down professionally. The distinction that marked his earlier academic career in France puts into perspective the accusations of ambition and pride so often leveled against him.

After he arrived in Switzerland, Zébédée was close to Calvin, Farel, and Viret, but he became increasingly concerned about the Calvinists' move away from Zwinglian theology, particularly on the nature of the ministry and of the sacraments, and he started to befriend the Calvinists' enemies in the Pays de Vaud. His relatively slow move away from Calvin, however, demonstrates that friendships and existing ties were at least as important as theology in forging the Calvinist and anti-Calvinist networks. If these networks had been shaped by theological commitment alone, Zébédée would have joined the anti-Calvinists soon after his arrival in Switzerland. Instead, his break from Calvin took nearly a decade. Nevertheless, by the time he became the arts professor at the Lausanne Academy in 1547, his relationship with the Calvinists was already strained. Soon afterward, it snapped. A bitter quarrel the following year with Viret and the other Lausanne ministers and professors led to Zébédée's thorough vilification among the Calvinists. Over the next decade, Zébédée would become the leading voice of dissent against Calvinist hegemony.

de documents inédits (Paris: Sandoz et Fischbacher, 1874), 84; (2) Jean Barnaud, Pierre Viret: Sa vie et son oeuvre (1511–1571) (Saint-Amans: G. Carayol, 1911), 332; (3) ibid., 339; (4) Herminjard 8:42n1; (5) Caroline Ruutz-Rees, Charles de Sainte-Marthe (1512–1555), Studies in Romance Philology and Literature (New York: Columbia University Press, 1910), 20; (6) Jules Le Coultre, Maturin Cordier et les origines de la pédagogie protestante dans les pays de langue française (1530–1564), Mémoires de l'Université de Neuchâtel 5 (Neuchâtel: Secrétariat de l'Université, 1926), 231.

[3] Calvin made little secret of his ambition to be welcomed into the elite circle of French humanist scholars from his first (largely self-funded) publication, the commentary on Seneca's De clementia. Likewise, his dedication to King Francis I of the Institutes while still an almost completely unknown scholar was typical of those seeking to place themselves among the intellectual elite. See Szczech, Calvin en polémique, 275. And as Calvin painted his opponents as "ambitious," so they applied the label to him. A contemporary text, most likely written by Jerome Bolsec, describes Calvin as follows: "J'entens qu'il ha trois qualitez notables / Qui sont vertus les plus propres des diables. / En premier lieu il est ambitieux / S'il en fut ung jamais dessoubs les cieux /. . . . De son orgueil encor plus oultre on dict, / Qu'homme n'y a tant soit docte en ce monde / A son advis qui l'approche ou seconde." [Jerome Bolsec], Le double des lettres envoyées à Passevent Parisien, par le noble et excellent Pasquin Romain, contenant en verité la vie de Jehan Calvin (Paris: Pierre Gaultier, 1556), Ci^r–Ci^v. Bolsec's authorship of this text is ascribed by Chiara Lastraioli, "D'un texte inconnu de Jérôme Bolsec contre Calvin," Reformation & Renaissance Review 10 (2008): 157–74.

4.2.1. Zébédée at the Collège de Guyenne,
1533/34–1538

Zébédée's early life is obscure. We know that he came from Brabant in the Low Countries, but not exactly where or when he was born.[4] He probably was not a native French speaker, but he spent his entire career in franco-phone lands and no doubt spoke the language fluently. He may have studied at the Universities of Louvain and Paris, but this is an educated guess based on his origin, contacts, and first teaching post.[5] Finally, in 1533 or 1534, he enters the public record as a teacher (or "regent") at the Collège de Guyenne in Bordeaux.[6] Since his appointment in Bordeaux probably came soon after he completed his university education, and since we know that he died some-time between 1570 and 1572, it seems likely that Zébédée was born some-time around 1510, making him roughly the same age as Calvin and Viret.

In Bordeaux, Zébédée was surrounded by learned men at a newly flourishing humanist school under the direction of André de Gouveia, a Portuguese humanist who had previously been the principal of the Collège Sainte-Barbe in Paris and whom Michel de Montaigne called "incomparably the greatest principal of France."[7] Several of the teachers in Bordeaux had

---

[4] He self-identifies as "And. Zebed. Brabeandri" in his poetic preface to Celio Secundo Curione, *Pasquillus Ecstaticus, una cum aliis etiam aliquot sanctis pariter et lepidis Dialogis, quibus praecipua religionis nostrae Capita elegantissime explicantur* ([Geneva]: [Jean Girard], 1544), α5ᵛ. Pierrefleur, the chronicler of Orbe, describes him as a "natif de Flandres"; [Guillaume de] Pierrefleur, *Mémoires de Pierrefleur: Édition critique avec une introduction et des notes*, edited by Louis Junod (Lausanne: La Concorde, 1933), 139. A French official who intercepted some of his letters describes him as "ung Allemant"; Gabrielle Berthoud, "Lettres de Réformés saisies à Lyon en août 1538," in *Etudes et documents inédits sur la Réformation en Suisse romande*, 87–111, Revue de théologie et de philosophie (Lausanne: La Concorde, 1936), 95, Jehan Tignac to [Chancellor Antoine du Bourg], Lyon, August 8, 1538. And Rudolph Gwalther describes him as a "vir doctus natione Geldrus"; HBBW 9:261, no. 1336, Gwalther to Bullinger, December 12, 1539. A note—seemingly added later—in Henri Vuilleumier's manuscript list of pastors of the Pays de Vaud indicates that Zébédée was from Bois-le-Duc ('s-Hertogenbosch, Netherlands). BCU, ms. IS 4511 (document nonpaginated, arranged al-phabetically), but the source of this information is not indicated. There is an "Andreas Zeberti" from 's-Hertogenbosch listed as enrolling at the University of Louvain on January 31, 1524, who may have been Zébédée. A. Schillings, *Matricule de l'Université de Louvain* (Brussels: Palais des Académies, 1903–), 3.1:720. A document in the Bordeaux archives which specifies his salary there refers to him as "Zobeder." Ariste Ducaunnés-Duval, *Inventaire sommaire des registres de La Jurade 1520 à 1783*, Archives Municipales de Bordeaux 8 (Bordeaux: F. Pech, 1905), 3:400, July 29, 1534.

[5] "Nous supposons qu'après avoir fait ses premières études à Louvain, il les termina à l'université de Paris." Herminjard 5:98n7. Herminjard does not indicate the basis on which he supposes this to be the case.

[6] He probably arrived there toward the end of 1533 (Herminjard 5:98n7), for he seems to have been there when the new principal, André de Gouveia, was appointed in 1534. Ernest Gaullieur, *Histoire de la Réformation à Bordeaux, et dans le ressort du Parlement de Guyenne* (Paris: H. Champion, 1884), 1:24. The archival note from July 29, 1534 (n. 4) seems to be the first mention of him there.

[7] "notre Principal, André de Gouvéa, se montra alors, sans comparaison possible, le meilleur Principal de France." Michel de Montaigne, *Essaies*, I.xxv.119.

evangelical leanings. The humanist Robert Britannus sent letters to Zébédée and mentioned him in others.[8] André de Gouveia's brother Antonio also taught in Bordeaux and addressed three epigrams to Zébédée.[9] Mathurin Cordier, Calvin's teacher and later Zébédée's colleague in Lausanne, arrived at the school not long after the Affair of the Placards. Claude Budin, whom Cordier would later recommend for a post in Geneva, also taught at the school and knew Zébédée.[10] Noted evangelical poet Charles de Sainte-Marthe taught for some time in Bordeaux. His stay briefly overlapped with Zébédée's, and the two men may later have exchanged letters.[11] Zébédée also had connections to several important political figures in the Bordeaux area, many with evangelical leanings. These included Guillaume de Longa and François Rabelais's friend Briand de Vallée, both *conseillers* in the parlement of Guyenne; Jehan de Ciret, city secretary; Charles de Candeley, lawyer and later *conseiller*; and a certain unnamed "lieutenant" who may well have been Michel de Montaigne's father.[12] All this is to say that during his time in France, Zébédée was surrounded by French humanists and evangelicals and was, thus, attached to Marguerite of Navarre's evangelical network, if only peripherally.[13]

Furthermore, Zébédée was by no means the dimmest light in his circle. His salary, at sixty *livres* per year, was one of the highest among the teachers at the Collège de Guyenne[14] and allowed him to afford what was apparently a lovely house on the banks of the Garonne River.[15] Despite making more money than many of his colleagues, he does not seem to have been the object of jealously or resentment. On the contrary, in 1535, when he expressed

---

[8] Letters to Zébédée: Robert Britannus, *Orationes quatuor: De parsimonia liber, Epistolarum libri tres, De virtute et voluptate colloquium, Eiusdem carminum liber unus* (Toulouse: Nicolas Vieillard, 1536), 49^r–49^v, 59^v–60^r; Robert Britannus, *Epistolarum libri duo* (Paris: Gullelmus Bossozelus, 1540), 16^v.

[9] Antonio de Gouveia, *Epigrammaton libri duo, ad mortalitatem* (Lyon: Sebastian Gryphius, 1539), 10, 23, 35–36.

[10] "Mathurin Cordier aux Seigneurs de Genève, 1541," *BSHPF* 15 (1866): 414–18.

[11] Britannus wrote to Sainte-Marthe, "Tuas literas Corderio et Zebedeo reddidi." Britannus *Epistolarum libri duo*, 13^r. On Zébédée and Sainte-Marthe, see Ruutz-Rees, *Charles de Sainte-Marthe*, 19–22.

[12] Berthoud, "Lettres de Réformés saisies à Lyon," 91–92.

[13] The closest connections between the Bordeaux humanists and Marguerite were through Mathurin Cordier and the poet Charles de Sainte-Marthe, whom Marguerite later employed as her secretary and who delivered a funeral oration for her. She also intervened with the Guyenne parlement a number of times on behalf of suspected heretics. See Reid, *King's Sister*, 63n60; 77–78; 480n54.

[14] Gaullieur, *Histoire du Collège de Guyenne*, 82. Britannus earned 48 *livres*; Joachim Polite, 42 *livres*; Pierre Tiercelin, 36 *livres*; and Jehan Binet, 30 *livres*.

[15] Gaullieur, *Histoire du Collège de Guyenne*, 82–83; Britannus, *Orationes quatuor*, "Epistolarum libri tres," 49^r.

a desire to leave the city for Spain, his colleagues pressed him to promise to return to the school after his visit.[16]

To be sure, Zébédée had enemies in Bordeaux as well, but their identities and the basis for his conflict with them are unclear.[17] The Guyenne parlement began to crack down on evangelical books and ideas at the end of 1534 and into 1535.[18] Thus, one surmises that perhaps Zébédée left Bordeaux for Spain because of the threat of religious persecution, but this is by no means certain. He did, in fact, return to Bordeaux at some point and was still there at the end of 1536. From that point, however, the trail is lost until we find him in Geneva in 1538.

4.2.2. Zébédée as a "Zwinglian Calvinist" While Pastor of Orbe and Yverdon, 1538–1547

Zébédée arrived in Geneva, via Lyon, probably sometime just before the expulsion of Calvin and Farel, and he clearly allied himself with them rather than with their replacements, Antoine Marcourt and Jean Morand.[19] Indeed, almost all of Zébédée's early career in Switzerland shows him to have been in league with the Calvinists. Farel reported to Calvin that "Zébédée is teaching

---

[16] "Existimare potes, ex quo Burdigalam appulimus, quantam de tua eruditione opinionem conceperim: neque ego solum, sed multo magis mei collegae, cum universi hinc parantem abire atque Hispaniam cogitantem omnibus verbis, omni copiarum et facultatum genere retinendum censuerint." Britannus, *Orationes quatuor*, "Epistolarum libri tres," Britannus to Zébédée, August 30, [1535?], 59ᵛ.

[17] Britannus wrote to Zébédée while he was gone, "Habes hic amicum fide, officio, gratia singulari Thomam Gentilem: is et te admodum diligit et tam doluit inimicorum tuorum iniuria, quam omnibus rebus quas unquam aut acerbas expertus est in vita aut tristeis. Huius opera et consilio in tuis rebus multum utor maximeque in defensione honoris et existimationis tuae." Britannus, *Orationes quatuor*, "Epistolarum libri tres," 49ʳ–49ᵛ.

[18] In November 1534, the parlement of Guyenne forbade "the school to hold any books forbidden by the Sorbonne." In December the court called for a general procession "for the preservation of the Christian faith." In March 1535, the parlement discovered and confiscated a shipment of several censured books to the city. Thus, the authorities were aware of growing evangelical dissent in the area and were beginning to take steps against it. Gaullieur, *Histoire de la Réformation à Bordeaux*, 26–27.

[19] The first documents we have from Zébédée's time in Geneva are three letters dated July 31, 1538. We know he passed through Lyon, for he wrote to Arnaud de Verteuil, "Iam tertias ad te literas mitto, vir ornatissime. In primis, quas Lugduno misi, nihil erat magni momenti; illud tantum scripseram me salvum pervenisse Lugdunum." Berthoud, "Lettres de Réformés saisies à Lyon," 102. Zébédée's positive attitude toward Calvin and Farel is revealed in another letter that was seized on its way to Charles de Candeley. Jehan Tignac, the French officer who passed the seized letters on to Antoine du Bourg, only summarized this letter from Zébédée. In his summary, Tignac wrote, "Il [Zébédée] respond qu'il faict plus dangereux là où il est que là où est ledit de Cante [Candeley], car il n'i a plus de pasteurs depuis que Farel et Caulvin sont esté expulsez et qu'on leurs faict la guerre plus forte qu'on ne feit oncq aux moynes et evesques et crie on là: 'Au Rhosne!' comme icy: 'Au feu!' " Berthoud, "Lettres de Réformés saisies à Lyon," 110.

in Orbe with great effect: both his piety and his learning have earned him the respect of even the impious and papists."[20] In 1539, Zébédée stood beside Farel and Viret when they met with Pierre Caroli at La Neuveville. Afterward, he and Viret traveled together to Bern to report on the conference and to plead on behalf of the persecuted Waldensians in southeastern France.[21] In 1540, Zébédée was one of the first to entreat Calvin to return to Geneva.[22] Three years later, Viret and Zébédée traveled together to Neuchâtel to confer about what advice to give the Reformed pastors of Montbéliard in the face of Lutheran reforms being imposed there.[23] Finally, through 1544, the reformers' correspondence demonstrates that Zébédée was a member of the Calvinist network and decidedly not among the anti-Calvinist group led by Marcourt, Thomas Malingre, and Jean Lecomte.

From early on, however, Zébédée showed signs of frustration with both his position and his friends. In 1538, he was appointed pastor at Orbe, a significant step down from his academic post in Bordeaux. Having taught at one of the centers of French humanism, Zébédée was likely disheartened by his role as pastor in a small town in the Vaud. In Bordeaux, he had rubbed shoulders with the likes of Sainte-Marthe, Cordier, Britannus, and the Gouveia brothers. In Orbe, he no doubt missed the company of other intellectuals, and he would have been forced to set aside his humanist studies in order to fulfill the demanding but pedestrian duties of a pastor, at a much reduced salary.[24]

There are also early signs of theological tension, for Zébédée's Zwinglianism occasionally clashed with his friends' new Calvinian ideas. In 1539, Zébédée circulated two poems praising Zwingli.[25] The first was his Latin translation

---

[20] "Zebedeus magno fructu Orbae docet: tum pietas, tum eruditio reddunt eum etiam impiis et pontificiis commendabilem." Herminjard 5:235, no. 768, Farel to Calvin, Neuchâtel, February 5, 1539. Orbe was a common lordship governed jointly by Bern and Catholic Fribourg that had not yet voted to abolish the Mass; thus, there was still active Catholic worship in the town.

[21] Herminjard 5:355n4; Vuilleumier, 1:441.

[22] Herminjard 6:321–24, no. 896, Zébédée to Calvin, Neuchâtel, October 1, [1540].

[23] Herminjard 9:97–98, no. 1303, Viret to Calvin, [Lausanne], November [3 or 4, 1543]; Vuilleumier, 1:568.

[24] Pastors in the Pays de Vaud generally earned around eighty florins per year (see, e.g., the 1550 accounts of Bern's bailiff of Morges, which list the salaries of the five pastors in the area as ranging from 60 to 90 florins. ACV, BP 33/2; copy in ACV, P Meylan, 44, "Prédicants du bailliage de Morges"). Pastors in larger cities like Lausanne earned more; many in rural areas earned less. Eighty florins would be approximately the equivalent of 32 livres tournois. Thus, it seems likely that Zébédée's position in Orbe paid little more than half what he had earned at the Collège de Guyenne.

[25] The poems were transcribed by Rudolf Gwalther in a letter to Heinrich Bullinger. See Paul Boesch "Zwingli-Gedichte (1539) des Andreas Zebedeus und des Rudolph Gwalther," Zwingliana 9, no. 4 (1959): 208–20. The text of Gwalther's letter with the poems is in HBBW 9:260–65, no. 1336, Lausanne, December 12, 1539.

of a German poem praising Reuchlin, Oecolampadius, Erasmus, Luther, and Zwingli.[26] The second was an original poem, which reads as follows:

Zébédée on Zwingli:
Impossible to hope for one greater. Perhaps we must beseech
    Our times to give us one equal.
His learned mouth, his upright heart, his zealous spirit
    All press toward the praises of the one God
Acclamation:
O strongest defender of the evangelical word,
    O you who dared to die bravely for Christ and country![27]

Thus, from the beginning of his time in Switzerland, Zébédée showed himself to be a staunch supporter of Zwingli even as he aligned himself for several years with Calvin's circle. Although he probably was aware that Marcourt, Malingre, and their anti-Calvinist allies shared his own Zwinglian inclinations, he seems to have made no move to join them. His early allegiance to a group with whom he was often at odds offers a reminder that theological conviction alone did not determine alliances; social connections and personal affinity also played important roles.

Still, Zébédée's unapologetic Zwinglianism affected his relationship with Calvin as early as 1539. Calvin bridled at Zébédée's ode to Zwingli,[28] and Zébédée, in turn, appears to have criticized Martin Bucer's influence on Calvin in Strasbourg. Just one year earlier, in 1538, Bucer had drawn the ire of almost all of the Swiss Reformed by encouraging them to sign the Wittenberg Concord, a formula of agreement with the Lutherans on the Eucharist.[29]

---

[26] The German version, possibly written by Leo Jud, can be found on a woodcut portrait of Zwingli from 1540 or 1550 by Augustin Mellis. Boesch, "Zwingli-Gedichte," 214. Zébédée's Latin translation of the verses on Zwingli are the following: "Hoc ad opus pretii vir summi Zvinglius unus / E paucis certo mittitur ore dei. / Qui nihil ostendens animo subit omnia prompto, / Quae Christi servos et pia corda decent." The poem continues, "Instat verbis armis et sancta voce senatus, / Aenea contra acres induit arma lupos / Pro Christi caussa quidvis tentare paratus / Et promptus Christi nomine cuncta pati. / Qui dum munus obit summa pietate fideque, / Hic obit, imo abit hinc, et meliora tenet." *HBBW* 9:263, no. 1336.

[27] "De Zvinglio Zebedeus: / Maiorem sperare nefas, fortasse petendum, / Ut dent vel unum saecula nostra parem. / Os doctum, pectus sincerum, spiritus acer / Unius in laudes incubuere dei. / Acclamatio: / O evangelici vindex fortissime verbi, / O Christo, o patriae fortiter ause mori!" *HBBW* 9:264, no. 1336.

[28] "Itaque mihi minime placuit Zebedaei carmen, in quo non putabat se pro dignitate laudare Zuinglium, nisi diceret: 'Maiorem sperare nefas.'" Herminjard 6:191, no. 854, Calvin to Farel, Strasbourg, February 27, [1540].

[29] See Bruening, *Calvinism's First Battleground*, 77–91.

Particularly galling to the Zurichers was that Bucer had published, at Luther's prompting, a book of *Retractions*,[30] which the Swiss understood as Bucer's recantation of his Zwinglian ideas on the Lord's Supper.[31] In a lost 1539 letter to Calvin, Zébédée seems to have referred disparagingly to Bucer's book. Calvin's response to Zébédée survives, and it is a vigorous defense of himself and of Bucer, and a harsh indictment of Zwingli:

> In truth, I dare to say that we perfectly and firmly agree with Bucer, abandoning no part of sound doctrine.... You have no reason to take such great offense at Bucer's *Retractions*. Since he had erred in his teaching concerning the use of the sacraments, he rightly retracted that part. If only Zwingli had made up his mind to do the same! For his opinion on this subject was both false and pernicious.[32]

By claiming that Bucer had acted appropriately while Zwingli's doctrine was "false and pernicious," Calvin shows how far he had moved from the theology held not just by Zwingli and the Zurichers, but also initially by Farel and the vast majority of French-speaking evangelicals in the Suisse romande. In his early works, Farel had adopted a Zwinglian understanding of the Eucharist, and he had done much to spread that view throughout his early network in Switzerland. Calvin had by this point developed his own theology of the Eucharist to emphasize "the true efficacy of our participation" in the Supper.[33] In the wake of this disagreement, Zébédée and Calvin were able to continue their good relationship—a year later, Calvin referred in a letter to *optimus Zebedaeus*[34]—but Zébédée never abandoned his preference for Zwingli's theology over that of Bucer or, indeed, Calvin.

---

[30] Text in *BDS* 6.1:303–88.

[31] Bucer *Retractions* were ambiguous, however. As Hastings Eells comments, "In the same breath Bucer retracted all his errors and refused to admit that he had ever made any to retract by failing to name them." Hastings Eells, *Martin Bucer* (New Haven, CT: Yale University Press, 1931), 211.

[32] "Verum audeo dicere, optimam nobis ac solidam concordiam cum Bucero, ut nihil de sana doctrina nobis depereat . . . Buceri retractionibus non est ut tantopere succenseas. Quia in tradendo sacramentorum usu erraverat, iure eam partem retractavit. Atque utinam idem facere Zwinglius in animum induxisset, cuius et falsa et perniciosa fuit de hac re opinio!" Herminjard 5:316–18, no. 790, Calvin to Zébédée, Strasbourg, May 19, [1539]. Translation adapted from Bonnet, ed., *Letters of John Calvin*, 4:402.

[33] "Siquidem videre promptum est [Zwinglius], ut nimium occupatus in evertenda carnalis praesentiae superstitione, veram communicationis vim aut simul disiecerit, aut certe obscurarit." Herminjard 5:318, no. 790.

[34] "Miseret me supra modum optimi Zebedaei, vel potius conditionis nostrae, quod nulla hodie disciplina est." Herminjard 6:240, no. 868, Calvin to Farel, Strasbourg, June 21, [1540].

Although there is no early evidence of Zébédée joining the anti-Calvinists, his position as pastor of Orbe placed him in the chapter of Yverdon, and thus in close contact with Malingre, Lecomte, and de Glant. Zébédée evidently got along with his colleagues in the area well enough that they elected him dean of the chapter in 1542. This election, in turn, led to his next conflict with his Calvinist friends. As we saw in Chapter 3, 1542 was the year when Farel and Viret tried to initiate Calvinist reforms in Neuchâtel and Lausanne. During the same year, the Bernese swung from a Bucerian to a Zwinglian theology of the Eucharist. Thus, when the deans of the francophone chapters were summoned to Bern in August to hear the new decrees, Zébédée was among them, representing Yverdon. He accepted Bern's decisions without question, a move bemoaned by Calvin, who complained bitterly about both the decrees[35] and Zébédée's response to them: "Who compelled the deans to give that response, to the prejudice of all their colleagues? If only Zébédée had not been there, or had brought a different heart and opinion to this affair!"[36]

Also in 1542, Zébédée ran into trouble with the people of biconfessional Orbe. During holy week, the Catholics of the town accused him of preaching too long, thereby continuing the Protestant service well past the time when the Catholics were supposed to have the parish church for Mass.[37] Moreover, he clashed publicly with the town's Catholic vicar, Claude Guyot.[38] The

---

[35] See 93.

[36] "Verum decanos quis coëgit responsum illud dare, quo praeiudicium collegis suis omnibus afferrent? Utinam vel abfuisset Zebedaeus, vel aliud cor aliudque consilium ad hanc causam attulisset!" Herminjard 8:121, no. 1156, Calvin to Viret, Geneva, September 11, 1542.

[37] The 1532 religious ordinances for Orbe stated that in the winter, until Easter, the Protestant service would take place from 7:00 until 8:00 (and from 6:00 to 7:00 in the summer). Catholics would be able to celebrate Matins and Lauds before the Protestant service and Mass afterward. In 1542, Zébédée was accused of preaching from 7:00 until 11:00. Pierrefleur, *Mémoires*, 61–62, 153.

[38] There are two contemporary accounts of this conflict. First, the Catholic chronicler Pierrefleur describes the events as follows: "Le jour de Pâques flories [Palm Sunday], le prédicant nommé Zébédée . . . alla à la messe perrochiale, et ainsi que le vicaire était au prône, faisant les commandemans de l'Eglise, entre autres se mit à faire remontrances au peuple pour comparaître et venir à la réception de son Créateur au jour de Pâques. Dont le dit prédicant le démenti, et sur ce eut grand bruit à l'église . . . Non content de ce, le dit prédicant, se sentant avoué du seigneur bailli, lequel était de Berne, pensa mettre empêchement au service divin qui se faisait ordinairement le jour du vendredi saint, à savoir qu'il se mit à sermonner son sermon depuis sept heures jusques à onze, et toujours eût sermonné, si ne fût que le gouverneur de la ville le fit à descendre de la chaire, disant qu'il passait l'heure ordonnée par les seigneurs. Le dimanche de Pâques et le lundi suivant, le dit prédicant et tous ses complices furent à vêpres; la raison, je ne la sais, mais il est bien à penser que ce n'était pas pour bien, car après les dites vêpres cerchaient tous moyens pour avoir question et différend avec les prêtres, leur disant beaucoup d'injures, usant toujours de leurs façons coutumières." Pierrefleur, *Mémoires*, 152–53.

Second, in Zébédée's apology before the Bernese magistrates, he lists three accusations against him: "Le primier point. J'ay esté trop long au sermon, le dimenche de Pasques flory et au sermon du grand vendredy sainct, et que je fasoye cela par certaine malice, pour empescher le service de prestres, et que toutes les dimenches je fasoye aultant, et que, quelques remonstrances qu'on me fait, je ne veulx aulcunement obeïr. Le second point. Ainsi que le vicaire faisoit son office, ce dimenche

Catholics denounced Zébédée to the Fribourg authorities, who imprisoned him and forced him to make an *amende honorable*, "crying mercy to God, to the Virgin Mary, and to all the saints of paradise."[39] In addition to demanding the *amende honorable*, the Fribourg magistrates attempted to banish Zébédée from Orbe. The banishment was overturned on appeal to Bern,[40] but the Bernese thought it prudent for Zébédée and Malingre to switch posts for a time. Thus, during most of the rest of 1542, Malingre preached in Orbe, and Zébédée in Yverdon. They reverted to their original positions by the end of the year.

Although he was restored to his former position, Zébédée appears never again to have been happy in Orbe (if, indeed, he ever had been). Even before he returned to Orbe, he had begun to seek a position in Geneva,[41] and much of the surviving record on Zébédée over the next three years documents his efforts to escape Orbe.[42] Finally, in 1545, he once again took Malingre's place as pastor in Yverdon.[43] Although the evidence from these last unhappy years in Orbe is sparse and ambiguous, it shows his relationship with

mesme, je suis venu audacieusement, voulant faire ung grand tumulte, le démentir publiquement, et qu'on n'a tenu à moy que n'aye eu une grande effusion du sang. Le troisiesme point. Le vendredy après l'Ascension, en plaine rue, j'ay appellé le vicaire *abuseur*." Herminjard 8:43, no. 1127, Zébédée to the Bern Council, [end of May 1542]. Zébédée essentially confessed to doing all of these things, but claimed that it was necessary to preach longer when the biblical text was longer, that the vicar Guyot was falling back on custom and tradition instead of the Scriptures in his instructions for holy week, and that Guyot was demanding unjust payment from his parishioners. Herminjard 8:43–48.

[39] "Et quant au prédicant Zébédée, c'est qu'il voulut faire quelque réponse qui ne fut agréable aux dits seigneurs [de Fribourg]. Finalement, après avoir ouï les propos du dit vicaire [Guyot] et de lui, fut condamné d'être mis en forte et étroite prison, et y demeura 24 heures. Au sortir, il fit amende honorable, à savoir crier merci à Dieu, à la Vierge Marie, à tous les saints et saintes de paradis." Pierrefleur, *Mémoires*, 153. Viret would later use this coerced appeal to Mary and the saints in his complaints about Zébédée: "Deinde quo nobis voluit [Zebedaeus] obtrudere de iureiurando praestando per aliorum nomina quam Dei unius? Nimirum ut defenderet, quod Friburgi peccarat, iurans per Deum et sanctos." *Epistolae Vireti*, 125, no. 23, Viret to Gwalther, Lausanne, July 23, 1548.

[40] "[les] seigneurs de Fribourg, lesquels acceptèrent ainsi la dite merci, le [Zébédée] bannissant de leurs terres et seigneuries, sur peine de vie. . . . Au réciproque, les seigneurs de Berne donnèrent citation personnelle à devoir comparaître par-devant eux le dit vicaire, et après plusieurs propos lui fut défendu de non plus se mêler des affaires de la cure jusques à ce qu'il eût trouvé grâce envers eux, et ce était en revanche du dit prédicant [Zébédée], et dura la dite défense jusques à Noël, que chacun fut remis en son office." Pierrefleur, *Mémoires*, 154.

[41] "Ioannes bibliopola, nuper istac reversus, mecum de Zebedaeo locutus est. Dicebat paratum esse hunc [*or* huc?] venire, si locus foret. Nihil aliud respondi nisi me tibi scripturum." Herminjard 8:145, no. 1163, Calvin to Viret, Geneva, [October 5, 1542].

[42] See, for example, Herminjard 9:35–36, no. 1283, Calvin to Viret, Geneva, [September 16–20, 1543]; Herminjard 9:108, no. 1307, Viret to Calvin, Lausanne, November 11, 1543; Herminjard 9:317, no. 1385, Viret to Calvin, Lausanne, August 9, 1544; Herminjard 9:334 no. 1395, Farel to Calvin, Neuchâtel, October 2, 1544; *CO* 12:84, no. 646, Viret to Calvin, Lausanne, May 30, 1545.

[43] For reasons that are unclear, Malingre had been forced to abdicate his position in Yverdon in August 1545. He soon found a position in Aubonne, and ten years later, he would return to Yverdon.

the Calvinists beginning to fray. The rift was driven in part by Zébédée's belief that his friends should have been able to find him a better position but were either unable or unwilling to do so.[44] Additionally, however, Zébédée had been working ever more closely with the Calvinists' enemies. We have noted that he was in the anti-Calvinist Yverdon chapter. Moreover, in 1544, he hosted Sebastian Castellio as the latter was on his way to Basel after his bitter fight with Calvin in Geneva.[45] In 1545, Farel noted that Zébédée had sided with Castellio in his dispute with Calvin over the Song of Songs.[46] Farel also complained that Zébédée had become too bellicose, favoring armed resistance by the French Waldensians.[47]

4.2.3. Zébédée's Appointment to the Lausanne Academy, 1547

Despite these frictions, the Calvinists still generally counted Zébédée as one of their own. Thus, when a position opened up at the Lausanne Academy in 1546, Viret, on behalf of the Lausanne chapter, nominated Zébédée to fill it; Viret later claimed, "I hoped that by your presence and erudition you would be an ornament for our school."[48] Given Zébédée's background at the Collège de Guyenne, his appointment in Lausanne should not be surprising. Indeed, in 1542, Viret was already thinking of Zébédée for the Academy,[49] but the position had gone instead to the famed Italian humanist Celio Secondo Curione.[50] In 1546, the Bernese banished Curione from their territories after he was caught in a sexual scandal with

---

[44] Viret wrote, for example, "Ex Zebedaei literis colliges quid de me sentiat, quoque animo exceperit Farelli monita et consilia, quae qualia fuerint non potui nisi ex Zebedaei literis conjicere. Vides in qua persistat sententia de mutando loco." Herminjard 9:108, no. 1307, Viret to Calvin, Lausanne, November 11, 154.

[45] Ferdinand Buisson, *Sébastien Castellion: Sa vie et son oeuvre (1515–1563)*, 2 vols. edited by Max Engammare (Geneva: Droz, [1892] 2010), 1:235; on Castellio, see Chapter 5.

[46] "Scis eum [Zebedaeum] cum Sebastiano sentire, aut non procul esse, super Cantico." *Epistolae Vireti*, 37, no. 4, Farel to Viret, Neuchâtel, June 14, 1545.

[47] "Timeo non parum Zebedaeo, nam, ut audio, nunc Sonerii sententiam tuetur, damnando eos qui dissuaserunt bellum et resistendum." *Epistolae Vireti*, 37, and n. 7, no. 4.

[48] "Sperabam enim fore ut tua praesentia et eruditione nostris esses scholis ornamento." *CO* 13:253, no. 1180, Viret to Zébédée, [Lausanne], [March to June 1549].

[49] "Cogitare coepimus de praeficiendo Zebedaeo huic Collegio: quem spero ad diem dominicum huc concessurum ac de rebus necessariis nobiscum deliberaturum." Herminjard 8:70–71, no. 1136, Viret to Calvin, Lausanne, July 21, 1542.

[50] Crousaz notes, however, that Curione did not really become famous until after his arrival in Lausanne. Crousaz, *L'Académie de Lausanne*, 81–82, 237.

his nine-year-old servant girl.[51] The following January, Zébédée began his fateful stint as Curione's successor.[52] As arts professor, he also served as "Master of the Twelve" (*maître des douze écoliers*) at the Lausanne Academy. This role put him in charge of a select group of scholarship students chosen for their academic promise and funded by the Bernese government in the hope that they would eventually be able to serve as pastors or teachers in Bern's territories.[53] No doubt Zébédée was gratified by the prestige of his new position, and he must have been pleased by the salary increase; he received the substantial sum of four hundred florins annually, an amount that was initially twice as much as that earned by the next highest paid professor[54] and probably around four times as much as his salary in Orbe. Within a year, however, Zébédée and Viret would be at each other's throats in a debate over the Eucharist and the power of the ministry.

Zébédée's early career, however, demonstrates how important earlier friendships were in forging the opposing evangelical networks in Switzerland. Like Zébédée, the reformers discussed in Chapter 3 tended to prefer Zwingli to Bucer or Calvin. Their anti-Calvinist network, built on friendships established earlier in France, developed in opposition to Calvin and continued in Switzerland in support of Caroli and Marcourt. Zébédée, although also attached tangentially to Marguerite's network in France, came from a different geographical region of the kingdom. The humanists of Bordeaux were not generally well acquainted with those in the Meaux circle; consequently, when Zébédée came to Geneva in 1538, he associated himself not with Marcourt but with Calvin, an alliance that likely developed from their shared connection to Mathurin Cordier, Calvin's teacher in Paris and Zébédée's colleague in Bordeaux. Thus, for several years, Zébédée's friendship with Calvin and his supporters could mask their theological differences. As Zébédée developed new relationships with the Yverdon pastors and Castellio, however, and as he nursed resentment over his friends' failure to secure for him the desired transfer from Orbe, his theological disagreements with the Calvinists became more difficult to set aside. In 1548, as Zébédée settled into his position at the Lausanne Academy, those differences surfaced in dramatic fashion.

---

[51] Crousaz, *L'Académie de Lausanne*, 251–53.

[52] The Bern council approved the nomination of Zébédée in December (*Epistolae Vireti*, 48, no. 7, Bern Council to Viret, [Bern], December 15, 1546), and the next month Farel noted that Zébédée had been welcomed in Lausanne: "Rescivisti ex Vireto, ut arbitror, ut fuerit exceptus Zebedaeus cum collega misso a classe." CO 12:476, no. 876, Farel to Calvin, Neuchâtel, January 24, 1547.

[53] On the Twelve, see Crousaz, *L'Académie de Lausanne*, 164–72, 255–310.

[54] Crousaz, *L'Académie de Lausanne*, 138–49.

4.3. Zébédée and the Fight for the Future of the Lausanne Academy

Soon after Zébédée's appointment to the Lausanne Academy, he became embroiled in a theological struggle with his friend Viret and with many of his new colleagues. The main issues at stake were the interpretation of the Eucharist and the understanding of pastoral power and authority. Zébédée defended the traditional Zwinglian position. Viret and most of the Academy's faculty adopted Calvin's interpretation. The fight spilled over into Bern, where it resulted in the expulsion of three pastors from the city. In Lausanne, this was nothing short of a fight for the future of the Lausanne Academy, at the time the only Protestant institution of higher learning in francophone Europe. Zébédée came within a hair's breadth of winning this struggle, but in the end, practical consider-ations on the part of the Bernese led them to keep Viret and the Calvinists in place—at least for the time being. Zébédée was transferred from Lausanne, but it would be a mistake to say that he lost the fight. The Bernese identified more with Zébédée's theology than with Viret's, but Zébédée was politically incon-venient. Nevertheless, he would emerge from the fight stronger among the anti-Calvinists of the Vaud. The debate in Lausanne helped promote Zébédée to the leadership of the anti-Calvinist faction through the 1550s.

4.3.1. Disputes on the Ministry at the Lausanne Colloquies, Autumn 1547

In February 1548, Zébédée had had enough. For months, as he listened to the colloquies and student examinations conducted by his colleagues at the Lausanne Academy, he heard repeated attacks on the doctrines taught by Zwingli and other participants in the celebrated 1528 Bern Disputation. He finally felt compelled to report to the Bernese pastors these diversions from what he viewed as the true, evangelical religion. Zébédée's report would set in motion a lengthy process of evaluating the theological teaching and views of the pastors and professors in both Lausanne and Bern itself.

The problems started in October 1547, when the Lausanne colloquies began to debate issues related to the power of the ministry.[55] The colloquies

---

[55] On these colloquies and for the full text of all the theses debated, see Michael Bruening, "The Lausanne Theses on the Ministry and the Sacraments," *Zwingliana* 44 (2017): 417–43.

were meetings held approximately every other week at which the Lausanne pastors and professors would discuss theological issues before an audience of students and most likely members of the public as well. They functioned similarly to the *Prophezei* in Zurich and the *congrégations* in Geneva.[56] For the October 19 colloquy, the Lausanne theology professor Jean Ribit had drawn up several theses for debate, five of which proved controversial and would later be condemned by some of the Bernese pastors:

1. Ministers are above and below all humans: above, because they are the ambassadors of Almighty God; below, because they are obliged to all.
2. He who does not know that he has the power of binding and loosing, of retaining and forgiving sins, can in no way fulfill the duty of a minister, since he is unaware of the fundamental nature of his position.
3. The minister should not introduce any doctrine of his own but should put forth the truth without any taint of falseness, in such a way that, by the example of the prophets and apostles, he can affirm without any doubt that what he says, the Lord has said.
4. Those who despise this type of minister utterly reject and repudiate their own salvation.
5. Since ministers bestow spiritual gifts and strengthen the faithful, those who reject them, reject not men but gifts of the Spirit that have been offered, and they despise God who gives them.[57]

---

[56] On the colloquies in the Vaud, see Vuilleumier, 1:285–88. On the Zurich *Prophezei*, see Fritz Büsser, *Die Prophezei: Humanismus und Reformation in Zürich: Ausgewählte Aufsätze und Vorträge*, Zürcher Beiträge zur Reformationsgeschichte 17 (Bern: Peter Lang, 1994). On the Geneva *congrégations*, see Erik de Boer, *The Genevan School of the Prophets: The Congrégations of the Company of Pastors and Their Influence in 16th Century Europe*, THR 512 (Geneva: Droz, 2012).

[57]

    6. Ministri sunt supra et infra omnes homines: supra quidem, quia Dei prepotentis legati, infra, quia omnium debitores.

    7. Qui nescit se habere potestatem ligandi et solvendi, peccata retinendi et remittendi, is ministri munus tueri nullo modo potest, cum suae functionis ignoret rationem....

    9. Nullam suam doctrinam minister afferre debet, sed veritatem sine ulla falsitatis admistione sic proponere, ut prophetarum et apostolorum exemplo non dubitanter affirmare possit quae dicat, dominum dixisse.

    10. Huiusmodi ministrum qui contemnit, is prorsus suam aspernatur et repudiat salutem.

    11. Dona spiritualia cum impertiant ministri, confirmentque fideles, qui eos aspernatur, non homines sed oblata dona spiritus aspernatur, deumque donantem contemnit.

Bruening, "The Lausanne Theses," 430–31, October 19, 1547. The numbering of the theses in the main chapter text reflects the numbering (1–10) of the Ten Theses that the Bernese would condemn in 1548. The numbering in the notes is the numbering of the theses during each meeting of the colloquy, as given in the text of all the theses in "The Lausanne Theses."

The theology of these theses reflects a decidedly Calvinian break from the traditional Zwinglian understanding of the ministry. Earlier in 1547, a debate had broken out in Bern's German-speaking lands over the same issue.[58] The Zwinglian pastors of Zurich weighed in on the affair as follows:

> Concerning the ministry and ministers, the Scriptures say this: Only God through the Spirit gives, increases, and confirms faith; in short, every saving virtue comes from Christ. The minister only announces the external word, and offers or administers the symbol, not the thing signified. . . . The ministers and the sacraments confer nothing; they simply announce. God confers everything.[59]

Thus, the Lausanne theses contradicted the claims of the Zurich pastors that the ministers "merely announce" and "confer nothing." The Calvinian position that pastors, in fact, have the power to "retain and forgive sins" and to "bestow spiritual gifts," represented a significant departure, indeed.

In November 1547, the Lausanne colloquies started to debate the sacraments as well, and once again the theses reflect a Calvinian position that clashed with the traditional Zwinglian interpretation. The controversial theses that emerged from this colloquy were the following:

6. Just as the external circumcision which the law prescribes profits nothing without internal circumcision brought about by the Holy Spirit, so also baptism that wets on the outside is utterly useless without an internal ablution.
7. The same thing applies to all other things that happen outwardly in the flesh.
8. But we cannot rashly affirm that these two interior matters and similar things do any good without the externals.[60]

---

[58] This quarrel had arisen between a Zwinglian pastor of Aarburg, Peter Schnyder, and two Lutheran pastors in Zofingen, Johannes Göppel and Benedikt Schürmeister. On this affair, see Hans Rudolf Lavater, "Johannes Goeppel: Prädikant zu Rohrbach 1527–1545 und zu Zofingen 1545–1548," *Jahrbuch des Oberaargaus* 21 (1978): 149–76; esp., 164–69.

[59] "De ministerio et ministris sic pronunciat scriptura: solum Deum per spiritum dare fidem, augere, confirmare fidem, breviter omnem virtutem salvificam esse Christi; ministrum tantum annunciare verbum externum, offerre aut administrare symbolum, non rem significatam. . . . Ministri et sacramenta nihil conferunt, sed annunciant. Deus confert omnia." *CO* 12:471–72, no. 875, Zurich Pastors to Jodocus Kilchmeyer, Eberhard von Rümlang, Nikolaus Artopoeus, and Johannes Weber, Zurich, January 17, 1547.

[60] 6. Ut circuncisio exterior, quam lex docet, nihil prodest sine interiore, eaque quam Spiritus Sanctus efficit, sic baptismus foris tingens sine interiore ablutione prorsus inutilis est.

These three theses must be viewed together, for the first two alone would not have stirred controversy with Zébédée or the Zwinglians, but the third suggests—contrary to the Zwinglian position—that the external sacraments may, in fact, assist in the internal regeneration of the Christian.

In addition to the debates at the colloquies, Viret was adding fuel to the fire by circulating the early manuscript of his book *On the Power and Use of the Ministry of the Word of God and of the Sacraments (De la vertu et usage . . .)*.[61] The conception of the ministry asserted in the book matched that expressed in Ribit's theses for the colloquies and, thus, likewise differed markedly from the doctrine of the Zurich pastors.[62] Viret's new treatise also expounded a doctrine of the Eucharist that departed from that held in Zurich. He wrote, "We recognize, therefore, that we truly, and not just in the imagination, eat the flesh and the body of Jesus Christ and drink his blood in the Supper."[63] Viret's challenges to Zwinglian doctrine troubled the anti-Calvinists in the Vaud. Viret reported to Calvin, "I do not know whether you have heard about the complaints against me on account of that book in which I have opposed those who are a disgrace to the ministry. Around here the complaints are great, sometimes coming with threats as well."[64]

---

7. In caeteris omnibus quae foris in carne fiunt eadem est ratio.
8. At interiora haec duo et similia sine exterioribus prodesse semper non temere possumus affirmare.

Bruening, "The Lausanne Theses," 432, November 16, 1547.

[61] Pierre Viret, *De la vertu et usage du ministere de la Parolle de Dieu, et des Sacremens dependans d'icelle* ([Geneva]: [Jean Girard], 1548). Although the book was not published until summer 1548, he appears to have completed or nearly completed the manuscript by August 1547, when Calvin told Viret, "Librum de ecclesia et sacramentis, quum voles, mitte." *CO* 12:582, no. 941, Calvin to Viret, Geneva, August 25, 1547.

[62] For example, "Nous ne pouvons semblablement nier, que nostre Seigneur Jesus Christ n'ait appellé le ministere de l'Evangile, la clef de science, et les clefz du Royaume des cieux, et qu'il n'ait donné la puissance et la commission d'icelles à ses Apostres, et à tous leurs vrais successeurs, et la puissance et commission de lier, et de deslier, de pardonner les pechez, et de les retenir, par le moyen de ce ministere et de ces clefz, et de gouverner et conduire son Eglise par icelles." Viret, *De la vertu et usage du ministere*, 166.

[63] Nous recognoissons donc, que nous mangeons vrayement la chair et le corps de Jesus Christ, en la Cene, et que nous y beuvons son sang, et non seulement par imagination." Viret, *De la vertu et usage du ministere*, 536. This stands in contrast to what the Zurich ministers had written in regard to the dispute between the Aarburg and Zofingen pastors: "Si illi addant: vere adest, sed non corporaliter, quantitave, localiter, qualitative, iubemus ut a verborum monstris abstineant, et oculos simplicibus perstringere desinant . . . Caeterum manducare corpus Christi non est aliud quam credere." *CO* 12:474, no. 875.

[64] "Nescio an quidquam audiveris de querelis adversum me, eius libelli causa in quo nonnihil aspersi eos qui ministerio sunt dedecori. Magnae sunt hic in vicinia querelae cum minis etiam coniunctiae." *CO* 12:616, no. 965, Viret to Calvin, Lausanne, November 13, 1547.

4.3.2. Disputes on the Eucharist at the Houbraque
Examination, December 1547

The event that set Zébédée and Viret directly against one another was the examination of Guillaume Houbraque,[65] a student at the Academy who was being examined for his suitability for a ministerial post.[66] The examination took place over two days just before Christmas 1547.[67] During its course, Zébédée and Viret, two of the examiners, entered into a bitter quarrel about the nature of the Eucharist. Viret argued that one must think philosophically and not naturally about the body of Christ in the Eucharist. Referring to the statement in the Creed, he argued that "the article on the ascension of Christ's body does not preclude the bodily presence of Christ in the Supper."[68] Viret referred to the passage in John 6 about eating the flesh of the Son of Man, but Zébédée argued that the passage does not prove a bodily eating. "He [Viret] said that it shows a spiritual and bodily eating. I said, to the contrary, that

---

[65] Houbraque would go on to have a distinguished career, as pastor of churches in Paris, Frankfurt, Strasbourg, and Heidelberg. A future study of Houbraque would be useful. He appears frequently in Denis, *Les églises d'étrangers en pays rhénans*, and he will appear several times in the chapters that follow. But, as with Zébédée, there do not seem to be any biographies or encyclopedia entries on him.

[66] The best information on this debate comes from a lengthy, 212-page German manuscript in Bern, StAB ms. A V 1457 (U.P. 82.2), no. 100. This is a multiple-author text. The citations that follow are mostly from section 3, an account of a deposition of Zébédée, probably by a Bernese official. Note that the manuscript is not paginated; the pages given here have simply been counted, starting with the title page and omitting blank pages. The sections of the manuscript that contain information on the Houbraque examination and the dispute between Viret and Zébédée are the following: section 2: "Span des Capittels ze Losannen wider Zebedeum . . . " (pp. 75–77); section 3: "Entschuldigung Zebedei gegen dem Capittel ze Losanna" (pp. 78–93); section 4: "Die ursach warumb Petrus Viret vom hervogtt von Losannen demütiglich begertt hatt das er Lodovico Corbelio ein tag bestimpte . . . " (p. 94); and section 5: "Anttwortt Ludovici Cordelii [*sic*] . . . " (pp. 95–97). The rest of the manuscript deals with the ten theses from the Lausanne colloquies that were condemned by the Bernese: section 1: Defense of the Ten Lausanne Theses, "Vorred" and ten "Schlußreden" (pp. 2–74); and section 6: "Antwurt über ettlich ussgesezten Schlussreden . . . (response to the Lausanne theses by Zwinglian pastors Kilchmeyer, Wäber, Rümlang, and Pfister, pp. 98–212). The next document in the manuscript volume is the response to the Lausanne theses by Sulzer, Gering, and Schmid, StAB, ms. A V 1457, no. 101.

[67] Most accounts have mistakenly dated this exam to January 1548, but the Bern manuscript is clear: "dem nach hatt der dechen das Colloquium geendet, das die ding also geredt unnd ergangen sigendt am mittwuchen vor dem wienachtag verschinen." AV 1457, no. 100, p. 96.

[68] "Alss heiterlich vom leser der Theology, das der lyb Christi liblich an einen ort were gerett, do sprach Viretus do es an inne kam under anderen, man sölte yetz nitt naturlich aber philosophisch vom lyb Christi redenn . . . darzu er ouch gerett heitterlich der artickel der uffart des lybs Christi ist nitt zewider aber liplichen gegenwürtigkeitt Christi im Nachtmal." StAB, ms. AV 1457, no. 100[, p. 85]. This was the point that Viret's former colleague in the Lausanne ministry, Béat Comte, seized on in describing the conflict to the Zurich pastors, CO 12:662, no. 996, Baden, February 23, 1548: "nimirum quod ausus fuerit [Zebedaeus] repugnare asserenti Vireto locum illum Lucae, qui est de ascensione Christi in coelos, nihil facere contra realem ac corporalem eiusdem Christi in coena praesentiam."

if it is spiritual it cannot be bodily."[69] Herein lies the crux of the difference between Viret's Calvinian understanding of the Eucharist and Zébédée's Zwinglian interpretation. To Viret there was nothing contradictory in talking about the spiritual, bodily presence of Christ in the sacrament. To Zébédée, however, spirit and body were opposites, and thus, one had to choose: The bodily presence of Christ, he believed, precluded a spiritual presence.

The Lausanne professors continued the debate on the sacraments at the next colloquy, on January 4, 1548. Ribit, the theology professor, made a late addition to the theses that were already set to be debated: "Those who teach that the power of the sacraments must be attributed to justifying action, or that they are only bare signs, or that they must be used only for the sake of discretion, do not agree with the Apostolic teaching."[70] This would become the ninth of ten theses that would ultimately be condemned in Bern, and it was perceived to be a clear attack on the Zwinglian interpretation of the Eucharist.[71]

4.3.3. Zébédée's Denunciation of Viret to the Bernese, Spring–Summer 1548

Seeing Zwingli's teaching on both the ministry and the sacraments being undermined by his colleagues, Zébédée notified a colleague in Bern, most likely the Zwinglian pastor Jodocus Kilchmeyer, who took his complaints to the Bern city council.[72] The council asked Viret and his colleagues to submit

---

[69] "Aber das dem lyb Christi dem selbenn warlich unnd lyplich zügefügtt werde, uß dem ein anderer domalenn ein lyplich essenn des fleischs Christi erwaren wolt mitt dem Ioannis 6. Es sye dann das ir essenn werdenn das fleisch des Suns des menschenn etc., dem ich offentlich widerredt und sprach das diß ort nitt zum liplichen essen brëchte. Sprach er das es geistlich unnd liplich gescheche. Redt ich witer so es geistlich so wer es nit lyplich." StAB, ms. AV 1457, no. 100, [pp. 85–86].

[70] "Qui sacramentorum actioni iustificandi vim tribuendam docent, aut nuda tantum signa esse dicunt, aut discretionis tantum causa adhiberi, cum doctrina non consentiunt Apostolica." We know that this is a late addition, because in Ribit's manuscript of the theses, he added just before this one: "Hoc etiam pronunciatum superioribus coniungi potest." Bruening, "Lausanne Theses," 435, January 4, 1548.

[71] The last of the ten theses, debated February 22, 1548, likewise put too great an emphasis, according to Zébédée and the Zwinglians, on the sacrament itself: "Bona Christi in baptismo fidelibus communicari sine ulla dubitatione confiteri debemus, in quo nunquam fallaciter spiritus sancti gratia promittitur ac offertur, quam sibi fideles recipiunt, impii a se repellunt." Bruening, "Lausanne Theses," 438.

[72] Viret later wrote of Zébédée, "Neque id solum fecit apud vulgus fratrum, sed scriptis etiam literis Bernam, quae nobis fuerunt causa et fons horum malorum, et huius tragoediae proaemia, quam nunc agere cogimur, maximo omnium nostrorum offendiculo." *Epistolae Vireti* 122, no. 23, Viret to Rudolf Gwalther, Lausanne, July 23, 1548. Kilchmeyer was the pastor who took Zébédée's complaints to the Bern council in March 1548. Crousaz, *L'Académie de Lausanne*, 93.

all the theses from their recent colloquies for review, and upon examination, ten of them were deemed contrary to Bern's reformation theology, including all of those quoted earlier.[73] Viret and his colleagues submitted a lengthy defense of the theses, and the Bern pastors weighed in as well.[74] The Zwinglian pastors in Bern—Kilchmeyer, Eberhard von Rümlang, Nikolaus Pfister, and Johannes Wäber—rejected the Lausanne pastors' defense. Simon Sulzer, Beat Gering, and Konrad Schmid, however, supported them and were exiled from the city.[75] Zwinglianism would hold sway in Bern.

4.3.4. Supporters of Both Zébédée and Viret, and Bern's Final Decision

When Viret and his Calvinist colleagues were summoned to Bern soon afterward, they feared they might be expelled, just as their allies in Bern had been.[76] Two months later, Viret still anticipated banishment at any time.[77] The reason why the Bernese chose not to expel Viret and his fellow Calvinists is not entirely clear, but it seems to have had more to do with practical considerations than with theology. The expulsion of Sulzer, Gering, and Schmid indicated clearly that the theological inclinations of the Bernese magistrates were decidedly opposed to those of the Lausanne Calvinists. The Bernese had invested heavily in the Lausanne Academy, however, and summarily dismissing nearly the entire teaching staff could not have been an attractive option. Moreover, the pastor Johannes Haller came to Bern in the wake of the expulsions of Sulzer and his friends. Haller was a Zwinglian from Zurich, but he was perhaps more diplomatic than his new colleagues, and he urged all sides to resolve their differences. The impetus toward cooperation was strengthened by the negotiations on the Eucharist between Calvin and Bullinger that were just beginning in earnest and that would eventually

---

[73] I refer to these as the "Ten Theses" in my article "The Lausanne Theses."

[74] See n. 66.

[75] See Hundeshagen, *Die Conflikte*, 207–9.

[76] "Nam causa nostra ita implicita est cum causa ministrorum Bernensium, ut vix videam qua ratione qui eos eiecerunt suo honori consulere possint si nos retineant, nisi ipsi velimus quod semel proposuimus abnegare." *CO* 12:699, no. 1019, Viret to Calvin, Lausanne, May 9, 1548.

[77] "Quod ad me quidem attinet, tantum abest ut mihi acerbum futurum existimem hinc emigrare, si ita sors ferat et ita Domino visum sit, ut nulla mihi merito dies optatim advenire possit, si me magis quam ecclesiam respicio." *Epistolae Vireti* 110, no. 23.

result in the *Zurich Agreement* (*Consensus Tigurinus*).[78] In addition, the debate between Zébédée and Viret took place not long after Emperor Charles V's defeat of the Schmalkaldic League in Germany. This was a time for Protestants to work together, not to bicker among themselves. Thus, Zébédée was fighting an uphill battle. He had the remaining Bern pastors on his side, but the tide of Reformed history was rising toward cooperation rather than conflict. Consequently, Viret and his Calvinist colleagues were saved by historical coincidence, not by Bernese support for their theological position.

One must also remember that although Zébédée was outnumbered in Lausanne, he had supporters there, as well as in the rest of the Pays de Vaud. In Lausanne itself, he found support from a former pastor, Béat Comte. In 1538, Comte had replaced Pierre Caroli as pastor of Lausanne but had been forced by his colleagues to resign in 1545.[79] For Comte, as for Zébédée, personal resentment of the Lausanne pastors was coupled with a theological affinity for Zwinglian doctrine and frustration with the Calvinist efforts to undermine it.[80] In addition, Zébédée received support from Louis Corbeil, a Lausanne student who came into conflict with Viret during this affair and was later admonished by Viret to abstain from communion.[81] Corbeil would long remain an ally of Zébédée and a thorn in the side of Viret and the Calvinists. Unfortunately, few of Zébédée's other allies are named specifically in the course of his conflict with Viret, and evidence of the positions taken by pastors outside of Lausanne is sparse. There can be little doubt, however, that many of the Vaud pastors would have sided with Zébédée rather than Viret, and Viret frequently refers to his enemies in the plural.[82]

[78] On the *Consensus Tigurinus*, see Emidio Campi and Ruedi Reich, eds., *Consensus Tigurinus (1549): Die Einigung zwischen Heinrich Bullinger und Johannes Calvin über das Abendmahl: Werden—Wertung—Bedeutung* (Zurich: Theologischer Verlag, 2009).

[79] Comte seems to have gotten along with Viret initially. In 1542, however, the two fell out over accusations that Comte spoke and acted too loosely with regard to certain women and girls. His resignation was prompted by accusations of dereliction of duty and the scandalous spending habits of his wife. See Herminjard 8:247–49, no. 1198, Bern Consistory to Viret, Bern, January 19, 1543; Barnaud, *Pierre Viret*, 302–4.

[80] In denouncing Viret and Calvin to the pastors of Zurich, he wrote, "Huic novo antagonistae supra fidem favet Calvinus, archiepiscopus Gebenensis, qui non ita pridem ausus est in haec verba de doctissimo atque beatae memoriae viro, D. Zuinglio, scribere: 'Alii,' inquit, 'in eo sunt toti ut salvus sit Zuinglius: falsa tamen eius et perniciosa fuit de re eucharistiae opinio, ut qui verum eius usum disiecerit et dissiparit.' Haec ille. Quae quam sint impia et blasphema, vos, o venerandi episcopi, iudicate ac cogitate, ut sancto Christi spiritu impiis istis daemonibus resistatur." *CO* 12:662, no. 996, Comte to the Zurich Pastors, Baden, February 23, 1548.

[81] See his deposition in the matter in the long Bern manuscript described in n. 66: "Anttwortt Ludovici Cordelii [*sic*]." StAB, ms. AV 1457, no. 100, [pp. 95–97]. On the "affaire Corbeil," see Crousaz, *L'Académie de Lausanne*, 95–97.

[82] See especially his long letter to Gwalther from July 1548: "Nam eo res devenerunt malis *quorundam* artibus, improbitate et perfidia ... At longe intolerabilius est, quod qui praecipui ac velut

In the end, the Bernese asked Zébédée rather than Viret to leave Lausanne, but they merely transferred him back to Yverdon. They did not banish him from their lands, for they did not believe he had done anything wrong; he was simply in an untenable position in Lausanne. Ultimately, it was simply easier for the Bernese to dismiss one professor rather than several. Still, it is worth pondering what might have happened to the Lausanne Academy—and thus to the training of many of the second-generation francophone Reformed pastors—if in 1549 the Bern council had, in fact, banished Viret and the Calvinists instead of Zébédée. Many of the Academy's students and professors would go on to careers in the French Reformed churches. How would their story—and that of French Protestantism more broadly—have been different if they had been trained by Zébédée and his allies instead of by Viret and the Calvinists?

4.4. Jerome Bolsec, the Seigneur de Falais, Zébédée, and the Consolidation of the Anti-Calvinist Party in the Suisse Romande

BOLSEC (Jérome Hermès), famous slanderer who, in the example of Herostratus, wanted to pass to posterity with a note of infamy. Let us briefly recount his life. Bolsec belonged to the Carmelite Order. The Carmelites never passed for being devoted to wholesome studies; they enjoyed an entirely different reputation.[83]

So begins the entry for Jerome Bolsec in *La France Protestante*; what follows is no less contemptuous.[84] In Calvinist historiography, few figures (except perhaps Caroli) have been quite as reviled as Bolsec. Much of the hostility

---

coryphaei in ecclesia haberi volunt et ipsius velut vitalia viscera, *horum pestilentissimorum hominum* se duces et antesignanos, proh dolor, aperte et impudenter nimis profitentur . . . Atque utinam vobis quoque *huiusmodi homines* nullum fecissent fucum, et vestros animos in tam sinistram de nobis suspicionem non deduxissent." *Epistolae Vireti*, 109, 110–11, 112, no. 23. Viret to Gwalther, July 23, 1548, emphasis added. See also Viret's letter to Calvin from Bern, "Occasio ex nostris disputationibus nata est, quas ideo *multis* offendiculo esse videmus, quod quo sint a nobis sensu propositae non satis nobis videantur assequuti." *CO* 12:694, no. 1015, Viret to Calvin, Bern, May 3, 1548. Recall, too, Viret's report that he was hearing great complaints about his manuscript and receiving threats in the fall of 1547. See n. 64.

[83] Haag 2:360.
[84] Note, however, that the entry in the second edition is much more evenhanded. Haag² 2:745–76.

stems from his bitterly negative biography of Calvin, written to counter what he saw as the hagiographic hogwash of Beza's *Life of Calvin*.[85] During the time when Bolsec lived in Romandie, however, Calvin may have been more widely despised.

In 1551, Bolsec openly challenged Calvin on the doctrine of double predestination. Calvin's response was fierce; Bolsec was arrested, imprisoned, and finally banished from Geneva. This part of the story is well known and spectacularly well documented.[86] Rarely, however, have scholars paid much attention to the long and important aftermath of Bolsec's trial in Geneva.[87] Bolsec did not leave Geneva quietly. He had the support of his employer, Jacques de Bourgogne, Seigneur de Falais. Falais was the great-grandson of Philip the Good, Duke of Burgundy, and he had grown up at the court of Charles V. Fear of persecution drove Falais and his wife to leave the Low Countries in late 1543 or early 1544. They took refuge first in Cologne and then Strasbourg, before moving in 1548 to Veigy, where he hired Bolsec as his personal physician. Falais and Bolsec soon drew into their circle Zébédée and many others, including—by correspondence at least—Sebastian Castellio. Moreover, Bolsec, Falais, and Zébédée joined forces with the anti-Calvinists discussed in Chapter 3, bringing together all the currents of anti-Calvinist sentiment in the Suisse romande. Their attacks centered on Calvin's doctrine of predestination; increasingly, however, their criticism extended as well to Calvin's iron-fisted efforts to quash debate when disagreement arose, and they started to portray him as the "pope of Geneva." Indeed, by the 1550s, the two factions had moved well beyond the Zwinglian/Calvinist disagreements

[85] "J'ay maintenans esté contrainct de mettre la main à la plume pour obvier, et refuter les mensonges dudict de Beze trop prejudiciable à la gloire de Dieu, et edification de l'Eglise de nostre Seigneur Jesus Christ, par lesquelles il veult affirmer un tres-vitieux ministre de Sathan avoir esté un syncere et excellent serviteur de Dieu." Jerome Bolsec, *De la vie, moeurs, actes, doctrine, constance et mort de Jean Calvin* (Paris: Guillaume Chaudiere, 1577), Aii^v–Aiii^r. Beza's *Vie de Calvin* is in *CO* 21:1–50. Of course, Bolsec's biography is no less partisan than Beza's. Moreover, it was instrumental in the development of the negative caricature of Calvin in Catholic historiography. See Frank Pfeilschifter, *Das Calvinbild bei Bolsec und sein Fortwirken im Französischen Katholizismus bis ins 20. Jahrhundert* (Augsburg: FDL-Verlag, 1983); Irena Backus, *Life Writing in Reformation Europe: Lives of Reformers by Friends, Disciples and Foes*, St. Andrews Studies in Reformation History (Burlington, VT: Ashgate, 2008), 153–62.

[86] Most of the pertinent primary documents on the Bolsec affair are in *CO* 8:85–248 and *RCP* 1:80–131. The congregation of December 18, 1551, "Sur l'élection éternelle de Dieu" is in Erik de Boer, ed., *Congrégations et disputations*, COR ser. 7, vol. 1 (Geneva: Droz, 2014), 56–131. The affair is narrated most fully in Roget, 3:157–206; Philip C. Holtrop, *The Bolsec Controversy on Predestination from 1551 to 1555: The Statements of Jerome Bolsec, and the Responses of John Calvin, Theodore Beza, and Other Reformed Theologians* (Lewiston, NY: Edwin Mellen Press, 1993); and Pfeilschifter, *Das Calvinbild bei Bolsec*, 14–30.

[87] Even Holtrop's lengthy study, despite the title's promise to take the story to 1555, focuses almost entirely on the few months of Bolsec's imprisonment and trial at the end of 1551.

that had characterized the 1547–1548 debates between Zébédée and Viret. Instead, the identities of both networks centered almost entirely on their attitudes toward Calvin himself and his claims to religious truth.

4.4.1. The Bolsec Affair in Geneva, 1551

Little is known of Jerome Bolsec's early life.[88] He seems to have been from Paris or the surrounding region, and at some point he became a Carmelite monk. In 1545 or 1546, he preached a controversial sermon at the church of St. Barthélemy and afterward thought it prudent to leave France. He found refuge in Renée de France's court in Ferrara, Italy. Around this time, he began to style himself a medical doctor, but it is unclear whether he studied medicine in France, Italy, or the monastery. When he arrived in the Geneva area in 1550, he soon found employment as doctor to Falais, then still a friend of Calvin. Falais lived in Bernese territory; his estate at Veigy lay approximately twelve kilometers from Geneva on the south shore of Lake Geneva. For several months in 1551, Bolsec also maintained a household in the Vaud town of Vevey, just east of Lausanne.[89] This fact appears to have escaped the notice of most scholars, yet it is significant, for it helps to explain why the pastors of Vevey, François de Saint-Paul and Augustin Marlorat, were more supportive of Bolsec than were their colleagues in Lausanne. Already in May 1551, Vevey's proximity to Lausanne brought Bolsec into conflict with Viret and Theodore Beza,[90] but it may also have brought him into contact with Viret's enemies.

In October 1551, Bolsec's well-known fight with Calvin erupted in Geneva. At one of the weekly *congrégations*, Bolsec criticized Calvin's doctrine of double predestination. In essence, Bolsec argued that, by claiming

---

[88] For Bolsec's biography, see Haag² 2:745–76; Pfeilschifter, *Das Calvinbild bei Bolsec*, 9–60; Holtrop, *The Bolsec Controversy*, esp. 767–76.

[89] See *Epistolae Vireti*, 245n2; *Bèze Cor.* 1: 71–72, no. 20, Beza to Bullinger, Lausanne, October 29, [1551]: "Reprehensus et admonitus a Calvino ut sanior esset, Viviacum abiit, quod oppidulum quatuor a nobis miliaribus tantum distat, in Bernensi ditione. Ibi egregiam illam paraphrasin et axiomata conscripsit quae apud te reliqui, minime tunc quidem cogitans fore ut haec Tragoedia ab illo excitaretur. Vocatus a nobis, correptus, monitus, doceri nunquam voluit." The Swiss mile was around five English miles, so Beza's estimate of Vevey being four miles from Lausanne translated to about thirty-two kilometers, which is close to the actual distance between the two city centers.

[90] "Medicus Viviacensis de quo ad me nuper scripseras proximis diebus apud nos fuit. Collocuti sumus de ea parte doctrinae in qua a nobis et ab omnibus doctis viris qui sunt nostrarum partium apertissime dissidet. Sibi mire placet in suo hoc errore." *Epistolae Vireti* 245, no. 67, Viret to Farel, Lausanne, May 10, 1551.

that God predestined not only the elect for heaven but also the reprobate for hell, Calvin made God a tyrant and an idol as nefarious as Jupiter among the pagans, as well as the author of evil.[91] The predestination of the elect was not controversial among Protestants. Bolsec and many others, however, had doubts about Calvin's teaching that God also predestined the reprobate to damnation. To Bolsec, this made Calvin's God "hypocritical, lying, perfidious, unjust, a promoter and patron of wickedness, and worse than the devil himself."[92] Certainly, Bolsec believed, God foreknew who would be damned, but the reprobate earned their damnation by their own wickedness; they were not condemned on a divine whim. In this regard, at least, Bolsec's position was not far from that of many other Protestants, even Reformed Protestants, in Europe.[93]

Calvin was outraged by Bolsec's critique. He vigorously defended his position and demanded that Bolsec be arrested and imprisoned. What Calvin wanted the Genevan authorities to do with Bolsec is not entirely clear, but Philip Holtrop argues convincingly that he wanted Bolsec executed for heresy. There was not enough support from the Swiss churches, however, to carry out such a plan.[94] The Genevans sought the opinions of the other churches in the region.[95] Only the Neuchâtel pastors denounced Bolsec with the vigor Calvin sought; all the others counseled moderation in dealing with him. Most declined even to condemn Bolsec's position. Thus, the Genevan authorities were in no position to do more than banish him from their own territory. Since he had not been living in the city anyway, he did not find this

[91] "ceux qui mettent une volonté eternelle en Dieu par laquelle il ait ordonné les uns à vie et les autres à mort en font un tyrant, voire une idole comme les payens ont faict de Jupiter: 'sic volo sic iubeo sit pro ratione volontas' [Juvenal, *Satires* 6.223], disant que c'estoit heresie, et que telle doctrine emportoit grand scandale . . . Après il [Bolsec] a adjousté encore plus, qu'en disant que Dieu a predestiné à vie ou à mort ceux qu'il a voulu, que nous le faisons autheur du mal et de l'iniquité." *RCP* 1:81, 86 (*CO* 8:145, 149).

[92] Cited in a letter from Calvin: "'Deus Calvini est hypocrita, mendax, perfidus, iniustus, fautor et patronus scelerum, et Diabolo ipso peior.'" John Calvin, *Lettres à Monsieur et Madame de Falais*, edited by Françoise Bonali-Fiquet, Textes Littéraires Français (Geneva: Droz, 1991), 206, no. 53, Calvin to M. de Falais, [Geneva], [June 1554] (*CO* 14:448, no. 1692, letter misdated 1552 in *CO*).

[93] See, for example, Bullinger's letter to Oswald Myconius shortly after the Bolsec affair: "Credo et doceo, una cum omnibus piis, Deum ab aeterno in Christo elegisse omnes credentes ad salutem, ideoque electos esse qui credunt, reprobos qui non credunt. Addo, fidem non esse ex nobis, sed merum Dei donum. Quod autem non omnes credunt, non Dei sed nostra fieri culpa." *CO* 14:283, no. 1603, Zurich, February 10, 1552.

[94] Holtrop, *The Bolsec Controversy*, 291–95.

[95] The responses to the Company of Pastors from the churches of Basel, Zurich, and Neuchâtel, along with individual letters from Oswald Myconius and Simon Sulzer are in *RCP* 1:119–30; additional letters to the Geneva council, as well as Bern's response, are in *CO* 8:229–42.

banishment a tremendous hardship; he simply returned to Falais's estate in Bernese territory.

4.4.2. Falais's Break from Calvin, 1551–1552

Falais's relationship with Calvin was one of the first casualties of the Bolsec affair.[96] From 1543, Calvin had corresponded with both Falais and his wife Yolande van Brederode, and he had been instrumental in the process of helping them immigrate to Veigy.[97] From the beginning of the Bolsec affair, however, Falais supported his doctor against what he saw as the Genevans' heavy-handed attempt to quash doctrinal debate: "The reason for his detention is nothing other than that he had spoken freely at the congregation about doctrine, which should certainly be permitted to all Christians without being imprisoned for it."[98] Herein lies a second aspect of the debate, less commonly addressed in the scholarship: Calvin's opponents objected not only to specific doctrines, but more broadly to the implied prohibition in Geneva on debate over controversial doctrines that lacked unequivocal biblical or patristic support. Disagree with Calvin, it seemed, and one would end up in jail. For humanists such as Zébédée and especially Castellio (as we will see in the next chapter), the suppression of debate was a betrayal of the intellectual honesty and openness fostered by the Renaissance. Such hide-bound thinking, they believed, had been the mark of the scholastics and *Sorbonnistes* whom the reformers were supposed to have left behind. Calvin, they charged, was creating a new kind of "papism." Bolsec wrote of Calvin a few years later, "Although he does not yet have miter or cope, yet he already mimics the pope . . . and one day he will require kissing his slipper."[99] Falais, too, who had already been in contact with Spiritualists and supporters of religious toleration, shared this view and abandoned his old friend.[100] In December 1551,

---

[96] On the breakdown in their relationship, see Mirjam van Veen, "'In excelso honoris gradu': Johannes Calvin und Jacques de Falais," *Zwingliana* 32 (2005): 5–22.

[97] Their correspondence began in 1543, well before Falais's move to Veigy. On Falais, and on Calvin's relationship with him and his wife, see the lengthy introduction to Jean Calvin, *L'Excuse de Noble Seigneur Jacques de Bourgogne, Seigneur de Falais et de Bredam*, edited by Alfred Cartier (Paris: Alphonse Lemerre, 1896), i–lxvi; also, Calvin, *Lettres à Monsieur et Madame de Falais*, 7–34.

[98] "la cause de sa detention n'est que pour avoir parlé à la congregation librement de la doctrine, ce qui doit estre bien permis à tous chrestiens sans pour cela estre emprisonné." *RCP* 1:83, Falais to the Geneva council, Veigy, November 9, 1551.

[99] "Combien qu'il n'ay encore mitre ne chape,/ Desjà pourtant il contrefaict le Pape/ . . . Baiser fera quelque jour sa pantoufle." [Bolsec], *Le double des lettres envoyées à Passevent Parisien*, Biiʳ.

[100] See Van Veen, "'In excelso honoris gradu.'"

even before Bolsec's sentence had been handed down in Geneva, Johannes Haller in Bern described Falais as "completely alienated from" Calvin on account of the controversy.[101]

4.4.3. Falais's Estate as Center of Opposition to Calvin, 1551–1554

This break between Calvin and Falais had lasting repercussions, for Falais's frustration with his former friend led him to make his estate a center of anti-Calvinist sentiment in the Léman region. The local pastor, Michel Porret, appears to have supported Bolsec against Calvin.[102] Jean Lange, pastor at Bursins in the Morges chapter, was accused of mocking the Genevans when he visited Falais's estate.[103] As we will see, Genevan pastor Philippe de Ecclesia and Vevey pastor François de Saint-Paul both discussed their reservations about Calvin's doctrine there. Jean Colinet, the schoolmaster in Geneva, kept his friend Castellio updated on events at Veigy, and Zébédée visited there as well.

From the very beginning of Bolsec's exile from Geneva, the anti-Calvinists of the Vaud rallied to his cause. Calvin complained that once expelled from Geneva, Bolsec was publicly welcomed into Bern's lands by several ministers there.[104] Bolsec himself would later claim, "Several ministers in Bern's lands raised up their spirit and understood well that Calvin and his supporters erred greatly in this matter of predestination."[105] These pastors' reception of Bolsec is further evidence that their opposition to Calvin was not simply a matter of embracing Zwinglian theology rather than Calvinism. Bullinger and the Zurich theologians may have differed somewhat from Calvin on

---

[101] "mitto tibi exemplar supplicationis illustrissimi principis D. Iacobi a Burgundia pro Hieronymo illo scriptae vel propositae nostro senatui. Qui, ut hactenus intimus fuit Calvino, in hac tamen causa iam prorsus alienatus est ab eo." *CO* 14:216–17, no. 1568, Haller to Bullinger, Bern, December 5, 1551.

[102] Calvin, *Excuse de Jacques de Bourgogne*, li.

[103] "Item de certaines parolles dictes par le predicant de Bursin à Veygier au chasteaulx sus le Sgr. de Falex touchant la clefz et l'aigle de ceste cité et de l'ors de Berne et de François de Cassinis teinturier." *CO* 21:507, April 25, 1552.

[104] "Conquestus est [Calvinus] deinde quod a multis ditionis nostrae ministris publice traducatur [Bolsecus]." *CO* 14:291, no. 1606, Haller to Bullinger, Bern, [soon after February 19, 1552].

[105] "plusieurs ministres des terres de Berne, leverent l'esprit et bien entendirent que ledict Calvin et ses adherents erroient grandement en ceste matiere de la predestination." Jerome Bolsec, *Histoire de la vie, moeurs, doctrine et deportements de Theodore de Beze, dit le Spectable, grand Ministre de Geneve, selon que l'on a peu voir et cognoistre jusqu'à maintenant, en attendant que luy mesme, si bon luy semble, y adjouste le reste* (Paris: Guillaume Chaudiere, 1582), 26ʳ.

the theology of predestination, but they continued to discuss it with him. Zébédée, Bolsec, and their circle rejected Calvin's position outright. They had moved too far in their opposition to Calvin to listen when they perceived him to be unreasonable, which they did most of the time. Calvin's denunciation of them all as slanderers (or worse) only exacerbated the division.

4.4.4. Philippe de Ecclesia and Jean Trolliet against Calvin, 1552–1553

The dispute over predestination continued for years after Bolsec's expulsion from Geneva. In 1552, in the immediate aftermath of Bolsec's confrontation with Calvin, two Genevans—the pastor Philippe de Ecclesia and a Genevan notary named Jean Trolliet—kept the controversy alive.[106] Calvin accused de Ecclesia of supporting Bolsec's doctrines and meeting with him at Falais's home.[107] Later, de Ecclesia was also accused of having preached the Lutheran doctrine of the ubiquity of Christ's body,[108] a charge that clearly demonstrates the dispute had moved well beyond a simple Zwinglian/Calvinist split. De Ecclesia denied this charge, among others.[109] The other Genevan ministers continued to pursue the case against him, however, and concluded that he had not shown signs of proper repentence. The Geneva council urged the pastors to reconcile with him, but the pastors refused, and in the end the council deposed de Ecclesia.[110]

As the case against de Ecclesia was proceeding, another opened in Geneva against Jean Trolliet, a native of Geneva and a former monk who had become a friend both of de Ecclesia and of Calvin's political opponent Ami Perrin. In 1545, Calvin had opposed Trolliet's application to become a pastor in the city, and Trolliet would forever hold a grudge against him, much as Castellio would do for the same reason. Calvin also rankled many of the city's leading politicians by refusing to provide the city council with a reason

---

[106] On these disputes, see Roget, 3:231–75.

[107] "Les ministers par l'organe de M. Calvin hont proposé que cependant ilz se sont apperceuz de l'infidelité de Ph. de Ecclesia, lequel treige en la maison du Sr de Fallex avecque Hieronyme Borset qu'est esté icy condampné et adhery à son opinion et soubtient sa doctrine." CO 21:505, April 7, 1552.

[108] "Item que led. de Ecclesia avoit presché le jour de Pasques que le corps de Jesus Christ n'estoit point en certain lieu, mais partout." RCP 1:134, April 25, 1552.

[109] "Respond premier: de avoir presché de l'occupation du lieu du corps de Crist [sic] comment luy imposé, il le nye et requiert que l'on examine les parroches et gens de biens qui y estoient." CO 21:509–10, June 9, 1552. He was also accused of usury.

[110] RCP 1:146–48.

for his rejection of Trolliet.[111] Later, in June 1552, Calvin accused Trolliet of having publicly criticized his *Institutes* and his teaching on predestination.[112] Trolliet acknowledged that he had received from Bolsec himself a text against Calvin and that he had shown it to others.[113] Soon, Trolliet was joined by Philibert Berthelier and Jean Philibert Bonna, both enemies of Calvin in Geneva.[114] Later in the year, the pastors asked de Ecclesia if he supported Trolliet's view that "we make God the author of evil," the same phrase used earlier by Bolsec. Clearly, the cases of Bolsec, de Ecclesia, and Trolliet were connected. In the end, the Geneva council settled the dispute with Trolliet by affirming that Calvin's teaching was sound but also acknowledging that Trolliet was a good citizen.[115]

4.4.5. François de Saint-Paul against the Calvinists on Predestination, 1552–1553

Before the Trolliet and de Ecclesia cases were settled in Geneva, François de Saint-Paul joined the fray from the Vaud. A pastor of Vevey, the town where Bolsec had once lived, Saint-Paul criticized Calvin's teaching on predestination and became a frequent guest at Falais's estate at Veigy. Even before Bolsec was arrested in Geneva, Viret expressed optimism to Calvin that Saint-Paul might come around on "that controversy you are aware of," but he had given up hope for Bolsec.[116] Soon after Bolsec's banishment from Geneva, however, when the Lausanne ministers sought to prevent his ideas from spreading

---

[111] Naphy, *Calvin and the Consolidation of the Genevan Reformation*, 94–96.

[112] "ledit M. Calvin a proposé comment ledit Troilliet au logis de la teste noyre l'auroit blasonné tant en sa doctrine que ès choses dictes en ses sermons et mesmement qu'il aye dict qu'il aye presché que le dyable ayt emporté ung enfant de ville et qu'il avoit menty etc., et qu'il se gloriffioit troup et que en son *Institution* il se soyt grandement contraire, etc., et qu'il a parlé aussy du livre de la predestination qu'il y auroit des choses dignes de reparer." *CO* 21:511, June 14, 1552.

[113] "Estant aoys ledit Troilliet respondant . . . qu'il y a quelcung qui luy en a donné escript qu'il a exhibé non pour les alleguer luy mais pour monstrer qu'elles luy sont opposées d'où il s'en decharge . . . L'on a demandé audit Trolliet qui luy a baillié tel escript. Il a respondu que c'est Me Hieronyme Holzet, mais quand à luy il ne les veult soubstenir." *CO* 21:511, June 14, 1552.

[114] Naphy, *Calvin and the Consolidation of the Genevan Reformation*, 174. As Robert Kingdon discovered, more than a dozen Genevans were summoned before the Geneva consistory for their alleged sympathy for Bolsec. R. M. Kingdon, "Popular Reactions to the Debate between Bolsec and Calvin," in *Calvin: Erbe und Auftrag, Festschrift für Wilhelm Heinrich Neuser zum 65. Geburstag*, edited by Willem van 't Spijker, 138–45 (Kampen: Kok Pharos, 1991), 143.

[115] Naphy, *Calvin and the Consolidation of the Genevan Reformation*, 174–75.

[116] "Franciscus Sampaulinus hodie nobiscum familiariter contulit de illa quam nosti controversia. Spes est bona de ministris, quia quaerunt Christi gloriam, non suam. De medico [Bolsec] nihil mihi boni polliceor." *CO* 14:136, no. 1501, Viret to Calvin, June 21, 1551.

through the Pays de Vaud, Saint-Paul protested their efforts. In January 1552, the Lausanne chapter tried to adopt Calvinist resolutions on predestination, but Saint-Paul refused to accept them.[117] These resolutions were again put forth in November 1552, and again Saint-Paul withheld his support,[118] deeming the theses on reprobation too harsh.[119] The Bern ministers tried to distance themselves from the theological dispute and encouraged the two sides to bury the hatchet. They warned the Lausanne ministers not to propose new doctrines that would become an excuse to harass those who did not subscribe to them.[120] Here we see the Bernese trying to remain neutral but expressing increasing frustration with the Calvinists in their lands.

4.4.6. Zébédée Enters the Fray, 1553–1554

In 1552 and 1553, the dispute on predestination seems to have been confined to the areas around Geneva, Lausanne, and Veigy.[121] Soon, however, Zébédée entered the picture once again, and tensions increased throughout the region. After his transfer from Lausanne in 1549, Zébédée had returned temporarily to Yverdon as a schoolmaster.[122] His time in that position was short,

---

[117] Barnaud, *Pierre Viret*, 406–7; Vuilleumier, 1:648.

[118] "Lausannenses tria constituerunt axiomata, quibus quum omnes praeter Franciscum S. Paulinum Viviacensem ministrum subscripserint, ipsum vix ferre possunt. Sunt autem axiomata haec: 1) Deus ab aeterno non tantum praecognovit sed etiam decrevit, non tantum indefinite, ut quicunque crederent servarentur, sed definite, ut certi homines nascerentur quos servaret per fidem in Christum, quique nunquam desciscerent a fide. 2) Eadem ratione Deus ab aeterno etiam decrevit definite ut certi homines nascerentur ad interitum, quos nunquam donaret spiritu regenerationis et fidei πληροφορία. 3) Damnationis culpa in solo homine quaerenda est, et tamen dicimus decretum Dei praecedere, quum sit aeternum, sine culpa tamen: quia, etsi causa aeterni decreti est nobis incognita, iusta tamen est, quum Dei voluntas sit certa et sola iustitiae regula." *CO* 14:440, no. 1688, Haller to Bullinger, Bern, December 14, 1552.

[119] "Supererat tantum de reprobationis causa quaestio . . . Non ita multo post in conventu fratrum praeter exspectationem nostram rursum ea causa vexata est, nobisque tum aliquot pronunciata, ut eis assentiremur, proposita sunt: sed quum duriora nobis viderentur iam tum confirmare detrectavimus . . . Sed tamen progrediente tempore, nescio qua occasione, vetus illa de causa reiectionis impiorum contentio, quam iam dudum sepultam arbitrabar, postremo conventu recruduit, atque multis ultro citroque habitis tres illae propositiones, quibus propter asperitatem anno superiore assentiri recusaveramus, rursum mihi obtrusae sunt ut obsignarem." *CO* 14:419, no. 1677, Saint-Paul to the Bern Ministers, Vevey, December 1, 1552.

[120] "Nos et ad classem et ad Franciscum scripsimus, et utramque partem ad concordiam cohortati sumus, indigne ferentes ipsos nova constituere pronunciata, quibus qui non subscriberent vexare vellent. Non esse hanc pacis sed multarum turbarum viam." *CO* 14:440, no. 1688.

[121] After a visitation to all the chapters in the Vaud in August 1553, Haller commented, "Controversia de praedestinatione in nulla alia praeterquam in Lausannensi classe fuit agitata." *CO* 14:608, no. 1789, Haller to Bullinger, Bern, September 6, 1553.

[122] The final decision in Bern was made on September 2, 1549; Crousaz, *L'Académie de Lausanne*, 97n96. Viret first reported the decision to Calvin on September 10: "Zebeaeus ludimagister Iverdunensis constitutus est, donec ei aliter prospici possit." *CO* 13:383, no. 1259, Lausanne.

but he was well liked among his colleagues there. The city's pastor, Pierre Byse, and Zébédée's own successor as schoolmaster (a figure we know only as Gobat) saw his transfer from Lausanne as retribution for his valiant defense of "sounder doctrine" against the "Lutherans and Bucerians,"[123] as the Calvinists were frequently described. After Yverdon, Zébédée served briefly as pastor of Bière (1551–1552) and then for many years as pastor of Nyon. In Nyon, Zébédée was only about twenty-five kilometers from Geneva, so he could keep abreast of events there relatively easily. He was also only about twenty kilometers from Aubonne, where Thomas Malingre was pastor. Zébédée was present on one occasion when Malingre criticized Calvin's catechism even while using it to teach the local youth.[124] Zébédée also became closely associated with Jean Lange, pastor of Bursins. Malingre, Lange, and Zébédée together ensured that the Morges chapter, which was already anti-Calvinist, remained steadfastly so.

From Nyon, Zébédée was also a short boat ride across Lake Geneva to Falais's estate at Veigy, and we find him there more frequently after 1552, associating with Bolsec and Falais. He also continued to maintain ties to Castellio. Zébédée and Castellio had been in friendly contact while Castellio was in Geneva; recall that in 1544 he had welcomed Castellio into his home as the latter traveled to Basel.[125] In the early 1550s Castellio was circulating a document on "How to understand the Holy Scriptures," which he would include as the preface to his French translation of the Bible.[126] In August 1553, a Geneva school teacher, Jean Colinet, reported to Castellio that Falais had taken much pleasure in hearing Zébédée read to him that preface.[127] After

---

[123] "Cum nuper illac transiret Scorus [Antoine van Schore] vir doctissimus, qui hic agit apud nos, audivit a ministro Iverdunensi et ludimagistro magna Zebedaei elogia; quibus addebant a Lausanensibus expulsum, quod saniorem tueretur doctrinam adversus Lutheranos et Buceranos." *Epistolae Vireti*, 206, no. 54, Viret to Farel, Lausanne, May 21, 1550.

[124] "Commendavi iterum paucis hanc causam Hallero: cui adieci quod mihi de Malingrio heri narratum est a quodam Morgiensis classis ministro, qui id ipsum audiverat quod narrabat. Quum pueros doceret tuum catechismum, libelli illius autorem coepit sugillare, non expresso nomine tuo sed circumscripto ut qui eius sit autor libelli. Lapsus vero tuus, dignus scilicet qui publice traduceretur, maxime praesente Zebedaeo qui aderat." *CO* 14:175–76, no. 1527, Viret to Calvin, Lausanne, September 4, 1551.

[125] See n. 45.

[126] The preface is printed in *CO* 14:727–39, no. 1889. Castellio's French Bible was not printed until 1555, but the preface appears to have circulated in manuscript form well before the publication. *CO* 14:586, n.7, no. 1769. Castellio's French Bible also included a prefatory letter addressed to King Henri II, but this seems not to have been the letter referred to here.

[127] "Et mesme est de cette opinion M. Zebedee, lequel a leu vostre espitre en la presence de M. de Phalaise, lequel M. de Pha[laise] prend fort grand plaisir à vostre escripture." *CO* 14:587, no. 1769, Colinet to Castellio, [Geneva], August 6, 1553 (textual corrections from Michael Bruening, et al., eds., "Castellio Correspondence Project," online at https://web.mst.edu/~bruening/Castellio%20 Project/Index%20Page.htm). On Colinet, see also the complaint made against him by Pelloquin to

Michael Servetus's execution in Geneva in October 1553, Castellio's influence on the group seems to have increased the animosity toward Calvin that had already been emanating from Veigy.[128] Although Zébédée and other anti-Calvinists associated with Falais did not generally support Servetus's antitrinitarian doctrine, they shared Castellio's disgust with his execution. Zébédée was alleged to have said, "The French fire defeated the Spanish fire (Servetus), but God's fire will overcome the French fire."[129] Sebastian Foncelet who joined Zébédée in his complaints against Calvin, circulated a poem "against the abominable Sodom" of Geneva: "Your cruel Calvin . . . / worse than a Caiphas or priest of the law, / pursues Christians under the guise of good zeal / and you [Geneva] support his unjust quarrel."[130] Summoned to Geneva to give an account of his faith, Foncelet replied that "he would not kiss the slipper."[131]

4.4.7. Calvin, "Heretic," 1554–1555

From this point on, Zébédée also took over leadership of the fight over Calvin's doctrine of predestination. Bolsec himself would later write, "Zébédée fought sharply against the Calvinists on this false doctrine, issued from the forge of the Manichaeans."[132] Tensions between the two sides boiled over in September

Calvin. *CO* 14:499–504, no. 1713, [Geneva], March 15, 1553. Zébédée and Falais were both from Brabant; it is impossible to say whether they had known each other previously—it seems unlikely— but they may have found that their common geographical origin only strengthened their connection.

[128] On Servetus's execution and Castellio's reaction to it, see Chapter 5.
[129] "Dixit etiam Zebedaeus: 'Ignis gallicus vicit ignem hispanicum (Servetum innuens), sed ignis Dei vincet ignem gallicum.'" *CO* 15:565, no. 2184, Haller to Bullinger, [ca. April 15, 1555].
[130] "Contre la Sodome abhominable qui maintient leurs bourdelaiges retenantz avec ce les femmes d'aultruy. . . . Ton cruel Chaulvin homme de faulx aloy/ Pire qu'ung Cayphe ou prebstre de la loy/ Poursuit chrestiens soub umbre de bon zelle/ Et tu maintains son injuste querelle." *CO* 15:182, no. 1982, Foncelet to Nicole Regnaudot (his wife), [July 1554]. The fact that this poem circulated beyond the readership of his wife is demonstrated by the charges against him brought by the Genevans: "Quant à l'article proposé par les Seigneurs de Geneve contre Sebastien Fonsselet, qu'est tel qu'il avoit dit et escrit leur ville estre une Sodome et Gomorre." *CO* 15:403, no. 2095, Bern council to the Geneva council, January 26, 1555, appendix. B. There is also a German translation of the poem in the dossier on Foncelet in the Geneva archives, AEG, p.h. 1503.
[131] "auxquels respondit ledit Fonsselet qu'il ne baiseroit le pantoufle." *CO* 15:404, no. 2095, appendix. B. See also John Calvin, *Oeuvres*, edited by Francis Higman and Bernard Roussel, Bibliothèque de la Pléiade ([Paris]: Gallimard, 2009), 1194–95n37.
[132] "Zebedee . . . vivement combattoit contre les Calvinistes sur ceste fausse doctrine yssue de la forge des Manicheens." Bolsec, *Histoire de la vie . . . de Beze*, 26ᵛ. In the same text, he defended Zébédée against Beza's criticisms as follows: "Il [Bèze] ment aussi impudemment escrivant dudict Zebedee, l'appellant turbulent et disant qu'il estoit infame par beaucoup de jugements. Car beaucoup de gens de bien sçavent le contraire. Vray est qu'il estoit chaud zelateur de la verité, et ennemy des vicieux. A ceste cause il leur resistoit aigrement." Ibid., 28ᵛ–29ʳ.

1554, when Zébédée, Lange, and Bolsec accused Calvin publicly of not just error but heresy.[133] Calvin and the Geneva pastors were outraged and complained bitterly to the Bernese,[134] but this gambit backfired. The Bern council refused to entertain their complaints, much less offer its support to the Calvinists. Rather, the Bern councilors warned the Geneva pastors not to "publicly or secretly offend, defame, or despise us, our ministers, or any of our subjects."[135] Even the Bern minister Johannes Haller, once a voice of accommodation, grew weary of Calvin's complaints[136] and began to refer to the Pays de Vaud as "our Africa,"[137] an allusion to the bitter struggles there in the early church. François de Saint-Paul joined the debate again as well, composing a short treatise on predestination, which he wanted (but never received permission) to publish in Bern.[138]

4.4.8. The Condemnation of Calvinism in Bern, 1555

In January 1555, Zébédée, Lange, and Bolsec brought to Bern a list of complaints that went well beyond the dispute over predestination,[139] and they presented as well passages from Calvin's books that they found "heretical, or at least scandalous and as wicked as the Mass."[140] This time, their efforts were rewarded. The

---

[133] On this series of events, see Bruening, *Calvinism's First Battleground*, 218–21; Vuilleumier, 1:648–54.

[134] Calvin's earliest extant complaint seems to be from September 18, 1554: "Nam agri Bernensis concionatores me haereticum papistis omnibus deteriorem pro suggestu proclamant." *CO* 15:233, no. 2011, Calvin to Bullinger, Geneva. The Genevans lodged official complaints with the Bernese a few weeks later. AEG, ms. CL 4, 13ʳ, Geneva Council to the Bern Council, October 2, 1554; *CO* 15:250–42, no. 202, Geneva Pastors to the Bern Council, October 4, 1554; *CO* 15:256–58, no. 2023, Geneva Pastors to the Bern Pastors, Geneva, October 6, 1554.

[135] "vous admonestans que de vostre costé vous y mettez bon ordre, pourvoyés, et ayés advis que vous et vous ministres par leurs parolles, livres, escriptures, publiquement ny secretement offensent, diffament, ne mesprisent nous ne nous ministres, Esglises, ne aulcuns de nous soubjectz, ains tiennent et ambrassent comme membres de Jhesu Christ et freres Chrestiens," *CO* 15:313–14, no. 2047, Bern council to the Geneva council, November 17, 1554.

[136] "Veremur ne Calvinus huc veniat, iniuriam suam persequuturus. Parum enim illi satisfactum etiam proxime, quod Zebedaeus et ille alter de gradu deiecti non fuerint." *CO* 15:347, no. 2062, Haller to Bullinger, Bern, December 12, 1554.

[137] "Novi nihil habemus nisi quod nostra semper nobis novi aliquid affert Africa. Fuere hic legati classis Lausannensis Iacobus Valerius et Theodorus Beza." *CO* 15:314, no 2048, Haller to Bullinger, Bern, November 17, 1554.

[138] The manscript of this treatise by Saint-Paul is in StAB, ms. A V 1457, no. 125 (misdated 1558 on the title page). Haller wrote to Bullinger about the treatise, indicating no objection to it, but saying he thought it imprudent to have it published at the time. *CO* 15:315, no. 2048, Bern, November 17, 1554.

[139] See *CO* 15:400–404, no. 2095, Bern council to the Geneva council, January 26, 1555.

[140] "Zébédée et L'Ange sont à Berne et comme M. Pierre d'Yverdun m'a raconté, que Benoit de Montaigni luy avoit dit (car ilz avoient passé vers luy) que Zeb. avoit plus de trente articles extraictz des oeuvres de M. J. Calvin tous heretiques, ou les moindres scandaleux, autant meschans que la

Bern council sided unequivocally with the anti-Calvinist faction. On January 26, 1555, the Bern councilors sent letters to their pastors and bailiffs prohibiting "innovations," disputes over predestination, and the celebration of communion according to "Calvinist ceremonies."[141] Zébédée rejoiced,[142] the Calvinists were livid,[143] and the Genevans appealed again to Bern.[144] The Bernese agreed to hold a hearing with all parties present,[145] but once more, Zébédée and his allies prevailed. On April 3, 1555, the Bern council officially refused to endorse Calvin's doctrine and instead indicated that it would not tolerate books or people found in its lands with messages "contrary to our Reformation."[146] Indeed, the

Messe." AEN, 1PAST 9.40, Gaspard de Vèze to Farel, Grandson, January 30, 1555. See also StAB, ms. A II 331, 72 (RM, January 21, 1555), 92–93 (January 26, 1555).

[141] "est ilz venuz à notice que aulcuns entre vous . . . encore tousjours soyent apres et ne cessent de mouver questions, parties, et pretendre innovations contraires à nous ordonnances, status, et ceremonies jusque à present en nous Eglises observées, voire aussy suyvants et se adjoingnans à certaines haultes et soubtiles doctrines, opinions, et conditions des hommes, principalement touchant la matiere de la divine predestination . . . A ceste cause derrecheff tresacertes vous admonestons de vous depourter de telles choses et sans contradictions suyvre et observer nostre susdicte rescription et advertissement." CO 15:405, no. 2096, Bern council to the Pastors in the Pays de Vaud, January 26, 1555; "Nous sommes advertiz que plusieurs de nos subjectz et aultres estrangers habitants riere nos terres . . . sont allez participer et prendre la Cene de nostre seul saulveur à Geneve jouxte les ceremonies Calvinistes, et pource que à nous appartient pourvoir sur ce . . . , vous commendons doyviez tresacertes admonester nosdictz subjects et habitans en nos terres . . . ne ayent ne doyvent plus ainsy user, ains suyvre jouxte l'ordre sur ce par nous establiz." CO 15:406, no. 2097, Bern council to its Bailiffs, January 26, 1555.
[142] "Zebedaeus hac transiit valde elatus et inflatus, ut solet, eorum quidem iudicio qui hominem viderunt. Dicitur iactare magnas victorias, et gloriari se effecisse Bernae omnia ex animi sententia." CO 15:414, no. 2102, Viret to Calvin, Lausanne, January 29, 1555.
[143] "Qui me haereticum vocitaverant, eos non solum absolvit senatus ac liberos dimisit, sed in me quoque et hanc ecclesiam emisit maiore ferocia armatos. Nos interim tot et tam graves iniurias perpessi in crimen vocamur." CO 15:449, no. 2120, Calvin to Bullinger, [Geneva], February 24, 1555.
[144] CO 15:478–82, no. 2136, Geneva council's instructions to its Ambassadors to Bern, March 5, 1555.
[145] CO 15:500–501, no. 2147, Bern council to the Genevan Ambassadors, March 13, 1555.
[146] The Bernese, of course, urged all sides to live in harmony and cease to defame others, but then added, "prians et admonestans fraternellement noz dictz combourgeoys de Geneve que de leur costé y pourvoyent et tiennent main que leurs ministres usent de telle modestie et se depourtent de composer livres contenantz si haultes choses pour perscruter les secretz de Dieu à nostre advys non necessaires et qui donnent occasion de telz differens, dissensions, contentions, et troublemens plus destruans que ediffians. Laquelle nostre amyable pronunciation et ordonnance auxdictz ambassadeurs pour responce donnée et declairée n'ont voulsus accepter ny d'ycelle soy contenter, nous prians de faire en ce plus ample declaration et donner sentence et mesmement touchant la doctrine dudict maistre Jehan Calvin, à icelle nous soubscripre et approuver, ce que pour bonnes et justes raisons en ladicte responce contenues avons reffusé faire et nous arresté entierement à icelle. Et davantaige faict advertissement auxdictz ambassadeurs de Geneve, cas advenant que en noz pays trouvions livres contrarians et repugnans à nostre dicte disputation et reformation, iceulx ne souffrirons: pareillement tous personnaiges passants et hantans en et par noz pays, parlants, devisants, disputants, escripvants, tentants propos contrayres à nostre disputation et reformation, iceulx punirons en sorte qu'ilz entendront que ne voulons cela souffrir." CO 15:548–49, no. 2176, Bern council to its Pastors, April 3, 1555.

council indicated that such books should be burned.[147] The Bernese insisted that their own officially approved catechism be used, rather than Calvin's,[148] and they forbade the use of Calvin's *Institutes* at the Lausanne Academy.[149] In Bernese territory, the anti-Calvinists' victory was nearly complete.

When it was issued, Bern's decree was a bombshell. In the centuries since, however, scholarship has minimized or ignored it, thus significantly distorting the narrative of the Swiss Reformation. Here was the most powerful Protestant canton in the Swiss Confederation, the city chiefly responsible for spreading Protestantism throughout the Suisse romande, effectively dismissing Calvin as a legitimate church leader. Moreover, news of this decision spread, and Calvin's enemies remembered it for many years. François Bauduin referred to it in his 1562 treatise against Calvin.[150] Three years later, in 1565—a full decade after the event—Charles Du Moulin mentioned it approvingly in his treatise *Against the Calumnies of the Calvinists*, indicating that he had received a copy of the decree while he was in Montbéliard.[151] Futhermore, an unpublished manuscript copy of a Du Moulin text in the Bibliothèque Nationale de France contains a reproduction of Bern's letter.[152] This copy is addressed to the pastors of Yverdon,

[147] "Toutteffoys, luy [Calvin] et tous les ministres de Geneve, par ces presentes, expressement advertissons, cas advenant que nous trouvions aulcungs livres en noz pays, par luy ou aultres composés contrariants et repugnants à nostre dite disputation et reformation, que non seullement ne les souffrirons, ains aussy les bruslerons." CO 15:545, Bern's Sentence in the Zébédée Affair, April 3, 1555.

[148] "vous tresacertes encor ung bon copt admonestans en cest endroict estre souvenans des serementz et soubscriptions qu'avez faictz en suyvant la doctrine du commencement jusques à present usitée, train et maniere et ordonnances de l'esglise au contenu du formulaire et catechisme à vous nagueres envoyez, et vous despourter de vous soubscripre à personne que soit." CO 15:549, no. 2176.

[149] Bruening, *Calvinism's First Battleground*, 220; French text of decree in ibid., 220n35, German in ACV, ms. Ba 14.1, 70ʳ, also dated April 3, 1555.

[150] "testantur ea quae postea tanto vehementius contra scripsisti, et in quibus sic tumultuatus es, ut ne quidem tui alioqui foederati ferre potuerint tuam in hoc genere intemperiem, et suos ministros tibi subscribere vetuerint. Testis est ipsius Senatus Bernensis sententia data III. Aprilis, M. D. LV. quae tua illa axiomata procul ex suis ditionibus facessere iussit. Nolo plura obiicere, quae te gravius vulnerent." François Bauduin, *Responsio altera ad Ioan. Calvinum* (Paris: Guil. Morelium, 1562), 112.

[151] "au contraire [les Bernois] leur [the Genevans] declarerent, que tous ceux qu'ils trouveroient en leurs pays contrevenans à ladite sentence, ils les puniroient, et commanderent à tous leurs sujets et officiers d'entretenir le formulaire de la doctrine et catechisme establay à Berne, et non celuy de Geneve, prohibans sur grandes peines à tous leurs sujets, voire aux estrangers venans en leurs pays, de tenir propos des secrets de Dieu imperscrutables, ny du contenu esdits quinze articles condamnez par ladite sentence, dattée du troisiéme Avril 1555 . . . Laquelle sentence avec copie des plaidoyers, fut incontinent apporté audit du Molin, estant lors à Montbeliart, lequel le tout veu, declara aux assistans que ladite sentence estoit tres-juste, et sainte, et chrestienne." [Charles du Moulin], *La Defense de Messire Charles du Molin ancien Docteur, et autres gens de scavoir, et pieté, contre les calomnies des Calvinistes, et Ministres de leur secte, abus, usurpations, et erreurs d'iceux. Par Maistre Simon Challudre* [anagram of Charles du Molin], *Professeur des Saintes Lettres* [1565], in Du Moulin, *Opera*, 5:607–620; here, 613–14.

[152] BNF ms. lat. 12,717, fols. 134–157. This manuscript has a misleading title: "Plaidoyé du Sʳ du Moulin, avec la sentence de Mʳˢ de Berne donnée sur ledict plaidoyé." There is a *plaidoyer* by Du Moulin in the manuscript, but the Bern sentence is the one on Calvin from 1555 and has nothing to

which suggests that Du Moulin likely received his copy from the anti-Calvinists there.[153] The Bern decree was a staggering blow to Calvin, who protested it repeatedly and vigorously,[154] but it was a source of great and lasting delight to his evangelical enemies.

4.5. The Critical Year of 1555: Calvinist Victory or Defeat?

Scholars of Calvin and Geneva have generally portrayed 1555 as the year of Calvin's great victory, when he and his allies successfully extended the vote to the French refugees in Geneva and drove Ami Perrin and his allies from the city, thereby securing Calvin's authority. Such a laudatory assessment of Calvin's fortunes at that point is possible, however, only if one focuses solely on Geneva. Beyond that city's walls, 1555 was a disaster for Calvin. He was vilified by Bern, which also ended its political alliance with Geneva the same year. His teaching was effectively banned from the Lausanne Academy. His relationship with Zurich took a turn for the worse.[155] Finally, theologians everywhere were attacking his doctrine of predestination and painting him as a bloodthirsty tyrant. Calvin's newly comfortable position in Geneva must have been cold comfort indeed.

Perhaps nothing illustrates better than the conflicts described here the fragility of the Calvinists' hold on the francophone Reformed community in the

do with Du Moulin's *plaidoyer* in the document. The manuscript also seems to contain at least some of the articles brought by Zébédée and Lange to Bern in January 1555 (see n. 140): "Les Passages extraictz par Zebedee des livvres tant latins que françois de Jean Calvin les quelz sont ça et la semez par plusieurs portepanniers et voyageurs et principalement en cestuy vostre pais de Savoye avec grande honte et ignominie. . . . 1) Les pechez qui sont perpetrez se font non seulement par la permission de dieu mais aussy par sa volonté. . . . 2) Tous crimes qui sont commis par quelquuongs homme que ce soit sont bonnes et justes oeuvres de dieu. Voylà unne maxime de leur theologie. 3) Si aucun commet adultere, homicide, larcin, ou autre detestable crime, il le commet non seulement par la permission mais aussi par la volonté de dieu et toulx ceux qui disent le contraire sont heretiques." BNF ms. lat. 12,717, fols. 142^v–143^r.

[153] The copy is addressed "Aux honorables, doctes, sçavants, discrets, nos chers feaulx et bien aymez doien, ministres, maistres d'ecolles, et bacheliers de la classe d'Yverdon." BNF, ms. Lat. 12,717, fol. 145^r.
[154] *CO* 15:550–51, no. 2177, Calvin to the Bern council, [Bern], [on or soon after April 3, 1555]; *CO* 15:600–604, no. 2199, Calvin to the Bern council, Geneva, May 4, 1555; *CO* 15:605–608, no. 2200, Calvin to the Bern pastors, Geneva, May 5, 1555; see also *CO* 15:585–91, no. 2195, Lausanne chapter to the Bern council, Lausanne, May 2, 1555; *CO* 15:608–13, no. 2201, Geneva council to the Bern council, Geneva, May 13, 1555.
[155] For example, after this episode, Calvin's correspondence with Bullinger ceased for nearly a year. Gordon, *Calvin*, 207.

1550s. The Pays de Vaud was the largest officially Protestant, French-speaking territory in Europe, yet Calvin and his allies there had failed to win it over. At the same time, the Comté of Montbéliard, another significant francophone Protestant territory, was becoming increasingly resistant to Calvinist doctrine, as we will see in Chapter 6. Indeed, at the time it must have looked like the Calvinists were on the ropes, struggling simply to stay in the fight. Their ultimate victory was anything but a foregone conclusion.

4.6. Epilogue: The Collapse of Calvinism in the Vaud

The Calvinists, led by Viret and Beza, were still active in the Vaud in the late 1550s, but their influence was rapidly waning. They began to focus with renewed energy on another pillar of Calvinism: the right of the church to exercise ecclesiastical discipline and the power of excommunication.[156] Although the anti-Calvinist French pastors offered no enthusiastic support for this initiative, they did not oppose it with the same vigor as they had the Calvinist doctrines of predestination and the Eucharist. Meanwhile, the predestination debate continued unabated. In April 1558, four pastors from the Thonon chapter were expelled from Bern's lands for preaching Calvin's doctrine of predestination.[157] They were initially denounced by the schoolmaster of Hermance, Pierre Mussard, who was none other than Castellio's brother-in-law.[158] Later that year, in August 1558, Beza complained to Calvin of Jean Davion, calling him the "destroyer of our churches," because he shared Bolsec's views on predestination and had presented to the Bernese a book against the Calvinists' doctrine. Davion was subsequently appointed pastor in Grandson, in Bern's territories.[159] A month later, the Bern council received a tract by Paul Le Comte against Calvin's and Beza's views on predestination.[160]

---

[156] See Bruening, *Calvinism's First Battleground*, 237–55.

[157] The pastors were Veran David, pastor of Douvaine; Antoine Chanorrier, pastor of Massongy; Michel Mulot, pastor of Hermance; and Barthélemy Corredon, pastor of Collonges. On the affair, see Henri Meylan, "L'affaire des quatre pasteurs du Chablais, champions et victimes de la prédestination (1558)," *Revue Historique Vaudoise* 80 (1972): 15–31.

[158] Meylan, "L'affaire des quatres pasteurs," 16.

[159] See Henri Meylan, "En marge de la correspondance de Théodore de Bèze: Un hérétique oublié," *Revue de Théologie et de Philosophie* ser. 3, 9 (1959), 177–81.

[160] "Pauli Comitis libellus de praedestinatione contra Calvinum et Bezam," StAB, ms. A V 1457, no. 124. In 1551, Viret mentions to Calvin a French secretary living in Lausanne named Paul Le Comte: "Paulus Comes scriba Gallus qui apud nos agit rogavit me ut tibi commendarem sororis suae uxoris causam, quae nupsit Nicolao Thiebeleio qui apud vos agit." *CO* 14:13, no. 1433, Lausanne,

Meanwhile, throughout 1558, Viret was locked in a struggle with the Bernese over excommunication. Finally, when he delayed the administration of the Christmas Eucharist, the Bernese had enough. They banished Viret, and most of his colleagues in Lausanne followed him to Geneva, and from there into France.[161] Few pastors from outside the Lausanne chapter followed suit. Viret himself would never return to his native Pays de Vaud. With his exile from Lausanne, the last bastion of Calvinism in the Vaud had fallen.

In place of the departed Lausanne pastors and professors, the Bernese selected pastors from their German-speaking lands to teach theology and Greek, and they hired Zébédée's supporter Béat Comte as arts professor.[162] Even before Viret's banishment, the Bernese considered Castellio as a replacement for Beza, who had departed a few months before Viret and the others. In 1562, the Bernese again considered Castellio for a post in Lausanne but eventually decided he was too controversial.[163] The very fact that Calvin's nemesis was a candidate for such a position reveals just how far the pendulum had swung in the Vaud. Calvinism there had collapsed; the anti-Calvinists had won.

One name has recurred peripherally throughout this chapter: Sebastian Castellio. He was associated with Falais, Zébédée, Colinet, Bolsec, and, of course, the Servetus affair. He appeared in connection with the expulsion of the Thonon chapter pastors, and he was a candidate for professor at the Lausanne Academy. Thus, he was tied closely to the network of anti-Calvinists in the Vaud. His connections, influences, and thought, however, extended far beyond the concerns that animated that faction. Castellio deserves his own chapter, and it is to him that we now turn.

January 10, 1551. Louis Guiraud identifies the individual mentioned by Viret with a Paul Le Comte who served as regent in the school of Montpellier in the early 1530s. L. Guiraud, *Études sur la Réforme à Montpellier*, 2 vols. (Montpellier: Louis Valat, 1918), 1:47–48. I have found no discussion in the correspondence of the period, however, of Le Comte's treatise on predestination.

[161] See Crousaz, *L'Académie de Lausanne*, 107–19.

[162] The new theology professor was Adrian Blauner, previously pastor of Spiez, and the new Greek professor was Hans Knechtenhofer. For a short time, the Bernese had grand designs on attracting Andreas Hyperius, Girolamo Zanchi, or even Philip Melanchthon himself to the Lausanne Academy, but all these plans fell through. Crousaz, *L'Académie de Lausanne*, 119–26.

[163] See Buisson, 2:249–50.

5

Sebastian Castellio's Liberal Challenge

5.1. Introduction

At first glance, the rift between Calvin and Jacques de Bourgogne, Seigneur de Falais, seems to have opened when Falais defended his personal physician Jerome Bolsec against the Genevans' charges against him. As Mirjam van Veen has noted, however, a deeper consideration suggests that the break may have been a long time coming, precipitated by Falais's long association with Spiritualists and advocates of religious toleration, including Sebastian Castellio.[1] Calvin told Falais that Castellio "is so perverse in every impiety that I would prefer a hundred times over to be a papist."[2] Calvin viewed most of his Protestant enemies as deeply misguided, mistaken, or unenlightened by the Spirit. Castellio, by contrast, represented a greater threat, for he seemed to call into question the objective truth of Christianity itself. Castellio's ideas were radical for his time and included not only his well-known support for religious toleration but also an abiding conviction in the opacity of Scripture, a commitment to a rationalist biblical hermeneutic, a Zwinglian understanding of the Eucharist, and seemingly Catholic ideas about justification and the relationship between faith and good works.

Because of his lasting influence, Castellio has fared better in modern scholarship than, for example, Caroli or Bolsec, and a study of his role does not present the same challenge of an unremittingly antagonistic historiography. While other opponents have been treated chiefly by hostile Calvinist authors, Castellio has won the admiration of modernists who have seen him as a forerunner of modern theology, liberal thought, and the Enlightenment's

---

[1] Van Veen, "'In excelsis honoris gradu,'" esp., 18–22.

[2] "j'aurois moins d'accointance avec vous qu'avec tous ennemis manifestes, puis qu'en vous monstrant ainsi famillier vous estiez, selon qu'on m'avoit rapporté depuis, le prescheur des louanges de Castalio, lequel est si pervers en toute impieté, que j'aimerois cent fois mieus estre papiste." Calvin, *Lettres à Monsieur et Madame de Falais*, 206–7, no. 53, Calvin to M. de Falais, [Geneva], [June 1554].

Refusing to Kiss the Slipper. Michael W. Bruening, Oxford University Press (2021). © Oxford University Press.
DOI: 10.1093/oso/9780197566954.003.0006

embrace of rationalism and religious toleration. Ferdinand Buisson's magisterial study of Castellio was originally subtitled *Study of the Origins of Liberal French Protestantism.*[3] Stefan Zweig's over-the-top polemic *The Right to Heresy: Castellio against Calvin*, written in the shadow of Nazi Germany, portrays Calvin as a totalitarian dictator whom the lowly, courageous, and freedom-loving Castellio dared to resist.[4] Recent work, by contrast, has resisted the image of Castellio as a liberal Protestant *avant la lettre*. Max Engammare's 2010 re-edition of Buisson's biography, for example, omits the original subtitle,[5] and on the very first page of his Castellio biography, Hans Guggisberg critiques Buisson for his "tendency to idealize Castellio and to view him as a forerunner of nineteenth-century liberal Protestantism."[6]

Historical scholarship is right to leave behind the hagiographical tradition for both Calvin and Castellio, but there is still value in viewing Castellio as a forerunner of liberal Christianity. He represents perhaps in its purest form an attitude shared by many of the anti-Calvinists we are meeting in this book, for whom Calvin's ecclesiastical authoritarianism (Calvin himself would probably say "prophetic calling") rendered him odious. Instead, they sought the freedom to discuss and debate religious issues absent the surveillance of an inquisitorial Protestant authority. We saw in Chapter 1, for example, how the early French evangelicals insisted on *le seul nécessaire* of preaching the Gospel. Chapter 4 described how Falais criticized the Genevans for not allowing free debate over predestination. It also showed how Zébédée and his allies in the Vaud lambasted Calvin's role in the death of Servetus, whose ideas they may have rejected but whose expression of those ideas, they firmly believed, should not have gotten him killed.

Castellio established his reputation in the wake of the Servetus execution and would remain a steadfast opponent of the Calvinists throughout his life. At the root of his opposition lay the foundational liberal principle of tolerance for ambiguity. While the Calvinists insisted on precise theological definitions for nearly everything, Castellio insisted on leaving theological difficulties open to debate, and this stance informed most of his thought.

---

[3] Ferdinand Buisson, *Sébastien Castellion: Sa vie et son oeuvre (1515–1563), Étude sur les origines du Protestantisme libéral français*, 2 vols. (Paris: Hachette, 1892).

[4] Stefan Zweig, *The Right to Heresy: Castellio against Calvin*, translated by Eden and Cedar Paul (New York: Viking Press, 1936).

[5] Ferdinand Buisson, *Sébastien Castellion: Sa vie et son oeuvre (1515–1563)*, edited and introduced by Max Engammare (Geneva: Droz, 2010).

[6] Hans R. Guggisberg, *Sebastian Castellio, 1515–1563: Humanist and Defender of Religious Toleration in a Confessional Age*, edited and translated by Bruce Gordon, St. Andrews Studies in Reformation History (Aldershot, UK: Ashgate, [1997] 2003).

It emerged from his conviction that Scripture is often impenetrable, which rendered contemporary exegetical methods outdated, precise theological definitions impossible, and executions for heresy especially heinous.

5.2. Castellio's Early Life, Schooling in Lyon, and Move to Geneva, 1515–1543

Castellio (1515–1563) was born Sébastien Chastillon or Chasteillon in Saint-Martin-du-Fresne in the duchy of Savoy.[7] He was from a large peasant family, and we know practically nothing about his education as a boy. When he was twenty years old, he went to Lyon to study at the Collège de la Trinité, where he received a humanist education and adopted the Latinized name Castalio.[8] While he stood out as an excellent student of Greek and Latin, he was not a member of Lyon's elite humanist circle, which included Rabelais, Clément Marot, and Etienne Dolet. Nevertheless, he was immersed in the general humanist culture of the city and the school.[9] In religious matters, Castellio adopted the attitude of the French humanists in Marguerite's network who hesitated to break definitively from the French church. Castellio was in Lyon during the five years immediately following the Affair of the Placards, suggesting that he initially had no plans to embrace Farel's radical vision of reform.

Nevertheless, in May 1540, he moved to Strasbourg, where Calvin was living during his exile from Geneva. Around this time, Castellio also came into contact with Farel, who recommended him for a teaching post at the Collège de Rive in Geneva.[10] Castellio accepted the position and began his duties on June 20, 1541, thus, after Antoine Marcourt and Jean Morand had left the city but before Calvin's return from Strasbourg.[11]

---

[7] This was in the portion of Savoy taken by the French, not the Bernese, in 1536. On his early life, see Guggisberg, *Sebastian Castellio*, 9–11.

[8] On his education in Lyon, see Guggisberg, *Sebastian Castellio, 1515–1563*, 15–17. On the Collège de la Trinité, see J. L. Gerig, "Le collège de la Trinité à Lyon avant 1540," *Revue de la Renaissance* 9 (1908): 76–95, 10 (1909): 137–57, 204–15; Georgette Brasart de Groër, "Le Collège, agent d'infiltration de la Réforme: Barthelémy Aneau au Collège de la Trinité," in *Aspects de la propagande religieuse*, THR 28 (Geneva: Droz, 1957), 167–75.

[9] It is possible, but only theoretically, that he met Zébédée there in 1538.

[10] Guggisberg, *Sebastian Castellio, 1515–1563*, 25.

[11] Pierre Viret was the interim leading pastor in Geneva at that time. Castellio seems to have developed a friendly relationship with Viret and left behind a short, undated piece of verse addressed to him, which to my knowledge, has never been published. It runs as follows: "Pastor Christiadum gregis Virete, / Nostram tibia quae viam morata est / Haec iam nunc properat valere, postquam / Praescriptum medicamen a Beato / E membris nervos trahat liquores. /

He remained in Geneva well after Calvin's return, and the two men appear to have gotten along well for a while. In Geneva, Castellio published his first and most commercially successful book, the *Sacred Dialogues*.[12] This was essentially a textbook that contained dialogues between biblical characters. It was intended to teach both Latin and Christian morals through biblical history and figures. Perhaps surprisingly, given his later reputation as a theological liberal, Castellio believed that using the pagan texts of antiquity was inappropriate for the education of young boys. He wrote in the prefatory letter to Mathurin Cordier,

> Certainly, in my opinion, these [pagan] authors, however correct and refined they may be, must only be studied by those who are stronger and of a more learned age. Nothing is more important than that the young be led to moral discernment. For this reason, I have taken excerpts of certain familiar passages and beautiful conversations from the sacred books of the Hebrews and translated them into Latin speech. In this way, we might shape the tongues of our pupils in Latin and their spirits in good morals.[13]

Importuna quidem mala illa Psora, / Si portus fuit unde me avocavit. / Sed si non animus referre gressum / (Vitaretne bonum an malum, deus scit)/ Iussisset, si qua spes fuisset, / Empusae potuit pedem tulissem, / Quam non visa foret Sebastiano / Quam diu postulat a deo, Rebecca." The letter was addressed, "D. Petro Vireto Lausannensis ecclesiae pastori fidelissimo, fratri amantissimo." BGE, ms. lat. 111a, 41. The text refers to Castellio's bad leg and helpful medicine prescribed by "Beatus," probably Viret's Lausanne colleague Béat Comte. It seems likely, therefore, that the letter dates to around the time of Castellio's break with Calvin, possibly around February 1544, when Castellio went to Lausanne hoping to find a position at the Academy. See Buisson, 1:197–204.

[12] *Dialogi sacri, latino-gallici, ad linguas moresque puerorum formandos* ([Geneva]: [Jean Girard], [1543]). A critical edition of Book One has been published: David Amherdt and Yves Giraud, eds., *Dialogues sacrés/Dialogi Sacri (Premier Livre)*, Textes Littéraires Français 571 (Geneva: Droz, 2004). Initially, Castellio published just book one, but books two and three followed in 1543. A fourth and final book was introduced in 1545: *Dialogorum sacrorum ad linguam simul et mores puerorum formandos, libri quatuor* (Basel: R. Winter, 1545). The work went through more than twenty editions in Castellio's lifetime and many more after his death. Guggisberg, *Sebastian Castellio, 1515–1563*, 32. See the list of editions in Buisson, 2:341–52.

[13] "Quare hi authores, mea quidem sententia, utut tersi sint et politi, non nisi et confirmatiore iam et eruditiore aetate sunt pertractandi. Quippe nihil tanti est, ut sint in discrimen mores adducendi. His ego de causis familiaria quaedam, et iucunda Colloquia de sacris Hebraeorum libris excerpseram et in Latinum sermonem converteram, quibus discipulorum nostrorum et linguas Latinitate et animos bonis moribus eadem opera informaremus." Castellio, *Dialogues sacrés/Dialogi sacri*, 46–47, ll.41–48, textual corrections from Michael Bruening, "Castellio Correspondence Project," online at https://web.mst.edu/~bruening/Castellio%20Project/Index%20Page.htm.

Thus, although Castellio may have adopted liberal theological views, he was no secularist. He believed deeply in Christian education and lamented the absence of schoolbooks that taught Christian history, stories, and morals.[14]

5.3. Castellio's Break with Calvin, 1543–1544

As rector of the Collège de Rive in Geneva, Castellio was responsible for teaching, and he often preached on Sundays, but he was not a member of the Company of Pastors. In 1543, following an outbreak of plague, the Geneva city council decided that Castellio should, in fact, become a full-time preacher.[15] This proposal led to the breakdown in Castellio's relationship with Calvin, for the pastors, led by Calvin, rejected the appointment.[16] They cited two main concerns: First, they suggested that Castellio did not believe the Song of Songs to be canonical but rather profane love poetry. Second, they noted that Castellio disagreed with Calvin's interpretation of Christ's descent into hell.[17] Thus, he was rejected for the Genevan ministry. The city

---

[14] Later, Castellio renewed this position in an attack on Beza and the extensive use of pagan authors at the Lausanne Academy: "Avise, Bèze, qu'il ne semble que soyez plustost ceux qui voulez renverser la religion, veu que vous lisez, enseignez, interprétez et apprenez par coeur en voz académies les autheurs toutalement contraires à la religion chrestienne. J'entens les filosofes et poètes desquelz les uns enseignent plusieurs choses contre la vérité, les autres monstrent la manière de pécher, paillarder et séduire les femmes d'autruy, comme Térence, Ovide, Martial et Théodore de Bèze en ses épigrammes. Penses-tu que nous soyons tant déporveuz de sens de penser que par telz ennemys de Christ sa dottrine soit avancée, ou que vous ayés la religion chrestienne à coeur, qui portez telz autheurs au sein et les proposez aux enfans pour faire apprandre par coeur?" Sebastian Castellio, *De l'Impunité des hérétiques, De Haereticis non puniendis*, edited by Bruno Becker and M. Valkhoff, THR 118 (Geneva: Droz, 1971), 295.

In a related vein, Castellio would blast Beza and Viret for using humor and mockery in their works, believing these tactics inappropriate in the discussion of religious topics: "Car je te [Bèze] prie, qu'est-ce scurrilité et plaisanterie, si ton Passavant, ta Zoografie, les Dialogues de Viret et l'Anatomie de la Messe ne le sont? De sorte que maintenant en France Viret est appelé le Pantagruel des théologiens, en quoy donnez à cognoistre que la théologie (laquelle vous souillez vilainement par ces livres scurriles et diffamatoires) ne vous est point plus à coeur, ne aggréable, qu'à ceux qui sont assiz au banc des moqueurs. Au moins, si vous plaisantiez seulement ès choses profanes; mais plaisanter et gaudir en la chose plus grande et plus sainte de toutes, qu'est-ce autre sinon se moquer de Dieu?" Castellio, *De l'Impunité des hérétiques*, 284.

[15] "Me Bastian Chastillon, pource qu'il est savant homme et est fort propice pour servyr à l'église, ordonne que il luy soyt provheu en l'église, et cependant que l'aultre maystre d'eschole viendra debvra toutjour exercyr son office." CO 21:326–27, December 17, 1543.

[16] "Sur ce que M. Calvin a rappourter que Me Bastian est bien sçavant home, mes [read: mais] qu'il ast quelque opignion dont n'est capable pour le ministere." CO 21:328, January 14, 1544.

[17] "Nam quum ex more inquireremus num in tota doctrinae summa inter nos et illum conveniret, duo esse respondit, in quibus non posset nobiscum sentire: quod Salomonis canticum sacris libris adscriberemus, et quod descensum Christi ad inferos acciperemus in Catechismo pro eo quem sustinuit conscientiae horrore, quum pro nobis sisteret se ad Dei tribunal, ut peccata nostra, poenam ac maledictionem in se transferendo, sua morte expiaret." CO 11:675, Testimony of the Genevan Ministers on Castellio. On Castellio's and Calvin's positions on the Song of Songs, see

council indicated that he was to remain as rector of the school and without a raise. The councilors also told Castellio and Calvin to settle in private their disagreements on the Song of Songs and Christ's descent into hell.[18] Growing frustrated, Castellio sought a new position at the Lausanne Academy; his bid was unsuccessful, however, and he had to remain in Geneva.

Castellio's annoyance boiled over at the *congrégation* held on May 30, 1544. After Calvin finished speaking on the difficulties of the preaching office, Castellio arose and "unleashed a storm of criticism of the Geneva ministers."[19] According to Calvin's narration of the meeting, Castellio painted a picture of dichotomies that contrasted St. Paul with the Geneva ministers: "He [Paul] devoted his nights to building the Church, we spend the night playing games; he was sober, we are drunks; he was threatened by seditions, we raise them; he was chaste, we are fornicators."[20] Castellio then moved to a theme that would come to define his future relations with Calvin and his followers: their eagerness to persecute anyone who disagreed with them: "He [Paul] was imprisoned, we imprison anyone who offends us with a word. He used the power of God, we use another [worldly] power. He suffered on account of others, we persecute the innocent."[21] Thus, ten years before the publication of *Concerning Heretics*, Castellio was already attacking the Genevan ministers' intolerance and persecution of the innocent. Castellio's harangue caused an uproar in Geneva, and he was pressured to resign.[22]

Max Engammare, *Le Cantique des Cantiques à la Renaissance: Étude et Bibliographie*, THR 277 (Geneva: Droz, 1993), 9–18.

[18] "M. Calvin et Mᵉ Bastian Chastillon. Sur ce que entre eulx sont en dubie sus l'approbation du livre de Salomon, lequel M. Calvin approve sainct et ledit Bastian le repudie, disant que quant il fist le capistre septieme il estoyt en folie et conduyct par mondaienetés et non pas du sainct Esperit. Et sur ce, hont demandé ledit Sʳ Calvin estre aoys en dispute et daventage ledit Sʳ Bastian a diest qu'il laysse tel livre pour tel qu'il est. Et quant au passage du symbole là où diest que Jhesus descendit aux enfers, il n'est pas encore fort resoluz approvant touteffois la doctrine estre de Dieu et saincte. Et sur ce ordonne que entre eulx secretement ayent à fere dispute, sans publier telles choses." CO 21:329, January 28, 1544.

[19] Guggisberg, *Sebastian Castellio*, 36.

[20] "Contexuit perpetuam antithesin, ut prorsus omni ex parte contraria omnia in nobis et Christi ministris ostenderet. Lusit ergo in hunc modum: Paulum fuisse servum Dei, nos servire nobis. Fuisse illum patientissimum, nos impatientissimos. Vigilasse illum de nocte ut ecclesiae aedificationi se impenderet, nos ludendo vigilare. Sobrium illum fuisse, nos ebriosos. Illum vexatum fuisse seditionibus, nos eas commovere. Illum fuisse castum, nos esse scortatores." CO 11:721, no. 554, Calvin to Farel, [May 31, 1544].

[21] "Illum carcere fuisse inclusum, nos includere si quis verbo nos laedat. Illum usum fuisse potentia Dei, nos uti aliena. Illum ab aliis passum fuisse, nos persequi innocentes." CO 11:721, no. 554.

[22] His resignation was accepted on 14 July 1544. As Buisson indicates (1:214), he was not banished from Geneva, as Beza implies in his *Life of Calvin*: "convaincu de manifeste malice et calomnie, la justice luy ordonna de sortir apres avoir recognu sa faute." CO 21:26.

Castellio's tenure in Geneva ended in bitterness and colored the mutual feelings of Calvin and Castellio for the rest of their lives. Castellio had witnessed Calvin's uncompromising nature firsthand. In the pastors' testimony on Castellio, they indicated that the church could not tolerate the uncertainty that Castellio would bring to the Company of Pastors: "This was our only concern: that great evil might arise from various interpretations. He responded that he did not want to accept anything that he could not support in good conscience."[23] This disagreement over multiple interpretations of doctrine set the terms of their lifelong debate: Calvin would always insist on clearly defined doctrines, while Castellio demanded freedom of conscience and the right to doubt. Their differences on the biblical text also had their roots in Geneva. In addition to their disagreement on the Song of Songs, Castellio had begun working on a French translation of the Bible. Calvin corrected it, but Castellio refused to incorporate his suggestions; consequently, it was not printed at the time.[24] Doctrine, doubt, and divergent biblical interpretation: these were the seeds planted in Geneva that would lead to the growth of conflict and recrimination between two of the greatest minds of the sixteenth century.

5.4. Castellio's Early Publications in Basel, 1545–1551

After his departure from Geneva, Castellio spent at least a little time with his friend André Zébédée in Orbe. As noted in the previous chapter, Castellio seems to have convinced Zébédée to accept his position on the Song of Songs.[25] It was around this time that Zébédée's relationship with the Calvinists started to fray, and Castellio's visit may have played a role in that development. After Orbe, Castellio passed through Yverdon—the main stronghold of anti-Calvinist sentiment in the Vaud—before proceeding to Basel, the city that would remain his home for the rest of his life.

Basel was a great center of humanist learning at the time: Erasmus had made it his home during his last years; the wealthy Amerbach family

---

[23] "Tantum id nobis curae esse, ne quod ex variis expositionibus grave malum nasceretur. Respondit, nolle se recipere, quod praestare nisi repugnante conscientia non posset." *CO* 11:675, no. 531. See also Guggisberg, *Sebastian Castellio*, 35.
[24] Guggisberg, *Sebastian Castellio*, 29–30.
[25] See 111–12.

supported a variety of humanist endeavors there; and the city was a center of humanist printing, led in the 1520s and 1530s by Johannes and Hieronymus Froben and later by Pietro Perna and Johannes Oporinus.[26] Castellio found employment with the latter, working for a pittance as a corrector.[27]

Although Castellio's work for the Basel printer may have paid meager wages, the position gave him access to a press that was not under Calvin's thumb. And so he began to publish—translations chiefly—at a furious rate. In three years, he published eight new titles, as well as three new editions of his *Sacred Dialogues*.[28] No doubt, he had prepared at least a few of these texts in Geneva but feared to publish them (or was prohibited from doing so) on account of Calvin's censure. None of these early Basel works caused much of a stir, however; most were traditional humanist editions and translations.

In 1551, however, Castellio published a complete new Latin translation of the Bible. He had already published portions of the Bible in his earlier works. In the *Latin Moses*, he stated that his objective in producing a new translation was to replace the Hebraisms contained in most existing versions with good Latin that any Roman would have recognized.[29] In other words, he would have Moses speak the Latin that he would have spoken had he been educated by Cicero or Quintillian.[30] Thus, for example, he used "to wash" (*lavare*)

---

[26] On Basel during this time, see Hans R. Guggisberg, *Basel in the Sixteenth Century: Aspects of the City Republic before, during, and after the Reformation* (St. Louis, MO: Center for Reformation Research, 1982); Peter G. Bietenholz, *Basle and France in the Sixteenth Century: The Basle Humanists and Printers in their Contacts with Francophone Culture*, THR 112 (Geneva: Droz, 1971).

[27] On Castellio's early years in Basel, see Guggisberg, *Sebastian Castellio*, 37–48.

[28] *Ionas Propheta, heroico carmine Latino descriptus* (Basel: Oporinus, September 1545); *Bernhardini Ochini Senensis Expositio epistolae divi Pauli ad Romanos, de italico in latinum translata* (Augsburg: Philippus Ulhardus, [1545]); *Xenophontis philosophi ac historici excellentissimi opera quae quidem extant omnia tam graeca quam latina* (Basel: Nicol. Brylingerum, 1545); *Sirillus, Ecloga de nativitate Christi* (Basel: Oporinus, March 1546); *Mosis institutio reipublicae graeco-latina, ex Josepho in gratiam puerorum decerpta* (Basel: [Oporinus], [1546]); *Sibyllina oracula de graeco in latinum conversa* (Basel: Oporinus, August 1546); *Moses latinus ex hebraeo factus* (Basel: Oporinus, August 1546); *Psalterium, reliquaque sacrarum literarum carmina et precationes* (Basel: Oporinus, September 1547). Two editions of the *Sacred Dialogues* were published in 1545 and a third by Oporinus in 1547.

[29] On Castellio's Latin Bible, see Josef Eskhult, "Castellion, traducteur de la Bible latine: Image de soi et réception durant la Renaissance et l'Âge classique," in *Sébastien Castellion: Des Écritures à l'écriture*, edited by Marie-Christine Gomez-Géraud (Paris: Classiques Garnier, 2013), 109–38; Irena Backus, "Moses, Plato and Flavius Josephus: Castellio's Conceptions of Sacred and Profane in His Latin Versions of the Bible," in *Shaping the Bible in the Reformation: Books, Scholars and Their Readers in the Sixteenth Century*, edited by Bruce Gordon and Matthew McLean (Leiden: Brill, 2012), 143–65.

[30] "Quia nonnullos a sacrarum literarum lectione sermonis absterret impolitia, alios obscuritas et ignoti latinis auribus hebraismi, conatus sum Mosem . . . in latinum sermonem tanta facilitate atque elegantia transferre, quanta ipsum, si latinus fuisset, usurum fuisse, ex ipsius Hebraeo sermone coniicio, ut neque iam peregrinitate quenquam, neque obscuritate possit offendere." Castellio, *Moses latinus*, α2r.

instead of "to baptize" (*baptizare*), "college" (*collegium*) instead of "syna-gogue" (*synagogum*), and "sect" (*secta*) instead of "heresy" (*haeresis*). Calvin and Beza would later criticize Castellio's translation harshly,[31] but there is no evidence of their reactions immediately after the 1551 publication.

More controversial was Castellio's prefatory letter in the full Latin Bible, addressed to the young King Edward VI of England. Here, he introduced several themes that would recur throughout his later works, in particular, the failure of Christians actively to pursue virtue, the opacity of Scripture, and the plea for religious toleration. At the beginning of his letter, Castellio ponders why there are so many quarrels and disagreements in his day, especially since learning—which Renaissance humanists tied closely to virtue—had never been stronger. The culprit? "Vice and impiety." He continues, "If we want to know the secrets hidden in these books [of the Bible], we must worship and fear God, obey him and be his disciples. This is the true path toward under-standing divine matters; this is the one key for opening the door of divine secrets."[32] Virtue and obedience are necessary precisely because Scripture is so difficult to understand, "for the things contained in it are given obscurely and often in enigmas and inscrutable questions, which have been in dispute for more than a thousand years without any agreement."[33] Because of this ob-scurity and lack of agreement on Scripture, the resulting uncertainty about religion renders abhorrent the act of killing in its name:

> We envy and revile and return not merely evil for evil, but often evil for good, and if anyone disagrees with us on a single point of religion we condemn him and pursue him to the corners of the earth with the dart of tongue and pen. We exercise cruelty with the sword, flame, and water

---

[31] Especially in Beza's preface to his own 1556 translation of the New Testament, in Calvin and Beza's 1560 Bible translation, and in Beza's 1563 *Responsio ad defensiones et reprehensiones Sebastiani Castellionis, quibus suam Novi Testamenti interpretationem defendere . . . conatus est* ([Geneva]: Henri Estienne, 1563). See Guggisberg, *Sebastian Castellio*, 136, 183.

[32] "Itaque cum attentius hanc rem considerarem, visus sum mihi huius ignorantiae unam verissimamque causam invenisse, vitiositatem ac impietatem. . . . Quod si Iovae arcana in his libris occultata nosse volumus, metuendus nobis, et colendus Iova est, eique obediendum, ut decet eius discipulos. Haec vera ad divinarum rerum cognitionem via, haec una ad hoc divinorum arcanorum sigillum aperiendum clavis est." Sebastian Castellio, ed. *Biblia* (Basel: Oporinus, 1551), α2v. Castellio's use of "Jove" for God, rather than "Yahweh" or "Jehovah," is another example of his translation of the Bible into classical Latin without Hebraisms.

[33] "Cum sint enim haec obscure et saepe per aenigmata tradita et de his iam per mille amplius annos disputetur, necdum componi res potuerit." Castellio, ed., *Biblia*, α4v. Translation from Roland H. Bainton, ed. and trans., *Concerning Heretics, Whether They Are to Be Persecuted and How They Are to Be Treated, A Collection of the Opinions of Learned Men both Ancient and Modern* (New York: Columbia University Press, 1935), 215.

and exterminate the destitute and defenseless. We declare that we are not allowed to kill anyone, yet we deliver him to Pilate and if he releases him we say that he is no friend of Caesar. And what is far worse, we declare that all this is done through zeal for Christ and at his command and in his name. . . . Wherefore, let us not condemn one another, for if we condemn, we will be condemned.[34]

Castellio would carry this core argument throughout his writings on religious toleration. Scripture is obscure and religious truth uncertain. Consequently, killing over religious disagreement is unjustified.

5.5. The Servetus Affair and *Concerning Heretics*

Ultimately, Castellio's works on religious toleration were what brought him international recognition and the lasting enmity of the Calvinists. His rise to prominence began with the Servetus Affair. The events that led to the 1553 execution of Michael Servetus in Geneva have been discussed many times, and there is no need to rehearse the details here.[35] Suffice it to say that Servetus was a Spanish medical doctor who cast doubt on the Christian doctrine of the trinity. After an initial arrest by the Inquisition in Lyon—aided by evidence supplied by Calvin—Servetus escaped and went to Geneva. There he was recognized and imprisoned "at my instigation," as Calvin boasted to Simon Sulzer.[36]

Servetus's trial in Geneva is meticulously documented.[37] Central to his eventual conviction were the opinions on the case received from the Swiss

---

[34] "Invidemus, maledicimus, non solum malum malo, sed saepe bonum malo pensamus, et si quis a nobis in aliquo religionis vel puncto dissidet, eum damnamus, et per omnes terrarum angulos linguae stilique iaculo petimus, et ferro et flamma et undis saevimus, et ex rerum natura indefensos et inopes tollimus; et nobis non licere quenquam interficere dicimus, et tamen Pilato tradimus, et si hunc dimittat, amicum esse Caesaris negamus. Et quod est omnium indignissimum, haec omnia Christi nos studio et iussu et nomine facere clamamus. . . . 'Quamobrem ne iam damnemus alius aliam' [Rom. 14:13]. Nam si damnabimus, damnabimur." Castellio, *Biblia*, α3v–α4r. Translation adapted from Bainton, ed., *Concerning Heretics*, 212–214. In the last sentence Bainton uses the traditional "let us not judge one another," but Castellio here uses *damnare*.

[35] The literature on Servetus is copious, but for a general biography, it is still hard to do better than Roland H. Bainton, *Hunted Heretic: The Life and Death of Michael Servetus, 1511–1553* (Boston: Beacon Press, 1953).

[36] "Tandem huc malis auspiciis appulsum unus ex Syndicis me autore in carcerem duci iussit." *CO* 14:614–15, no. 1793, Calvin to Sulzer, Geneva, September 9, 1553. Translation from Bonnet, ed., *Letters of John Calvin*, 2:410.

[37] *CO* 8:721–872.

churches, all of which harshly condemned him.[38] These responses stood in contrast to those received in Bolsec's case, for, while Bolsec had embraced a not uncommon position on the much disputed doctrine of predestination, Servetus seemed to undermine the very foundations of Christian doctrine by rejecting the Nicene understanding of God—and, one should add, by adopting Anabaptist positions on the sacraments.[39] He was found guilty and sentenced to be burned at the stake. The execution was carried out on October 27, 1553.[40]

5.5.1. Opposition to Servetus's Execution

Although the official line from the Swiss churches was supportive of Geneva's position, many individuals opposed the execution. Soon after Servetus's arrest, Calvin complained to Sulzer in Basel, "Would that your old disciples were animated by the same spirit" as those vigorously against Servetus.[41] Dispiriting to the Calvinists were the reservations of Pierre Toussain, the pastor of Montbéliard and formerly a staunch ally. Toussain wrote to Farel that he had heard "a certain Spaniard" was imprisoned in Geneva on account of religion and commented, "I do not think we should put anyone to death for the sake of religion, unless sedition or other aggravating circumstances are present."[42] Similarly, Pier Paolo Vergerio wrote to Bullinger, "Certainly I abhor Servetus and monsters of that sort. But I do not think that fire or

---

[38] See the following: (1) Geneva's request for advice on the case, *CO* 8:802–803, September 21, 1553; (2) response from the Zurich council, *CO* 8:808, October 2, 1553; (3) response from the Zurich pastors, *CO* 8:555–58, October 2, 1553; (4) responses from the council and pastors of Schaffhausen, *CO* 8:809–10, October 6, 1553; (5) Bern pastors on Servetus, *CO* 8:811–817; (6) responses of Bern council and pastors, *CO* 8:818–19, October 6, 1553; (7) responses of Basel council and pastors, *CO* 8:820–23, October 12, 1553.

[39] Indeed, in the sentence given by the Genevans, he was told that he had "for a long time promulgated false and thoroughly heretical doctrine . . . [and had] with malicious and perverse obstinacy sown and divulged even in printed books opinions against God the Father, the Son, and the Holy Spirit, in a word, against the fundamentals of the Christian religion." Quoted in Bainton, *Hunted Heretic*, 208–9.

[40] See Bainton, *Hunted Heretic*, 207–12.

[41] "Utinam veteres tui discipuli eodem modo animati forent." *CO* 14:615, no. 1793. Translation from Bonnet, ed., *Letters of John Calvin*, 2:411. Sulzer expressed confusion about who these lukewarm disciples might be, guessing perhaps the Genevan magistrates Caspar Favre and Jean-Baltasar Sept. *CO* 14:623, and n. 3, no. 1801, Sulzer to Calvin, Basel, September 18, 1553.

[42] "Scriptum est ad me Basilea Hispanum quendam Genevae ob religionem in vincula coniectum esse de vitaque periclitari. Quod an verum sit et quis sit scire cupio. Quanquam non putem nobis quemquam ad mortem religionis causa persequendum, nisi seditio aut aliae magnae causae adsint, ob quas magistratus iure officio suo fungatur." *CO* 20:416, no. 4166, Toussain to Farel, September 21, [1553].

the sword should be used against them."[43] Vergerio also informed Bullinger that Servetus had supporters in Basel.[44] Toussain told Farel that his information about "the Spaniard" had come from Basel. And it was from Basel that the most vociferous opposition to Servetus's execution came. David Joris, an Anabaptist and associate of Castellio, sent perhaps the strongest letter of opposition to Servetus's prosecution:

> I have heard how the good, pious Servetus was delivered into your hands through no kindness and love, but rather through envy and hate, as will be made manifest at the last judgment to those whose eyes are now darkened by base cunning, and to whom the truth is unknown. . . . I hope that the bloodthirsty counsel of the learned will not weigh with you. Consider rather the precepts of our only Lord and Master Christ, who taught not only in human and literal fashion in Scripture, but also in a divine manner by word and example that we should crucify and kill no one for his faith, but should rather be crucified and killed ourselves."[45]

Most shocking in this letter is Joris's description of Servetus as "good and pious." Unlike Toussain or Vergerio, Joris seems to defend Servetus himself, not just to argue against the death penalty for heretics.

News of Servetus's execution galvanized opposition to Calvin. Although the death penalty had been decreed by the Geneva city council, Calvin himself was widely blamed, especially in Basel.[46] Several members of Castellio's circle had been in Geneva for the execution but left soon afterward to report

---

[43] "Nunc tantum dixerim, me abhorrere quidem a Servetis, et id genus monstris. Interea tamen non putarem igne aut ferro contra ea utendum." *CO* 14:633, no. 1814, Chur, October 3, 1553.

[44] "Scribit ad me amicus e Basilea Serveto illic non deesse fautores." *CO* 14:641–42, no. 1828, Vergerio to Bullinger, Chur, October 14, 1553.

[45] "Na dat Ick . . . den Handel (so den ghoeden vromen Serveto wedervaren) gehoort heb, der deur gheen vrundeliikheit unde liefde in in U. E. E. Handen unde Macht, maer net enckelder nijt unde haat overghlevert is, ghelijk aen den Jongsten Gerichte wel openbaer sal werden den genen, dien het nu deur scholcke list in een ooch verdonkert, den grondt der Waerheijt alles onbewust is, Godt geve tyliick die sacke t' ervaren . . . . Un of sy U. E. E. Ooren . . . te veel deur bloetgierighe benijdinghe moeyliick maken, un daer toe porren oder reytsen wilden, die selve doch inghedenck sijn willen onses alleroversten Heeren unde Leermeysteren, Christi: Dat is, niet alleen in die Schrift letterlijck op Menschen, maer Godlijcker wijse, geliick by ons gheleert unde voorghetreden heft, niemants te cruijzigen of te dooden om sijns Gheloofs oder Leere willen: maer self daer om gekruijziget unde gedoodet te werden." Johann Lorenz von Mosheim, *Anderweitiger Versuch einer vollständigen und unpartheyischen Ketzergeschichte* (Helmgeaede: Christian Friederich Weygand, 1748), 1:421–22, no. XIV. Translation from Bainton, *Hunted Heretic*, 206–7. On this letter, see also Uwe Plath, *Calvin und Basel in den Jahren 1552-1556*, Basler Beiträge zur Geschichtswissenschaft 133 (Basel: Helbing & Lichtenhahn, 1974), 73–75.

[46] On the opposition to Calvin in Basel after Servetus's execution, see Plath, *Calvin und Basel*, 80–93; Gordon, *Calvin*, 224–32.

on it. The schoolmaster Jean Colinet, who had reported on Zébédée reading Castellio's letter to Falais,[47] left a month after the execution. Calvin attempted to block the city council from giving Colinet an attestation, claiming that he held "several unbearable opinions, principally that one should not punish people for their opinions . . . and that he received and showed several people a certain preface of Sebastian Castellio, even though it contained bad doctrine."[48] Léger Grymoult, who would later help to edit Castellio's works, left Geneva for Zurich, where he complained to the mayor about the execution, but he was forced to leave by the hostile clergy there.[49] In reporting on his visit, Zurich pastor Rudolf Gwalther complained that Servetus had "more supporters among our people (I'm talking about the Italians and the French) than you might think."[50] And Pieter Anastasius de Zuttere, the "South-Netherlands Apostle of Tolerance" also known as Petrus Hyperphragmus, was in Geneva for the execution and wrote a *History of the Death of Servetus.*[51] He wrote verses in French condemning the burning and went to Falais's estate at Veigy. From there, he, too, moved to Basel.[52]

5.5.2. Castellio's First Criticism of the Execution, December 1553

Another written description of Servetus's death that appeared in Basel in late December 1553 was probably the work of Sebastian Castellio.[53] In it, Castellio

---

[47] See 131–32.

[48] "Icy M. Calvin accompagné de Guill. Chiccand a remonstré sus ce que luy est esté dict de la part du Conseil que Iehan Colinet pedagogue demandoit actestation de sa loyaulté: que ledit Colinet a plusieurs opinions non portables, mesmement que l'on ne doibt punir les gens pour les oppinions . . . . Item et qu'il a receupt et monstré certaine preface de Bastian Chastellion à plusieurs, combien qu'elle contenusse choses de maulvaises doctrine." CO 21:562, November 21, 1553.

[49] Plath, *Calvin und Basel*, 85–86. On Grymoult, see 186.

[50] "Nec sine numine factum est, quod communi fere omnium ecclesiarum Helvetiae consensu pestis haec sublata est, quae fautores inter nostros (de Italis et Gallis loquor) plures iam invenerat quam putasses. Apud nos certe totius anni spatio egit puerorum quorundam Genevensium paedagogus, Gallus natione, et Calvino parum propitius (fortassis in Maecenatum suorum gratiam) qui quaestionem hanc apud Consulem Habium movere non est veritus." CO 14:683, no. 1860, Gwalther to Haller, Zurich, November 26, 1553.

[51] Only a short excerpt of the text survives. See Plath, *Calvin und Basel*, 86–87; Stanislas Kot, "L'Influence de Michel Servet sur le mouvement antitrinitarien en Pologne et en Transylvanie," in *Autour de Michel Servet et de Sébastien Castellion*, edited by B. Becker, 72–115 (Haarlem: H. D. Tjeenk Willink & Zoon, 1953), 109–11.

[52] See Plath, *Calvin und Basel*, 86–87.

[53] Plath, *Calvin und Basel*, 88–93. The untitled work was first published along with Castellio's *Contra libellum Calvini, in quo ostendere conatur haereticos iure gladii coercendos esse* ([Amsterdam]: [Reiner

lays the blame for Servetus's imprisonment squarely at Calvin's feet: "Calvin brought the accused to the magistrate and made sure that Servetus would be thrown in jail for heresy."[54] He claims, "Servetus was held in prison in such a way that no one could meet with him unless he was a friend of Calvin."[55] Castellio notes that the final responsibility for the death sentence lay with the city council but comments, "Some say that when Calvin saw Servetus led to the stake, he gave a subtle smile and that his dejected face became brighter beneath his cloak."[56]

The negative reactions to Servetus's execution, from Castellio and others, demonstrate that opposition to the death sentence was mounting. Calvin's defenders often explain that Calvin was simply acting as a "man of his time" with regard to Servetus's execution.[57] The opposition we have seen here reveals the weakness of this defense; in fact, many people of that time were appalled by the execution.

Calvin himself saw that his opponents would not be easily dismissed and, therefore, began to prepare his defense. It would be published in 1554 and is commonly known as *The Defense of the Orthodox Faith in the Holy Trinity against the Prodigious Errors of Michael Servetus*.[58] But the subtitle of the work is important, too: *Where It Is Shown That Heretics Rightly Are to Be Coerced by the Sword*. Indeed, Calvin starts the treatise not by discussing the trinity but by defending the magistrate's right to punish heretics.[59]

Telle], 1612), M2^r–M4^v. Uwe Plath has recently published the first modern edition of *Contra Libellum Calvini*, including the additional texts that were in the 1612 publication. Sebastian Castellio, *Contra Libellum Calvini: A New Critical Edition Supplemented by the Text of the Basle Manuscript-Fragment*, edited by Uwe Plath, Cahiers d'Humanisme et Renaissance 160 (Geneva: Droz, 2019). Subsequent references will refer to this new edition.

[54] "Calvinus e vestigio ad magistratum [Plath: *magistrum*] reum detulit, aut deferendum, curavit, ut Servetum propter haeresim in vincula petant." Castellio, *Contra Libellum Calvini*, 220.

[55] "Servetus in vinculis sic habitus est, ut eum convenire nemo (nisi magna authoritate praeditus) posset, nisi qui Calvini amicus esset." Castellio, *Contra Libellum Calvini*, 220.

[56] "Sunt, qui affirmant Calvinum, cum vidisset ad supplicium duci Servetum, subrisisse vultu sub sinu vestis leviter deiecto." Castellio, *Contra Libellum Calvini*, 222.

[57] See Émile Doumergue's discussion on "L'erreur du temps," in *Jean Calvin: Les hommes et les choses de son temps*, 7 vols. (Lausanne and Neuilly-sur-Seine, 1899–1927), 6:373–96.

[58] *Defensio orthodoxae fidei de sacra trinitate contra prodigiosos errores Michaelis Serveti Hispani, ubi ostenditur haereticos iure gladii coercendos esse et nominatim de homine hoc tam impio iuste et merito sumptum Genevae fuisse supplicium*. In CO 8:453–644.

[59] On Calvin's treatise, see Plath, *Calvin und Basel*, 120–27.

5.5.3. *Concerning Heretics*, 1554

Soon after Calvin's treatise was published, a book appeared in Basel that would become the most important text produced during this conflict: *Concerning Heretics, Whether They Are to Be Persecuted and How They Are to Be Treated*.[60] This was a collection of texts by various authors, both contemporary and ancient, edited by the pseudonymous "Martin Bellius."[61] "Bellius" was, in fact, Castellio, who almost certainly wrote the chapters written by "Basil Montfort" and who may also have had a hand in composing those by "George Kleinberg."[62] Few were fooled by the pseudonyms. Calvin immediately recognized Castellio's hand behind the text.[63] In addition to his own original but pseudonymous contributions, Castellio cleverly included many well-known authors in his collection, including an excerpt of his own prefatory letter to King Edward VI and a selection from Calvin himself.

Castellio dedicated the work to Duke Christoph of Württemberg, who had previously governed the French-speaking region of Montbéliard for his father Duke Ulrich. Christoph was eager to establish in his lands a religious peace that would be welcoming to both Lutherans and Calvinists, and perhaps to others as well. His irenic attitude helps to explain Castellio's decision to dedicate the work to him,[64] for achieving religious peace in his lands would require his pastors to overlook some of the theological differences that separated the confessions. The pointlessness of this theological wrangling forms the starting point of Castellio's preface:

---

[60] *De Haereticis, an sint persequendi, et omnino quomodo sit cum eis agendum . . .* (Magdeburg: Georg Rausch [Basel: Oporinus], 1554); modern facsimile edition: *De haereticis, an sint persequendi . . . : Reproduction en fac-similé de l'édition de 1554*, edited by Sape van der Woude (Geneva: Droz, 1954); English translation in Bainton, ed., *Concerning Heretics*. Since the 1954 edition is a facsimile and since the original edition is widely available online, I will cite page numbers from the original 1554 edition. The dates of *De Haereticis* and Calvin's text are too close together for *De Haereticis* to have been written in response to Calvin's text. As we will see, Castellio wrote *Contra Libellum Calvini* in direct response to Calvin's treatise.

[61] The pseudonym seems to be a play on the name *Mars*, the Roman god of war, and *bellum*, the Latin word for "war," hence, a "war on war." Buisson, 1:358.

[62] The identity of the pseudonymous author, "George Kleinberg," is harder to pin down. For a long time, scholars agreed that this, too, was probably Castellio, but Mirjam van Veen has convincingly revived the argument that it was probably Castellio's associate David Joris. Mirjam van Veen, "'Contaminated with David Joris's Blasphemies': David Joris's Contribution to Castellio's *De Haereticis an sint Persequendi*," *BHR* 69 (2007): 313–26.

[63] "Furtim etiam nuper excusus est liber Basileae falsis nominibus, in quo disputant Castalio et N., non esse gladio coercendos haereticos." *CO* 15:95–96, no. 1935, Calvin to Bullinger, Geneva, March 28, 1554.

[64] Eugénie Droz, "Castelloniana," in idem, *Chemins de l'hérésie: Textes et documents*, 4 vols. (Geneva: Slatkine, 1970–1976), 2:325–432, here, 329.

We dispute, not as to the way by which we may come to Christ, which is to correct our lives, but rather as to the state and office of Christ . . . ; likewise with regard to the trinity, predestination, free will; so also of God, the angels, the state of souls after this life and other like things, which do not need to be known for salvation by faith. . . . Although opinions are almost as numerous as men, nevertheless, there is hardly any sect which does not condemn all others and desire to reign alone. Hence arise banishments, chains, imprisonments, stakes, and gallows and this miserable rage to visit daily penalties upon those who differ from the mighty about matters hitherto unknown, for so many centuries disputed, and not yet cleared up.[65]

Here Castellio revives one of the key arguments in his prefatory epistle to Edward VI, namely, that too many theological issues remain unclear to justify persecuting anyone for them.[66] Even more dangerous, Castellio argues, is that persecuting heretics will result in putting innocent people to death. It often happens, he notes, that "he is held for a heretic who is not a heretic"; indeed, the best examples are Christ himself and his disciples, who were deemed heretics by the authorities in their day.[67] In seeking to explain what a heretic is, Castellio notes wryly, "After a careful investigation into the meaning of the term *heretic*, I can discover no more than this: that we regard as heretics those with whom we disagree."[68]

[65] "Disputatur non de via, qua ad Christum veniri possit, hoc est, de vitae correctione, sed de ipsius Christi statu et officio. . . . Item de trinitate, de praedestinatione, de libero arbitrio, de Deo, de angelis, de statu animarum post hanc vitam, et caeteris huiusmodi rebus, quae neque ad salutem per fidem obtinendam usque adeo cognitu necessariae sunt. . . . Cumque non plures fere sint hodie homines quam sententiae, tamen nulla fere secta est, quae non alias omnes damnet, et sibi soli regnum vendicet. Hinc exilia, hinc vincula, hinc ignes et cruces, et miserabilis quotidianorum suppliciorum facies, ob invisas potentioribus opiniones de rebus adhuc ignotis, et inter homines per tot iam secula disputatis, necdum tamen certo conclusis." Castellio, *De haereticis, an sint persequendi*, 5–6; translation from Bainton, ed., *Concerning Heretics*, 122–23.

[66] One can see this argument repeated later in the text by "Kleinberg": "Non ego hic homicidas, aut adulteros, caeterosque eius generis maleficos defendo: scio, magistratui contra tales datum esse divinitus gladium. Sed propter intelligentiam locorum Scripturae, de quibus nondum certo constat (si enim constaret, disputari desisset, nec ullus tam insanus esset, qui mori sustineret, quo rem certam negaret)." Castellio, *De haereticis, an sint persequendi*, 127–28; Bainton, ed., *Concerning Heretics*, 218.

[67] "Primum, ne quis pro haeretico habeatur, qui non sit haereticus: quod cum hactenus acciderit (nam et ipse Christus, et sui, pro haereticis interfecti fuerunt) est non levis causa, cur hoc nostro seculo (quod certe nihilo sanctius est illo, ne dicam sceleratius) metuendum sit ne idem accidat." Castellio, *De haereticis, an sint persequendi*, 13; English translation from Bainton, ed., *Concerning Heretics*, 126.

[68] "Equidem cum quid sit haereticus, saepe quaesiverim, nihil aliud depredendi, nisi haereticum haberi, quisquis a nobis dissentit." Castellio, *De haereticis, an sint persequendi*, 19; English translation adapted from Bainton, ed., *Concerning Heretics*, 129.

Those who persecute, "Basil Montfort" argues, do so to defend not Christ but their own power: "The oppressors are actuated rather by the desire to defend their power and worldly kingdom by the arms of the world. This appears from the fact that when they were poor and powerless, they detested persecutors, but now, having become strong, imitate them."[69] This power-hungry bloodlust has a further unwelcome consequence, according to Castellio; it encourages false teaching and blind obedience, for it prohibits doubt, the single most important tool of critical analysis:

> This violence brings it about that men are constrained to approve of what-ever the violent assert. Nothing is too monstrous to teach the people when doubt is prohibited, since if you doubt or do not believe, you are put to death. Hence, the power of the Scribes and Pharisees, who exclude from their synagogue those who dare to speak of Christ. Hence, the tyranny of him who in our day has been unmasked and is rightly held in detestation. He could never have attained to this tyranny if he had left religion free, nor would he have introduced so many errors had he not deprived men of the power of judgment.[70]

Castellio seems here to be referring to Calvin, and he condemns not only religious persecution but also "so many errors" that he has introduced by quashing freedom in religion and by depriving individuals of the power of judgment.

Castellio disagreed with Calvin on many issues that went beyond their early disagreement about the Song of Songs and their later conflict over per-secuting heretics. Like the anti-Calvinists in the Vaud, Castellio almost al-ways opposed Calvin's view. He went much further than Marcourt, Zébédée, or Bolsec in his ideas, however, and created a theological program that could

---

[69] "Id quod mihi non Christi instinctu . . . facere videntur, sed ut potentiam suam, mundanumque regnum mundanis possint armis defendere. Hoc ita esse, perspicitur ex eo, quod principio cum pauperes essent, et sine potestate, detestabantur persecutores: iisdem vires nacti imitantur persecutores." Castellio, *De haereticis, an sint persequendi*, 138; English translation from Bainton, ed., *Concerning Heretics*, 226.

[70] "Hac enim violentia efficitur, ut quicquid illi dicunt, id homines approbare metu cogantur. Hinc fit, ut nihil tam monstrosum sit, quod non populis obtrudatur, dum dubitare non licet; cum si dubites, aut non credas, moriendum tibi sit. Hinc illa scribarum et pharisaeorum potentia, qui eos ex synagoga sua excludebant, qui de Christo loqui auderent. Hinc illa illius, qui nostro tempore detectus est, et quem merito abominamur, tyrannis; quam profecto nunquam assecutus fuisset, si religionem liberam reliquisset, nec unquam tot errores invexisset, nisi iudicandi potestatem hominibus ademisset." Castellio, *De haereticis, an sint persequendi*, 166; English translation from Bainton, ed., *Concerning Heretics*, 248.

be followed by individuals across Europe, especially individuals who did not fully agree with the dominant religion in their area. Castellio did not really have an ecclesiology; his theology was personal, spiritual, and moral. This is one reason Calvin found him so dangerous; thousands of individuals could be "infected" by his views while outwardly conforming to the Reformed Church. They could be Calvinists institutionally but Castellionists inwardly. They were the enemy within, a strange new type of Nicodemite within Calvin's own church.

5.6. The Castellian Theological Program

Castellio, like Lefèvre and many other humanists, was not a trained theologian, but he had developed a keen interest in theology. In the years following the publication of *Concerning Heretics*, new quarrels with Calvin and Beza led Castellio to think more deeply about the contested issues of the day. Over time he developed a theological program different from all others in the sixteenth century, a set of core beliefs far ahead of their time that served as a rallying point for him and his followers. This program was an almost wholesale rejection of Calvinist thought, particularly its teachings on the persecution of heretics, predestination, the clarity of Scripture, biblical hermeneutics, total depravity, and justification by faith alone. In its place, Castellio embraced ideas of religious toleration, free religious debate, relativism and doubt, a rationalist biblical hermeneutic, and an emphasis on works cooperating with faith in justification. The result was a theology that was neither traditionally Catholic nor Protestant, but one that found followers both in his own day and in the succeeding generations.

5.6.1. "To kill a man is not to defend a doctrine, but to kill a man": Castellio on Religious Toleration

The debate on religious toleration continued vigorously after the publication of *Concerning Heretics*. First, Castellio read Calvin's *Defense of the Orthodox Faith* against Servetus and fired back in *Contra Libellum Calvin* (*Against Calvin's Pamphlet*). Soon after that, Beza wrote *On Punishing Heretics by the Civil Magistrate, against Martin Bellius's Collection and the Sect of the New*

Academics, a book commonly referred to as the *Anti-Bellius*.[71] Castellio responded to Beza's text in *On Not Punishing Heretics*, a work that remained unpublished, in both Latin and French versions, until the twentieth century.[72]

In *Contra Libellum Calvini*, Castellio quoted passages directly from Calvin's *Defense of the Orthodox Faith* and then offered his rebuttals in the persona of "Vaticanus."[73] These responses constituted a blistering attack on Calvin: "If Christ himself came to Geneva, he would be crucified. One must not go to Geneva for Christian freedom, for there is another pope there, who burns people alive while the Roman pope at least strangles them first."[74] He also brushes aside Calvin's attempts to defend his actions with regard to Servetus's execution and instead ascribes thoroughly nefarious motives to him: "I want to show that Calvin brought forth no firm reason or authority for proving [that heretics can be punished], and that everything he says, he says from a desire to rule and from an unquenchable thirst for blood."[75] This sets the tone of the whole work and likely explains why it was not published in 1554 when Castellio wrote it; the open hostility toward Calvin would not have made it past Basel's book censors. While *Concerning Heretics* presented theoretical arguments against punishing heresy, *Contra Libellum Calvini* is specific and a direct ad hominem attack on Calvin. Here Castellio explicitly blames Calvin for Servetus's death: "Tell me, Calvin, when you accused Servetus, did you not seize the sword as a private individual? For he who accuses, kills. Not perhaps with your own hand, but not even Herod killed John [the Baptist] with his own hand."[76]

[71] Théodore de Bèze, *De Haereticis a civili Magistratu puniendis Libellus, adversus Martini Belli farraginem, et novorum Academicorum sectam* ([Geneva]: Robert Étienne, 1554).

[72] Castellio, *De l'Impunité des hérétiques*. Castellio dated the completion of the work March 11, 1555, ibid. 197. There are two separate manuscripts of this text in the Rotterdam Library (Remonstrants Library, mss. 508 and 509), both with corrections in Castellio's hand. The French version was likely completed near the end of Castellio's life, ibid., 203.

[73] On the various interpretations of the meaning of this name, see Plath's introduction to Castellio, *Contra Libellum Calvini*, 20–24. Plath plausibly (I believe) suggests that Castellio combined the Latin words *vates* (prophet) and *canere* (to sing) to come up with *Vaticanus*. Hence, the text pits the lowly, all-too-human Calvin against the singing prophet Castellio.

[74] "Si Christus ipse Genevam veniret, fore, ut crucifigeretur: Non esse iam eundum Genevam ad Christianam libertatem. Ibi enim esse alterum Papam, sed qui vivos torreret, cum Romanus prius suffocaret." Castellio, *Contra Libellum Calvini*, 42–43.

[75] "*Calvinus, 21*: An Christianis iudicibus haereticos punire liceat. *Vaticanus*: Quaeso vos, lectores, ut utriusque dicta benigne audiatis. Hoc volo ostendere nullam a Calvino ad hoc probandum firmam rationem aut authoritatem adduci, eumque sola regnandi cupidine, sanguinisque inexhausta siti omnia haec dicere, quae dicit." Castellio, *Contra Libellum Calvini*, 55–56.

[76] "Sed dic mihi, Calvine, cum Servetum accusasti, nonne privatus homo gladium arripuisti? Nam qui accusat, interficit. Non tu quidem tua manu, sed ne Herodes quidem Ioannem sua manu." Castellio, *Contra Libellum Calvini*, 136.

In *Contra Libellum Calvini*, Castellio also introduces a new level of doctrinal relativism that demands restraint in dealing with heretics: "All sects hold their religion as established by the Word of God and call it certain. Therefore all sects are armed by Calvin's rule for mutual persecution."[77] Castellio was shocked that anyone could be so arrogant as to presume that he alone possessed the truth:

> Who ever thought that he held a false religion? The Jews erred in perse-cuting Christ and the apostles. The Gentiles erred who persecuted the Christians. The pope erred in persecuting Lutherans and Zwinglians. Henry, king of England, erred in killing Papists, Lutherans, Zwinglians, and Anabaptists. Luther erred when he called the Zwinglians devils and damned them to hell. Will the Zwinglians and Calvinists alone be free from error? Will they alone sit in the tribunal of Christ to pass judgment on heretics and kill them?[78]

By Calvin's argument, Castellio points out, Catholic officials are entirely jus-tified in killing Protestants: "Therefore, the pious papist magistrate can judge in religious matters no less than the Genevans can. But if he is pious and this is permitted him, he can by his own judgment kill those he deems heretics. Therefore, he can kill Calvin and all the Calvinists, since he holds them for heretics."[79] By the same token, if Calvin is serious in his argument, and "if

---

[77] "Omnes sectae religionem suam verbo Dei tuentur, certamque esse dicunt. Itaque omnes sectae, hac Calvini norma armatae, alias persequentur." Castellio, *Contra Libellum Calvini*, 149, English translation from Bainton, ed., *Concerning Heretics*, 281.

[78] "Quis unquam putavit se tenere falsam religionem? Errarunt Iudaei, qui Christum et Apostolos persecuti sunt. Errarunt gentiles, qui Christianos persecuti sunt. Erravit Papa, qui Lutheranos et Zvinglianos persecutus est. Erravit Henricus Anglius Rex, qui Papistas et Lutheranos, et Zvinglianos, et Anabaptistas interfecit. Erravit Lutherus, qui Zvinglianos diabolos appellavit et in gehennam damnavit. An soli Zvingliani et Calviniani non errabunt? An soli hi in Christi tribunali sedebunt, ut eis solis liceat de haereticis iudicare, et eos occidere?" Castellio, *Contra Libellum Calvini*, 128; English translation from Bainton, ed., *Concerning Heretics*, 278–79. See also the almost identical argument in *De L'Impunité des hérétiques*, where Castellio blames the German peasants and Münster Anabaptists, too: "Ceux qui trouvent entre eux quelques-uns contraires à leur religion et pensent toutes choses leur estre claires et certaines, ne mettent-ilz pas souventes foys à mort les bons et innocents? Les anabaptistes de Munster n'ont-ilz pas grandement failly, pensans que le royaume terrien leur estoit donné de Dieu? Les rustiques d'Almaigne ne se sont-ilz pas mis eux-mesmes la corde au col, pensans que le glaive leur feüst donné de Dieu (comme jadis à Gédéon) pour destruire tous les tyrans de la terre? N'i ha-il pas certains princes lesquelz voulans estre chef de leur église et juger toutes choses et maintenant mettans à mort les papistes, tantost les luthériens, les zwingliens ou anabaptistes, sont tombez en homicides irréparables? Quoi, Bèze, estes-vous donc seulz lesquelz ne pouvez faillir?" Castellio, *De l'Impunité des hérétiques*, 225–26.

[79] "Ergo Papisticus magistratus pius est, potestque de religionis causis non minus iudicare quam Genevensis. Quod si pius est et hoc ei licet, potest iudicio suo, hoc pio, interficere eos, quos iudicat haereticos. Potest ergo et Calvinum ipsum et Calvinianos omnes occidere, quoniam eos habet pro haereticis." Castellio, *Contra Libellum Calvini*, 184.

Calvin regards heretics as apostates and considers the papists to be heretics, he should raise an army in Geneva and invade France, which has fallen away from the true religion of the apostles."[80] Thus, the only logical outcome of Calvin's reasoning would be religious warfare leading to a European-wide bloodbath. The century following Castellio seems to have proved him right.

The only acceptable response to the religious turmoil of the day, according to Castellio, is to withhold judgment, which properly belongs to God on the Last Day: "Today, I do not think that so many religions should all be called heretical. . . . Therefore, we must await Christ the Judge and not rashly announce, 'It's God's judgment!' beforehand."[81] In response to Calvin's argument on the parable of the wheat and the tares,[82] he writes,

> To root out the tares is to pronounce someone to be reprobate and cut off forever from the body of Christ. This should not be done before the day of the Lord. . . . The tares are those whom the devil sowed by false doctrine after the coming of the Gospel. Of this sort are the heretics and hypocrites who deceive men through the guise of the Christian religion and lie concealed among the godly as the tares among the wheat until the fruit appears. Christ commands that they be left until the harvest lest perchance the good be destroyed with them, for it is better that all the bad live until the judgment than that one good man should be destroyed in keeping out the bad.[83]

Moreover, in his response to Beza, Castellio makes the radically relativist claim that all who confess Christ—including Catholics—are part of the

---

[80] "Quod si haereticos habet Calvinus pro apostatis, cum Papistas haereticos iudicet, deberet eos in primis persequi et coacto Genevensium exercitu Galliam in primis invadere, quae a vera Apostolorum religione defecerit." Castellio, *Contra Libellum Calvini*, 151–52; English translation from Bainton, ed., *Concerning Heretics*, 282.

[81] "Sic hodie tot sectas non puto debere omnes haereticas appellari. . . . Itaque exspectandus est iudex Christus nec temere 'Dei iudicio' praeeundum." Castellio, *Contra Libellum Calvini*, 71.

[82] "Calvinus 96: 'Adducunt etiam scripturae testimonia, in quibus unum videtur habere aliquid coloris: Sinite, inquit Christus, zizania cum tritico crescere, 'ne simul evellatur et triticum.' Si praecise nobiscum agunt ex verborum formula, non tantum prohibentur magistratus ab usu gladii, sed omnem disciplinam e medio tolli oportet.'" Castellio, *Contra Libellum Calvini*, 124 (*CO* 8:472).

[83] "Igitur evellere zizania est iudicare aliquem esse reprobum, et eum ex Christi corpore in sempiternum abscindere. Id quod fieri non potest ante diem Domini. . . . Sed videtur zizania appellare eos, quos Diabolus sevit falsa doctrina post Evangelium. Cuiusmodi sunt haeretici et hypocritae, qui per speciem religionis Christianae decipiunt homines et sic inter pios latent, quomodo herbae latent in segete, donec fructum ediderint. Haec iubet Christus usque ad messem relinqui, ne quis forte bonus una cum eis interficiatur." Castellio, *Contra Libellum Calvini*, 125–27; English translation from Bainton, ed., *Concerning Heretics*, 277.

church.[84] No one who confesses Christ should be put to death, he argues, even if that person errs in the understanding of the faith.

Moreover, Castellio starts to go beyond a call for mere religious toleration; he begins to argue for open debate and even religious freedom: "Why did Jerome [Bolsec], [Matteo] Gribaldi, and Servetus not have the right to discuss their views freely? Is there freedom in your prisons?"[85] In his response to Beza, he explains further,

> Because we want Christians to have the freedom to say what they feel, you cry out that we want to introduce monsters. But what is more likely to feed monsters: those who want tongues to be free, or those who want to be the only ones allowed to speak? Who would have discovered the errors of our century if they had not been free to speak against the Scribes and Pharisees? Why do you cut off people's tongues, unless you do not want your own deeds to be discovered?"[86]

Thus, we find in Castellio the roots of not only religious toleration but the modern idea that free speech (and, by implication, a free press) is useful as a check on those in authority by uncovering misdeeds and corruption.

Above all, for Castellio, one must never think that killing can be a pious act. Beza's arguments in favor of punishing heretics, he says, are "totally contrary to the doctrine of Christ."[87] Faith, he argues instead, "is not to burn a

---

[84] "Mais quant à ce que tu dis que vous supportez et endurez le [sic] papistes, pource qu'ilz sont dehors, c'est-à-dire, qu'ilz ne sont de l'Eglise, premièrement je suys émerveillé de vostre audace, qui estes si hardi de forclorre de l'Eglise ceux qui confessent le nom de Christ. Mais ilz sont idolâtres, diras-tu. Aussy estoient les juifz idolâtres et avoient fait de la maison de Dieu une caverne de brigans, et ce néantmoins Christ les appelle filz du Royaume." Castellio, De l'Impunité des hérétiques, 336.

[85] "Cur ergo Hieronymo, cur Gribaldo, cur Serveto (ut multos alios taceam) non fuit apud vos libera ex aequo loco disceptandi potestas? Estne apud vos libertas in carcere?" Castellio, Contra Libellum Calvini, 69. Matteo Gribaldi, who wrote the Apologia pro Michaele Serveto, had been an early ally of the Calvinists (see, e.g., Epistolae Vireti 30–33, no. 2), but he later developed antitrinitarian ideas. In 1555, Calvin refused to shake his hand when offered and instead had him summoned before the Geneva council to explain his views. Gribaldi left town soon thereafter. Buisson, 1:344–45.

[86] "Car pource que nous voulons que les chrestiens ayent liberté de dire ce qu'ilz sentent, vous criez que nous voulons introduire des monstres. Mais desquelz est-il plus probable vouloir nourrir monstres: ou ceux qui veulent que les langue [sic] soient libres, ou ceux qui veulent estre licite à eux seulz de parler. Qui eüst descouvert les erreurs de nostre siècle, s'il n'eüst esté libre de parler contre les scribes et farisiens? Pourquoy couppés-vous la langue aux gens, sinon afin que voz faitz ne soient descouvers?" Castellio, De l'Impunité des hérétques, 327–28.

[87] "Et si je donne à cognoistre les choses lesquelles je reprens au livre de Bèze estre contraires à la vérité de Christ, je n'entens pas qu'elles soient mises en avant par le commun consentement des prescheurs, beaucoup moins de l'Eglise, veü qu'elles sont toutalement contraires à la doctrine de Christ et aux exemples de la primitive église et conviennent à la fureur et arrogance des puissantz de ce dernier siècle." Castellio, De l'Impunité des hérétiques, 222.

person, but to be burned."[88] Or as he puts it most succinctly, "To kill a man is not to defend a doctrine, but to kill a man."[89]

5.6.2. "Reason, I say, is a sort of eternal word of God": Doubt, Belief, and Exegesis

The root of Calvin's and Beza's errors, Castellio suggests, is their inability to admit they might be wrong. Nor would they even admit doubt where Scripture or doctrine is unsure. To Castellio, these are literally fatal errors:

> Not without great cause do I assert that some things ought to be doubted, for I see no fewer evils arising from not doubting where there should be doubt than from not believing where there should be belief.... Today in the Christian churches some of the most saintly persons are put to death indiscriminately. If the Christians entertained a doubt about what they are doing, they would not perpetrate such dreadful homicides for which they will have to repent soon after.[90]

We have already seen Castellio's views on the obscurity of Scripture, and he would continue to repeat this assertion. If Scripture is so clear, he asks Calvin and Beza, "Why do you write so many—and such long—Biblical commentaries? Is it to provide clarity on clear matters and to uncover perfectly obvious things?"[91] He also mocks Beza for holding such contentious colloquies that

---

[88] "Fidem suam asserere non est hominem cremare, sed potius cremari." Castellio, *Contra Libellum Calvini*, 81.

[89] "Hominem occidere non est doctrinam tueri, sed est hominem occidere." Castellio, *Contra Libellum Calvini*, 103, English translation from Bainton, ed., *Concerning Heretics*, 271.

[90] "Quod autem interdum dubitandum esse doceo, id non sine magna causa facio. Video enim non minus malorum ex non dubitando, ubi dubitari debet, existere quam ex non credendo, ubi credi debet.... Et hodie, cum in Christianis ecclesiis sanctissimi quique passim interficiuntur, si Christiani de facto suo dubitarent, nunquam tot tam nefanda homicidia (quorum paulo post eos poenitere necesse erit) perpetrarent." Sebastian Castellio, *De arte dubitandi et confidendi, ignorandi et sciendi*, edited by Elisabeth Feist Hirsch, SMRT 29 (Leiden: Brill, 1981), 50–51, ll. 55–57, 69–72; English translation from Bainton, ed., *Concerning Heretics*, 290.

[91] "En après, pourquoy vous escrivez tant de commentaires—et si longs—sus icelles? Est-ce point pour donner clarté aux choses claires et découvrir les choses manifestes?" Castellio, *De l'Impunité des hérétiques*, 264. He also noted Zwingli's criticism of Luther for saying that the Scriptures were perfectly clear: "Bellie et les siens disent que les questions desquelles aujourduy on débat sont oscures; davantage, ilz nient que les saintes lettres soient encores assez entendues. Mais elles te semblent claires et manifestes, Bèze? Que s'il est ainsy, je te demande en premier lieu pourquoy c'est que Zwingle, vostre parangon et capitaine, ha dit qu'elles estoient oscures et en ce ha reprins Luther qui disoit qu'elles estoient manifestes?" Ibid., 264. He says essentially the same thing against Calvin: "Indignatur [Calvinus] esse aliquem, qui dicat sacras literas esse obscuras, ipse putat

the Bernese city council had to step in to settle religious matters: "Certainly, if the sacred letters are clear and manifest, it appears that you who so obstinately debate such clear matters are either blind or malicious."[92]

In his later and arguably most interesting work, *The Art of Doubting and Believing, of Knowing and Not Knowing* (*De arte dubitandi et confidendi, ignorandi et sciendi*), Castellio takes a more theoretical approach, not only to the question of the clarity of Scripture but also to doubt in religious matters more generally. He rejects out of hand the Calvinist position that leaves almost nothing to doubt:

> There are some who are unwilling to doubt anything, to be in ignorance of anything. They assert everything unreservedly, and if you dissent from them, they damn you without hesitation. Not only do they doubt nothing themselves, but they will not permit others to doubt, and if you do doubt, they do not hesitate to call you an Academician, who thinks nothing certain and assured. . . . The reason for doubting is this: To hold the uncertain for certain and to entertain no doubt on the point is rash and dangerous.[93]

Since "Academician" was the label Beza applied to Castellio in the *Anti-Bellius*, there is little doubt whom Castellio had in mind here. In essence, Castellio argues that if a topic is subject to "innumerable books and disputations . . . and perpetual contentions," then one must leave room for uncertainty and doubt, for "so long as men are in their right minds, they do not contend about matters which are certain and assured."[94] The trick is to

apertas. In quo pugnat contra Zvinglium, qui putat obscuras; pugnat contra seipsum, qui ad has tam apertas literas aperiendas, paene innumeros edidit commentarios. . . . Ipsemet in praefatiuncula in suas Institutiones dicit suum Institutionum librum esse ad scripturas intelligendas 'instrumentum necessarium.'" Castellio, *Contra Libellum Calvini*, 60.

[92] "Davantage, pourquoy est-ce qu'en voz congrégations, esquelles vous interprétez les saintes escritures, on amène souventesfoys sept opinions sus un passage, voire avec telle opiniastrise que le plus souvent vous donnez tant d'affaire à voz magistratz qu'il faut accorder les différens des prédicans avec ordonnances et éditz. Certes, si les saintes lettres sont tant clères et manifestes, il apert que vous estes aveugles ou malicieux qui des choses si apertes débatez tant ostinément." Castellio, *De l'Impunité des hérétiques*, 264.

[93] "Est enim genus quoddam hominum, qui nihil dubitari, nihil nesciri volunt, omnia audacter affirmant et, si ab eis dissentias, sine ulla dubitatione damnant neque solum ipsi nihil dubitant, sed ne quidem ab aliis dubitari patiuntur et, si dubites, non dubitant Academicum appellare, qui nihil certi, nihil explorati haberi posse putes. . . . Ac dubitandi quidem ratio est haec. Incerta pro certis habere deque eis nihil dubitare et temerarium est et plenum periculi, id quod nemo negabit." Castellio, *De arte dubitandi*, 49, ll. 6–11, 26–28; English translation from Bainton, ed., *Concerning Heretics*, 289.

[94] "Esse autem incerta quaedam, quis opus est, ut planum faciam? Cum id aperte ostendant innumeri libri et disputationes contentionesque quotidianae et perpetuae summorum doctissimorum virorum. Neque enim profecto de rebus certis exploratisque contendunt, nisi plane

learn which matters can be doubted and what needs to be known without doubt.[95] The answer to this, he suggests, is simple: "We may be ignorant of those matters which man does not need to know for salvation."[96]

Since what one needs to know for salvation is found in the Bible, Castellio's answer leads once again to the question of Scriptural interpretation. Here, Castellio takes his argument on the opacity of Scripture a step further, arguing that God "desired to leave obscurity as an exercise to human industry that the mind, like the body, might gain its bread by the sweat of its brow."[97] But this still leaves the problem that "all opinions are defended out of Scripture. Each defends his views tenaciously and will not be dislodged."[98] One of the root problems that led to this impasse, he believed, was the commonly accepted hermeneutical principle that Scripture explains Scripture. In other words, it is the idea that one can best explain one passage of the Bible by referring to a different passage. This tactic does not work, Castellio argues, because "he who cites one passage incorrectly can easily find others to cite incorrectly by way of support."[99] Thus, Castellio concludes, "Unless some other rule is discovered, I see no way here of attaining concord."[100]

From his first biblical translation in 1546, the *Latin Moses*, Castellio revealed that he did not view the exact words of Scripture as sacrosanct, for he had no problem replacing the Bible's "Hebraisms" with "good Latin." For

mente capti sunt." Castellio, *De arte dubitandi*, 49, ll. 29–34; English translation from Bainton, ed., *Concerning Heretics*, 289.

[95] "Primum sciendum est quaedam esse, de quibus sit dubitandum, alia, quae sint citra ullam dubitationem credenda. Item quaedam esse, non dicam quae sint ignoranda, sed quae ignorari liceat et nonnumquam necesse sit, alia, quae sciri et possint et debeant." Castellio, *De arte dubitandi*, 49, ll. 1–4.

[96] "De ignorando quoque hoc dico: Ignorare nobis ea licet, quae homini non sunt ad salutem necessaria." Castellio, *De arte dubitandi*, 50, ll. 44–45; English translation from Bainton, ed., *Concerning Heretics*, 290.

[97] "dicamus et in sacris literis et doctrina eandem esse rationem atque causam, nimirum voluisse deum, ut ea esset obscura, quo haberet humana industria, ubi se exereret et hunc animi quasi panem cum sudore non minus quam corporis pabulum sibi compararet." Castellio, *De arte dubitandi*, 59, ll. 76–79; English translation from Bainton, ed., *Concerning Heretics*, 294.

[98] "Denique, ut in pauca conferam, pleraeque omnes opiniones sacrarum literarum authoritate defenduntur et, qui eas mordicus retinent, ii ab opinionibus suis divelli nequeunt." Castellio, *De arte dubitandi*, 56, ll. 35–37; English translation from Bainton, ed., *Concerning Heretics*, 293.

[99] "Neque vero illud ad rem conponendum satis est, quod quidam tradunt, videlicet literas per literas, hoc est alios locos per alios esse interpretandos. Quamquam enim id commodum est, tamen aliquid desideratur. Nam idem sectae omnes faciunt nec tamen invenitur concordia. Qui enim locum aliquem male citat, idem et alios locos ad illum interpretandum facile invenit, quos aeque male citet." Castellio, *De arte dubitandi*, 56, ll. 37–43; English translation from Bainton, ed., *Concerning Heretics*, 293.

[100] "Proinde nisi alia ineatur ratio, nullam hic adhuc video rationem concordiae." Castellio, *De arte dubitandi*, 56, ll. 43–44; English translation from Bainton, ed., *Concerning Heretics*, 293.

Castellio, it was not the specific words of Scripture but the spirit and overall message of the Bible that were significant. He also emphasized the primacy of the New Testament over the Old. Calvin and Beza based much of their argument for punishing heresy on the Mosaic law against blasphemy. Castellio wrote, "I see, Beza, that you completely ignore the difference between the Old and New Testament, since you, still clinging to the Old Testament with the Jews, have a heart of stone."[101] He painted an even starker difference in *Contra Libellum Calvini*: "Who will allow Christ to be snatched away from himself in order to return to Moses with Calvin? Let Calvin be the disciple of Moses with his Jews; for us, the Messiah, our Legislator, has come. We want to obey *his* law."[102] Indeed, Calvin and Beza did not make nearly as sharp a distinction between the Old and New Testaments, seeing essential continuity, with God as the author of both.[103]

For Castellio, the authorship of the Bible was more complicated, and his approach to it demonstrates the radical nature of his hermeneutics. Scripture, he argues is divided into three types of passage: revelation/prophecy, knowledge, and instruction. Here he departs perhaps most markedly from the Calvinists, and indeed from most Christians of the time, for he viewed only the revelation/prophecy texts as the actual Word of God, or as "oracles," as he put it: "In considering the sacred authors, we must not confuse these three things: revelation, knowledge, and instruction. Let us hold those things that have been passed down by revelation for oracles, those by knowledge as testimonies, and those by instruction for human opinion."[104] Only the oracles, he argues, require us to adapt our thinking until all the passages agree with one another. Knowledge and instruction are decidedly less important than the revelations and are subject to human interpretation.[105] According to

---

[101] "Je voy, Bèze, que tu ignores toutalement la différence du Viel et Nouveau Testament, parce que demourant encores au Viel Testament avec les juifz, tu has un coeur de pierre." Castellio, *De l'Impunité des hérétiques*, 373.

[102] "Quis sibi Christum eripi patiatur, ut ad Mosem cum Calvino redeat? Sit Calvinus Mosis discipulus cum suis Iudaeis: Nobis Messias iam venit Legislator noster, cuius legi obedire volumus." Castellio, *Contra Libellum Calvini*, 158.

[103] On Calvin's hermeneutical principles of the two testaments, see T. H. L. Parker, *Calvin's Old Testament Commentaries* (Louisville, KY: Westminster/John Knox, 1986), esp. 42–82.

[104] "Quae cum ita sint, nobis ita versandum est in sacris authoribus, ut haec tria, videlicet patefactionem et cognitionem et doctrinam, non confundamus, sed quae patefactione tradita sunt, ea pro oraculis, quae cognitione, pro testimoniis, quae doctrina, pro hominum sententiis habeamus." Castellio, *De arte dubitandi*, 40, ll. 36–40.

[105] "Igitur, si quae occurrent in sacris literis vel discrepantiae vel repugnantiae, diligenter considerandum erit, utrum eae sint in oraculis an in testimoniis an in hominum sententiis. Nam si erunt in oraculis oportebit circumstantias omnes et locorum et temporum et personarum et occasionem et causarum sedulo perpendere, ut in ea, quae videbitur discordia, concordiam inveniamus. Quod si ne sic quidem invenerimus, tribuendum id erit ignorantiae nostrae et

Castellio, the biblical authors themselves viewed their own roles according to this tripartite scheme: "What I said about testimonies, I also say about human opinions, namely, that only so much authority ought to be given to them as to holy individuals or as much as these holy persons attribute to themselves. But they should not be given the same standing as the oracles, since not even they demand that of us."[106]

Castellio uses an analogy that sees the biblical authors not as prophets or oracles into whom God breathed the Holy Spirit, but as ambassadors to whom Christ gave a message but who delivered it in their own way. Just as an ambassador sometimes reads the very words of the prince who sent him and sometimes provides his own narrative and interpretation, so also, Castellio suggests, did the biblical authors sometimes relate the words of God himself but sometimes their own memories or understandings.[107] Even the Gospel writers, he claims, did not write everything from divine inspiration. Some things they wrote from memory, if they had been present at the events described; others they learned from eyewitnesses.[108] Paul himself explicitly distinguishes between his own instructions to the faithful and the precepts he has from the Lord.[109]

---

credendum aliquid ibi esse nobis ignotum, quod si perciperemus, summam ibi concordiam esse videremus. . . . Sin erunt in testimoniis, non oportebit nos minus esse superstitiosos neque singula verba curiosius observare atque inter sese componere, sed ea concordia, quae est in summa rei, contentos esse." Castellio, *De arte dubitandi*, 40–41, ll. 43–51, 53–56.

[106] "Ac quod dixi de testimoniis, idem dico de hominum sententiis, videlicet tantum eis tribuendum esse, quantum sanctorum hominum dictis tribui debet vel quantum ipsimet sibi tribuunt, non tamen, ut eodem cum oraculis loco habeantur, cum ne ipsi quidem hoc a nobis postulent." Castellio, *De arte dubitandi*, 41, ll. 65–69.

[107] "Ac primum quod ad rationem attinet, illud mihi negabit nemo, solere legatos, quae a principe mandata acceperunt, ea ut principis mandata exponere, quae in dubium vocari non liceat. Quae vero ipsi sua sponte dicunt, ea ipsos (si boni fidique sunt legati) non principi, sed sibi ascribere nec eandem his quam illis authoritatem poscere. . . . Erant Apostoli (ut ab his potissimum exemplum petamus) Christi legati, a quo quae mandata acceperant, ea ut Christi mandata atque oracula bene et fideliter (quippe sancti iustique viri) vel iis, qui ipsos praesentes audiebant, verbis vel absentibus et porro nobis scriptis exposuerunt ac de iis dubitare non licet. Sin aliquid non a Christo mandatum, sed ipsi sua sponte dicebant, id non Christo aut spiritui sancto, sed sibi ascribebant. . . . Iam cum et memoriae et intellectus vim a natura haberent, si qua erant vel memoriae vel intellectus ope scribenda, Christus eis ad illa scribenda memoriam aut intellectum non dabat, non magis profecto quam oculos aut manus aut chartam aut atramentum, quippe cum omnia illa iam haberent, sed ipsi sua memoria suoque ingenio illa scribebant." Castellio, *De arte dubitandi*, 42–43, ll. 21–25, 42–48, 59–64.

[108] "Scripsisse autem eos non omnia patefaciente spiritu sancto, sed quaedam ope memoriae, alia ingenii, patet ex ipsorum scriptis. Nam quod ad memoriam attinet, didicerunt Evangelistae evangelium non patefactione, ut Paulus, sed vel quia ipsi adfuerunt, ut Matthaeus et Iohannes, vel ex iis, qui adfuerant, cognoverunt, ut Marcus et Lucas, id quod ipsimet testantur." Castellio, *De arte dubitandi*, 43, ll. 67–73.

[109] "Item quod ad ingenium attinet, scribit disertis verbis Paulus in priore ad Corinthios epistola: 'Coniugibus praecipio non ego, sed dominus.' etc. et mox: 'Caeteris ego dico, non dominus.' Et paulo post: 'De virginibus autem Domini praeceptum non habeo, sed consilium do, ut qui is sim,

Castellio recognized that this hermeneutical principle of dividing the Bible into inspired and instructional passages would be shocking and offensive to his contemporaries: "They will cry out that this is blasphemy. 'The sacred letters were written by divine inspiration, brought forth by the will of God, not of men!'"[110] He believes, however, that he must be shocking, that he must be innovative: "But we must dare something new if we want to help humanity. . . . We see that advances in the arts, as in other things, are made not by those content with the status quo, but by those who dare to alter and correct those things that have been found defective."[111] Castellio saw himself in the avant-garde. Calvin and Beza, by contrast, he viewed as stuck in old, contentious, and ultimately unproductive methods of Scriptural interpretation.

By stripping many Bible passages of their divinely inspired nature, Castellio was free to offer an exegetical method just as radical: Scripture, he contends, should be interpreted according to sense and reason:

> For reason is, so to speak, the daughter of God. . . . Reason, I say, is a sort of eternal word of God, much older and surer than letters and ceremonies, according to which God taught his people before there were letters and ceremonies, and after these have passed away he will still so teach that humans may be truly taught of God. . . . According to reason Jesus Christ himself, the Son of the living God, lived and taught. In the Greek he is called *logos*, which means reason or word. They are the same, for reason is a sort of interior and eternal word of truth always speaking.[112]

---

cui Domini clementia fidentem esse datum sit.' Hic certe palam ostendit non omnia se ex Domini praecepto scribere, sed in nonnullis suam sententiam dicere." Castellio, *De arte dubitandi*, 44, ll. 81–87.

[110] "Non dubito quin hoc loco nonnulli offendantur. Clamabunt esse blasphemiam. Sacras enim literas esse divino afflatu conscriptas neque hominum." Castellio, *De arte dubitandi*, 41, ll. 1–3.

[111] "Sed audendum aliquid est, modo verum, si iuvare homines volumus. . . . Videmus tum artium tum caeterorum omnium incrementa fieri non per eos, qui usitatis contenti sunt, sed per eos, qui, si quid perperam comparatum est, corrigere ac mutare audent." Castellio, *De arte dubitandi*, 47–48, ll. 9–10, 18–21.

[112] "Nam ratio est ipsa, ut ita loquar, dei filia. . . . Ratio, inquam, est aeternus quidam sermo dei longe tum literis tum ceremoniis et antiquior et certior, secundum quam deus suos et ante ceremonias et literas docuit et post easdem ita docebit, ut sint vere divinitus docti . . . . Denique secundum hanc ipse Iesus Christus, viventis dei filius, qui Graeco sermone *Logos* dicitur, hoc est ratio aut sermo, quod idem est (nam ratio est quasi quaedam interior et aeterna semperque loquens veritatis oratio atque sermo)." Castellio, *De arte dubitandi*, 65–66, ll. 39–40, 44–47, 49–52; English translation adapted from Bainton, ed., *Concerning Heretics*, 297.

Castellio rejects the common proposition that reason was corrupted by the Fall, for "experience and history teach the contrary."[113] Instead, he argues that the real problem is close-mindedness:

> For example, if a Lutheran is wedded to his opinion on the Lord's Supper, he will scarcely be able to weigh dispassionately his opponent's opinion, or even to follow it. The same is true of other opinions. The judgment is beclouded by mental disturbances and above all by a closed mind, for this impedes judgment not of one only but of all matters. . . . A person whose mind is closed holds tenaciously to his opinion and prefers to give the lie to God himself and all the saints and angels if they are on the other side rather than to alter his opinion. Flee this vice as you would death itself.[114]

With an open mind, free of prejudice, one can discern properly, he felt, the meaning of cryptic or contested Scriptures, according to reason and the tenor of the passage.

In discussing the Lord's Supper, for example, Castellio adopts an essentially Zwinglian position, not because he was a disciple of Zwingli (he was most decidedly not),[115] but because Zwingli's symbolic understanding of the Eucharist was the only one, he believed, that reason supports. Castellio dismisses the argument of Luther and others that one must believe, against all evidence of sense and reason, that Christ's body and blood are truly in the sacrament simply because he said, "This is my body; this is my blood."[116]

---

[113] "Primum enim quaeritur, an hominis sensus et intellectus fuerit Adami peccato vitiatus. . . . Ac quod ad primum attinet, vereor, ne magis sit publicus et vetustate confirmatus error quam veritas. Primum enim nulla vel authoritate vel ratione dictum est. . . . Quae ratio doceat? Nulla. Quin imo et experientia et historia contra docet." Castellio, *De arte dubitandi*, 69, ll. 15–19, 22–23; English translation from Bainton, ed., *Concerning Heretics*, 298.

[114] "Exempli gratia, si quis Lutheri opinioni de Coena Domini sit addictior, is adduci vix poterit, ut adversantem opinionem aequo animo perpendat, nedum ut sequatur, quod idem dico de caeteris opinionibus, usque adeo perturbationibus impeditur animi iudicium . . . . Sic pertinax, homo, ubi semel quidpiam affirmavit, nihil iam quod contra sit videre aut audire sustinet adeoque mordicus opinioni suae adhaeret, ut, si deus ipse omnesque eius sancti atque angeli contra dicant, malit deumque sanctosque angelosque omnes condemnare quam opinionem suam recantare. Quocirca vitium hoc tanquam mortem ipsam fugito." Castellio, *De arte dubitandi*, 79, ll. 56–59, 64–69; English translation adapted from Bainton, ed., *Concerning Heretics*, 301.

[115] In *Concerning Heretics*, "George Kleinberg" (who could, however, have been David Joris) blames Zwingli for having started the policy of killing heretics and saw his death on the battlefield as simply his just deserts: "Ostendisse videtur ipse Deus, quantopere illa sibi placerent, cum effecit, ut ille ipse eius sententiae author, vir literatus, et toto orbe celebris, non multo post alios inermes interfectos, ipse in acie cum multis ceciderit: id quod ei propter illud commissum accidisse, multi pii credunt." Castellio, *De Haereticis*, 128; Bainton, ed., *Concerning Heretics*, 218–19.

[116] "Alii etiam docent fidei Christianae proprium officium esse credere incredibilia tantum propter hoc argumentum: Nullum verbum dei est impossibile deo. Hoc est verbum dei: 'Hoc est corpus meum, hic est sanguis meus.' Ergo hoc verbum non est impossibile deo et per consequens credendum

"These and similar arguments," Castellio explains, "are calculated to deceive. When people have been persuaded to shut their eyes and reject the evidence of the senses of the body and of the mind, to believe words, though all the senses refute the words, then nothing is so absurd, impossible, or false as not to be accepted. Why not believe that the white which you see is not white?"[117] This last phrase calls to mind Ignatius of Loyola, who in the *Spiritual Exercises* embraces the antithetical proposal: "To be right in everything, we ought always to hold that the white which I see is black if the hierarchical church so decides it."[118] Castellio's Calvinist enemies sometimes cast him as a closet Catholic for his insistence on the necessity of works for salvation. Castellio's insistence on the freedom to use reason to interpret the Bible and evaluate Christian doctrine, however, reveals the gulf that separated him from Ignatius and a Catholic Church that insisted on its own infallibility. The same insistence on freedom, reason, and open-mindedness opened a similar gulf between him and the Calvinists on other theological issues.

5.6.3. "God wants all to be saved through Christ": Predestination

In the last chapter, we saw that Castellio became tangentially involved in the Bolsec affair in Geneva and the Pays de Vaud.[119] His writings from this period, chiefly 1554–1555, show great familiarity with the situation there, for he refers several times to Zébédée and François de Saint-Paul, as well as to

---

est propter solam authoritatem loquentis dei nulla alia ratione requisita, etiam si et oculi et aures et nares et gustatus et tactus et ratio, universa denique rerum natura reluctetur." Castellio, *De arte dubitandi*, 60, ll. 33–40.

[117] "Haec sunt et alia in hanc sententiam, quae a quibusdam magna cum diligentia et scripta fuerunt et dici solent accommodate sane ad fallendum. Postquam enim semel hominibus persuaserunt, ut clausis oculis, hoc est remotis reiectisque tum corporis tum animi sensibus, credant verbis, quamvis omnes sensus verba refellant, nihil deinde tam absurdum, tam impossibile, tam falsum est, quod non persuadeant. Quid enim non credas ei, qui tibi persuasit id, quod album vides, non esse album?" Castellio, *De arte dubitandi*, 61, ll. 43–49; English translation adapted from Bainton, ed., *Concerning Heretics*, 295.

[118] "Debemus super omnia hoc servare, ut recte sapiamus, quod id quod ego album video, credam esse nigrum, si ita Ecclesia hierarchia ita diffiniret esse . . ." Ignatius of Loyola, *Exercitia Spiritualia: Textuum antiquissimorum nova editio lexicon textus Hispani*, edited by Iosephus Calveras and Candidus de Dalmases, Monumenta Historica Societatis Iesu 100 (Rome: Institutum Historicum Societatis Iesu, 1969), 411–12, section 364, rule 13; translation from Ignatius of Loyola, *The Spiritual Exercises*, translated by Elder Mullan, S. J. (New York: P. J. Kenedy & Sons, 1914), 192.

[119] See 131–32.

specific edicts issued by the Bernese against the Calvinists.[120] Soon, Castellio himself entered the predestination debate and unsurprisingly took a view entirely different from that of Calvin. He first addressed this issue with a long annotation on Romans 9 in the 1554 edition of his Latin Bible.[121] In the *Annotations on Romans 9*, Castellio counters several of the key arguments and biblical texts cited in favor of predestination. He announces his intention to interpret the scriptural passages according to the "sense and tenor" of Scripture,[122] thus laying down already in 1554 the exegetical principle he would develop later in the *Art of Doubting*. The first text he analyzes is the passage in which Paul quotes Malachi 1:2–3, "I have loved Jacob, but I have hated Esau." To Calvin, this passage proves that God's election is declarative, effective, and thus predestinarian; it is not simply a matter of foreknowledge, especially since God told Rebekah that "the elder shall serve the younger" (Gen. 25:23, Rom. 9:12) while they were still in the womb.[123] Castellio, by contrast, interprets the two brothers not as individuals whom God has arbitrarily elected, one to life and the other to death, but as types representative of the good (Jacob) and the wicked (Esau).[124] He then lays out the basic soteriological principle he would adhere to throughout his writings:

> It is clear that those who are loved and elected are elected by God's gratuitous benevolence, and salvation proceeds from this election, by moving

---

[120] For example, "Principio Bernenses a Genevensibus quantum dissideant videamus. Fuit quidam Lausannae concionator nomine [Saint-Paul], qui de praedestinatione semper contra docuit quam Calvinus." Castellio, *Contra Libellum Calvini*, 213. See also several passages in *De l'Impunité des hérétiques*, especially 241, and 329–33, where he refers to the conflicts of late 1554–1555 between Zébédée and the Calvinists, reproducing verbatim a number of letters and decrees.

[121] Sebastian Castellio, ed., *Biblia interprete Sebastiano Castalione, una cum eiusdem Annotationibus* (Basel: Oporinus, 1554). The annotation proved so controversial, however, that the Basel professor of theology, Martin Borrhaus, ordered the text expunged from at least some of the printings. However, see Mirjam Van Veen, "'. . . Stoica Paradoxa . . .': Sebastian Castellio's Polemic against Calvin's Doctrine of Predestination," *BHR* 77 (2015): 325–50. Van Veen raises the possibility that the 1554 edition was not tampered with, explaining that she has found several complete editions, and that the edition of the Bible in the Basel library that Buisson used may well have just had some missing quires. But it is clear that some copies of the 1554 edition were censored. The copy available on Google Books from the Bibliotheca Casanatense in Rome skips from Romans 8 to Romans 10 in the same column. Castellio, *Biblia* (1554), NT 451, VV1ᵛ. In any case, the expunged text circulated in manuscript form for many years before finally being printed again in the 1613 edition of the *Dialogi IV*. Sebastian Castellio, *Annotationes Sebastiani Castellionis in caput nonum ad Rom.*, in *Dialogi IV* (Gouda: Jaspar Tournay, 1613), 2nd numbering, 1–30.

[122] "Itaque quo revocantur, si fieri potest, in angustam viam, dicam ea ad quae me sensus ipse tenorque sacrarum literarum impellit." Castellio, *Annotationes*, 9.

[123] Calvin, *Institutes*, III.xxii.4–6.

[124] "Cur autem Esaum, hoc est malos, oderit, et Iacobum, hoc est bonos, amet Deus, patet ex Deut. 9 . . ." Castellio, *Annotationes*, 2.

individuals to a life worthy of his election. But those who are hated and rejected are rejected because of their own sins.[125]

Thus, for Castellio, salvation is chiefly due to God's grace and election, but reprobation is entirely the consequence of human sin.

With regard to the second proof text often used to support predestination, namely, "God hardened Pharaoh's heart" (Ex. 9:12), Castellio argues that God did no such thing. Instead, the text is Scripture's way of saying that God did not intervene to soften Pharaoh's heart, which was already hard to begin with.[126] In a similar way, he suggests that when one prays in the Lord's Prayer, "Lead us not into temptation," one knows very well that God does not actually lead anyone into temptation or cause anyone to sin, for that would be contrary to God's nature. The prayer is really asking God not to allow us to fall into or be conquered by temptation.[127]

Thus, Castellio comes close to the position held by Bolsec, who argued that Calvin made God the author of sin.[128] Central to Castellio's argument are two principles: First, God, as goodness itself, created all things good and wants only good for his creatures.[129] Second, he gave humans free will, and their improper use of it is the cause of sin.[130] In rejecting the idea that God created some humans for damnation, Castellio uses the analogy of the

---

[125] "Ex his apparet, eos qui amantur et eliguntur, eligi gratuita Dei benignitate, ex qua electione proficiscatur salus, hominibus vitam electione sua dignam agentibus: eos autem qui odio sunt, et repudiantur, repudiari propter sua peccata." Castellio, *Annotationes*, 2.

[126] "Quod si Pharaonis cor erat natura lapideum, non magis poterat vel a Deo, vel a seipso indurari, quam lapis, nisi prius fuerat mollitum, quod non fuit. Itaque quod dicitur a Deo indurari, id videtur idem esse quod non molliri, sed in sua duritate relinqui." Castellio, *Annotationes*, 3.

[127] "Hanc interpretationem neque a verbis, neque a sententia discrepare, sic ostendemus: Non inducas nos in tentationem, est, Ne patiare nos tentari, aut tentatione vinci. . . . Iam vero cum Deus neminem tentet, hoc est, ad peccandum impellat, sicut scripsit Iacobus, Pharaonem certe non tentavit aut induravit, sed tentari et durum manere passus est." Castellio, *Annotationes*, 3–4.

[128] Castellio does not use those precise words here, but he would in later writings. See, for example, his letter to Martin Borrhaus, who ordered the removal of Castellio's annotation on Romans 9 from his Latin Bible: "Iam ut ad rem veniam, duo sunt potissimum in tuis de Praedestinatione scriptis (a quibus caetera fere omnia pendent) quae quo pacto vera sint, nullo modo comprehendere possum, et quae nisi aliis quam hactenus fecisti rationibus defenderis, tibi assentiri nequeo. Unum est, quod *Deum* videris authorem facere peccati. Alterum quod eundem videris in suis praeceptis simulatorem, et aliud verbis praecipientem, aliud in animo gerentem facere. Sebastian Castellio, *De Praedestinatione scriptum*, in *Dialogi IIII* (Aresdorffii [Basel]: Theophil. Philadelph. [P. Perna], 1578), 332–445, here, 335–36; in *Dialogi IV* (1613), 254–339, here, 256–57.

[129] "Deus nullum hominem creavit, ut eum perderet, sed tantum perdit eos qui boni esse nolunt, cum tamen eos creasset, ut boni essent. Vellet enim omnes homines esse bonos et salvos fieri, cum sit ipse bonus et omnia bona creaverit." Castellio, *Annotationes*, 6.

[130] "Sed cum homo ad imaginem Dei, imperaturus orbi crearetur, oportuit eum (sicut filium Dei et orbis Imperatorem decebat) esse liberae voluntatis. . . . Ex his apparet Adamum pecasse, non destinatione Dei (qui peccatum non vult) sed voluntate culpaque sua, nulla necessitate cogente." Castellio, *Annotationes*, 12–13.

potter. The potter wants all of his pots to be good; it would be absurd for him to create some simply in order to destroy them. He only destroys them if flaws are found in them. Similarly, the magistrate wants all of his citizens to be good, but if some turn to crime, he does not hesitate to punish them.[131] In the same way, God elected all humans for life and salvation. It is absurd, Castellio claims, to assert that God created some for reprobation and damnation. Nevertheless, some humans turn away from God and are consequently consigned to destruction. He sums up:

> God wants all to be saved through Christ. Whoever wants to be saved, can be through Christ, if only they wish to fulfill the things necessary for obtaining salvation. Those who perish do so against God's will and design [*destinatio*] by their own fault and depraved free will.[132]

Thus, for Castellio, damnation has nothing to do with God's predestination.

Castellio developed his ideas further in the *Dialogi IV*, which was written no later than 1558,[133] and which he presents as a dialogue between Ludovicus, a Calvinist, and Federicus, who represents Castellio's own views. Here Castellio develops Bolsec's argument that Calvin's doctrine of predestination makes God the author of evil. He characterizes as absurd the notion that God both wanted and did not want humans to sin.[134] Moreover, he suggests, a God who wants people to sin is effectively the same as the devil.[135] In addition, Castellio places a new focus on Adam's creation in the image of God and concludes that Adam's will cannot have been forced by God's precept.[136] Castellio ends the section of the *Dialogi IV* on predestination by enumerating five evils in the Calvinist doctrine of predestination:

---

[131] "Dicet tibi figulus, 'Ego nullum vas vellem frangere, sed si quod malum esse contigit, ostendo potestatem meam id frangendo.' Dicit magistratus, 'Ego nullum civem vellem interficere, vellem enim omnes esse bonos, sed si quis latro est, ostendo meam potestatem eo interficiendo.'" Castellio, *Annotationes*, 7.

[132] "Deus vult omnes per Christum salvos fieri. Quicunque servari volunt, per Christum possunt, si modo ea praestare velint, quae ad salutem adipiscendam sunt necessaria. Qui pereunt, ii contra Dei destinationem et voluntatem pereunt, sua prava et libera voluntate et culpa." Castellio, *Annotationes*, 19.

[133] Guggisberg, *Sebastian Castellio*, 211.

[134] "*Fed.* Suntne inter sese contraria haec duo: velle peccatum, et nolle peccatum? *Lud.* Maxime. *Fed.* Si igitur nolle peccatum bonus est, velle peccatum malum est. Ita sit ut in Deo bonum sit et malum. Quid haesitas? *Lud.* Non succurrit mihi quod respondeam." Castellio, *Dialogi IIII* (1578), 7.

[135] "*Fed.* Si enim Deus vult peccatum, Diabolus non vult peccatum. Sin uterque vult, sunt unum et idem Deus et Diabolus." Castellio, *Dialogi IIII* (1578), 15.

[136] "*Fed.* Si homo, inquam, tam necessario voluntate ferretur ad peccandum, quam appetitu ad esuriendum, supervacaneum et absurdum, ne dicam iniustum esset, eius voluntati praecipere

1. It contradicts God the Father's nature to think that he created children for punishment, which not even wolves and tigers do.
2. It destroys God's mercy.
3. It turns God into a deceiver who wants one thing but orders another.
4. It eliminates zeal for religion and obedience, since it persuades humans there is nothing they can do for their own salvation.
5. It hinders prayer to God with certain faith, for one will always fear on some level that one has not been predestined for life.[137]

These, he argues, are the rotten fruits of Calvin's doctrine of predestination. Castellio concludes, by contrast, "If you believe that all humans were created for salvation, you will find all the opposites, namely God's paternal spirit for all things he created, a most generous mercy, and agreement between his commands and his will without any deceit. And thus it happens that true and serious zeal for piety and prayers and hope for salvation set forth for all are born."[138] Ultimately, Castellio was annoyed that he had to waste time discussing predestination and thought the whole controversy would hardly have been necessary if not for the "the audacity of certain individuals."[139]

---

ne peccaret. Quae cum ita sint, sic statuamus, ADAMI VOLUNTATEM DEI PRAECEPTO COGI NON POTUISSE." Castellio, *Dialogi IIII* (1578), 39, emphasis in original.

[137] "*Fed.* Igitur hoc statuamus, eos male et perniciose docere, qui docent a Deo creatos esse certos homines ad miseriam sempiternam, idque ob multa mala, quae inde consequuntur. Primum quia id naturae Dei adeo non convenit, ut nihil possit ei magis esse contrarim, quam creare filios (fuit enim Adamus et porro Adami semen universum filius Dei) ad poenam, cum id ne lupi quidem aut tigres faciant . . .

>   Alterum in ista praedestinatione malum est, quod tollitur misericordia Dei illa, quam ipse praedicat, dum dicit, se esse multae misericordiae, et ad iram tardum. . . .
>   Tertium malum in ea est, quod efficitur simulator Deus, qui aliud velit, aliud iubeat. In quo faciunt isti Deum longe deteriorem quam diabolum, sicuti iam demonstravimus. . . .
>   Quartum est, quod periculum est ne tollatur studium religionis, et obedientiae, cum sit persuasum non posse te id non facere, ad quod sis destinatus. . . . Ita fiet, ut nemo salutem suam procuret cum timore et tremore, sed aut dissolute vivant si credant electos esse se, aut desperent si reiectos. . . .
>   Quintum malum est, quod manente ista opinione, non possis certa fide vel pro te, vel pro quovis alio orare Deum. Semper enim metuere licebit, ne non sis praedestinatus ad salutem." Castellio, *Dialogi IIII* (1578), 76–81.

[138] "*Fed.* Haec sunt et alia multa istius praedestinationis mala, quae quoquo te vertas vitari nequeunt, nisi sublata sit ista opinio. At si credas a Deo creatos esse homines omnes ad salutem, invenies omnia contraria, videlicet, Dei paternum in omnes a se creatos animum, et misericordiam liberalissimam, eiusque praecepta cum voluntate sine ulla simulatione convenientia. Ita fiet, ut verum seriumque pietatis studium certaeque praeces, et omnibus expositae salutis spes nascantur." Castellio, *Dialogi IIII* (1578), 82.

[139] "*Fed.* Perdifficilis et ardua quaestio est, et eadem disputatio minime necessaria, nisi eam hoc tempore necessariam fecisset quorundam audacia." Castellio, *Dialogi IIII* (1578), 2.

Castellio insists that he would far rather have devoted his time to discussing what he saw as the core of the Christian faith: following Christ.[140]

5.6.4. "The way to salvation is to obey God's will": Faith, Works, and Justification

To Castellio, the path to salvation was clear:

> Be afraid of God's wrath inflamed against our sins. Turn with desire to obtain forgiveness. Come into hope of a life for the love of Christ. Trust in God's mercy promised in Christ. Give thanks in prosperity and invoke God in adversity. Praise God continually. Love God with all your heart. Love your neighbor as yourself. Be good to your enemies. Do not return evil for evil. Do not lie. Do not be envious. Do not slander, Do not be contentious or stingy, a fool, false witness, or usurer.[141]

These are the rules for a Christian life, Castellio suggests, and he asks Beza, "Why do you not treat these things on which salvation depends? Why do you focus instead on things that are in doubt and dispute," such as eternal election, predestination, and the trinity?[142] The Calvinists, he suggests, put so much emphasis on doctrine rather than on life that they

---

[140] See, for example, his response to Beza, referring to his alter ego Bellius: "Il [Bellius] nie que la cognoissance de ces choses, à sçavoir de la trinité, prédestination et autres desquelles coustumièrement on dispute soit si nécessaire à obtenir salut par la foy, et aymeroit mieux que les gens traitassent du moyen par lequel on peult parvenir à Christ, c'est-à-dire de l'amendement de vie." Castellio, *De l'impunité des hérétiques*, 252.

[141] "Et vous[, Bèze,] cependant estans empêchez à condamner les autres, à cause de ces questions oscures, ne tenez conte des commandemens de l'amour et crainte de Dieu, desquelz nul ne doute, et toutes sectes en sont d'accord, comme sont: Estre épouvantez cognoissans l'ire de Dieu enflambée contre noz péchez. Ardre du désir d'obtenir pardon. Venir en espérance d'une vie pour l'amour de Christ. Avoir fiance en la miséricorde de Dieu promise par Christ. Randre grâces en prospérité. Invoquer en adversité. Louer Dieu continuellement. Aymer Dieu de tout son coeur. Aymer son prochain comme soy-mesme. Bien faire aux ennemis. Ne randre à aucun mal pour mal. Ne mentir. N'estre envieux. Ne calomnier. N'estre contentieux, avare, plaisanteur, faux tesmoin, usurier. Ces choses et telles sont clères, apertes, et manifestes et ne viennent en débat entre ceux qui confessent les saintes lettres." Castellio, *De l'Impunité des hérétiques*, 267.

[142] "Pourquoy ne traités-vous de ces choses-cy, desquelles le Salut dépend et non de celles qui sont en doute et contention?" Castellio, *De l'Impunité des hérétiques*, 267. See also a similar passage in *Contra Libellum Calvini*: "Certa sunt pietatis praecepta de amando Deo et proximo, de amandis inimicis, de patientia, de misericordia, de benignitate et caeteris huiusmodi necessariis officiis. Sed nos haec, quae sunt officii nostri neglegentes, de Dei officio sumus solliciti, et perinde, ac si ei fuerimus a consiliis. De eius aeterna electione multa disputamus, et de predestinatione, et de trinitate, quae nunquam videmus affirmantes, et quae sunt ante pedes, omnia contemnentes" (63–64).

would prefer an immoral, lying, vicious, greedy fool, as long as he agreed with them on baptism and predestination and held their preachers in reverence, to a moral person who disagreed with them on some point of doctrine; the latter they would hold for a heretic who needed to be cut off from the Church.[143]

As these few passages make clear, on the subject of justification, Castellio departed sharply not just from Calvin, but from nearly all Protestant theologians of the time, including Luther, whose foundational principle of justification by faith alone (*sola fide*) he rejects entirely. For Luther, Calvin, and most other Protestants, the doctrine of justification *sola fide* was necessary because of their belief in humans' total depravity and, consequently, their inability to achieve anything meritorious by their own works. Castellio held no such reservations about human nature:

> Those who boast of being not only Christians but also the reformers of the church publicly and commonly . . . profess that they are inclined to evil and useless at doing good and that they constantly violate God's holy commands. . . . But we recognize that the true confession of true Christians is completely contrary to this, and we contend that it can be truly understood in these words, namely: We are inclined to doing good; we are suited to doing all good, and we will constantly obey God's holy commands. Certainly, we have sometimes been wicked, 'but we have been washed, sanctified, and justified' [1 Cor. 6:11], and we delight in the law of the Lord, and meditate on it day and night [Ps. 1:2].[144]

---

[143] "Parquoy, s'il y a quelcun envers eux, encores que ce feüst autrement un homme fort vicieux, avaricieux, moqueur, plaisanteur, médisant, calomniateur, insidiateur, envieux, ireux, cupide de vengeance, pourveu qu'il soit d'accord avec eux au baptesme, en la prédestination, serf arbitre et autres choses et qu'il fréquente les prêches et sacremens et aye en honneur et révérence les prédicants, iceluy est bon chrestien; Christ ha effacé ses péchez passez, présens et à venir. Mais si quelcun se garde de tous ces vices-là et se gouverne de sorte qu'ilz n'ayent que reprandre en sa vie et soit seulement différent d'eux en quelque point de leur doctrine, comme au baptesme, prédestination, franc arbitre et persécution, il est hérétique et membre pourry; il le faut retrancher du corps de l'Eglise." Castellio, *De l'Impunité des hérétiques*, 383.

[144] "De nostri vero temporis Christianis quid multis opus est? Cum ipsimet Christiani se improbos esse pene profiteantur: quid pene dixi? Cum ii qui non solum Christianos, verum etiam ecclesiarum reformatores esse iactant, publice et communiter . . . profiteantur se esse proclives ad malum et inutiles ad omne bonum suoque vitio sine ulla intermissione violare sancta praecepta dei?. . . Nos vero verorum Christianorum veram confessionem isti plane contrariam agnoscimus eamque his verbis vere concipi posse pugnamus, videlicet: Nos sumus ad bene faciendum proclives, ad omne bonum utiles et sine ulla intermissione sanctis dei praeceptis obediemus. Et fuimus quidem aliquando improbi, 'sed abluti sumus, sed sancti, sed iusti facti sumus' et 'dei lege delectamur deque ea dies noctesque cogitamus.'" Castellio, *De arte dubitandi*, 25–27, ll. 21–27, 58–63.

Thus, Castellio's starting point is antithetical to that of the magisterial reformers. Instead, he approaches justification from the perspective of a humanist with a high regard for the ability of humans to do good and to follow God's commandments.

Castellio does not, of course, deny the human tendency to sin, or claim that humans can fulfill God's law perfectly, but unlike the magisterial reformers, he believes that, with God's help, people can hew closely to his law. To begin with, recall Castellio's insistence that God created all humans for salvation. Now, "the way of salvation is to obey God's will, which has been declared in his commands. But God wants nothing impossible; if he commands something to humans which they cannot fulfill, he gives them the power to fulfill it."[145] Justification, therefore, involves human cooperation with God's election and will. To explain justification, Castellio uses the analogy of tree grafting. The unjustified are like wild, uncultivated trees that do not bear fruit. But when by God's power, the Holy Spirit is grafted onto them, they cease to be wild and will begin to produce fruit. "This change, by which the unjust individual becomes just, similar to how the uncultivated tree becomes cultivated, is called by Paul sometimes justification, sometimes the 'putting on of the new man,' sometimes the 'resurrection with Christ.'"[146] As with the tree, it might take time for the good fruits to appear, but this does not mean the person is not good:

> The tree which produces good fruit is good, even if some of its fruit is imperfect or does not ripen. In the same way, a person who performs works of justice is just, even if not all his deeds are free of vice or achieve perfection.... The farmer judges a tree good if it thrives and has good in it; in the same way, God judges the person good who is endowed with the spirit of justice and performs works of righteousness.[147]

---

[145] "Demonstravimus primum Deum velle omnes homines salvos fieri. Salutis via est obedire Dei voluntati, in eius praeceptis declaratae. Vult autem Deus nihil impossibile, quod si quid homini praecipit, quod homo praestare non possit, dat ei vires ad praestandum." Castellio, *Dialogi IIII* (1578), 192–93.

[146] "Ipsa autem mutatio qua homo ex iniusto iustus tanquam ex arbore sylvestri cicur efficitur, vocari solet a Paulo modo iustificatio, modo novi hominis indutio, modo cum Christo resurrectio." Castellio, *De arte dubitandi*, 150, ll. 13–15.

[147] "Neque non illud patet quemadmodum bona arbor est quae bonum fructum parit, etiam si non omnis eius fructus vitio careat, aut ad maturitatem perveniat. Ita et hominem iustum esse qui iusta faciat, etiam si non omnia eius facta vitio careant aut perfectionem adipiscantur.... Et de arbore ex eo iudicat agricola quod in ea bonum est et excellit, quod idem et de homine facit deus, hoc est hominem eum bonum iudicat qui iusticiae spiritu praeditus iusta facit." Castellio, *De arte dubitandi*, 152–153, ll. 22–26, 47–50.

Castellio, in essence, believes God has "lowered the bar" to a level that all humans are capable of leaping over. Luther and Calvin, by contrast, believe God's bar is so high that no one can possibly clear it unless borne over it by Christ. For them, "All have sinned and fallen short of the glory of God" (Rom. 3:23). For Castellio, by contrast, God says, "My yoke is easy and my burden is light" (Matt. 11:30). Castellio's position comes close to late medieval "semi-pelagianism," which held that as long as humans did their best (*facere quod in se est*), God would reward their efforts with the grace to achieve salvation.

At the same time, Castellio insisted that even if the fruit of justification is imperfect or delayed, the Christian must produce it eventually, for faith without works is not really faith. Eventually, the farmer will prune the cultivated trees that fail to produce fruit, and God likewise will cast down the human who produces no works of righteousness.[148] Those who boast that they are new men but bear no fruit are deluded. They claim to be new men, but since they bear no fruit, they conclude that the new man does not bear fruit. They ought to conclude instead, Castellio insists, that "the new man bears fruits of justice; I do not bear them. Therefore, I am not a new man."[149]

Castellio's emphasis on good works and Christian piety helps to explain his decision to publish editions of two popular late medieval devotional manuals: the anonymous *German Theology* (*Theologia Deutsch*) and Thomas à Kempis's *Imitation of Christ*. Castellio's preface to the *Imitation of Christ*, a work "full of piety," is brief and explains that he has, first, translated the work from "rustic to more refined Latin" and, second, cut off [*castrare*] certain parts which were inappropriate "after the light of Christ has so shined on our age that it has detected many errors and superstitions."[150] In essence, Castellio excised the sections on transubstantiation and sacramental adoration.

---

[148] "Utque nonnullae insitae arbores steriles sunt, ita et nonnulli Christiani ignavi sunt, et nemini nocent illi quidem neque flagitiosi sunt, sed neque prosunt aut recte faciunt. Ii diligenti doctrina et exercitatione redduntur interdum operosi. Sed si id non succedit, interdum a deo exciduntur. Non enim solum sylvestris arbor, sed etiam sterilis, quamvis cicur, displicet agricolae. Ita non solum improbus homo, verum etiam ignavus, quamvis improbitatis expers, displicet deo." Castellio, *De arte dubitandi*, 151, ll. 57–64.

[149] "Quoniam enim renati non sunt ideoque non novi, sed veteris hominis fructus ferunt, et tamen novi nomen sibi vendicant, sic statuunt: 'Ego sum novus homo et tamen iusticiae fructus non fero, ergo novus homo iusticiae fructus non fert.' Cum potius sic ratiocinari debeant: 'Novus homo fructus fert iusticiae, atqui ego non fero, ergo non sum novus homo.'" Castellio, *De arte dubitandi*, 152, ll. 69–74.

[150] "Hunc ego libellum, quia pietatis plenus, non mihi solum, sed et aliis piis multis visus est, putavi de latino in latinum, hoc est de agrestiore sermone in paulo mundiorem, sed tamen simplicem, esse convertendum. . . . Quod ad alterum attinet, postquam Christi lux nostro seculo sic affulsit, ut multos errores et superstitiones detexerit, puto non nefas esse nonnullos castrare libros, ut omnia probantes, quae bona sunt teneamus." Sebastian Castellio, ed., *De Imitando Christo, contemnendisque mundi*

The *German Theology*, which Castellio produced in both Latin and French editions and subtitled *How to Cast off the Old Man and Put on the New*, included a lengthy preface.[151] Eugénie Droz suggests that the French edition was instrumental in spreading Castellio's teachings to his followers, particularly in France. She notes that it was "intended for disciples obliged to live in an individual and mystical piety without a minister."[152] Her argument is largely based on a section Castellio appended to the original, entitled "Some serious sayings by which each diligent disciple of Christ can examine himself and know what he must study with regard to the true union and conjunction of the true and sovereign good."[153] Both the *Imitation of Christ* and the *German Theology* focus on individual, personal piety. This, for Castellio, was the only true piety. Although he did not entirely dismiss the external, institutional church, he regarded it as secondary. Moreover, he found that the visible church could often err or distract the faithful from this pursuit of piety. In his book against Beza, Castellio sets up a dichotomy between the visible and spiritual churches:

> Those constitute the true church who truly listen to the voice of the pastor [i.e., Christ]. That is to say, they obey him and adhere to the true use of the sacraments; that is, they are cleansed in the washing of rebirth and are new creatures, baptized by fire and spirit. They have truly eaten the body of Christ and have drunk his blood. In other words, they have put away the old man of sin and put on the new man."[154]

Here, Castellio takes an entirely spiritual view of the sacraments. *True* baptism and communion are not external acts but internal regeneration. "This

vanitatibus libellus authore Thoma Kempisio, interprete Sebastiano Castellione (Basel: [Oporinus], 1563), A2ʳ–A3ʳ.

[151] Johannes Theophilus [Sebastian Castellio], ed. and trans., *Theologia Germanica: Libellus aureus, hoc est, brevis et praegnans, Quo modo sit exuendus Vetus homo, induendusque novus* (Basel: Oporinus, 1557), preface, 3–13. [Sebastian Castellio, ed. and trans.], *La Théologie Germanique: Livret auquel est traicté comment il faut dépouiller le vieil homme, et vestir le nouveau* (Antwerp: Christofle Plantin, 1558), preface, 3–12.

[152] Eugénie Droz, "Castelloniana," 407.

[153] [Castellio], *La Théologie Germanique*, 100–103; [Castellio], *Theologia Germanica*, 121–25.

[154] "Ceux-là sont la vraye Eglise qui vrayement oyent la voix du pasteur, c'est-à-dire qui luy obéissent et qui ont la vray usage des sacremens, c'est-à-dire sont lavez au lavement de renaissance et sont nouvelles créatures baptizés de feu et d'esprit, qui ont vrayement mangé la chair de Christ et beü son sang, c'est-à-dire ayans dépouillé le viel homme de péché ont revestu le nouveau." Castellio, *De l'Impunité des hérétiques*, 366.

church," he claims, "is unknown to the Calvinists."[155] He draws a stark contrast between the "carnal" and spiritual churches:

> These two churches, namely the carnal and the spiritual, are so contrary to one another that the carnal, which is the elder and more powerful, persecutes the spiritual, as Cain persecuted Abel, Ishmael persecuted Isaac, Esau Jacob, the Pharisees Christ, and the flesh the spirit. . . . Thus, today, this carnal church, devoid of charity, puffed up with external signs of preaching and sacraments, and armed with the sword of the magistrate, assaults the spiritual church.[156]

Castellio was chiefly concerned with the spiritual church: those who have truly been reborn, put on the new man, and given their lives to Christ through their willingness to follow his commands. The spiritual church was everywhere, invisible, and often persecuted by the carnal church, which Castellio suggests could be seen most clearly in Calvin's persecuting church in Geneva.

5.7. Castellio and the Liberal Protestant Tradition

Because the spiritual church was invisible and everywhere, it did not have a hierarchy of authorities or a written confession of faith. Castellio's writings were among its guides and anti-Calvinist theology part of its creed. The fundamentals of this theology, outlined earlier, included, most importantly, opposition to religious persecution and the doctrine of double predestination, support for a radically new rationalist biblical exegesis, belief in the essential goodness of humanity and in humans' ability both to reason and to keep God's law, and the conviction that the path to salvation lay in following Christ's example and becoming a "new man." Behind all these ideas lay a liberal embrace of relativism, nuance, and tolerance for ambiguity that stood in stark contrast to Calvin's insistence on absolute truth, precise definitions, and adherence to his understanding of Christianity.

---

[155] "Ceste église est incogneüe aux calviniens." Castellio, *De l'Impunité des hérétiques*, 366.

[156] "Ces deux églises, à savoir la charnelle et spirituelle, sont tellement entre soy contraires que la charnelle (qui est l'aînée et la plus puissante) persécute la spirituelle, comme Caïn persécute Abel, Ismaël Isaac, Esaü Jacob, les farisiens Christ, et la chair l'esprit. . . . Ainsy aujourd'huy ceste église-là charnelle, vuide de charité, enflée des signes extérieurs des prêches et sacremens et armés du glaive du magistrat, assaut la spirituelle." Castellio, *De l'Impunité des hérétiques*, 367.

Castellio's ideas laid the groundwork for later liberal Christianity. His rejection of a literalist interpretation of Scripture, aversion to strict confessional statements, embrace of rationalist exegesis, openness to multiple theological possibilities, and emphasis on piety and devotion as opposed to doctrine remain to this day hallmarks of the liberal Protestant tradition. To be sure, historians must avoid the temptation to cast historical figures anachronistically as champions of modern values. Nonetheless, they have a duty to identify forerunners and originators of significant historical trends. Castellio is just such a figure. He was by no means a thoroughly modern man; like Calvin, Castellio was in many ways a man of his times. We have seen his antisemitism rise to the surface as he criticized Calvin's reliance on the Old Testament. And few Western liberals today would embrace his support for the thoroughly Christianized early education that he sought to advance through his *Sacred Dialogues*.[157] His legacy, however, is unmistakable.

The stark differences between Castellio and Calvin reflect the turmoil of the age and capture the many angry divisions emerging from a single geographical, educational, and religious milieu. Both men were French-speaking humanists who had broken from the Roman church, yet their prescriptions for replacing the old church could hardly have been more different. One sought to build a new institutional church with a clear set of newly defined beliefs. The other saw religion as an internal affair of the spirit with charity for all Christians and malice toward none. Both men and their visions had legions of followers. Calvin's are more visible and therefore familiar. Castellio's often remained hidden within the existing institutional churches of the time, but they formed distinct networks that stretched across Europe. We shall meet some of them in the next chapter.

---

[157] Indeed, by rejecting the use of pagan authors in early education, Castellio was far more "conservative" than most educators of his own time. See, for example, Karine Crousaz, "Les auteurs païens dans les *Colloques* d'Érasme et de Maturin Cordier," in *Crossing Traditions: Essays on the Reformation and Intellectual History in Honour of Irena Backus*, edited by Maria-Cristina Pitassi and Daniela Solfaroli Camillocci, 311–30, SMRT 212 (Leiden: Brill, 2017), 311–12.

6

Castellio's Long Shadow

6.1. Introduction

Sebastian Castellio never wanted to be the head of a church or sect. As Peter Bietenholz comments, "Nothing was farther from his mind than to surround himself with a sect of Castellionists."[1] His ecclesiology, as we saw in the previous chapter, was too spiritual to accommodate such a notion. Nevertheless, his ideas inspired numerous followers across a wide geographical area and a broad spectrum of backgrounds. Many of these individuals shared, if not all aspects of his theology, at least his antipathy toward Calvin—especially Calvin's doctrine of double predestination—and revulsion at the execution of Servetus. These shared ideas resulted in the construction of several networks of Castellionists, particularly near Basel in the Suisse romande and in Montbéliard. Some admirers formed networks further afield, such as the Remonstrants in the Netherlands and the Socinians in Poland, that remained influential well into the seventeenth century. In France, Castellio gained numerous individual followers, and a small community of disciples formed in Lyon. Castellio's followers in France, however, had little success in undermining the Calvinists. Indeed, fear of the Castellionists was a significant factor driving the creation of Geneva's missionary program in France and the institutionalization of a Calvinian French Reformed church.

6.2. Castellionists in the Suisse Romande and Montbéliard

As we saw in the previous chapters, Castellio's objections to the execution of Michael Servetus in Geneva found sympathetic audiences in the Suisse romande and Montbéliard.[2] Friends and family members there kept Castellio

---

[1] Bietenholz, *Basle and France in the Sixteenth Century*, 136.
[2] See 131–32, 149–51.

Refusing to Kiss the Slipper. Michael W. Bruening, Oxford University Press (2021). © Oxford University Press.
DOI: 10.1093/oso/9780197566954.003.0007

informed about local events, maintained a lively dissenting voice even within the Calvinist strongholds of Lausanne, Geneva, and Neuchâtel, and helped to keep Calvinist influence at bay in the Lausanne Academy after Viret's expulsion. Indeed, the county of Montbéliard would become a veritable refuge for supporters of Castellio and opponents of Calvin.

6.2.1. The Suisse Romande

Castellio's *On Not Punishing Heretics* refers several times to events in the Vaud, demonstrating that his supporters there kept him well informed, especially about Zébédée's conflicts with Calvin.[3] Castellio's correspondence also reveals contacts in the region beyond those mentioned in Chapter 5. In 1554, Hughes Caviot wrote to him from Lausanne and signed his letter, "Your humble servant who once stayed with you,"[4] suggesting that he had been a pupil or lodger with Castellio. We previously met Jean Colinet, the former schoolmaster in Geneva, who reported that Zébédée read Castellio's work to Falais.[5] In 1558, we find him—like many others expelled from Geneva—in the Vaud, whence he complained to Castellio bitterly about the Calvinists. He sent two messengers to Castellio who, he said, would bring him more news in person; one of them, he writes sarcastically, "will explain how sweetly and how humanely he was treated by the masters of the Sorbonne,"[6] by which he no doubt meant Calvin and his followers. He goes on to complain that "the Great One [i.e., Calvin] always tries great things and has now brought it about by his machinations that no one in all of France will be allowed to

---

[3] For example, (1) "Or l'occasion de ce feürent les propos tenuz en une congrégation de la classe de Morges contre la dottrine de Calvin. Car avertiz de ce, les sept ministres de Genève présentèrent requeste au magistrat de ce lieu-là, se plaignans en icelle d'aucuns ministres contredisans à Calvin. . . ."; (2) "Que diray-je de Zébédée, Bèze, et plusieurs autres? Que diray-je de Mélanthon, lequel vous tenez pour hérétique, combien que vous couvriez cela à cause de son authorité? Certes, vous avez jugé Jérôme le médecin et plusieurs autres hérétiques, lesquelz sont de l'opinion de Mélanthon"; (3) "Plus, quelques jours après, Zébédée feït la prédication ordinaire à Nion, en laquelle traitant de la permission et volonté de Dieu démonstra qu'il failloit distinguer ces choses-là. . . . Par ces choses Zébédée amonesta le peuple qu'il se donnast garde de ces confuses et diaboliques doctrines par lesquelles on enseigne que Dieu ne permet le mal qu'il ne le vueille. Zébédée demonstroit que Christ avoit permis aux mauvais espritz d'entrer ès pourceaux, et ne leur avoit commandé." Castellio, *De l'impunité des hérétiques*, 241, 323, 329–30.

[4] "Par le tout vostre humble serviteur Hugue Caviot qui a demouré autres foys avec vous." *CO* 15:211, no. 1997, Caviot to Castellio, Lausanne, August 10, 1554 (with slight corrections from Bruening, "Castellio Correspondence Project").

[5] See 131–32.

[6] "hic quam suaviter quamque humaniter tractatus fuerit a Sorbonae magistris tibi exponet." Buisson, 2:441, no. 71, Jean Colinet to Castellio, [Lausanne or Yverdon], November 4, 1558.

preach the Gospel unless he has been sent there by him: such is the power of the Beast!"[7]

Castellio very nearly found himself in a position to exert far more influence in the Vaud than he already had. As we have seen, he was considered for a teaching post at the Lausanne Academy on two occasions, first in 1558 to replace Beza, and a few years later in 1561–1562.[8] Although on both occasions Castellio was passed over, some of his followers did end up teaching at the Lausanne Academy after the 1559 expulsion of Viret and his allies. That year, Zébédée's ally Béat Comte became arts professor. In 1562, Comte was replaced by Jean Perrin, whom one of Bullinger's correspondents described as "a sworn student of Castellio, that is, a follower of Servetus and Pelagius."[9] Like Comte, Perrin had a long history of clashes with the Calvinists. He had been one of Bern's scholarship students at the Lausanne Academy in 1546,[10] and thus had studied under Zébédée while the latter was the arts professor there. Perrin then went to the University of Basel and in 1554 met Lelio Sozzini in Geneva.[11] In 1556, the Bernese named him deacon and schoolmaster in Aigle against the wishes of Viret and his colleagues in Lausanne.[12] Although Perrin's tenure at the Lausanne Academy was brief, he and Comte helped to keep the school free of Calvinist influence in the years following the expulsion of Viret and his colleagues from the city.

While Zébédée, Falais, Caviot, and Colinet kept Castellio informed about the Vaud, various family members were able to update him on Geneva itself. Castellio's brother-in-law Jacques Paquelon lived there in 1559; Castellio's nephew Michel Chastillon sent letters to him from Geneva in 1559 and 1561.[13] Michel's letter of 1561 reports that two Frenchmen accosted his cousin Jean in the city and told him that his relative Castellio was a heretic. A couple of days later Jean and his mother were brought before the consistory, and the interrogators tried to convince them that Castellio was "the wickedest devil of hell."[14] Castellio's relatives clearly faced hostility from Calvin's allies. The

[7] "Magnus magna semper molitur iamque suis artibus effecit ut per totam Franciam nulli ad Evangelium praedicandum admittantur, nisi ab eo missi: tanta est vis Bestiae!" Buisson, 2:441, no. 71.

[8] Guggisberg, *Sebastian Castellio*, 182; see also 138.

[9] Guggisberg, *Sebastian Castellio*, 104. The letter writer was Guglielmo Grataroli.

[10] Crousaz, *L'Académie de Lausanne*, 525.

[11] Guggisberg, *Sebastian Castellio*, 104.

[12] Crousaz, *L'Académie de Lausanne*, 285–86.

[13] Buisson, 2:449, no. 80, Jacques Paquelon to Castellio, Geneva, December 9, 1559; Buisson, 2:449–50, no. 81, Michel Chastillon to Castellio, [Geneva], December 9, 1559; CO 18:523–24, no. 3423, Michel Chastillon to Castellio, Geneva, June 20, 1561. Paquelon was the brother of Castellio's first wife, Huguine.

[14] "Or ledit Jean alloyt un jor sur les prins de la fusterie, là où se trouva deux franscoys qui devisoyt ensemble et disoyent que vous estes hereticque.... Quelques jours apres, ces deux Françoys menerent

mere fact that Castellio had such allies and informants living in Geneva well after Calvin is supposed to have gained control of the city in 1555 is a good reminder that Calvin's power was limited, even in Geneva itself. It was still quite possible for his detractors to maintain a dissenting presence there.

Guillaume Farel's Neuchâtel region was also home to at least one prominent Castellionist dissenter. Soon after the publication of *Concerning Heretics*, Jean L'Archer initiated contact with Castellio and would become one of his most frequent correspondents.[15] From 1552 to 1563, L'Archer was the pastor in Cortaillod, not far south of the city of Neuchâtel. In 1553, he published *The Canons of All the Councils* with Oporinus in Basel.[16] Viret censured this edition, although his reasons for doing so are unclear.[17] L'Archer was, therefore, yet another figure with ties to Basel who became a victim of the Calvinists. L'Archer's first letter to Castellio indicates that the two had met and that L'Archer knew Castellio's opinion of the Servetus affair.[18] Later letters reveal his interest in reading anti-Calvinist books, including those of François Bauduin, whom we will meet in the next chapter.[19] In 1563, L'Archer

M. Raimon vers Jan, et firent venir Jan et sa mere au Consistoyre, là où ils furent fort bien interrogué de beaucoup de poins par deux foys et mesme les menerent pour estre davantage interrogué en la maison de M. le Marqui et leur veulent faire croire que vous estes le plus meschant diable d'enfer." *CO* 18:524, no. 3423. The Geneva consistory records verify the essentials of the story; *CO* 21:745–46, March 27 and April 1, 1561.

[15] Often spelled "Larcher," and Latinized as either "Arquerius" or "Sagittarius." On him, see Haag², 1:320–33; *Epistolae Vireti*, 346n7. With nine extant letters between them, Castellio's surviving correspondence with L'Archer is second in size only to Castellio's exchanges with Niklaus Zurkinden of Bern.

[16] Jean L'Archer, *Canones Conciliorum Omnium, qui a primo Apostolorum Concilio, usque ad postremum sub Eugenio IIII. Pont. Max. celebratum, a S. Patribus sunt constituti* (Basel: Oporinus, 1553).

[17] See *Epistolae Petri Vireti*, 346n7.

[18] "Finalement, le bruict court qu'avez faict imprimer un livre contraire à ce que M. Calvin a traicté contre Servetus, c'est *De non comburendis haereticis*. Or touchant cest article, je sçay assez en quoy vous en estes, car nous en conferasmes par ensemble la dernière fois que je feus à Basle." Jules Bonnet, *Nouveaux récits du seizième siècle* (Paris: Grassart, 1870), 300, L'Archer to Castellio, [Cortaillod], July 30, 1554.

[19] "Je vous prie m'apporter ou envoyer Balduinus contre Calvin et m'en recouvrer ung." *CO* 20:46, no. 3970, L'Archer to Castellio, [Héricourt], June 26, 1563. "Je vous prie de cercher le livre de Heshusius et Nicolaus Gallus contre lesquelz Calvin a escript et les m'envoyer." *CO* 18:499, no. 3408, L'Archer to Castellio, [Cortaillod], June 1, 1561. François Bauduin wrote two books against Calvin in 1562: *Ad leges de famosis libellis et de calumniatoribus commentarius* (Paris: André Wechel, 1562) and *Responsio altera ad Ioan. Calvinum*; see Chapter 7 for more on Bauduin. The Heshusius book, no doubt, was Tilemann Heshusius, *De praesentia corporis Christi in Coena Domini* (Jena: Ritzenhain, 1560); the 1561 edition bore the subtitle *Contra Sacramentarios*. Calvin responded with *Dilucida explicatio sanae doctrinae de vera participatione carnis et sanguinis Christi in sacra Coena a discutiendas Heshusii nebulas* (*CO* 9:457–517), in the first paragraph of which he says, "Ecce ex altera parte Nicolaus Gallus bubonis stridorem in me quoque emisit." (*CO* 9:461), but Gallus does not seem to have published any books particularly against Calvin and is better known as a Gnesio-Lutheran opponent of Melanchthon.

quit the Neuchâtel region without permission and moved to the Castellio-
friendly region of Montbéliard.

6.2.2. Montbéliard

One need look no further than the county of Montbéliard (see Map 3.1) to
realize that the Calvinists failed to dominate francophone Protestantism
everywhere in Europe. Instead, that region became both a haven for Castellio
supporters and a testing ground for Lutheran-Reformed cooperation. Recall
that Castellio's prefatory letter to *Concerning Heretics* was dedicated to Duke
Christoph of Württemberg, former governor of Montbéliard. The dukes of
Württemberg struggled to prevent their bilingual territories—which included Montbéliard—from becoming biconfessional as well. It was a difficult
task, for the German speakers preferred Lutheranism, while the pastors in
francophone Montbéliard tended toward Reformed Protestantism. Among
the Reformed of Montbéliard, we find the same divisions that were present
in the Pays de Vaud.[20] Some of the pastors had either gone to school in Viret's
Lausanne or preached in Farel's Neuchâtel and embraced strict Calvinism.
Others supported Zwinglian and French notions about the supremacy of the
state church and were willing to seek compromise with the Württemberg
Lutherans. The latter found the Calvinists exasperating and discovered a kin-
dred spirit in Castellio.

For a long time, Montbéliard had been reliably Reformed. Farel himself had been one of the earliest evangelical missionaries there, and in the
early years, the region's pastors focused on abolishing the Mass rather than
fighting other Protestants. Moreover, the leading pastor of Montbéliard,
Pierre Toussain, was a long-time friend of the Calvinists, particularly Farel.[21]
The Servetus affair ruined this relationship. We saw earlier that during the
trial of Servetus, Toussain had expressed reservations about putting heretics
to death.[22] A few weeks after the execution, he had not changed his mind. He
wrote to his German colleague Mathias Erb, "I want to know what you think
about heretics, whether they should be subject to capital punishment by the
magistrate. Also, whether a minister of the Word of God can in good conscience go after them all the way to death and be the prod to the magistrate

---

[20] On the Reformation in Montbéliard, see Viénot.
[21] See 46.
[22] See 149–50.

for capital punishment."[23] Clearly this was not a hypothetical question, and Toussain's tone suggests that he thought the answer to all of these questions was "no."

Toussain's relationship with the Calvinists was further strained when he caught wind of rumors they had spread that he and his fellow Montbéliard pastors were disciples of Servetus who rejected ecclesiastical discipline. Moreover, he complained to Calvin that some of the staunchly Calvinist pastors in the region were introducing innovations in the administration of the sacraments without the approval of the prince, the superintendents, or the other pastors.[24] He was referring specifically to four pastors in the area who were refusing to conform to Montbéliard's church ordinances and were instead banning "the unworthy" from the Eucharist and refusing to give communion to people on their deathbeds.[25] Much to the annoyance of Calvin and his friends, these pastors were expelled from the region. Increasingly, Toussain became the object of criticism from his former friend Farel, who eventually accused him of trying to introduce Castellio and "Bellianism" throughout the region.[26] Toussain had the support of his princes, however. When the Calvinists solicited Ambrosius Blarer to complain to Count Georg, the governor of Montbéliard, that Toussain had not condemned Castellio's *Concerning Heretics*, Georg responded by telling them that Toussian had simply adhered to the count's bidding and that *his* pastors "were there to direct and feed their flocks; they have quite enough to do with

---

[23] "Sed scire cupio, quid de haereticis sentiatis, an per Magistratum extremo supplicio plecti debeant. Item, an Verbi Dei Minister illos ad mortem persequi bona conscientia possit Magistratuique author esse, ut capite plectantur." Viénot, 2:146, no. 104, Toussain to Mathias Erb, Montbéliard, November 21, [1553].

[24] "Est quidem facile, hoc praesertim tempore in tanta hominum licentia et perversitate, quidvis comminisci in proximos et spargere nos esse Serveti discipulos, reiicere disciplinam ecclesiasticam, contemnere literas et alia id genus. . . . Nec fuerat hic inter nos (ut sparsum quoque esse audio) ob Servetum aut eius doctrinam ortum dissidium, sed solum quod nonnulli ex nobis in administrandis sacramentis quaedam sine caeterorum consensu novaverant, quae nec Princeps nec superintendentes, nec caeteri fratres ad huius ecclesiae aedificationem facere iudicabant." *CO* 15:262–63, no. 2026, Toussain to Calvin, Montbéliard, October 9, 1554.

[25] The pastors were Etienne Noël (pastor at Blamont), Georges Laurent (St.-Julien), Humbert Artus (Valentigney), and either the pastor at Désandans or Louis Faucheux, pastor at Allanjoie. On this incident, see Viénot, 1:199–201.

[26] "Bonus vir [Ambrosius Blarer] nihil superesse videt nisi ut Dominum precemur, quandoquidem princeps totus sit in manu Tossani. . . . Blaurero aperui aliis quoque indicarem, nimirum de Belliana factione, ex qua tantum deligendos audimus qui in pulsorum locum introducantur, et quum coeperit, ut referebat pius aliquis, ita moliri piis mala, ubi eum vellet Castallionem introducere, et id non probaretur bonis (nam tunc ordo aliquis erat in eligendis et vocandis ministris et iuventutis formatoribus) nunc ubi solus omnia potest, omnibus probantibus quod ille censuerit, nihil nisi Castallionianum et Bellianum locum habebit." *CO* 17:124, no. 2844, Farel to Calvin, Neuchâtel, April 4, 1558.

this task, without being required to condemn books without our consent or that of our council."[27]

Toussain's sympathies for Castellio led to the establishment of Montbéliard as a francophone haven for Castellionists and other anti-Calvinist Protestants. The deacon in Montbéliard, Gérard Guillemin, was a follower of Castellio.[28] Jacques Gète, pastor of Bavans, was an "enthusiastic Castellionist and passionate admirer of Martin Bellius," in the words of Eugénie Droz, who believed Gète was the French translator of *Concerning Heretics*.[29] Uwe Plath has suggested that *Concerning Heretics* was translated instead by another pastor of Montbéliard, Léger Grymoult. We encountered Grymoult as one of the witnesses and critics of Servetus's execution.[30] Along with Nicolaas Blesdijk, he worked on the manuscript of Castellio's *On Not Punishing Heretics* and may have translated that work from Latin into French.[31]

Much of the support for Castellio and opposition to Calvin in Montbéliard centered on the two themes of persecution and predestination. Toussain and many of the Montbéliard pastors criticized the execution of Servetus and agreed with Bolsec that Calvin's doctrine of predestination made God the author of evil.[32] For many years, therefore, Montbéliard would remain a francophone Protestant region largely free of Calvinian doctrine.

6.3. Persecution, Predestination, and Piety: The Ties That Bound International Networks of Castellionists

The francophone areas of the Vaud, Geneva, Neuchâtel, and Montbéliard were all officially Protestant, and Castellio's friends and admirers had a strong presence in all of them. As we move away from Protestant francophone territories, Castellio's supporters become thinner on the ground but just as driven in their ideological opposition to the Calvinists. Beyond the Basel environs,

---

[27] "Zum andern, das auch der Tossanus ein buch in der predicanten Congregation oder sonst nit hab stracks condemnieren wöllen, daran hat er sich unserer ordnung nit ungemesz gehalten, dan unsere predicanten sindt dem volk iren schafflen fürzusteen und zu waiden, darmit sie auch genug zu thun haben, und nit die bücher zu condemniren, one uns und unsere räth, verordnet." CO 15:732, no. 2273, Count Georg of Monbéliard to Ambrosius Blarer, Montbéliard, August 19, 1555.

[28] Guggisberg, *Sebastian Castellio*, 121.

[29] See Droz, "Castellioniana," 325–354, esp. 341.

[30] See 150–51.

[31] Guggisberg, *Sebastian Castellio*, 117–18.

[32] Viénot, 1:196.

in areas where Castellio had relatively fewer supporters, it was more diffi-cult to forge networks based on personal friendships, and ideology became more important in creating bonds among his followers. Three issues in par-ticular galvanized support for Castellio and opposition to Calvin in the inter-national Protestant community: support for religious toleration, opposition to the doctrine of double predestination, and an emphasis on personal piety, together with criticism of the Calvinists' insistence on consistorial discipline.

6.3.1. Persecution and Toleration

As we have seen, support for "Bellianism," or Castellio's teaching on religious toleration, was embraced extensively in Basel and Montbéliard. Religious refugees and others under the threat of persecution likewise tended to em-brace Castellio's thought on the subject. With Castellio, they believed that the logical extension of Calvin's arguments was that Catholic political authorities were well within their rights to execute Protestants for heresy.

Philip Benedict and Nicolas Fornerod note that in the formative years of the French Reformed churches, Castellio's thought represented the only re-curring challenge to Calvinian orthodoxy. They point out that "only two het-erodox positions recur even a few times . . . : the Castellionist rejection of the use of force to punish false belief, and the refusal to restrict access to the Lord's Supper via a system of church discipline."[33] In Poitiers, as described in more detail at the end of this chapter, Jean Saint-Vertunien de Lavau, a friend of Castellio, was spreading several of Castellio's teachings, including those on religious toleration.[34] Not far from Poitiers, in Beaugency, a layman named Jean Bonneau was also spreading Castellionist ideas. Beza's *Ecclesiastical History* reports that Bonneau "held the opinion that it is not legal for the magistrate to punish heretics." It adds that "soon afterwards, this opinion was held by three other individuals with an excessively agitating spirit."[35] The

[33] Philip Benedict and Nicolas Fornerod, "Conflict and Dissidence within the Early French Reformed Churches," in *Crossing Traditions: Essays on the Reformation and Intellectual History, in Honor of Irena Backus,* edited by Maria-Cristina Pitassi and Daniela Solfaroli Camillocci, 15–31 (Leiden: Brill, 2018), 17.

[34] See 204–10.

[35] "Ceux de Baugency furent plus tardifs pour un temps, mais peu à peu s'esvertuans comme les autres, cuida advenir schisme entr'eux par le moyen d'un nommé Jean Bonneau, natif du lieu, homme de bien au demeurant et de sçavoir, mais ayant pour lors une opinion qu'il n'estoit loisible aux magistrats de punir les heretiques, ce qui fut aussi tost recue par trois personnes estans d'un esprit par trop fretillant." *Hist. eccl.* 1:191; see also Benedict and Fornerod, "Conflict and Dissidence," 21–22.

local consistory convinced Bonneau to abandon this belief. They found the other three to be less tractable (although the *Ecclesiastical History* reports that these too eventually renounced their former views).[36] Among the French humanists, François Bauduin commended Castellio's anti-Calvinist writings on persecution.[37]

Castellio's influence on the question of religious persecution was also significant among the communities of Dutch and Italian religious refugees. His Dutch associates had much experience with the Anabaptists, and many of the Italians had fled persecution by the Inquisition in Italy. Several of the latter would go on to embrace antitrinitarian doctrine and were therefore under almost constant threat of persecution, even in exile.

Castellio became associated with the underground Anabaptist leader David Joris, who had adopted the pseudonym Johann van Brugge after moving from Antwerp to Basel. Joris's deceit allowed him to escape the notice of Basel's authorities, who would not have admitted him had they known his true identity.[38] As we have seen, Joris wrote to the Swiss in favor of "the good and pious Servetus," and he may have been the pseudonymous author George Kleinberg in *Concerning Heretics*.[39] Joris's own (later estranged) son-in-law, Nicolaas Blesdijk, remained a lifelong correspondent of Castellio and fellow critic of the persecutions of Anabaptists, despite the fact that he himself left the Anabaptist community and became a Reformed pastor at Freinsheim in the Palatinate.[40] He and Castellio corresponded about the wisdom of holding

---

[36] "Bonneau quitta volontairement et sur le champ son opinion, protestant qu'il estoit entierement satisfait et souscrivant de sa main le contraire de ce qu'il avoit maintenu, fut peu après envoié au ministere en Bretagne par ceux d'Orleans. Quant aux trois autres, ils se monstrerent plus difficiles et toutesfois finalement se rengerent, après avoir conferé particulierement avec les ministres." *Hist. eccl.* 1:191.

[37] See 231.

[38] Joris had been a Dutch Anabaptist leader in the 1530s and 1540s. He tried to reconcile the more militant Anabaptist remnant from Münster with the peaceful Melchiorites, with whom his own affinities lay. His theology was deeply spiritual and emphasized spiritual rebirth, humility, and obedience to the Holy Spirit. There is too little evidence to say whether Joris's religious thought had any influence on Castellio's, or vice versa. Gary K. Waite, *David Joris and Dutch Anabaptism, 1524–1543* (Waterloo, ON: Wilfrid Laurier University Press, 1990), 182. On Joris's early career and time in Basel, see ibid., esp. ch. 10; Buisson, 2:133–65.

[39] See 149–50, 153 n.62.

[40] On Blesdijk (often spelled "Blesdyck"), see S. Zijlstra, *Nicolaas Meyndertsz. van Blesdijk: Een Bijdrage tot de Geschiedenis van het Davidjorisme*, Van Gorcum's Historische Bibliotheek 99 (Assen: Van Gorcum, 1983); Buisson, 2:141–51. Blesdijk had been a Mennonite before joining Joris and marrying Joris's daughter Susanna. He grew disillusioned with Joris, however, particularly over his emphasis on spiritual revelation over the Bible and his morally dissolute lifestyle—Joris had at least one lasting, adulterous affair with one of his followers. By the time of Joris's death, he and Blesdijk were completely estranged. In 1559, Blesdijk continued his assault on Joris by writing *The Life and Doctrine of the Arch-heretic David Joris*. [Nicolaas Blesdijk], *Davidis Georgii Holandi Haeresiarchae vita et doctrina, quandiu Basileae fuit: tum quid post eius mortem, cum cadavere, libris,*

debates with Anabaptists. Both deplored the violent persecutions of the sect's members,[41] but Castellio advised against publicly debating them at all,[42] while Blesdijk insisted that Christ would want him to "show the truth to both parties and refute false opinions."[43] Blesdijk was Calvin's worst nightmare: a Reformed pastor, eager to point out the faults of the Anabaptists—and thus to all appearances orthodox—but with close ties to his nemesis Castellio.

Castellio developed relationships with other scholars and ministers in the Low Countries who favored toleration as well. He addressed an early letter to the Flemish scholar and advocate of religious compromise George Cassander.[44] In addition, J. Lindeboom suggests that the pastor in the Dutch Stranger Church in London, Adrian van Haemstede, was one of Castellio's supporters.[45] Haemstede opposed all religious persecution and was accused of having "given the right hand of fellowship" to Anabaptists in London; moreover, he claimed that debates over Christology were "circumstantial" rather than "fundamental."[46]

As they had with the Dutch, Castellio's teachings on toleration resonated with Italian religious refugees. The Italians' experience with religious persecution, together with their exposure to Italian humanism, led many of them to support Castellio's ideas. Among the first Italians to come into contact with Castellio was one who nearly ruined him at the end of his life: Bernardino

---

ac reliqua eius familia actum sit. Per Rectorem et Academicam Basilien. in gratiam Amplissimi Senatus eius urbis conscripta (Wittenberg [Basel]: Haeredes Georgii Rhauu [Hieronymus Curio], 1559).

[41] "Quod istic sic passim saevitur in Anabaptistas doleo et persequutoribus sanam mentem opto." *CO* 19:587, no. 3880, Castellio to [Blesdijk], [Basel], November 22, 1562. "Venio nunc ad Anabaptistas, quorum calamitatem tu pie deprecaris optasque eorum interfectoribus meliorem mentem. Quod certe tecum facio toto ex animo." Buisson, 2:464, no. 98, Blesdijk to Castellio, Duisberg, January 31, 1563.

[42] "Et tu, frater, cave, per Deum te quaeso, cave ne te vel imprudens ulla persequutionis societate contamines. Non ego de sententia tua loquor quam ab istis persequutionibus abhorrere mihi persuasum est: sed de eventu qui vel invito te consequitur tuas cum Anabaptistis disputationes." *CO* 19:587, no. 3880.

[43] "Quare, dum haec omnia ad hunc modum perpendo dumque, ex tuo consilio, in mea conscientia apud Deum quid veri officii sit inquiro et mecum tacitus cogito quid hic faceret Jesus Christus: utrique parti veritatem ostenderet et falsas opiniones refutaret." Buisson, 2:466, no. 98.

[44] Petrus Bertius, ed., *Illustrium et clarorum virorum epistolae selectores, superiore saeculo scriptae vel a Belgis, vel ad Belgas* (Leiden: Ludovicus Elzeverius, 1617), 1:49, no. 8, Castellio to Cassander and Gualterus, Basel, August 23, 1546. In another letter to Cassander, Castellio asks him to greet Gualterus for him. Ibid., 1:173–74, no. 35, Castellio to Cassander, Basel, April 12, 1553. We will return to Cassander in Chapter 7.

[45] J. Lindeboom, "La place de Castellion dans l'histoire de l'esprit," in *Autour de Michel Servet et de Sébastien Castellion*, edited by B. Becker, 158–80 (Haarlem: H. D. Tjeenk Willink & Zoon, 1953), 174–75. Haemstede certainly knew Giacopo Aconcio, a known associate of Castellio.

[46] On the Haemstede affair, see Patrick Collinson, *Archbishop Grindal, 1519-1583: The Struggle for a Reformed Church* (Berkeley: University of California Press, 1979), 134–40.

Ochino.[47] After fleeing the Roman Inquisition, Ochino began his sojourn in Switzerland in the good graces of the mainstream reformers. He lived peacefully in Zurich from 1554 to 1563, but as time passed, his ideas strayed increasingly from Reformed orthodoxy. He maintained his ties to Castellio, and it was Castellio's translation of Ochino's *Thirty Dialogues*[48] that put Castellio at odds with the Basel authorities. Ochino had written questionable things about the trinity, but more importantly, he seemed to support polygamy.[49] Ochino was banished from Zurich, and in Basel, Adam Bodenstein (son of Andreas Bodenstein von Karlstadt) drew up accusations against Castellio.[50] In the end, however, Castellio's death cut short the case against him.

Castellio's closest Italian ally was probably his colleague at the University of Basel—and possible contributor to *Concerning Heretics*—Celio Secundo Curione. When Curione was forced to leave the Lausanne Academy,[51] there was no love lost between him and the Calvinists there. In Basel, he and Castellio discovered a shared antipathy for those who had driven them both out of the Suisse romande. Their Calvinist enemies frequently mentioned them together; Beza, for example, believed that Curione was the author behind the pseudonymous Basil Montfort in *Concerning Heretics*.[52]

Other Italians in Castellio's network included Matteo Gribaldi, a legal scholar who had early ties to the Calvinists but later defended Servetus and tended toward antitrinitarianism himself. He was in Geneva for Servetus's execution and was a main source of information to the Baslers about the event.[53] Giacopo Aconcio (frequently Latinized as Acontius), from Trent, came to Basel in 1557 and from there went to London, where he seems to have been an intermediary between Castellio and the Dutch pastor Van Haemstede.[54]

---

[47] Castellio met Ochino while they were both in Geneva. Castellio, who knew Italian, translated into Latin Ochino's *Exposition on Paul's Epistle to the Romans*. Ochino, *Expositio Epistolae divi Pauli ad Romanos*. On Castellio's relationship with Ochino, see Buisson, 1:221–29, 2:261–64.

[48] Bernardino Ochino, *Dialogi XXX, in duos libros divisi quorum primus est de Messia, continetque dialogos XVIII; secundus est, cum de rebus variis, tum potissimum de Trinitate* (Basel: Pietro Perna, 1563).

[49] Bullinger wrote of the work to Beza, "totus liber nil aliud est quam impia perversitas." *Bèze Cor.* 4:228, no. 297, Bullinger to Beza, November 28, 1563. On the Ochino affair in Zurich, see Mark Taplin, *The Italian Reformers and the Zurich Church, c.1540–1620*, St. Andrews Studies in Reformation History (Aldershot, UK: Ashgate, 2003), 111–69.

[50] The text of his accusations is printed in Buisson, 2:483–93.

[51] See 112–13.

[52] "Tertius [author] est Secundus qui bene ac nimium cognitus est nostrae scholae. Is adversus ea quae in Decadibus rectissime scripsisti de hoc argumento refutationem proprie scripsit, Basilii Monfortii nomine, te quidem nominatim non appellato, sed ita ut inficiari non possit, quia verba tua etiam usurpat et exagitat." *Bèze Cor.* 1:129–30, no. 45, Beza to Bullinger, Lausanne, June 14, [1554]. The other two he mentions as authors are Castellio and Lelio Sozzini.

[53] Guggisberg, *Sebastian Castellio*, 74.

[54] Lindeboom, "La place de Castellion dans l'histoire de l'esprit," 174.

Aconcio wrote *Satan's Strategems (Stratagemata Satanae),*[55] a treatise in favor of religious toleration and based on Castellio's thought.[56] Mino Celsi, another exile, wrote a treatise on religious toleration that quoted extensively from Castellio's writings, as well as from those of Erasmus, Aconcio, and others.[57] And Giovanni Bernardino Bonifacio, Marchese d'Oria, may have had a hand in financing the publication of *Concerning Heretics.*[58] Bonifacio was in Basel in 1557 and served as godfather (together with Blesdijk) to Castellio's son Bonifacius.[59] In 1561, Bonifacio was in Poland and asked Castellio to join him there. He painted a picture of a tolerant paradise for Castellio: "Here you would have great, no, the *greatest* freedom for living, writing, and publishing your thoughts and opinions. No one is censor. You would have people who would respect and defend you."[60]

Castellio, of course, declined Bonifacio's invitation to Poland, but his followers there would continue to advocate for religious toleration. Most important among them were two other Italians, Lelio and Fausto Sozzini,

[55] Giacopo Aconcio, *Stratagemata Satanae libri octo* (Basel: Perna, 1565). Modern edition: *Satanae Strategematum libri octo, Ad Johannem Wolphium eiusque ad Acontium Epistulae, Epistula apologetica pro Adriano Haemstede, Epistula ad ignotum quendam de natura Christi,* edited by Walther Köhler (Munich: Ernst Reinhardt, 1927).

[56] Guggisberg, *Sebastian Castellio,* 234. This work was reprinted several times and translated into multiple languages, including English. It influenced William Chillingworth and the Great Tew Circle of anti-Calvinists in seventeenth-century Oxfordshire. Chillingworth noted, "Let the reader be pleased to peruse the seventh book of Acont. de Strat. Satanae . . . and he shall confess as much." William Chillingworth, *The Works of William Chillingworth, M.A. in Three Volumes* (Oxford: Oxford University Press, 1838), 2:38, note i. For more on Aconcio's influence in seventeenth-century England, see Giorgio Caravale, *Storia di una doppia censura: Gli* Stratagemmi di Satana *di Giacomo Aconcio nell'Europa del Seicento* (Pisa: Edizioni della Normale, 2013), part 2.

[57] See Peter G. Bietenholz, "Mino Celsi and the Toleration Controversy of the Sixteenth Century," *BHR* 34 (1972): 31–47; Mino Celsi, *In haereticis coërcendis quatenus progredi liceat, Poems, Correspondence,* edited by Pieter G. Bietenholz, Corpus reformatorum italicorum (Naples: Prismi, 1982). In this edition of Celsi's work, Bietenholz carefully notes which passages Celsi took from Castellio and others. Castellio's *De haereticis* was Celsi's most important source; Bietenholz notes, "Celsi reproduced about one fifth of the contents of Castellio's collection without significant changes. He also used, and sometimes even identified, some of Castellio's other writings." Ibid., 616.

[58] This is, however, by no means certain. Manfred Welti comments, "Qu'il ait soutenu Castellion, Oporinus et leurs collaborateurs, me paraît probable. Dans quel but et de quelle manière il l'ait fait, je ne saurais cependant le dire concrètement." "La contribution de Giovanni Bernardino Bonifacio, marquis d'Oria, à l'édition princeps du 'De Haereticis an sint persequendi,'" *Bolletino della Società di Studi Valdesi* 90, no. 125 (1969): 45–49, here, 48. On Bonifacio generally, see Buisson, 2:14–18; Aldo Bertini, "Giovanni Bernardino Bonifacio: Sein Leben und seine Beziehungen zu Basel," *Basler Zeitschrift für Geschichte und Altertumskunde* 47 (1948): 19–84.

[59] Bietenholz, *Basle and France,* 126.

[60] "Magnam, immo maximam haberes hic libertatem tua sententia arbitratuque vivendi, item scribendi, et edendi. Nemo esset censor. Haberes homines qui te diligerent et defenderent." Giovanni Bernardino Bonifacio to Castellio, Kasimierz, Poland, June 30, 1561, in Delio Cantimori, *Eretici italiani del Cinquecento: Ricerche storiche,* Biblioteca storica Sansoni (Florence: G. C. Sansoni, 1939), 267n3.

who brought antitrinitarian Socinianism to the region.[61] Like so many of Castellio's friends, Lelio Sozzini had been appalled at the execution of Servetus, and Beza thought he was the second main author of *Concerning Heretics*.[62] Sozzini's 1562 *Brief Explanation of John 1* would influence both his nephew Fausto and the antitrinitarian movement in Poland and Transylvania.[63] Castellio's works, too, were popular among the Unitarians in Hungary and Transylvania.[64]

There is no evidence that Castellio was an antitrinitarian himself, but he certainly believed that questions about the trinity were of minor importance and could never be settled. For that reason, he and his followers believed that persecution on the basis of that doctrine was unacceptable. Castellio's influence among the antitrinitarian groups, therefore, stemmed less from shared theological conviction than from a shared opinion about either persecuting authorities or Calvinist churches. Castellio's works in favor of toleration and against Calvin offered support to the persecuted, whatever their beliefs. In this way, Castellio's status as Calvin's *bête noire* made him a hero among later opponents of the Calvinists. These groups, from the Dutch Remonstrants to the Socinians and Unitarians, differed widely in their confessions of faith, but they all shared Castellio's revulsion at Calvinist orthodoxy and religious persecution, and they celebrated his insistence on freedom, reason, and toleration.

Finally, perhaps the greatest of all early modern champions of religious toleration, John Locke, was well aware of Castellio's works. Locke owned Castellio's translation of the Bible, his *Four Dialogues* (the 1613 edition), his *Defense of His Own Bible Translation*, and perhaps most importantly, *Contra Libellum Calvini*.[65] By contrast, the only work of Calvin he owned was the *Institutes*.[66] In 1693, when Locke was asked by a Dutch Remonstrant pastor

---

[61] Lelio knew Castellio from trips to Basel, and he traveled in Poland to secure letters for safe passage to Italy. Bonifacio told Castellio to consult Sozzini about a move to Poland, for "Est homo ille qui te amat, et probe novit totam Sarmatiam." Cantimori, *Eretici italiani*, 268.

[62] See n. 52.

[63] Castellio knew Fausto Sozzini briefly, when the latter was in Basel in the winter of 1562–1563. More importantly, Castellio's works were instrumental in forging Fausto's own religious thought. Fausto was chiefly behind the publication of several of Castellio's manuscripts in the *Four Dialogues* of 1578. Buisson, 2:313–19. The dialogue "De fide" from this work was also later translated into Polish. See Janusz Tazbir, "Les échos de la persécution des hérétiques occidentaux dans les polémiques religieuses en Pologne," *BHR* 34 (1972): 125–36, here, 129. Fausto also wrote a prefatory letter to the edition in which he called himself Castellio's spiritual successor. Guggisberg, *Sebastian Castellio*, 236.

[64] Guggisberg, *Sebastian Castellio*, 245–46.

[65] John Harrison and Peter Laslett, *The Library of John Locke*, 2nd ed. (Oxford: Clarendon Press, [1965] 1971), 102, nos. 618–23.

[66] Harrison and Laslett, *The Library of John Locke*, 99, nos. 570–71 (the 1585 and 1654 editions of the *Institutes*).

whether there would be a market in England for a new edition of Castellio's Bible,[67] Locke replied:

> I am very glad that an edition such as you describe of Castellio's Bible is designed in your country, and do not doubt that the work will be welcome and acceptable to the *literati* here. . . . I shall consult others as opportunity offers, though it is hard to believe that a choice edition of so choice a translation, furnished in addition with notes and other writings relating thereto by so learned a man, will not be approved by all.[68]

"So choice a translation . . . by so learned a man." Clearly Locke knew Castellio's work. How many of his own ideas on religious toleration were taken from Castellio is impossible to say, but over a century after Castellio's death, his long shadow yielded to the *lumières* of a new age.

6.3.2. Predestination and Free Will

Jerome Bolsec's criticisms of Calvin's teaching on predestination kicked off a long debate within Reformed circles. As noted in the previous chapter, Castellio himself soon became involved in the larger quarrel and embraced a view that went so far as to embrace universal election.[69] Castellio's associates across Europe continued for years to criticize the Calvinian doctrine, a clash

---

[67] "Verum literis quibusdam meis (an illis quae interciderunt dubito) mentionem feci novae editionis Bibliorum Castellionis, quam hic quidam bibliopolae meditantur. Characterem mihi ostenderunt eximium; omnes notas adjicere, quin et defensionem suarum translationum, nec non descriptionem Reip. Judaicae ex Josepho concinnatam subjicere ad operis calcem, decreverunt; ut ita omnia quae Castellio in Scripturam commentatus est, hoc in volumine conjuncta prodeant. Rogarunt me, ut praefationem addam: quod non abnui. Antequam vero opus, quod sine magnis sumptibus perfici nequit, aggrediantur, per te doceri cupiunt, an existimes hoc opus in Anglia gratum fore, et emptores reperturum. Nam in ejusmodi operum editione solent bibliopolae nostrates vel maxime Angliam respicere." John Locke, *The Correspondence of John Locke*, edited by E. S. de Beer (Oxford: Clarendon Press, 1976–), 4:704, no. 1646, Philippus van Limborch to Locke, Amsterdam, July 25/ August 4, 1693.

[68] "Bibliorum Castellionis editionem qualem tu narras apud vos designari valde laetor et viris literatis apud nos gratum acceptumque fore opus non dubito. Post diuturnam rusticationem nuperus meus in urbem reditus nondum mihi concessit plurimorum doctorum colloquia, prout datur occasio alios consulam, quamvis vix credi potest Elegantem editionem tam elegantis versionis notis etiam aliisque scriptis eo spectantibus tam docti viri ornatum non omnibus non placituram." Locke, *Correspondence of John Locke*, 4:744, no. 1671, Locke to Van Limborch, [London], November 10, 1693. English translation from ibid. 4:744.

[69] See 168–73.

that culminated in the debates between the Remonstrants and Counter-Remonstrants in the Netherlands.

Within the French-speaking churches, the embrace of Calvin's doctrine of predestination was far from universal. We have already seen the opposition to it in the Pays de Vaud from Bolsec's allies and even otherwise good Calvinists, such as François de Saint-Paul. In Montbéliard, Pierre Toussain and most of the pastors in the region likewise opposed double predestination.[70] And Philippe Denis notes that among the many francophone refugee churches in the Rhineland, only in Strasbourg and the Val de Liepvre did the Calvinian doctrine take hold.[71] In the refugee church in Frankfurt in 1556, Calvin himself debated the subject with one of Castellio's Dutch associates, the "erudite but rambling prophet" from The Hague, Justus Velsius Haganus.[72] Velsius exchanged a number of letters with Castellio, and in his debate with Calvin, contended that "either there is free will, or God is a tyrant." After the debate, Calvin wrote to Melanchthon that Velsius was insane.[73]

In France itself, some of the anti-Calvinists of the Vaud had moved to the kingdom and continued to oppose their old enemies there. In 1555, Sebastien Foncelet had allied with Zébédée against Calvin.[74] Nine years later, he was in France, with powerful friends and a penchant for Castellio's thought. At the provincial synod of Ferté-sous-Jouarre, he was condemned "as an Anabaptist and Castellionist." The synod also determined to report his case to the Prince de Porcien, at the time Antoine III de Croÿ, a powerful Protestant nobleman.[75] Further south, in Bergerac, a pastor named Pierre Villeroche ran afoul of his old Calvinist friends due to his association with Castellio. Calvin himself had sent Villeroche to Antoine de Bourbon, king of Navarre and husband of Jeanne d'Albret, to represent the interests of French

---

[70] See Viénot, 1:195–99.

[71] Denis, Les églises d'étrangers en pays rhénans, 573.

[72] On Velsius, see Hans de Waardt, "Justus Velsius Haganus: An Erudite but Rambling Prophet," in Exile and Religious Identity, 1500–1800, edited by Jesse Spohnholz and Gary K. Waite (London: Pickering and Chatto, 2014), 97–109.

[73] "Quasi vero parum mihi esset in hac re negotii, insanus quidam Velsius, ad quem bis scripsisti, novis tricis nos implicuit." CO 16:281, no. 2531, Calvin to Melanchthon, Frankfurt, September 17, 1556; see also Waardt, "Justus Velsius Haganus," 103.

[74] See 131–32.

[75] "Quand à Samuel Le Febvre ou Sebastien Foncelet: sera declaré aux eglises à ce qu'on s'en donne garde comme d'un anabaptiste et castalioniste, et qu'on priera monseigneur de Bouillon escripre à monsieur de La Lande, où ledict Foncelet est, de s'en donner garde et le rejecter; et en semblable sera prié monseigneur le prince de Portian." Philippe Denis and Jean Rott, Jean Morély (ca. 1524–ca. 1594) et l'utopie d'une démocratie dans l'église, THR 278 (Geneva: Droz, 1993), 272. The identity of M. Lalande is unclear. On the Prince of Porcien, see Jules Delaborde, "Antoine de Croÿ, prince de Porcien," BSHPF 18 (1869): 2–26, 124–37, 513–29.

Protestants.[76] At some point, however, perhaps after a trip to Basel, he seems to have come under Castellio's influence. In 1559 or 1560, he sent Castellio a treatise he had written. Castellio's reply indicates that he knew and respected Villeroche,[77] even though Villeroche seems to have been critical of some of Castellio's positions. In 1561, Beza sent the church of Bergerac a letter against Villeroche. The letter is lost,[78] but Beza and Calvin insisted that Villeroche be deposed from the ministry, and eventually he was. The conflict seems to have arisen primarily from a scandal involving Villeroche's engagement to a rich woman, as well as from Villeroche's complaints that Calvin had written too harshly against Castellio.[79] But Villeroche's association with Castellio, together with a letter he wrote to Calvin, suggest that he may have been critical of Calvin's doctrine of predestination as well. His letter to Calvin acknowledges his previous faults in an attempt to return to the good graces of the Genevan reformer. In it he writes,

See, I report everything, practicing what I learned before about the doctrine of providence, by which the good heavenly Father and very admirable creator has been accustomed to convert evil into good for his elect and beloved children. I am certain he has placed me in their number before the creation of the world and will never take that away from me.[80]

[76] See Buisson, 2:452n2; CO 17:136–37, no. 2851, Villeroche to Calvin, Nérac, April 13, 1557.

[77] "Quod ad istum de Villeroche attinet, cuius tu scriptum mihi misisti, equidem partim memini eorum quae narrat, sed magnam partem oblivioni tradidi. Verum merae mentis et sententiae (contra quam certe non sum loquutus: amo enim veritatem) memini." Buisson, 2:452, no. 84, Castellio to Gaspar Herwagen, [Basel], February 26, 1560.

[78] Beza's letter is referred to here: "aussi nous traitasmes de l'afaire de Villeroche mais pour deux raisons nous rendimes sa cause en suspens jusques au prochain synode. La premiere qui babila et mena si bien sa cause qu'on luy donna quasi gaigné, l'autre que nous estions incertains de la verité du fait. Vray est qu'on nous monstra bien quelques lettres de Mr. de Beze, mais nous n'osions asoir jugement sur ycelles pour sa deposition." CO 18:586–87, no. 3464, Lucas Hobé to Colladon, Sainte-Foy-la-Grand, August 1, 1561.

[79] "ac me dixisse Calvinum ea in me scripsisse quorum vel scortum pudere deberet, cum quidem ipse de Villeroche mihi respondit, illa a doctis non probari. Nisi me fallit memoria, sic locuti sumus." Buisson, 2:453, no. 84, and Rotterdam Library, Remonstrants ms. 505, 22ʳ. See also Robert Kingdon, Geneva and the Coming of the Wars of Religion in France, 1555–1563, reprint edition, Cahiers d'Humanisme et Renaissance 82 (Geneva: Droz, [1956] 2007), 44; Benedict and Fornerod, "Conflict and Dissidence," 23 and n. 18.

[80] "Voilà où je rapporte le tout, pratiquant ce que par cydevant j'ay apprins de la doctrine de la providence par laquelle ce bon pere celeste et tres admirable ouvrier a accoustumé de convertir le mal en bien à ses esleus et bienaimés enfans, du nombre desquels je suis certain qu'il m'a mis devant la fondation du monde et que jamais il ne m'en ostera." CO 20:480, no. 4204, Villeroche to Calvin, Bergerac, September 19 [after 1561].

The statement has the tone of a repentant sinner trying to pass a test to show that he really has changed his ways. Furthermore, the allegation of following Castellio's doctrine of predestination seems to explain better than the questionable engagement the vehemence with which Beza and Calvin insisted on Villeroche's removal from the ministry.

Perhaps the most sensational controversy in France over predestination took place in Lyon and involved Calvin's friend Pierre Viret, on the one hand, and Castellio's good friend Jean Bauhin and Bauhin's son of the same name, on the other. Bauhin *père* and Castellio had become friends soon after the latter's arrival in Basel, and they remained close until Castellio's death. Bauhin was a native of Amiens who practiced medicine in Paris, possibly as a physician to Marguerite of Navarre.[81] He fled Paris for fear of religious persecution and went to Antwerp, where he met David Joris; Bauhin was probably responsible for introducing Castellio to the Anabaptist leader in Basel. Many letters addressed to Castellio ask him to greet Bauhin; Falais addressed a letter to the two of them.[82] In his will, Castellio named Bauhin guardian of his children.[83] Bauhin regularly traveled between Basel and Lyon and perhaps served as a liaison between Castellio and his group of followers there, whom we will meet shortly.[84]

In spring 1565, little more than a year after Castellio's death in December 1563, both Bauhins were in Lyon.[85] The son wanted his marriage to Denise Bornard approved and publicly announced in the Reformed church there.[86] The Lyon pastors, including Viret, were reluctant to do so since they knew

---

[81] Haag², 1:1017.

[82] Philippe Denis identified the anonymous author of this letter as Falais and printed the entire letter, of which Buisson included only an excerpt (Buisson, 2:428–29, no. 57). Denis, *Les églises d'étrangers en pays rhénans*, 644–45.

[83] "Premièrement donque j'ordonne pour tuteurs de ma femme et de mes enfans M. Jehan Bauhin médecin, M. Jehan Brandmiller predicant, les priant d'en prendre la charge, e par l'amitié que nous nous portons en Christ espérant qu'ils le feront." Buisson published the entire will, dated initially December 4, 1560 and reaffirmed on November 1, 1563. Buisson, 2:271–72; here, 271. "Jehan Brandmiller predicant" was probably Johannes Brandmüller, a German preacher who had studied in Tübingen before matriculating at the University of Basel in 1551. He later became known for his published sermon collections. See Amy Nelson Burnett, *Teaching the Reformation: Ministers and Their Message in Basel, 1529–1629*, Oxford Studies in Historical Theology (New York: Oxford University Press, 2006), 176–79.

[84] See 202–203.

[85] The son, at least, was there before October 3, 1564, on which date, his friend Conrad Gessner addressed a letter to him in Lyon. Ironically, Gessner commended to him Pierre Viret, who was in the city at that time. Conrad Gessner, *Vingt lettres à Jean Bauhin fils, 1563–1565*, edited by Claude Longeon (Saint-Etienne: Université de Saint-Etienne, 1976), 27. The sources for much of the conflict described are found in *Epistolae Vireti*, 445–59, nos. 151–53.

[86] "filius matrimonium suum a nobis comprobari et pro ecclesiae more publice enuntiari cuperet." *Epistolae Vireti*, 447–48, no. 151, Viret and Jean-François Salvard to Bullinger, Lyon, April 21, 1565.

Bauhin *père* to be Castellio's friend and "avowed disciple."[87] Thus, the pastors summoned father and son to the consistory and questioned them about their beliefs, "and especially those in which Castellio departs from the true doctrine accepted everywhere in the purer churches," in particular predestination.[88] The chief problem for the Lyon pastors was that the Bauhins subscribed to Castellio's doctrine of universal election.[89] After the pastors tried to refute them, Bauhin *père* left the city, but the son returned to the pastors in a second attempt to have his marriage recognized. In Castellian fashion, he argued that he should not be punished "when among all who profess the Gospel, there is no agreement on this question."[90] After being rebuked yet again by the pastors, Bauhin *fils* cried out that there were other churches he could go to that were not so peevish (*non tam morosas*).[91] The Bauhin affair soon involved the churches of Geneva and Zurich, for Viret sent their confession of faith to Beza in Geneva, and the Bauhins cited Melanchthon and the Zurich pastors Bullinger and Rudolf Gwalther as supporters of their doctrine. Bullinger and Gwalther rejected the Bauhins' attempts to enlist their support,[92] and Gwalther approved of the extra diligence taken by the Lyon pastors in their dealings with followers of Castellio.[93]

It is not entirely clear what Bauhin *fils* decided to do about his marriage. Probably, he made good on his promise to find another church "not so peevish" as that in Lyon to bless his union. Nevertheless, the episode illustrates how contentious the debate over predestination continued to be even after the deaths of Castellio and Calvin.

---

[87] "valde esset suspecta apud omnes bonos eorum doctrina et pietas (quod pater ex intimis semper fuisset Castellionis amicis et illius quasi iuratus discipulus)." *Epistolae Vireti*, 448, no. 151.

[88] "requirunt fratres ut suam illi sententiam (in iis praecipue in quibus Castellio a vera et passim in ecclesiis magis puris recepta doctrina dissentiebat) clare et dilucide explicent. Ac inter caetera de praedestinatione Dei, idest de aeterna tum piorum electione ad vitam tum impiorum reiectione ad mortem, quaestionem proponunt." *Epistolae Vireti*, 448, no. 151.

[89] "Tum illi suam illam universalem electionem (qua omnes promiscue ad salutem electos esse a Deo affirmant)." *Epistolae Vireti*, 449, no. 151.

[90] "Id vero non existimare sibi praeiudicium afferre debere, quo minus in ecclesia recipiatur et nuptiae publice celebrentur, quandoquidem apud omnes qui Evangelium profitentur de hac quaestione non conveniat." *Epistolae Vireti*, 450, no. 151.

[91] "Hic ille inflatos suos spiritus amplius non potuit cohibere, et suam hypochrisim satis detexerit. Esse alias ecclesias (inquit) non tam morosas ad quas confugiat, siquidem nos tam sanctum opus hic prohibemus." *Epistolae Vireti*, 450, no. 151.

[92] See *Epistolae Vireti*, 456–59, no. 153, Gwalther to Viret and Salvard, Zurich, May 17, 1565; *Bèze Cor.* 6:84, no. 394, Bullinger to Beza, May 17, 1565.

[93] "Nec immerito diligentius examinandi sunt qui sub praeceptore Castellione profecerunt, quem Anabapsticorum furorum et aliorum quolibet dogmatum absurdissimorum portenta fovisse et astutia singulari hinc inde sparsisse constat." *Epistolae Vireti*, 458, no. 153.

Castellio's influence among the Dutch only increased after his death as well, particularly on the question of predestination. The great Dutch free thinker Dirck Volkertszoon Coornhert—another enemy of Calvin— found Castellio's writings and translated some of them into Dutch.[94] But it was especially in the early seventeenth-century theological conflicts be- tween the Remonstrants (Arminians) and Counter-Remonstrants (or- thodox Calvinists) that Castellio's works saw a major revival. It was then that Castellio's *Contra Libellum Calvini* (1612) was first published, as well as an ex- panded edition of the *Four Dialogues* (1613), which included for the first time his anti-predestinarian *Annotations on Romans 9*. Moreover, the first edition of Castellio's collected works translated into Dutch was published in Haarlem in 1613.[95] Because of his opposition to the Calvinian teaching of predestina- tion and his advocacy of religious toleration, Castellio became a hero of the Remonstrant cause. Further, Earl Morse Wilbur notes, "Castellio was thus, after his death, the inspiration and effective source of the liberal develop- ment in Holland."[96] Although the Remonstrant cause was officially defeated in 1619 at the Synod of Dordrecht (or Dort), Castellio and the Remonstrants arguably had greater lasting influence in the Netherlands, which in the long run preferred Castellio's tolerant ideas to Calvinist orthodoxy.

6.3.3. Piety and Discipline

Castellio's emphasis on personal piety likewise found wide support among his associates across Europe. As noted in the previous chapter, his French translation of the *German Theology* may well have been instrumental in spreading his pietistic ideas to followers in underground religious commu- nities.[97] Certainly, Calvin found it a threat. In 1559, Calvin complained to

---

[94] Guggisberg, *Sebastian Castellio*, 241. Indeed, most of Castellio's works were eventually trans- lated into Dutch; even some of Castellio's own translations were translated once again into Dutch. The Dutch translation of Castellio's new Latin translation of the *Imitation of Christ*, for example, appears to have been quite popular, suggesting that his emphasis on individual devotional piety de- void of "papist superstitions" struck a chord among the people of Erasmus's native land. Guggisberg, *Sebastian Castellio*, 239. On Coornhert, see Gerrit Voogt, *Constraint on Trial: Dirck Volckertsz Coornhert and Religious Freedom*, Sixteenth Century Essays and Studies 52 (Kirksville, MO: Truman State University Press, 2000). Coornhert was the target of Calvin's *Response à un certain holandois, lequel sous ombre de faire les chrestiens tout spirituels, leur permet de polluer leurs corps en toutes idol- atries* (1562), in COR, ser. 4, vol. 1.

[95] *Opera Sebastiani Castellionis . . .* (Haarlem: Vincent Casteleyn and David Wachtendonck, 1613).

[96] Earl Morse Wilbur, *A History of Unitarianism*, 2 vols. (Boston: Beacon Press, 1945), 1:208.

[97] See 176–77.

the French church in Frankfurt that someone had introduced the translation there, which he described as containing "pleasantries forged by Satan's cunning for muddling up the simplicity of the Gospel. But if you look closer, you will find a venom hidden there that is so mortal that to support them is to poison the Church."[98]

The individual most likely responsible for circulating the book in the city was Castellio's friend François Perrussel.[99] Perrussel (spelled variously Perrucel, Perucel, or Peroucelle, and also known as De la Rivère) had been a Cordelier in Paris before embracing evangelicalism. His decision to remain in France and hide his true beliefs would have made him a Nicodemite in Calvin's eyes. He was a bachelor in theology and a master of novices when he came under suspicion by the Sorbonne in 1545. When he refused to make a public retraction of his views, he was expelled from the Faculty, and he left France the following year. Perrussel's first stop was Basel, where he met Castellio, and the two would correspond for many years. He then went to London, where he served as one of the first pastors of the French Church there. Jean Morély may have attended the church at the time; Morély would later clash with the Calvinists and would claim Perrussel as one of his supporters.[100] With Mary's accession to the throne of England, Perrussel fled with his flock to Wesel, whence he wrote friendly letters to both Calvin and Castellio. He asked Castellio for a copy of his French translation of the Bible and passed on the greetings of "many other brothers living here who do not know you personally but to whom you are known by name."[101] In 1557, Perrussel moved to Frankfurt, where he introduced Castellio's ideas and probably his *German Theology* to his congregants.

At the time Calvin wrote to the Frankfurt church to condemn the book, Perrussel was in the midst of a clash with his colleague Guillaume Houbraque.

---

[98] "Ce pendant je ne juge point de la cause, sinon d'autant qu'on parle de quelques livrets qu'on a voulu introduire ou bien qu'on a voulu approver, à sçavoir la *Théologie Germanique, et de l'homme nouveau*. Quant à cela si jamais j'ay rien cogneu ou gousté en la parolle de Dieu, je voudroye bien que les autheurs s'en fussent abstenus. Car encores qu'il n'y ait point d'erreurs notables, ce sont badinages forgez par l'astuce de Satan pour embrouiller toute la simplicité de l'Evangile. Mais si vous y regardez de plus pres, vous trouverez qu'il y a du venin caché si mortel que de les avancer, c'est empoisonner l'Eglise." *CO* 17:441–42, no. 3011, Calvin to the French Church of Frankfurt, Geneva, February 23, 1559.

[99] On Perrussel, see Haag, 8:262; Denis, *Les églises d'étrangers en pays rhénans, passim*.

[100] See 281–82.

[101] "Si la Bible en français de votre version estoit imprimée in-4, je désireroie que la m'envoiissiez par la voie de Francfort. . . . Ma femme [Buisson: *Mon père*] vous salue de bon cueur avec moy et maintz aultres freres vivans ycy qui n'ont point veue vostre face, mais leur estes cogneu de nom." Buisson, 2:424, no. 50, Perrussel to Castellio, Wesel, August 16, 1555, with correction from Bruening, "Castellio Correspondence Project."

Houbraque was generally a devoted Calvinist, whose 1547 examination in Lausanne had been the occasion of the dispute between Zébédée and Viret.[102] The conflict in Frankfurt started over the election of the church's elders, but it soon turned on the subject of ecclesiastical discipline, which also pitted Calvin's followers against those of Castellio. Both encouraged morality and piety, but while Castellio's ideas emphasized a voluntary, internal life of Christian piety, Calvin's insisted on the external enforcement of both moral behavior and doctrine. The Castellionists found the Calvinists' enforcement of doctrine by consistorial discipline to be a milder form of the religious persecution they had inflicted on Servetus. This struggle over discipline became a new front in the war between the Calvinists and their opponents. Increasingly, the anti-Calvinists saw this issue as part of Calvin's and Geneva's campaign to dominate francophone Protestant churches everywhere.[103]

In Frankfurt, Houbraque, who was attempting to impose Calvinist disciplinary measures, accused Perrussel of administering communion to unworthy communicants and refused to administer it himself to anyone as long as the divisions remained in the church. Perrussel, by contrast, continued to celebrate the sacrament every month. The case thus echoes that of the Calvinist pastors of Montbéliard who refused to administer the Eucharist to unworthy communicants.[104] Perrussel believed that the Calvinists' ideas about discipline sowed discord in the church and helped to construct a new "papism."[105]

The campaign in support of internal piety and against Calvinist discipline was being waged in France by other Castellio supporters, notably a number of his family members. Another of his brothers-in-law, Mathieu Eyssautier, was a pastor in Provence when he was censured by the synod of Lourmarin.[106] The complaint against him was that he was too lax in his discipline and had administered the Lord's Supper to individuals who had not been sufficiently catechized. Moreover, he was accused of saying that

---

[102] See 118–19. On his conflict with Perrussel in Frankfurt, see Denis, *Les églises d'étrangers en pays rhénans*, 362–69. We will see in the next chapter, however, that he had some association with and sympathy for the ideas of Jean Morély.

[103] See the objections to the Calvinists' consistories later by Charles Du Moulin (248–50) and Morély (278–79).

[104] See 185–86.

[105] Denis, *Les églises d'étrangers en pays rhénans*, 369.

[106] See Benedict and Fornerod, "Conflict and Dissidence," 27. Eyssautier was the husband of Castellio's third sister, Jeanne. Guggisberg, *Sebastian Castellio*, 162.

Christians should not go to the magistrate to punish sedition. To the pastors, this claim seemed to come "straight from Castellio's boutique."[107] Eyssautier left Provence and returned to the environs of Geneva, taking up the ministry in Saconnex, just outside the city in the Pays de Gex. While there, he was summoned to the Geneva consistory to answer the charges made by the churches of Provence.[108] The consistory also asked him why he had gone to France without a proper attestation. His reply: "If it were necessary for each one to take a letter from this city, that would turn Geneva into Rome, where one must kiss the slipper."[109]

Eyssautier gave as little deference to the Genevan consistory as he gave to Rome, and thus was soon summoned again, this time with the goal of making him confess that Castellio was a heretic. He refused, and the consistory excommunicated him.[110] A year later, Eyssautier was summoned to the Geneva consistory yet again, this time in connection with the publication of Castellio's *Conseil à la France désolée*. The consistory also complained that he was preaching to the people of Lancy, which was under Geneva's jurisdiction, even though in the Genevans' eyes he was excommunicate.[111] Eyssautier's case exposes a key weakness in the Calvinists' ability to enforce discipline, namely that outside Geneva, enforcement was dependent on the willingness

---

[107] "Nous avons pres et au milieu de nous ung personnaige lequel bien cognoissés, appellé Matthieu Yssautier, beau frere du venerable Castalio, lequel apres avoir (esté) à la Synode censuré de plusieurs trop lourdes faultes, tant s'en fault qu'il monstre quelque amendement, que plustost semble vouloir comme par despit empirer. Les dictes faultes furent telles: asçavoyr d'avoyr administré la S. Cene à deux personnes privéement jamais au paravant receues en aucune Eglise, cela sans assemblée quelconque: D'avoyr derechef administré la Cene à toute son Eglise qui est de trois ou quatre cens personnes (Dieu sçait quelle rudesse il y a selon le pais) sans les avoyr catechisez que pour l'espace de deux jours seulement. . . . D'avoyr tenu propos au frere ministre de Lormarin . . . que les Chrestiens ne doibvent recourir au magistrat pour la punition des seditieux, propos qu'a semblé audict remonstrant estre yssu de la Bottique Castallienne." *CO* 19: 534–35, no. 3854, Ministers of the Churches of Provence to the Ministers of Geneva, Lourmarin, September 20, 1562.

[108] Sacconex was in the contested *terres de St.-Victor et Chapitre*. Officially under the high jurisdiction of the Bernese, Basel's arbitration sentence of 1544 gave the Genevans most lower-level rights in the area, including over religious affairs.

[109] "Confesse bien avoir dict qu'il seroit faict de Geneve ung Romme au cas qu'il faillust que chascung vinst prendre lettre d'attestation en ceste cité, et mesmes comme baiser la pantoffle." Quoted in Benedict and Fornerod, "Conflict and Dissidence," 28n31.

[110] Benedict and Fornerod, "Conflict and Dissidence," 28.

[111] "Ledit Michel Chastillon le confesse, et qu'ilz luy ont esté envoyés par son cousin Ph. Chapuis, imprimeur, demourant à Basle; et sont intitulés: *la Consolation de la France désolée*, composée par Sebastien Castalleo son oncle demourant à Basle. Interrogué pourquoy il en fyt venyr deux, respond: l'un pour luy, et l'autre pour son oncle M. Mathieu Exsautier, qui luy en avoit donné charge. . . . L'advis est de . . . avertir dudit Essautier, qui est excommunié et toutes foys il presche et administre à ceulx qui sont habitans à Lancy subjects de ceste ville ainsi que l'on a rapporté." Cited in Buisson, 2:225n1. A new critical edition of the *Conseil* has recently been published: Sebastian Castellio, *Conseil à la France désolée*, edited by Florence Alazard et al., Textes Littéraires Français (Geneva: Droz, 2017).

of the local church to do Geneva's bidding. In many cases, the churches were disinclined to cooperate.

Perhaps no place in France had a greater concentration of Castellionists intent on living a life of internal piety, separate from the local Calvinist church, than Lyon.[112] Indeed, Droz suggests that Castellio's followers effectively created a clandestine church in the city.[113] The origins of this community lay among Castellio's family. His brother Michel Chastillon was a printer in Lyon who was arrested for publishing a now-lost work against Calvin's doctrine of predestination.[114] Castellio denied that he had written it, and Calvin was unsure of its authorship as well but wrote a short treatise against the text and its Castellionist assertion that God created everyone for salvation.[115] Droz believes that Chastillon was also the printer of the French translation of *Concerning Heretics*.[116] Chastillon died in 1558, but his widow, Marie Françoise Roybet, continued to associate with the Lyon printing community (indeed, she eventually remarried another printer) and with Castellio's friends and followers there. She also corresponded with Castellio himself.[117] She and Castellio knew Guillaume Constantin, who may have been Marie's cousin and who Droz suggests was the leader of the clandestine congregation of Castellionists in Lyon.[118] In 1557, Constantin wrote Castellio to ask for a confession of faith, and Castellio obliged, sending a lengthy letter summarizing his beliefs and defending himself against his accusers.[119]

Other individuals associated with the group in Lyon appear in Castellio's correspondence. In 1561, Thomas Lafarge, a former student in Basel, wrote

[112] See Droz, "Castellioniana," esp. section 3: "Castellionistes et Calvinistes lyonnais," 373–97.

[113] Droz, "Castellioniana," 376.

[114] Guggisberg, *Sebastian Castellio*, 138. See Beza's report to Farel on Chastillon's arrest, as well as news that Chastillon planned to publish an edition of Servetus with Castellio's notes: "Castalionis frater Lugduni interceptus est et in carcerem coniectus cum impurissimo fratris libello de praedestinatione, quem ibi exuderat. Aiunt ipsi fuisse in animo Servetum etiam recudere cum fratris scholiis adiunctis." *Bèze Cor.* 2:83, no. 102, Beza to Farel, Lausanne, August 2, [1557].

[115] See *Bèze Cor.* 2:84, n. 8. Calvin's response, entitled *Response à certaines calomnies et blasphemes, dont quelques malins s'efforcent de rendre la doctrine de la predestination de dieu odieuse*, is in *CO* 58:199–206. On Calvin's uncertainty: "En premier lieu, celui qui a composé l'escrit, soit Sebastian Chastillon, ou quelque semblable, pour monstrer que Dieu a créé tout le monde pour estre sauvé, allègue qu'il tasche de réduire à soy tout ce qui est esgaré." *CO* 58:199.

[116] Droz, "Castellioniana," 372.

[117] On Roybet, see Guggisberg, *Sebastian Castellio*, 163–64; Droz, "Castellioniana," 356–84, *passim*. Roybet's surviving letter to Castellio is in ibid., 358–59, and in excerpt in Buisson, 2:434–35.

[118] Droz, "Castellioniana," 375–76.

[119] Buisson, 2: 431–34, no. 61, Castellio to [Guillaume Constantin], [Basel], December 1557.

to Castellio from Lyon, regretting that he had not written earlier and had consequently missed out on Castellio's "Christian instruction."[120] Droz has identified a certain "Master Jean" who appears in some of the letters as the printer Jean de Tournes.[121] In 1557, Constantin complained to Castellio about Jean's defection; apparently, de Tournes had given in to the demands of the Calvinists and abandoned his devotion to Castellio.[122] Castellio sent de Tournes a letter (now lost), chastising him for following the crowd instead of his own convictions. A repentant de Tournes responded, thanking him for his correction and apologizing for his weakness.[123] As a printer, De Tournes would end up causing no end of trouble for the Calvinists: It was he who published Jean Morély's controversial *Treatise on Christian Discipline and Polity*.[124]

Throughout this section, we have seen how far Castellio's influence extended beyond the Suisse romande and Montbéliard. Followers in France, the Netherlands, Eastern Europe, and refugee churches all admired him and took inspiration from one or more of his central ideas. To conclude this chapter, however, we shall examine the case of one little-known French associate of Castellio, Jean Saint-Vertunien de Lavau. Lavau embraced nearly all of Castellio's ideas. And when he sought to introduce them in Poitiers, he unwittingly changed the course of the French Reformation.

---

[120] "Monsieur, j'ai différé jusques astheure [read: à cette heure] de vous escrire, et ce à mon grand desadvantage seullement, car se plustost je vous eusse escrit plustost aussi eussiés contenté mon esprit par quelque vostre lettre pleine de chrestienne instruction." He also recalls visits he had made in Basel with Castellio, as well as with Bauhin and Blesdijk: "Tant je m'asseure bien de vostre privauté envers moi, de laquelle me donnastes un assés certain tesmoignage par de là, tant en vostre maison qu'avec Messieurs Bouin et Blesdic." Buisson, 2:457, no. 91, Thomas Lafarge to Castellio, Lyon, [end of 1561].

[121] Droz, "Castellioniana," 378–84.

[122] "Quant au retretement que maître Jehan a faict, il est tout obeisang à l[e]ur volonté, bref se est [c'est] un autre heus mesme, car il a cherchié tout moen de leur complaire et a faict une confection de foy qu'[il] avoet promis de me montre[r], mais il ne l'a pas faict." Buisson, 2:431, no. 60, Guillaume Constantin to Castellio, [Lyon], [ca. August 10, 1558].

[123] "Frere et ami, nous vous remercions du soin que vous avez de nous en nous advertissant de nostre devoir si nous ne voulons estre accablez avec la multitude. . . . Il y a en moy une pusilanimité qui gaste tout, laquelle ostée il n'y auroit affexion si contraire que le Seigneur par son filz Jesus Christ ne desracinast. Mais ceste lascheté faict que je ne m'oppose pas vaillamment à l'encontre des assaults tellement que je ne me puis vanter que de la connaissance qui n'est aultre chose qu'une attente de plus grande condamnation dont le Seigneur me veuille garder en me faisant prandre la matiere à cueur." *CO* 17:297–98, no. 2937, also in Droz, "Castellioniona," 381, [Jean de Tournes ("anonymous" in *CO*)] to Castellio, [Lyon?], August 20, 1558.

[124] Jean Morély, *Traicté de la discipline et police chrestienne* (Lyon: Jean de Tournes, 1562).

6.4. The Pivotal Case of a Castellionist in France: Jean Saint-Vertunien de Lavau

In 1555, Calvin wrote a long letter to the evangelicals in Poitiers.[125] He was deeply concerned about a "savage beast," "driven by Satan," who was spreading dangerous ideas among them. This "beast" was Jean Saint-Vertunien de Lavau (or La Vau). While in Geneva, Lavau had been a supporter of Calvin, but he was also a correspondent of Servetus and later a disciple of Castellio.[126] He is listed as a suspected heretic at the very first proto-synod of the French Reformed Churches at Poitiers in 1557 and at the first national synod two years later. We know next to nothing about Lavau's personal life, education, or profession. What information we have about him comes from his opponents, but from their criticisms and accusations, we can discern the outlines of his beliefs.[127] His case is crucial for understanding the early organization of the French Reformed Churches and Calvin's strategic shift away from encouraging emigration from France and toward supporting the creation of established Reformed churches within the kingdom.[128] Lavau's role in this shift reveals that Castellio's influence was ironically, albeit indirectly, responsible in part for both the Genevan missionary venture into France and the formal organization of the French Reformed churches.

6.4.1. The Charges against Lavau

Beza's *Ecclesiastical History* explains the occasion for the first national synod in Paris in 1559: The year before, Antoine de Chandieu had been sent to Poitiers "for some affair and to give testimony about a certain individual

---

[125]   CO 15:435–46, no. 2118, Calvin to the Church of Poitiers, Geneva, February 20, 1555. See also the significant annotations on the letter in Calvin, *Oeuvres*, 1189–1198.

[126]   A letter from the bookseller Enguilbert Chapitre to Castellio verifies their common acquaintance with Lavau: "Par la présente je vous averti que ma demeurance est pour ce jourduy à Poictiers, là où est Monsieur de Lavaut. Lequel me bailla une pere de lettres pour vous faire tenir seurement, desquelles lettres me suis bien volu efforcer à ce faire pour l'amour de M. de Lavault lequelt est bien mon amy." Buisson, 2:442–43, no. 73, Lyon, November 8, 1558.

[127]   With the exception of Higman and Roussel's lengthy annotations on Calvin's letter to Poitiers (see n. 125), Reformation scholarship has largely ignored Lavau. Buisson devotes a single paragraph to him (Buisson, 2:248–49); Guggisberg does not mention him at all. Benedict and Fornerod discuss his case at greater length than Buisson but do not go into the details about his teaching as contained in Calvin's letter. Benedict and Fornerod, "Conflict and Dissidence," 20–21.

[128]   The Genevans distinguished between *églises plantées*—nascent evangelical communities in France that lacked a regular pastor—and *églises dressées*, which had a regular pastor, consistory, and worship services.

about whom those in Poitiers were having difficulty."[129] The text is vague—with the author employing a *damnatio memoriae* technique to preserve the anonymity of the enemy—but we know from other contemporary sources that the "certain individual" about whom Chandieu gave testimony was Jean Saint-Vertunien de Lavau. The "difficulty" the church was having with Lavau was that he was a follower of Castellio. According to Calvin's 1555 letter, Lavau had been circulating a letter, in which he complained about Calvin and his followers. Calvin believed the letter would "clearly show them [the evangelicals in Poitiers] that Satan drives and guides him."[130]

Earlier, Lavau had been in Geneva and, according to Calvin, he had initially been a zealous opponent of Castellio.[131] Like so many others, however, Lavau turned against Calvin. Calvin tended to blame such defections, as he does in the case of Lavau, on Satanic influence. By contrast, Calvin's letter to Poitiers reveals his conviction about his own divinely sanctioned prophetic calling. He explains to the church that he is zealous in defense of his own doctrine "because," as he writes, "I know it is from God."[132] This absolute certitude in the truth of his own teaching stands in sharp contrast to everything Castellio believed.

For Lavau, as for so many others, it was probably Servetus's execution that turned him against Calvin and toward Castellio. Lavau and Servetus had carried on an extensive correspondence.[133] It is hardly surprising, then, that Lavau soon turned to the anti-Calvinists of the Vaud; Calvin complains that "he joined all those he knew to have a bad reputation, going so far as to cross the lake to seek out a heretic who was banished from here."[134] Thus, Lavau

---

[129] "L'occasion de ceste assemblée fut, que sur la fin de l'année precedente, 1558, estant Antoine de Chandieu, envoyé par l'Eglise de Paris à l'Eglise de Poitiers pour quelque affaire, et mesme pour rendre tesmoignage de certain personnage dont ceux de Poitiers estoient en peine." *Hist. eccl.*, 1:199.

[130] "Combien que ce pauvre homme, La Vau, naict que sa folle gloire, qui luy esblouit les yeux, sans qu'il sente le mal et dommage qu'il faict, toutefois en bien poisant une certaine letre qu'il a escrite par delà, vouz verrez clairement que Satan la poulse et conduit." *CO* 15:437, no. 2118, Calvin to the Church of Poitiers, Geneva, February 20, 1555.

[131] "Mais je vouldrois bien sçavoir depuis quel temps il s'est advisé d'adherer à Castallio en cest article, veu qu'estant par deça sans en estre requis, il faisoit du grand zelateur contre luy." *CO* 15:441, no. 2118.

[132] "Mais si fault il que je dise ce mot qu'il m'est aultant licite, et me doit estre aussi bien permis d'estre zelateur pour maintenir la doctrine que je porte, puis que je la congnois estre de Dieu." *CO* 15:442, no. 2118. On Calvin's sense of his own status as "prophet," see Balserak, *John Calvin as Sixteenth-Century Prophet*.

[133] Joseph Scaliger would later claim to have seen around fifty letters from Servetus to Lavau: "Monsieur [François] de la Vau, medecin à Poictiers a une cinquantaine d'epistres de Michel Servet, qu'il escrivoit au pere [i.e., Jean] de Monsieur La Vau, estant à Vienne en Dauphiné; j'ay veu ces lettres là." Joseph Scaliger, *Scaligeriana, sive excerpta ex ore Josephi Scaligeri*, 2nd ed. (The Hague: Adrian Ulacq, 1668), 197.

[134] "Il ne dict pas aussi qu'il s'estoit frotté parmy toutes les brebis rongneuses, qu'il alloit flairant çà et là toutes les ordures pour y mettre le nez, qu'il s'accouploit à tous ceux qu'il congnoissoit estre mal

apparently sought out Bolsec at Falais's estate. There he likely met Zébédée and seems to have been put in touch with Castellio. Indeed, he likely stayed with Castellio in Basel before moving on to Poitiers.[135] Subsequently, Calvin complains, "he alleges as his accomplices a dreamer [*un fantastique*] named Sebastian Castellio and two others [probably Curione and Martin Borrhaus] who he says are professors in Basel."[136]

Calvin then explains his specific accusations against Lavau. These can be broken down into three fundamental charges: first, continued Nicodemism or, as it increasingly appeared in the 1550s, a willingness to compromise between Catholicism and Protestantism; second, resentment at Calvin's and Geneva's dominance in French affairs, and third, agreement with Castellio's teachings on toleration and the pursuit of holiness. These charges, indeed, paint Lavau as a follower of Castellio, but they also present a useful summary of the key issues that would bind together Calvin's enemies in France for years to come.

On the question of Nicodemism, Lavau believed that exposure to Catholic rites did not have the polluting effect that Calvin insisted it had. Calvin wrote, "one of the articles he disagreed with was that I had written that fathers pollute their children by introducing them to the superstitions that reign in papism." After Calvin had further explained his position to Lavau, the latter responded, according to Calvin, "like a cocky doctor, 'there you go; it seems otherwise to me.'"[137]

Next, as we saw among the Vaud pastors and will see again with Charles Du Moulin and Jean Morély in the next chapters, Lavau resented the power that Calvin and Geneva claimed over Protestant churches in France. "He says," Calvin complains, "that everyone here has to kiss my slipper."[138] The phrase *baiser la pantoufle*, "kiss the slipper," is precisely that used by Bolsec,

---

renommez, jusques à traverser le lac pour chercher ung heretique qui a esté banny d'icy." *CO* 15:438, no. 2118.

[135] Buisson, 2:248n6.

[136] "Il allegue pour ses complices ung fantastique nommé Sebastian Castallio, auquel il en conjoinct deux aultres qu'il dict estre lecteurs publiques à Basle." *CO* 15:440, and n. 10, no. 2118.

[137] "Or à l'opposite, pource que l'ung des articles estoit qu'il ne trouvoit pas bon que j'eusse escrit que les peres polluent leurs petitz enfants, les presentant aux superstitions qui regnent en la Papaulté, on luy amena des raisons qui le debvoient contenter tant et plus: asçavoir que le nom de Dieu, son Temple et les Sacremens sont bien polluez par ceux qui en abusent. Et comme le pere sanctifie son enfant, le dediant à Dieu, aussi il le souille en le prostituant aux superstitions qui sont à condamner, et aultres semblables. Luy comme ung docteur superlatif respond: 'Voilà, il me semble aultrement.'" *CO* 15:439, no. 2118.

[138] "Il dict qu'il fault que tout le monde me baise icy la pantoufle." *CO* 15:442, no. 2118.

Foncelet, and Eyssautier, and it reflects the same indignation felt among Calvin's enemies toward Geneva as a new Rome, and Calvin as a Protestant pope. Lavau claimed not only that everyone had to bow down to Calvin, but also that Calvin and the Genevans were trying strenuously to encourage emigration from France to Geneva: "In order to rattle you and bring you over to his faction, he points out that we think of nothing else than of bringing everyone to Geneva—as if this would bring us any great advantage."[139] Calvin's last comment is truly ironic, for just a few months later, he would, in fact, derive immense advantage from the presence of French refugees in Geneva, when the electoral defeat of Ami Perrin and his allies allowed the pro-Calvin faction to pack the Genevan electorate with their supporters among the refugees. Moreover, Lavau had a point. As Etienne Trocmé and, more recently, Jonathan Reid have argued, before 1555, Calvin was not enthusiastic about starting Reformed churches in France and, indeed, may even have played a retarding role.[140] Furthermore, as Kenneth Woo has recently argued, in the years just before 1555, Calvin was encouraging French evangelicals more strongly than ever to emigrate rather than to remain in France and endure persecution.[141] For Lavau, Calvin's uncompromising position on participating in Catholic worship served only to drain evangelicals from France.

Finally, Lavau seems to have adopted Castellio's ideas on more than just toleration. Certainly, he agreed with Castellio on the subject of persecuting heretics. His affinity ran deeper, however, for he also embraced Castellio's emphasis on the pursuit of moral perfection. To Calvin, this was as dangerous as his teaching on toleration, if not more so: "Above all, guard yourselves, my brothers, from Satan's snares when such people speak to you of the perfection of life. For their intention is to nullify the grace of our Lord Jesus. . . . This wiseacre [preudhomme] Castellio, whom Lavau canonizes among you,

---

[139] "Pour vous picquer et attirer à sa cordelle, il specifie que nous n'avons aultre regard, ny estude, sinon d'attirer tout le monde à Geneve. Voire comme si en cela nous y avions grand profict et advantaige." CO 15:443, no. 2118.

[140] Etienne Trocmé, "Une révolution mal conduite: À propos d'un centenaire et d'un livre," Revue d'histoire et de philosophie religieuses 39 (1959): 160–68; Jonathan Reid, "French Evangelical Networks before 1555: Proto-churches?," in La Réforme en France et en Italie: Contacts, comparaisons et contrastes, edited by Philip Benedict, Silvana Seidel Menchi, and Alain Tallon, 105–24, Collection de l'École française de Rome 384 (Rome: École française de Rome, 2007), 123–24.

[141] Specifically, Woo argues that in his 1552 work Quatre Sermons, Calvin made a decided shift in his preference for flight rather than enduring persecution. Kenneth J. Woo, Nicodemism and the English Calvin, 1544–1584, Brill's Series in Church History and Religious Culture 78 (Leiden: Brill, 2019), 30–57. Calvin's text in CO 8:369–452.

tries hard to spread this deadly poison."[142] Calvin was clearly worried not only about what he saw as Lavau's heresy but also and especially about the possibility that Lavau and Castellio were trying to spread it: Lavau tries to "bring you over to his faction" and "canonizes Castellio" to the people, while Castellio "tries hard to spread this deadly poison." To Calvin, these were not merely solitary individuals who had wandered off the path; they were Satan's instruments, sent to spread the deadly poison of heresy among the people. Thus, he believed, they must be stopped.

6.4.2. Impact of the Lavau Affair on French Church Organization and Geneva's Missionary Program

The combination of Calvin's confidence in the righteousness of his own cause, together with his fear that others might be infected with heretical notions, drove Calvin and his supporters in France to take steps to consolidate their control and stop the spread of dangerous doctrines. Lavau did, in fact, draw followers to his side, and his case seems to have led to the first proto-synod of the French Reformed churches, which took place, not at all coinciden- tally, in Poitiers in 1557. There, the "partisans of Lavau" were condemned, along with the usual suspects: Anabaptists, Servetists, libertines, atheists, and Epicureans.[143] The next year, Chandieu went to Poitiers to deal with the Lavau affair; there, the *Ecclesiastical History* relates, the ministers "began to understand what good there would be if it pleased God for all the churches of France to create of one accord a confession of faith and an ecclesiastical disci- pline." Just as important, they saw "how, on the contrary, if they do not do this, great evils could arise and cause divisions in both doctrine and discipline."[144]

---

[142] "Sur tout, mes freres, gardez vous de l'astuce de Satan, quant telles gens vous parleront de per- fection de vie. Car leur intention est d'aneantir la grace de nostre Seigneur Jesus. . . . ce preudhomme Castellio, que La Vau vous canonize tant, s'est efforcé de semer ceste poison mortelle." *CO* 15:445, no. 2118.

[143] "Prendront garde qu'aucun n'ayt opinion particuliere contre la saine doctrine de nostre Seigneur Jesus-Christ, ne qu'aucun face division ou secte à part pour rompre l'union de l'Eglise du Seigneur, comme Anabaptistes, Servetistes, Libertins, Atheistes et Epicuriens, Sadduciens, Quintions et ceux qui sont sectateurs de Lanau (*sic*), lequel a esté condamné d'heresie par apres la premiere et seconde admonition, sachant qu'ils sont condamnez par eux-mesmes." Philip Benedict and Nicolas Fornerod, eds., *L'organisation et l'action des Églises Réformées de France (1557–1563): Synodes provinciaux et autres documents*, Archives des Églises Réformées de France 3, THR 504 (Geneva: Droz, 2012), 3. The "Quintions" were followers of Quintin Thiery, a spiritualist in Marguerite of Navarre's circle against whom Calvin wrote in *Contre la secte phantastique et furieuse des libertins qui se nomment spirituelz*, COR, ser. 4, vol. 1.

[144] "les ministres estans assemblés, communiquerent par ensemble tant de la doctrine que de l'ordre et discipline entre eux observée, et par les choses qu'ils traitoient commencerent à apprehender quel

In 1559, at the first national synod in Paris, Lavau was admonished again. The synod cited his "strange doctrines, schisms, and notorious heresies," noting in particular his belief that "a heretic is not to be punished as a heretic but as a disturber of the civil government."[145] Although the synod did not think Lavau should be excommunicated solely for this belief, it cited his opposition to the synod, ministers, and consistory, and his continued relationship with a certain (unfortunately unidentified) schismatic heretic.[146]

This lengthy treatment of a fairly obscure follower of Castellio demonstrates several points. First, Lavau's case reveals that Castellio's influence reached far into France, and at a relatively early stage; Calvin's letter to Poitiers was written just a year after the publication of *Concerning Heretics*. The Pays de Vaud and Montbéliard were both within easy reach of Basel. Poitiers, by contrast, is more than seven hundred kilometers away, yet Castellio's teachings had an effective spokesperson there as well. Second, in 1555, Geneva was only just starting to send missionaries into France. Before this time, as Lavau suggested, Calvin had been encouraging French Protestants to flee persecution in France, and initially, he was not fully supportive of creating Protestant churches (*églises dressées*) in the kingdom. Calvin's deep concern about Lavau and the timing of Geneva's first missionary efforts suggest that the initial foray of Genevan missionaries into France was directly related to the Lavau affair. The very first missionary, Jacques L'Anglois, was sent just a couple of months after Calvin composed his letter to Poitiers; his

---

bien ce seroit s'il plaisoit à Dieu que toutes les Eglises de France dressassent d'un commun accord une confession de foy et une discipline Ecclesiastique; comme au contraire, cela ne se faisant, les grands maux qui pourroyent survenir et divisions tant en la doctrine qu'en la discipline, les Eglises n'estans liées ensemble et rengées sous un mesme joug d'ordre et de police Ecclesiastique." *Hist. eccl.*, 1:200.

[145] "Sur le recit du Ministre de Poictiers il fut dit, que quant à Lavau qui fait des schismes et dogmatise, enseignant et écrivant dès long-tems pour établir des heresies manifestes, les freres l'appelleront au prochain synode provincial, s'ils le trouvent bon, où confereront avec lui. . . . Touchant ce que le frere de Poictiers a soutenu, à celui qui disoit que l'heretique ne devoit être puni comme heretique, mais comme perturbateur de l'ordre politique, s'il n'y avoit autre faute que celle-là, il sera exhorté de ne point troubler l'Eglise lui-même, et de se moderer sur cela avec reverence et crainte de Dieu." Jean Aymon, *Tous les synodes nationaux des églises reformées de France*, 2 vols. (The Hague: Charles Delo, 1710), 1.2: 8–9, art. 4–5. English translation adapted from John Quick, *Synodicon in Gallia reformata, or the Acts, Decisions, Decrees, and Canons of those Famous National Councils of the Reformed Churches in France* (London: For T. Parkhurst and J. Robinson, 1692), 17.

[146] "Mais pour cela il ne doit pas être retranché de la Cene. Toutefois pour les circonstances qui ont été jointes à cela, et entre autres, parce qu'il s'est élevé orgueilleusement contre le synode, et qu'il a injurié et calomnié les ministres avec tout le consistoire, l'appellant le conducteur des aveugles, et que nonobstant les remontrances à lui faites de ne frequenter un certain heretique schismatique, néanmoins il a toujours été à sa compagnie. Pour ces causes, nous donnons conseil qu'un tel homme soit retranché de la compagnie des fideles." Aymon, *Tous les synodes*, 1.2:9, art. 5.

destination: Poitiers.[147] Calvin seems to have realized that if Geneva did not actively support the creation of churches in France according to the Genevan model, the Castellionists could gain the upper hand and be better able to "spread their poison." Finally, Lavau's case shows how intertwined the networks of Calvin's enemies were. Lavau was a correspondent of Servetus; after Servetus's execution, he became associated with Bolsec and presumably Falais and Zébédée; from there, he went to Basel where he forged ties with Castellio and Curione; and finally he went to France. These connections were not accidental. We saw earlier that Bolsec allied with Zébédée and Falais, who were, in turn, in contact with Castellio. Lavau was simply wending his way through the networks of anti-Calvinists from Geneva to Veigy to Basel and taking their message into France.

---

[147] Kingdon, *Geneva and the Coming of the Wars of Religion*, 2; *RCP* 2:62, [April or May 1555].

7

The Gallican Evangelicals

State-Sponsored French Religious Reform Revisited

7.1. Introduction

In 1904, Antoine Degert published an article on a group of bishops accused of heresy by the Inquisition. He entitled the article "The Trial of Eight French Bishops Suspected of Calvinism."[1] The title is striking: Calvin's uncompromising position on Nicodemism renders the notion of "Calvinist bishops" oxymoronic. Earlier, we saw Calvin and Farel harshly criticize Gérard Roussel and Michel d'Arande for accepting French bishoprics. How could these eight bishops, accused by the Roman Inquisition in 1563, possibly have been Calvinists?

The short answer: they weren't. Degert's title instead reflects the ingrained habit at the beginning of the twentieth century of equating French evangelicals, Huguenots, and Calvinists.[2] To be sure, several of the bishops cited by the Inquisition held religious views that could be characterized as evangelical or Protestant. The fact that they maintained their episcopal titles, however, distinguishes them from true Calvinists.

The historian will do better, I suggest, to label such individuals "Gallican evangelicals." While imperfect, this term has the advantage of avoiding more polemical descriptors, the most common of which emerged from Geneva as derogatory labels, such as *moyenneurs*, mediators, temporisers,

---

[1] Antoine Degert, "Procès de huit évêques français suspects de Calvinisme," *Revue des questions historiques*, n.s. 32 (July 1904): 61–108. The eight bishops were Jean de Monluc, bishop of Valence; Louis d'Albret, bishop of Lescar; Antonio Caracciolo, bishop of Troyes; Jean du Chaumont/de Saint-Romain, archbishop of Aix; François de Noailles, bishop of Dax; Claude Régin, bishop of Oloron; Charles Guillart, bishop of Chartres; and Jean de Saint-Gelais, bishop of Uzès. For Roman records on their cases, see Cesare Baronio et al., eds. *Annales ecclesiastici*, 37 vols. (Bar-Le-Duc: L. Guerin, 1864–1883), 22:256–60.

[2] Of course, the Catholic authorities also did not nitpick about heretical designations. Early in the Reformation, all French evangelicals were designated "Lutherans." By the 1560s, suspects of heresy in the kingdom were indiscriminately labeled "Calvinists" or "Huguenots."

Refusing to Kiss the Slipper. Michael W. Bruening, Oxford University Press (2021). © Oxford University Press.
DOI: 10.1093/oso/9780197566954.003.0008

or compromisers. Moreover, it appropriately characterizes these figures, who were the heirs of Roussel and Arande: evangelicals in belief who continued to insist that the Gallican church should be reformed from within. In addition to bishops and priests, the group included humanists and legal scholars who continued to seek religious reform without taking the Calvinist path of rejecting France's existing institutions. Far from being Calvinists themselves, they saw Calvin as an obstacle to reform in France. His intractable stubbornness on the Nicodemite question, Geneva's dominance of the French Reformed synods, and Calvinist control over consistories left no room for the kind of change that they believed could bring religious unity and reform—and consequently, peace—to France. In theology and practice, they generally sought to restore the primitive church, thereby maintaining the continuity of the early church's episcopal system, while eliminating "superstitions" and adopting Protestant views on the primacy of Scripture and sometimes on justification and the Eucharist as well.

The Calvinists derisively labeled such individuals *moyenneurs* (translated perhaps most literally but inelegantly as "middle-ground-ers").[3] They argued that such people were trying to serve both Christ and Belial, mixing the things of God with those of the devil. Thus, they had little time for either the *moyenneurs* or official attempts to reach a religious settlement. Commenting two decades after the failed Colloquy of Poissy, which had sought just such a settlement, the *Ecclesiastical History* noted, "If on the one side the prelates showed themselves to be open enemies of those who follow the true religion, there were several others who tried to do even worse, seeking a middle way where there was none, that is, a religion mixed up and composed of two things, which is all the more dangerous in religion as there is more appearance of rightness and similarity, which lulls the ignorant to sleep."[4] For this Calvinist author, possibly Beza himself, the *moyenneurs* were even worse

---

[3] See, for example, Calvin's treatise against François Bauduin: *Response à un cauteleux et rusé moyenneur, qui sous couleur d'appaiser les troubles touchant le faict de la Religion, a tenté tous les moyens d'empescher et rompre le cours de l'Evangile par la France* ([Paris]: [Nicolas Edouard], 1561); Latin text (*Responsio ad versipellem quendam mediatorem*) in CO 9:525–60. Viret also entitled the first dialogue in his *Interim*, "Les Moyenneurs." Pierre Viret, *L'Interim fait par dialogues*, edited by Guy R. Mermier, American University Studies, ser. 2, 14 (New York: Peter Lang, 1985), 17–65.

[4] "Mais si d'un costé les prelats se monstrerent ennemis ouverts de ceux de la religion, il y en eut bien d'autres qui tascherent de faire encores pis, cherchans un milieu où il n'y en a point, c'est à dire une religion, meslée et composée des deux choses d'autant plus dangereuses en la religion, qu'il y a en cela plus d'apparence de droiture et d'equité pour endormir les ignorans." *Hist. eccl.* 1:715.

than the hardline "papists."[5] For the Gallican evangelicals, however, seeking the middle ground was the only sensible solution to France's religious unrest.

In the middle of the sixteenth century, many individuals fell into this category of Gallican evangelical,[6] but this chapter will focus on three of them: Jean de Monluc, the Bishop of Valence (one of the bishops cited in 1563 by the Inquisition); François Bauduin, the original *moyenneur* for whom Calvin coined the term; and Charles Du Moulin, the great jurisconsult and defender of Gallican liberties—and also a convinced evangelical who came to detest the Calvinists. These three men were connected to each other, and each was connected as well as to one or more of the networks we have discussed previously. Perhaps most importantly, all had connections among the French nobility, including those who would become the principal Huguenot leaders during the Wars of Religion. For pragmatic reasons, these nobles eventually sought the support of the rank-and-file members of the Calvinian French Reformed churches, but many would have preferred the moderate path proposed by the Gallican evangelicals.

7.2. Jean de Monluc, François Bauduin, and the Colloquy of Poissy

We ended Chapter 1 with a discussion of the reforming work of Gérard Roussel in the diocese of Oloron. Roussel, we saw, was essentially continuing the work of Briçonnet and the Meaux group to bring evangelical doctrine and reform to his own diocese. We resume that story here with the career of Jean de Monluc, bishop of Valence. Roussel was killed in 1555 by a Catholic zealot. Monluc, after spending time in Marguerite's court, became bishop in 1554 and turned his efforts almost immediately to reforming his own diocese. Like Roussel, Monluc was opposed by Catholic hardliners. Thus, in terms of both chronology and religious views and strategies, Roussel's story flows directly into that of Monluc. François Bauduin's relationship with French evangelicals likewise extends back to the 1540s when, as a professor in Bourges, he was connected with Marguerite's network. The continuity

---

[5] Later Calvinists followed that lead, with the French Reformed synods repeatedly condemning any effort at compromise and reconciliation with the Catholics. See, for example, Aymon, *Tous les synodes*, 1.2:190, matières particulières, no. 4 (Quick, *Synodicon*, 169, no. 6.4); Aymon, *Tous les synodes*, 1.2:222, matières générales, no. 2 (Quick, *Synodicon*, 196, no. 5.4); also, Quick, *Synodicon* 196, no. 5.2 (not in Aymon).

[6] See, especially, the individuals discussed by Wanegffelen in *Ni Rome ni Genève*.

between Marguerite of Navarre's early network and that of later Gallican evangelicals like Monluc and Bauduin is significant, for it demonstrates that French evangelical reform-from-within did not die with Marguerite, Lefèvre, and Roussel, to be replaced by Calvinism; rather, it survived, and continued to compete vigorously with Calvinism.

7.2.1. Jean de Monluc in Roussel's Footsteps, 1554–1560

In the mid-1530s, Jean de Monluc spent at least some time in Marguerite's court at Nérac and may have met Roussel there. Although his stay in Nérac was short, his contact with Marguerite's network seems to have made a lasting impression on him.[7] In 1554, Monluc was named bishop of Valence and Die. As bishop, he strove to implement reform among the clergy and people of his diocese. Between 1558 and 1561, he published five works, all of which had a pastoral or reforming character.[8] His goal in writing appears to have been similar to that of Roussel in his *Forme de visite*.[9] That is, he set forth instructions for the clergy in his jurisdiction and provided sermons that his priests could use, as well as simple explanations of the sacraments and articles of faith. There is little that is strikingly heterodox in these works. Indeed, they seem intended to serve as testimony to his own orthodoxy.[10] He

---

[7] On Monluc's life, see Hector Reynaud, *Jean de Monluc, Évêque de Valence et de Die: Essai d'histoire littéraire* (Geneva: Slatkine Reprints, 1971 [Paris, 1893]), here, 17–18; Philippe Tamizey de Larroque, *Notes et documents inédits pour servir à la biographie de Jean de Monluc, évêque de Valence* (Paris: Auguste Aubry, 1868).

[8] The works were the following: (1) Jean de Monluc, *Cleri Valentini et Dyensis Reformatio, restitutioque, ex sacris Patrum Conciliis excerpta* (Paris: Federici Morelli, 1558); (2) Monluc, *Sermons de l'Evesque de Valence sur certains poincts de la religion, receuillis fidelement, ainsi qu'ilz ont esté prononcez. Autres Sermons du mesme aucteur, servans à descouvrir, par tesmoignage de l'Escriture saincte, les fautes qu'on commet sur les Dix Commandemens de la Loy. Plus un Sermon à son Clergé fait au Sene de Juillet 1557* (Paris: M. Vascosan, 1558); (3) Monluc, *Deux Instructions, et Trois Epistres, faictes, et envoyées au Clergé et peuple de Valence, et de Dye, par leur Evesque* (Paris: M. de Vascosan, 1558); (4) Monluc, *Familere explication des articles de la foy* (Lyon: Guillaume Regnoult, 1561); (5) Monluc, *Sermons de l'evesque de Valence sur l'Oraison Dominicale* (Lyon: Guillaume Regnoult, 1561).

[9] See 31–33.

[10] Note, for example, his comments to the Cardinal of Lorraine in the dedicatory letter to his *Sermons*: "quelques uns de mon clergé (combien qu'en petit nombre) peult estre pour entretenir l'ancienne et universelle inimitié qu'il y a entre le moien et le menu ordre de l'Eglise, et les prelatz et superieurs, m'auroient avec leur mauvaise langue (sans que je l'eusse merité) voulu mettre au reng de ces bons peres, qui en leur temps furent troublez et empeschez en leur estat. . . . D'autre costé beaucoup de gens de bien, de lettres et de vertu, pour convaincre la menterie qui estoit si mal fondée, publierent de main en main, et en divers endroitz, un nombre de mes sermons, qu'ilz avoient recueillis soubz moy, et fidelement mis par escript. Desquelz (apres les avoir retirez et recognuz) j'en

realized that if he wanted to maintain his position and be effective at encouraging reform, he would have to be more circumspect than his predecessors in Marguerite's network had been. Consequently, the teaching in his works was not overtly evangelical, yet it contained hints of heterodoxy, and its omissions were significant.

These subtleties were not lost on his critics in the Paris Faculty of Theology. In 1561, the Faculty censured eighteen propositions from Monluc's works.[11] He was accused of supporting the Calvinist doctrine of purgatory, questioning the necessity of hearing Mass, giving the cup to the laity during communion, and teaching Protestant doctrine on faith and good works.[12] The Faculty also cited him for proposing a new vernacular liturgical rite for the Eucharist,[13] and they censured Monluc's *Christian Instructions* for containing "false, schismatic, erroneous, and heretical propositions," noting that in a book on the sacraments, the author failed to discuss confession, holy orders, and confirmation, as well as the precepts of the Church, the veneration of the saints, and prayers for the dead.[14] They also cited his *Sermons on the Lord's Prayer* for supporting Lutheran teaching on good works; specifically, Monluc had written: "We do not take account of all the good works we have done but recognize that it is he [God] who wanted to work in us."[15]

---

ay baillé à faire imprimer une partie, à fin que ceux qui avoient (peult estre trop facilement) presté l'oreille aux detracteurs, eussent de quoy juger, quelle doctrine j'avoy presentée aux auditeurs qui sont soubz ma charge." Monluc, *Sermons . . . sur certains poincts de la religion*, 11–13.

[11] D'Argentré, 2:297–301.

[12] "Conclusiones Sacra Facultatis quibus damnantur plures libri D. de Monluc Episcopi de Valence qui in colloquio Bisciaco et passim dicebatur favere haeresi Calvinianorum de Purgatorio, de libertate per Christi gratiam sublata prop. 4, de Missa audiendae necessitate, praecipue poenitentibus, tempore ab Ecclesia praescripto prop. 5, et calicis cuius usum laïcis concedebat, novam ad hoc formam praescribens more haereticorum, prop. 6, de iustitia imputativa et bonis operibus, de spe Christiana, et gratia actuali in peccatore nondum converso prop. 1, 2, 3, 4, et 5." D'Argentré, 2:297 [misnumbered as a second p. 296].

[13] "Haec nova forma publice laïcis administrandi sacramentum Eucharistiae lingua vernacula verbis consecrationis, et sub utraque specie duplicem continet errorem, explicite quidem Nestorii damnatum in Concilio Ephesino, ante 1100 annos celebrato, et Hussitarum et Bohemorum in Concilio Constantiensi; implicite vero videtur continere haeresim Lutheri et sequacium existimantium praesentiam corporis Christi in sacramento in solo eius usu contineri." D'Argentré, 2:298.

[14] "Hic ergo liber, cuius titulus, *Instructions Chrétiennes de l'Evêque de Valence, etc.*, continens propositiones falsas, schismaticas, erroneas, et haereticas, in qua multa etiam nacta opportunitate omittuntur instructioni Christianorum necessaria, ut in praeparatione ad sacramentum Eucharistiae, nulla fit mentio confessionis auricularis, in tractatu de infirmis in agonia visitandis, nulla similiter fit mentio confessionis sacramentalis, in quo libro etiam nihil de sacramento confirmationis et ordinis, et proinde non satisfacit autor titulo, in quo proposuit se dicturum de sacramentis, in quo etiam libro nusquam fit mentio praeceptorum Ecclesiae, venerationis sanctorum, precum faciendarum pro defunctis, est perniciosus." D'Argentré, 2:298.

[15] "Prima propositio: 'Nous ne mettons point en compte les bonnes oeuvres que nous avons faites, ains reconnoissons que c'est lui qui a voulu operer en nous. . . .' Censura: Prima pars illius

In addition to his literary and diocesan efforts, Monluc hoped to influence national reform as well. In August 1560, the Queen-mother Catherine de Medici summoned a council to meet at Fontainebleau in an effort to reduce tensions between the increasingly hostile religious factions in France. She was aided in this endeavor by the religiously moderate chancellor, Michel de l'Hôpital.[16] Monluc was among the delegation of reform-minded bishops and spoke on the need for church reform in France. Nowhere in the speech does Monluc explicitly identify with the Protestants, but he makes it clear that he understood why so many people had embraced the new doctrine, namely because the Catholic clergy in France had failed to act as proper shepherds to their flock:

> The doctrine, Sire, that diverts your subjects has been sown over thirty years, not in one, two, or three days. It has been carried by three or four hundred diligent ministers trained in letters, with great modesty, seriousness, and appearance of sanctity . . . , always having Jesus Christ in their mouths, which is a word so sweet that it opens the most stopped-up ears and flows smoothly in the most hardened of hearts. And these preachers, having found the people without the guidance of a pastor or shepherd, nor anyone who bothered to instruct or teach them, were easily received and willingly heard and heeded.[17]

These are the words of neither a zealous Calvinist nor a hardline Catholic. Monluc speaks officially on the Catholic side, but his sympathy for the preachers of the "new doctrine" is obvious. Importantly, Monluc indicates that the preaching of this doctrine has been going on "for over thirty years," and he notes the presence in France of "three or four hundred diligent

propositionis est contra Sacram Scripturam, 2. pars captiosa est, conspirans errori Lutheri, olim damnato, qui asserit in omni opere bono hominem mere passive se habere." D'Argentré, 2:299.

[16] On this council, see Bernerd Weber, "The Council of Fontainebleau (1560)," *ARG* 45 (1954): 43–62; Daussy, *Le Parti Huguenot*, 178–81. On L'Hôpital, see Seong-Hak Kim, *Michel de L'Hôpital: The Vision of a Reformist Chancellor During the French Religious Wars*, Sixteenth Century Essays and Studies 36 (Kirksville, MO: Sixteenth Century Journal Publishers, 1997).

[17] "La doctrine, Sire, qui amuse vos subjects, a esté semée en trente ans, non pas en un ou deux ou trois jours, a esté apportée par trois ou quatre cens ministres diligens et exercez aux lettres, avec une grande modestie, gravité et apparence de saincteté . . . , ayans tousjours Jesus-Christ en la bouche, qui est une parole si douce, qu'elle fait ouverture des oreilles qui sont les plus serrées, et découle facilement dans le coeur des plus endurcis. Et ayans lesdicts prédicans trouvé le peuple sans conduicte de pasteur ni de berger, ni personne qui print charge de les instruire ou enseigner, ils ont esté facilement receus, volontiers ouys et escoutez." *Mémoires de Condé* 1:558–59.

ministers." Clearly, he was not thinking of the few dozen missionaries sent into France from Geneva, who started showing up only five years before. Instead, he must have had in mind earlier evangelical humanists, "trained in letters," going back to the Meaux group. Thus, Monluc perceived in French evangelical preaching a clear line from Marguerite's circle in the 1520s to the evangelicals of his own day. As we will see, he was not alone.

In his speech at Fontainebleau, Monluc continues by highlighting more of the failings of the Catholic clergy. He starts at the top, with the pope, about whom he comments ambiguously, "I protest that I do not want to talk about this See except with the honor and reverence I owe it."[18] He blames bishops for being lazy, greedy, and ignorant, claiming that all are eager to live in Paris while their own dioceses burn, "and so the eyes of the church, which are the bishops, are blindfolded."[19] Monluc then offers several remedies to help correct these problems. After acknowledging God's deserved wrath against France, he suggests, first, that the king must see to it that "God's Scripture be published and interpreted sincerely and purely, and that henceforth, it not be torn apart by the heretics on the one hand, or by those who would use it to cover their avarice, abuses, and superstitions" on the other.[20] Once again, we see Monluc in the middle, blaming Protestants for misinterpreting Scripture and Catholics for using it to hide their "avarice, abuses, and superstitions." His proposed remedy also includes the preaching of daily sermons in the king's household, and he tells the queens (Catherine de Medici and Mary of Guise, wife of Francis II and better known as Mary, Queen of Scots) to have those around them sing the Psalms instead of silly songs.[21] He notes

---

[18] "commençant par le Pape (je proteste que je ne veux parler de ce Siege, qu'avec l'honneur et la reverence que je luy doibs)." *Mémoires de Condé*, 1:559.

[19] "Les evesques (j'entends pour la pluspart) ont esté paresseux, n'ayans devant les yeux aucune craincte de rendre compte à Dieu du troupeau qu'ils avoyent en charge, et leur plus grand soulci a esté de conserver leur revenu, en abuser en folles despences et scandalleuses: tellement qu'on en a veu quarante resider à Paris, pendant que le feu s'allumoit en leurs dioceses. Et en mesme-temps l'on voit bailler les eveschez aux enfans, et à personnes ignorantes, et qui n'avoyent le savoir ni la volonté de faire leur estat. Et enfin les yeux de l'Eglise, qui sont les evesques, ont esté bandez: les colomnes ont fleschi, et sont tombées à terre sans se relever." *Mémoires de Condé*, 1:560.

[20] "Il vous fault donc humilier, Sire, devant Dieu, et recognoistre que les punitions viennent de luy et de son juste et certain jugement. Il fault mettre peine de l'appaiser, avec continuelles prieres et changement de vie. . . . Que son escripture soit publiée et interpretée sincerement et purement, et qu'elle ne soit d'ici en avant deschirée d'un costé par les hérétiques, ni usurpée sans propos par ceux qui s'en aident à couvrir leur avarice, abus et superstitions." *Mémoires de Condé*, 1:562.

[21] "et qu'en vostre maison il y ait sermon tous les jours, qui servira à clorre la bouche de ceux qui disent qu'on ne parle jamais de Dieu à l'entour de vous. Et vous, mesdames les roines, pardonnez-moy, s'il vous plaist, si j'ose entreprendre vous supplier qu'il vous plaise ordonner qu'au lieu des chansons folles, vos filles et tout vostre suitte ne chantent que les Psalmes de David, et les chansons spirituelles qui contiennent louange de Dieu." *Mémoires de Condé*, 1:562.

that he finds "extremely strange the opinion of those who want to prohibit Psalm singing" in the vernacular, for David wrote the Psalms in Hebrew, the common language of his own people.[22]

The other major remedy Monluc proposes is to hold a general council. He means a council different from Trent, one that would truly welcome and listen to Protestants. In true Gallican fashion, he suggests that if a general council could not be convened, the king should summon a national council, following the examples of Charlemagne and other early French kings.[23] Monluc's speech at Fontainebleau leaves little question that he wanted to see a French church reformed along evangelical lines but not subject to Calvin's leadership in Geneva. His proposal recalls the reform efforts of the 1520s: preach the word of God, and make the Bible available in the vernacular. And he shows the same optimism for national reform that the early evangelicals showed around the time of Roussel's Lenten sermons of 1533.

Over the next year, Monluc's hopes for national reform continued to grow. At Easter 1561, he was at court, preaching to the new king, Charles IX; the king's mother, Catherine de Medici; and Francis II's widow, Mary. The Spanish ambassador to France worried that Monluc was pouring poison into the royal ears and considered him an outright heretic. "In his first sermon," he reported, "he made no invocation of God, nor of the saints, although that was the ordinary custom. At the end he proposed that Holy Scripture should be read in every language and the Psalms chanted, and infinite other fantasies."[24] The ambassador also reported that Monluc "gave a booklet to the

---

[22] "Et sur ce je ne me puis tenir de dire que je trouve extremement estrange l'opinion de ceux qui veulent qu'on defendre le chant des Pseaumes, et donnent occasion aux seditieux de dire qu'on ne fait plus la guerre aux hommes, mais à Dieu, puis qu'on veult empescher que ses louanges soyent publiées et entendues d'un chacun. Si l'on veut dire qu'il ne les faut traduire en nostre langue, il fault donc qu'on nous rende raison pourquoy David les composa en la langue hebraïque, qui estoit la langue commune et vulgaire à tout le païs." *Mémoires de Condé*, 1:562.

[23] "Pour le second remede, Sire, je vous supplie de vouloir promettre un concile général, qui est le moyen que nos anciens ont suivy pour mettre en paix la Chrestienté, qui a esté à plusieurs fois divisée par les hérésies plus pernicieuses que ne sont celles du jourd'huy. . . . Toutesfois s'il advenoit qu'il y eust empeschement au concile général, vous deschargerez vostre conscience, s'il vous plaisoit en faire un national, à l'exemple de vos predecesseurs le Roy Gonltran, Charlemaigne Roy, Roy Loys III, lesquels à moindre necessité que ceste cy ont faict convoquer tous les evesques de ce royaume." *Mémoires de Condé*, 1:564.

[24] "L'Evesque de Valence, à solicitation de plusieurs, a obtenu de prescher devant le Roy Très-Chrestien et les Roynes; en quoy il ha monstré plus de venin, qu'il n'a donné de contentement, ny de tesmoignage de sçavoir, et grace à ceulx mesmes qui sont de sa secte; car ses sermons ont esté sans ordre, ni queue ny teste. Pour donner quelque tesmoignage de son intention, au premier sermon, il ne feit invocation ny de Dieu ny de sainctz, combien que ce soit la coustume ordinaire . . . sur la fin, proposa que la Saincte Escriture debvoit estre leuë à chasqung, en toute langaige, et les Pseaulmes chantées, et une infinité d'aultre resveries." *Mémoires de Condé*, 2:4–5, Moret-sur-Loing, April 13, 1561. The ambassador was Thomas Perrenot de Granvelle, sieur de Chantonnay, brother of the more famous advisor of Charles V, Antoine de Granvelle.

Most Christian King in which were found several heretical propositions."[25] It is difficult to know how well Monluc was received at court. What is most significant, however, is that he was invited at all. After his conciliatory speech at Fontainebleau, Catherine knew his position and was at least partly inclined toward it herself. For Monluc, the opportunity to preach before the king must have seemed like validation of the entire French evangelical movement to that point and an opportunity for that movement to gain traction on a national scale. The opportunity was particularly significant since the Huguenot leader and first prince of the blood, Antoine of Navarre, was inclined to adopt a similar compromise solution, which he was working to develop with François Bauduin.

7.2.2. François Bauduin's Path from Calvinism to Religious Concord, 1545–1558

François Bauduin (1520–1573) was from Arras in the Low Countries.[26] He was the countryman of Jacques de Falais, and he helped Calvin with the Latin translation of the *Apology* for Falais.[27] Bauduin received a humanist education from Gabriel Mudée, who had been in direct contact with both Erasmus and Juan Luis Vivès.[28] He attended university at Louvain, earning his law degree in 1538 at the age of nineteen. The next year, he went to Paris for further studies with Charles Du Moulin, the jurisconsult we will meet again later in this chapter. Bauduin served as Du Moulin's secretary in Paris for three years and stayed in his household along with two other students, François Hotman and Jean Crespin, who would become notable Protestants. Together they formed a Nicodemite, humanist household of lawyers, as they all grew increasingly committed to the evangelical faith.[29]

---

[25] "[il] bailla un livret au Roy Très-Chrestien, dans lequel furent trouvez plusieurs propositions hérétiques." *Mémoires de Condé*, 2:5, report of Perrenot de Chantonnay, Moret-sur-Loing, April 13, 1561.

[26] Today, Arras is in northeastern France, about fifty kilometers southwest of Lille. On Bauduin generally, see Mario Turchetti, *Concordia o tolleranza? François Bauduin e i "Moyenneurs"* THR 200 (Geneva: Droz, 1984); Michael Erbe, *François Bauduin (1520–1573): Biographie eines Humanisten*, Quellen und Forschungen zur Reformationsgeschichte 46 (Gütersloh: Gerd Mohn, 1978); Jenkins, *Calvin's Tormentors*, 93–107; Wanegffelen, *Ni Rome ni Genève*, 101–14; Joseph Duquesne, "François Bauduin et la Réforme," *Bulletin de l'Académie delphinale*, ser. 5, t. 9 (1914–1917): 55–108.

[27] Turchetti, *Concordia o tolleranza*, 69; Erbe, *François Bauduin*, 49–50. The Latin translation, *Apologia illustris D. Iacobi a Burgundia Fallesii Bredanique domini qua apud Imperatoriam Maiestatem inustas sibi criminationes diluit fideique suae confessionem edit*, is in CO 10/1:269–94.

[28] Turchetti, *Concordia o tolleranza*, 37; Erbe, *François Bauduin*, 36.

[29] On this period, see Turchetti, *Concordia o tolleranza*, 40–46; Erbe, *François Bauduin*, 37–42.

As early as 1545, Mario Turchetti argues, Bauduin began to develop a theory to defend his Nicodemite position, distinguishing sharply in his *Prefaces on Civil Law* between "interior mandates" (*interiora mandata*) and "external prescriptions" (*externa praescripta*).[30] He may well have internalized this distinction long before, following his early teacher, the student of Erasmus. Around the same time, in 1545, Bauduin and Crespin (also from Arras) came under suspicion of heresy in the Low Countries. Bauduin was in Paris at the time, but back home he was banished and his goods confiscated.[31] He worried that word of his condemnation would be passed to the French authorities and thought it prudent to leave the country. Calvin may also have urged him to do so; the correspondence between the two began around this time.[32] In late summer 1545, Bauduin arrived in Geneva.[33] This first sojourn in that city lasted only two months, but it left an impression on him. Later—after his break from Calvin—he would write to the Genevan reformer, "I thought you were a good and religious man and that you were seriously undertaking the work of reforming the Church. By this opinion I was turned into a true 'Calvinolater.'"[34] Bauduin was back in Paris by December, but he continued to write to Calvin, wondering aloud whether he should become a Reformed pastor.[35] In the summer of 1547, Bauduin returned to Geneva, this time serving as Calvin's secretary and assisting him with Falais's *Apology*. Once again, his stay was short. He left for Lyon, probably to deal with a family matter, and found work as a corrector for the great Lyonnais printer Sebastian Gryphius.[36] It is an interesting coincidence that Bauduin

---

[30] Turchetti, *Concordia o tolleranza*, 54–55. Bauduin's book was *Francisci Balduini Atrebatii Iuriscons. in suas Annotationes in libros quatuor Institutionum Iustiniani Imp.* προλεγόμενα *sive Praefata de iure civili* (Paris: Jean Loys, 1545).

[31] Tuchetti, *Concordia o Tolleranza*, 57–58; Erbe, *François Bauduin*, 44–45. Bauduin and Crespin were named in the proceedings against Pierre Brully. Most of the information about his banishment is found in the 1563 text overturning his ordered exile, published in Erbe, *François Bauduin*, 286–88.

[32] In Bauduin's first extant letter to Calvin, he apologizes for his delay, which suggests that the two had previously discussed his move from France: "Quod ad rationem nostrae morae attinet, piget certe, pudetque nos cessationis nostrae. Sed nos infinitis difficultatibus Satan implicat." *CO* 12:109, no. 663, [Paris], July 20, 1545. Bauduin used the pseudonym Petrus Rochius when writing to Calvin, and addressed Calvin as Charles Despeville. Unfortunately, none of Calvin's epistolary responses to Bauduin survive.

[33] Turchetti, *Concordia o Tolleranza*, 62; Erbe, *François Bauduin*, 47.

[34] "Probabis, me adolescentem, . . . putasse, te virum bonum esse et religiosum: te Ecclesiae reformandae curam serio suscepisse. Denique probabis me hac opinione factum fuisse prope Calvinolatram." Bauduin, *Responsio altera ad Ioan. Calvinum*, 45.

[35] "Et fortassis Dominus aliquando nos inde avocaturus est ad ministerium ecclesiae, ut olim Chrysostomum a causis forensibus, Ambrosium a profana praefectura evocavit. Fac, mi pater, obsecro, ut resciscam quid tibi videatur. Tu enim unus es a cuius consilio totus pendeo." *CO* 12:229, no. 738, Bauduin to Calvin, [Paris], December 5 [1545].

[36] Turchetti, *Concordia o Tolleranza*, 71.

and Sebastian Castellio were doing essentially the same work at the same time for two of the greatest printers of humanist books in Europe.[37]

In Lyon, Bauduin once again adopted a Nicodemite position. His decision to dissemble religiously led to the initial breakdown in his relations with Calvin. Although we do not have Calvin's letters, Bauduin's responses to him grow increasingly defensive.[38] Rather than heed Calvin's advice to flee France, Bauduin took a position as professor of law at the University of Bourges. There he was surrounded by other evangelicals connected to Marguerite of Navarre.[39] Bauduin continued to correspond with Calvin, but after his move to Bourges, their letters become more sporadic and formal.

Into the mid-1550s, Bauduin continued to seek Calvin's approval, to little avail. In 1555, he followed his former master Du Moulin to Strasbourg. From there, he wrote Calvin, "I finally fled when I was able."[40] Far from congratulating Bauduin for heeding his advice or forgiving him for remaining so long "in idolatry," Calvin wrote to Peter Martyr Vermigli that he wished Bauduin had remained in Bourges.[41] Calvin had become completely estranged from Bauduin. Increasingly, the feeling became mutual.

After two years in Strasbourg, Bauduin found a new position at the University of Heidelberg. At this point, he became close to George Cassander, who would be instrumental behind the scenes of the Colloquy of Poissy by writing *The Duty of the Pious and Peace-Loving Man in this Religious Schism* (referred to hereinafter as *De officio*);[42] this was the treatise that would prompt Calvin to denounce the *moyenneurs*. Cassander was also among Castellio's

---

[37] On Castellio's work in Basel with Oporinus, see 145–46.

[38] See, for example, his letter of January 2, 1548: "Quod ad nos [Bauduin and Crespin] attinet, multa hic nos cogunt ad aliquot haerere dies. . . . Multi hic nobis occurrunt amici, et pii et ingenui. Ad eorum synaxin vocatus accessi, et Domino gratias egi qui suum ubique semen habet, suas reliquias, ne tota plane terra instar Sodomorum sit et Gomorrhae." *CO* 12:650, no. 987, Bauduin to Calvin, [Lyon]. This was followed by a letter of March 25, 1548: "Quod mones, mi pater, ne haec mora aut ignava desertio, aut nescio cuius periculi fuga esse videatur, faciam ut memorem monuisse scias. Sed illud molestum est quod subverearis ne mihi molesta sit admonitio, nisi iocosa. Serio et severe si castigares, nec tam mihi placeo quin merito fieri agnoscerem, nec tam ingratus sum quin magnas tibi gratias agerem." *CO* 12:670, no. 1002, Bauduin to Calvin, [Lyon].

[39] On the evangelical community in Bourges, and especially evangelical preaching there by members of the Catholic clergy before the Wars of Religion, see Reid, "French Evangelical Networks before 1555," 108–16.

[40] "Eripui me tandem aliquando ut potui, vir clarissime." *CO* 15:434, no. 2116, Bauduin to Calvin, Strasbourg, February 20 [1555].

[41] Bauduin had brought with him a controversial individual named Pierre Boquin, leading Calvin to comment, "Atque utinam Balduinus apud Bituriges potius mansisset quam huius hirci foetore inquinasset gregem Christi." *CO* 15:724, no. 2266, Calvin to Vermigli, Geneva, August 8, 1555. On Boquin and his conflict in Strasbourg, see Denis, *Les églises d'étrangers en pays rhénans*, 103–106.

[42] [George Cassander], *De officio pii ac publicae tranquillitatis vere amantis viri, in hoc religionis dissidio* (Paris: Hercule François, 1562).

acquaintances. Although only two letters from Castellio to Cassander survive, from 1546 and 1553, the dates and tone of both, especially the latter, suggest that the two men were in regular contact with one another.[43] Cassander was convinced that the religious schism of the Reformation could be ended only by restoring the structures and practices of the early church.[44] In this way, the church's basic episcopal structure would remain, but the later accretions to which Protestants objected would be purged. Cassander's vision, therefore, was not far from that of the early French reformers, and he exerted great influence on Bauduin.

Bauduin and Cassander also disapproved of Calvin's actions in the Servetus case. In 1557, Bauduin published *On the Edicts of the Ancient Emperors*, ostensibly as a commentary on Roman religious laws, but more importantly as an argument from an historical and legal perspective for religious toleration.[45] He published the work with Castellio's favored publisher in Basel, Johannes Oporinus.[46] The next year, he wrote Cassander, "I have shown how averse to shedding blood [Emperor] Theodosius was, and how those times did not permit such capital punishments. . . . Few understand the ancient ecclesiastical law of this public judge, yet many nevertheless rashly subscribe to the bloody punishment."[47] Cassander responded by lamenting the fact that so many people "praise that notorious Genevan crime in burning Servetus."[48]

---

[43] Bertius, *Illustrium et clarorum virorum epistolae selectiores*, 49, no. I.8, Castellio to Cassander and Cornelius Gualther, Basel, August 23, 1546; ibid., 173–74, no. I.35, Castellio to Cassander, Basel, April 12, 1553. In the 1553 letter, Castellio addresses Cassander as his "amicus charissimus," shares news of his completed French Bible, and sympathizes with Cassander's illness, all of which seem to suggest a larger correspondence between the two than the extant record indicates.

[44] See, for example, George Cassander, *Liturgica de ritu et ordine dominicae coenae celebrandae, quam celebrationem Graeci Liturgian, Latini Missam appellarunt, ex variis monumentis et probatis scriptoribus collecta* (Cologne: Arnold Birckmann, 1558). On Cassander, see John Patrick Dolan, *The Influence of Erasmus, Witzel and Cassander in the Church Ordinances and Reform Proposals of the United Duchies of Cleve during the Middle Decades of the 16th Century*, Reformationsgeschichtliche Studien und Texte 83 (Münster: Aschendorffsche Verlagsbuchhandlung, 1957), 87–108. Like Bauduin, Cassander would become a bitter enemy of the Calvinists after Calvin harshly rejected his *De officio*. See Cassander, *Traditionum veteris ecclesiae et sanctorum patrum defensio, adversus Io. Calvini importunas criminationes* (Cologne: Arnold Birckmann, 1564).

[45] See Turchetti, *Concordia o tolleranza*, 86–87.

[46] François Bauduin, *Ad Edicta Veterum Principum Rom. de Christianis* (Basel: Oporinus, [1557]).

[47] "et ostendi quam et Theodosius ille a sanguine fuerit alienus, et illa tempora tam capitales non tulerint animadversiones. . . . Nunc quam sit hoc necesse, vides, cum et pauci intelligant antiquam et Ecclesiasticam huius publici iudicii Legem, et multi tamen temere sanctionibus sanguinariis subscribant." Michael Erbe, "François Bauduin und Georg Cassander: Dokumente einer Humanistenfreundschaft," *BHR* 40 (1978): 537–60, here, 540–41, no. 2, Bauduin to Cassander, Heidelberg, January 5 [1558].

[48] "Miror sane hos non videre quo praeiudicio se suosque passim per varia regna et provincias dispersos gravent, cum huiusmodi leges ferant, cum praeclarum illud Genevensium facinus in Serveto cremando laudibus efferant." Erbe, "François Bauduin und Georg Cassander," 541, no. 3, Cassander to Bauduin, Cologne, January 27, 1558.

As Turchetti has shown, Bauduin would go beyond arguments for religious toleration to support for religious concord. Although earlier scholars generally used "toleration" and "concord" interchangeably, Turchetti points out that there is, in fact, a profound difference between the two.[49] Indeed, he argues that the ultimate goals of toleration and concord are fundamentally opposed to one another. Sixteenth-century authors such as Castellio who sought religious toleration wanted the state to permit the practice of multiple religions. They argued, in essence, for freedom of religion. Those who sought concord, as Bauduin ended up doing, wanted the state to come to an agreement on one particular religion. Compromise would inevitably be necessary and would entail at least temporary toleration until an agreement could be made, but the ultimate goal was the elimination of competing religious bodies within the state. Concord had been the goal of French evangelicals since the Meaux experiment. The Calvinists, by contrast—and strangely in closer agreement with Castellio on this issue—sought religious toleration, at least for themselves. They wanted to be left alone to practice their religion in what they conceived to be its purity, free of "papist pollution." They were convinced, of course, that God would eventually lead French Catholics to embrace the "truth," but there could be no compromise in that process. Toleration, they believed, would eventually lead to a single state religion, namely *their* religion, not a perverse, compromise position.

7.2.3. Bauduin and Antoine of Navarre's Plan for Reform, 1558

In 1558, Bauduin sought to put his views on religious concord into practice, as he again became involved in French affairs. Marguerite of Navarre's son-in-law, Antoine de Bourbon, King of Navarre, sent representatives to meet with Bauduin about the growing religious turbulence in France. Bauduin wrote to Cassander, describing his meeting with Antoine's legates as follows:

> He said that certain ignorant zealots were stirring up trouble, but it did not please the prudent individuals in France to overthrow the whole form and

---

[49] For a succinct English presentation of Turchetti's thesis, developed at greater length in *Concordia o tolleranza*, see his "Religious Concord and Political Tolerance in Sixteenth- and Seventeenth-Century France," *SCJ* 22 (1991): 15–25; see also idem, "Concorde ou tolérance? Les Moyenneurs à la veille des guerres de religion," *Revue de théologie et de philosophie* 118 (1986): 255–67.

appearance of religion, because that could neither be accomplished nor attained without great sedition and the wretched confusion of everything. Instead, some compromise is required, which does not arrogantly repudiate what can be tolerated in matters now long received and which does not scornfully reject what remains from the ancient church. He indicated that wise and sensible moderation of this type can be heard in the king's court.[50]

Taking the long view, we see that Bauduin's report shows that the hopes of Marguerite's network were being revived with vigor through her son-in-law and successor, the new king of Navarre. Reform of the French church from within was as close to reality as perhaps it had ever been in the kingdom, promising the adoption of evangelical doctrine while retaining most of the external forms and anything that agreed with the ancient church. Moderate voices prevailed at court, Gallican independence was on the rise, and the need for reform continued to be widely perceived. Herein lay the roots of the Colloquy of Poissy.

Antoine of Navarre is routinely castigated in Calvinist historiography—and even in more neutral studies—as indecisive, self-interested, and weak.[51] In the political realm, he may, in fact, have been so.[52] Most condemnation, however, has stemmed primarily from his refusal to support strongly the Calvinist cause in France. Of course, this condemnation only makes sense if Antoine was a Calvinist. He was not. Certainly, he maintained cordial relations with Calvin, Beza, and their associates, for he knew he needed the

---

[50] "Dominus Vendosmius inter proceres primus, qui nunc et est et appellatur Rex Navarrae, bonis partibus et palam et vehementer favet. Legatum huc quendam misit, qui me convenit. Dixit multa miscere quosdam ardeliones rerum imperitos: sed non placere hominibus in Gallia cordatis, totam et religionis formam, et religionis faciem inverti, quia neque id impetrari possit, neque possit obteneri sine magna seditione et misera rerum omnium confusione. Sed temperationem aliquam requiri, quae quod in rebus iamdiu receptis tolerari potest, superbe non repudiet, quodque ex antiquitate Ecclesiastica reliquum est, fastidiose non respuat. Sapientem et sanam eius generis moderationem posse audiri in consilio Regio." Erbe, "François Bauduin und Georg Cassander," 542, no. 4, Bauduin to Cassander, Frankfurt-am-Main, April 1 [1558].

[51] See, for example, the entry in Haag: "Les Protestants estimèrent cette conquête [i.e., Antoine's conversion] plus haut qu'elle ne le méritait. Flattés de voir Antoine de Bourbon toujours escorté de plusieurs ministres, donnant audience aux Huguenots des provinces qu'il traversait, leur promettant sa protection . . . ils s'aveuglèrent complètement sur le caractère de ce prince. Aussi faible qu'inconstant, le roi de Navarre se laissait mener par des favoris vendus aux Guise, en sorte que son alliance était plus propre à compromettre leur cause qu'à le servir. Il était d'ailleurs très ambitieux, et l'ambition devait toujours faire taire en lui la voix assez peu écoutée de la conscience." Haag 2:430.

[52] His unwillingness to challenge Catherine de Medici for the regency of young King Charles IX, despite the overwhelming support of the nobility for him to do so, is perhaps the best evidence for this. See Daussy, Le Parti Huguenot, 188–93.

support of their followers for his political and religious goals. As we see from Bauduin's letter, however, as early as 1558, Antoine believed the best solution for France was the one that French evangelicals had been pursuing since the early 1520s and that Calvin found repugnant: a moderate solution that would reform the church but retain the traditional institutional structures. Thus, one can, of course, disagree with Antoine's assessment of the situation, but one should not criticize him as a "weakling" for taking the path he believed in mostly strongly.

7.2.4. The Colloquy of Poissy, 1561

After Monluc's 1561 Easter sermons before the court, momentum continued to build for a compromise religious solution for France. By May, Bauduin was back in France, at the urging of Antoine of Navarre. Soon after his arrival, he wrote to Cassander and described enthusiastically his meetings with the greatest courtiers, who spoke to him "about the religious constitution and the reformation of the Church," and he noted that "many things were said about some compromise formula and form of ecclesiastical peace."[53] Bauduin reported that he told them about Cassander's ideas, and he begged Cassander to write his "advice concerning the way to establish the Church, by returning as much as possible to the ancient ecclesiastical laws and remnants."[54] This request was the origin of Cassander's *De officio*.

A compromise religious formula was the last thing Calvin and his followers wanted. When they learned of Bauduin's return to France and his influence over Antoine of Navarre, they tried to thwart him. The friendship between Bauduin and Navarre stung the Calvinists all the more because Calvin himself had tried for years to curry favor with Antoine, seeing him as the best hope for the Reformation in France. As first prince of the blood, Antoine wielded great official authority, and Calvin saw him as the most legitimate leader of

---

[53] "Statim atque in Aulam Regis venissem, summi quique proceres, qui Regio Consilio praesunt, familiarissime atque humanissime mecum sunt locuti de constitutione religionis, Reformatione Ecclesiae, et partium iam dissidentium quadam conciliatione, huiusque conditione: et cum ultro citroque multa dicta essent de media aliqua formula atque adeo forma pacis Ecclesiasticae." Erbe, "François Bauduin und Georg Cassander," 545, no. 6, Bauduin to Cassander, Paris, May 30 [1561].

[54] "Ego (quod alias sepe feceram), te nominavi, iisque ostendi quas tunc forte mecum habebam literas tuas. . . . Sed iterumque petam, ut si venire ipse non possis (quod valde vellem ut posses), saltem ad illos proceres pios, atque inprimis ad Regem Navarrae, praescribas consilium tuum de ratione Ecclesiae constituendae, retentis, quantum fieri potest, antiquitatis Ecclesiasticae legibus et reliquiis." Erbe, "François Bauduin und Georg Cassander," 545, no. 6.

a possible Calvinist insurrection against the Catholic monarchy.[55] Bauduin's 1558 report that Antoine saw compromise as the best solution for France, however, reveals that Calvin's hopes for him had long been deeply misplaced. Nevertheless, Antoine's open friendship with Bauduin infuriated Calvin. He wrote Antoine to warn him of "a boorish apostate named Bauduin," who might try to trick the king of Navarre.[56] For his part, Bauduin expressed optimism to Cassander that "all the bishops with the king's councilors and some other learned men deliberate about the reformation. . . . The more rational among them really seek and want to hear your advice, with me as sponsor, even though the Lemannic lord's faction howls."[57] Calvin's letter to Navarre and Bauduin's reference to the "Lemannic lord's faction" reveal that well before the Colloquy of Poissy opened, the Calvinists and Gallican evangelicals understood that they were operating at cross-purposes, and each sought the upper hand with the royal family and nobility.

When the colloquy opened on September 9, 1561, the factions had come no closer together. From the first day of the meeting, it was apparent that disagreement over the interpretation of the Eucharist would doom the effort to bring the sides together.[58] Nevertheless, Monluc participated in an effort to draft language on the Eucharist that would be acceptable to both sides. Their proposal, which leaned more toward the Reformed doctrine, went nowhere with the hardline Catholics. And so, after a month of negotiations— and before Bauduin was able to arrive with Cassander's book—the colloquy disbanded.

The Colloquy of Poissy is usually described as an utter failure, and in a way, of course, it was. From another perspective, however, its very failure meant that each of the three sides got at least part of what it wanted. The Calvinists successfully withstood pressure to compromise, and just three months later, the crown's 1562 Edict of January granted them limited recognition of their

---

[55] See Balserak, *John Calvin as Sixteenth-Century Prophet*, 118–25.

[56] "Il y a un aultre rustre aposte qui se nomme Baudouin, qui a desjà esté trois ou quatre fois apostat de Jesus Christ, et possible toutesfois se sera insinué tellement vers vous, Sire, que vous en seriez trompé, si vous n'en estiez adverti." CO 18:660, no. 3502, Calvin to Antoine of Navarre, [Geneva], [August 1561].

[57] "Episcopi omnes cum Regiis Consiliariis et aliquot doctis hominibus deliberant de Reformatione, eoque nomine convenerunt in oppido Poissy prope aulam et Lutetiam. Qui inter eos saniores sint, mirabiliter expetunt et expectant tuum consilium, me sponsore, fremat licet factio Lemannici reguli." Erbe, "François Bauduin und Georg Cassander," 548, no. 8, Bauduin to Cassander, Paris, July 31 [1561]. "Lemannic" is a reference to *lac Léman*, the French name for Lake Geneva.

[58] On the course of events at Poissy, see Christopher Nugent, *Ecumenism in the Age of the Reformation: The Colloquy of Poissy*, Harvard Historical Studies 89 (Cambridge, MA: Harvard University Press, 1974).

faith. The hardline Catholics, in turn, successfully resisted pressure from the crown to compromise with the Calvinists. Although the grant of limited toleration for the Huguenots in the Edict of January was a blow, it soon became moot as the Wars of Religion began with the massacre of Wassy on March 1, 1562, five days before the Paris parlement officially registered the Edict. Probably the biggest losers coming out of Poissy were the Gallican evangelicals themselves. The colloquy was called with the intent to reach religious concord, and that effort failed. Poissy had been the anti-Calvinist French evangelicals' best chance at implementing their vision of reform at the national level. For a brief moment, the regent Queen-mother, the first prince of the blood, the chancellor, and even Charles de Guise, the Cardinal of Lorraine, were all working toward a religious compromise solution for France. Although it failed, the dream of concord continued. The Edict of January specified that the decree was a temporary provision for peaceful coexistence "while waiting for God to give us the grace and ability to reunite and come back to the same sheepfold, which is our entire desire and principal intention."[59] Thus, the conflict between the Calvinists' desire for biconfessional toleration and the Gallican evangelicals' goal of uniconfessional concord continued. In the years following Poissy, this conflict only grew more bitter, as evidenced by the series of attacks launched by Bauduin and the Calvinists against one another.

7.3. Bauduin versus The "Lemannic Lord," 1561–1565

In October 1561, just after the Colloquy of Poissy, Calvin published a *Response to a Certain Cunning "Moyenneur," Who under the Guise of Bringing Peace Endeavors to Break the Course of the Gospel in France.*[60] The treatise was

---

[59] "pour entretenir noz subjectz en paix et concorde en attendant que Dieu nous face la grace de les pouvoir reunir et remectre en une mesme bergerie, qui est tout nostre desir et principale intention." "Édit de Janvier," Saint-Germain-en-Laye, 17 janvier 1562, in Bernard Barbiche, et al., eds., *L'édit de Nantes et ses antécédents (1562–1598)*, I, [03], online at http://elec.enc.sorbonne.fr/editsdepacification/edit_01.

[60] Calvin, *Responsio ad versipellem quendam mediatorem*, in CO 9:525–60. A French translation of the text appeared less than two months later: Calvin, *Response à un cauteleux et rusé moyenneur*, also printed in Jean Calvin, *Recueil des opuscules, c'est à dire, Petits traictez de M. Jean Calvin* (Geneva: Baptiste Pinereul, 1566), 1885–1918. An edition in modern French is available in Calvin, *Oeuvres*, 573–621. Higman and Roussel note that the 1566 French edition is somewhat different from the 1561 French version and that the later one is actually closer to Calvin's language. Calvin, *Oeuvres*, 1291–93. The date of the 1561 translation is established by a letter from Bauduin to Cassander on

a response to Cassander's *De officio*, but Calvin believed that Bauduin had authored the text.

Calvin's *Response* was the opening salvo in a lengthy polemical battle between Bauduin, on the one hand, and Calvin and Beza, on the other.[61] These debates, in effect, extended the one held at Poissy and serve as a reminder that the religious violence between Calvinists and Catholics was not the inevitable consequence of the colloquy. Although the war certainly disrupted their efforts, the Gallican evangelicals persisted and continued to influence the upper nobility and push for the reformation of the French church. Indeed, *reformation* was the term that Bauduin seized upon to characterize his program, accusing the Calvinists of pursuing instead a *transformation* of the church, along the same lines as the Donatists of the fourth century.

7.3.1. Calvin's Argument

In his *Response*, Calvin charges the author of *De officio* with trying "to forge a kind of neutral religion." He accuses Bauduin of claiming both that "the true religion is found as much among the papists as among us," and that after the errors of each are removed, the remnants are to be sewn together to form "a new church out of two different ones."[62] By this reasoning, Calvin charges, one must conclude that "the neutrals who falsely call themselves

---

December 1, 1561: "Declamationem illam Lemannicam, hic etiam Gallicam ediderunt." Erbe, "François Bauduin und Georg Cassander," 551, no. 10, Paris.

[61] In chronological order of composition, the texts were the following: (1) Calvin, *Responsio ad versipellem quendam mediatorem*, (2) Bauduin, *Ad leges de famosis libellis*; (3) Jean Calvin, *Responsio ad Balduini Convicia* (1561), in *CO* 9:561–80; (4) Bauduin, *Responsio altera ad Ioan. Calvinum*; (5) Theodore de Bèze, *Ad Francisci Balduini apostatae Ecebolii convicia responsio* (Geneva: [Jean Crespin], 1563); (6) François Bauduin, *Optati Afri, Milevitani episcopi, Libri sex de schismate Donatistarum, Adversus Parmenianum, multo quam antehac emendatiores, cum praefatione Fr. Balduini* (Paris: Claude Fremy, 1563), esp. avi[v]–dvii[v], prefatory letter to "Ioanni Lucanio" (anagram of Ioanni Caluino); (7) François Bauduin and Michael Fabricius, *Responsio ad Calvinum et Bezam, pro Francisco Balduino juriscons., cum refutatione calumniarum, de scriptura et traditione. Adiecimus eiusdem Fr. Balduini alteram responsionem ad Io. Calvinum* (Cologne: Wernerus Richwinus, 1564), esp. 1[r]–33[v] (two letters from Bauduin to Calvin, October 24 and November 1, 1563) and 134[r]–170[r], "Ex Fr. Balduini commentariis rerum ecclesiasticarum," directed mostly against Beza.

[62] "Nostre bon reformateur donc est tellement moyen, que par une ruse secrete il forge une maniere de religion neutre. La vraye religion est tant entre les Papistes qu'entre nous, et toutesfois il dit que les uns et les autres sont entachez de plusieurs erreurs. Que reste-il, sinon que d'un costé et d'autre une partie de la doctrine estant abolie, on couse ensemble les pieces qui seront de demeurant, et que de là on voye sortir une nouvelle Eglise composée de deux diverses?" Calvin, *Response à un cauteleux et rusé moyenneur*, in *Recueil des opuscules*, p. 1912 (*CO* 9:554–55).

Nicodemites are alone wise and remain on the right path."[63] Calvin's use of the term *Nicodemite* shows that he saw Bauduin and his fellow *moyenneurs* of the 1560s as the same enemy he had been fighting since the 1530s.

Much of Calvin's treatise focuses on Cassander's fundamental argument in *De officio* that understanding the Scriptures requires the common consent of the church. Cassander argues that this consent is found in the universal catholic tradition, which is "nothing other than the explanation of Scripture itself."[64] Calvin argues, by contrast, that insistence on common consent would mean that "Scripture would have no weight unless aided by men's determination,"[65] and it would undermine the Protestant teaching on salvation.[66] Thus, he comes to the conclusion that the goal of the author of *De officio* was "to break up the good accord that the faithful have together in order to halt the advance of the Gospel."[67] Calvin concludes that the author, whom he believed to be Bauduin, "having apostasized many times, deserves no more credit than a dog and an enemy of Christ's cross."[68]

7.3.2. Bauduin's Response

Bauduin soon responded in several publications to the "furious and slanderous book of the Lemannic lord."[69] His arguments focused on the

[63] "Il est bien vray que par ce moyen il faudra tenir pour resolu, que ceux qui font des neutres, lesquels à fausses enseignes se nomment Nicodemites, sont seuls sages, et seuls tiennent le droit train." Calvin, *Response à un cauteleux et rusé moyenneur*, in *Recueil des opuscules*, p. 1913 (*CO* 9:555).

[64] "Atque haec est, quae catholica traditio et veritas non scripta a nonnullis appellatur. Quamquam in iis quae fidei quaestiones attingunt, nihil est quod scripturis sacris non aliquo modo contineatur: cum haec traditio nihil aliud sit, quam Scripturae ipsius explicatio et interpretatio." Cassander, *De officio*, 6.

[65] "Mais cest habile reformateur nous tire bien d'un autre costé par ses circuits: c'est que l'Escriture n'ait nul poids, sinon estant aidée des determinations des hommes." Calvin, *Response à un cauteleux et rusé moyenneur*, in *Recueil des opuscules*, p. 1888 (*CO* 9:532).

[66] "Cependant s'il nous faut puiser de leur tradition et enseignement la doctrine de salut, toute nostre fiance sera sans vigueur. . . . Ainsi si on en veut croire ce nouveau maistre, tous les poincts desquels la cognoissance est plus necessaire à salut, non seulement demeureront à demi ensevelis, mais n'auront plus de certitude, pource que nulle tradition ne les conferme." Calvin, *Response à un cauteleux et rusé moyenneur*, in *Recueil des opuscules*, p. 1891 (*CO* 9:535).

[67] "Et pour certain du commencement il avoit dressé toutes ses flesches envenimées pour parvenir à un poinct, qui estoit son but: c'est à savoir, de desunir le bon accord qu'avoyent les fideles ensemble, à fin de rompre le cours de l'Evangile." Calvin, *Response à un cauteleux et rusé moyenneur*, in *Recueil des opuscules*, p. 1913 (*CO* 9:555).

[68] "car ayant esté tant de fois apostat, il ne merite d'avoir non plus de credit, qu'un chien et ennemi de la croix de Christ." Calvin, *Response à un cauteleux et rusé moyenneur*, in *Recueil des opuscules*, p. 1918 (*CO* 9:560).

[69] "mitto ad te furiosum et famosum libellum Lemannici Reguli, et responsionem aliquam meam." Erbe, "François Bauduin und Georg Cassander," 551, no. 10.

Calvinists' encouragement of radical religious change, rather than a true reformation, of the church, on Calvin's assumption of pope-like authority, and on his moral character in slandering Bauduin.

Bauduin insisted on the need for a reformation that would bring peace and unity to the French church. He praises the Colloquy of Poissy, telling Calvin it was "more religious than any discussion I ever had with you."[70] He asks Calvin, "Why are you so riled up against such colloquies, which seek to find religious methods of restoring the church and establishing concord?"[71] And he pleads with Calvin, "I urge you to be the author and promoter of unity rather than of disorder. I speak of Christian unity and peace, which can follow the reformation of the church. . . . For we seek no other peace and unity than that which is of Christ."[72] By contrast, he charges that the Calvinists seek not to reform but to transform the Church.[73]

The theme of reformation versus transformation is central to Bauduin's writings against the Calvinists; a reformation of the church, he argues, would seek to fix problems and abuses; the Calvinists' transformation of the church, by contrast, would entail the complete dismantling of the Apostolic church. The Calvinists' goal of transformation rather than reformation makes them no different, Bauduin charges, from the Donatists of the early church. Like the Donatists, he argues, the Calvinists insist that the problems of the Catholic Church render the existing church illegitimate and in need not just of reform but of replacement by a purer church:

> Do you not dare to sprinkle with infamy and to burden with atrocious crime not only so many thousands of pious and Christian people of this age who dissent from you, but also the entire ancient church and its religious

---

[70] "Anno superiori Rex ille [Antoine de Bourbon], in cuius clientela sum, iussit, ut magnis de rebus convenirem Principem Cardinalem [the Cardinal of Lorraine], qui tunc erat Lutetiae. Colloquium de religionis quaestionibus controversis fuit, quod, Deo teste, dico et affirmo religiosius fuisse, quam ullum fuerit unquam, quod tecum aliquando habuerim." Bauduin, *Responsio altera ad Ioan. Calvinum*, 37–38.

[71] "Cur te tam valde urunt talia colloquia, in quibus de religiosis rationibus Ecclesiae restituendae et concordiae constituendae quaeritur?" Bauduin, *Responsio altera ad Ioan. Calvinum*, 38.

[72] "Interea te obtestor, ut unitatis potius quam (Pauli verbo utar [1 Cor. 14:33]) ἀκαταστασίας suasor auctorque esse velis. Unitatem dico et pacem Christianam, quae Ecclesiae reformationem consequi potest. . . . Nam (ut iterum dicam) non aliam aut pacem aut unitatem quaerimus, quam quae Christi sit." Bauduin, *Responsio altera ad Ioan. Calvinum*, 90–91.

[73] "Caeterum obtestor omnes sapientes, ut considerent, quale sit hoc totum artificium religionis transformandae atque inflectendae." Bauduin, *Responsio altera ad Ioan. Calvinum*, 87.

moderation? You with the Donatists often exclaim, "The whole world has apostatized!" You say that everyone errs except for you and your followers.[74]

Echoing Castellio, Bauduin charges that Calvin wants to murder all who disagree with him: "You condemn almost all as heretics. You want to burn the condemned, and by a similar sentence you would slay those who do not approve of these things. So who, therefore, would you leave alive?"[75] Bauduin explicitly thanks Castellio for writing against the Calvinists' understanding of heresy,[76] but denies ever having met or corresponded with him.[77]

Bauduin's second main line of attack on Calvin is the same one that we have seen repeatedly from others, namely that Calvin has effectively made himself a tyrannical pope of a new church. "Tyranny," Bauduin insists to Calvin, "is intolerable in the church. . . . You would be wise to contain yourself. For there are others who also understand what religion is. You err over and over again if you think that whatever pleases you is right. Having been set up on that throne, you scoff at all and order all to silence, so that you alone might reign, command, and hurl thunderbolts."[78] He notes that, by contrast with Calvin, "there are some serious, dedicated, and wise men, with true zeal for the true religion . . . who see much farther and know what needs to be done and what should be copied, and who want both church and state to be safe."[79] He mentions, in particular, Antoine of Navarre and Antoine's late mother-in-law, Marguerite, noting the Queen of Navarre's low estimation of

---

[74] "Itane vero audes, non dico tot huius aetatis piorum et Christianorum hominum milia, qui abs te dissentiunt, sed et universam Ecclesiam veterem, eiusque religiosam moderationem, non iam dico infamia aspergere, sed tam atroci crimine onerare? Tu cum Donatistis saepe exclamas, 'Totus mundus apostatavit.' Tu cum omnes, praeter te et tuos, errare dicas." Bauduin, *Responsio altera ad Ioan. Calvinum*, 71.

[75] "haereseos prope omnes damnas: damnatos ardere vis: rursusque eos, quibus haec non probantur, simili sententia iugulas. Cui igitur vitam relinquis?" Bauduin, *Responsio altera ad Ioan. Calvinum*, 71.

[76] "Credo te tam hebetem non esse, quin videas talem definitionem, et eius auctori et tibi esse periculosam, et propterea gratias agas Castalioni, qui de utroque solicitus, eam esse vitiosam ostendit." Bauduin, *Responsio altera ad Ioan. Calvinum*, 73.

[77] "neque Castalionem (ne iterum fingas me eius causam agere) unquam vel vidi vel audivi: ac ne per literas quidem unquam sum allocutus." Bauduin, *Responsio altera ad Ioan. Calvinum*, 110. He would soon meet Castellio, on his return trip from the Council of Trent. Erbe, *François Bauduin*, 150.

[78] "et intolerabilis in Ecclesia res est, tyrannis. . . . Ergo si te contineas, feceris sapienter. Nam et alii quid religio sit, sciunt. Erras vero iterumque erras, si in eo iam te solio collocatum putas, ut tibi quod libet, liceat: ut omnibus insultes, silentium omnibus indicas, solus regnes, imperes, fulmines." Bauduin, *Ad leges de famosis libellis*, 53.

[79] "Imo vero omnium ordinum aliqui viri graves, cordati, sapientes supersunt, qui cum verae religionis vero studio retinent suum illud (ut recte dictum olim est) incoctum generoso pectus honesto, qui longius prospiciunt, quid agatur, quid simuletur: qui Ecclesiam cum Republica salvam esse volunt." Bauduin, *Ad leges de famosis libellis*, 53.

Calvin.[80] Bauduin repeatedly assaults what he sees as Calvin's arrogance in claiming to speak for Christ. "What?" he asks, "Do you think that I was ever so lost that I would put you in Christ's place? Try to persuade others, if you can, that those who depart from you also abandon Christ. I, for one, know just how much distance there is between you and Christ. So that I might draw nearer to him, my conscience compels me to withdraw from your newfangled counsels and conspiracies."[81] As we have seen, Calvin's prophetic sense of self led him to believe that he was, in fact, speaking as God's prophet in his theological determinations.[82] Bauduin did not buy it.

Finally, and perhaps most interestingly, Bauduin accused Calvin of calumny and libel. His first response to Calvin was entitled *Commentary on the Laws about Defamatory Books and Calumniators*. Bauduin accuses Calvin of having committed libel himself by accusing Bauduin of writing *De officio*, which, of course, he had not: "A master of great authority (as I hear), but a dictator of greater intemperance and impotence (as I see), has violently attacked that book by publishing a defamatory declamation against it. He has also fashioned me as its author . . . and has poured out terrible bile in a blind rage."[83] Calvin's ultimate crime in Bauduin's eyes, however, and the reason that Bauduin composed the treatise around the theme of calumny, is that Calvin pretends there is a theological gulf between them, when, Bauduin insists, there is not: "You and I were fellow students for so many years in the same school of piety. . . . You hold forth your doctrine to me with arrogant disdain. But doctrine is not in question; we understand perfectly well from where you draw it. You litigate matters about which there is no case between us."[84] In essence, Bauduin is saying that he and Calvin agree perfectly well on

---

[80] "Ego cum et veteres et novos in Gallia multos possim patronos laudare, viros clarissimos atque amplissimos, tum vero unum imprimis agnosco, ad quem me Deus, cum primum huc redii, applicuit, optimum dico et nobilissimum Regem illum, apud cuius antea socrum, Reginam lectissimam atque sanctissimam, (cuius alias de te iudicium tibi opponam) honestissimo me loco fuisse, olim etiam doluisti." Bauduin, *Ad leges de famosis libellis*, 58.

[81] "Quid? An me tam perditum esse unquam putasti, ut te Christi loco locarem? Aliis si potes, persuadeas, quod impudentissime iactas, eos, qui a te desciscunt, abs Christo desciscere. Ego quidem certe, quantum inter te et eum intersit, scio: et ut ad illum propius accederem, conscientia mea me coëgit ab novis tuis consiliis et conspirationibus secessionem facere." Bauduin, *Responsio altera ad Ioan. Calvinum*, 49.

[82] See 205.

[83] "magnae (ut audio) magister auctoritatis, verum maioris (ut video) intemperantiae atque adeo impotentiae Dictator, non modo libellum illum terribiliter, edita adversaria declamatione famosa, exagitat, sed et me eius libelli auctorem esse fingit . . . et . . . caeco furore effundit suam (quod quidam dixit) terribilem bilem." Bauduin, *Ad leges de famosis libellis*, 44–45.

[84] "Tu mihi condiscipulus tot annis in eadem pietatis schola fuisti . . . Tu mihi magno supercilio tuam doctrinam ostentas. Atqui de ea non quaeritur: neque tamen nescimus unde eam hauseris. Tu litigas de iis, de quibus inter nos lis nulla nunc est." Bauduin, *Ad leges de famosis libellis*, 59, 62–63.

doctrine. This was a daring statement. In effect, Bauduin was legitimating Calvin's basic theology in France, even though they disagreed sharply about ecclesiology. Thus, he reveals his desire for a true *via media* solution, like that adopted by Elizabeth I in England: an external, traditional hierarchy coupled with Protestant doctrine. Indeed, Alexander Russell has shown that Bauduin was, in fact, involved in discussions with the English about the Elizabethan settlement and attempted to use it as the basis for a similar agreement between Protestants and Catholics in France.[85]

In the end, Bauduin, believed that posterity would have the last word on Calvin: "What will posterity say, not about me whose name will perhaps be unknown in the future, but about you, the memory of whom you boast will be great and eternal? You might be and might be held to be the greatest theologian, but certainly, unless you become a good man, you cannot even claim to be a theologian."[86] Bauduin indicates that he himself will not go into the details of Calvin's life, "but I leave that to your colleague and associate [André] Zébédée to describe, if it is to be done."[87] We do not know whether Bauduin knew Zébédée personally;[88] he certainly could have met him on one of his trips to Geneva. Regardless, Bauduin's reference to Zébédée here shows that he knew very well the enmity that existed between him and Calvin. In his pamphlet war with Calvin, therefore, Bauduin associated himself with both Zébédée and Castellio, thus situating himself within the network of anti-Calvinists that had been forming for decades across francophone Europe.

7.3.3. Bauduin's Postwar Efforts at Religious Concord

After the First War of Religion, Bauduin continued to push for Gallican evangelical reform, and his efforts captured the attention of Louis de Bourbon, Prince of Condé and brother of Antoine of Navarre. The prince seems to have been planning a religious colloquy to discuss the

---

[85] Alexander Russell, "The Colloquy of Poissy, François Baudouin and English Protestant Identity, 1561–1563," *Journal of Ecclesiastical History* 65 (2014): 551–79, esp. 568–73.

[86] "Quid dicet posteritas, non de me, cuius fortasse nomen erit ignotum posteritati, sed de te, cuius magnam et sempiternam fore memoriam gloriaris? Sis sane vel habearis summus Theologus: at certe ni vir bonus sies, verus non eris Theologus." Bauduin, *Responsio altera ad Ioan. Calvinum*, 17.

[87] "Ego vitam tuam non describam (non enim id est pudoris mei) sed eam familiari et collegae tuo Zebedaeo describendam relinquo, si ita agendum sit." Bauduin, *Responsio altera ad Ioan. Calvinum*, 145.

[88] On Zébédée, see Chapter 4.

doctrine of the early church. His intention was to bring together some of the most moderate voices from both sides of the religious divide in France, with Bauduin and Jean de Monluc representing one side, and François Perrussel and Jean de l'Espine the other.[89] We met Perrussel earlier as one of Castellio's associates.[90] Jean de l'Espine was closer to Calvin, but he had long been a Nicodemite in France and, as we will see in the next chapter, some retained doubts about his attachment to the Geneva church.[91] In the end, the proposed colloquy did not take place, but the proposal itself and the individuals who were to be involved reveal that, even following the First War of Religion, hope remained for a middle way in France.

Whether Condé had been in contact with Bauduin regarding the possibility of a colloquy is uncertain, but Bauduin's most significant later activities certainly brought the two together. Condé had been captured during the first war and, like his brother before him, sought a peaceful way to settle the religious question in France. He called on Bauduin to draw up articles for the Reformation of the Church. The result was Bauduin's *Discourse on Reforming the Church*.[92] According to the posthumous preface by "a friend," possibly Papire Masson,[93] Bauduin composed the text "in order voluntarily to obey the wish of the Prince of Condé, who, at the end of the first troubles, was displeased and annoyed by the mutinies and seditious suggestions of the new

[89] "Hic denuo agitur de instituendo colloquio de controversiis religionis, in quo, quantum coniicio, magis disputabitur de statu veteris Ecclesiae, quam de ipsa doctrina. Dicitur Condaeus exhibuisse Reginae quosdam articulos, qui in eo colloquio examinentur. Delecti sunt ad illud colloquium ab una parte, Episcopus Valentinus et Balduinus, ab altera Franciscus Perrucellus . . . et de Spina." Hubert Languet, *Arcana seculi decimi sexti, Huberti Languet legati, dum viveret, et consiliarii Saxonici Epistolae secretae*, edited by J. P. Ludwig (Halle (Saale): J. F. Zeitlerus and H. G. Musselius, 1699), 2.260–61, no. 92, Languet to Ulrich Mordeisen, August 23, 1563.

[90] See 199–200.

[91] See 295–96. On L'Espine generally, see Louis Hogu, *Jean de l'Espine, moraliste et théologien (1505?–1597): Sa vie, son oeuvre, ses idées* (Paris: H. Champion, 1913); Bernard Roussel, "Jean de l'Espine (c. 1505–97): écrire dans un temps de troubles," in *The Sixteenth-Century French Religious Book*, edited by Andrew Pettegree, et al., 138–56, St. Andrews Studies in Reformation History (Aldershot, UK: Ashgate, 2001).

[92] This was first published in François Bauduin, *Discours sur le faict de la Reformation de l'Eglise par Françoys Balduin, et par luy envoyé à un grand Seigneur de France, avec la response dudit Seigneur* (s.l.: s.n., 1564). The titular "grand Seigneur" was, in fact, Condé. This publication, however, came from a hostile press. The preface, "Au lecteur chrestien," sought to distance Condé from Bauduin, whom it describes as a "minister of Satan" (Aii^r). Condé's alleged response to Bauduin's text was entirely forged. To rectify this, Bauduin's text was later republished under the title, *Advis de François Balduin jurisconsulte, sur le faict de la reformation de l'église, avec response à un predicant calomniateur, lequel sous un faux nom et tiltre d'un Prince de France s'opposa à l'Advis susdict* (Paris: Nicolas Chesneau, 1578). Bauduin's text can also be found in *Mémoires de Condé*, 5:139–45.

[93] Turchetti, *Concordia o Tolleranza*, 558, n.4.

preachers and who desired a reformation by another method more gentle than by force of arms."[94]

From the outset of the treatise, Bauduin acknowledges the substantial problems with the Catholic Church: "We are very much in agreement that it has never been more necessary to discuss and bring about the Reformation of the church, for there is a horrible corruption."[95] Nevertheless, he again draws a sharp distinction between the reformation that he and his fellow moderates wanted and the transformation that the Calvinists were urging.[96] The apostles, he argues, received the command from Christ to make a transformation of the church, altering it entirely from Judaism to Christianity.[97] Bauduin continues: "Today," however, "those who are responsible for providing order have a duty similar rather to the prophets than to that of the apostles, that is, to restore things to their original state and not to change them otherwise."[98] He suggests, as had Cassander before Poissy, that the model on which to base this reformation is the early church as it existed around the time of Ambrose, Augustine, and Chrysostom.[99] Thus, he suggests, there is no need "to introduce a completely new form of church, which would be, as it were, a third," after the churches of Moses and the apostles.[100]

---

[94] "bref, pour avoir volontairement obey à la priere . . . du feu illustre Prince de Condé, à l'issue des premiers troubles, qui estoit desplaisant et ennuyé des mutineries et suggestions seditieuses des predicants nouveaux, et desiroit une reformation par autre voye et plus douce que de faict et par armes." Bauduin, *Advis sur le faict de la reformation* (1578), 5.

[95] "Nous sommes bien d'accord, qu'il ne fut jamais plus necessaire de parler et traitter de la reformation de l'Eglise, car il y a une horrible corruption." *Mémoires de Condé* 5:139.

[96] "Cela presupposé, pour parler de la reformation exterieure de l'Eglise, nous disons en premier lieu, qu'il faut observer la difference qu'il y a entre une reformation et une transformation. Nous appelons maintenant *transformation*, quand on efface du tout une forme visible, pour en introduire une autre toute nouvelle. Nous appelons *reformation*, quand on tasche à reparer et establir la forme premiere." *Mémoires de Condé*, 5:139.

[97] "Après Jesus-Christ, les Apostres ont plustost eu charge d'une transformation, c'est-à-dire, d'abolir ladite forme Mosaïque, avec ses ceremonies, et en introduire ou subroguer une toute autre, que nous appelons *Chrestienne*, en laquelle le service de Dieu seroit moins ceremonial, et à laquelle tous peuples seroyent conviez, et laquelle seroit espandue par toute la terre." *Mémoires de Condé* 5:140.

[98] "Ainsi aujourd'huy . . . ceux qui ont la charge d'y donner ordre, ont une charge plustost semblable aux Prophetes, qu'aux Apostres, c'est-à-dire, de reduire les choses à leur premier estat, et non pas de les changer autrement." *Mémoires de Condé* 5:140.

[99] "il semble qu'elle [la forme de l'église] ne se trouve plus vivement et amplement representée, qu'en ce que nous lisons de Saint Ambroise en Italie, Saint Augustin en Affricque, Saint Chriosostome en Orient. Car aussi semble, que lors a esté la conclusion finalement arrestée et conclue de ce que requerons, voire que ça esté l'estat magnifique jadis prédit par les Prophetes parlans de la majesté, gloire, et magnificence visible de l'Eglise Chrestienne, dont les Rois et Empereurs seroyent nourrissiers, ainsi que les nomme Jesaye, et tels, qu'un Constantin ou un Theodose a esté." *Mémoires de Condé* 5:141.

[100] "nous disons que ladite forme est comme le patron et pourtrait, auquel nous devrions aujourd'huy compasser la reformation, plustost que de dresser ou introduire une toute nouvelle forme d'Eglise, qui seroit comme la tierce." *Mémoires de Condé* 5:143.

Both Bauduin and Calvin saw each other as inventing a totally new, perverse, third-way church. For Calvin, there was the true church of Christ, the false church of Antichrist, and Bauduin's monstrous mixture of the two. For Bauduin, there was the Mosaic Jewish church, the Apostolic Christian church, and Calvin's newly invented, Donatistic church. Restore the church of the Fathers, he suggests, and all will be well.

Unfortunately, we do not know how Condé received Bauduin's proposal. It is no stretch, however, to assert that the prince's appeal to Bauduin would have vexed Calvin had he lived to hear of it.[101] As Jon Balserak has argued, Calvin hoped that a Protestant Prince of the Blood—first Antoine of Navarre and then his brother Condé—would lead the Huguenots in a Reformed insurrection against the Catholic establishment in France in order to establish the "true religion" in the kingdom.[102] Antoine, by working with Bauduin before the Colloquy of Poissy, had deeply disappointed Calvin. Condé's appeal to "the apostate" Bauduin would have been just as disheartening, as indeed it was to Calvin's successor, Beza.

The year after Bauduin's *Discourse on Reforming the Church*, Beza published his Latin New Testament, with a preface addressed to Condé that alluded clearly to Bauduin: "Here, the proposals come to mind of certain very subtle individuals (as they think themselves), who think that we must not transform the church but reform it. . . . As an example, we recall the vain and futile collections of such things made by George Cassander and his disciple—I am talking about that crazy apostate whose very name I do not want to soil these pages."[103] Beza worried that Bauduin was pulling Condé away from the Reformed cause, and virtually the entire New Testament preface was Beza's attempt to keep Condé firmly in place as the champion of the Calvinist churches. Most dangerous, he believed, were not the "open enemies of the truth," but the "new Sinons"—a reference to the treacherous Greek Sinon who persuaded the Trojans to bring in the famous Greek

---

[101] The Genevan reformer had died, however, on May 27, 1564, probably before Condé approached Bauduin. The date of Condé's request to Bauduin is unknown, but in Beza's correspondence, there does not seem to be any reference to Bauduin's contact with Condé until December 1564: "Cardinalis totus est in eo ut Condensem oblata in matrimonium nepti Scotiae regina a nobis avertat, strenuam operam etiam navante impuro apostata Balduino." *Bèze Cor.* 5: 174, no. 372, Beza to Bullinger, Geneva, December 30, 1564.

[102] Baserak, *John Calvin as Sixteenth-Century Prophet*, 118–24.

[103] " Icy me vient en memoire le propos de certains personnages des plus subtilz (ce leur semble) qui pensent qu'il ne fault pas transformer l'Eglise, mais la reformer. . . . Dont nous serviront pour exemple ces vains et futiles ramas de telle chose de G. Cassander et de son disciple—je dy de ce fol apostat du nom duquel je n'ay voulu souiller ces escripts." *Bèze Cor.* 6:262, Annexe II, Beza to the Prince de Condé and the Reformed Nobility of France, Geneva, February 20, 1565.

horse—"who forge for themselves some new alloy-religion" and take advantage of the Eucharistic quarrels to sow discord.[104] Thus, even in 1565, Beza was afraid that the *moyenneurs* still held too much influence over the Huguenot nobility, and he made every effort to keep the nobles in line with Geneva's uncompromising religious position.

In the end, Beza would get his wish, and Condé would stay faithful to the Huguenot cause. In 1567, Condé attempted to seize King Charles IX in the "Surprise of Meaux," which reignited hostilities in France. Although the dream of religious concord in France never died completely, the Second War of Religion—and later the St. Bartholomew's Day massacre—effectively put to rest the possibility of an Elizabethan-style religious *via media* that Bauduin had been encouraging over the previous years. Bauduin himself continued to push for peace in his native Netherlands and remained active in France as well. But he would never again play such a prominent role as a negotiator in the pursuit of religious compromise in France.

7.4. Charles Du Moulin: Idiosyncratic Prophet for a Syncretistic Religion in France

"You have publicly dogmatized and spread everywhere," complained Charles Du Moulin to the Calvinists, "this new article of your faith, namely that one must be either a Papist or a Huguenot."[105] The great French jurisconsult, and one-time teacher of François Bauduin, rejected this stark choice. Du Moulin's religious beliefs are nearly impossible to classify using standard terminology. A great defender of the Gallican church's traditional liberties with regard to Rome, he spent several years among the Reformed of Switzerland and Germany before returning to France and ostensibly to the Catholic Church. Meanwhile, he continued to associate with evangelicals and to write books with ever more theological focus, most containing much Protestant doctrine. He expressed admiration for the Lutheran Augsburg Confession yet held a Zwinglian view of the Eucharist. He turned completely, however,

---

[104] "Je ne parle poinct de ces ennemys ouvertz de la verité, mais j'entens de ces Sinons-là, lesquelz se forgeant en partie je ne sçay quelle religion metive, en partie aussi prenent occasion de ces malheureuses contentions de la Cene du Seigneur pour semer entre vous des discordes." *Bèze Cor.* 6:268, Annexe II.

[105] "[Vous] avez publiquement dogmatisé et semé par tout ce nouveau article de votre foi, qu'il faut estre papiste ou huguenot." Du Moulin, *Contre les calomnies des Calvinistes*, in Du Moulin, *Opera*, 5:607.

against his former Calvinist friends, for he despised the foreign influence of Geneva's consistories in France. And his Gallican principles led him to reject any ecclesiology that deferred to Rome and the papacy. Indeed, although he was for a time firmly in the Reformed camp, a survey of Du Moulin's career as a whole demonstrates that he perfectly typifies those whose outlook Wanegffelen characterizes as "ni Rome ni Genève." The only terms that one absolutely cannot apply to him during his last years in France are "Papist" and "Calvinist."

Du Moulin's early Catholic biographers sought to emphasize his "reconversion" to Catholicism after a flirtation with Protestantism and used his late writings against the Calvinists as evidence of his return to Rome.[106] More recent scholars have downplayed any attachment Du Moulin had to the Protestants, calling it "ephemeral" or arguing that he had never truly joined them at all.[107] To discount Du Moulin's Protestant sympathies, however, is to misunderstand his theological trajectory. In fact, Du Moulin adhered firmly to the Reformed faith for several years, and his attachment to its doctrine was far from ephemeral. Toward the end of his life, Du Moulin saw himself as no less than a prophet for the restoration of religion in France. His vision was similar to that of other Gallican evangelicals we have seen; he aimed to combine Protestant doctrine with the existing Gallican church structure. He did not fit precisely the model laid out by his student Bauduin; indeed, he was far more openly Protestant in his doctrine than Bauduin was in the 1560s. But like both Bauduin and Monluc, Du Moulin saw himself in the line of French evangelical reformers going back to Meaux, who sought to reform the French church from within.

---

[106] Note the last part of the title of the earliest full biography: Julien Brodeau, *La vie de Maistre Charles du Molin, advocat au Parlement de Paris, tirée des titres de sa maison, de ses propres escrits, de l'histoire du temps, des registres de la Cour, et autres monuments publics. Et sa mort Chrestienne et Catholique* (Paris: Jean Guignard, 1654). Brodeau's biography is also printed in Du Moulin, *Opera*, 1:1–60; see esp. 52 on testimonies about his death.

[107] Jean-Louis Thireau notes, "Ce bref séjour parmi les calvinistes eut une influence certaine, quoique éphémère, sur les idées religieuses de notre juriste." Thireau, *Charles Du Moulin (1500–1566): Étude sur les sources, la méthode, les idées politiques et économiques d'un juriste de la Renaissance*, THR 176 (Geneva: Droz, 1980), 39. Wanegffelen is even less convinced of Du Moulin's attachment to the Reformed: "il y a sans doute de l'exagération à dire, comme Jean-Louis Thireau à la suite de Julien Brodeau, qu''il se convertit à la Réforme.' . . . Au fond, comme tant d'autres, Du Moulin, croyant intensément à l'absolue gratuité du salut et animé d'un très profond désir de Réforme de l'Eglise, a été conduit à manifester de l'intérêt pour la réformation protestante, sans y adhérer." Wanegffelen, *Ni Rome ni Genève*, 134.

7.4.1. Du Moulin Among the Reformed,
1552–1556

Charles Du Moulin (1500–1566) was born near Paris to a family among the lower nobility. After initial studies at the University of Paris, he studied law at Orléans and Poitiers. In 1522, he became a lawyer with the Paris parlement. In 1539, he rose to prominence by publishing a massive commentary on Paris customary law.[108] It was around this time that Du Moulin became interested in evangelical ideas, and for more than a decade he appears to have lived a Nicodemite life in France, occasionally housing, as we saw earlier, Bauduin, Crespin, and Hotman.[109] In 1552, however, he wrote a *Commentary* on King Henri II's edict against *petites dates* (taxes paid to Rome on ecclesiastical benefices), which led to his exile.[110] Du Moulin no doubt intended this text as a support for Henri II's Gallican tendencies, but the Paris Faculty of Theology and Parlement thought he went too far, straying well beyond traditional Gallicanism into outright Protestantism.[111] Du Moulin fled France, leaving behind his wife, Louise de Beldon, and children. He would not see them again for several years.

In July 1552, Du Moulin arrived in Basel. For the next year, he moved around among the Calvinists in Geneva, Lausanne, and Neuchâtel. He hoped initially to find a teaching position at the Lausanne Academy, but the Bernese could not accommodate him. In Lausanne, he stayed with his former lodger Hotman, who reported that he was becoming a "great devourer" of Calvin's books.[112] In his late writings against the Calvinists, Du Moulin would protest that he had always opposed them, even during this stay in francophone Switzerland, but as Jean-Louis Thireau correctly points out, this version of events deserves no credit.[113] All of the evidence from his contemporary

---

[108] Charles Du Moulin, *Prima pars commentariorum in Consuetudines Parisienses* (Paris: Poncetum le Preux, 1539). The very first text following the title page of this edition is an epigram by François Bauduin praising the work. Du Moulin would expand on the work throughout his career. The full, final text is in Du Moulin, *Opera*, 1:1–934 (second numbering).

[109] Thireau, *Charles Du Moulin*, 32; see also 215.

[110] Charles Du Moulin, *Commentarius ad edictum Henrici Secundi contra parvas datas, et abusus curiae Romanae, et in antiqua edicta et senatusconsulta Franciae, contra Annatarum, et id genus abusus, multas decisiones iuris et praxes continens*, in idem, *Opera*, 4:297–368.

[111] The Faculty of Theology condemned the work as "toti orbi Christianissimo perniciosus, scandalosus, seditiosus, schismaticus, impius, blasphemus in sanctos, conformis haeresibus Waldensium, Wiclefistarum, Hussitarum et Lutheranorum, et maxime conspirans erroribus Marsilii Patavini." D'Argentré, 2:205–206. A copy of the parlement's proceedings may be found in BNF, ms. DuPuy 488, 7ʳ–12ʳ (digitized: https://gallica.bnf.fr/ark:/12148/btv1b103164401/f23.image).

[112] "Et a Domino Molinaeo scriptorum tuorum helluone tuique ut videtur cupidissimo valebis." *CO* 14:414, no. 1675, Hotman to Calvin, Lausanne, November 25, 1552.

[113] Thireau, *Charles Du Moulin*, 39.

correspondence suggests that he had perfectly amicable relations with Calvin and his allies at the time.

Indeed, the evidence from his correspondence, much of which either remains unpublished or has been published only relatively recently,[114] suggests that, contrary to the claims of some modern scholars,[115] Du Moulin saw himself during these years as a full adherent to the Swiss Reformed churches. This is most abundantly clear during Du Moulin's stay in Tübingen. In September 1553, Du Moulin left Neuchâtel, where he had been staying, for Strasbourg, and from there he went to Tübingen, where found a position teaching law. Earlier scholarship has entirely misrepresented Du Moulin's time in Tübingen. His early biographer Julien Brodeau claimed that his enemies there labeled him an Ubiquitist, that is, someone who followed the Lutheran doctrine of the ubiquity of Christ's resurrected body.[116] Others have suggested that Du Moulin could not distinguish clearly between "Papists" and "Lutherans."[117] Neither claim has merit.

Far from being an Ubiquitist himself, Du Moulin noted to Bullinger that he had argued vigorously against the doctrine of ubiquity, calling it "not only false but also monstrous and not to be endured."[118] He wondered how anyone who adopted this doctrine would dare to "condemn so many holy churches, such as those in Lausanne, Geneva, Neuchâtel, Basel, and the church of our princes at Montbéliard"[119] Further, Du Moulin explained to Bullinger, "The next Sunday, when they administered the Supper, I did not want to commune,

---

[114] See, esp. his correspondence with Heinrich Bullinger. Thireau lists fourteen unpublished letters between Du Moulin and Bullinger between 1553 and 1555. See also Du Moulin's correspondence from 1552 to 1556, mostly with Boniface Amerbach, in the *Amerbachkorrespondenz*, nos. 3558, 3565, 3628, 3643, 3672, 3693, 3822, 3838, 3847, 3860, 3866, 3891, 3893, 3926, 3927, 3955, 3956, 3990, 4012, 4026, 4027, 4029, 4043, 4046, 4055, 4059, 4060; vol. 8, Anhang 11; vol. 10.2, Anhang 1, 2, 3, 6. None of the *Amerbachkorrespondenz* letters were published at the time of Thireau's inventory: *Charles Du Moulin*, 437–41.

[115] Especially Wanegffelen, see n. 107.

[116] Du Moulin, *Opera*, 1.1:29.

[117] Du Moulin wrote to Calvin, "Papistae hic, quae tota fere schola est, omnium theologorum me excludere voluerunt," to which the editors noted, "Deest vocabulum. Papistas vocat Lutheranos." *CO* 15: 86, and n.6, no. 1932, [Tübingen], March 31, 1554. Likewise, Thireau writes, "les deux termes [luthériens et papistes] [étaient] alors pour lui à peu près synonymes." *Charles Du Moulin*, 42. Jean Carbonnier helped fix some of the problems with Brodeau's narrative, but he, too, notes, "papistes, schismatiques, ce sont les qualificatifs les plus doux qu'il applique à ses collègues luthériens." Jean Carbonnier, "Dumoulin à Tubingue," *Revue générale du droit, de la législation et de la jurisprudence en France et à l'étranger* 60 (1936): 194–209; here, 201.

[118] "Excepi tamen articulum de ubiquitate, quem non solum falsum, sed etiam prodigiosum esse dixi, et merito non ferendum." ZZb, ms. F62, 369ᵛ, Du Moulin to Bullinger, Tübingen, [February 1554]; a contemporary copy is also in AEN, 1PAST 9.68a.

[119] "Rogavi quanam fronte tot sanctas ecclesias, Losannensem, Genevensem, Neocomensem, Basiliensem, et principis nostri Mompelgardensem damnare auderet?" ZZb, ms. F62, 369ᵛ. At the time, Tübingen and Montbéliard both lay within the jurisdiction of the Dukes of Württemberg.

since I did not want to seem to condemn the holy churches by which I have communed and to adhere to a schismatic church."[120] Five months later, he repeated to Bullinger his concern about taking communion in Tübingen, writing that he did not want to seem to condemn "your churches in which I communed and with whom I remain in spirit."[121] These are not the words of someone who "showed an interest in the Protestant Reformation without adhering to it."[122] Indeed, it shows that he adhered not just to the Protestant Reformation but to one specific branch of Protestantism, communing with the Reformed but refusing to do so among the Lutherans.

Similarly, Du Moulin's alleged inability to distinguish between Lutherans and Catholics in Tübingen is entirely unfounded. He wrote to Bullinger, "Some here are clear and obstinate papists. Others are Lutherans, but not pure Lutherans, for they hold to an Augsburg Confession corrupted by horrible pseudo-adiaphora. Others are of the two religions, and others have no religion."[123] Certainly, someone who could discern the difference between "pure Lutherans" and "pseudo-adiaphora" Lutherans was fully capable of distinguishing between Lutherans and Catholics. In fact, the evidence from this period reveals clearly that Du Moulin was not confusing Lutherans and Catholics; rather, he was involved in entirely distinct disputes with each. His fights with the Lutherans were over the doctrine of the Eucharist, as we have just seen, while his conflicts with the Catholics revolved around graduation ceremonies at the university.

On the graduation issue, Du Moulin criticized the Dean of the Arts Faculty for announcing the graduations of students "by Apostolic authority," which to him implied a Catholic connection, instead of on the authority of the princes and the university itself.[124] He explained:

This academy is and ought to be Christian. Thanks to God and to the support of our illustrious prince, we have a Christian church in which the

---

[120] "Sed dominica proxima, cum coena Domini celebraretur, communicare nolui, quia non potui, ne viderer sanctas ecclesias quibus communicavi damnare, et schismati adherere." ZZb, ms. F62, 369ᵛ.

[121] "nolo enim communicare, tum ne consensum schismate, tum ne sanctas vestras ecclesias (quibus communicavi, et quocum semper spiritu maneo) aliquatenus reprobem." ZZb, ms. F62, 366ʳ, Du Moulin to Bullinger, Tübingen, July 31, 1554.

[122] Wanegffelen, Ni Rome ni Genève, 134.

[123] "Alii hic papistae manifesti et obstinati . . . , alii Lutherani, non puri, sed confessionem Augustanam fermentati horrendis pseudadiaphoris, alii utriusque, alii nullius religionis." CO 15:225, no. 2006, Du Moulin to Bullinger, Tübingen, September 4, 1554.

[124] See Carbonnier, "Dumoulin à Tubingue," 204.

Gospel and the Word of God are preached and administered purely. The frauds, deceits, and idolatries of the Roman Antichrist have been uncovered, and after they have been destroyed, we must not bring them back. . . . I said many other things in the school senate, and I warned them frankly that they must not do anything against the Reformation of the Gospel. Thus, to conduct the promotions of Masters or Doctoral students, or to do any other acts in this school, on the basis of Apostolic authority, which is of the Roman pope, who is true Antichrist, is a truly papist and antichristian act.[125]

Thus, in his struggles with the Lutherans over the Eucharist and with the Catholics over graduation, Du Moulin was hardly one of the "faithful between two pulpits," but instead identified definitively with the antipapal "Reformation of the Gospel," as it was preached in Protestant Switzerland.

Du Moulin's struggles in Tübingen led him to seek a post elsewhere, and Duke Christoph of Württemberg invited him to move to Montbéliard, which was under the jurisdiction of Christoph's uncle Georg. Du Moulin welcomed the opportunity and moved to the city in October 1554. Montbéliard was francophone, and it was geographically closer to his wife and children, whom he had not seen for more than two years and with whom, his correspondence reveals, he very much wanted to be reunited. Around this time, he also learned that King Henri II was agreeable to the possibility of his return to France. Du Moulin wrote to Boniface Amerbach, "If I would be willing to dissimulate in the matter of religion—far be it from me to do so!—it would happen immediately."[126] Thus, at this point, Du Moulin was not even willing to return to his former Nicodemite position in France in order to be reunited with his family. He also believed that with the right support from the Württembergers, he could turn Montbéliard into a religious refuge for jurists. He asked Bullinger to "intervene with Prince Georg for

[125] "Haec academia Christiana est et esse debet. Habemus, Dei gratia, et Illustriss. principis nostri tuitione ecclesiam Christianam in qua pure predicatur et administratur evengelium et verbum Dei. Detectae sunt fraudes, imposture, idolomaniae Romani antichristi, et hinc profligata non debent reduci. . . . Ego pluries in senatu scholae et hic examinatur ne quid contra reformationem evangelii fueret. Porro authoritate apostolica quae est papae Romani, qui verus est antichristus . . . facere promotiones doctorum vel magistrorum, aut alios actus publicos in schola est antichristianum et verum opus papisticum." Du Moulin, "Exemplum declarationis et confessionis datae Principi et Universitati Tubingensi initio Septembris 1554," AEN, 1PAST 9.68b.

[126] "Si in causa religionis dissimulare vellem (quod absit!), iamdudum actum esset." *Amerbachkorrespondenz* 9.2:515, no. 3860, Du Moulin to Boniface Amerbach, Montbéliard, February 22, 1555.

the establishment of a school here, where a new asylum might be created for the French who have suffered under the cross for so long, more than thirty years."[127] Here we see—as we did with Monluc and will yet again with Du Moulin—the French evangelicals of the 1550s and 1560s identifying with those of the 1520s.

Du Moulin's grand vision, however, was never realized. Count Georg never built the school, established a printing press, or secured permission for Du Moulin's family to move to Montbéliard. From his initial enthusiasm, Du Moulin shifted to fury. In May 1555, he signed a letter to Amerbach, "from the barbarian land of Montbéliard."[128] Over the following year, Du Moulin became increasingly frustrated with his situation. Finally, he decided that he was, in fact, willing to dissimulate in the matter of religion. In June 1556, he fled Protestant Montbéliard and went first to Catholic Dole in the imperial Franche-Comté, and from there to Paris, arriving on January 21, 1557. His first wife, Louise, had already died.[129]

7.4.2. Du Moulin's Continued Evangelicalism in France, 1557–1565

In 1558, Du Moulin was reinstated to the bar[130] and remarried, this time to a widow, Jeanne du Vivier, who would play a role in Du Moulin's hostility toward the Calvinists. His hatred of the Calvinists did not, however, stem from a newfound devotion to Catholicism. On the contrary, Du Moulin's religious beliefs hardly changed upon his return to France. The first clue we have of his continued evangelicalism is found in the dedications in his newly published works; upon his return to France he dedicated books to Antoine of Navarre, Jeanne d'Albret, Gaspard de Coligny, François de Coligny d'Andelot, Odet de Coligny, and Antoine de Croÿ, Prince de Porcien,[131] in other words, virtually the entire Huguenot upper nobility.

---

[127] "Desino te rogare ut apud Principum Illustriss. Georgium intercedas, de schola hic instruenda, quo novum asylum ecclesiae Dei in Galliis, sub longissimi temporis plusquam tringinta annorum cruce laboranti, hic institueretur." StAZ, ms. E II 356, 141ʳ, Du Moulin to Bullinger, March 1, 1555.

[128] "Vale. 10. Cal. Iunii 1555. In barbaro pago Montbelgardensi." *Amerbachkorrepondenz* 9.2, 594, no. 3893, Du Moulin to Boniface Amerbach, Montbéliard, May 23, 1555.

[129] On his journey from Montbéliard back to Paris, see Thireau, *Charles Du Moulin*, 44–45.

[130] The text of the Paris parlement's decision to reinstate him can be found in AN, U//2046, vol. 26, 340ᵛ–341ᵛ, January 14, 1558.

[131] Thireau, *Charles Du Moulin*, 46. Thireau does not mention Odet, but Du Moulin's *In commentaria Philippi Decii in ius pontificium annotationes solemnes* (*Opera* 5:297–346) was dedicated to him.

Beyond the simple matter of the dedications, his works began to take on a more religious character and one that was decidedly evangelical. In 1561, he published the *Treatise on the Origin, Progress, and Excellence of the Kingdom and Monarchy of the French and the Crown of France*.[132] The title suggests that the text is a typical defense of the Gallican privileges of the French king—and much of it is—but Du Moulin inserted many evangelical ideas in the text. He dedicated the work to the "very noble and Christian Queen of Navarre," Jeanne d'Albret. On the first page of the dedication, he refers to Jesus Christ as "sole Savior, Mediator, and Redeemer," and he notes that his studies "have been employed for the defense of the truth and Word of God."[133] Here, he begins to present himself not just as a jurist but as a "defender of the Word of God," who, by referring to Christ as "sole mediator," seems to reject the idea of the intercession of the saints. In the text, Du Moulin also criticizes the use of images in the churches[134] and praises Charlemagne's orders to up-root the "superstitions surrounding the dead,"[135] a scarcely disguised attack on purgatory, indulgences, and related Catholic "superstitions." He supports communion in both kinds,[136] and he defends the Waldensians, criticizing the 1545 attack on them at Mérindol and Cabrières and pinning the blame for the attack on the "papists." He suggests that they had used King Francis I as the Jews had used Pilate to cover their crimes.[137] Perhaps most surprising

---

[132] Charles Du Moulin, *Traicté de l'origine, progrez, et excellence du royaume et monarchie des François et couronne de France*, in idem, *Opera*, 2:1025–1050.

[133] "Il y a une trop plus haute, et préexcellente cause, qui attire et oblige à vous tous loyaux serviteurs, et amateurs de Dieu, et de Jesus-Christ, son Fils seul Sauveur, Mediateur et Redempteur.... [C]e petit mien labeur est inscrit et dedié à vous et à vostre Royale Majesté, qui sçait bien de long-temps ma ju-risprudence, et anciennes études des Ecritures Saintes, et des histoires et choses politiques, avoir esté employées pour la defense de la verité et parole de Dieu." Du Moulin, *Opera*, 2:1026.

[134] "il ne faut pas que le Royaume de France se blandisse sous ombre qu'il a déjà deux fois plus duré que les regnes d'Israël et Juda: mais faut qu'il ensuive les exemples des bons Rois de Juda Ezechias, et Josias, qui ont restitué la religion sous la parole de Dieu, abbatans et chassans les idoles, et les sacrificateurs d'icelles; car il n'y a autre moyen d'eviter l'ire de Dieu assez imminente." Du Moulin, *Opera*, 2:1038, §97.

[135] "Et au mesme livre [one of the books of the *Capitularies* of Charlemagne] a étably une très-sainte, et très-chrestienne loy de la predication de la parole de Dieu ... en ces termes, 'Les Evesques ... nourrissent le Clergé à eux commis en sobrieté et chasteté, et desracinent les superstitions qu'aucuns font en aucuns lieux ès obseques des trépassez." Du Moulin, *Opera*, 2:1039, §107.

[136] "Il est notoire que l'usage de ce saint sacrement entier tant ès hommes laiz, qu'ès femmes, a esté gardé publiquement, et ordinairement en France, jusques au Concile de Constance.... Ledit usage ès deux especes de pain et vin au saint sacrement a esté indifferemment administré." Du Moulin, *Opera*, 2:1039, §110.

[137] "Il est clair à entendre de quels esprits ledit Louys XII ... fut meu dresser et envoyer une armée pour mettre à feu et à sang, les habitans de la vallée et villages de Merindol et Cabrieres.... Les Papistes luy persuadoient que c'estoient sorciers et incestueux, et qu'il auroit grand merite, et grands biens de Dieu, et du Siege de Rome, s'il les détruisoit.... Autres, mesmes Jean Sleidan, ont assez écrit comme ils furent cruellement occis l'an 1545. Et parce que l'on tenoit pour certain que c'estoit par

of all is that he includes in this treatise the full text of the 1544 Waldensian Confession of Faith,[138] which contained beliefs similar to those of the Swiss Reformed churches. He includes the text not to criticize their doctrine but, in fact, to demonstrate its thoroughly Christian nature and, consequently, the evil of the "papists" who encouraged their slaughter. Thus, in an ostensibly Gallican treatise on royal privileges, we find Du Moulin continuing to encourage Protestant ideas in France.

He did the same thing a few years later in his *Advice on the Council of Trent*,[139] another ostensibly Gallican text containing much evangelical doctrine. On the title page of this work, Du Moulin began to style himself, "Professor of Sacred Letters,"[140] revealing his increasing sense of religious vocation. No one was surprised that Du Moulin discouraged the reception of the decrees of Trent in France; any good Gallican would have done the same. The bases for his rejection, however, went well beyond traditional Gallican arguments and embraced specifically Protestant ideas. For example, he rejects Trent outright on the basis of its rejection of the doctrine of *sola scriptura*:

In the third session, the alleged Council mixes up and equates Holy Scripture and the traditions and unwritten matters alleged to have been handed on from hand to hand. . . . Therefore, one must not receive the Council of Trent, which is made up only of those devoted and sworn to the pope, on whom alone it depends and to whom it attributes everything, excluding all others. It mixes up and equates the Holy Scriptures and traditions written by neither the Apostles nor the Evangelists. Such a decree and council is heretical.[141]

le commandement du Roy [Francis I], duquel les Papistes se vouloient couvrir, comme les Juifs de Pilate, combien qu'un Cardinal gouvernoit lors les affaires, le feu Roy Henry non seulement desavoua le faict, mais fit publiquement plaider en Parlement l'innocence desdits occis." Du Moulin, *Opera*, 2:1043–1044, §§154, 159.

[138] Du Moulin, *Opera*, 2:1043–1044, §158.
[139] Charles Du Moulin, *Conseil sur le Fait du Concile de Trente*, in Du Moulin, *Opera*, 5:349–64.
[140] "Docteur ès droits, professeur des saintes Lettres, Jurisconsulte de France et Germanie, Conseiller et Maistre des Requestes de l'Hostel de la Royne de Navarre." Du Moulin, *Opera*, 5:347.
[141] "car ledit pretendu Concile en la tierce session . . . mesle et égale avec l'Ecriture sainte les traditions et choses non écrites pretendues baillées, comme de main en main. . . . Partant ne faut recevoir ledit Concile de Trident, qui n'est que d'aucuns tous sacrez et jurez au Pape, duquel seul il depend, auquel il attribue tout, et tous autres exclus, et qui mesle et égale aux saintes Escritures traditions non écrites par les Apostres ny par les Evangelistes. Tel Decret et Concile est heretique." Du Moulin, *Opera*, 5:354–55, §§26, 29.

Du Moulin's ideas, together with the fact that he had published the work without a proper royal privilege, led to his imprisonment for a month. After appeals on his behalf from Jeanne d'Albret and Renée de France, King Charles IX released him, but ordered him not to publish any more works on theology.[142]

Du Moulin completely ignored the royal command and, in fact, dedicated to the king what he saw as his theological *magnum opus*, the *Union and Harmony of the Four Evangelists*.[143] In his dedicatory letter to Charles IX, he notes, "The foundations of all Christian piety are considered here. . . . Of all my works, none is more distinguished, none more worthy of Your Majesty. Moreover, this work is such that it can soon be translated into all languages, and consequently, your name, O Most August King, will be celebrated in all tongues as well."[144] Of course, the work was never translated into any other language, much less all tongues, but Du Moulin's dedication to the king provides a sense of both his grand hopes for the book and of his new vocation as "Professor of Sacred Letters," as he once again styled himself on the title page.

Like the two works discussed earlier, Du Moulin's *Union and Harmony* contains a great deal of Protestant doctrine. Indeed, one could characterize it as a Protestant biblical commentary. On justification, he writes, "Nothing benefits us except Christ's death, the only thing accepted by God for the expiation of our sins and justly for eternal life. . . . Therefore, we must give thanks for his death and hope only in its merits, and we must not count on any other remedy for salvation, or we shall perish eternally."[145] On the Eucharist, Du

---

[142] Thireau, *Charles Du Moulin*, 51–52; Brodeau, *Vie*, in Du Moulin, *Opera*, 1.1: 46–47.

[143] Charles Du Moulin, *Collatio et unio quatuor Evangelistarum Domini nostri Iesu Christi, eorum serie et ordine, absque ulla confusione, permixtione vel transpositione servato, cum exacta textus illibati recognitione* (s.l.: s.n., 1565) in idem, *Opera* 5:447–606. Note that there are several additions to the original 1565 edition which are published in Du Moulin's 1681 *Opera*. There is no extant evidence of a second edition of the *Collatio*, and the additions are not present in the 1658 edition of his collected works: Charles Du Moulin, *Caroli Molinaei Franciae et Germaniae celeberrimi iurisconsulti et in supremo Parisiorum Senatu antiqui Advocati, Opera* (Paris: Mathurin du Puis, 1658), 3:1125–1422. The source of the additions in the 1681 text, therefore, is unclear. The original 1565 publisher notes at the end of the text that many annotations were missing due to Du Moulin's illness at the time, but that his son had his papers and had helped his father with the text ("Lectori," in Du Moulin, *Opera* [1681] 5:606). It is possible that those papers were used to prepare the additions, but this is by no means clear.

[144] "Deinde totius Christianae pietatis fundamenta hic versantur. . . . Postremo, omnium operum meorum nullum est insignius, nullam regia Maiestate dignius. Et insuper tale est hoc opus, ut mox in omnes linguas verti possit, et consequenter nomen tuum, ô Rex augustissime, omnibus linguis celebrari." Du Moulin, *Opera* 5:450.

[145] "Nihil haec omnia proderant nobis, nihil poterant, sed sola mors Christi, sola a Deo acceptata pro expiatione nostrorum peccatorum, et iure vitae aeternae. . . . Ideo necesse est gratitudinem habere illius mortis et in solo eius merito sperare, nec ab ullo alio salutis remedio pendere, vel in aeternum perire." Du Moulin, *Opera* 5:585–86, part 51.

Moulin presents not just a Protestant but a Reformed understanding of the sacrament. Commenting on the biblical words "This is my body," Du Moulin writes,

> The controversial words of the sacrament do not refer to the real presence of the body itself, nor to the real presence of the blood . . . , but they refer to the truth of the bloody sacrifice of the true body of Christ and the pouring out of his blood, which happened one time, the virtue and efficacy of which are truly received by the faithful in this sacrament. . . . Thus, there is no corporal presence in it, for Christ himself said that it profits nothing, but everything refers to the true sacrifice of his body.[146]

Following Du Moulin's early biographer Brodeau, historians often characterize Du Moulin as favoring the Augsburg Confession.[147] He does, indeed, have good things to say about the Lutheran confession, but one must understand that he never abandoned the Reformed understanding of the crucial issue of the Eucharist. He had fought against the Lutheran Ubiquitists in Tübingen, and his views did not change when he was in Paris ten years later.

7.4.3. Du Moulin's Assault on the Calvinists

Despite his adherence to a Reformed understanding of the Eucharist, by 1562, Du Moulin had become completely alienated from the Calvinists in France. The breakdown in his relations with them began during the First War of Religion, when he found himself once again living among them in Orléans, which had been seized by the Huguenots. While there, he composed a catechism, which is unfortunately lost, and began to give lessons in theology. The local Calvinist pastors, however, forced him to stop, claiming that he had no calling to do so.[148] In 1563, his quarrels with the Calvinists

---

[146] "ea verba controversa sacramenti non referuntur ad realem praesentiam ipsius corporis, sicut nec ad realem praesentiam sanguinis, seu potius cruoris extra corpus effusi; sed referuntur ad veritatem mactationis realis corporis Christi, et effusionis sanguinis eius semel factae, cuius virtus et effectus a fidelibus in hoc sacramento vere recipitur. . . . Ergo nec praesentia corporalis per se: ipse Christus ait, quod non prodest quicquam, sed totum refertur ad veram immolationem corporis et sanguinis sui." Du Moulin, *Opera* 5: 601, part 95.

[147] Brodeau, *Vie*, in Du Moulin, *Opera*, 1.1:14, 48–49; Thireau, *Charles Du Moulin*, 48–49.

[148] On July 6, 1562, Du Moulin was at Ferté, "où estoient deux ministres, Marandé et Miremont, ils furent bien si hardis de s'attacher incontinent audit du Molin, pour le cuider par leur haut babil, comme estant sur leur fumier, faire confesser qu'il ne luy appartenoit pas de traiter de la sainte

continued in Lyon, where the city's Reformed pastors condemned his catechism.[149] He was also imprisoned briefly in Lyon, accused of having written
the scandalous *Défense civile et militaire des Innocents de l'Eglise du Christ*,
which advocated open revolt against the king and tyrannicide.[150] The local
governor, the Seigneur de Soubise, ordered all copies of the *Défense civile*
burned, and it is, in fact, no longer extant. Du Moulin's *Apology* against the
work[151]—dedicated to Jean de Monluc—contains our best information
about the contents of the lost book. Another factor that soured Du Moulin's
relations with the French Calvinists around this time was that, according
to Du Moulin, a Reformed consistory told his wife, Jeanne du Vivier, that
she should divorce him and remarry "someone from their sect."[152] Finally,
the 1565 National Synod of the French Reformed Churches condemned Du
Moulin's *Union and Harmony of the Evangelists* and warned the faithful not
to attend his sermons or take the sacraments from him.[153]

Du Moulin was, therefore, constantly at odds with the French Reformed
churches for three years. He took his revenge in a bitter, pseudonymous dia-
tribe *Against the Calumnies of the Calvinists*, written at the end of his life.[154]

Ecriture, mais de l'oüir et apprendre d'eux, comme de ses superieurs, ausquels seuls appartenoit, luy
disant qu'ils n'avoient [*sic*, read: il n'avoit] point de vocation." Du Moulin, *Opera* 5:615, §68.

[149] Du Moulin, *Opera* 5: 617–18, §§82–91.

[150] Thireau, *Charles Du Moulin*, 48.

[151] Charles Du Moulin, *Apologie de M. Charles Du Moulin contre un livret, intitulé La deffense civile
et militaire des innocens et de l'Eglise de Christ*, in idem, *Opera* 5:xv–xxii.

[152] "Ils ont voulu persuader à la femme dudit Complaignant [Du Moulin] qu'elle se pouvoit
et devoit remarier à un de leur secte, parce que comme ils disent, il a délaissé la foy et l'Eglise, ce
qu'ils entendent de leur secte." "Copie des articles presentez par Maistre Charles du Molin, contre les
Ministres de la Religion pretendue Reformée de son temps, pour en faire informer," in Du Moulin,
Opera 5:622, art. XVII. See also the testimony of Robert Trehet: "Et outre dit ledit deposant, que la
femme dudit du Molin luy a dit que les Ministres luy avoient dit qu'elle se pouvoit remarier, attendu
que ledit du Molin n'estoit de mesme Religion qu'elle." "Copie de l'Information faite à la Requeste de
Maistre Charles du Molin, de l'Ordonnance de la Cour, en vertu de la Commission d'icelle, du 20.
jour de Février 1565, par Boutherouë, Huissier en la Cour," in Du Moulin, *Opera*, 5:628.

[153] "Les Eglises seront averties de se donner de garde du livre de Monsieur Charles du Moulin,
intitulé, *Unio quatuor Evangelistarum*, parce qu'il contient plusieurs erreurs, et entr'autres, touchant
les Limbes, le franc arbitre, le péché contre le Saint Esprit et la Cene, et specialement contre la vocation des ministres de l'Eglise et l'ordre d'icelle, lequel il meprise, et confond entierement. Tous
les fideles seront aussi avertis de ne se trouver point aux exhortations dudit Sieur du Moulin, ni à
la participation des sacremens qu'il entreprend d'administrer contre l'ordre ecclesiastique de nos
assemblées de pieté." Aymon, *Tous les synodes*, 1.2:70, avertissemens generaux, art. IX. Soon afterward, the Calvinist author Étienne de Malescot wrote a pseudonymous tract critiquing Du Moulin's
Collatio et unio in greater detail: "Annibal d'Auvergne" [Étienne de Malescot], *Censure des erreurs
de M. Charles Du Moulin de n'agueres mis en lumiere en un certain livre qu'il a intitulé Union ou
Harmonie des quatre Evangelistes* (s.l.: s.n., 1566). On the authorship of this text, see Julien Goeury, *La
Muse du Consistoire: Une histoire des pasteurs poètes des origines de la Réforme jusqu'à la révocation de
l'édit de Nantes*, Cahiers d'Humanisme et Renaissance 133 (Geneva: Droz, 2016), 426–27.

[154] Du Moulin, *Opera*, 5:607–20. The stated author, "Simon Challudre," is an anagram of "Charles
Du Molin," the spelling he used to sign his name. Du Moulin appears to have written the text at the

His chief complaint in the treatise was that the Reformed consistories in France had unjustifiably usurped ecclesiastical power in the kingdom. He begins the work as follows:

> If ever there was arrogance joined with ambition, avarice, and insatiable greed to subjugate all, it is revealed today in abundance among the ministers and consistories of the highly dangerous sect spread throughout France, in which it strives not only to nest but also to reign by usurping all ecclesiastical power.[155]

Later in the text, he continues,

> Your goal is to acquire a new reign, under the shadow of religion, and to dominate over the faith of others, over consciences, over treasuries, forces, and faculties. To these ends, you first had to introduce new doctrine, destructive of all others, and, secondly, a new authority, surpassing all others, which you can neither accomplish nor maintain without your accursed consistories.[156]

For Du Moulin, a jurist with a speciality in customary law, the Calvinists' consistories had no basis whatsoever in the history of French law. They were

---

very end of his life. No copy of the original work survives, and the printing history of the text is difficult to decipher. Almost all available references indicate that it was published in 8° format in 1565, but a letter to Beza in late 1566 seems to indicate that it was published only in part in 1565 and that Du Moulin was working with Claude D'Espence and Bauduin to have the full text published outside of France: "nous voions que ce malheureux Du Moulin continue à desgorger son venein et ne tache qu'à semer ses meschantes calomnies par tout. . . . J'ay recouvré aussi l'aultre livre où son nom est torné, imprimé en partie, lequel il seme aussi par tout. Il n'a peu le faire achever en cette ville à cause que par le moien de Mr le Mareschal, tant lui que les imprimeurs furent visités, toutesfois on s'i porta si mal que, ne fouillant où il faloit, pas un des exemplaires ne fut trouvé, mais l'impression cessa. Maintenant, par le moien de Despence et Balduin, avec lesquels il s'est r'alié, il le faict imprimer complet hors cette ville, et ne sçavons où." *Bèze Cor.* 7:235, no. 503, Marin Delamare to Beza, La Forest (outside Paris), September 25, 1566. Another letter from Delamare to Beza in January 1567 attests that the book referred to here was Du Moulin's *Against the Calumnies of the Calvinists*. The letter refers to several items contained in Du Moulin's book. *Bèze Cor.* 8:26, no. 525, January 5, 1567.

[155] "Si jamais y eut orgueil conjoint avec ambition, avarice et cupidité insatiable de tout subjuguer: Il se demontre tres-débordement aujourd'huy ès ministres et consistoires de ladite tres-pernicieuse secte épandue en France, en laquelle elle s'efforce non seulement nicher, mais aussi regner avec usurpation de toute puissance Ecclesiastique." Du Moulin, *Opera.* 5:607, no. 1.

[156] "Mais vostre but est d'acquerir un regne nouveau, sous ombre de religion, et dominer sur la foy d'autruy, sur les consciences, sur les bourses, forces, et facultez, ausquelles fins, vous faut premierement nouvelle doctrine, destructive de toutes autres. Secondement nouvelle authorité, surpassant toutes autres: ce que ne pouvez faire ny maintenir sans vos maudits consistoires." Du Moulin, *Opera*, 5:618, no. 87.

entirely new and, therefore, indefensible. He also bore no small amount of personal ill will toward the consistories, due to their attempt to break up his marriage.

The 1565 Synod of Paris had condemned Du Moulin, in part, because he wrote "against the vocation of the ministers of the church." Du Moulin had never forgiven the Calvinist ministers who first told him he had no right to preach. On the contrary, he believed it was the Calvinist ministers who had no proper vocation:

> For you say that it pertains to no one but you to treat Holy Scripture, as if you have already stripped all of France of that ability: all the bishops, archbishops, curates, all the universities, all the doctors and learned men there who are much more capable and experienced at it, and who have a legitimate vocation. You, by contrast, have in France no vocation or charge, nor any ecclesiastical or civil commission from any king, parlement, magistrate, body, or university.[157]

As we have seen, Du Moulin's theology—on justification, on *sola scriptura*, on the Eucharist—was clearly evangelical. As with so many other reformers, we see his continued attachment to the existing French church, citing the proper ecclesiastical authority residing in the bishops, universities, king, and magistrate. Note that his argument for the continued existence of the ecclesiastical hierarchy differs from that of Cassander and Bauduin. While their claims rested on the need to preserve the structure of the early church, Du Moulin says virtually nothing about early Christianity and instead argues in defense of the long-term customs of the French Church. Bauduin had argued principally that the Calvinists were transforming rather than reforming the church, thereby creating a schismatic church like that of the Donatists. Du Moulin, by comparison, argues that the Calvinists have usurped traditional French ecclesiastical authority through their consistories.

Du Moulin, like Bauduin and Monluc, saw himself as standing in a line of French evangelicals that long predated Calvin. Much like the anti-Calvinists of the Vaud (to whom he refers repeatedly in this

---

[157] Car vous dites qu'il n'appartient à autres qu'à vous de traiter de l'Ecriture sainte: comme si en aviez jà depossedé toute la France, tous les Evesques, Archevesques, et Curez, toutes les Universitez, et tous les Docteurs et gens doctes qui y sont, et qui en sont trop plus capables et experimentez, et qui en ont leur vocation legitime: et non pas vous qui n'avez en France aucune vocation, charge ny commission Ecclesiastique, ny civile, ny du Roy, ny d'aucun Parlement ou Magistrat, ny d'aucun Corps ou Université." Du Moulin, *Opera*, 5:609, no. 18.

treatise),[158] he sees Calvin as having undermined the original French evangelical message. He says to the Calvinists,

> It was not so much to teach the Gospel as to force everyone to receive and believe all the hyperboles and errors of Calvin, and to extinguish every other light and knowledge of the Gospel, which a great many people of learning and piety held who were in France long before you, without having learned it from Calvin's books, and without adhering to his heresies. Under the guise of religion and of ruining and dragging down papal superstitions and idolatries, your goal was to establish a new regime in France, worse than the papal one, by means of your consistories, which you have built and multiplied in imitation and subordinate dependence on the consistory of Geneva.[159]

As he had done in Montbéliard when he referred to those who had suffered for the Gospel in France for more than thirty years,[160] here, too, Du Moulin refers to the "light of the Gospel" that had come to France well before anyone had heard of Calvin. Far from advancing the cause of the Gospel, the Calvinists, he suggests, were instead destroying it by erecting a new "papism" even worse than the old.

Charles Du Moulin was a complicated reformer who defies easy categorization. A Gallican jurist who accused the Calvinists of usurping ecclesiastical authority in France, he did not hesitate himself to preach and administer the

---

[158] "Messire Jacques de Bourgogne, Seigneur de Falaiz . . . n'alloit à Geneve pour apprendre, mais pour y vivre en paix à l'exercice de la pure religion, qu'il avoit apprise de ces excellens docteurs Philippes Melancthon et Martin Bucer. Mais si tost qu'à la bonne foy il s'en fut declaré à Geneve, faisant doute de quelques points, qu'il y ouït prescher, discordans à ce qu'il avoit bien appris il fut deferé en leur Consistoire . . . , et outre se servoit d'un sçavant medecin [Bolsec], condamné au Consistoire de Geneve, il fut declaré rebelle à l'Eglise. . . . [E]t cependant deux fideles ministres de Nyon et Bursin [André Zébédée and Jean Lange], sous Berne près Geneve du costé du lac, ne pouvans plus endurer les pernicieuses heresies de la doctrine de Calvin, qui estoient non seulement preschées dedans Geneve, mais aussi jusques au pays de Berne, semées par les merciers ou portepanniers de livres, et par les tavernes, hostelleries, et foires publiques, contre la doctrine et reformation de la religion, faite et establie à Berne, . . . declarerent en pleins sermons lesdites nouvelles propositions venans de Geneve . . . estre heretiques." Du Moulin, *Opera*, 5:608, nos. 10–12; 613, no. 51.

[159] "Je vous fais trop d'honneur: ce n'estoit pas tant pour enseigner l'Evangile, que pour faire recevoir et croire toutes les hyperboles et erreurs de Calvin, et pour esteindre toute autre lumiere et connoissance de l'Evangile, que grand nombre de gens de sçavoir et pieté estans en France avoient long-temps devant vous, sans l'avoir apprinse des livres de Calvin, et sans adherer aux heresies d'iceluy. Vostre but estoit sous un ombre de la religion, et de ruiner et traisner en pompe les superstitions et idolatries papales: establir un nouveau regne en France, pire que le Papal, par le moyen de vos Consistoires, qu'avez incontinent erigez et multipliez à l'imitation et dependance subalterne du Consistoire de Geneve." Du Moulin, *Opera*, 5:614, no. 60–61.

[160] See n. 127.

sacraments without episcopal authorization. An admirer of Melanchthon and the Augsburg Confession, his view of the divisive issue of the Eucharist owed far more to Bullinger's Zwinglianism. Perhaps it is best to see him as he saw himself: a free-thinking heir of Erasmus[161] and a nonsectarian Christian,[162] who believed that his understanding of Christianity could provide a path forward for the French church. Although his religious thought was idiosyncratic, it bore the marks of the evangelicals before him and with whom he identified, who sought to reform the French church extensively, but from within.

7.5. The External Attack on the French Evangelical Movement

Robert Kingdon identified Charles Du Moulin as one of the chief instigators of the "external attack" on the nascent French Reformed Churches. Du Moulin represented, he argued, powerful Gallican interests in the kingdom who were critical of the Catholic Church but hesitant to break fully from it and who constituted much of the upper nobility.[163] The Calvinists faced the constant threat that these nobles would side with Du Moulin and the *moyenneurs* instead of with them. The three principal individuals considered in this chapter, Jean de Monluc, François Bauduin, and Charles Du Moulin, did, indeed, have powerful allies. Among the three of them, they had ties to every member of the elite Huguenot nobility. Bauduin was closely allied with Antoine of Navarre, and Charles Du Moulin was employed by Antoine's wife, Jeanne d'Albret, in the early 1560s.[164] Monluc had ties to the royal court and the Cardinal of Lorraine while the latter was amenable to compromise. Condé sought Bauduin for his advice on reforming the church after the First War of Religion. Du Moulin dedicated works of the early 1560s to all of the major Huguenot nobles and had ties as well to Renée de France,

---

[161] "Tu es heres optimi et eruditissimi Erasmi, qui hereticis et schismaticis nunquam coniungi voluit, sed ecclesiae catholicae adhaesit. Quare aequior esse mihi debes, si ita facio." *Amerbachkorrespondenz* 10.1:156, no. 4055, Du Moulin to Boniface Amerbach, Dole, June 20, 1556.

[162] "les leçons publiques qu'il [Du Moulin] avoit faite à Tubingue, où il s'estoit declaré Chrestien non sectaire et schismatique: mais vray Catholique." Du Moulin, *Opera*, 5:614, no. 57.

[163] Robert Kingdon, *Geneva and the Consolidation of the French Protestant Movement, 1564– 1572: A Contribution to the History of Congregationalism, Presbyterianism, and Calvinist Resistance Theory* (Madison: University of Wisconsin Press, 1967), 138.

[164] In several of his published works of the period he describes himself as "Conseiller et Maistre des Requestes ordinaires de l'hostel de la Royne de Navarre."

who appealed on his behalf during his imprisonment in 1564.[165] Monluc was close to the chancellor Michel de l'Hôpital, whom the papal nuncio accused of sponsoring secret conventicles at his residence attended by Monluc, Condé, and Odet de Coligny.[166] Finally, of course, Bauduin, Monluc, and Du Moulin knew each other well, and all were also connected to another well-known Gallican evangelical, Claude d'Espence.[167]

Indeed, so well connected were these evangelicals that we should not be at all surprised that there were many others like them who still hoped for internal reform and had not yet joined the Calvinist French Reformed Churches. In the early 1560s, they were the reformers on the inside who had the best access to the political players in the kingdom. The surprise really should be that the Calvinists ultimately succeeded in winning over the Huguenot nobility. Kingdon described Du Moulin as the one making the "external attack," on the French churches, but one could as easily argue that it was the Genevans who launched an external attack on the original French evangelical movement. Previously content to criticize them from afar as Nicodemites, the Calvinists moved into the realm and assaulted them from within the French halls of power. As we have seen, Monluc and Du Moulin both referred positively to the French evangelical preachers of thirty years before, clearly referring to those in Marguerite's network and not to the Calvinists. From Meaux to Du Moulin, there was an unbroken line of evangelical reform in France, and this line remained in constant tension with the Calvinists from Farel in the 1520s to Beza in the 1560s.

By the 1560s, a clear network of anti-Calvinist evangelicals had developed across francophone Europe. Although those considered in this chapter may not have been as deeply enmeshed in that network as were some others

[165] Brodeau, Vie, in Du Moulin, Opera, 1.1:46.

[166] Kim, Michel de L'Hôpital, 92.

[167] On D'Espence, see Alain Tallon ed., Un autre catholicisme au temps des Réformes? Claude d'Espence et la théologie humaniste à Paris au XVIe siècle, Nugae humanisticae 12 (Turnhout: Brepols, 2010); Wanegffelen, Ni Rome ni Genève, 181–94. As we saw, Du Moulin dedicated his Apology to Monluc (see §7.4.3) and also had praise for him, whom he sees as a fellow victim of the Calvinists: "ce grand vertueux et tres sçavant personage Messire Jean de Montluc, Evesque et Comte de Valence . . . a esté le premier des Prelats de France, qui dès plus de quinze ans a commencé et continué à bien prescher et instruire son peuple en la doctrine de l'Evangile et benefice de Jesus Christ, et en a fait imprimer plusieurs sermons et saintes instructions, que premier il avoit voulu faire. Mais quoy? Sitost qu'avez eu entrée en ce royaume, et en Dauphiné, c'est le premier sur lequel vous estes ruez, et intrus en son saint labourage, non pas pour le continuer, mais pour y semer vos mechantes heresies Calvinistes, et vous faire superieurs, et avez seduit et gagné le peuple, par ledit de Montluc son pasteur preparé et instruit, lequel peuple vous avez emeu et concité contre son evesque et pasteur, jusques à luy courir sus à coups de traits et pistolets, et par terre, et par eau sur le Rhosne, pour le tuer: ainsi le chasserent." Du Moulin, Opera 5:609, no. 22.

considered in this book, they certainly knew about them and used their negative experiences with the Calvinists to bolster their own cause. Bauduin
mentioned both Castellio and Zébédée positively. Du Moulin also referred
to Zébédée, as well as to Falais, Bolsec, and Lange. He noted that Bern's April
1555 decree against Calvin was "immediately brought to him [Du Moulin] in
Montbéliard," and he approved.[168] Du Moulin also criticized the Calvinists'
condemnation of "Pierre Perrucelli," by whom he probably meant Castellio's
friend François Perrussel, simply for praising the Augsburg Confession.[169]
And he defends Jean de Salignac, a fellow Gallican evangelical. Salignac
openly joined the Reformed Church in 1565 but was almost immediately
chastized for criticizing Beza's New Testament.[170] According to Du Moulin,
Salignac was "prohibited by the authority of your consistory from preaching
or teaching the Word of God, even though you could find nothing in his
doctrine to reproach."[171] Thus, the Gallican evangelicals embraced Calvin's
enemies from the past and sought to keep the reform-minded nobility devoted to internal French religious reform. Nearly all their efforts were intended to fend off the external attack from Geneva on the French evangelical
movement.

In his attacks on the Calvinists, Du Moulin mentions one additional individual, whom Kingdon identifies as representing the "internal attack" on
the French Reformed churches: Jean Morély. Du Moulin noted, "One Jean
Morély, a native of Paris who belongs to their sect, was excommunicated
by them and his book burned in Geneva because he had written that the
ministers had taken over the [ecclesiastical] government and that their

---

[168] "Laquelle sentence avec copie des plaidoyers, fut incontinent apportée audit du Molin, estant
lors à Montbeliart, lequel le tout veu, declara aux assistans que ladite sentence estoit tres-juste, et
sainte, et chrestienne." Du Moulin, *Opera*, 5:614, no. 54. This copy of Bern's decree and the accompa-
nying "plaidoyers" referred to here constitute a substantial portion of the Du Moulin manuscript in
the BNF, ms. lat. 12,717, fols. 134–57.

[169] "L'an mil cinq cent soixante deux, au commencement de l'occupation de la ville d'Orleans, avez-
vous pas voulu excommunier, et retrancher Maistre Pierre Perrucelli homme tres-docte et modeste,
seulement pour avoir dit que la confession d'Auguste estoit bonne et sainte?" Du Moulin, *Opera*,
5:608, no. 14. On the confusion about the first name, see *Bèze Cor.* 8:28n13.

[170] In 1561, Calvin encouraged him to join the Protestants openly (*CO* 19:118–19, no. 3615).
Salignac responded by saying, "Miles vero Christi ego sum," but that he was not as free as Calvin to
fight openly (*CO* 19:165–66, no. 3646, Paris, December 1, 1561). On Salignac's criticism of Beza's
Bible translation, see *Bèze Cor.* 6:118–120, no. 406, Jean Lasicki to Beza, Paris, July 25, 1565. On
Salignac's early career, see Farge, *Biographical Registry*, 401–2.

[171] "Et en l'an 1564, vous avez bien esté si hardis d'assaillir un ancien docteur en theologie, fort
renommé pour son eminent sçavoir, et vie honneste, Maistre Jean de Sallignac, Prieur de Morées, où
il enseignoit purement et saintement la parole de Dieu, selon son office et vocation publique . . . après
qu'il vous avoit trop bien traitez, vous par grande ingratitude luy avez prohibé et defendu par
l'authorité de vostre Consistoire, de prescher ou enseigner la parole de Dieu: combien que ne puissiez
rien reprendre en sa doctrine." Du Moulin, *Opera*, 5:608, no. 15.

consistories were illicit usurpations."[172] Du Moulin and Morély do not seem to have known each other personally,[173] and their convictions diverged on many points. Du Moulin argued for the preservation of the traditional ecclesiastical hierarchy, while Morély wanted to see the Calvinists' more limited hierarchy flattened. As the next chapter demonstrates, however, they found a common enemy in what they saw as the pernicious, foreign influence of the Calvinists from Geneva.

---

[172] "Un Jean Morelli natif de Paris, qui estoit de leur secte, pour avoir écrit que les Ministres entreprenoient sur la police, et que leurs Consistoires estoient usurpations illicites, a esté par eux excommunié et retranché, et son livre brûlé à Geneve." Charles Du Moulin, *Copie des articles presentez par Maistre Charles du Molin, contre les Ministres de la Religion pretendue Reformée de son temps, pour en faire informer*, in idem *Opera*, 5:621–25; here, 623, art. XXII

[173] Indeed, Du Moulin appears not to have realized that Morély and "de Villiers," whom he cites in the article following that cited in the previous footnote were, in fact, the same person. Du Moulin, *Opera*, 5:623, art. XXIII.

8

Jean Morély's Assault
on Calvinist Ecclesiology

8.1. Introduction

In the mid-1560s, no challenger attracted more attention from the
Calvinists in Geneva than a minor French nobleman named Jean Morély.
Robert Kingdon was one of the first to highlight Morély's importance,[1]
and the volumes of the *Correspondance de Bèze* published since Kingdon's
study support his assessment.[2] Largely because of Kingdon's work,
English-language scholarship invariably describes Morély as a "congregationalist" who challenged the presbyterian-synodal ecclesiology of the
French Reformed churches. Scholars owe an enormous debt of gratitude
to Kingdon, as well as to Philippe Denis and Jean Rott, who have written
the most important study on Morély to date.[3] Nevertheless, a closer look at
the evidence suggests that Morély's vision was neither as strictly congregationalist as Kingdon suggests nor as utopian as Denis and Rott's subtitle—
The Utopia of a Democracy within the Church—indicates. Instead, Morély
presented a practical program that called for control of the French church,
not from afar by Genevan pastors, but locally by the leading French nobility, clergy, and laity, while permitting all church members to vote on
major issues. Morély strikes a strong patriotic note of resentment against
Geneva's foreign dominance of French church affairs, a theme that ties him
to Du Moulin and several Huguenot nobles, a number of whom Morély
counted among his supporters.

Historians have generally failed to acknowledge the patriotism
that shaped Morély's thought. This is somewhat surprising since several recent studies of French Reformed churches have appropriately

---

[1] Kingdon, *Geneva and the Consolidation of the French Protestant Movement*, 43–120.
[2] See, in particular, *Bèze Cor.*, vols. 6–8.
[3] Denis and Rott, *Jean Morély*.

Refusing to Kiss the Slipper. Michael W. Bruening, Oxford University Press (2021). © Oxford University Press.
DOI: 10.1093/oso/9780197566954.003.0009

sought to emphasize native French developments that were not necessarily influenced by Geneva.[4] Nevertheless, few have conveyed Morély's deep resentment of Geneva, an attitude shared by at least some French Protestants. Undoubtedly, most Huguenots were happy to receive support and guidance from Geneva. Morély and others, however, sought to exclude Geneva from French affairs, with some going so far as to charge the Genevans with instigating the French wars by actively encouraging disloyalty to the Crown.

Among those who saw Genevan influence on French Protestantism as nefarious was Pierre Charpentier, a former professor at the Geneva Academy. Soon after the Saint Bartholomew's Day massacre, he blamed Beza and the Genevans for prompting the horrific event.[5] His work has routinely been dismissed as Catholic propaganda, but Charpentier remained unequivocally Protestant even after the massacre, and several of his arguments deserve a second look. In particular, he identifies several "God-fearing ministers who detest 'the Cause,'" which he identifies as Theodore Beza's Geneva-based wing of francophone Protestantism. External evidence confirms that Charpentier's list of "God-fearing ministers" who opposed Beza's faction is basically accurate and consists in large part of Morély's supporters.

Throughout this book, we have been exploring the extent of the opposition to the Calvinists and Geneva among francophone Protestants. The fact that, in 1572, Charpentier would continue the long tradition of Reformed anti-Calvinism should not be the least bit surprising. Indeed, his argument, coming on the heels of Morély's challenge to Calvinist ecclesiology in the kingdom, encapsulates the fundamental theme of this entire book: there was far more to francophone Protestantism than Calvin and Geneva.

---

[4] See, for example, Benedict and Fornerod, "Conflict and Dissidence"; Karen E. Spierling, Erik A. de Boer, and R. Ward Holder, eds., *Emancipating Calvin: Culture and Confessional Identity in Francophone Reformed Communities* (Leiden: Brill, 2018); Glenn Sunshine, *Reforming French Protestantism: The Development of Huguenot Ecclesiastical Institutions, 1557–1572*, Sixteenth Century Essays and Studies (Kirksville, MO: Truman State University Press, 2003).

[5] Pierre Charpentier, *Lettre de Pierre Charpentier Jurisconsulte, adressée à François Portes Candiois, par laquelle il montre que les persécutions des Eglises de France sont advenues, non par faute de ceux qui faisaient profession de la Religion, mais de ceux qui nourrissaient les factions et conspirations, qu'on appelle la Cause* (s.l: s.n., 1572). On Charpenier, see John Viénot, "Un Apologiste de la Saint-Barthélemy: Pierre Charpentier," in *Séance de rentrée des cours de la Faculté libre de théologie protestante de Paris le lundi 3 novembre 1902*, 19–42 (Paris: Fischbacher, 1902).

8.2. Morély's Controversial Book: *The Treatise on Christian Discipline and Polity*

In 1562, Morély published his most famous work, dedicating it to Pierre Viret, one of Calvin's closest friends and allies. This intriguing dedication, however—to which we will return—was insufficient to win over church leaders. In April, the National Synod of the French Reformed churches meeting at Orléans decreed the following:

> As to that book entitled *A Treatise of Christian Discipline and Polity*, com-
> posed and published by Jean Morély, the council judges that as to the points
> concerning the discipline of the church, by which he aims to condemn and
> subvert the order received in our churches, founded upon the Word of God,
> the said book contains wicked doctrine, and tends to the confusion and dis-
> sipation of the church; and therefore the said council cautions the faithful
> to take heed of the aforesaid doctrine.[6]

The synod found the work dangerous because it seemed to overturn the French *Discipline* established at the first national synod in 1559, as well as the long tradition of pastoral control over church matters established by the Calvinists.[7]

8.2.1. The Calvinist Status Quo

The system threatened by Morély's program developed in the wake of events that opened one of the earliest rifts between the Calvinists and their opponents. In Chapter 3, we saw that Antoine Marcourt and Jean Morand were appointed to the Genevan ministry without the consultation of the other pastors in the city and region.[8] The conflict that followed gave rise to the

---

[6] "Quant au livre intitulé, *Traité de la discipline et police chrétienne*, composé et publié par Jean Moreli, le concile est d'avis, quant aux points concernant la Discipline de l'Eglise (par lesquels il pretend condanner et renverser l'ordre accoutumé des Eglises, et fondé sur la parole de Dieu) que ledit livre contient une mauvaise doctrine et tendante à la dissipation et confusion de l'Eglise: C'est pourquoi ledit concile exhorte tous les fideles de se donner de garde de la susdicte doctrine." Aymon, *Tous les synodes*, 1.2:29; translation adapted from Quick, *Synodicon*, 27.

[7] The forty articles of the French *Discipline* can be found in Aymon, *Tous les synodes*, 1.2:1–7. A critical edition can also be found in Faulenbach et al., eds., *Reformierte Bekenntnisschriften*, 2/1:74–83.

[8] See 77–78.

Calvinist practice for electing pastors, known as "cooptation." Most franco-phone Reformed churches followed the model for cooptation established by the 1541 Geneva ordinances, establishing what was normally a two- or three-step process, depending on whether there was a confessionally sympathetic magistrate in charge. First, the local pastors selected a candidate (sometimes together with the consistory); second, the secular magistrate approved the candidate; and third, the candidate was formally accepted by the people.[9] The final stage served as a check to make sure the candidate did not have any disqualifying characteristics that had been missed in the first two steps, but it was not intended to be a free and open debate by the people on the desirability of the proposed candidate. In 1558, the pastors of the Lausanne chapter, while acknowledging that the right of election "pertains to the en-tirety of the church,"[10] downplayed the role of the laity, "seeing the rudeness of the people and the confusion that could come about if the entire com-munity were summoned to hold elections."[11] They added a preliminary step to Geneva's process, requiring that all candidates be examined at a school, thereby reinforcing the role of the Lausanne Academy in the process.[12] The pastors likewise limited the role of the laity in all other ecclesiastical matters:

> All of this [ecclesiastical] government cannot be committed to the gener-ality of the church, that is to say to the entire body of the faithful as it is

---

[9] "S'ensuit à qui il appartient d'instituer les pasteurs. Il sera bon en cest endroict de suyvre l'ordre de l'esglise ancienne, veu que ce n'est que practique de ce qui nous est monstré par l'escripture. C'est que les ministres eslisent premierement celluy qu'on doibvra mettre en l'office. Apres, qu'on le presente au conseil. Et s'il est trouvé digne, que le conseil le reçoive et accepte, luy donnant tesmonage pour le produyre finablement au peuple en la predication, affin qu'il soit receu par consentement commun de la compagnye des fidelles. S'il estoit trouvé indigne et demonstré tel par probations legitime, il fauldroit lors proceder à nouvelle election pour en prendre un aultre." *CO* 10:17–18.

[10] "Quant au droict d'election, il est aysé à veoir par ce qui est escrit, Act. 2 et 6, et par l'ancienne coustume de l'eglise que ce droict apartient à tout le corps de l'eglise, selon qu'elle est distincte en paroisses et troupeaux." Michael W. Bruening, "'La nouvelle réformation de la Lausanne': The Proposal by the Ministers of Lausanne on Ecclesiastical Discipline (June 1558), *BHR* 68 (2006): 21–50, here, 46–47.

[11] "Mais d'autant que tout se doibt faire par bon ordre en la maison du Seigneur, ainsy que S. Pol a escrit, 1 Cor. 14, il fault qu'il y ayt certain ordre et forme d'election. Or quant à nous, à dire en con-science, veu la rudesse des peuples et la confusion qui pourroit advenir si toute la communaulté estoit incontinent appellée à faire les elections . . . nous ne saurions, quant aux ministres, trouver aultre meilleure maniere d'election ny plus conforme à la parole de Dieu, que celle qui a esté dressée aux eglises de par deçà." Bruening, "'La nouvelle réformation de Lausanne,'" 47.

[12] "en premier lieu une escole ordonnée là où il y ayt certains personages, autant que possible sera, qui soyent diligemment enseignez et sur la vie desquels on ayt ordinairement grand regart, comme vous avez estably cest ordre en vostre ville de Lausanne." Bruening, "'La nouvelle réformation de Lausanne,'" 47.

distributed in parishes or communities. For all are not appropriate to hold the charge, and it would not be possible for all to assemble when required.[13]

The following year, the first national synod of the French Reformed churches issued the *Discipline*, which required that a minister be chosen "by two or three ministers with the consistory, or by the provincial synod, if it can be done, and then he shall be presented to the people to be received."[14] The text goes on to explain that if there is opposition to the candidate from the people, "the consistory shall judge thereof."[15]

Thus, while the details varied according to context—for example, the presence of the Academy in Lausanne or the absence of a Protestant magistrate in France—the procedures developed throughout the francophone Reformed territories gave most of the authority in pastoral elections to the ministers and consistories. The regular church members served only as a final check on the selection; in most cases, they were expected to approve what the pastors and consistories had already decided.

8.2.2. Morély's Program

Jean Morély sought to overturn this system. Driving Morély to publish his book was his belief that "none of the churches today use a discipline that promises us long enjoyment of this pure doctrine of the Gospel."[16] His criticism included the Calvinist model, which he attacks head-on:

---

[13] "Tout ce gouvernement ne peut estre commis à la generalité de l'eglise, c'est-à-dire, à tout le corps des fideles, selon qu'ils sont distribuez en paroisses ou communautez. Car tous ne sont pas propres à avoir charge, et ne seroit possible que tous s'assemblassent quand il seroit requis." Bruening, "'La nouvelle réformation de Lausanne,'" 32. The exact authorship of this text is uncertain. It was submitted by Jean Reymond Merlin in the name of the entire Lausanne chapter, which included the colloquies of Lausanne, Vevey, and Aigle (ibid., 50). Since Pierre Viret was head pastor of Lausanne at the time and exerted great influence within the chapter, it seems reasonable that he supported the ideas in the text. One should note, however, that the text continues, "D'aultre part aussi, il n'est ne bon ny raisonable ny ordonné de Dieu que la generalité de l'eglise n'ayt nulle authorité par dessus les membres d'icelle," suggesting that there is some role for the generality of the church in ecclesiastical affairs.

[14] "Ung ministre ne peult estre esleu pour le présent par ung seul ministre avecques son consistoire, mais par deux ou trois ministres avecques le consistoire, ou par le synode provincial si fere se peult, puys sera présenté au peuple pour estre receu." Faulenbach, *Reformierte Bekenntnisschriften* 2/1:75, n.7; cf. Aymon, *Tous les synodes*, 1.2:2; Quick, *Synodicon*, 3.

[15] "et s'il y a opposition ce sera au consistoire de la juger." Faulenbach, *Reformierte Bekenntnisschriften* 2/1:75; cf. Aymon, *Tous les synodes*, 1.2:2; Quick, *Synodicon*, 3.

[16] "Car je peux veritablement dire qu'il n'y a aujourd'huy discipline en usage en toutes les Eglises, qui nous puissent promettre longue jouïssance de ceste pure doctrine de l'Evangile." Morély, *Traicté de la discipline*, 25.

> For to permit the ministers to elect the consistories, elders, and also pastors
> and to coopt for themselves the right to discern doctrine in their council,
> to remove scandals from the communion of the church at their whim, even
> where the magistrate's authority intervenes, that is too dangerous.[17]

As the range of pastoral privileges listed here makes clear, Morély's work had
implications well beyond pastoral elections. Indeed, he suggests that virtually all major decisions in the church be decided not hierarchically by the
synods, pastors, and consistories, but by the generality of the local church.
Behind his argument is the fundamental principle "that what affects all must
be heard by all. Therefore, the understanding and judgment of such things
must pertain to the church in general."[18]

Morély organizes his work in four books, which treat, first, doctrine, then
moral discipline, followed by elections, and finally, other matters of church
order. On doctrine, he writes, "There is no doubt that the power to judge
doctrine according to the Word of God, to eliminate disagreements over it,
and to interpret it is given to the church."[19] It is not, he specifies, "proper to
a certain ecclesiastical estate but given to all to whom God's Spirit has given
understanding, and the judgment on it pertains not to one or to a few but to
the whole church in general."[20] When it comes to making decisions on doctrine, Morély prescribes the following:

> The ministers and elders will hold the initial council, for matters that per-
> tain to the church should be reported to them. They will place all matters
> under deliberation, and if it turns out to concern the state of the church and
> to merit consideration, they will hold a council and come to a conclusion.
> Then all will be reported to the church. Where there is a great multitude, in
> order to avoid confusion and to settle the matter more quickly, the assembly

---

[17] "Car de permettre à l'advenir aux ministres de elire les consistoires, et senieurs, comme aussi les
pasteurs, et se coopter, de decerner de la doctrine en leur conseil, de retrencher de la communion de
l'eglise les scandales à leur phantasie, bien que l'authorité du magistrat y entrevienne, c'est chose par
trop dangereuse." Morély, *Traicté de la discipline*, 39.

[18] "Je pense donc que ce qui touche tous, doit estre entendu de tous. Parquoy que la cognoissance et
jugement de telles choses doit appartenir à l'Eglise en general." Morély, *Traicté de la discipline*, 41.

[19] "Or il n'y a doute que ceste puissance de juger de la doctrine selon la parole de Dieu, de vuider
tous differens par icelle, de l'interpreter, ne soit donnee à l'Eglise." Morély, *Traicté de la discipline*, 77.

[20] "De quoy nous devons inferer que ceste puissance de traitter l'Escriture, n'est seulement propre
à un certain estat Ecclesiastic, mais qu'elle est donnée à tous, à qui l'Esprit de Dieu et intelligence sont
données: et que le jugement n'en appartient à un ne à peu, mais à toute l'Eglise en general." Morély,
Traicté de la discipline, 78.

should subdivide by neighborhoods or by parishes. . . . The church thus dispersed, one of the ministers should explain the matter at hand.[21]

After that, anyone who wishes to speak to the matter should be free to do so, preferably in order of age, excluding women and boys under fifteen.[22] Even in large cities, he argues, the opinions and voices gathered would help the church come to a conclusion. In an attempt to address objections to his model, Morély cites his own city of Paris as an example: "As for the city of Paris and other similar cities . . . , it would not be difficult to be able to avoid the confusion that some fear if the church is divided into several neighborhoods or parishes."[23]

Here, we should consider what exactly Morély means by "the church." Kingdon routinely translates Morély's *église* with the English *congregation*. As the earlier statements make clear, however, Morély did not have in mind a single congregation or parish, as the word is normally understood in English. For Morély, the entire area around Paris, for example, constituted a single church. Thus, while he was critical of the hierarchical presbyterian-synodal structure of the French Reformed churches, he clearly was not suggesting a system in which individual parishes or congregations should make their own decisions. Instead, "the church" included all the parishes within a metropolitan area. Indeed, he explicitly rejects the idea of strict congregationalism:

As to the election of ministers of such cities, the matter similarly can be debated in the general assembly, then the opinions gathered by the parishes.

---

[21] "Quant à l'ordre externe, qui y doit estre tenu, nous avons desjà declairé que les ministres et senieurs tiendroyent le premier conseil; à iceux on rapporteroit les affaires qui appartiendroyent à l'Eglise. Là le tout seroit mis en deliberation. Et si c'estoit chose qui concernast l'estat d'icelle, et le meritast, le conseil tenu, et la conclusion prinse, le tout seroit rapporté à l'Eglise. Laquelle, où il y auroit grande multitude, pour eviter confusion, et pour vuider l'affaire plus tost, pour moins aussi retenir l'assemblee, seroit departie par les quartiers de la ville, ou par paroisses. . . . L'Eglise donc ainsi departie, un des ministres (tel qu'on l'entendra cy apres) declareroit l'affaire dont il seroit question." Morély, *Traicté de la discipline*, 112.

[22] "Adonc si aucun vouloit user de remonstrance pour l'instruction plus ample et exhortation, il le pourroit faire en toute liberté; et doit l'Eglise donner audience à quiconque il soit, mais qu'il ayt tesmoignage et ayt voix et droict de suffrage. . . . Quant à l'ordre qu'il faudroit tenir en opinant, je seroye d'advis qu'on commençast tousjours par les plus anciens, et que par ce moyen on vinst jusques aux jeunes. . . . Pourtant ces personnes sont à exclure. Premierement les enfans, et ceux qui seroyent au dessous de quinze ans, pour l'incertitude de leur jugement. . . . Gens aussi retrenchés de l'Eglise sont à exclure comme sont aussi les femmes, ausquelles sainct Paul defend de parler en l'assemblee." Morély, *Traicté de la discipline*, 112–13, 119–20.

[23] "Quant à la ville de Paris, et quelque autre semblable . . . , il ne seroit mal-aisé de pourvoir à la confusion que l'on craint, si on departoit l'Eglise, en plusieurs quartiers ou paroisses." Morély, *Traicté de la discipline*, 121.

For it would be a dangerous situation if one parish had its own ministers, separate and apart. If the councils, ministers, and order were diverse within one town, this would give rise to schism.[24]

Hence, Morély was not, strictly speaking, a congregationalist.

As with the determination of doctrine, Morély believed that the local church should control the correction of morals. The theological discussion of moral discipline during the Reformation most commonly turned on the interpretation of Matthew 18:15–17, which prescribes, first, individual admonition and, second, reproach by two or three individuals. Finally, if the sinner fails to heed both, the passage says, "Tell it to the church" (v.17). The Calvinists generally interpreted this phrase to mean, "Tell it to the consistory"; Zwinglian theologians instead interpreted it to mean, "Tell it to the magistrate."[25] This difference of opinion was one of the bases for the Calvinist-Zwinglian debates on discipline, first in the Pays de Vaud, and later in the Erastian controversy in Heidelberg.[26] Morély, by contrast, took the phrase quite literally. To him, "Tell it to the church" meant literally, tell it to the whole church and not just a representative body of it:

This power of rejection from the church, prohibiting communion, cutting off from the body of the Lord, and restoring to the company and community is a sovereign power that comes under each individual church, as to the mother of the family in her house. Therefore, it does not pertain to the rights of the pastors.[27]

---

[24] "Quant à l'election des ministres en telles villes, l'affaire pourroit pareillement estre debatu en l'assemblee generale, puis les opinions se pourroyent recueillir par les paroisses. Car ce seroit chose pernicieuse qu'une paroisse eust ses ministres comme peculiers, et à part. Ce qui donneroit occasion de schisme, si les conseils, les ministres, et les ordres estoyent divers en une ville." Morély, *Traicté de la discipline*, 122.

[25] See, for example, Robert M. Kingdon, "La discipline ecclésiastique vue de Zurich et Genève."

[26] On the conflicts in the Pays de Vaud, see Bruening, *Calvinism's First Battleground*, 160–65, 179–82, 237–55; on Heidelberg, see Charles D. Gunnoe, *Thomas Erastus and the Palatinate: A Renaissance Physician in the Second Reformation*, Brill's Series in Church History 48 (Leiden: Brill, 2010), ch. 6.

[27] "Mais ceste puissance de rejetter de l'Eglise, interdire de sa communion, retrencher de ce corps du Seigneur, ou recevoir en ceste Eglise, et remettre en ceste compagnie et communauté, est une puissance souveraine, qui compete à une chacune Eglise, comme à une mere de famille en sa maison. Pourtant elle ne peut appartenir aux pasteurs de leur droit." Morély, *Traicté de la discipline*, 168. In his manuscript treatise, *De ecclesiae ordine*, written later in England, Morély criticizes the Calvinist interpretation of *Dic ecclesiae*: "Nam ipsorum opinione Dominus his verbis, 'Dic ecclesiae,' omnem vim ordinis ecclesiastici ad consistorium detulisset: Apostolus autem multis locis sed maxime eo quam paulo ante commemoravimus, scilicet cap 1 ad Chorinthios omnem huius disciplinae vim traducit ad ecclesias." Jean Morély, *De ecclesiae ordine et disciplina*, BNF, ms. lat. 4361, bk. II, 30.

The pastors, he claims, have the right and duty to execute the decisions of the church, but they do not possess the right to determine the will of the church.[28] "I conclude," he continues, "that the consent of the church is necessary in excommunication and in reception into this body."[29]

The same principle applies to the election of pastors. Of the questions Morély addresses, this was perhaps the most controversial, as it had been since early in the Swiss Reformation, when the city councils sought jurisdiction over the appointment of pastors. It continued to be so in France, where many places initially lacked established consistories or groups of local pastors to conduct elections. Arguably, Geneva won one of its greatest victories in the French Reformation by moving quickly to ensure that the French Reformed churches adopted the Geneva model for pastoral elections, rather than allowing an alternative system to take root. Morély believed the Calvinist model employed in France lacked both Scriptural support and early-church precedent. In particular, he thought the final step of presenting the selected candidate to the church for a rubber-stamp approval failed to give church members their due: "By these means, the minister is presented to the church, not in order to be approved or rejected by it, but in order to be placed in possession of his office, as if the church were unworthy of having better understanding."[30]

Instead, Morély proposes a process that would involve the whole church. First, any candidate would need to have positive external recommendations. Morély suggests that these might come from "any faithful outsider who has good testimony from his church,"[31] rather than only from other pastors or consistories. The church should also "give freedom and a hearing to anyone" who wants to testify to a candidate's morals and domestic life.[32] Morély would also permit anyone to nominate candidates for the position, in addition to

---

[28] "Car bien qu'ils [les pasteurs] soyent ambassadeurs de Dieu, et interpretes de sa volonté, si n'ont-ils pas ceste domination en l'Eglise, mais ils ont seulement l'execution de la puissance et ordonnance d'icelle, non pas toute la jurisdiction pour en definir et determiner à leur volonté." Morély, *Traicté de la discipline*, 168.

[29] "je concluray le consentement de l'Eglise estre necessaire en l'excommunication, et reception en ce corps." Morély, *Traicté de la discipline*, 168–69.

[30] "Par ce moyen le ministre est presenté à l'Eglise, non pas pour estre approuvé ou rejetté par icelle, mais pour estre mis en possession de son office, comme si elle estoit indigne d'en avoir plus grande cognoissance." Morély, *Traicté de la discipline*, 185.

[31] "Premierement puis qu'il requiert que le ministre ayt bon tesmoignage de ceux qui sont de dehors, il ne faut exclure de ceste election aucun estranger fidele, qui ayt bon tesmoignage de son Eglise, et vueille advertir l'Eglise qui seroit assemblee pour elire." Morély, *Traicté de la discipline*, 193.

[32] "Item que voulant qu'il soit irreprehensible en ses moeurs, et gouvernement domestique, il faut donner liberté et audience à quiconque voudra donner advertissement sur cela, ou faire complaintes." Morély, *Traicté de la discipline*, 193.

those nominated by the pastors and elders.[33] Perhaps taking a cue from time he spent in Lausanne, he also suggests that each province have a university and each county (*bailliage*) a good school, which could provide suitable candidates for the ministry.[34]

Morély's focus on these central schools further challenges the characterization of him as a congregationalist. He proposes that pastoral elections be held not in each parish or even in each town, but in the "mother church" (*église matrice*) that would be in the "county seat" (*siège du bailliage*) of the territory, partly because of the schools that would be established there:

> One should conduct the election in the county seat for all the churches of the region that are dependent on it. For the schools would be there; the crowds of learned and notable individuals would be there; and the seat of the consistory and the principal ecclesiastical order would be there.... It is a reasonable practice and a very ancient custom to defer some advantage to the mother churches, seeing as there would be a very good order, two councils legitimately assembled, a great number of intellectuals and of persons tested over a long time.[35]

Morély's emphasis on the urban "mother church" again calls into question the characterization of his model as congregationalist. One should also note Morély's mention of the "two councils" assembled there. As one might expect, one council was the consistory, made up of the pastors and elders. The other, however, was to be a council of "the most God-fearing and learned men who were well versed in Scripture."[36] He, thus, gives the local lay notables an

---

[33] "En apres puis que tant de graces sont requises au pasteur et senieur, qu'il doit estre permis à quiconque voudra de nommer autres qu'il estimera estre plus suffisans et capables outre ceux qui auront esté nommés par les ministres et senieurs." Morély, *Traicté de la discipline*, 193.

[34] Quant aux villes où telles elections se feroyent, je seroye d'advis qu'en chacune des provinces, lesquelles sont de grande estendue et ressort, comme aussi il est expedient pour beaucoup de raisons, comme Dieu aydant nous le declairerons, il y eust une université, et une bonne eschole en chacun bailliage: on prendroit les plus propres et commodes tant de l'université, que des escholes pour servir au ministere des Eglises." Morély, *Traicté de la discipline*, 200.

[35] "Es sieges desdicts bailliages, on feroit l'election pour toutes les Eglises des lieux qui en dependroyent. Car là seroyent lesdictes escholes, là seroit une affluence de gens notables et doctes, là seroit le siege du consistoire, et le principal ordre ecclesiastique.... Car c'est chose raisonnable et coustume tresancienne de deferer quelque advantage aux Eglises matrices, veu qu'en icelles il y auroit un si bonne ordre, deux conseils si legitimement assemblés, un si grand nombre de gens de sçavoir, et de personnes esprouvées par un long temps." Morély, *Traicté de la discipline*, 200–201.

[36] "Davantage il y auroit un conseil moderateur de ceste sainte assemblee, composé des pasteurs et senieurs eleus legitimement selon la vocation de Dieu, ausquels les affaires se rapporteroyent, lesquels veilleroyent diligemment sur le troupeau du Seigneur, qui consulteroyent prealablement entre eux pour digerer le tout à l'Eglise, et luy esclarcir ce qui seroit obscur: outre lequel qui se desfieroit encores

additional role beyond their mere participation in the votes of the church, a provision inconsistent with strict congregationalism.

As with the election of pastors, their removal also requires approval of the whole church. According to Morély, "No individual person, order, or estate can depose a minister other than the church itself that elected and ordained him."[37] As might be expected, Morély suggests that the council of elders also be elected by the church and should be based in the mother church.[38] He tentatively suggests that deacons be elected by the church as well, although he admits he could be convinced otherwise.[39] Intriguingly, Morély suggests that deaconesses could be restored in the church and "would be a great comfort to the ministry of the poor and would be highly appropriate for the order and dignity of the church."[40]

The last section of Morély's treatise deals with miscellaneous questions of church order and polity and was not as controversial as the earlier sections. The model of local church order and structure that he proposes is remarkably similar to that which was in use in the Pays de Vaud.[41] In the Vaud, a dean (doyen) headed each chapter, and a juror (juré) represented each colloquy within the chapter. Similarly, Morély suggests that groups of approximately twenty pastors meet every week or two in colloquies, headed by a dean and assisted by jurors elected in the mother church.[42] Morély also believes that

de la constance et jugement de l'Eglise, elle eliroit des plus sages, plus craignans de Dieu, et mieux versés en l'Escriture." Morély, *Traicté de la discipline*, 33; see also Denis and Rott, *Jean Morély*, 167–68.

[37] "Mais ceste deposition est tant propre de l'Eglise, que aucune personne, ne ordre, ne estat, quel qu'il soit, ne peut deposer un ministre, que l'Eglise mesme qui l'a eleu et ordonné." Morély, *Traicté de la discipline*, 209–10.

[38] "Ce conseil donc est principalement institué pour deux fins. Premierement pour veiller sur l'Eglise du Seigneur.... En second lieu ce conseil a esté institué, à ce qu'on evite en l'Eglise la confusion qui advient ordinairement en une commune et estat populaire.... Et n'y a doute que l'election de ce conseil n'appartienne pareillement à l'Eglise, à qui est la souveraineté. Car si elle est libre, il est necessaire qu'elle elise son conseil." Morély, *Traicté de la discipline*, 247–48.

[39] "Je seroye donc d'advis, sous correction de meilleur jugement, que diacres fussent eleus par les Eglises avec prieres et jeusnes, et que, jouxte l'admonition des Apostres, personnes pleines du sainct Esprit et de sapience fussent eleus pour avoir esgard sur le gouvernement et solicitude du traictement et moeurs des povres." Morély, *Traicté de la discipline*, 253–54.

[40] "L'Eglise ancienne a eu des Diaconisses, comme nous avons dit, pour le traictement des povres et malades.... Lequel estat, si estoit repurgé et restitué en l'Eglise en sa premiere institution, il seroit un grand soulagement pour le ministere des povres, et appartiendroit grandement à l'ordre et dignité de l'Eglise." Morély, *Traicté de la discipline*, 255–56.

[41] On the ecclesiastical structure of the Pays de Vaud, see Bruening, *Calvinism's First Battleground*, 169–72; Vuilleumier, 1:267–305.

[42] "je desireroye que l'ordre des Eglises de par deça fust observé: c'est à sçavoir que les Eglises de chacun bailliage fussent departies en certaines congregations, assemblées ou colloques, tant pour l'interpretation de l'escriture ... que pour leur communiquer des affaires des Eglises de leurs corps.... En quoy on auroit esgard que les lieux ne fussent trop distans, à ce que les ministres se peussent commodement assembler une fois la sepmaine. . . . Si seroit-il à souhaiter (si le païs le pouvoit

provincial synods should be held every year or two;[43] the Bernese likewise initially recommended annual synods in the Vaud but soon abandoned them. Morély believed that the synods, unlike those of French Reformed churches, should be chiefly advisory. Their role, he insists, was to provide advice to the local churches, which should retain sovereignty.[44]

Morély allows for national as well as provincial synods, but he expresses fear that these too often become occasions for "hatred, discord, and schisms" in the church.[45] They can do some good, he believes, if they "assemble to discuss together the affairs of the church, with the intention of advising about the best way to extirpate heresies and remove scandals."[46] The national synod must not, however, "seek to usurp the power Jesus gives to his church, by determining obscure parts of Scripture according to its will, or by cutting off from the body of the church or receiving into it whomever it likes."[47] Even so, he doubts their utility: "Since no council has ever been pure, is it not a great prejudice against God's truth to want to trust in and receive any council as holy and sacred, seeing as they have all so grievously erred?"[48] Far better, he believes, for matters to be settled by the local churches.

souffrir) qu'il y eust en chacune telle assemblee environ vingt pasteurs. . . . En chacune telle assemblee un de ces ministres que nous pouvons appeler surveillans, presideroit (iceux sont communement appelés par deça doyens), outre lesquels pour leur soulagement, et à ce que l'Eglise ne soit jamais sans personne grave et propre pour presider, et pour beaucoup d'autres affaires, on a coustume d'elire des jurés, ce que je loue grandement, et est chose digne d'imitation. . . . Iceux seroyent eleus en l'Eglise matrice du bailliage." Morély, *Traicté de la discipline*, 284.

[43] "Ce qui doit estre appliqué au synode provincial, que je trouveroye bon, suyvant la coustume ancienne, confermée par un Concile de Carthage, qu'il se tinst tous les ans une fois, ou selon l'ordonnance du Concile de Nicee, pour moins qu'il fust tenu de deux ans en deux ans." Morély, *Traicté de la discipline*, 286.

[44] "Quant aux autres cas, nous avons cy dessus dit, que ces synodes n'auroyent puissance de determiner, ne de decreter aucune chose qui despendist de la puissance de l'Eglise, mais de communiquer par ensemble des causes susdictes, esplucher les passages de l'escriture, puis remettre le tout en son entier au jugement des Eglises." Morély, *Traicté de la discipline*, 289.

[45] "Il est donc ordinairement advenu que ce qui devoit estre le lien de paix et de concorde, a esté le feu qui a allumé les inimitiés, les discords, et schismes en l'Eglise." Morély, *Traicté de la discipline*, 293.

[46] "Bien confesseray-je que où bon nombre de personnes craignantes Dieu, remplies du sainct Esprit et de sapience, sera assemblé pour communiquer par ensemble des affaires de l'Eglise, avec intention d'adviser aux moyens plus convenables pour extirper les heresies, qui s'eleveroyent, et retrencher les scandales, non pas pour en ordonner à leur fantasie, mais pour conseiller fidelement les Eglises: je confesse, dy-je, que le Seigneur Jesus Christ se trouvera entre eux." Morély, *Traicté de la discipline*, 295–96.

[47] "Mais je nie que si telle assemblee vouloit usurper la puissance que Jesus donne en ce passage à son Eglise, en determinant des poincts obscurs de l'Escriture saincte à sa volonté, en retranchant du corps de l'Eglise, recevant en icelle, qui bon leur sembleroit, qu'il y aye promesse qui les asseure que Jesus Christ soit au milieu de telle compagnie." Morély, *Traicté de la discipline*, 296.

[48] "En outre puis qu'ainsi est que nul concile n'a onques esté pur, n'est-ce pas un grand prejudice à la verité de Dieu, de vouloir adjouster foy et recevoir aucun concile comme chose saincte et sacrée, veu qu'ils ont tous bien lourdement erré?" Morély, *Traicté de la discipline*, 297.

8.2.3. Reassessing Morély's Model

Taking the entire treatise together, we see that Morély's vision for the church was neither congregationalist nor even truly democratic. Instead, he presents a vision of the church that is nearly as aristocratic as that of the Calvinists. Morély advocates much wider participation of all the members of the church than do the Calvinists, but his emphasis on the centrality of the county seats, mother churches, schools, universities, and the council of "God-fearing men" would have granted much power to the local notables and intellectual elites.[49] The key difference between the Genevan model and Morély's mixed aristocratic model, then, is that the former favors the clerical elite and the latter is biased toward the local secular elite. This distinction helps to explain why Morély's model might have been so attractive to the French nobility. Indeed, it would have been appealing to anyone who did not want the French churches to take orders from either the national synods or Geneva.

Having called into question the long-accepted notion that Morély was a congregationalist, we may reasonably revisit as well Denis and Rott's characterization of his model as utopian. They conclude, "The institutions such as Morély describes them could never have worked, if only because they were conceived for small territories, not for a state as vast as the kingdom of France.... It is a utopian work: the church whose operation he describes meticulously did not exist anywhere."[50] One must, of course, concede the point that Morély's vision was never implemented in francophone Europe, but one can challenge the notion that Morély's *Treatise* was a utopian work. The book contains detailed descriptions about how the church order would function in a variety of cases, none of which are particularly far-fetched. Morély constantly seeks to make practical what might at first glance seem impractical: Is the church or city too big? Break up the assemblies by neighborhoods or parishes. Are the members of the rural parishes too unruly or ignorant? Hold elections and disciplinary proceedings in the urban mother churches. And so on.

Denis and Rott are certainly correct to note that Morély's vision was intended for a territory much smaller than France. Far from betraying utopian

---

[49] Henry Heller noted this perceptively, writing, "In practice, the application of Morély's proposals would have put the Reformed church at the mercy of its aristocratic protectors." Henry Heller, *Iron and Blood: Civil Wars in Sixteenth-Century France* (Montreal: McGill-Queen's University Press, 1991), 74.

[50] Denis and Rott, *Jean Morély*, 208.

ideals, however, Morély's focus on smaller territories in fact demonstrates his pragmatism; he seems to have realized that a nation-wide Protestant church was not practical and that any ecclesiastical structure in such a large kingdom would have to be broken up into provinces and counties. As we will see later, Morély moved around a great deal after his conversion to Protestantism, and he was well aware of the many regional differences among the Protestant churches all over Europe. His ecclesiology sought to translate those differences into strengths. Only by tapping into local communities, local elites, and local mindsets could the Gospel flourish to its full potential, whether in Paris, Montbéliard, or Lausanne. Morély's book offers a striking contrast between his approval of provincial synods and his disapproval of national ones. Provincial synods, he believed, could play an important unifying role in the church, but national synods would invariably give rise to a self-righteous clerical elite who would attempt to flatten the very local differences that he believed would allow the church to thrive. Perhaps most importantly, Morély's program gave a prominent role in the church to the local nobility and intellectual elites. These were the people, he believed, who should be responsible for the success or failure of a local ecclesiastical community. Whether in the kingdom of France or the comté of Neuchâtel, the local elites must be allowed to guide the church as they thought best, and not have to take orders from a distant authority—much less a foreign regime, in the case of Geneva—with no understanding of the local situation. As we will see, several of the elites in France believed likewise. In a way, Morély's emphasis on the regional, metropolitan churches mirrored the emphasis on diocesan reform that had been a mainstay of French evangelicalism from Briçonnet to Roussel and Monluc.

Moreover, parts of Morély's model were not without precedent even among the Calvinists. The model that was perhaps closest to Morély's was that of the Pays de Vaud, a fact that may explain why Morély dedicated the treatise to Viret. It was not so much that Viret inspired or shared Morély's quasi-democratic beliefs, as one historian has suggested,[51] but that Morély saw in the Pays de Vaud, and perhaps in discussions with Viret, a model that he preferred to that of Geneva. We have seen that Morély's proposed ecclesiastical structure, with annual provincial synods and local colloquies with deans and jurors, mimicked that of the Vaud. Moreover, Viret's dealings with the Bernese while he was in Lausanne may well have informed Morély's

---

[51] Philippe Denis, "Viret et Morély: Les raisons d'un silence," *BHR* 54 (1992): 395–409.

work. Just as Viret was distrustful of orders coming from a hierarchically superior and external entity, namely the Bern city council, so also Morély distrusted the national synods and the external influence of Geneva. Viret repeatedly demanded that the Bern council not interfere in the appointment of pastors, and he asked that candidates for the ministry be sought from the Lausanne Academy. Morély gives no role to the magistrate in the appointment of pastors[52] and suggests that schools and universities be set up in France for the same purpose. Viret fought against the anti-Calvinist churches in the Vaud when they tried to appoint pastors without consulting the Lausanne church. Similarly, Morély gives great authority to the "mother churches," among which he might have counted Lausanne, in the election of pastors and the administration of discipline. Thus, it is not so much the democratic element that ties Viret and Morély together, but Morély's regional, metropolitan ecclesiastical structure that closely echoes the model in Viret's Lausanne.

Morély's model was never implemented exactly as he imagined, but few prescriptive ecclesiological programs ever are. More importantly, Morély drew on his own experiences in various Protestant territories, as well as on the long tradition of local, diocesan reform in France itself, to present a model that would not have looked utopian to his readers. On the contrary, there was much that would have been familiar to them, and much that would have been attractive. Finally, as we shall see later, Calvin's succesor, Theodore Beza, denounced Morély's work at every opportunity. Perhaps this obsessive condemnation is the most important evidence that Morély's ideas presented a real threat to the Calvinist system. Utopias rarely elicit such worried condemnation.

8.3. Morély's Path to Fame (or Infamy)

Jean Morély was an unlikely rabble-rouser in the francophone Reformed world. In contrast to most of the other key individuals we have met in this book, Morély was neither a pastor, nor a professor, nor even a notable

---

[52] Morély criticizes the practice in Geneva and other Reformed territories of having the magistrate approve the pastoral candidates recommended to them by the consistories: "Enquoy y a double faute: L'une, que ce n'est l'estat ne la vocation d'iceluy magistrat, et est confondre les deux gouvernemens. . . . Le seconde faute en cecy est, que quand ainsi ne seroit, le magistrat ne pourroit rejetter le ministre eleu, sinon pour cause bien notable." Morély, *Traicté de la discipline*, 184.

humanist. Like many of the others, however, Morély did not start out as the Calvinists' opponent. Indeed, even at the time he wrote the *Treatise on Christian Discipline*, he still had reasonably good relations with them. In dedicating his book, he describes Viret as "the principal" among the "excellent individuals in piety, knowledge, and judgment."[53] His book also mentions Calvin favorably, describing him as "one of the most excellent apostles the Lord has raised up in this time, not only for the restoration of his church but also for the illustration of doctrine and its preservation in perpetuity."[54] Controversies in Geneva related to the Conspiracy of Amboise, however, had begun to damage his relationship with Beza, and it was Beza who would be his chief adversary in the 1560s. Furthermore, although Morély was on good terms with the Calvinists, he developed ties to several of the anti-Calvinists in francophone Switzerland. As Beza and the Genevans turned ever more sharply against him, Morély increasingly sought refuge in the circles of their opponents. The anti-Calvinists, in turn, found that Morély's ecclesiology gave them a new avenue by which to harass their old enemies. As Morély returned to France and challenged the Reformed churches there over church governance issues, the conflict raised tensions between national identity and confessional loyalty. Particularly controversial was the question of how dependent the French churches should be on Geneva.

8.3.1. Morély among Calvinists and Anti-Calvinists, 1545–1560

Morély grew up in the Paris region and was the son of a minor nobleman, also named Jean.[55] His education is difficult to piece together, but he mentions studying in the Collège de Guyenne in Bordeaux, where Zébédée

---

[53] "et [je] confesse franchement avoir beaucoup apprins et avoir eu facile ouverture en cecy par la conference et devis d'excellens personnages en pieté, sçavoir, et jugement. Entre lesquels, vous, mon treshonoré pere en nostre Seigneur, estes le principal." *Epistolae Vireti*, 422, no. 143, Morély to Viret, Lyon, March 29, 1562.

[54] "comme aussi l'expose Maistre Jean Calvin, un des plus excellens apostres que le Seigneur a suscités en ce temps, non seulement pour la restauration de son Eglise, mais aussi pour l'illustration de la doctrine et conservation d'icelle à perpetuité." Morély, *Traicté de la discipline*, 257. In his later *De ecclesiae ordine* he says of Calvin, "Quid de Jo. Calvino dicam, qui iudicium suum, et suis veris fidelibusque interpretationibus toties declarat suis in commentariis, quoties ea de re agitur, et in confessione novi Gallicanarum Ecclesiarum scripta, cuius edenda princeps fuit apertissime docuit qui de ea re tota sentiret?" Morély, *De ecclesiae ordine et disciplina*, BNF, ms. Lat. 4361, bk. I, 16. Denis and Rott describe and analyze this manuscript in *Jean Morély*, 324–45, annexe XI.

[55] On his early life, see Denis and Rott, *Jean Morély*, 17–20.

had taught and, indeed, recalls hearing about him there.[56] Morély may have received some education in law as well, for in 1545, he is listed as an *avocat au parlement*.[57]

Around this time, he converted to Protestantism and began a peripatetic lifestyle, traveling among various Protestant regions while occasionally returning to France. He spent time in both Wittenberg and Zurich, with significant stretches in francophone Switzerland as well. As we have seen, he knew Viret and spent time in Lausanne and the Vaud. In Lausanne, he sided with Viret in his quarrels with Zébédée, and he seems to have studied for a time at the Academy there.[58] He also exchanged letters with Calvin and Farel. Through the 1550s, we can situate him within the Calvinist network.

All the while, however, he was consorting with some of the region's anti-Calvinists. He was in contact with Jean Morand, Marcourt's colleague in Geneva during Calvin's exile.[59] Jerome Bolsec's supporter Jean Davion helped Morély with some financial transactions.[60] Morély also became friends with Benoît de la Coste and was the brother-in-law of Vevey pastor François de Saint-Paul, both critics of the Calvinists on the question of predestination.[61] Despite these connections to their opponents, Morély remained on good terms with the Calvinists through the 1550s and was welcomed as a resident (*habitant*) of Geneva in January 1559.

Morély's first major breakdown with the Calvinists came in 1560, when he was accused of spreading rumors that Beza had supported the Conspiracy of Amboise.[62] The Geneva council concluded that Morély was guilty of having

---

[56] "Nam accepisse me, abesse urbe dominum Zebedaeum, quem Burdegalae de nomine cognitum, postea vero sua doctrina celebrem visum Lausannae ante annos aliquot convenire voluisse, tristari sublatam esse mihi facultatem; sed tamen arbitrari me, non inanem esse profectionem et suo more laborare de Ecclesia." Jean Rott, "Un réfugié français en Suisse romande en 1550: Deux lettres inédites de Jean Morély à Guillaume Farel," in Jean Rott, *Investigationes Historicae, Églises et société au XVIe siècle, Gesammelte Aufsätze zur Kirchen- und Sozialgeschichte*, 2 vols., edited by Marijn de Kroon and Marc Lienhard, 2:83–92, Société savante d'Alsace et des regions de l'Est, Collection "Grandes Publications" 32 (Strasbourg: Oberlin, 1986), 86, [Morély] to Farel, Lausanne, [middle of June 1550].

[57] Denis and Rott, *Jean Morély*, 20.

[58] See Denis and Rott, *Jean Morély*, 27–28.

[59] Denis and Rott, *Jean Morély*, 23; on Morand, see 77–78.

[60] Denis and Rott, *Jean Morély*, 24; on Davion, see 137.

[61] Denis and Rott, *Jean Morély*, 35–36.

[62] See Denis and Rott, *Jean Morély*, 44–49. The Amboise conspiracy was a failed attempt to kidnap the young king Francis II and marginalize the influence of the powerful Catholic Guise family. Philip Benedict's recent work demonstrates that "if Calvin and the other Genevan pastors did not baldly lie when they sought to distance themselves from the conspiracy of Amboise after its failure, they at the very least engaged in lawyerly evasion." Philip Benedict, *Season of Conspiracy: Calvin, the French Reformed Churches, and Protestant Plotting in the Reign of Francis II (1559–60)*, Transactions of the American Philosophical Society 108, pt. 5 (Philadelphia: American Philosophical Society Press, 2020), 5. Later in 1560, Calvin and Beza were even more directly involved in the plotting around the Maligny Affair, an abortive attempt to seize Lyon. Ibid., *passim*.

"highlighted the calumny that the ministers of the church of Geneva had consented" to the subversive action in France.[63] Even at this point, though, there were no indications of disagreement between Morély and the Calvinists over ecclesiology. Nevertheless, Morély's sympathy for Calvin's critics on predestination and the official accusations against him in Geneva were pushing him away from his former allies.

8.3.2. Possible Influences on Morély's Ecclesiology

On the ecclesiological controversy, it is possible that Morély was mulling over ideas long before he set them down on paper. Of the places he passed through in the 1550s, London may have had a particularly strong influence on his later thinking.[64] In 1553, Morély crossed the English Channel and likely met Castellio's friend François Perrussel, who, with Richard Vauville, was one of the first pastors of the French Strangers' Church in London, where Morély undoubtedly would have worshiped while there. Later in France, Morély would claim Perrussel as a supporter.[65] Perhaps most importantly, however, the London Strangers' Church, which included French and Dutch congregations, was presided over by Jan Łaski (or John a Lasco), whose *Forma ac ratio* established the church's structure and order.[66] On the key question of pastoral elections, Łaski's text maintained the laity's right to nominate and approve candidates. It also required full participation of the congregation in disciplinary matters.[67] There are significant differences between Łaski's and Morély's programs. In the *Forma ac ratio*, the church's most important role comes at the beginning, in nominating candidates for the ministry, but the pastors and elders make the final decision. The selected candidate is then presented to the people only for their final approbation, as in

---

[63] Denis and Rott, *Jean Morély*, 48.
[64] Denis and Rott, *Jean Morély*, 32.
[65] See 281–82.
[66] See Michael S. Springer, *Restoring Christ's Church: John a Lasco and the* Forma ac Ratio, St. Andrews Studies in Reformation History (Aldershot, UK: Ashgate, 2007); Judith Becker, "La constitution ecclésiastique de Jean a Lasco pour l'Eglise néerlandaise de Londres et son influence en France," in *Entre Calvinistes et Catholiques: Les relations religieuses entre la France et les Pays-Bas du Nord (XVIe-XVIIIe siècle)*, edited by Yves Krumenacker and Olivier Christin, 59–75 (Rennes: Presses Universitaires de Rennes, 2010).
[67] Springer, *Restoring Christ's Church*, 120; Becker, "La constitution ecclésiastique," 62.

the Calvinist system.[68] Nevertheless, Łaski's system allowed for greater congregational participation than did the Geneva model.

It is unclear how long Morély was in London or whether he read Łaski's
church ordinance. Morély, of course, knew Latin, but a French version of
the text was also published a year after the Latin,[69] and that translation may
have influenced francophone Reformed communities before anyone had
heard of Morély. Disputes over related issues arose in several places well before Morély published his controversial book. In 1554, the French church
members in Strasbourg successfully fought their pastor, Jean Garnier, for the
right to elect the church's elders.[70] In 1555 and 1556, in the French church in
Frankfurt, the pastor Valérand Poullain tried to appoint elders and deacons
without the laity's approval. The people were outraged and deposed Poullain;
they elected Perrussel to replace him.[71] In France, the Reformed church
of Le Mans elected its own church officials before the first national synod
met.[72] Indeed, in the shadowy years before the first synods, when the French
churches remained largely hidden and there were no established consistories
or bodies of pastors to govern them, most congregations seem to have established a system of popular election of local church officials. The first national
synod sought to change that and to make the Calvinist presbyterian-synodal
model normative for all of France.

8.3.3. Publication and Condemnation of Morély's Treatise

Not long after the first national synod, Morély wrote his *Treatise on Christian
Discipline and Polity*,[73] and he published the text in Lyon with Jean de

---

[68] Jan Łaski, *Toute la forme et maniere du Ministere Ecclesiastique, en l'Eglise des estrangers, dressée à Londres en Angleterre* . . . ([Emden]: [Gellius Ctematius], 1556), 17ᵛ–21ᵛ.

[69] Jan Łaski, *Forma ac ratio tota ecclesiastici ministerii, in peregrinorum, potissimum vero Germanorum Ecclesia: instituta Londini in Anglia* . . . ([Frankfurt], [1555]); Łaski, *Toute la forme et maniere*.

[70] Denis, *Les églises d'étrangers en pays rhénans*, 91–92.

[71] Denis, *Les églises d'étrangers en pays rhénans*, 334–49.

[72] Philip Conner, "Huguenot Identities during the Wars of Religion: The Churches of Le Mans and Montauban Compared," *Journal of Ecclesiastical History* 54 (2003): 23–39; here, 27.

[73] The exact date is, of course, uncertain, but we know that he had completed a draft of it before September 1561, for he claims in the preface to have shown the manuscript to Viret before his departure for France that month: "vostre authorité ne m'a servi d'un petit aiguillon de mettre en avant le
traicté que j'en avois escrit. Lequel mesmement je my alors entre vos mains; à ce qu'il fust examiné par
vous en toutes ses parties, et qu'aucune chose ne m'eschappast par legereté et imprudence, qui peust
troubler l'eglise du Seigneur. Ce que, toutesfois, pour vos autres occupations et departement soudain,

Tournes, who, as we saw in Chapter 6, was associated with the circle of Castellionists in the city.[74] If Morély's goal was to angrily confront the French synods, his prefatory letter to Viret does not reflect that motivation. Instead, he claims to have been looking forward to presenting his book to the synod of Orléans, hoping that Viret would be present there.[75] On the other hand, he seems to have expected some resistance to his ideas; he ends the book with a quotation from Psalm 119: "*Redime me a calumniis hominum*: Redeem me from the malicious accusations of men."[76] No doubt, that was exactly what he felt he faced in Orléans: malicious accusations, brought not by Viret, who was not present, but by Beza and Antoine Chandieu, who presided at the synod. Both came prepared to denounce Morély's book and successfully convinced the synod to condemn it.

When Morély returned to Geneva later in 1562, he was summoned to the consistory, but he refused to appear and instead returned quickly to Lyon.[77] In July 1563, he once again returned to Geneva, and this time appeared before the consistory, which excommunicated him and referred him to the city council. Morély left town and returned to France before the council could take further action against him. The Geneva council ordered a copy of his book to be burned, forbade its sale in the city, and published an *Excerpt of the Procedures against Jean Morély*.[78] These actions indicate that the Genevans believed Morély's book constituted a considerable threat to their own ecclesiology.

Beza and Chandieu would exert much energy over the next four years trying to prevent Morély's ideas from taking root among the French churches. For his part, Morély sought to be readmitted to the French churches, which

ne m'advint comme je l'avois souhaitté. Car il ne vous fut possible de le veoir tout à faict." *Epistolae Vireti*, 422–23, no. 143, Morély to Viret, Lyon, March 29, 1562.

[74] See 202–203.

[75] "Partant, ayant entendu que de toutes parts pasteurs et anciens deputés par les eglises se devoyent assembler pour pourveoir aux affaires d'icelles, je n'ay voulu defaillir à ceste oportunité que j'avois tant souhaittée. Auquel synode ayant esté adverti que vous deviez trouver, je vous ay envoyé ce livre, à ce que poursuyviez la lecture que vous avez encommencée et soyez autheur au synode d'entendre à cest affaire par grande maturité de jugement." *Epistolae Vireti*, 423–24, no. 143. He also sent a copy to Calvin and expressed similar optimism about his reaction. Rudolphe Peter and Jean Rott, eds., *Les lettres à Calvin de la collection Sarrau* (Paris: Presses Universitaires de France, 1972), 71–75, Lyon, April 10 [1562].

[76] Morély, *Traicté de la discipline*, 349.

[77] Denis and Rott, *Jean Morély*, 59.

[78] Geneva consistory and council, *L'Extrait des procedures faites et tenues contre Jean Morelli, natif de Paris et n'agueres habitant en la ville de Geneve, touchant un livre composé par luy, De la discipline ecclesiastique* . . . (Geneva: François Perrin, 1563). The full text is reproduced in Denis and Rott, *Jean Morély*, 261–65.

were hesitant to overturn a sentence of excommunication issued by the Geneva consistory. In 1564 and 1565, Morély appeared several times at provincial synods of the churches of the Île de France.[79] In April 1564, the provincial synod of Ferté-sous-Jouarre stated clearly that the governing power in the French churches did not belong to the church as a whole, as Morély argued, but to the consistory:

> The sovereign dominion that Morély says pertains to the whole body of the church in general, composed of the people and others who preside in the church, cannot be attributed to the whole body. Instead, the government of the church pertains and ought to pertain to the consistory of the church which represents the whole body in order to govern according to the Word of God. Likewise, the elections and interpretation of doctrine, excommunication, and the dependencies, corrections, and discipline pertain to the consistory.[80]

The Calvinists' emphasis on the power of the consistory had enraged Charles Du Moulin, and it would have the same effect on Morély. Nevertheless, Morély agreed at Ferté-sous-Jouarre to sign the French *Confession of Faith* and the *Discipline*, and to publish a correction regarding the errors the pastors had found in his book.[81] He also wrote to the Genevans seeking reconciliation,[82] but much to his annoyance, the Genevans refused to accept his overtures.[83]

Morély failed to publish his retractions, and in February 1565, he was summoned to another provincial synod to explain why. Instead of explaining or apologizing, Morély initially insisted that his book contained nothing

---

[79] See Kingdon, *Geneva and the Consolidation of the French Protestant Movement*, 67–76; Denis and Rott, *Jean Morély*, 60–64.

[80] "Et oultre que le souverain empire que ledict Morelly dict appartenir à tout le corps de l'eglise en general composé du peuple et autres qui resident en l'eglise, ne peult estre attribué à tout le corps, mais que le gouvernement de l'eglise appartient et doibt appartenir au consistoire de l'eglise representant tout le corps pour gouverner selon la parolle de Dieu. Et en semblable que les eslections et cognoissance de la doctrine, excommunication et ses deppendances, corrections et discipline appartiennent au consistoire." Denis and Rott, *Jean Morély*, 269, annexe V.

[81] "on ne peult le recepvoir en l'eglise, que premier il n'aict donné tesmoignage de sa repentance, qu'il aict signé la confession de foy des eglises et discipline d'icelles et promis à se retracter par escript des erreurs et faultes qu'a faictes contenues audict livre, et icelles corrections faire publier imprimées, ayant premier l'advis de l'eglise de Clermont en Beauvoisis à prochain colloque du lieu. Ce que ledict Morelly a promis faire, comme il appert par ses promesses et declaration signée de sa main." Denis and Rott, *Jean Morély*, 270, annexe V.

[82] *Bèze Cor*. 6:227–30, Annexe 1a, Morély to the Geneva Pastors, Paris, May 8 [1564].

[83] Kingdon, *Geneva and the Consolidation of the French Protestant Movement*, 69.

contrary to the word of God, and he added an implicit threat, noting that the synod was meeting illegally.[84] Nevertheless, he soon changed his tune. By the end of the synod, he had once again retracted his errors and was readmitted to communion.[85] The synod also ordered that "a book be published as soon as possible that will refute comprehensively Morély's heresies and warn the church to beware of this most wicked man."[86] This mandate was the origin of Antoine Chandieu's *Confirmation of the Ecclesiastical Discipline Observed in the Reformed Churches of the Kingdom of France*,[87] which was an extended response to Morély's *Treatise*. After the February synod, Morély wrote to the Genevans once again, seeking reconciliation,[88] but once again he was rebuffed,[89] for Beza and the Genevans doubted—with good reason—the sincerity of his repentence. Morély, in fact, continued to circulate copies of his book and to advocate for his vision of church governance in opposition to the approved French *Discipline*.[90] In July 1565, he was summoned once again to the provincial synod, where, under pressure from his most powerful ally, Odet de Coligny, the Cardinal of Châtillon, the synod allowed him to continue to receive communion but insisted once again that he reconcile with the Genevans.[91] Finally, on Christmas Day 1565, a national synod of

---

[84] "Mais il monstra bien de quel esprit il estoit mené, car il manifesta ouvertement que son livre ne contenoit rien qui fust contraire à la parolle de Dieu. . . . et creignant qu'on ne procedast à la censure de son oppinion, menaça ladite compagnie avec haultes et braves parolles, disant qu'elle estoit assemblée contre les editz du Roy." *Bèze Cor.* 8:220, Annexe Ie, "Discours des procedures tenues et gardées tant ès Synodes provinciaux des pasteurs de l'Isle de France et colloques, qu'au Synode national dernier . . . a l'endroict de Me Jehan Morely."

[85] Kingdon, *Geneva and the Consolidation of the French Protestant Movement*, 69. His retraction at the synod is printed in *Bèze Cor.* 6:231–32, Annexe Ib, Paris, February 12, 1565.

[86] "Decretum vero fuit omnium consensu, ut liber primo quoque tempore excudatur, quo Morelli haereses locupletissime refutantur, Ecclesiae vero admonitae ut sibi ab iniquissimo homine caveant." *Bèze Cor.* 6:29, no. 357bis, Theophile de Banos to Beza, Paris, February 16 [1565].

[87] [Antoine de Chandieu], *La confirmation de la discipline ecclesiastique, observée ès eglises reformées du royaume de France, avec la response aux objections proposées alencontre* ([Geneva]: [Henri Estienne], 1566). For a detailed discussion of Chandieu's text and an analysis of its structure, see Theodore G. Van Raalte, *Antoine de Chandieu: The Silver Horn of Geneva's Reformed Triumvirate*, Oxford Studies in Historical Theology (New York: Oxford University Press, 2018), 123–39, 309–16.

[88] *Bèze Cor.* 6:233–34, Annexe Ic, Morély to the Pastors and Elders of Geneva, Paris, April 18, 1565.

[89] *Bèze Cor.* 6:234–36, Annexe Id, Church and Consistory of Geneva to Morély, Geneva, May 17, 1565.

[90] "Mais encores fust elle [the church of Paris] plus ennuyée, estant advertie qu'il donnoit à quelques personnes des coppies de son livre, semant par ce moyen son oppinion, et qu'il conferoit avec plusieurs de sa nouvelle discipline tachant à la faire valoir, et desprisant, contre sa promesse, celle qui est gardée ès Eglises." *Bèze Cor.* 8:221, Annexe Ie, "Discours des procedures."

[91] Denis and Rott, *Jean Morély*, 62–63; *Bèze Cor.* 8:221–22, Annexe Ie, "Discours des procedures." In the "Discours," the author notes that that synod's lenient decision was made in part, "ayant . . . esgard au repos des Esglises de par deçà" (222), suggesting that a harsher decision could well have caused trouble, perhaps stirred by the Protestant Cardinal.

the French Reformed churches convened in Paris, where Morély's book was again condemned.[92]

Thus, the official story of the Morély affair is one of repeated condemnations by the French Reformed synods and of a series of thwarted efforts to reconcile with the Genevans. The story behind the scenes is more complicated, for Morély had supporters among both the Reformed pastors and the Huguenot nobility. This extensive and powerful support drove Beza and his allies to see Morély as a real threat. Even after the condemnation by the 1565 national synod, one French pastor complained to Beza, "since [Morély] is supported by some of the lords and already has a large number of ministers as companions, I have no doubt that he will soon start to trouble the church again like never before."[93]

8.4. Morély's Network

In the summer of 1566, Beza's allies broke into the home of Hughes Sureau du Rosier, a Reformed pastor in Orléans who was in prison at the time.[94] In Sureau's study, they discovered a cache of letters written by Jean Morély.[95] Sureau had been suspected of supporting Morély; the letters confirmed those suspicions. In them, Morély set aside the diplomatic language he used when seeking reconciliation with the Genevans and set forth his true feelings. The letters made clear what the Genevans had suspected, namely, that his efforts at reconciliation were insincere and that he had not truly retracted the views he had expressed in his book. Like Du Moulin, Morély lashed out

[92] "les ministres et anciens deputés . . . , apres avoir vu diligemment les livres et autres ecrits de Monsieur Jean de Moreli touchant la police et discipline de l'Eglise . . . ont condanné ses livres et ecrits, comme contenant de mauvaises et dangereuses opinions, par lesquelles il renverse la *Discipline*, conforme à la parole de Dieu, qui est aujourd'hui receu dans les Eglises Reformées de ce roiaume; car en attribuant le gouvernement de l'Eglise au peuple, il veut introduire une nouvelle conduite tumultueuse et pleine de confusion populaire." Aymon, *Tous les synodes*, 1.2:58. See also the account of the synod in the "Discours des procedures," *Bèze Cor.* 8:224, Annexe Ie.

[93] "estant supporté de quelques seigneurs, ayant pour compagnons desjà quelque grant nombre de ministres, je ne doubte point qu'il ne recommencent au plus tost de troubler l'Eglise plus que jamais." *Bèze Cor.* 7:191, no. 486, Le Maçon, Sieur de la Fontaine, to Beza, Orléans, August 4, 1566.

[94] He was suspected as the author of the *Défense civile et militaire des Innocents de l'Eglise du Christ*, the same text Du Moulin was accused of writing (see 247–48). On Sureau, see Robert M. Kingdon, "Genève et les Réformés français: Le cas d'Hughes Sureau, dit Du Rosier (1565–1574)," *Bulletin de la Société d'histoire et d'archéologie de Genève* 12 (1962): 77–87; Robert M. Kingdon, "Problems of Religious Choice for Sixteenth Century Frenchmen," *Journal of Religious History* 4 (1966): 105–12.

[95] Excerpts from the letters, in Latin, have been preserved, some of which were also translated into French for presentation to Jeanne d'Albret. These excerpts are published in Denis and Rott, *Jean Morély*, 279–95, Annexe VII.

at the power the consistories had assumed for themselves in France, saying that they, not he, were responsible for the schisms in the church, "for the consistories have raised themselves against their pastors, and the churches are split from their consistories."[96] He saved most of his fire for the Genevans, however. Echoing Bauduin's descriptions of Calvin, Morély refers to Beza as the "Lemannic Jove"[97] and exclaims, "May God free his church from the tyranny of the new Antichrist! . . . May the Lord God look down from heaven on his church, redeemed by his blood. Having recently recovered from the tyranny of the Roman Antichrist, it will be overcome by the Genevan one!"[98] Morély thus continued the anti-Calvinist tradition of portraying Geneva as the new Rome, and its church leader as the new pope.[99] Just before the 1565 national synod, Morély wrote to Sureau, "I think you have understood from my last letters how great is the Genevans' insolence, or rather tyranny. . . . As for me, I am at the point where I want to demonstrate my confidence, relying on God's mercy and his word in order to tear down their primacy."[100]

Perhaps most galling to Morély was that he, a Frenchman, had to answer to the Genevans at all. Here we see the patriotic element of Morély's arguments that likely appealed to other French evangelicals and nobles. "I was born in," he exclaims, "and am a native of France, not of Geneva. I am a subject of the king. . . . I cannot submit to the judgment of another without offending my prince."[101] Like Du Moulin who lamented the foreign influence of Geneva on French evangelicals,[102] Morély casts the city as a foreign power that tyrannizes the French churches and has no business demanding apologies from him.

---

[96] "Iceluy [the provincial synod of February 1565] m'accusoit que j'estoit autheur de scismes et tumultes en l'Eglise, et pourtant me citoit au siège judicial de Dieu. Car les consistoires s'eslevoyent contre leurs pasteurs, et les églises estoyent divisées de leurs consistoires, que (c)es schismes me devoyent estre imputez." Denis and Rott, *Jean Morély*, 284, no. V, Paris, August 29 [1565]; see also ibid., 305, n. 56 and 306.

[97] "Quaeris quibus expiationibus Jovem istum Lemanicum placare conentur?" Denis and Rott, *Jean Morély*, 285, no. 19, [late October/early November 1565].

[98] "Velit de(us E)cclesiam suam liberare ab ista novi Antichristi tyrannide! . . . Videat vero dominus Deus noster de coelo sancto suo Ecclesiam suam, suo redemptam sanguine, summo imperio receptam modo a Romani Antichristi tyrannide, vindicet a Genevensi!" Denis and Rott, *Jean Morély*, 286, no. 19.

[99] For example, "Je ne receux les lettres de ceux de Genève comme si elles fussent venues de Rome." Denis and Rott, *Jean Morély*, 284, no. V.

[100] "Tu as, je pense, entendu par mes dernières lettres, combien est grande l'insolence ou plustôt la tyrannie de ceux de Genève. . . . Quant à moy, je suis là, que je veux monstrer mon assurance, estant appuyé en la miséricorde de Dieu et sa parolle pour abattre la primauté de ceux-cy." Denis and Rott, *Jean Morély*, 286, no. 17, [end of Decemer 1565].

[101] "Je suis nay et natif de France, non pas de Genève; je suis subject du Roy. . . . Je ne me puis submettre au jugement d'autruy sans offencer mon Prince." Denis and Rott, *Jean Morély*, 285, no. V.

[102] See 248–50.

8.4.1. Morély's Supporters among the
Reformed Pastors

This French nativist pride, probably even more than his controversial eccle-siology, helped Morély win supporters in France. His anti-Genevan stance would have played well in certain evangelical circles in the kingdom. First, in Orléans, Morély found support with Sureau himself, as well as with an-other local pastor, Pierre Baron. Sureau's origins are difficult to discern, but his connections with the Reformed movement extend back to the days be-fore Calvin, when he worked as a corrector for Pierre de Vingle's press in Neuchâtel.[103] He may have studied in Geneva for a time before being sent first to France, possibly to Paris, and then certainly to Orléans.[104] The best evidence for Sureau's support is in Morély's correspondence with him. Although we do not have any letters from Sureau, Morély's tone and frank-ness throughout his own letters suggests that he saw Sureau as a friend and supporter. Sureau's colleagues likewise reported him to Geneva as belonging to Morély's party.[105] In addition, Sureau was reported to have converted Pierre Baron to Morély's views.[106] Baron had studied law at Bourges; his time there overlapped with that of Bauduin, and so he may well have studied under him.[107] Soon afterward, Baron openly adopted the Reformed faith and in 1560 was ordained by Calvin himself. He was preaching in Orléans by 1564. After the St. Bartholomew's Day massacre, he fled to England, where he taught at Cambridge and adopted the anglicized name Peter Baro. At Cambridge he publicly held anti-Calvinist views on predestination and

---

[103] E. Droz, "Pierre de Vingle, l'imprimeur de Farel," in *Aspects de la propagande religieuse*, 38–78, THR 28 (Geneva: Droz, 1957), 73–74.

[104] Kingdon, "Genève et les Réformés français," 78.

[105] "Le premier [problem affecting our church] est touchant la doctrine de Morely. Vous avez peu conoistre que desjà de long tems Monsieur Du Rozier suyvoit ceste partie. Toutesfois pour ce qu'il s'est tousjours teu et s'est rangé en l'exercice de l'ordre que nous avons commun avec les aultres Eglises, nous avons estimé que le mal ne glissoit point davantage, mays depuis peu de tems, j'ay cogneu, et pour certain, sus tout depuis la prison dudit sieur Du Rozier, qu'il a familiarité et communication très frequente avec Morely, lequel sans cela se manieroit plus aiseement." *Bèze Cor.* 7:191, no. 486, Le Maçon to Beza, Orléans, August 4, 1566.

[106] "Depuis peu de tems il [Sureau] a attiré en ceste opinion un de nos compagnons, M. Baron." *Bèze Cor.* 7:191, no. 486. See also Beza's reprimand to the two ministers of Orléans: "Sans user de plus grands circuits, c'est de vous, Monsieur Du Rosier, et de vous, Monsieur Baron, desquels nous nous pleignons, devant la compagnie de laquelle vous estes membres de par Dieu, et toutesfois par nostre moyen, puis qu'il luy a pleu." *Bèze Cor.* 7:309, annexe I.g., Beza in the name of the Geneva Pastors to the Church of Orléans, [Geneva], [September 25, 1566].

[107] Baron graduated from Bourges in 1556; Bauduin left the city in 1555. On Baron, see C. S. Knighton, "Baro, Peter," in the *Oxford Dictionary of National Biography*, online at https://doi.org/10.1093/ref:odnb/1492. This dictionary entry mentions nothing, however, about Baron's connection to the Morély affair.

has been described as "the most prominent of those who have been called Arminians *avant la lettre*."[108] Thus, despite ordination in Geneva, Baron/ Baro had a long history of conflict with the Calvinists in both France and England.

Morély's letters provide the names of several other individuals he identified as his supporters. In one letter, he lists as allies Bernard de Montméja, Jean Mallot, Hermès de La Haye, Matthieu d'Olivier, Guillaume Houbraque, François Philippi, Juan Pérez, and François Perrussel.[109] Little is known about some of these individuals, especially d'Olivier.[110] Among the better known figures on this list are Houbraque and Perrussel, whom we have already met. Perrussel's presence is not surprising, for he and Morély may have met earlier in London. As noted in Chapter 6, Perrussel was among Castellio's friends and correspondents.[111] He argued for a looser disciplinary system in the French church in Frankfurt, and Du Moulin cited him as a victim of the Calvinists for his praise of the Augsburg Confession.[112] At the time of Morély's letter, Perrussel was a pastor in Condé's household. Bernard de Montméja was a poet and pastor of the church of Chauny (not far from Calvin's hometown of Noyon) and also tied to Perrussel and Condé.[113] In addition, Perrussel seems to have introduced to Morély a small network of associates from his days in Frankfurt. François Philippi, originally from Bourges, had been Perrussel's colleague in Frankfurt before moving to Aix-la-Chapelle.[114] Juan Pérez de Pineda (or Pierins in French) was also connected to both Perrussel and Condé, as well as to Renée de France. He was a Spaniard who had been chased out of Seville by the Inquisition.[115] Through much of the 1550s, Pérez

---

[108] Knighton, "Baro, Peter."

[109] "Je suis après pour attirer à ma cause Momméjan et ay bon espoir. . . . Je t'escriray quelz ministres trouvent bonne ma cause, j'entend des voisins. En cas de Mallot, de la Haye et d'Olivier, je croy que là n'en fais aucuns doubte. Houbraque est nostre, nostres sont François Phelippes, bon et honorable vieillard, Pierius et Parrocely." Denis et Rott, *Jean Morély*, 289, no. X, Paris, March 16, 1566.

[110] D'Olivier had been a pastor in the Chablais before being sent to Grenoble. *Bèze Cor.* 7:230n4.

[111] See 199–200.

[112] See 253–54.

[113] See *RCP* 2:111. On Montméja's career as a poet, see Goeury, *La Muse du Consistoire*, 166–204.

[114] Denis and Rott, *Jean Morély*, 303n43; Denis, *Les églises d'étrangers en pays rhénans*, 374–77. Denis suggests that in the 1550s, Philippi was secretary to the English chancellor Thomas Goodrich, in which capacity he produced a French translation of the *Book of Common Prayer* (1553). Just before 1560, he seems to have been preaching for Louis de Barbançon in Varesnes-lez-Noyon in Picardie. He arrived in Frankfurt in April 1560. In 1562, he published *Defense des eglises estrangieres de Francfort en Allemagne* (Denis, 397). Philippi's location in 1566, however, is unknown.

[115] On Pérez, see A. Gordon Kinder, "Juan Pérez de Pineda (Pierius): A Spanish Calvinist Minister of the Gospel in Sixteenth-Century Geneva," *Bulletin of Hispanic Studies* 53 (1976): 283– 300; Edward Boehmer, *Bibliotheca Wiffeniana: Spanish Reformers of Two Centuries from 1520* (Strasbourg: Trübner, 1883), 2:55–100.

was pastor to the small Spanish population in Geneva, where he published a Spanish translation of the New Testament, a catechism, and other religious works.[116] In 1556, he accompanied Calvin to Frankfurt to help resolve the disputes involving Valérand Poullain but stayed there for at least two years during the time when Perrussel served as pastor.[117] In 1563, he was serving as minister in Blois, when Condé called on him, together with Chandieu, to discuss terms ending the First War of Religion.[118] In early 1565, Pérez was at Montargis, serving as chaplain to Renée de France alongside fellow Spaniard—and noted Calvinist opponent and Castellio supporter—Antonio del Corro.[119] Soon after Pérez's arrival, Renée dismissed the hardline Calvinist minister François Morel, Sieur de Collonges.[120] Despite his numerous associations with members of Perrussel's circle, Morély later felt betrayed by Perrussel himself, noting that he "wickedly fled the [1565 Paris national] synod, seeing that they were going to treat my case."[121]

Houbraque's presence on Morély's list is more surprising, for he and Perrussel had fought bitterly against one another in Frankfurt, where Houbraque defended the strict Calvinist cause.[122] Beza's allies certainly doubted that Houbraque supported Morély.[123] Nevertheless, Morély and Houbraque had a long-standing personal connection. In 1553, Morély reported that "our Houbraque" was among a group of Reformed prisoners who had recently been freed.[124] The same year, the two men may also have been

---

[116] See Kinder, "Juan Pérez de Pineda," 286–88.

[117] Kinder, "Juan Pérez de Pineda," 288–89.

[118] Kinder, "Juan Pérez de Pineda," 292–93.

[119] Kinder, "Juan Pérez de Pineda," 293–95. On Del Corro, see Rady Roldan-Figueroa, "Antonio del Corro and Paul as the Apostle of the Gospel of Universal Redemption," in *A Companion to Paul in the Reformation*, edited by R. Ward Holder, 389–426 (Leiden: Brill, 2009). At this time, Pérez and Del Corro were likely working together, alongside Casiodor de Reina, on the famous *Inquisitionis Hispanicae Artes*, which also incorporates some of Castellio's ideas in the prologue. See "Reginaldus Gonsalvius Montanus" [pseudonym: Antonio del Corro, Casiodoro de Reina, and Juan Pérez de Pineda], *Inquisitionis Hispanicae Artes: The Arts of the Spanish Inquisition*, edited by Marcos J. Herráiz Perja, et al., Heterodoxia Iberica 2 (Leiden: Brill, 2018), 13–31.

[120] Kinder, "Juan Pérez de Pineda," 293.

[121] "Parrocely s'en est enfuy villainement du synode, voyant qu'on vouloit traitter de mon fait." Denis and Rott, *Jean Morély*, 288, no. 11, [end of December 1565 or beginning of January 1566]

[122] See 197–200.

[123] See, for example, Nicolas Des Gallars' letter to Beza, describing the content of Morély's letters. He doubted Perrussel's support, as well as that of Jean de l'Espine, who is not named in the Morély's letters, but to whom we will return. *Bèze Cor.* 7:257, no. 509, Orléans, [October 24, 1566]: "De aliis multis idem sibi persuadebat ille fanaticus, veluti de Spinaeo, Holbracho, Perrucellio aliisque nonnullis quos nominat in literis suis."

[124] "Olbracus noster sponsione data liberatus est et emissus e morte certissima gratia et autoritate suorum eodem profectus." *CO* 20:413, no. 4164, Morély to Calvin, [Paris], [shortly before March 26, 1553].

in England together.[125] Later, in 1566, Houbraque would testify to Morély's orthodoxy on the subject of predestination.[126] Despite generally being a loyal Calvinist, Houbraque offered alternatives to the procedures presented in the French *Discipline* regarding church structure. Nicolas Fornerod and Christian Grosse recently brought to light Houbraque's *Treatise Demonstrating How to Proceed in the Correction of Vices and Scandals, and to Excommunication in the Christian Church*,[127] which they describe as a "third way" between Geneva's presbyterian-synodal system and Morély's proposals. In particular, with regard to discipline, Houbraque's treatise permits the church to approve the disciplinary decisions recommended by the consistory. Like Morély, Houbraque writes that "one must not so strictly interpret 'the church' to mean 'the consistory.'"[128] He also directs that decisions on excommunication be announced three times during the church service, a step that would allow anyone with additional information to bring it to the consistory "so that the liberty of the whole church and of each individual be preserved."[129]

As for the other supporters on Morély's list, Jean Mallot was Gaspard de Coligny's personal chaplain. He sought to help Morély mend fences with the Genevans,[130] but the minister Le Maçon denounced Mallot as a supporter of Morély,[131] and Beza wrote to blast him for his conciliatory

---

[125] Christian Grosse and Nicolas Fornerod, "Une troisième voie entre le 'modèle' genevois de discipline ecclésiastique et celui de Jean Morély? Guillaume Houbraque et son traité sur la correction des vices et l'excommunication (1567)," *Revue de théologie et de philosophie* 148 (2016): 713–31, here, 721.

[126] Grosse and Fornerod, "Une troisième voie," 721.

[127] Grosse and Fornerod, "Une troisième voie." The treatise in question is Guillaume Houbraque, *Traité monstrant comme il faut proceder à la correction des vices et scandales, et à l'excommunication en l'Eglise chrestienne* (Orléans: Loys Rabier, 1567).

[128] "ne faut pas si estroictement entendre par l'Eglise le consistoire." Cited in Grosse and Fornerod, "Une troisième voie," 723.

[129] "s'il y a quelque particulier ou plusieurs de l'Eglise qui ayent quelque chose à dire, pourquoy ils ne peuvent consentir à l'excommunication qu'ils ayent à le venir proposer au consistoire . . . afin que la liberté soit gardee à toute l'Eglise, et à chacun particulier." Cited in Grosse and Fornerod, "Une troisième voie," 723.

[130] After the July 1565 provincial synod, Mallot wrote to Beza, "Aderant autem in eo concilio provinciali Verbi Dei ministri supra triginta, quorum omnium et quidem bonorum et doctorum suffragia, exceptis paucis, eo venerunt ut censuerint non rejiciendum esse eum qui semel fuisset admissus, quandoquidem promissa servasset. Sperandum esse ut pergat in melius, si secus fecerit, penes nos semper esse ad extrema venire, ubi deploratus erit morbus. Rogandos esse fratres Genevenses ut pari, si possunt, misericordia utantur. . . . Hic [Morély] vero erravit quidem in multis, sed non in fidei doctrina." *Bèze Cor.* 6:124, no. 407, Châtillon-sur-Loing, August 8, 1565.

[131] "Et ceux cy aussi ont gagné et M. Malot et ses compagnons, et mesme rendu autant qu'ilz ont peu nostre discipline odieuse aux seigneurs lesquels portent nostre cause." *Bèze Cor.* 7:191, no. 486, Le Maçon, Sieur de la Fontaine, to Beza, Orléans, August 4, 1566.

attitude toward Morély.[132] Finally, Hermès de La Haye was the personal pastor of Odet de Coligny, Cardinal of Châtillon.[133] In 1556, La Haye intervened several times with the churches of the Île-de-France on Morély's behalf—likely at Odet's behest.[134] Like Morély, La Haye wanted to keep Geneva from meddling in French religious issues. In 1566, he was accused of summoning an assembly in Lyon without the permission of the other pastors and treating "with sharp and bitter words" a long series of issues, including "the affair of the minister Mercure . . . , a point on the Supper, Morély's book on ecclesiastical discipline and [Antoine Chandieu's] *Confirmation of the Ecclesiastical Discipline,* [and] attacking the ministers of Lyon and those of Geneva both in the assembly and in the other places he went."[135] We will return to the pastor Mercure, whose attitude toward Morély is unknown but who was decidedly contemptuous of the Genevans. La Haye seems also to have been able to consolidate support for Morély in the churches around Châtillon-sur-Loing. In June 1566, Jean Mallot, seeking to return to the Genevans' good graces, reported to Beza, "On my return from Moulins, what should I find here but that at Monsieur de La Haye's persuasion, all the members of our entire consistory, except for two ministers . . . , were opposed to what had been decided [about Morély] at the last synod held at Paris."[136]

---

[132] "Dico igitur, mi frater, nullo exemplo, nullo neque novo neque vetere canone vestrum hoc factum defendi posse. Obsecro enim quo jure vobis licet ab una Ecclesia publice ligatum hominem prius solutum pronunciare quam illi satisfecerit?" *Bèze Cor.* 6:162, Beza to Mallot, Geneva, September 6, 1565.

[133] Although De La Haye's name appears repeatedly in the volumes of the *Correspondance de Bèze* regarding Morély—always as one of his supporters—his first name is almost never used. Bernard Roussel notified me that a contemporary manuscript and old copies of the synodal acts likely identify him as Hermès. On him, see esp., *Bèze Cor.* 7:350–54, annexe X, "Avis de MM. de Chatillon sur la pasteur de La Haye," [September or October 1566].

[134] See, for example, *Bèze Cor.* 7:150–51, no. 478; ibid. 7:297, annexe Ia.

[135] "il ha assemblé aucuns de ceulx de l'Eglise, sans en parler aux ministres d'icelle ne les y appeller, ny ceux qui en matieres d'assemblee le debvroient estre, et neantmoings avec ceux qu'il avoit ainsi convoquez, il a traicté du faict du ministre Mercure, de l'affaire d'Alamanus du poinct de la Cene, du livre de la Police eclesiasticque imprimé soubz le nom de Morelli et d'un autre intitulé 'la confirmation de la discipline eclesiasticque,' blasmant tant en ladite assemblee qu'en assez d'autres lieux où il a passé les ministres de Lyon et ceulx de Geneve, avec propos d'aigreur et vehemence." *Bèze Cor.* 7:350, annexe X, "Avis de MM. de Châtillon sur le pasteur De La Haye," [September or October 1566].

[136] "A mon retour de Moulins, ne trouvay je pas icy qu'à la suasion de Monsieur de La Haye tout nostre Consistoire, excepté deux des ministres, assavoir Messieurs Des Roches et Mellet (mais la pluralité l'emporte), estoit opposé à ce qui avoit esté arresté au dernier synode tenu à P[aris]?" *Bèze Cor.* 7:151, no. 478, Mallot to Beza, Châtillon-sur-Loing, June 27, 1566.

8.4.2. Morély and the Huguenot Nobility

Connecting several of the pastors among Morély's circle were their ties to the Huguenot nobility. Perrussel and Montméja were in Condé's household, Mallot was Gaspard de Coligny's personal chaplain, Pérez was chaplain to Renée de France, and La Haye was household minister to Odet de Coligny, Cardinal of Châtillon. Moreover, Morély himself was reasonably well connected to the French elites. He was the brother-in-law of Baptiste Du Mesnil, the *avocat du roi au parlement* in the 1550s and 1560s.[137] He also seems to have known the chancellor Michel de l'Hôpital, for he indicated on one occasion to Sureau, "I wrote a clear and concise treatise about the matter itself [ecclesiastical discipline], which I sent to the most honorable chancellor. I pray that he conveys his judgment to the Cardinal of Châtillon."[138]

Probably more than anyone else, the Cardinal of Châtillon tried to defend Morély from his detractors. We saw earlier that he intervened at the July 1565 provincial synod on behalf of Morély. He intervened once again after the 1565 national synod, prodding his local church of Châtillon-sur-Loing to oppose the decisions made at the Paris national synod and warning the church not to slide under "tyrannical ambition,"[139] presumably that of the Genevans. At the same time, La Haye wrote to the Orléans provincial synod, notifying them that if Chandieu's response to Morély (the *Confirmation de la Discipline*) were published, a response to Chandieu would be published very quickly.[140] Odet himself wrote to the Paris consistory attempting to halt publication of Chandieu's book. According to the consistory's report, he argued "that it is not reasonable for two, three, or a few people to impose law on others, and that the discipline that we want to be observed by all the churches

---

[137] See the note on Du Mesnil in Denis and Rott, *Jean Morély*, 213–14, annexe C.

[138] "Scripsi tractatum ipsa de re (disciplina ecclesiastica) bene firmum et succinctum quem misi ad Cancellarium cl. v. Oro ut conferat judicium suum cum cardinali Castilioneo." Denis and Rott, *Jean Morély*, 288, no. VIII, Morély to Sureau, Paris, February 18 [1566].

[139] "receurent entre autres choses une lettre des freres de l'Eglise de Chastillon sur Loin, au nom de toute leur Eglise, pour se opposer à toute l'assemblee qui avoit esté dernierement faite à Paris sur la fin de decembre. . . . Adjoustant avec ce qu'il se falloit bien garder qu'une ambition tyrannique soubs laquelle nous avons esté ne glisçast en l'Eglise, dont cela en estoyent des commencemens, et de telles façons de parler estoit abrevé Monsieur le comte de Beauvois [i.e., Odet]." *Bèze Cor.* 7:296, Annexe Ia, Provincial Synod of Orléans to Chandieu, La Charité, March 11, 1566.

[140] The author of the letter from the synod to Chandieu notes that the synod received a letter from La Haye "par laquelle il nous declaroit persister constamment en son opposition, faisant mention de Monsieur ledit comte de Beauvois [Odet], et notamment d'un livre que avez dernierement escript touchant la Police ecclesiastique contre celuy de Morelli, auquel il disoit que s'il estoit imprimé et publié, que dans cinq ou six jours, quelcun y pourroit responde à l'encontre, comme depuis il ne nous dissimula pas en nostre presence." *Bèze Cor.* 7:297, Annexe Ia.

must first be received and approved by all the churches after long and serious deliberation."[141] A letter from the Paris consistory twice refers to the displeasure of the "seigneurs de Châtillon,"[142] with the plural implying that Odet's brother Gaspard de Coligny was also displeased by the church's persecution of Morély. Indeed, the admiral's early support for Morély is confirmed by his later explanation to Beza: "As for Morély, I confess certainly that I was deceived."[143]

As both Kingdon and Hughes Daussy have noted, Odet de Châtillon considered the Genevan ecclesiastical model too rigid and too radical a departure from the existing French church to provide any hope for religious unity in France.[144] He might easily have been included in the previous chapter as one of the Gallican evangelicals who sought a compromise religious solution for the kingdom.[145] Du Mesnil and L'Hôpital were in the same camp. These religious moderates may have found in Morély's ecclesiastical model an alternative both to that of Geneva and to the more traditional Gallican proposal favored by Bauduin. After the failure at Poissy and then the First War of Religion, Bauduin's compromise solution was increasingly seen as unworkable and ultimately rejected by both sides. Perhaps these noble supporters found in Morély's vision a new possibility for reform, a model that allowed for both local variation and elite lay dominance of French religion. By giving

---

[141] "Mais on nous a proposé plusieurs inconvenients, mesme Monsieur le cardinal de Chastillon s'estant persuadé que nous le voulions faire imprimer en ceste ville, nous escrivit une lettre pour empescher l'édition, disant qu'il n'estoit pas raisonnable que deux ou trois ou peu de gens baillassent la loy aux autres, et qu'il falloit que la discipline que on vouloit estre observée par toutes les Eglises eust esté premièrement receu et approuvée par toutes les Eglises, voire après longue et meure délibération." A. Coquerel, *Précis de l'histoire de l'Église Réformée de Paris d'après des documents en grande partie inédits, Première époque, 1512–1594, de l'origine de l'église à l'Édit de Nantes* (Paris: Librairies Protestantes, 1862), lxxxii, Annexe VI, Paris Consistory to Chandieu, Paris, April 2, 1566.

[142] "Je ne parle pas du mescontentement des seigneurs de Chastillon, qui nous ont advertis de ne le faire imprimer et qui pourroyent penser que nous aurions tout à propos emprunté le nom des Eglises voisines pour mieux couvrir nostre jeu. . . . Monsieur de Saules nous escrivit il y a environ trois sepmaines qu'il estoit d'advis qu'on ne fist encores imprimer, pour ce qu'il voyoit que cela ne plairoit guères à Messeigneurs de Chastillon." Coquerel, *Précis de l'histoire de l'Église Réformée de Paris*, lxxxiii, Annexe VI. The "Discours des procedures" likewise notes that Morély sought refuge "à Messieurs de Chastillon," but with the qualification, "et principallement à Monsieur le cardinal." *Bèze Cor.* 8:221, Annexe Ie.

[143] "Quant à Morelly, je confesse certainement que j'ay esté deceu." *Bèze Cor.* 8:52, no. 532, Coligny to Beza, Châtillon, January 21 [1567].

[144] See, for example, Daussy, *Le parti huguenot*, 498; Kingdon, *Geneva and the Consolidation of the French Protestant Movement*, 75.

[145] On his efforts at compromise, see Alain Tallon, "Gallicanism and Religious Pluralism in France in the Sixteenth Century," in *The Adventure of Religious Pluralism in Early Modern France: Papers from the Exeter Conference, April 1999*, edited by Keith Cameron, Mark Greengrass, and Penny Roberts, 15–30 (Oxford: Peter Lang, 2000), 19–22.

power to the local churches, and especially to the mother churches, where the nobility and intellectual elite would dominate, Morély's system allowed greater flexibility to find the best solution for each area. Odet's response to the Paris consistory cited earlier suggests that the Protestant cardinal seems to have understood some of Morély's basic principles. By arguing that the form of discipline should be approved by all the churches, rather than dictated by a select few, he shows his sympathy for Morély's argument that authority should reside in the local churches rather than with the national synod. Gaspard de Coligny seems to have shared his brother's interest in locating authority within local churches. Daussy suggests that the admiral may have seen Morély's model as a way to support the Huguenot nobility in the face of the Reformed pastorate.[146]

8.4.3. Morély and Jeanne d'Albret

Morély's most important connection among the Huguenot nobility was his appointment as tutor to the young Prince Henri of Navarre (the future King Henri IV) by Queen Jeanne d'Albret. Jean de Salignac, whom Du Moulin defended against the Calvinists, was instrumental in his appointment.[147] It is difficult to know whether Jeanne knew of Morély's prescriptions for ecclesiastical organization, or of their rejection by the Reformed synods. From her perspective, what mattered was that he was an outstanding teacher. She claimed that "he is the most appropriate and skilled teacher she has ever seen, and that her son has profited more in three months with him than he had in eight years" with his previous tutor.[148] To the Calvinists, Morély's appointment as tutor to the future King of Navarre was deeply troubling. Beza and several others complained bitterly to Jeanne.[149] In November 1566, the

---

[146] Daussy, *Le parti huguenot*, 505.

[147] Des Gallars noted to Beza that he was glad Béroald led the hearing at Jeanne's court on Morély, "pour la familiarité qu'il a avec monsieur Salignac, duquel Morely est porté et favorisé. Car c'est luy qui a rendu tesmoignage de la suffisance dudit Morely pour le mettre en ceste charge." *Bèze Cor.* 7:290, no. 521, Des Gallars to Beza, Orléans, December 20, 1566.

[148] "Adjoustant qu'elle [Jeanne] estoit fort fachée qu'il [Morély] n'estoit bien d'accord avec les Eglises, et qu'au demeurant il est le plus propre et le mieux adroit à bien enseigner qu'homme qu'elle ait jamais veu, et que son fils avoit plus profité en trois mois avec luy qu'il n'avoit fait en huit ans avec feu Monsieur de La Gaucherie." *Bèze Cor.* 8:30, no. 526, Pierre Merlin to Beza, Longueville, January 10, 1567. Cf. Jeanne's own letter to Beza: "Car je feray isy une parenthaise pour vous dire que les sept ans que feu monsieur de la Gaucherie a tenu mon filz, il les a perdus . . . de fasson que en troys ou catre moys que Morely l'avoit entre mains, il avoit plus profité qu'en ses sept ans." *Bèze Cor.* 7:281–82, no. 518, Jeanne d'Albret to Beza, Paris, December 6, 1566.

[149] See *Bèze Cor.* 7:241, no. 504, Des Gallars to Beza, Orléans, September 30, 1566.

queen assembled a group of pastors and nobles that included Coligny, Odet de Châtillon, Houbraque, Jean de L'Espine, and others. Matthieu Béroald, professor of Hebrew at the Academy of Orléans, presented the case against Morély, which included the letters stolen from Sureau's study.[150] In addition to the bitter language against Beza and the Genevans, the letters revealed that Morély supported Benoît de La Coste, an anti-Calvinist from Yverdòn who had been deposed from the ministry in France for his views on predestination. The position of La Coste, and of Morély himself, came closer to Bolsec's view, with Morély expressing fear that the hardline Calvinist interpretation of the doctrine would lead to schism with the German churches.[151] The letters were too damning, and Jeanne agreed to dismiss Morély, but only after she was able to find a suitable replacement as the prince's tutor. The search seems to have taken some time, for Morély remained in Jeanne's service for weeks, if not months."[152]

Morély's hearing at Jeanne's court turned the tide against him. Soon afterward, Coligny assured Beza that he had abandoned his support for Morély and was fully on the Genevan side.[153] Beza, meanwhile, sought to bring the French churches in line with Geneva. He wrote to Viret, encouraging him to distance himself from Morély, particularly given Morély's dedicatory letter to him.[154] And he wrote to Morély himself, accusing him of having "violated the virginity of the French churches."[155] At this point, Morély disappears for a few years from the historical record.

[150] On the meeting, see Denis and Rott, *Jean Morély*, 65–66; also Béroald's description, in ibid., 296–312, annexe VIII; *Bèze Cor.* 7:272–74, no. 515, Pierre Hesperien to Beza, Saint-Maur-lès-Paris, November 26–27, 1566; *Bèze Cor.* 8:29–31, no. 526, Pierre Merlin to Beza, Longueville, January 10, 1567.

[151] See, for example, Morély's letters to Sureau from February 1565: (1) "Mitto ad te Costani confessionem de providentia, quae mihi ita probatur, ut subscribere, si roger, non dubitem, nec unquam D. Calvino, Farello Viretoque aliter sentire prae me tuli." (2) "A quocumque sint illa conventu proposita, multa sunt quae reprehendam: primum illud est quod affirmatur: 'Deus ab aeterno pro suo arbitrio quos voluit (id est non pro praescientia sua aut pro ratione peccati subsecuti) liberasse aeternae morti et devovisse exitio et perditioni' . . . Par quoy je ne chercheroy plus loing la cause de la damnation qu'en l'arrest éternel de Dieu, car je ne puis. . . . Summa sit, te, si mihi credis, authorem fore istis nostris, ut scriptum molliant, ne inducant in ecclesiam novum schisma, distrahantque germanicas ecclesias a nostris, alieno praesertim tempore ac ne nostrorum cetuum concordiam scindant." Denis and Rott, *Jean Morély*, 280, no. I, Paris, February 2, 1565; ibid., 281–82, no. II, Paris, February 7, 1565.

[152] As late as 1571, Morély was describing himself as the "teacher of Monseigneur, the Prince of Navarre." It was not uncommon, however, for individuals to continue to claim a title long after the official duties that went with it had ended. Denis and Rott, *Jean Morély*, 71–72.

[153] *Bèze Cor.* 8:52–54, no. 532, Coligny to Beza, Châtillon, January 21 [1567].

[154] *Bèze Cor.* 8:78–80, no. 541, Beza to Viret, Geneva, [ca. March 1, 1567].

[155] "Car c'est vous qui avés violé la virginité des Eglises françoyses, et ceux qui se sont rengés avec vous monstrent assés et de quel esprit [ils ont] esté seduits." *Bèze Cor.* 8:91 no. 545, Beza to Morély, Geneva, March 26, 1567.

8.4.4. French Churches with Morellian Ecclesiology

Although we temporarily lose sight of Morély himself after 1566, his ideas continued to circulate. In 1571, the national synod of La Rochelle still saw them as a threat. This was the most important French Reformed synod to meet since the first one in 1559. Orders were given that both the *Confession of Faith* and the *Discipline*, as revised by the Synod of La Rochelle, were to be written on parchment and deposited in La Rochelle, Geneva, and Béarn.[156] Presiding at the synod was Beza himself, which ensured that Geneva's ideology would continue to dominate in the French Reformed churches. Nevertheless, the evidence from the synod suggests that some churches in France had continued to adopt practices that lined up closely with Morély's suggestions. The deputy from Brie brought a complaint from the elders and people of the church of Meaux "that they are deprived of their freedom in elections of the consistory." The synod responded that this matter had been settled by the provincial synod of Ferté-sous-Jouarre (which had censured Morély) and ordered the church "to acquiesce in the order of discipline received in our churches of France."[157] At La Rochelle, the synod was also informed that "certain churches in Languedoc practice various things contrary to our *Discipline*," specifying that "in the election of elders, and in the sending and lending of ministers, they gather the people's vote one after another." The synod ordered the Languedoc churches "to conform themselves to that order established and observed by us, according to the *Discipline*."[158] Whether or not Morély inspired these democratic practices, either personally or through his book, is unknown and largely irrelevant. More important is that there remained an

---

[156] Kingdon, *Geneva and the Consolidation of the French Protestant Movement*, 96–97.

[157] "Sur l'Article 1, Mr. Viret [Quick: "Vercelle"; note that this could not have been Pierre Viret, who died shortly before the opening of the synod], député de la Brye, a remontré que les anciens et peuple de Meaux, ne se contentent pas de cet article, disant qu'il leur ôte la liberté de l'élection des consistoires; sur quoi il a été resolu que puisqu'on a déjà examiné plusieurs fois leur prétendu grief, et qu'ils ont même reçu de très amples instructions sur cette matiere, par des lettres fondées très expressément sur la parole de Dieu, qui leur furent adressées par le synode de la Ferté sur Loire [Quick: "Ferté under Jouarre"], cette compagnie les exhortera derechef par quelque lettre de se soumettre aux regles de la discipline ecclesiastique reçue dans nos eglises de France." Aymon, *Tous les synodes*, 103; translation adapted from Quick, *Synodicon*, 95.

[158] "Le synode étant averti qu'il y a quelques eglises en Languedoc, qui agissent d'une maniere contraire à notre *Discipline*, pour l'élection des anciens, pour l'envoi et le prêt des ministres, recueillant les voix du peuple, l'une après l'autre, ledit synode rejette et improuve cette façon de faire, exhortant lesdites eglises de se conformer à l'ordre accoutumé entre nous, suivant l'article de la *Discipline* sur cela." Aymon, *Tous les synodes*, 111; translation adapted from Quick, *Synodicon*, 101.

appetite in the French churches for a more participatory system of ecclesiastical elections. It is also interesting that the churches of Languedoc were singled out at La Rochelle. Almost all of Morély's early support came from the north, in the areas around Paris and Orléans. The Languedoc example shows that those favoring congregational elections had made gains in the south as well.

8.4.5. Petrus Ramus, Nicolas Bergeron, and the 1572 Synod of Nîmes

After the synod of La Rochelle, Petrus Ramus enters the picture as a key supporter of Morély. Ramus is, of course, well known as a controversial scholar and teacher who was critical of Aristotelian logic.[159] He was famous across Europe and corresponded with some of the individuals featured in this book, including Jean de Monluc and Giacopo Aconcio, on whose Castellio-inspired *Satan's Stratagems* he bestowed high praise.[160] In 1568, Ramus openly embraced Protestantism. During the next two years, he traveled through Protestant Germany and Switzerland. He taught briefly in Geneva, but he and Beza did not get along.[161] He fared better with Bullinger. After the synod of La Rochelle, Ramus complained to Bullinger about the synod's decisions, noting that jurisdiction over doctrine, discipline, and election

---

[159] On Ramus generally, see his early biography by Charles Waddington, *Ramus (Pierre de la Ramée): Sa vie, ses écrits et ses opinions* (Paris: Meyrueis, 1855). On his career as a logician, see Walter J. Ong, *Ramus, Method, and the Decay of Dialogue: From the Art of Discourse to the Art of Reason* (Cambridge, MA: Harvard University Press, 1958). On his theology, see P. Lobstein, *Petrus Ramus als Theologe: Ein Beitrag zur Geschichte der Protestantischen Theologie* (Strasbourg: C. F. Schmidt's Universitäts-Buchhandlung, 1878). James Skalnik seeks to bring both sides of his career together in *Ramus and Reform: University and Church at the End of the Renaissance*, Sixteenth Century Essays and Studies 60 (Kirksville, MO: Truman State University Press, 2002).

[160] "Interea bibliopolae nostri Francoforto Lutetiam reversi, attulerunt octo libros Stratagematum, quorum lectione non solum recreatus sum vehementer, sed quibusdam apud nos melioris et notae et literaturae theologis legendos proposui, qui modestiam orationis et disputationis prudentiam mirifice conprobarunt." Petrus Ramus and Omer Talon, *Praefationes, Epistolae, Orationes* (Paris: apud Dionysium Vellensem, 1577), 203, December 19, 1565. The letter to Monluc is in ibid., 199–203, December 19, 1565.

[161] See, for example, the following note in the registers of the Company of Pastors from May 31, 1570: "Le mesme jour, M. de Besze et le recteur [Jean Le Gasgneux] parlerent à M. Ramus de changer sa façon qu'il tenoit à enseigner et faire leçons en l'auditoire publiq. Ce qu'on pense qu'il n'approuva pas, comme estimant savoir aussi bien qu'ung aultre la maniere qu'il faloit suivre. Tant y a qu'il ne poursuivit plus à lire, ains desista du tout. Dont aucuns escoliers furent marris et afficherent certains vers en l'honneur dudit M. Ramus et blasmant ceulx qu'ils pensoyent luy avoir defendu de continuer ses leçons." *RCP* 3:26.

"was practically reduced to the ministers."[162] Ramus continues in a fashion reminiscent of Morély:

> The argument does not concern ordinary and everyday cases, which are granted to and remitted without objection to the consistory, but it concerns public matters, in the decisions on doctrine and discipline, on election and deposition, on excommunication and absolution, namely, whether all the church makes a decision first, which is then ratified by the consistory, or the reverse, as has been done till now in France.[163]

Ramus clearly preferred to give the right to the whole church first, since "Christ gave the keys to the entire church," and he describes the ideas in Chandieu's book against Morély as "false."[164]

In 1572, Ramus was back in France, and he worked with Morély himself to encourage the adoption of Morély's ideas at the provincial synod of the churches of the Île-de-France at Lumigny-en-Brie. Morély planned to attend the synod but could not. Ramus, however, was there and advocated greater lay participation in church governance. The synod proved amenable to compromise. It determined that churches could hold *congrégations* where laymen could speak; it also allowed the people to nominate pastors and permitted the people to vote on the final nominee.[165]

---

[162] "Ecclesiastica est disciplina, quae antea per senatum e ministris, senioribus, diaconis compositum administrata est ab anno 1559, cum interea reliquus populus administrationis huius nonnihil conscius fieret in gravioribus praesertim caussis, ut in decisione doctrinae et disciplinae, in electione senatorum, in excommunicatione fratrum. At nunc nuper Rupellana synodo tota iuris huius dictio ad solos ministros propemodum est reducta." Waddington, *Ramus*, 433, no. 14, Ramus to Bullinger, Paris, September 1, 1571.

[163] "Thesis igitur est, non de quotidianis et ordinariis caussis (quae senatui sine controversia conceduntur et committuntur) sed de publicis illis in decisione doctrinae et disciplinae, in electione et destitutione, in excommunicatione et absolutione, utrum primo sit ecclesiae totius statuere, deinde separati senatus approbare, an contra (sicut adhuc in Francia factum est)." Waddington, *Ramus*, 433–34, no. 14.

[164] "Pro prima quaestione profertur claves ecclesiae a Christo datas esse, primo per manus Petri, XIV. Matth., ut Augustinus ait Homilia in Ioannem L; deinde per manus discipulorum omnium, Matth. XVIII. et Ioan. XX; denique communi omnium fidelium nomine, cum Christus ipse profiteatur (Ioan. X): Ovium esse de voce boni pastoris iudicare, eumque sequi, contra distinguere vocem mali pastoris, et ab eo refugere. Contra autem quae reponuntur pro senatus supra ecclesiam principatu, ut ecclesiae nihil hic sit, nisi erudiri et assentiri, libro *De confirmatione disciplinae* inscripto, et gallice publicato, continentur: falsa illa quidem, aut certe nihil concludentia, sed tamen nixa authoritate ingeniosorum hominum, et in vulgus gratiosorum, quibus idcirco difficilius sit obsistere." Waddington, *Ramus*, 434, no. 14. Waddington is greatly mistaken when he identifies Chandieu's book as having been written by Morély! He notes after Chandieu's title in the quotation earlier, "Le livre de Morelli, sans doute" (ibid. 434n1). In doing so, he makes it appear that Ramus disapproved of Morély, when, in fact, they were allies.

[165] See Kingdon, *Geneva and the Consolidation of the French Protestant Movement*, 105–7. The synod's decrees were later ordered to be burned and do not exist. The information we have about

Ramus was supported in his proposals, both at Lumigny and later at the national synod of Nîmes by a certain Bergeron. None of the literature on Morély has been able to identify this individual,[166] but Grégoire Holtz has shown that he was Nicolas Bergeron, an *avocat au parlement* and student of Ramus, who also served as executor of Ramus's will.[167] Moreover, Bergeron had collaborated with Charles Du Moulin.[168] Holtz presents him as another example of an individual between Rome and Geneva, and he demonstrates how his parlementary *arrêts* reveal a strong Gallican position similar to that of Du Moulin.[169] Thus, with Bergeron, we see—as we did with Odet de Châtillon, Du Mesnil, and de L'Hôpital—the close affinity between Morély's supporters and the Gallican evangelicals.

Beza and the Genevans were outraged at the decisions of the Lumigny synod, and the next national synod, at Nîmes, placed "the democratic question" at the top of the agenda.[170] The acts of the national synod indicate that "the deputies of the Île-de-France asked our advice concerning these points of the *Discipline* of the church now debated by Monsieur Ramus, [Hughes Sureau] du Rosier, Bergeron, and some others."[171] Morély himself returned to the stage in Nîmes. He had written a refutation—unfortunately lost—of Chandieu's *Confirmation of the Discipline*, and the representatives of the Île-de-France presented it to the synod.[172] The synod had no desire to give

them comes largely from a letter from the pastor Jean de Lestre to Beza, *Bèze Cor.* 13:96–101, no. 909, Wy-dit-Joli-Village, March 19 [1572].

[166] The editors of *Bèze Cor.* note, "Bergeron n'est pas connu autrement que par sa mention au synode de Lumigny." They point to a Laurent Bergeron who was a servant to a Reformed merchant named Nicolas Croquet. *Bèze Cor.* 13:100n5. Denis and Rott likewise refer to "Laurent(?) Bergeron" in the index to *Jean Morély*, 376.

[167] Grégoire Holtz, *L'ombre de l'auteur: Pierre Bergeron et l'écriture du voyage à la fin de la Renaissance*, THR 480 (Geneva: Droz, 2011), 58–61. On Bergeron, see also Grégoire Holtz, "Nicolas Bergeron (1584/1588) et la construction de la culture gallicane," *Revue de l'histoire des religions* 3 (2009): 429–43. Ramus's will states, "Bibliothecam et suppellectilem reliquam nominaque omnia lego semisse altero pauperibus alumnis Praelei gymansii: altero procuratoribus executoribusqe mei testamenti Nicolao Bergeronio et Antonio Loyselo discipulis quondam meis, modo advocatis in Senatu." Petrus Ramus, *Testamentum Petri Rami cum senatus consulto et promulgatione professionis institutae ab ipso testatore* (Paris: Ioannis Richerius, 1576), 8–9.

[168] Holtz, "Nicolas Bergeron et la construction de la culture gallicane," 431–32.

[169] Holtz, "Nicolas Bergeron et la construction de la culture gallicane."

[170] "Hodie unas accepi a fratribus Nemausensibus ad vestrum collegium scriptas quas vobis gratas fore confido. Illuc indicta est Synodus generalis, in qua Democratici audientur, et quibus altera Synodus Rupellana non satisfecit." *Bèze Cor.* 13:37, no. 891, Beza to Bullinger, Geneva, February 3, 1572.

[171] "Les députés de l'Isle de France ont demandé notre avis touchant ces points de la *Discipline* de l'Eglise maintenant debatus par Monsieur Ramus, du Rosier, Bergeron, et quelques autres." Aymon, *Tous les synodes*, 1.2:122; Quick, *Synodicon*, 111.

[172] "il a été ordonné que Monsieur de Chambrun liroit dans cette assemblée l'abregé fait par nos frères de l'Isle de France, et l'extrait de la Reponse de Morellius au livre de la *Confirmation de la*

Morély's new book against Chandieu a fair hearing, and so it gave the book to Beza and Chandieu himself for judgment![173]

After examining Morély's texts and the decisions of the provincial synod of Lumigny, the synod of Nîmes made the following decree:

> The *Discipline* of our church will remain in the future as it has always been practiced and observed to this day, without making the slightest change or innovation, since it is founded on the word of God. And as for the propositions advanced by Ramus, Morély, Bergeron, and others . . . , not one of these propositions will be received among us, since they are not founded on the word of God and would have very dangerous consequences for the church.[174]

The synod ordered the representatives from the synod of Lumigny "to destroy all accounts of their synod."[175] Further, it ordered the colloquy of Beauvoisin to demand the attendance of Morély, Ramus, and Sureau at the next synod, commanding that "if they reject [the synod's] good counsel and advice, one should proceed against them as against rebels and schismatics."[176]

The synod of Nîmes in March 1572 was the last act in the Morély affair. Six months later, Ramus was killed during the Saint Bartholomew's Day Massacre, Morély fled to England, and Sureau du Rosier converted—albeit temporarily—to Catholicism; he would reconvert to Protestantism several months later. After the massacre, there were no further major efforts to

---

Discipline, envoié par eux à ce Synode, avec le livre dudit Morellius, qui est la reponce à ce livre *de la Confirmation de la Discipline*, pour decider des points et arguments qui sont contenus dans le livre dudit Morellius, et de ceux de Ramus et du Rosier." Aymon, *Tous les synodes*, 1.2:122.

[173] "Et en cas que l'on y trouve quelques autres argumens, outre ceux qui ont déjà été pesés par Morellius, on y fera reponse. Messieurs de Beze, de Roche-Chandieu et de Beaulieu sont choisis pour y repliquer." Aymon, *Tous les synodes*, 1.2:122–23.

[174] "la *Discipline* de notre Eglise resteroit à l'avenir comme elle avoit toujours été pratiquée et observée jusqu'aujourd'hui, sans qu'on y fit le moindre changement ou innovation, comme étant fondée sur la parole de Dieu. Et pour ce qui est des propositions que Messieurs Ramus, Morellius, Bergeron, et autres ont avancées . . . , pas une de ces propositions ne sera reçue parmi nous, parcequ'elles ne sont pas fondées sur la parole de Dieu, et qu'elles sont d'une consequence très-dangereuse pour l'Eglise." Aymon, *Tous les synodes*, 1.2:123; Quick, *Synodicon*, 112.

[175] "Les deputés au colloque de Limmigni seront avertis de faire suprimer tous les memoires de leur Synode, et qu'ils ne peuvent faire aucun canon de leur chef, mais qu'ils doivent se regler sur ceux de notre *Discipline*." Aymon, *Tous les synodes*, 1.2:123; Quick, *Synodicon*, 112.

[176] "et en cas qu'ils voulussent rejetter leurs bon conseils et avertissements, on procedera contr'eux, comme contre des rebelles et schismatiques." Aymon, *Tous les synodes*, 1.2:124; Quick, *Synodicon*, 113.

democratize the French church. The Calvinists' presbyterian-synodal model had won the day, but Morély and his allies had made it a hard-fought battle.

8.5. Epilogue: Pierre Charpentier's "God-Fearing Ministers Who Detest 'The Cause' "

A little-known epilogue to Morély's story encapsulates the divisions among French Protestants at the time of the St. Bartholomew's Day Massacre. Not long after the slaughter, a former law professor from the University of Geneva named Pierre Charpentier published a controversial book. The book's title is long but revealing: *Letter of Pierre Charpentier, Jurisconsult, addressed to François Portus, in which he Demonstrates that the Persecutions of the Churches of France came about, not by the Fault of Those who Profess the Religion, but of Those who Nourish Factions and Conspiracies, who are called "The Cause."*[177] The title reveals his basic argument, namely that there were two factions of Protestants in France, one whose members "profess the religion" and who had nothing to do with the recent killings, the other called "The Cause," who effectively brought the massacre on themselves by their "wicked and seditious rebellion."[178] Charpentier identifies "The Cause" with the faction of Huguenots led by Beza and the Genevan foreigners. Early in the treatise, he defines it as "nothing other than an illicit assembly and faction of certain ones of ours who have not wanted to pursue peace and live quietly, but interrupt the public repose and break and violate the ordinances of our prince."[179] For Charpentier, it was, in fact, the Genevan-based Calvinists who constituted this secondary—and dangerous—sect of French Protestants.

---

[177] Charpentier, *Lettre*. This was published first in Latin in 1572 as *Petri Carpentarii I. C. Epistola ad Franciscum Portum Cretensem in qua docetur persecutiones ecclesiarum Galliae, non culpa eorum qui religionem profitentur: sed eorum qui factionem et conspirationem (qua Causa appellatur) fovebant, accidisse*; a 1573 edition of the Latin is available at Google books, published together with Portus's response: *Ad Petri Carpentarii causidici virulentam epistolam responsio Francisci Porti Cretensis; pro Causiorum, quos vocat, innocentia* (1573). The addressee, François Portus, was a native of Crete and held the chair in Greek at the Geneva Academy.

[178] "Mais soudain que j'ay cogneu que ceste damnable Cause ne tendoit au service de Dieu, mais au contraire à une meschante et seditieuse rebellion, je m'enfuis du tout retiré." Charpentier, *Lettre*, 2ᵛ.

[179] "ceste Cause (qui n'est autre chose qu'une illicite assemblée et faction de quelques uns des nostres qui ne ont voulu user de la paix et vivre paisiblement, pour interrompre le repos public, enfraindre et violer les ordonnances de nostre prince)." Charpentier, *Lettre*, 2ᵛ.

In opposition to the Cause, writes Charpentier, "we have several of our ministers, good, learned, and God-fearing men who detest the Cause, whom we set up like a wall in opposition to their efforts."[180] In the first place, he names Ramus, whom he describes as "a good man, and far removed from the Cause."[181] Charpentier has nothing but praise for Ramus and his opposition to the Genevans: "Petrus Ramus was preparing a book full of doctrine and piety against [Beza's] faction and rashness, by which he showed that [Beza] had come to France in secret to force on us the Talmud of Savoy in order to light fires and sow seditions instead of the true and holy religion. Ramus would soon have published this book had he not been killed in the course of these miseries."[182] Charpentier's use of the phrase "Talmud of Savoy" is striking and was likely intended to emphasize both the foreign origins and what he saw as the Judaizing legalism of the Calvinism being imposed on France.

Next to Ramus, Charpentier names several other "God-fearing ministers who detest the Cause," namely, "de l'Espine, du Rosier, Houbraque, Capel, La Haye, Mercure, and many others whom your sovereign Pontiff hates and detests and has designated with his censure as deserters of the Cause."[183] We have already met nearly all of the individuals in Charpentier's list, most of them in association with Morély. Sureau du Rosier and La Haye were clearly among Morély's friends and allies. Morély also counted as a supporter Houbraque, who had, in fact, suggested a middle way between the system proposed by Morély and that adopted by the Genevans.[184] We met Mercure briefly in association with La Haye.[185]

---

[180] "Au contraire nous avions plusieurs de noz ministres gens de bien, sçavans, et craignans Dieu, et detestans la Cause, lesquelz nous opposions comme une muraille à leur entreprise." Charpentier, *Lettre*, 14ʳ.

[181] "Autre fois Pierre Ramus, homme de bien, et fort eslongné de la Cause." Charpentier, *Lettre*, 13ʳ⁻ᵛ.

[182] "Mesmes Pierre Ramus apprestoit un livre plain de doctrine et pieté contre sa faction et temerité, par lequel il enseignoit qu'il estoit venu en France en cachette, et comme par une gouttiere, pour nous donner par force le talmud de Savoye, et nous semer des feux et seditions au lieu de la vraie et saincte religion. Ce livre eust esté bien tost mis en lumiere par Ramus, s'il ne fust mort en ces miseres." Charpentier, *Lettre*, 17ᵛ⁻18ʳ.

[183] "Au contraire nous avions plusieurs de noz ministres gens de bien, sçavans, et craignans Dieu, et detestans la Cause, lesquelz nous opposions comme une muraille à leur entreprise. Sçavoir est d'Espina, des Rosiers, Albrac, Capel, de la Haye, Mercure, et plusieurs autres, lesquelz vostre souverain Pontife . . . hayssoit et detestoit, et les avoit notez de sa censure comme deserteurs de la Cause." Charpentier, *Lettre*, 14ʳ.

[184] See 282–83.

[185] See 283–84.

He was the Sieur de Mercure, a pastor in Provence.[186] In 1567, Coligny informed Beza that Mercure was complaining about "the pre-eminence and prerogative that he says the church of Geneva wants to usurp and attribute to itself over the other churches."[187] The 1571 synod of La Rochelle also noted "the calumnies with which [Mercure] blackened the Church of Geneva."[188] Capel appears to have been a minister in the Paris region, perhaps Louis Capel. In a letter to Bullinger, Ramus mentions a certain Capel; he expresses a wish that one of the Zurich ministers could have been at one of their recent synods "so that one of our ministers, Capel by name, might have freely denounced the ambiguity inherent in the word 'substance' [in regard to the Supper] and might have attacked Beza by name, who has so imperiously assaulted his opinions."[189] Jean de l'Espine is the most surprising name on Charpentier's list. By most accounts, he was a loyal Calvinist, fully in line with the official French Reformed churches. Nevertheless, we met him in the previous chapter as one of the moderates selected to debate, alongside Perrussel, with Monluc and Bauduin.[190] Moreover, there seems to have been some evidence in Sureau's study that Morély believed L'Espine to be a supporter.[191] Thus, Charpentier's list of "God-fearing ministers who detest the Cause" appears to be a reasonably accurate list of French pastors associated in some way with Morély who did, in fact, resent Geneva's influence on the French churches.

---

[186] On Mercure, see *Bèze Cor.* 7:353–54n5.

[187] "Et en tant que touche le fait de Mercure, je ne sçays si avez entendu comme il s'addressa à moy et avec quelle façon et contenance je parlay à luy. De quoy, d'autant qu'il feist ses plainctes et doleances en plusieurs endroits, et que je ne voulois estre remarqué seul en cela qui en feisse instance, j'en escrivy à Monsieur d'Aix, affin qu'il s'informast du tout, ne blasmant rien au reste de ce qu'il me feist entendre de l'Eglise de Geneve, sinon la preeminence et prerogative qu'il disoit qu'elle vouloit usurper et s'attribuer sur les autres Eglises." *Bèze Cor.* 8:52, no. 532, Coligny to Beza, Châtillon, January 21 [1567].

[188] "Sur ce qui a été proposé par le frere Monsieur de Beze touchant le frere Mercure, la compagnie est d'avis que le prochain synode prendra connoissance des causes de sa deposition, et comment il a été rétabli au ministere, et quelles sont les calomnies dont on pretend qu'il a noirci l'eglise de Geneve." Aymon, *Tous les synodes*, 1.2:110; Quick, *Synodicon*, 101.

[189] "Utinam vestrum aliquis adfuisset, qui de vestris laudibus testis nequaquam suspectus esset . . . ut deinde minister e nostris, Capellus nomine, ambiguitatem substantiae vocabulo inclusam libere detestatus sit, utque sit in Bezam nominatim invectus, qui tam imperiose non solum opiniones suas, sed sua etiam vocabula Francis obtruderet." Waddington, *Ramus*, 439, no. 19, Ramus to Bullinger, Paris, March 19, 1572.

[190] See 233–34.

[191] See n. 123.

Charpentier's book has been routinely dismissed by historians as "a masterful stroke of Catholic propaganda."[192] It is not difficult to see why. John Viénot has demonstrated that Charpentier was working as a spy for the Spanish ambassador to France, Frédéric Perrenot, Sieur de Champagney, one of the Cardinal de Granvelle's brothers.[193] To Viénot, Charpentier's spying disqualified him as a real Protestant. He lamented the fact that "Champagney's miserable spy has succeeded to our day to pass himself off as a Huguenot."[194] And he criticized contemporary scholars for describing Charpentier as a "Protestant" author.[195]

Despite Viénot's objections, it is clear that Charpentier remained a Protestant throughout his life. To be sure, there is little doubt that he did, in fact, spy for Champagney; Viénot demonstrates that effectively. Nevertheless, the very document that proves his guilt as a spy—a memoir written by Champagney himself—also proves Charpentier's steadfast refusal to abjure his Protestant faith. About Charpentier, Champagney wrote, "The wretch still persists in his heresy, from which I never knew how to turn him, even though he served me faithfully and diligently. I believe that he only did [the spying] for the money."[196] For Viénot's generation, someone who hated Beza could not possibly be considered a Protestant. It has been the central purpose of this book to demonstrate that this view is no longer tenable. Protestants from Antoine Marcourt to André Zébédée to Sebastian Castellio to Jean Morély all detested the Calvinist domination of francophone reform from Geneva. To them, first Calvin and then Beza had taken on the role of Protestant pope—note Charpentier's reference earlier to Beza as the "sovereign pontiff." Thus,

---

[192] Scott Manetsch, *Theodore Beza and the Quest for Peace in France, 1572–1598*, SMRT 79 (Leiden: Brill, 2000), 48.

[193] Viénot, "Un Apologiste de la Saint-Barthélemy." On Champagney, see Hugo de Schepper, "Frederick Perrenot van Champagney (1536–1602), het 'enfant terrible' van de Familie Granvelle," in *Les Granvelle et les anciens Pays-Bas*, edited by Krista De Jonge and Gustaaf Janssens, 233–44 (Leuven: Leuven University Press, 2000). See also Champagney's published memoirs: Frédéric Perrenot, *Mémoires de Frédéric Perrenot, Sieur de Champagney 1573–1590, avec notice et annotations*, edited by A. L. P. de Robaulx de Soumoy (Brussels: Société de l'histoire de Belgique, 1860).

[194] Viénot, "Un Apologiste de la Saint-Barthélemy," 40.

[195] "le savant Wuttke, naïf sur ce point, cite et étudie Charpentier parmi les auteurs *protestants* qui ont écrit sur la Saint-Barthélemy. Il va jusqu'à dire qu'il peut y avoir des choses vraies dans son témoignage. Plus près de nous enfin, M. Hector de la Ferrière regarde encore Charpentier comme un auteur protestant." Viénot, "Un Apologiste de la Saint-Barthélemy," 41.

[196] "le misérable persistait encore en son hérésie, de laquelle je ne le sus jamais retirer, malgré qu'il servit très fidèlement et diligemment. Je crois bien, que c'était pour le gain qu'il faisait." Quoted in Viénot, "Un Apologiste de la Saint-Barthélemy," 23.

far from a "masterful stroke of Catholic propaganda," Charpentier's book offers a more accurate picture of the divided religious loyalties among French Protestants than do the acts of the national synods or the voluminous correspondence of Beza. In 1572, as in 1526, francophone evangelicals remained deeply divided.

Conclusion

The Calvinists faced opposition at every turn, and their ultimate dominance of francophone Protestantism was far from inevitable. Before Calvin himself appeared on the scene, the early French reform movement set goals very different from those that Calvin and his followers would later pursue. Those who led that movement sought an internal, state-sponsored reform of the French church along evangelical lines. It was Guillaume Farel who set the stage for what would become the Calvinist agenda, namely a decisive break from the old church with an emphasis on following the Reformed doctrine of the Eucharist. Calvin himself would further establish a range of uncompromising theological views, deviation from which invariably brought down the Genevan reformer's wrath. Calvin's opponents saw such reactions as self-righteous indignation and led them to view Calvin as little different from the pope, tolerating no debate and demanding submissive obedience.

Many francophone evangelicals, however, refused to submit. The anti-Calvinists in the Suisse romande believed that Calvin and his disciples went too far in their alterations to Zwingli's doctrine of the Eucharist and in their insistence on consistorial discipline and excommunication. They also believed that Calvin was too rigid in his doctrine of predestination and too harsh in his condemnation of Michael Servetus. On these two issues, they were joined by Sebastian Castellio and his network of humanist allies. These opponents of Calvin instead plotted a course forward that included a commitment to religious toleration as well as the pursuit of holiness that they believed other Protestants had largely abandoned in defense of the doctrine of *sola fide*. Meanwhile, the goal of internal reform of the French church established by Marguerite of Navarre's network continued unabated and was taken up by later Gallican evangelicals such as Jean de Monluc, François Bauduin, and Charles Du Moulin. They still saw hope for an approach to evangelical French reform that would neither upend the entire French church nor require the church to take orders from Geneva. Jean Morély and his allies shared a sense of revulsion toward Genevan dominance of the French evangelical movement and sought a way to ensure that the kingdom

Refusing to Kiss the Slipper. Michael W. Bruening, Oxford University Press (2021). © Oxford University Press.
DOI: 10.1093/oso/9780197566954.003.0010

would remain the locus of religious authority. Sympathetic to both these French nativist groups were the elite Huguenot nobility, who were similarly uneasy with the Calvinists' uncompromising and confrontational attitudes.

C.1. Overlapping Networks of Opposition

Although this book has treated these groups distinctly in separate chapters, there was extensive overlap among them. Each group may have been based in a different geographical area or focused on a different topic of contention with the Calvinists, but of central importance to them all, and binding all of them together, was hostility to Calvin and his disciples. Thus we see, for example, that members of the Meaux group, such as Jean Lecomte and Pierre Caroli, came to the Suisse romande and joined with Antoine Marcourt in his fights against the Calvinists in Geneva and the Pays de Vaud. André Zébédée came from the humanist circle in Bordeaux to align with the Zwinglians in the Vaud and later with Castellio and Bolsec. Jacques de Falais broke with Calvin over the Bolsec affair and welcomed to his estate Calvin's enemies from all around Lake Geneva, as well as some, like Castellio, from farther away. Falais's friend and fellow countryman François Bauduin spent his early career in Marguerite's university town of Bourges before allying with Castellio's friend Cassander and Marguerite's son-in-law Antoine of Navarre. Charles Du Moulin was acquainted with Zébédée and the anti-Calvinists of the Vaud, moved to Castellio-friendly Montbéliard, and returned to France where he worked for Jeanne d'Albret and developed relationships with Jean de Monluc, Renée de France, and the rest of the Huguenot nobility, while reuniting with his former student Bauduin. Jean Morély associated with Calvin critics Benoît de La Coste, Jean Morand, and Jean Davion in the Pays de Vaud, printed his controversial book with Castellio sympathizer Jean de Tournes, and was supported by Castellio's correspondent François Perrussel and Huguenot nobles Odet and Gaspard de Coligny, as well as Jeanne d'Albret. The interconnectedness of these groups reveals that opposition to Calvin was neither localized nor individualistic. Instead, as shown in Figure C.1,[1] Calvin's francophone opponents created a web of relations that cut across geographical and ideological borders.

---

[1] This figure was created using Stanford University's Palladio program (https://hdlab.stanford. edu/palladio/) and is based on known positive personal connections, correspondence, or citations in sources. It is not weighted by number of contacts or other data, as these are not plentiful enough to facilitate meaningful analysis. Thus, the figure is intended simply to indicate which of the Calvinists' opponents were connected positively in some way.

Figure C.1 Overlapping networks of individuals treated in this book

What tied these individuals together? First and foremost—and at the risk of stating the obvious—hatred of Calvin. This point is worth emphasizing because antipathy toward Calvin was often precisely what drew together disparate opponents. Zébédée's opposition to Calvin began over his Zwinglian objections to the Calvinists' doctrines of the Eucharist and the ministry, but he then found common cause with Bolsec on predestination and with Castellio on Servetus's execution. Bauduin may or may not have known Zébédée personally and claimed not to have met Castellio before 1562, but he clearly recognized both as part of the anti-Calvinist brotherhood and cited them approvingly. Du Moulin may never have met Perrussel or Morély, but his knowledge of their ill treatment by the Calvinists led him to write supportively of them. Thus, we repeatedly see that individuals who broke from Calvin over one issue then joined with the larger network of his opponents, often adopting the grievances of others in that network.

Apart from personal animosity toward Calvin, resentment of his role as self-appointed leader of the Reformed movement was the most common criticism. From the early references to Calvin, Farel, and Viret as the "three patriarchs" and Castellio's denunciation of the "pope of Geneva," to Bauduin's and Morély's mockery of the "Lemannic lord" and repeated references to "kissing the slipper," Calvin's (and later Beza's) enemies everywhere saw him as a new, Protestant pope. From their perspective, they had not broken away from Rome to fall under the dominance of a new ecclesiastical lord in Geneva. To many of them, such submission was a betrayal of the core evangelical principle of *sola scriptura*. Calvin, they believed, was saying, "Scripture alone, but as interpreted by me alone!" How, they wondered, was this different from Martin Luther's "second wall of the Romanists," that "only the pope may interpret the Scriptures"?[2]

Many of Calvin's opponents had first-hand knowledge of Calvin's exegetical arrogance, for many—including Zébédée, Falais, Castellio, Bauduin, Du Moulin, Toussain, and Morély—had been friends before becoming foes of the Calvinists. In most cases, their relationships ruptured over a doctrinal disagreement in which Calvin insisted that the other yield to his interpretation. Zébédée's break from Calvin arose from disagreement over the interpretation of the Eucharist and the ministry. With Castellio and Toussain, the execution of Servetus led to a split over the magistrate's right to administer capital punishment for heresy. In Castellio's case, the divide

---

[2] Martin Luther, *To the Christian Nobility of the German Nation*," in LW 44:115–217, here, 126.

widened further over a whole range of doctrinal disputes, from predestination to justification to basic biblical hermeneutical principles. Bauduin and Du Moulin were driven away by Calvin's uncompromising position against Nicodemism, for they saw no biblical support for such a narrow view of the church, no patristic precedent for separating from the "one, holy, catholic, and apostolic church," and no realistic way to apply the Calvinist model in France. With Morély, ecclesiological differences based on competing biblical interpretations related to moral discipline and pastoral elections led to lasting and bitter personal enmity between him and the Genevans. All these individuals had developed an understanding of Christianity based on their own reading of Scripture. Their interpretations, however, were not Calvin's, and Calvin would suffer no opposition. For him, deviation from his own doctrinal position was evidence of a deficient understanding of Scripture, or possibly the influence of Satan.

Another theme that bound many, although not all, of Calvin's enemies was criticism of the execution of Servetus. This was more controversial even at the time than Calvin's apologists have portrayed it. Although not all of Calvin's enemies would go as far as Castellio in his advocacy for religious freedom, a great many criticized Calvin's role in the event. Not only Castellio and his colleagues in Basel, but also Pierre Toussain and his associates in Montbéliard, distanced themselves from Calvin over this issue and were never able to repair the relationship. Bauduin wrote *On the Edicts of the Ancient Emperors* as a historical argument for religious toleration. Several individuals in France, such as Jean Saint-Vertunien de Lavau and Jean Bonneau, sided with Castellio in the debate. Those in France no doubt saw, as Castellio did, the logical consequences of Calvin's defense of the right to persecute heretics. In France, they themselves were the "heretics"; therefore, Calvin's arguments supported the king's right to persecute French evangelicals. In the Vaud, Zébédée and Falais criticized the Servetus execution. To them, it was an extension of the Bolsec affair. The Calvinists' persecuting tendencies, made manifest during Bolsec's imprisonment, reached their culmination with Servetus at the stake. Moreover, the Servetus execution provided yet more evidence that Calvin's true aim was to become a new pope. He insisted that his interpretation of Scripture was alone correct, required that ministers and missionaries be approved by him, demanded that ecclesiastical authority remain distinct from the secular magistrate, and urged heretics be put to death. How, his opponents wondered, could this not be interpreted as a new "papism"?

C.2. Why Did the Calvinists Win?

Despite their similarity to the old "papists," the Calvinists won, in the sense that their theology endured, their documents survived, and their influence continued to extend for generations, while their opponents have been largely forgotten. Because scholars have never appreciated the extent of the anti-Calvinist networks in francophone Europe, the question of how the Calvinists defeated them has never been posed. Certainly, historians have analyzed the reasons why Calvinism spread, considering why it was appealing and to whom, and other, related questions. No one, however, has ever tried to explain why the Calvinists defeated their francophone evangelical opponents. There are several plausible reasons: The Calvinists dominated major early Protestant towns, printing presses, educational institutions, and synods. Their dominance in large urban areas gave them political power as well. In addition, their uncompromising position on doctrinal issues and their black-and-white worldview were likely appealing to many rank-and-file members of the church who were not immersed in the fine points of biblical interpretation and theology. Finally, the Calvinists maintained an unremittingly hostile polemical program against all their opponents in an attempt to demonize them.

Before discussing each of these points more fully, however, we must note that the anti-Calvinists' defeat was by no means inevitable, nor was it, in the end, total. Almost every group we have encountered in this book had some advantage over the Calvinists. In the Pays de Vaud, the governing Bernese magistrates favored the Zwinglian theology followed by most of Calvin's opponents in the region. Against the Calvinists, the Bernese insisted on Zwinglian doctrines of the Eucharist, the ministry, church–state relations, and moral discipline. They banned Calvin's catechism and the use of his *Institutes* at the Lausanne Academy, and in 1559, they banished Viret and his Calvinist colleagues from the Vaud. The anti-Calvinists remained in the region. In Montbéliard, Pierre Toussain and his moderate, Castellio-friendly colleagues worked with the Lutheran Dukes of Württemberg to ensure that hardline Calvinism was forever kept at bay in the region. From Basel, Castellio had access to a European-wide network of sympathetic humanists, religious reformers, and refugees who did not want to see a new Calvinist Inquisition replace the Roman one that many had fled. Castellio's followers were able to establish significant dissenting communities across Europe, especially in the Netherlands and Eastern Europe. In France, first Marguerite of Navarre's network and then their Gallican evangelical heirs had access to the highest reaches of political power in the kingdom. The project for internal reform of the French church that had started in Meaux reached its peak just before the Colloquy of Poissy, with Catherine de Medici, Antoine of Navarre, Michel de l'Hôpital, the Cardinal of Lorraine, Monluc, Du Moulin, and Bauduin all striving toward a compromise solution that would adopt Protestant theological principles while preserving the external form of the French church. When that failed, at least some prominent members of the Huguenot nobility were sympathetic to Morély's proposals, which would have placed responsibility for religious reform largely in the hands of the local nobility and intellectual elites. It is not too far-fetched to imagine a scenario in which Calvin's opponents won significant power, the French church adopted an Elizabethan-style *via media*, and Geneva faded into a haven for marginalized religious zealots.

But now let us examine more closely how the Calvinists managed not only to avoid the dustbin of history but also to become the winners who would write that history. As noted earlier, on perhaps the most practical level, the Calvinists dominated the largest, most important cities in francophone Switzerland. Calvin in Geneva, Farel in Neuchâtel, and Viret in Lausanne formed the Calvinist triumvirate that wielded enormous influence in the region. Meanwhile, their opponents Lecomte, Malingre, Zébédée, and Marcourt were relegated to the smaller towns. Moreover, the Calvinists' dominance of the larger cities depended at least in part on chance and was not the result of sheer merit. Had the political situations in Geneva and Bern unfolded differently, it is entirely possible that Marcourt could have remained in Geneva (or indeed Neuchâtel), and Caroli and Zébédée stayed in Lausanne. With the main cities largely under their influence, the Calvinists had a their disposal two related institutions that reinforced their control in the region: the printing press and the academies. The Geneva printing press allowed the Calvinists to control the dissemination of Protestant books throughout francophone Europe, at least in the crucial early years of the Reformation. Moreover, the kinds of books that they produced were important. Nearly all the early catechisms, the biblical commentaries, and, of course, Calvin's *Institutes* presented a Calvinian worldview and theology to the literate francophone world. Their opponents occasionally went to Basel to publish, and Lyon and Paris later emerged as printing centers of Calvinist and anti-Calvinist literature alike. By that point, however, the wave of Calvinist printing could not be checked. Similarly, before

1559, the Lausanne Academy and later that of Geneva were almost entirely in the hands of the Calvinists, which meant that they were able to train nearly the entire second generation of francophone Reformed pastors. One must wonder how the francophone Reformed world would have been different had the publishing field been more evenly balanced in the 1540s and 1550s, or had Caroli, Du Moulin, and Zébédée rather than Cordier, Beza, and Viret led the Lausanne Academy through the same period.

In France, it was not dominance of the leading cities that allowed the Calvinists to shape Protestantism in the kingdom; the churches in the Île de France and Orléans, for example, were among the most sympathetic to Morély. Rather, it was their early control of the national synods, seized in the wake of the Lavau affair in Poitiers, that gave the Calvinists a leg up. From the very earliest proto-synod of Poitiers (1557) to the first full national synod of Paris (1559) to La Rochelle (1571) and Nîmes (1572), the Calvinists saw the need to organize, set the agenda, and preside at the meetings. They created the *Confession of Faith* and the *Discipline*. They identified the early heretics, apostates, and *coureurs*. These *coureurs* (literally "runners") were preachers without an official call, but no one can say how many of them were the wandering, wild-eyed, ranting street preachers the Calvinists made them out to be and how many could have been classified among Pierre Charpentier's "God-fearing ministers who detest the Cause." No doubt, several were among the latter.

We noted earlier how politically well-connected many of the anti-Calvinists were. Of course, this was true of the Calvinists as well. Ideologically, the Bernese magistrates may have preferred the Zwinglianism of the anti-Calvinists in the Vaud, but they recognized the importance of maintaining good relationships with the Calvinists, especially given Calvinist dominance of the Lausanne Academy. The Bernese saw their francophone school as not just a training ground for pastors but also for teachers in the region and for future civil servants who would need to know French. Thus, in the clashes between Viret and Zébédée, the Bernese allowed Viret to stay in Lausanne and relocated Zébédée. Although they eventually banished Viret, even then they gave him every chance to repent and return to his post. Likewise, with the Genevans, the Bernese exercised great political influence in the city but realized that in order to maintain such influence, they had to preserve good relations with Calvin and his colleagues. The Bern councilor Niklaus Zurkinden, for example, was an advocate for religious toleration and a friend of Castellio, but he also maintained a regular correspondence with Calvin. Thus, the Bern magistrates needed the Calvinists in Romandie to maintain their political influence in the region. The same was true of the Huguenot nobility in France. Most of them likely would have preferred religious reform along the lines advocated by Bauduin, Du Moulin, or Morély. To maintain their base of support among the French evangelicals, however, they were forced to work with Calvin and Beza. In short, the Calvinists made themselves indispensable to the Protestant authorities, while the anti-Calvinists could never apply similar levels of political pressure, even if their ideas might have been more appealing to the elites.

Despite the broad appeal of the anti-Calvinists' ideas among intellectuals and the nobility, the Calvinists' binary worldview, framed by Calvin's absolute confidence in his own righteousness and exegesis, would likely have been more attractive to the church membership more broadly. In essence, the very thing that drove so many of Calvin's enemies away from him—his tendency to speak prophetically in stark, black-and-white, good-versus-evil terms—undoubtedly drew many others to him. Today, leadership seminars teach that "people want to be led"; employees want a supervisor who will make decisions and set agendas. In the religious realm, this translates roughly to "people want a pope," not necessarily the pope in Rome, but some religious authority, whether an individual or a body who will make clear decisions and offer an unambiguous doctrinal program and worldview. The grand failing of many anti-Calvinists—and indeed of many efforts to challenge an established authority figure—is the misconception that people want to think for themselves. For the most part, this is not so; they want someone who provides unambiguous explanations to support belief and imposes a clear structure to inform action, thus binding the group together within a common cultural and ideological framework. Calvin did exactly that.

Not only did Calvin tell francophone evangelicals what to believe, he also made it quite clear what a "true Christian" should not believe. His extensive corpus of polemical writings, many against the groups or individuals presented in this book, represents another strategy the Calvinists used to defeat their rivals. Starting with the beginning of the Farellian publishing program in Neuchâtel in the 1530s, a substantial proportion of the books produced by the Calvinists could be classified as polemical.[3] At first,

---

[3] On Calvin's polemical writing, see especially Szczech, *Calvin en polémique*. She counts forty-eight polemical works penned by Calvin himself between 1538 and 1564. Ibid., 530. One should note that many of Viret's works from the same period could also be classified as polemical, although he generally targeted Catholicism broadly rather than evangelical rivals.

the chief target was the Catholic Church. As we have seen, however, even some of these early anti-Catholic works seem to have been aimed in part at evangelicals in France, in an effort to "provoke to piety" those among them who were hesitant to break from the old church. As we move through the 1540s and 1550s, however, an increasing number of Calvinist polemical texts are aimed specifically at fellow evangelicals—including, for example, Pierre Caroli, the Nicodemites and "libertines," Castellio, and Lutherans like Joachim Westphal. By the 1560s, the French Wars of Religion led to a revival of anti-Catholic Calvinist propaganda, which also targeted those who would "water down the true church" by seeking compromise with the Catholics. We see this in Calvin's and Beza's writings against Bauduin and the *moyenneurs*, as well as in the attack on Morély for questioning the ecclesiology of the French *Discipline*. In short, wherever the Calvinists saw a threat to their authority, theology, or practice, they attempted to quash it through a war of words. Their dominance of the printing press allowed them to do so effectively. In the process, Calvinist religious polemic aided the establishment of francophone Protestant religious identity.

Finally, with victory in hand, Beza ensured that the Calvinists' opponents would be forgotten for generations by writing them out of history. For his own generation, Beza's *Life of Calvin* and his *Ecclesiastical History of the Reformed Churches in the Kingdom of France* created a common history and identity for French Protestants.[4] This history presented Calvin and his allies as the heroes who followed the true religion, while those treated in this book are either ignored or presented as heretics. For later generations, no works have done more than these two to secure the image of the Calvinists as the dominant wing of francophone Protestantism. Moreover, the deliberate focus on the French Reformed churches in Beza's *Ecclesiastical History* helps to explain why the francophone churches outside the kingdom—in the Vaud, Montbéliard, the Rhineland, and elsewhere—have received far less scholarly attention than those in Geneva and France. For centuries, "French reform" in the historiographical context has meant not francophone reform broadly but, literally, reform in the kingdom of France.

---

[4] See Marianne Carbonnier-Burkard, "*L'Histoire Ecclésiastique des Églises Réformées . . .* : La construction Bèzienne d'un 'Corps d'histoire,'" in *Théodore de Bèze (1519–1605): Actes du Colloque de Genève (septembre 2005)*, edited by Irena Backus, 145–61, THR 424 (Geneva: Droz, 2007).

C.3. The Anti-Calvinists and the Protestant Principle

The title of this book, *Refusing to Kiss the Slipper*, is intended to be ambiguous. Mostly, of course, the phrase refers here to Calvin, perceived by his enemies to be a new pope. But Calvin's opponents among the reformers were no more eager to kiss the slipper of a Roman than a Genevan pope. No matter how earnestly individuals such as Lefèvre, Roussel, Monluc, Bauduin, and Du Moulin sought compromise with the existing church, none supported strong ties to Rome; these were not "papists," despite the efforts of Calvin and his allies to portray them as such. Instead, every individual featured in this book supported a flattening of religious hierarchy and encouraged the freedom to criticize dominant religious authorities and doctrine.

As such, they can be understood to be among the first true practitioners of the "Protestant principle," as explained by twentieth-century theologian Paul Tillich. For Tillich, the enduring legacy of the Reformation lay not in the doctrines of the Protestant reformers, all of which he suggests had lost their urgency by the twentieth century, but in the protest itself against existing religious institutions. "The Protestant principle," Tillich writes, "contains the divine and human protest against any absolute claim made for a relative reality, even if this claim is made by a Protestant church. The Protestant principle is the judge of every religion and cultural reality, including the religion and culture which calls itself Protestant."[5] In other words, it is the need constantly to test, evaluate, and judge all human religious institutions. This is, of course, what so many of the individuals treated here were doing. They saw and challenged absolute claims for what they believed was a relative reality, whether those claims came from Calvin or the pope. Tillich explains further, "The Protestant principle . . . is the guardian against the attempts of the finite and conditional to usurp the place of the unconditional in thinking and acting. It is the prophetic judgment against religious pride, ecclesial arrogance, and secular self-sufficiency and their destructive consequences."[6] No doubt most of the reformers of the sixteenth century saw themselves as just that prophetic voice against religious pride and ecclesial arrogance. For Calvin it was the pride and arrogance of the Catholic Church. Calvin's opponents initially

---

[5] Paul Tillich, *The Protestant Era*, abridged edition, translated by James Luther Adams (Chicago: University of Chicago Press, 1957), 163.

[6] Tillich, *The Protestant Era*, 163.

noted the pride of Calvin himself; later, as the francophone Reformed Church became institutionalized, they highlighted the ecclesial arrogance of the Reformed synods and consistories.

The individual we have encountered here who best anticipates Tillich is, of course, Castellio. His insistence on the relativity of historical claims to Christian truth, his realization that today's heretic is often tomorrow's hero, and his desire to downplay institutional religion while emphasizing the personal pursuit of piety make him perhaps the best exemplar of the proto-liberal wing of the Protestant Reformation. We see a tendency toward this in others as well, as in Falais's complaints that one could not even debate predestination in Calvin's Geneva. We note it in Du Moulin's self-proclaimed status as professor of Sacred Scriptures and his insistence on his own ability to preach and administer the sacraments despite lacking ordination from any established church, and in Morély's repeated false claims of repentance to the Genevans while continuing to circulate his book and spread his anti-Genevan ideas. All these actions reflect to some extent Tillich's Protestant principle and embrace the freedom to judge those who claimed religious authority.

Such critics often gain followers but rarely lasting power. Leaders of movements need not only to attack the old institutions but to build new ones. This is what the Calvinists were able to do and what the anti-Calvinists, with rare exceptions, were unable to accomplish. Nevertheless, neither the construction of new institutions nor the reform of existing ones is intelligible without an understanding of the obstacles and opposition faced along the way. The legacy of those in the sixteenth century who refused to kiss the slipper of either Calvin or the pope may be largely hidden, but it was the anvil against which Calvin and his disciples forged a new Protestant identity. The legacy of these critics endures as a cautionary warning against religious pride and ecclesial arrogance and a call for the constant reform of the church.

Glossary of Key Individuals

Aconcio (Acontius), Giacopo (ca. 1520–ca. 1566). Italian refugee tied to Castellio and author of *Satan's Strategems*, which was influenced by Castellio's thought. He probably was an intermediary between Castellio and the pastor of the Dutch church in London, Adrian Van Haemstede.

Arande, Michel d'. Member of the Meaux group, almoner for Marguerite of Navarre, and later bishop of Saint-Paul-Trois-Châteaux. In 1522, he was denounced by the Sorbonne for attacking the veneration of the saints and for defending Luther.

Baron, Pierre/Baro, Peter (1534–1599). Pastor in Orléans and, along with his colleague Hughes Sureau du Rosier, supporter of Morély. Baron studied law at Bourges and was ordained to the ministry in 1560 by Calvin. After St. Bartholomew's Day, Baron moved to England and taught at Cambridge under the anglicized name Peter Baro. There, he supported proto-Arminian views on predestination.

Bauduin, François (1520–1573). Native of Arras, legal scholar, and student of Charles Du Moulin. He joined the Calvinists and served briefly as Calvin's secretary, but he fell away from them when he returned to France to teach in Bourges. He worked with Antoine of Navarre and George Cassander to push for a religious settlement at the Colloquy of Poissy. Afterward he engaged in a literary war with Calvin and Beza. Calvin coined the term *moyenneur* to refer to Bauduin.

Bauhin, Jean (*père*) (1511–1582). Medical doctor from Amiens and Castellio's best friend in Basel. He seems to have supported Castellio's views on universal election.

Bauhin, Jean (*fils*) (1541–1613). Son of Castellio's friend, he was interested in science, especially botany, and was friends with Conrad Gessner in Zurich. He came into conflict with Viret and his colleagues in Lyon, when he wanted to get married there, but the pastors insisted he conform to the teachings of the French Reformed Churches.

Bergeron, Nicolas. Student of Petrus Ramus, *avocat au parlement*, collaborator with Charles Du Moulin, and supporter of Morély. He appeared together with Ramus and Morély at the 1572 Synod of Nîmes.

Blesdijk, Nicolaas (ca. 1520–1584). Initially a Dutch Mennonite and son-in-law of David Joris in Basel. He later attacked Joris for both his doctrine and adulterous lifestyle, and he became a Reformed pastor while maintaining ties to Castellio. He also worked on the manuscript of Castellio's *De l'impunité des hérétiques*.

Bolsec, Jerome (d. ca. 1584). Native of Paris, he joined the Carmelite Order but fled France in 1545 or 1546 for Renée de France's court at Ferrara. Bolsec became Jacques de Falais's personal physician by 1550. In October 1551, he criticized Calvin's doctrine of predestination at a *congrégation* in Geneva. Banished from Geneva, he returned to

Falais's estate and continued to criticize the Calvinists. In 1555, he joined Zébédée in his denunciations of Calvin in Bern. Although the Bernese sharply criticized Calvin in response, they also banished Bolsec, who returned to France. The 1563 national Synod of Lyon condemned him as an apostate. He wrote one of the first negative biographies of Calvin, *De la vie, moeurs, actes, doctrine, constance et mort de Jean Calvin.*

Bonifacio, Giovanni Bernardino (1517–1597). Marchese d'Oria, friend of Castellio and godfather to his son Bonifacius. He may have had a hand in producing *Concerning Heretics*, and he later asked Castellio to join him in Poland.

Bonneau, Jean. French layman in Beaugency who agreed with Castellio's teachings on religious toleration.

Briçonnet, Guillame (1470–1534). Royal envoy to Rome for negotiations on the Concordat of Bologna. Commendatory abbot of Saint-Germain-des-Prés in Paris, where he welcomed Jacques Lefèvre d'Étaples. Bishop of Meaux and founder of the Meaux reform group, he established preaching stations around the diocese and encouraged Lefèvre and his colleagues in their work to "bring the Gospel to the people." In 1525, he yielded to Catholic demands to abandon his reforming work.

Byse, Pierre. Pastor of Yverdon (1547–1556) and supporter of Zébédée. Later served as pastor of Aubonne (Vaud), deacon of Yverdon, and pastor in the Dauphiné.

Capel, [Louis?]. In Pierre Charpentier's list of those who detested Beza's "Cause." Ramus also names a certain Capel as an opponent of Beza. It is unclear whether these are the same person or two different individuals both named Capel.

Caroli, Pierre (1480–1550). Sorbonne graduate, member of the Meaux group, and frequent target in the 1520s of the Paris Faculty of Theology. At the top of the wanted-heretics list following the Affair of the Placards, he fled to Switzerland, participated in the Lausanne Disputation (1536), and was named chief pastor of Lausanne. He clashed with Calvin, Viret, and Farel, accusing them of Arianism and being accused by them of advocating prayers for the dead.

Cassander, George (1513–1566). Flemish humanist, correspondent of Castellio, friend of François Bauduin, and author of *De officio*, which was prepared for the Colloquy of Poissy. The book sought to find religious compromise by focusing on the shared legacy of the Church Fathers but was bitterly attacked by Calvin, who believed Bauduin to be the author.

Caviot, Hughes. Correspondent and possibly former student of Castellio, he reported to Castellio from Lausanne in the 1550s.

Celsi, Mino (1514–1575). Italian refugee and author of *In haereticis coërcendis*, which quotes extensively from Castellio.

Chaponneau, Jean (d. 1545). Farel's colleague in Neuchâtel. After receiving a doctorate from the University of Louvain, he became an Augustinian monk in Bourges, where he preached evangelical sermons. In 1536, he arrived in Neuchâtel but clashed repeatedly with Farel. In 1543, he and Jean Courtois drew up articles denouncing Calvin's "heresies." In 1544, he opposed Farel on the subject of fraternal censures.

Charpentier, Pierre. Native of Toulouse, he was law professor in Geneva from 1566 to 1570. After returning to France, he spied on Huguenot leaders for the Spanish ambassador, and after St. Bartholomew's Day, he wrote a treatise that pinned blame for the massacre on Beza's faction, which he designated the "Cause." He distinguished the Cause from patriotic French Protestants who, he claims, detested the Cause. A list of these Protestant opponents of Beza includes several known associates of Morély.

Chastillon, Michel (the Elder) (d. 1558). Castellio's brother and a printer in Lyon. He was arrested for publishing a lost work against Calvin's doctrine of predestination. He may have been the printer of the French translation of *Concerning Heretics*.

Chastillon, Michel (the Younger). Castellio's nephew, who reported to him from Geneva.

Coligny, Odet de, Cardinal de Châtillon (1517–1571). Brother of Admiral Gaspard de Coligny and François d'Andelot, Odet refused to give up his title of Cardinal after joining the Protestants. Initially, he seems to have favored the path of religious compromise in France; later he was Morély's most prominent noble supporter.

Colinet, Jean. Schoolmaster in Geneva, he corresponded with Castellio and was associated with Zébédée and Falais. Calvin criticized him for denouncing religious persecution.

Comte, Béat (d. 1578). Native of the Dauphiné, he replaced Caroli as pastor in Lausanne (1538–1545), before being deposed for dereliction of duty and the spending habits of his wife. He was an ally of Zébédée in his conflicts with Viret, and he took over as Lausanne Arts professor in 1559, after the exile of most of the faculty.

Constantin, Guillaume. Possibly the leading Castellionist of Lyon, possibly a cousin of Michel Chastillon's wife, Marie Roybet. Several letters exist between him and Castellio.

Coornhert, Dirck Volkertszoon (1520–1599). Dutch free thinker who translated several of Castellio's works into Dutch. He was the object of Calvin's anti-Nicodemite attack in *Response à un certain holandois*.

Corbeil, Louis. Student supporter of Zébédée during his fight with Viret who continued to oppose the Calvinists throughout his career. In 1551, he was arrested in France and imprisoned with the five Lausanne students who were burned for heresy in Lyon. Corbeil was spared because he was not French himself. In 1554, became deacon of Morges.

Courtois, Jean. Jean Chaponneau's son-in-law, who assisted him in drafting the 1543 articles of Calvin's alleged heresies.

Curione, Celio Secondo (1503–1569). Italian humanist, arts professor in Lausanne and then in Basel, where he was close to his colleague Castellio.

Davion, Jean. From Milly, France (near Etampes), inhabitant of Lausanne in 1553, described by Beza as the "destroyer of our churches" for his support of Bolsec. He presented a book against the Calvinists' doctrine of predestination to the Bernese in 1558 and was pastor of Grandson in the 1560s. He was also an associate of Morély.

De Ecclesia, Philippe (Philippe Ozias). Native of Vierzon, near Bourges, and pastor of Geneva (1542–1553). He was tied to Falais and accused of supporting Bolsec and the doctrine of the ubiquity of Christ's body. He was deposed from the Genevan ministry.

Del Corro, Antonio (1527–1591). Spanish monk who embraced Protestantism in 1557, when he left Spain for Lausanne; he later worked in Béarn, Bergerac, and Montargis. In Montargis, he worked for Renée de France alongside Juan Pérez. In 1567, he moved to London, where he came into conflict with the Calvinist French church. He is perhaps best known for his controversial *Tableau de l'Oeuvre de Dieu*, which rejected the Calvinist understanding of predestination and embraced the Castellionist idea of universal election.

Du Moulin, Charles (1500–1566). Parisian jurisconsult who gained fame with his commentary on Paris customary law. In 1552, he fled France for Switzerland, where he initially was friendly with the Calvinists. He also maintained a regular correspondence with Bullinger. During his exile, he taught in Strasbourg, Tübingen, and Montbéliard. In 1556, he left Montbéliard for Dole before returning to Paris. He continued to embrace evangelical ideas during his later career but turned sharply against the Calvinists, particularly over the power of their consistories in France. His *Union and Harmony of the Four Evangelists* was condemned at the 1565 Synod of Paris. One of his last works, *Against the Calumnies of the Calvinists*, was a particularly harsh denunciation of his former allies.

Eyssautier, Matthieu. Castellio's brother-in-law, he was censured by provincial synod of Lourmarin for spreading Castellio's teachings. He was later excommunicated by Geneva while pastor in nearby Saconnex.

Falais, Jacques de Bourgogne, Seigneur de (d. 1556). Nobleman from Brabant. Early friend of Calvin, who encouraged him to immigrate to the Geneva area. The two fell out over the condemnation in Geneva of Jerome Bolsec, who was Falais's personal physician. Afterward, Falais established an anti-Calvinist center at his estate at Veigy, which welcomed Zébédée, François de Saint-Paul, and others. Falais also was friendly with Castellio.

Foncelet, Sebastian. Ally of Zébédée in the 1550s, he was later condemned at the 1564 French provincial synod of Ferté-sous-Jouarre as an Anabaptist and Castellionist.

Gète, Jacques. Pastor of Bavans (Montbéliard), he was a follower of Castellio who possibly played a role in translating *Concerning Heretics* into French.

Glant, Claude de. Native of Yverdon, Switzerland, he received clerical orders in Lausanne (1521) before serving as Protestant pastor of la Prévoté (1530), of Tavannes (1530–1531), in the territory of Biel/Bienne (1531–1536), and in Cudrefin (1536). He was deposed from the ministry at the Synod of Yverdon (1536) but was later restored and became rector of the Yverdon school (1539) and then deacon (1545–1550).

Gobat (first name unknown). Schoolmaster of Yverdon and supporter of Zébédée.

Gribaldi, Matteo (d. 1564). Italian legal scholar and later antitrinitarian, he was probably a main source for the Baslers of information about Servetus's trial and execution.

Grymoult, Léger. Montbéliard resident, he was a witness to and critic of the Servetus execution. He was also an editor of Castellio's *De l'impunité des hérétiques* and possibly the translator of *Concerning Heretics.*

Guillemin, Gérard. Deacon of Montbéliard and follower of Castellio.

Houbraque, Guillaume (d. ca. 1584). Graduate of Lausanne Academy; his final examination was the occasion of the major fight between Viret and Zébédée. He later served churches in Paris, Frankfurt, Strasbourg, and Heidelberg. Although he seems mostly to have been a faithful Calvinist, he was claimed by Morély as a supporter, and he proposed a compromise solution between Morély and the Calvinists on church order in his treatise *Traité monstrant comme il faut proceder à la correction des vices et scandales . . .* (1567).

Joris, David (or David George) (ca. 1501–1556). Dutch Anabaptist who lived in Basel under the pseudonym Johann van Brugge. He was a defender of Servetus and possibly the pseudonymous author "George Kleinberg" in *Concerning Heretics.*

La Coste, Benoît de. Pastor of Montagny near Yverdon in the Vaud, where he had conflicts with the Calvinists in Lausanne. He was deposed from the ministry in France for his views on predestination and was an associate of Morély.

Lafarge, Thomas. Student of Castellio and part of his Lyon group of followers.

La Haye, Hermès de. Personal pastor of Odet de Coligny and supporter of Morély.

Lange, Jean. From France, he was a student at the Lausanne Academy in 1544 and pastor of Bursins (Vaud) by 1552. He was accused of mocking the Genevans at Falais's estate in 1552 and was an ally of Zébédée in his complaints to Bern about the Calvinists.

L'Archer (or Larcher, Sagittarius), Jean (ca. 1516–1588). Native of Bordeaux, he was a friend and frequent correspondent of Castellio. He was pastor in Cortaillod (near Neuchâtel) and then Héricourt in Montbéliard. He published the *Canons of All the Councils* (Oporinus, 1553), which was censured by Viret.

Lavau, Jean Saint-Vertunien de. Correspondent of Servetus and follower of Castellio. Calvin's long letter in 1555 to the church of Poitiers was intended to warn them of Lavau, who was denounced at the 1557 proto-synod of Poitiers and again at the 1559 national synod of Paris.

Lecomte, Jean (ca. 1500–1572). Native of Picardy, student of Mathurin Cordier in Paris, and member of the Meaux group. Around 1532, he joined Farel's group of exiles in Switzerland. He was pastor of Grandson in the Pays de Vaud until his death. He was friendly with Caroli, whom he knew from Meaux, and a lifelong opponent of Calvin and his allies in the region.

Le Comte, Paul. Schoolmaster in Montpellier in the 1530s, he later moved to Lausanne and wrote an unpublished treatise against Calvin's and Beza's doctrine of predestination.

Le Coq, Jacques. Native of Paris, he fled by 1532 to Switzerland, where we find him as pastor of Corcelles (near Neuchâtel). He was pastor of Morges from 1536. An early Calvinist, he broke with them over a pastoral call to Metz, which Farel insisted on taking despite Le Coq's earlier call.

L'Espine, Jean de (ca. 1505–1597). French pastor generally in line with the Calvinists but possibly named by Morély as one of his supporters. Pierre Charpentier identified him as one of those opposed to Beza's "Cause."

Lefèvre d'Étaples, Jacques (a.k.a. Faber Stapulensis, ca. 1460–1536). Humanist scholar of Aristotle at the University of Paris and intellectual leader of the Meaux reform group. Author of the *Quincuplex Psalterium* (1509), a commentary of the letters of St. Paul (1512), and leading translator of the French New Testament (1524).

Malingre, Thomas (d. 1572). From a noble family of Normandy, he preached evangelical sermons in Blois in 1527. Around 1531, he moved to Switzerland and published books of evangelical poetry with the Neuchâtel printer Pierre de Vingle under his nom de plume Mathieu Malingre. He wrote the *Indice des principales matieres contenues en la Bible*, which appeared in Olivétan's 1535 French Bible. He was pastor of anti-Calvinist Yverdon in the Vaud from 1536 for most of his life, except for a decade from 1546 to 1556, when he was pastor of Aubonne.

Mallot, Jean. Gaspard de Coligny's personal chaplain and a supporter of Morély.

Marcourt, Antoine (ca. 1485–1561). From Picardy in France, he was author of the 1534 Placards, as well as of the *Livre des marchans* (1533), the *Petit traicté tres utile et salutaire de la saincte eucharistie* (1534), and the *Declaration de la Messe* (1534). Pastor in Neuchâtel, 1531–1538, then he and Jean Morand replaced Calvin and Farel in Geneva, 1538–1540. He supported the rights of the Christian magistrate and clashed with the Calvinists over his friendship with Caroli, his political appointment in Geneva, and the distribution of ecclesiastical goods in the Vaud. After Geneva, he served as pastor of Orzens-Essertine, Curtilles, Versoix, and finally Saint-Julien.

Marguerite of Navarre (1492–1549). Sister of King Francis I and leading protector of French evangelicals, her network was chiefly responsible for spreading evangelical ideas throughout the kingdom. She protected and found positions for individuals such as Lefèvre, Roussel, and Caroli, and she encouraged reform in Bourges, Nérac, and Béarn.

Mercure, Sieur de. Pastor in Provence and opponent of Geneva's dominance of the French churches. The 1571 Synod of La Rochelle condemned him for his "calumnies" against Geneva, and Charpentier lists him among those who detested Beza's "Cause."

Monluc, Jean de (ca. 1502–1579). Bishop of Valence who sought internal French reform. He was censured by the Paris Faculty of Theology for introducing a vernacular liturgy and for including Protestant teaching in his published works. He was a leading moderate figure at the Colloquy of Poissy.

Montméja, Bernard de (or Momméjan). Evangelical poet and pastor of the church of Chauny, he was associated with François Perrussel, Morély, and Condé.

Morand, Jean. Native of Vervins in Picardy, he earned a doctorate in theology from Paris (1530). He was named canon and vicar-general of Amiens (1533) but was denounced by the Faculty of Theology (July 1534). In 1537, he moved to Switzerland and was pastor first at Cully, then together with Marcourt was one of the replacements for Calvin and

Farel in Geneva in 1538. In 1540, he returned to the Vaud and was pastor of Nyon from 1540 to 1552. He disappears from the historical record after that.

Morély, Jean (ca. 1524–ca. 1594). Minor French nobleman whose *Traicté de la discipline et police chrestienne* (1562), argued that most ecclesiastical decisions should be made by the generality of the local churches, rather than by synods and consistories. Morély's position was seen by Beza as highly threatening, and he was condemned at three different national synods (Orléans, 1562, Paris, 1565, Nîmes, 1572). Morély gained support from several Huguenot nobles, and Jeanne d'Albret employed him as tutor to the future King Henri IV. Morély was also tied to critics of Calvin's doctrine of predestination Jean Davion and Benoît de La Coste.

Mussard, Pierre. Castellio's brother-in-law and schoolmaster of Hermance (Chablais), whose accusations against four pastors for preaching the Calvinist doctrine of predestination against Bern's orders led to their dismissal.

Ochino, Bernardino (1487–1564). Italian refugee who met Castellio in Geneva. His *Thirty Dialogues*, in which Ochino seemed to cast doubt on the Trinity and to support polygamy, led to his banishment from Zurich. Castellio's translation of the text into Latin led to an investigation in Basel at the end of his life.

Olivier, Matthieu. Pastor in the Chablais before moving to Grenoble. Morély listed him as one of his supporters.

Oporinus, Johannes (1507–1568). Basel printer for whom Castellio worked as a corrector and with whom he published many of his works, including *Concerning Heretics*. Oporinus also published François Bauduin's *Ad Edicta Veterum Principum* and Jean L'Archer's *Canons of All the Councils*.

Paquelon, Jacques. Brother of Castellio's first wife, Huguine, he reported to Castellio from Geneva.

Pérez de Pineda, Juan (Pierins, Pierius) (ca. 1500–1568). Spaniard who had been chased out of Seville by the Inquisition. In the 1550s, he was pastor to the Spanish congregation in Geneva, where he published a Spanish translation of the New Testament and a catechism. In 1556, he moved to Frankfurt, where he worked with Perrussel. In 1563, he was preaching in Blois and two years later was serving alongside Antonio del Corro as chaplain to Renée de France. Morély listed Pérez as a supporter.

Perrin, Jean. Student of Zébédée at the Lausanne Academy (1546) and possibly of Castellio in Basel. He was friendly with Castellio and Lelio Sozzini. His appointment as deacon in Aigle (Vaud) was opposed by the Lausanne professors (1556). He replaced Béat Comte as Arts professor in the Lausanne Academy (1562).

Perrussel, François (De la Rivère). Early Nicodemite, he was one of the first pastors of the French church in London, then in Frankfurt, and finally chaplain to the Prince de Condé. He was a friend of Castellio and a supporter of Morély. Du Moulin also cites him as a victim of the Calvinists for his praise of the Augsburg Confession.

Philippi, François. Native of Bourges, he was likely the author of a French translation of the *Book of Common Prayer*. He was Perrussel's colleague in Frankfurt before moving to Aix-la-Chapelle. He was also author of *Defense des eglises estrangieres de Francfort en Allemagne* (1562). Morély lists him as one of his supporters.

Porret, Michel. From Neuchâtel, he was pastor of Veigy and a supporter of Falais and Bolsec.

Ramus, Petrus (Pierre de la Ramée) (1515–1572). Renowned dialectician, critic of Aristotelian logic, and supporter of Morély, he appeared together with Morély at the 1572 Synod of Nîmes, before being killed in the St. Bartholomew's Day massacre.

Roussel, Gérard (1500–1550). Early follower of Lefèvre at Saint-Germain and then Meaux, he was later almoner for Marguerite of Navarre and bishop of Oloron. His Lenten sermons at the Louvre in 1533 marked a high point for evangelical French reform. His *Forme de visite de diocèse* and *Familiere exposition du simbole, de la loy et oraison domincale* reveal his continued push for evangelical reform after his appointment as bishop.

Roybet, Marie Françoise. Castellio's sister-in-law, wife of Michel Chastillon. She corresponded with Castellio and associated with other Castellionists of Lyon.

Saint-Paul, François de (d. 1580). From Picardy, possibly Soissons, he was professor of Greek at the Lausanne Academy (1547–1549) and then pastor of Vevey (Vaud), 1549–1559. He was allied to the Calvinists on most issues and went into exile with Viret in 1559, but he opposed the Calvinist view of reprobation and was associated with Falais after the Bolsec affair. In 1554, he wrote an unpublished treatise on predestination. He later served the French churches of Poiters (1559) and Montélimar (1559–1560), moved to Dieppe and England, and finally returned to Vevey (1572–1580).

Sozzini, Fausto (1539–1604). Nephew of Lelio and founder of the Socinian movement. He was largely responsible for the 1578 publication of Castellio's *Four Dialogues*.

Sozzini, Lelio (1525–1562). Friend of Castellio who was influential on his nephew Fausto's antitrinitarian views.

Sureau du Rosier, Hughes (d. ca. 1578). Pastor of Orléans and friend of Morély. The discovery of Morély's letters in Sureau's study helped Beza's allies condemn Morély to Jeanne d'Albret and the Huguenot nobility. Charpentier lists Sureau as one of the French ministers opposed to Beza and the Genevans. After St. Batholomew's Day, he abjured the Reformed faith but soon afterward espoused it once again.

Tournes, Jean de (1504–1564). Lyon printer associated with the Castellionists in the city, he printed of Morély's controversial treatise.

Toussain, Pierre (1499–1573). Early friend and ally of Farel, he was the leading pastor of Montbéliard for most of his career. He turned against the Calvinists during the Servetus Affair. He had to negotiate differences between the Lutheran rulers and pastors of Württemberg and the French-speaking pastors who were inclined toward Reformed Protestantism.

Trolliet, Jean. Genevan notary, former monk, friend of Philippe de Ecclesia, and associate of Bolsec. Calvin opposed his admittance to the ministry. He was also accused of criticizing Calvin's *Institutes* and his doctrine of predestination.

Van Haemstede, Adrian (ca. 1525–ca. 1562). Pastor of the Dutch Strangers' Church in London, he was an advocate of religious toleration and possibly an associate of Castellio.

Villeroche, Pierre. Reformed pastor sent by Calvin to appeal to Antoine of Navarre, he was also an associate of Castellio. He was deposed from ministry by the church of Bergerac. He was a critic of Calvin and probably his doctrine of predestination

Zébédée, André (ca. 1510–ca. 1570). Native of Brabant. He studied perhaps at Louvain and Paris before becoming a professor at the Collège de Guyenne in Bordeaux (1533/34–1538). He was allied to the Calvinists as pastor Orbe and Yverdon (1538–1547) but was a staunch supporter of Zwinglian theology. He broke decisively with the Calvinists in his quarrels with Viret over the sacraments and the power of the ministry while Arts professor at the Lausanne Academy (1547–1549). Later, as pastor in Nyon, he supported Bolsec's arguments against Calvin's doctrine of predestination (1552–1555), and he successfully led the effort to have Calvinism condemned by the Bernese in 1555. He was friends with Castellio and is mentioned positively by both François Bauduin and Charles Du Moulin.

Bibliography

Archival Sources

ACV	(Archives cantonales Vaudoises)
Ba 14.1	Mandats et ordonnances souveraines pour le bailliage de Lausanne
BP 33/2	Comptes du bailliage de Morges
P Meylan	Archives privées, Henri Meylan
AEG	(Archives de l'État de Genève)
CL	Lettres du Conseil
p.h.1503	Sebastien Fonselet dossier
AEN	(Archives d'État de Neuchâtel)
1PAST	Lettres des Réformateurs
AN	(Archives nationales de France)
U//2046	Collection Le Nain, Registres du parlement, vol. 47, juillet 1557–juillet 1558
BCU	(Bibliothèque cantonale et universitaire de Lausanne)
Ms. IS 4511	Henri Vuilleumier, "Ministres du Saint-Evangile qui ont été au service à l'église évangélique réformée du Pays de Vaud," nonpaginated, arranged alphabetically by last name
BNF	(Bibliothèque nationale de France)
Ms. DuPuy 488, fols. 7^r–12^r (digitized)	Plainte des gens du Roy, pour faire censurer ung livre de Du Molin
Ms. fr. 419 (digitized)	Gérard Roussel, *Familere exposition du simbole, de la loy, et oraison dominicale, en forme de colloque*
Ms. lat. 12,717, fols. 134–157	Plaidoyé du Sr du Moulin, avec la sentence de Mrs de Berne donnée sur ledict plaidoyé
Ms. Lat. 4361	Jean Morély, *De ecclesiae ordine et disciplina*
BGE	(Bibliothèque de Genève)
Archives Tronchin, vol. 64	Bèze, Apology for the Lausanne pastors and professors

Ms. lat. 111a	Correspondance de Calvin
BRott	(Bibliotheek Rotterdam)
Remonstrants, ms. 508, ms. 509	Castellio, *De Haereticis a civili magistratu non puniendis* (ms. 508 in Latin, ms. 509 in French)
Remonstrants ms. 505	Castellio, Opera varia (epistolae, tractatus)
StAB	(Staatsarchiv des Kantons Bern)
Ms. AV 1457 (UP 82.2)	Kirchliche Angelegenheiten, 1547–1559
Ms. A II (RM)	Ratsmanuale Bern
StAZ	(Staatsarchiv des Kantons Zürich)
Mss. E II	Antistitialarchiv
ZZb	(Zurich Zentralbibliothek)
Mss. F	Thesaurus Hottingerianus, original letters
Mss. S	Simler Manuscript Collection: Copies of reformers' letters

Primary Sources

Aconcio, Giacopo. *Stratagemata Satanae libri octo*. Basel: Perna, 1565.

Aconcio, Giacopo. *Satanae Strategematum libri octo, Ad Johannem Wolphium eiusque ad Acontium Epistulae, Epistula apologetica pro Adriano Haemstede, Epistula ad ignotum quendam de natura Christi*. Edited by Walther Köhler. Munich: Ernst Reinhardt, 1927.

Amerbach, Johannes, et al. *Die Amerbachkorrespondenz*. 11 vols. Edited by Afred Hartmann, et al. Basel: Universitätsbibliothek, 1942–1995.

Anonymous. "Pierre Caroli, Clément Marot, Mathurin Cordier, et quarante-six autres, ajournés par les gens du Roi comme suspects d'hérésie." *BSHPF* 10 (1861): 34–39.

Anonymous. *La visite des églises du diocèse de Lausanne en 1416–1417*. Mémoires et documents publiés par la société d'histoire de la Suisse romande ser. 2, 11. Lausanne: Georges Bridel & Cie, 1921.

Aymon, Jean. *Tous les synodes nationaux des églises reformées de France*. 2 vols. The Hague: Charles Delo, 1710.

Bainton, Roland H., ed. and trans. *Concerning Heretics, Whether They Are to Be Persecuted and How They Are to Be Treated, A Collection of the Opinions of Learned Men Both Ancient and Modern*, by Sebastian Castellio. New York: Columbia University Press, 1935.

Barbiche, Bernard, et al., eds. *L'édit de Nantes et ses antécédents (1562–1598)*. Available at http://elec.enc.sorbonne.fr/editsdepacification/.

Baronio, Cesare et al., eds. *Annales ecclesiastici*. 37 vols. Bar-Le-Duc: L. Guerin, 1864–1883.

Bauduin, François. *Francisci Balduini Atrebatii Iuriscons. in suas Annotationes in libros quatuor Institutionum Iustiniani Imp. προλεγόμενα sive Praefata de iure civili*. Paris: Jean Loys, 1545.

Bauduin, François. *Ad Edicta Veterum Principum Rom. de Christianis*. Basel: Oporinus, [1557].

Bauduin, François. *Ad leges de famosis libellis et de calumniatoribus commentarius*. Paris: André Wechel, 1562.

Bauduin, François. *Responsio altera ad Ioan. Calvinum*. Paris: Guil. Morelium, 1562.

Bauduin, François. *Optati Afri, Milevitani episcopi, Libri sex de schismate Donatistarum, adversus Parmenianum, multo quam antehac emendatiores, cum praefatione Fr. Balduini.* Paris: Claude Fremy, 1563.

Bauduin, François, and Michael Fabricius. *Responsio ad Calvinum et Bezam, pro Francisco Balduino jurisc*ons., *cum refutatione calumniarum, de scriptura et traditione. Adiecimus eiusdem Fr. Balduini alteram responsionem ad Io. Calvinum.* Cologne: Wernerus Richwinus, 1564.

Bauduin, François. *Discours sur le faict de la Reformation de l'Eglise par Françoys Balduin, et par luy envoyé à un grand Seigneur de France, avec la response dudit Seigneur.* S.l.: s.n., 1564.

Bauduin, François. *Advis de François Balduin jurisconsulte, sur le faict de la reformation de l'Eglise, avec response à un predicant calomniateur, lequel sous un faux nom et tiltre d'un Prince de France s'opposa à l'Advis susdict.* Paris: Nicolas Chesneau, 1578.

Bedouelle, Guy, and Franco Giacone, eds. *Epistres et Evangiles pour les cinquante et deux dimanches de l'an: Texte de l'édition de Pierre de Vingle, édition critique avec introduction et notes.* Leiden: Brill, 1979.

Benedict, Philip, and Nicolas Fornerod, eds. *L'organisation et l'action des Églises Réformées de France (1557–1563): Synodes provinciaux et autres documents.* Archives des Églises Réformées de France 3, THR 504. Geneva: Droz, 2012.

Berthoud, Gabrielle. "Lettres de Réformés saisies à Lyon en août 1538." In *Etudes et documents inédits sur la Réformation en Suisse romande,* 87–111. Revue de théologie et de philosophie. Lausanne: La Concorde, 1936.

Bertius, Petrus, ed. *Illustrium et clarorum virorum epistolae selectores, superiore saeculo scriptae vel a Belgis, vel ad Belgas.* Leiden: Ludovicus Elzeverius, 1617.

Bèze, Théodore de. *De Haereticis a civili Magistratu puniendis Libellus, adversus Martini Belli farraginem, et novorum Academicorum sectam.* [Geneva]: Robert Étienne, 1554.

Bèze, Théodore de. *Ad Francisci Balduini apostatae Ecebolii convicia responsio.* Geneva: [Jean Crespin], 1563.

Bèze, Théodore de. *Responsio ad defensiones et reprehensiones Sebastiani Castellionis, quibus suam Novi Testamenti interpretationem defendere . . . conatus est.* [Geneva]: Henri Estienne, 1563.

Bèze, Théodore de. *Vie de Calvin,* in *CO* 21:1–50 and *Vita Calvini,* in *CO* 21:119–72.

Bèze, Théodore de, ed. *Histoire ecclésiastique des Églises Réformées au royaume de France.* New edition. 3 vols. Edited by G. Baum and E. Cunitz. Paris: Fischbacher, 1883–1889.

Bèze, Théodore de. *Correspondance de Théodore de Bèze.* 43 vols. Edited by Hippolyte Aubert, et al. THR. Geneva: Droz, 1960–2017.

Blesdijk, Nicolaas. *Davidis Georgii Holandi Haeresiarchae vita et doctrina, quandiu Basileae fuit: tum quid post eius mortem, cum cadavere, libris, ac reliqua eius familia actum sit. Per Rectorem et Academicam Basilien. in gratiam Amplissimi Senatus eius urbis conscripta.* [Basel]: [Hieronymus Curio], 1559.

Boer, Erik de, ed. *Congrégations et disputations.* COR ser. 7, vol. 1. Geneva: Droz, 2014.

[Bolsec, Jerome]. *Le double des lettres envoyées à Passevent Parisien, par le noble et excellent Pasquin Romain, contenant en verité la vie de Jehan Calvin.* Paris: Pierre Gaultier, 1556.

Bolsec, Jerome. *De la vie, moeurs, actes, doctrine, constance et mort de Jean Calvin.* Paris: Guillaume Chaudiere, 1577.

Bolsec, Jerome. *Histoire de la vie, moeurs, doctrine et deportements de Theodore de Beze, dit le Spectable, grand Ministre de Geneve, selon que l'on a peu voir et cognoistre jusqu'à maintenant, en attendant que luy mesme, si bon luy semble, y adjouste le reste.* Paris: Guillaume Chaudiere, 1582.

Bonnet, Jules ed. *The Letters of John Calvin, Compiled from the Original Manuscripts and Edited with Historical Notes.* 4 vols. Translated by David Constable, et al. Edinburgh and Philadelphia, 1855–1858.

Boyve, Jonas. *Annales historiques du Comté de Neuchâtel et Valangin depuis Jules-César jusqu'en 1722.* 5 vols. Bern: Edouard Mathey, 1854–1861.

Briçonnet, Guillaume, and Marguerite d'Angoulême. *Correspondance (1521–1524).* 2 vols. Edited by Christine Martineau and Michel Veissière. THR 141, 173. Geneva: Droz, 1975, 1979.

Britannus, Robert. *Orationes quatuor: De parsimonia liber, Epistolarum libri tres, De virtute et voluptate colloquium, Eiusdem carminum liber unus.* Toulouse: Nicolas Vieillard, 1536.

Britannus, Robert. *Epistolarum libri duo.* Paris: Guillaume de Bossozel, 1540.

Bruening, Michael, et al., eds. "Castellio Correspondence Project." Available at https://web.mst.edu/~bruening/Castellio%20Project/Index%20Page.htm.

Bucer, Martin. *Martin Bucers deutsche Schriften.* Martini Buceri Opera Omnia, series 1. Gütersloh: Gerd Mohn, 1960–.

Bullinger, Heinrich. *Heinrich Bullinger Briefwechsel.* Heinrich Bullinger Werke, 2nd Abteilung. Zurich: Theologischer Verlag, 1972–.

Calvin, Jean. *Response à un cauteleux et rusé moyenneur, qui sous couleur d'appaiser les troubles touchant le faict de la Religion, a tenté tous les moyens d'empescher et rompre le cours de l'Evangile par la France.* [Paris]: [Nicolas Edouard], 1561.

Calvin, Jean. *Recueil des opuscules, c'est à dire, Petits traictez de M. Jean Calvin.* Geneva: Baptiste Pinereul, 1566.

Calvin, Jean. *Tracts Relating to the Reformation,* 4 vols. Translated by Henry Beveridge. Edinburgh: Calvin Translation Society, 1844–1851.

Calvin, Jean. *Ioannis Calvini Opera quae supersunt omnia. Ad fidem editionum principum et authenticarum ex parte etiam codicum manu scriptorum, additis prolegomenis literariis, annotationibus criticis, annalibus Calvinianis indicibusque novis et copiosissmis.* 59 vols. Edited by G. Baum, E. Cunitz, and E. Reuss. Corpus Reformatorum. Braunschweig: C. A. Schwetschke and Sons, 1863–1900.

Works Cited within the *CO*

Calvin, Jean, and François Bauduin. *Apologia illustris D. Iacobi a Burgundia Fallesii Bredanique domini qua apud Imperatoriam Maiestatem inustas sibi criminationes diluit fideique suae confessionem edit. CO* 10/1:269–94.

Calvin, Jean. *Defensio orthodoxae fidei de sacra trinitate contra prodigiosos errores Michaelis Serveti Hispani, ubi ostenditur haereticos iure gladii coercendos esse et nominatim de homine hoc tam impio iuste et merito sumptum Genevae fuisse supplicium. CO* 8:453–644.

Calvin, Jean. *Dilucida explicatio sanae doctrinae de vera participatione carnis et sanguinis Christi in sacra Coena a discutiendas Heshusii nebulas. CO* 9:457–517.

Calvin, Jean. *Discours d'adieu aux ministres. CO* 9:891–92.

Calvin, Jean. *Instruction et confession de foy dont on use en l'église de Genève. CO* 22:25–74.

Calvin, Jean. *Response à certaines calomnies et blasphemes, dont quelques malins s'efforcent de rendre la doctrine de la predestination de dieu odieuse. CO* 58:199–206.

Calvin, Jean. *Responsio ad Balduini Convicia. CO* 9:561–80.

Calvin, Jean. *Responsio ad versipellem quendam mediatorem. CO* 9:525–60.

Calvin, Jean. *L'Excuse de Noble Seigneur Jacques de Bourgogne, Seigneur de Falais et de Bredam.* Edited by Alfred Cartier. Paris: Alphonse Lemerre, 1896.

Calvin, Jean. *Joannis Calvini opera selecta.* Edited by Peter Barth. Munich: C. Kaiser, 1926–36.

Calvin, Jean. *Epistolae duae. OS* 1:287–362.

Calvin, Jean. *Institutes. OS* vols. 3–5.

Calvin, Jean. *Calvin's Commentary on Seneca's De Clementia.* Edited and translated by Ford Lewis Battles and André Malan Hugo. Renaissance Text Series 3. Leiden: Brill, 1969.

Calvin, Jean. *Lettres à Monsieur et Madame de Falais.* Edited by Françoise Bonali-Fiquet. Textes Littéraires Français. Geneva: Droz, 1991.

Calvin, Jean. *Ioannis Calvini Opera omnia: denuo recognita et adnotatione, critica instructa, notisque illustrata.* Edited by Helmut Feld et al. Geneva: Droz, 1992–.

Calvin, Jean. *Contre la secte phantastique et furieuse des libertins qui se nomment spirituelz. Response à un certain holandois.* Edited by Mirjam van Veen. COR, ser. 4, vol. 1. Geneva: Droz, 2005.

Calvin, Jean. *Défense de Guillaume Farel et de ses collègues contre les calomnies du théologastre Pierre Caroli par Nicolas Des Gallars.* Translated by Jean-François Gounelle. Etudes d'histoire et de philosophie religieuses 73. Paris: Presses universitaires de France, 1994.

Calvin, Jean. *Epistolae.* Edited by Cornelis Augustijn et al. COR ser. 6. Geneva: Droz, 2005–.

Calvin, Jean. *Oeuvres.* Edited by Francis Higman and Bernard Roussel. Bibliothèque de la Pléiade. [Paris]: Gallimard, 2009.

Calvin, Jean. *Pro G. Farello et collegis ejus, adversus Petri Caroli theologastri calumnias, defensio Nicolai Gallasii.* Edited by Olivier Labarthe. COR ser. IV, vol. 6, 1–143. Geneva: Droz, 2016.

Campi, Emidio, and Ruedi Reich, eds. *Consensus Tigurinus (1549): die Einigung zwischen Heinrich Bullinger und Johannes Calvin über das Abendmahl: Werden—Wertung—Bedeutung.* Zurich: Theologischer Verlag, 2009.

Caroli, Pierre. *Refutatio blasphemiae Farellistarum in sacrosanctam Trinitatem.* Metz: Jean Palier, 1545.

Caroli, Pierre. *Refutatio blasphemiae Farellistarum in sacrosanctam Trinitatem.* Edited by Olivier Labarthe and Reinhard Bodenmann. COR, ser. IV, vol. 6, 145–242. Geneva: Droz, 2016.

Cassander, George. *Liturgica de ritu et ordine dominicae coenae celebrandae, quam celebrationem Graeci Liturgian, Latini Missam appellarunt, ex variis monumentis et probatis scriptoribus collecta.* Cologne: Arnold Birckmann, 1558.

[Cassander, George]. *De officio pii ac publicae tranquillitatis vere amantis viri, in hoc religionis dissidio.* Paris: Hercule François, 1562.

Cassander, George. *Traditionum veteris ecclesiae et sanctorum patrum defensio, adversus Io. Calvini importunas criminationes.* Cologne: Arnold Birckmann, 1564.

Castellio, Sebastian. *Dialogi sacri, latino-gallici, ad linguas moresque puerorum formandos.* [Geneva]: [Jean Girard], [1543].

Castellio, Sebastian. *Dialogorum sacrorum ad linguam simul et mores puerorum formandos, libri quatuor.* Basel: R. Winter, 1545.

Castellio, Sebastian, ed. *Ionas Propheta, heroico carmine Latino descriptus.* Basel: Oporinus, 1545.

Castellio, Sebastian, ed. *Xenophontis philosophi ac historici excellentissimi opera quae quidem extant omnia tam graeca quam latina*. Basel: Nicol. Brylingerum, 1545.

Castellio, Sebastian, ed. *Sirillus, Ecloga de nativitate Christi*. Basel: Oporinus, 1546.

Castellio, Sebastian, ed. *Mosis institutio reipublicae graeco-latina, ex Josepho in gratiam puerorum decerpta*. Basel: [Oporinus], [1546].

Castellio, Sebastian, ed. *Sibyllina oracula de graeco in latinum conversa*. Basel: Oporinus, 1546.

Castellio, Sebastian, ed. *Moses latinus ex hebraeo factus*. Basel: Oporinus, 1546.

Castellio, Sebastian, ed. *Psalterium, reliquaque sacrarum literarum carmina et precationes*. Basel: Oporinus, 1547.

Castellio, Sebastian, ed. *Biblia, interprete Sebastiano Castalione*. Basel: Oporinus, 1551.

Castellio, Sebastian, ed. *Biblia interprete Sebastiano Castalione, una cum eiusdem Annotationibus*. Basel: Oporinus, 1554.

[Castellio, Sebastian, ed.] *De Haereticis, an sint persequendi, et omnino quomodo sit cum eis agendum. . . .* [Basel]: [Oporinus], 1554.

[Castellio, Sebastian, ed. and trans.] *Theologica Germanica: Libellus aureus, hoc est, brevis et praegnans, Quo modo sit exuendus Vetus homo, induendusque novus*. Basel: Oporinus, 1557.

[Castellio, Sebastian, ed. and trans.] *La Théologie Germanique: Livret auquel est traicté comment il faut dépouiller le vieil homme, et vestir le nouveau*. Antwerp: Christofle Plantin, 1558.

Castellio, Sebastian, ed. *De Imitando Christo, contemnendisque mundi vanitatibus libellus authore Thoma Kempisio, interprete Sebastiano Castellione*. Basel: [Oporinus], 1563.

Castellio, Sebastian. *Dialogi IIII*. [Basel]: [P. Perna], 1578.

Castellio, Sebastian. *De Praedestinatione scriptum*, in *Dialogi IIII*, 332–445. [Basel]: [P. Perna], 1578.

Castellio, Sebastian. *Contra libellum Calvini, in quo ostendere conatur haereticos iure gladii coercendos esse*. [Amsterdam]: [Reiner Telle], 1612.

Castellio, Sebastian. *Dialogi IV*. Gouda, Jaspar Tournay, 1613.

Castellio, Sebastian. *Annotationes Sebastiani Castellionis in caput nonum ad Rom*. In idem, *Dialogi IV*, 2nd numbering, 1–30. Gouda: Jaspar Tournay, 1613.

Castellio, Sebastian. *Opera Sebastiani Castellionis. . . .* Haarlem: Vincent Casteleyn and David Wachtendonck, 1613.

Castellio, Sebastian. *De haereticis, an sint persequendi . . .: Reproduction en fac-similé de l'édition de 1554*. Edited by Sape van der Woude. Geneva: Droz, 1954.

Castellio, Sebastian. *De l'impunité des hérétiques, De haereticis non puniendis*. Edited by Bruno Becker and Marius F. Valkhoff. THR 118. Geneva: Droz, 1971.

Castellio, Sebastian. *De arte dubitandi et confidendi, ignorandi et sciendi*. Edited by Elisabeth Feist Hirsch. SMRT 29. Leiden: Brill, 1981.

Castellio, Sebastian. *Dialogues sacrés/Dialogi Sacri (Premier Livre)*. Edited by David Amherdt and Yves Giraud. Textes Littéraires Français 571. Geneva: Droz, 2004.

Castellio, Sebastian. *Conseil à la France désolée*. Edited by Florence Alazard, et al. Textes Littéraires Français. Geneva: Droz, 2017.

Castellio, Sebastian. *Contra Libellum Calvini: A New Critical Edition Supplemented by the Text of the Basle Manuscript-Fragment*. Edited by Uwe Plath. Cahiers d'Humanisme et Renaissance 160. Geneva: Droz, 2019.

Celsi, Mino. *In haereticis coërcendis quatenus progredi liceat, Poems, Correspondence*. Edited by Pieter G. Bietenholz. Corpus reformatorum italicorum. Naples: Prismi, 1982.

Chandieu, Antoine de la Roche. *La Confirmation de la discipline ecclesiastique, observée ès eglises reformées du royaume de France, avec la response aux objections proposées alencontre.* [Geneva]: [Henri Estienne], 1566.

Charpentier, Pierre. *Lettre de Pierre Charpentier Jurisconsulte, adressée à François Portes Candiois, par laquelle il montre que les persécutions des Eglises de France sont advenues, non par faute de ceux qui faisaient profession de la Religion, mais de ceux qui nourrissaient les factions et conspirations, qu'on appelle la Cause.* S.l.: s.n., 1572.

Charpentier, Pierre, and François Portus. *Petri Carpentarii I. C. epistola ad Franciscum Portum Cretensem, in qua docetur persecutiones ecclesiarum Galliae non culpa eorum qui religionem profitentur, sed eorum qui factionem et conspirationem (quae Causa appellatur) fovebant, accidisse, et Ad Petri Carpentarii causidici virulentam epistolam responsio Francisci Porti Cretensis, pro Causariorum, quos vocat, innocentia.* S.l.: s.n., 1573.

Chillingworth, William. *The Works of William Chillingworth, M.A. in Three Volumes.* Oxford: Oxford University Press, 1838.

Condé, Louis de Bourbon, prince de. *Mémoires de Condé.* 5 vols. London: [The Hague?], 1743.

Cordier, Mathurin. "Mathurin Cordier aux Seigneurs de Genève, 1541." *BSHPF* 15 (1866): 414–18

[Corro, Antonio del, Casiodoro de Reina, and Juan Pérez de Pineda]. *Inquisitionis Hispanicae Artes: The Arts of the Spanish Inquisition.* Edited by Marcos J. Herráiz Perja et al. Heterodoxia Iberica 2. Leiden: Brill, 2018.

Curione, Celio Secundo. *Pasquillus Ecstaticus, una cum aliis etiam aliquot sanctis pariter et lepidis Dialogis, quibus praecipua religionis nostrae Capita elegantissime explicantur.* [Geneva]: [Jean Girard], 1544.

D'Argentré, Charles du Plessis. *Collectio judiciorum de novis erroribus, qui ab initio duodecimi saeculi post incarnationem verbi, usque ad annum 1735 in ecclesia proscripti sunt et notati.* 3 vols. Paris: André Cailleau, 1728–1736.

Dufour, Théophile ed. *Un opuscule inédit de Farel: Le Résumé des Actes de la Dispute de Rive (1535).* Geneva: Charles Schuchardt, 1885.

Du Moulin, Charles. *Prima pars commentariorum in Consuetudines Parisienses.* Paris: Poncetum le Preux, 1539.

Du Moulin, Charles. *Collatio et unio quatuor Evangelistarum Domini nostri Iesu Christi, eorum serie et ordine, absque ulla confusione, permixtione vel transpositione servato, cum exacta textus illibati recognitione.* S.l.: s.n., 1565.

Du Moulin, Charles. *Caroli Molinaei Franciae et Germaniae celeberrimi iurisconsulti et in supremo Parisiorum Senatu antiqui Advocati, Opera.* Paris: Mathurin du Puis, 1658.

Du Moulin, Charles. *Caroli Molinaei Franciae et Germaniae celeberrimi jurisconsulti, et in supremo Parisiorum Senatu antiqui advocati, omnia quae extant opera.* 5 vols. Edited by François Pinsson. Paris: Charles Osmont, 1681

Works Cited in Du Moulin, *Opera* (1681 ed.)

Du Moulin, Charles. *Apologie de M. Charles du Moulin contre un livret, intitulé La deffense civile et militaire des innocens et de l'Eglise de Christ. Opera,* 5:xv–xxii.

Du Moulin, Charles. *Collatio et unio quatuor Evangelistarum Domini nostri Iesu Christi, eorum serie et ordine, absque ulla confusione, permixtione vel transpositione servato, cum exacta textus illibati recognitione. Opera,* 5:447–605.

Du Moulin, Charles. *Commentarii in consuetudines Parisienses. Opera*, 1.

Du Moulin, Charles. *Commentarius ad edictum Henrici Secundi contra parvas datas, et abusus curiae Romanae, et in antiqua edicta et senatusconsulta Franciae, contra Annatarum, et id genus abusus, multas decisiones iuris et praxes continens. Opera*, 4:297–368.

Du Moulin, Charles. *Conseil sur le fait du Concile de Trente. Opera*, 5:349–64.

Du Moulin, Charles. *Copie des articles presentez par Maistre Charles du Molin, contre les Ministres de la Religion pretendue Reformée de son temps, pour en faire informer. Opera*, 5:621–25.

[Du Moulin, Charles]. *La Defense de Messire Charles du Molin ancien Docteur, et autres gens de scavoir, et pieté, contre les calomnies des Calvinistes, et Ministres de leur secte, abus, usurpations, et erreurs d'iceux, par Maistre Simon Challudre, Professeur des Saintes Lettres. Opera*, 5:607–620.

Du Moulin, Charles. *In commentaria Philippi Decii in ius pontificium annotationes solemnes. Opera*, 5:297–346.

Du Moulin, Charles. *Traicté de l'origine, progrez, et excellence du royaume et monarchie des François et couronne de France. Opera*, 2:1025–50.

Erbe, Michael. "François Bauduin und Georg Cassander: Dokumente einer Humanistenfreundschaft." *BHR* 40 (1978): 537–60.

Farel, Guillaume. *La maniere et fasson qu'on tient en baillant le sainct baptesme . . . .* Neuchâtel: Pierre de Vingle, 1533.

Farel, Guillaume. *Le Sommaire de Guillaume Farel, réimprimé d'après l'édition de l'an 1534.* Edited by J.-G. Baum. Geneva: Jules-Guillaume Fick, 1867.

Farel, Guillaume. *Un opuscule inédit de Farel: Le résumé des actes de la Dispute de Rive (1535).* Edited by Théophile Dufour. Geneva: Charles Schuchardt, 1885.

Farel, Guillaume. *Confession de la foy, laquelle tous bourgeois et habitans de Genève et subjets du pays doivent jurer de garder et tenir. CO* 22: 77–96.

Fatio, Olivier, et al., eds. *Registres de la compagnie des pasteurs de Genève.* THR. Geneva: Droz, 1962–.

Faulenbach, Heiner, et al., eds. *Reformierte Bekenntnisschriften.* Neukirchen-Vluyn: Neukirchener Verlag, 2002–.

Geneva Consistory and Council, *L'Extrait des procedures faites et tenues contre Jean Morelli, natif de Paris et n'agueres habitant en la ville de Geneve, touchant un livre composé par luy, De la discipline ecclesiastique . . . .* Geneva: François Perrin, 1563.

Gessner, Conrad. *Vingt lettres à Jean Bauhin fils, 1563–1565.* Edited by Claude Longeon. Saint-Etienne: Université de Saint-Etienne, 1976.

Gouveia, Antonio de. *Epigrammaton libri duo, ad mortalitatem.* Lyon: Sebastian Gryphius, 1539.

Herminjard, A.-L. *Correspondance des Réformateurs dans les pays de langue française.* 9 vols. Geneva: H. Georg, 1866–1897.

Heshusius, Tilemann. *De praesentia corporis Christi in Coena Domini.* Jena: Ritzenhain, 1560.

Hochuli Dubui, Paule, et al., eds. *Registres du Conseil de Genève à l'époque de Calvin.* THR. Geneva: Droz, 2003–.

Houbraque, Guillaume. *Traitté monstrant comme il faut proceder à la correction des vices, et scandales: et à l'excommunication, en l'Eglise chrestienne.* Orléans: Loys Rabier, 1567.

Ignatius of Loyola. *The Spiritual Exercises.* Translated by Elder Mullan, S. J. New York: P. J. Kenedy & Sons, 1914.

Ignatius of Loyola. *Exercitia Spiritualia: Textuum antiquissimorum nova editio lexicon textus Hispani.* Edited by Iosephus Calveras and Candidus de Dalmases. Monumenta Historica Societatis Iesu 100. Rome: Institutum Historicum Societatis Iesu, 1969.

Jussie, Jeanne de. *Petite chronique: Einleitung, Edition, Kommentar.* Edited by Helmut Feld. Veröffentlichungen des Instituts für europäische Geschichte Mainz, Abteilung abendländische Religionsgeschichte 167. Mainz: Philipp von Zabern, 1996.

Jussie, Jeanne de. *The Short Chronicle: A Poor Clare's Account of the Reformation of Geneva.* Edited and translated by Carrie F. Klaus. The Other Voice in Early Modern Europe. Chicago: University of Chicago Press, 2006.

Languet, Hubert. *Arcana seculi decimi sexti, Huberti Languet legati, dum viveret, et consiliarii Saxonici Epistolae secretae.* Edited by J. P. Ludwig. Halle (Saale): J. F. Zeitlerus and H. G. Musselius, 1699.

L'Archer, Jean. *Canones Conciliorum Omnium, qui a primo Apostolorum Concilio, usque ad postremum sub Eugenio IIII. Pont. Max. celebratum, a S. Patribus sunt constituti.* Basel: Oporinus, 1553.

Łaski, Jan. *Forma ac ratio tota ecclesiastici ministerii, in peregrinorum, potissimum vero Germanorum Ecclesia: instituta Londini in Anglia....* [Frankfurt], [1555].

Łaski, Jan. *Toute la forme et maniere du Ministere Ecclesiastique, en l'Eglise des estrangers, dressée à Londres en Angleterre....* [Emden]: [Gellius Ctematius], 1556.

Lefèvre d'Etaples, Jacques *S. Pauli Epistolae XIV. ex Vulgata editione, adiecta intelligentia ex Graeco, cum commentariis Jacobi Fabri, Stapulensis.* Paris: Henri Estienne, 1512.

Lefèvre d'Etaples, Jacques. *Quincuplex Psalterium.* THR 170. Geneva: Droz, 1979.

Locke, John. *The Correspondence of John Locke.* Edited by E. S. de Beer. Oxford: Clarendon Press, 1976–.

Luther, Martin. *Luther's Works, American Edition.* Edited by Jaroslav Pelikan, et al. St. Louis: Concordia, and Philadelphia: Fortress, 1955–.

[Malescot, Étienne de]. *Censure des erreurs de M. Charles du Moulin de n'agueres mis en lumiere en un certain livre qu'il a intitulé Union ou Harmonie des quatre Evangelistes.* "Annibal d'Auvergne," author's pseudonym. S.l.: s.n., 1566.

Malingre, [Thomas]. *Moralité de la maladie de Chrestienté, à xiii personnages: en laquelle sont monstrez plusieurs abuz, advenuz au monde, par la poison de peche et l'hypocrisie des hereticques.* [Neuchâtel]: [Pierre de Vingle], 1533.

Malingre, [Thomas]. *Noelz nouveaulx.* [Neuchâtel]: [Pierre de Vingle], [1533?].

Malingre, [Thomas]. *S'ensuivent plusieurs belles et bonnes chansons, que les chrestiens peuvent chanter en grande affection de cueur.* [Neuchâtel]: [Pierre de Vingle], 1533.

Malingre, [Thomas]. *Chansons nouvelles demonstrantz plusieurs erreurs et faulsetez, desquelles le paovre monde est remply par les ministres de Satan.* [Neuchâtel]: [Pierre de Vingle], [1534?].

Malingre, [Thomas]. *Indice des principales matieres contenues en la Bible.* Geneva: Jean Girard, 1543.

Malingre, [Thomas]. *L'Epistre de M. Malingre envoyée à Clement Marot, en laquelle est demandée la cause de son departement de France.* Basel: Jacques Estauge, 1546.

Marcourt, Antoine. *Le livre des marchans, fort utile à toutes gens.* [Neuchâtel]: [Pierre de Vingle], 1533.

Marcourt, Antoine. *Articles veritables sur les horribles, grandz et importables abuz de la Messe papalle.* [Neuchâtel]: [Pierre de Vingle], 1534.

Marcourt, Antoine. *Petit traicté tres utile et salutaire de la saincte eucharistie de nostre Seigneur Jesuchrist.* [Neuchâtel]: [Pierre de Vingle], 1534.

Marcourt, Antoine, and "Cephas Geranius." *Declaration de la Messe, le fruict dicelle, la cause et moyen pourquoy et comment on la doibt maintenir.* [Neuchâtel]: [Pierre de Vingle], [1534].

Marcourt, Antoine. *Le Livre des marchans d'Antoine Marcourt: Une satire anticléricale au service de la Réforme.* Edited by Geneviève Gross. Textes littéraires de la Renaissance 17. Paris: Honoré Champion, 2016.

Monluc, Jean de. *Cleri Valentini et Dyensis Reformatio, restitutoque, ex sacris Patrum Conciliis excerpta.* Paris: Federici Morelli, 1558.

Monluc, Jean de. *Deux Instructions, et Trois Epistres, faictes, et envoyées au Clergé et peuple de Valence, et de Dye, par leur Evesque.* Paris: M. de Vascosan, 1558.

Monluc, Jean de. *Sermons de l'Evesque de Valence sur certains poincts de la religion, receuillis fidelement, ainsi qu'ilz ont esté prononcez. Autres Sermons du mesme aucteur, servans à descouvrir, par tesmoignage de l'Escriture saincte, les fautes qu'on commet sur les Dix Commandemens de la Loy. Plus un Sermon à son Clergé fait au Sene de Juillet 1557.* Paris: M. Vascosan, 1558.

Monluc, Jean de. *Familere explication des articles de la foy.* Lyon: Guillaume Regnoult, 1561.

Monluc, Jean de. *Sermons de l'evesque de Valence sur l'Oraison Dominicale.* Lyon: Guillaume Regnoult, 1561.

Montaigne, Michel de. *Essaies.* 3 vols. Edited by Pierre Michel. Paris: Librairie Générale Française 1972.

Morély, Jean. *Traicté de la discipline et police chrestienne.* Lyon: Jean de Tournes, 1562.

Ochino, Bernardino. *Expositio Epistolae divi Pauli ad Romanos, de italico in latinum translata.* Translated by Sebastian Castellio. Augsburg: Philippus Ulhardus, [1545].

Ochino, Bernardino. *Dialogi XXX, in duos libros divisi quorum primus est de Messia, continetque dialogos XVIII; secundus est, cum de rebus variis, tum potissimum de Trinitate.* Translated by Sebastian Castellio. Basel: Pietro Perna, 1563.

Olin, John C., ed. *A Reformation Debate: Sadoleto's Letter to the Genevans and Calvin's Reply.* New York: Fordham University Press, 2000. [New York, 1966].

Olivétan, Pierre, ed. *La Bible, qui est toute la saincte escripture.* Neuchâtel: Pierre de Vingle, 1535.

Perrenot, Frédéric, Sieur de Champagney. *Mémoires de Frédéric Perrenot, Sieur de Champagney 1573–1590, avec notice et annotations.* Edited by A. L. P. de Robaulx de Soumoy. Brussels: Société de l'histoire de Belgique, 1860.

Piaget, Arthur ed. *Les actes de la Dispute de Lausanne 1536, publiés intégralement d'après le manuscrit de Berne.* Mémoires de l'Université de Neuchâtel 6. Neuchâtel: Secrétariat de l'Université, 1928.

Pierrefleur, [Guillaume de]. *Mémoires de Pierrefleur: Édition critique avec une introduction et des notes.* Edited by Louis Junod. Lausanne: La Concorde, 1933.

Peter, Rudolphe, and Jean Rott, eds. *Les lettres à Calvin de la collection Sarrau.* Paris: Presses Universitaires de France, 1972.

Portus, François. *Response de Francois Portus Candiot, aux lettres diffamatoires de Pierre Carpentier Advocat, pour l'innocence des fideles serviteurs de Dieu, et obeissans subjets du Roy, massacrez le 24. jour d'Aoust 1572, appellez factieux par ce plaidereau.* S.l.: s.n., 1574.

Quick, John. *Synodicon in Gallia reformata, or the Acts, Decisions, Decrees, and Canons of those Famous National Councils of the Reformed Churches in France.* London: For T. Parkhurst and J. Robinson, 1692.

Ramus, Petrus. *Testamentum Petri Rami cum senatus consulto et promulgatione professionis institutae ab ipso testatore.* Paris: Ioannis Richerius, 1576.

Ramus Petrus, and Omer Talon. *Praefationes, Epistolae, Orationes.* Paris: apud Dionysium Vellensem, 1577.

[Rhellican, Johannes, and Antoine Morelet du Museau, trans.]. *La Maniere, ordre et fasson d'espouser et confirmer les mariages devant la compaignie et assemblee des fideles . . . .* Geneva: Wigant Köln, 1537.

Rice, Eugene F., Jr., ed. *The Prefatory Epistles of Jacques Lefèvre d'Etaples and Related Texts.* New York: Columbia University Press, 1972.

Roussel, Gérard. *Forme de visite de diocese.* In Charles Schmidt, *Gérard Roussel, Prédicateur de la Reine Marguerite de Navarre: Mémoire servant à l'histoire des premières tentatives faites pour introduire la Réformation en France,* 226–39. Strasbourg: Schmidt & Grucker, 1845.

Roussel, Gérard. *Familiere exposition du simbole, de la loy et oraison dominicale en forme de colloque.* In Paul J. Landa, "The Reformed Theology of Gérard Roussel, Bishop of Oloron (1536–1555)," 269–599. PhD diss., Vanderbilt University, 1976.

Scaliger, Joseph. *Scaligeriana, sive excerpta ex ore Josephi Scaligeri,* 2nd ed. The Hague: Adrian Ulacq, 1668.

Sources du Droit Suisse/Sammlung Schweizerischer Rechtsquellen. Aarau: Sauerländer, 1902–. Available at https://www.ssrq-sds-fds.ch/online/cantons.html.

Viret, Pierre. *De la vertu et usage du ministere de la Parolle de Dieu, et des Sacremens dependans d'icelle.* [Geneva]: [Jean Girard], 1548.

Viret, Pierre. *Disputations chrestiennes, touchant l'estat des trepassez, faite par dialogues.* [Geneva]: [Jean Girard], 1552.

Viret, Pierre. *L'Interim fait par dialogues.* Edited by Guy R. Mermier. American University Studies, ser. 2, 14. New York: Peter Lang, 1985.

Viret, Pierre. *Epistolae Petri Vireti: The Previously Unedited Letters and a Register of Pierre Viret's Correspondence.* Edited by Michael Bruening. THR 494. Geneva: Droz, 2012.

Vuilleumier, Henri. "Quelques pages inédites d'un réformateur trop peu connu." *Revue de théologie et de philosophie* 19 (1886): 313–39.

Wildermann, Ansgar, ed. *La visite des églises du diocèse de Lausanne en 1453.* 2 vols. Mémoires et documents publiés par la société d'histoire de la Suisse romande ser. 3, 19–20. Lausanne: Société d'histoire de la Suisse romande, 1993.

Secondary Sources

Backus, Irena. *Life Writing in Reformation Europe: Lives of Reformers by Friends, Disciples and Foes.* St. Andrews Studies in Reformation History. Burlington, VT: Ashgate, 2008.

Backus, Irena. "Moses, Plato and Flavius Josephus: Castellio's Conceptions of Sacred and Profane in His Latin Versions of the Bible." In *Shaping the Bible in the Reformation: Books, Scholars and Their Readers in the Sixteenth Century,* edited by Bruce Gordon and Matthew McLean, 143–65. Leiden: Brill, 2012.

Bähler, Edouard. "Petrus Caroli und Johannes Calvin: Ein Beitrag zur Geschichte und Kultur der Reformationszeit." *Jahrbuch für schweizerische Geschichte* 29 (1904): 39–168.

Bähler, Edouard. *Jean Le Comte de la Croix: Ein Beitrag zur Reformationsgeschichte der Westschweiz.* Biel: Ernst Kuhn, 1895.

Bainton, Roland H. *Hunted Heretic: The Life and Death of Michael Servetus, 1511–1553.* Boston: Beacon Press, 1953.

Balserak, Jon. *John Calvin as Sixteenth-Century Prophet*. Oxford: Oxford University Press, 2014.

Barnaud, Jean. *Pierre Viret: Sa vie et son oeuvre (1511-1571)*. Saint-Amans: G. Carayol, 1911.

Becker, Judith. "La constitution ecclésiastique de Jean a Lasco pour l'Eglise néerlandaise de Londres et son influence en France." In *Entre Calvinistes et Catholiques: Les relations religieuses entre la France et les Pays-Bas du Nord (XVIe–XVIIIe siècle)*, edited by Yves Krumenacker and Olivier Christin, 59–75. Rennes: Presses Universitaires de Rennes, 2010.

Bedouelle, Guy. *Lefèvre d'Etaples et l'intelligence des Ecritures*. THR 152. Geneva: Droz, 1976.

Bedouelle, Guy. *Le Quincuplex Psalterium de Lefèvre d'Etaples: Un guide de lecture*. THR 171. Geneva: Droz, 1979.

Benedict, Philip. "Global? Has Reformation History Even Gotten Transnational Yet?" *ARG* 108 (2017): 52–62.

Benedict, Philip. "The Spread of Protestantism in Francophone Europe in the First Century of the Reformation." *ARG* 109 (2018): 7–52.

Benedict, Philip, and Nicolas Fornerod. "Conflict and Dissidence within the Early French Reformed Churches." In *Crossing Traditions: Essays on the Reformation and Intellectual History, in Honor of Irena Backus*, edited by Maria-Cristina Pitassi and Daniela Solfaroli Camillocci, 15–31. Leiden: Brill, 2018.

Benedict, Philip. *Season of Conspiracy: Calvin, the French Reformed Churches, and Protestant Plotting in the Reign of Francis II (1559-60)*. Transactions of the American Philosophical Society 108, pt. 5. Philadelphia: American Philosophical Society Press, 2020.

Berthoud, Gabrielle. *Antoine Marcourt: Réformateur et pamphlétaire du 'Livre des Marchans' aux Placards de 1534*. THR 129. Geneva: Droz, 1973.

Bertini, Aldo. "Giovanni Bernardino Bonifacio: Sein Leben und seine Beziehungen zu Basel." *Basler Zeitschrift für Geschichte und Altertumskunde* 47 (1948): 19–84.

Besson, Edouard. "Jean Le Comte de la Croix: Un réformateur peu connu." *Berner Taschenbuch* 26 (1876): 139–68.

Bietenholz, Peter G. *Basle and France in the Sixteenth Century: The Basle Humanists and Printers in their Contacts with Francophone Culture*. THR 112. Geneva: Droz, 1971.

Bietenholz, Peter. "Mino Celsi and the Toleration Controversy of the Sixteenth Century." *BHR* 34 (1972): 31–47.

Bodenmann, Reinhard. "Le réformateur Jean Le Comte (1500-1572): De l'oublie à une mémoire remodelée." *Zwingliana* 42 (2015): 177–93.

Bodenmann, Reinhard. *Les Perdants: Pierre Caroli et les débuts de la Réforme en Romandie*. Nugae humanisticae. Turnhout: Brepols, 2016.

Boehmer, Edward. *Bibliotheca Wiffeniana: Spanish Reformers of Two Centuries from 1520*. Strasbourg: Trübner, 1883.

Boer, Erik de. *The Genevan School of the Prophets: The congrégations of the Company of Pastors and their Influence in 16th Century Europe*. THR 512. Geneva: Droz, 2012.

Boesch, Paul. "Zwingli-Gedichte (1539) des Andreas Zebedeus und des Rudolph Gwalther." *Zwingliana* 9, no. 4 (1959): 208–20.

Bonnet, Jules. *Nouveaux récits du seizième siècle*. Paris: Grassart, 1870.

Bouwsma, William. *John Calvin: A Sixteenth Century Portrait*. New York: Oxford University Press, 1988.

Brodeau, Julien. *La vie de Maistre Charles du Molin, advocat au Parlement de Paris, tirée des titres de sa maison, de ses propres escrits, de l'histoire du temps, des registres de la Cour, et autres monuments publics. Et sa mort Chrestienne et Catholique.* Paris: Jean Guignard, 1654.

Brodeau, Julien. *La vie de Maistre Charles Du Molin, advocat en parlement.* In Charles Du Moulin, *Opera*, 1:1–60.

Bruening, Michael. *Calvinism's First Battleground: Conflict and Reform in the Pays de Vaud, 1528–1559*, Studies in Early Modern Religious Reforms 4. Dordrecht: Springer, 2005.

Bruening, Michael. "'La nouvelle réformation de la Lausanne': The Proposal by the Ministers of Lausanne on Ecclesiastical Discipline (June 1558)." *BHR* 68 (2006): 21–50.

Bruening, Michael. "Pierre Viret and Geneva." *ARG* 99 (2008): 175–97.

Bruening, Michael. "Triumvirs, Patriarchs, or Friends? Evaluating the Relationship between Calvin, Viret, and Farel." *Reformation & Renaissance Review* 10 (2008): 125–36.

Bruening, Michael. "The Lausanne Theses on the Ministry and the Sacraments." *Zwingliana* 44 (2017): 417–43.

Bruening, Michael, ed. *A Reformation Sourcebook: Documents from an Age of Debate.* Toronto: University of Toronto Press, 2017.

Bruening, Michael. "Before the *Histoire Ecclésiastique*: Theodore Beza's Unknown Apologetic History of the Lausanne Pastors and Professors." In *Beza at 500: New Perspectives on an Old Reformer*, edited by Kirk Summers and Scott Manetsch, 57–77. Göttingen: Vandenhoek & Ruprecht, 2020.

Bruening, Michael. "Guillaume Farel et les réformateurs de langue allemande: Les origines de la doctrine réformée dans l'espace romand." In *La construction internationale de la Réforme et l'espace romand à l'époque de Luther*, edited by Daniela Solfaroli Camillocci et al. Paris: Classiques Garnier, forthcoming.

Buisson, Ferdinand. *Sébastien Castellion: Sa vie et son oeuvre (1515–1563), Étude sur les origines du Protestantisme libéral français.* 2 vols. Paris: Hachette, 1892.

Buisson, Ferdinand. *Sébastien Castellion: Sa vie et son oeuvre (1515–1563).* 2 vols. in 1. Edited by Max Engammare. Geneva: Droz, (1892) 2010.

Burnett, Amy Nelson. *Teaching the Reformation: Ministers and their Message in Basel, 1529–1629.* Oxford Studies in Historical Theology. New York: Oxford University Press, 2006.

Burnett, Amy Nelson. *Karlstadt and the Origins of the Eucharistic Controversy: A Study in the Circulation of Ideas.* Oxford Studies in Historical Theology. New York: Oxford University Press, 2011.

Büsser, Fritz, *Die Prophezei: Humanismus und Reformation in Zürich: Ausgewählte Aufsätze und Vorträge.* Zürcher Beiträge zur Reformationsgeschichte 17. Bern: Peter Lang, 1994.

Campi, Emidio. *Shifting Patterns of Reformed Tradition.* Reformed Historical Theology 27. Göttingen: Vandenhoeck & Ruprecht, 2014.

Cantimori, Delio. *Eretici italiani del Cinquecento: Ricerche storiche.* Biblioteca storica Sansoni. Florence: G. C. Sansoni, 1939.

Caravale, Giorgio. *Storia di una doppia censura: Gli* Stratagemmi di Satana *di Giacomo Aconcio nell'Europa del Seicento.* Pisa: Edizioni della Normale, 2013.

Carbonnier, Jean. "Dumoulin à Tubingue." *Revue générale de droit, de la législation et de la jurisprudence en France et à l'étranger* 40 (1936): 194–209.

Carbonnier-Burkard, Marianne. "'L'Histoire Ecclésiastique des Églises Réformées . . . : La construction Bèzienne d'un 'Corps d'histoire.'" In *Théodore de Bèze (1519–1605): Actes du Colloque de Genève (septembre 2005)*, edited by Irena Backus, 145–61. THR 424. Geneva: Droz, 2007.

Carbonnier-Burkard, Marianne. "Une cène inconnue: Morceau choisi de la liturgie bernoise en version française (1537)." In *Bible, Histoire et Société: Mélanges offerts à Bernard Roussel*, edited by R. Gerald Hobbs and Annie Noblesse-Rocher, 323–44. Bibliothèque de l'École des Hautes Études, Sciences Religieuses 163. Turnhout: Brepols, 2013.

Chevalier, Bernard. *Guillaume Briçonnet (v. 1445–1514), un cardinal-ministre au début de la Renaissance: Marchand, financier, homme d'État et prince de l'Église*. Collection 'Histoire'. Rennes: Presses universitaires de Rennes, 2005.

Collinson, Patrick. *Archbishop Grindal, 1519–1583: The Struggle for a Reformed Church*. Berkeley: University of California Press, 1979.

Comité Farel. *Guillaume Farel 1489–1565: Biographie nouvelle écrite d'après les documents originaux par un groupe d'historiens, professeurs et pasteurs de Suisse, de France et d'Italie*. Neuchâtel: Delachaux & Niestlé S.A., 1930.

Conner, Philip. "Huguenot Identities during the Wars of Religion: The Churches of Le Mans and Montauban Compared." *Journal of Ecclesiastical History* 54 (2003): 23–39.

Coquerel, A. *Précis de l'histoire de l'Église Réformée de Paris d'après des documents en grande partie inédits, Première époque, 1512–1594, de l'origine à l'église à l'Édit de Nantes*. Paris: Librairies Protestantes, 1862.

Crousaz, Karine. *L'Académie de Lausanne entre Humanisme et Réforme (ca. 1537–1560)*. Education and Society in the Middle Ages and Renaissance 41. Leiden: Brill, 2012.

Crousaz, Karine. "Les auteurs païens dans les *Colloques* d'Érasme et de Maturin Cordier." In *Crossing Traditions: Essays on the Reformation and Intellectual History in Honour of Irena Backus*, edited by Maria-Cristina Pitassi and Daniela Solfaroli Camillocci, 311–30. SMRT 212. Leiden: Brill, 2017.

Crouzet, Denis. *La Genèse de la Réforme française*. Regards sur l'histoire 109. Paris: Sedes, 1996.

Damasio, Antonio. *Descartes' Error: Emotion, Reason, and the Human Brain*. New York: Putnam, 1994.

Daussy, Hughes. *Le Parti Huguenot: Chronique d'une désillusion (1557–1572)*. 2nd ed. Titre courant 54. Geneva: Droz, 2015.

Degert, Antoine. "Procès de huit évêques français suspects de Calvinisme." *Revue des questions historiques*, n.s. 32 (July 1904): 61–108.

Delaborde, Jules. "Antoine de Croÿ, prince de Porcien." *BSHPF* 18 (1869): 2–26, 124–37, 513–29.

Denis, Philippe. *Les églises d'étrangers en pays rhénans, 1538–1564*. Bibliothèque de la Faculté de Philosophie et Lettres de l'Université de Liège 242. Paris: Les Belles Lettres, 1984.

Denis, Philippe. "Viret et Morély: Les raisons d'un silence." *BHR* 54 (1992): 395–409.

Denis, Philippe, and Jean Rott. *Jean Morély (ca. 1524–ca. 1594) et l'utopie d'une démocratie dans l'église*. THR 278. Geneva: Droz, 1993.

Dictionnaire historique de la Suisse. Available at https://hls-dhs-dss.ch/fr/.

Dolan, John Patrick. *The Influence of Erasmus, Witzel and Cassander in the Church Ordinances and Reform Proposals of the United Duchies of Cleve during the Middle Decades of the 16th Century*. Reformationsgeschichtliche Studien und Texte 83. Münster: Aschendorffsche Verlagsbuchhandlung, 1957.

Doumergue, Émile. *Jean Calvin: Les hommes et les choses de son temps*. 7 vols. Lausanne and Neuilly-sur-Seine, 1899–1927.

Droz, Eugénie. "Pierre de Vingle, l'imprimeur de Farel." In *Aspects de la propagande religieuse*, 38–78. THR 28. Geneva: Droz, 1957.

Droz, Eugénie. "Castelloniana." In E. Droz, *Chemins de l'hérésie: Textes et documents*, 4 vols., 2:325–432. Geneva: Slatkine, 1970–1976.

Du Plessis, Toussaints. *Histoire de l'Église de Meaux, avec des notes ou dissertations, et les pièces justificatives*. 2 vols. Paris: Julien-Michel Gandouin and Pierre François Giffart, 1731.

Ducaunnés-Duval, Ariste. *Inventaire sommaire des registres de La Jurade 1520 à 1783*. Archives Municipales de Bordeaux 8. Bordeaux: F. Pech, 1905.

Dufour, Théophile. *Notice bibliographique sur le Catéchisme et la Confession de foi de Calvin (1537) et sur les autres livres imprimés à Genève et à Neuchâtel dans les premiers temps de la Réforme (1533–1540)*. Geneva: Jules-Guillaume Fick, 1878.

Duquesne, Joseph. "François Bauduin et la Réforme." *Bulletin de l'Académie delphinale*, ser. 5, t. 9 (1914–1917): 55–108.

Eells, Hastings. *Martin Bucer*. New Haven, CT: Yale University Press, 1931.

Ehrman, Bart. *The Orthodox Corruption of Scripture: The Effect of Early Christological Controversies on the Text of the New Testament*. New York: Oxford University Press, 1993.

Ehrman, Bart. *Lost Christianities: The Battle for Scripture and the Faiths We Never Knew*. New York: Oxford University Press, 2003.

Eire, Carlos. *War against the Idols: The Reformation of Worship from Erasmus to Calvin*. New York: Cambridge University Press, 1986.

Engammare, Max. *Le Cantique des Cantiques à la Renaissance: Étude et Bibliographie*. THR 277. Geneva: Droz, 1993.

Erbe, Michael. *François Bauduin (1520–1573): Biographie eines Humanisten*. Quellen und Forschungen zur Reformationsgeschichte 46. Gütersloh: Gerd Mohn, 1978.

Eskhult, Josef. "Castellion, traducteur de la Bible latine: Image de soi et réception durant la Renaissance et l'Âge classique." In *Sébastien Castellion: Des Écritures à l'écriture*. Edited by Marie-Christine Gomez-Géraud, 109–38. Paris: Classiques Garnier, 2013.

Estes, James. "*Officium principis christiani*: Erasmus and the Origins of the Protestant State Church." *ARG* 83 (1992): 49–72.

Farge, James K. *Biographical Register of Paris Doctors of Theology 1500–1536*. Subsidia Mediaevalia 10. Toronto: Pontifical Institute of Mediaeval Studies, 1980.

Ganoczy, Alexandre. *The Young Calvin*. Translated by David Foxgrover and Wade Provo. Edinburgh: T&T Clark, 1987 [Wiesbaden, 1966].

Gaullieur, Ernest. *Histoire du Collège de Guyenne, d'après un grand nombre de documents inédits*. Paris: Sandoz et Fischbacher, 1874.

Gaullieur, Ernest. *Histoire de la Réformation à Bordeaux, et dans le ressort du Parlement de Guyenne*. Paris: H. Champion, 1884.

Gerig, J. L. "Le collège de la Trinité à Lyon avant 1540." *Revue de la Renaissance* 9 (1908): 76–95, 10 (1909): 137–57, 204–15.

Gilliard, Charles. *La conquête du Pays de Vaud par les Bernois*. Histoire Helvétique. Lausanne: L'Aire, 1985 [Lausanne, 1935].

Gilmont, Jean-François. "L'Oeuvre imprimé de Guillaume Farel." In *Actes du Colloque Guillaume Farel, Neuchâtel, 29 septembre–1er octobre 1980*, 2 vols., edited by Pierre

Barthel, Rémy Scheurer, and Richard Stauffer, 2:105–45. Cahiers de la Revue de Théologie et de Philosophie 9. Geneva: Revue de théologie et de philosophie, 1983.

Gilmont, Jean-François. *Insupportable mais fascinant: Jean Calvin, ses amis, ses ennemis, et les autres.* Nugae humanisticae sub signo Erasmi. Turnhout: Brepols, Musée de la Maison d'Érasme, 2012.

Goeury, Julien. *La Muse du Consistoire: Une histoire des pasteurs poètes des origines de la Réforme jusqu'à la révocation de l'édit de Nantes.* Cahiers d'Humanisme et Renaissance 133. Geneva: Droz, 2016.

Gordon, Bruce. *Clerical Discipline and the Rural Reformation: The Synod in Zürich, 1532–1580.* Zürcher Beiträge zur Reformationsgeschichte 16. Bern: Peter Lang, 1992.

Gordon, Bruce. *The Swiss Reformation.* New Frontiers in History. Manchester, UK: Manchester University Press, 2002.

Gordon, Bruce. *Calvin.* New Haven, CT: Yale University Press, 2009.

Groër, Georgette Brasart de. "Le Collège, agent d'infiltration de la Réforme: Barthelémy Aneau au Collège de la Trinité." In *Aspects de la propagande religieuse,* 167–75. THR 28. Geneva: Droz, 1957.

Grosse, Christian. *L'excommunication de Philibert Berthelier: Histoire d'un conflit d'identité aux premiers temps de la Réforme genevoise, 1547–1555.* Geneva: Société d'histoire et d'archéologie de Genève, 1995.

Grosse, Christian, and Nicolas Fornerod. "Une troisième voie entre le 'modèle' genevois de discipline ecclésiastique et celui de Jean Morély? Guillaume Houbraque et son traité sur la correction des vices et l'excommunication (1567)." *Revue de théologie et de philosophie* 148 (2016): 713–31.

Gross, Geneviève. "Pratique du ministère et terrains d'activité de deux acteurs de la Réforme: Jean Reymond Merlin (1510–1578) et Jean Lecomte de la Croix (1500–1572)." PhD diss., University of Geneva, 2012.

Guggisberg, Hans R. *Basel in the Sixteenth Century: Aspects of the City Republic before, during, and after the Reformation.* St. Louis, MO: Center for Reformation Research, 1982.

Guggisberg, Hans R. *Sebastian Castellio, 1515–1563: Humanist and Defender of Religious Toleration in a Confessional Age.* Edited and translated by Bruce Gordon. St. Andrews Studies in Reformation History. Aldershot, UK: Ashgate, 2003 [Göttingen, 1997].

Guiraud, Louis. *Études sur la Réforme à Montpellier.* 2 vols. Montpellier: Louis Valat, 1918.

Gunnoe, Charles D. *Thomas Erastus and the Palatinate: A Renaissance Physician in the Second Reformation.* Brill's Series in Church History 48. Leiden: Brill, 2010.

Haag, Eugène and Emile. *La France Protestante, ou vies des Protestants français qui se sont fait un nom dans l'histoire.* 9 vols. Paris, 1846–1859.

Haag, Eugène and Emile. *La France Protestante,* 2nd ed. 6 vols. (incomplete). Edited by Henri Bordier. Paris, 1877–1888.

Haidt, Jonathan. "The New Synthesis in Moral Psychology." *Science* 316 (2007): 998–1002.

Haidt, Jonathan. *The Righteous Mind: Why Good People Are Divided by Politics and Religion.* New York: Pantheon, 2012.

Harrison, John, and Peter Laslett. *The Library of John Locke.* 2nd ed. Oxford: Clarendon Press, (1965) 1971.

Heller, Henry. "The Evangelicalism of Lefèvre d'Étaples: 1525." *Studies in the Renaissance* 19 (1972): 42–77.

Heller, Henry. *Iron and Blood: Civil Wars in Sixteenth-Century France.* Montreal: McGill-Queen's University Press, 1991.

Higman, Francis M. *Piety and the People: Religious Printing in French, 1511–1551.* St. Andrews Studies in Reformation History. Aldershot, UK: Ashgate, 1996.

Hillerbrand, Hans, ed. *Oxford Encyclopedia of the Reformation.* 4 vols. New York: Oxford University Press, 1996.

Hogu, Louis. *Jean de l'Espine, moraliste et théologien (1505?–1597): Sa vie, son oeuvre, ses idées.* Paris: H. Champion, 1913.

Holtrop, Philip C. *The Bolsec Controversy on Predestination from 1551 to 1555: The Statements of Jerome Bolsec, and the Responses of John Calvin, Theodore Beza, and Other Reformed Theologians.* Lewiston, NY: Edwin Mellen Press, 1993.

Holtz, Grégoire. "Nicolas Bergeron (1584/1588) et la construction de la culture gallicane." *Revue de l'histoire des religions* 3 (2009): 429–43.

Holtz, Grégoire. *L'ombre de l'auteur: Pierre Bergeron et l'écriture du voyage à la fin de la Renaissance.* THR 480. Geneva: Droz, 2011.

Höpfl, Harro. *The Christian Polity of John Calvin.* New York: Cambridge University Press, 1982.

Hughes, Philip Edgcumbe. *Lefèvre: Pioneer of Ecclesiastical Renewal in France.* Grand Rapids, MI: Eerdmans, 1984.

Hundeshagen, Karl Bernard. *Die Conflikte des Zwinglianismus, des Luthertums und des Calvinismus in der Bernischen Landeskirche 1532–1558.* Bern: C. A. Jenni, 1842.

Jenkins, Gary. *Calvin's Tormentors: Understanding the Conflicts That Shaped the Reformer.* Grand Rapids, MI: Baker, 2018.

Junod, Eric, ed. *La Dispute de Lausanne (1536): La théologie Réformée après Zwingli et avant Calvin.* Bibliothèque historique vaudoise 90. Lausanne: Bibliothèque historique vaudoise, 1988.

Jourda, Pierre. *Marguerite d'Angoulême, Duchesse d'Alençon, Reine de Navarre (1492–1549): Étude biographique et littéraire.* 2 vols. Bibliothèque littéraire de la Renaissance. Paris: Honoré Champion, 1930.

Kim, Seong-Hak. *Michel de L'Hôpital: The Vision of a Reformist Chancellor during the French Religious Wars,* Sixteenth Century Essays and Studies 36. Kirksville, MO: Sixteenth Century Journal Publishers, 1997.

Kinder, A. Gordon. "Juan Pérez de Pineda (Pierius): A Spanish Calvinist Minister of the Gospel in Sixteenth-Century Geneva." *Bulletin of Hispanic Studies* 53 (1976): 283–300.

Kingdon, Robert. *Geneva and the Coming of the Wars of Religion in France, 1555–1563.* Reprint edition. Cahiers d'Humanisme et Renaissance 82. Geneva: Droz, 2007 [1956].

Kingdon, Robert M. "Genève et les Réformés français: Le cas d'Hughes Sureau, dit Du Rosier (1565–1574)." *Bulletin de la Société d'histoire et d'archéologie de Genève* 12 (1962): 77–87.

Kingdon, Robert M. "Problems of Religious Choice for Sixteenth Century Frenchmen." *Journal of Religious History* 4 (1966): 105–12.

Kingdon, Robert M. *Geneva and the Consolidation of the French Protestant Movement 1564–1572: A Contribution to the History of Congregationalism, Presbyterianism, and Calvinist Resistance Theory.* Madison: University of Wisconsin Press, 1967.

Kingdon, Robert M. "Popular Reactions to the Debate between Bolsec and Calvin." In *Calvin: Erbe und Auftrag, Festschrift für Wilhelm Heinrich Neuser zum 65. Geburstag,* edited by Willem van 't Spijker, 138–45. Kampen: Kok Pharos, 1991.

Kingdon, Robert M. "La discipline ecclésiastique vue de Zurich et Genève au temps de la Réformation: L'usage de Matthieu 18, 15–17 par les réformateurs." *Revue de théologie et de philosophie* 133 (2001): 343–55.

Kingdon, Robert, and John Witte, Jr. *Sex, Marriage, and Family in John Calvin's Geneva*. Grand Rapids, MI: Eerdmans, 2005.

Kingdon, Robert M. "Confessionalism in Calvin's Geneva." *ARG* 96 (2005): 109–16.

Kingdon, Robert, and Thomas Lambert. *Reforming Geneva: Discipline, Faith, and Anger in Calvin's Geneva*. Cahiers d'Humanisme et Renaissance 103. Geneva: Droz, 2012.

Knecht, R. J. *Renaissance Warrior and Patron: The Reign of Francis I*. Cambridge: Cambridge University Press, 1996.

Knighton, C. S. "Baro, Peter." In *Oxford Dictionary of National Biography*. Available at https://doi.org/10.1093/ref:odnb/1492.

Kot, Stanislas. "L'Influence de Michel Servet sur le mouvement antitrinitarien en Pologne et en Transylvanie." In *Autour de Michel Servet et de Sébastien Castellion*, edited by B. Becker, 72–115. Haarlem: H. D. Tjeenk Willink & Zoon, 1953.

Kuhr, Olaf. "Calvin and Basel: The Significance of Oecolampadius and the Basel Discipline Ordinance for the Institution of Ecclesiastical Discipline in Geneva." *Scottish Bulletin of Theology* 16 (1998): 19–33.

Kuhr, Olaf. *"Die Macht des Bannes und der Buße": Kirchenzucht und Erneuerung der Kirche bei Johann Oekolampad (1482–1531)*. Basler und Berner Studien zur historischen und systematischen Theologie 68. Bern: Peter Lang, 1999.

Labarthe, Olivier. "Faut-il prier pour les morts? Un débat de pastorale entre Viret et Caroli." In *Pierre Viret et la diffusion de la Réforme: Pensée, action, contextes religieux*, edited by Karine Crousaz and Daniela Solfaroli Camillocci, 289–309. Lausanne: Antipodes, 2014.

Landa, Paul J. "The Reformed Theology of Gérard Roussel, Bishop of Oloron (1536–1555)." PhD diss., Vanderbilt University, 1976.

Lastraioli, Chiara. "D'un texte inconnu de Jérôme Bolsec contre Calvin." *Reformation & Renaissance Review* 10 (2008): 157–74.

Lavater, Hans Rudolf. "Johannes Goeppel: Prädikant zu Rohrbach 1527–1545 und zu Zofingen 1545–1548." *Jahrbuch des Oberaargaus* 21 (1978): 149–76.

Lavater, Hans Rudolf. "Kurzbiographien, II. Peter Cyro." In *Der Berner Synodus von 1532: Edition und Abhandlungen zum Jubiläumsjahr 1982*, edited by Gottfried Locher, 2 vols., 2:370–74. Neukirchen-Vluyn: Neukirchener Verlag, 1984.

Le Coultre, Jules. *Maturin Cordier et les origines de la pédagogie protestante dans les pays de langue française (1530–1564)*. Mémoires de l'Université de Neuchâtel 5. Neuchâtel: Secrétariat de l'Université, 1926.

Lindeboom, J. "La place de Castellion dans l'histoire de l'esprit." In *Autour de Michel Servet et de Sébastien Castellion*, edited by B. Becker, 158–80. Haarlem: H. D. Tjeenk Willink & Zoon, 1953.

Lipscomb, Suzannah. *The Voices of Nîmes: Women, Sex, and Marriage in Reformation Languedoc*. New York: Oxford University Press, 2019.

Lobstein, P. *Petrus Ramus als Theologe: Ein Beitrag zur Geschichte der Protestantischen Theologie*. Strasbourg: C. F. Schmidt's Universitäts-Buchhandlung, 1878.

Manetsch, Scott. *Theodore Beza and the Quest for Peace in France, 1562–1598*. SMRT 79. Leiden: Brill, 2000.

Mentzer, Raymond, ed. *Sin and the Calvinists: Morals Control and the Consistory in the Reformed Tradition*. Sixteenth Century Essays and Studies 32. Kirksville, MO: Sixteenth Century Journal Publishers, 1994.

Mentzer, Raymond, et al., eds. *Dire l'interdit: The Vocabulary of Censure and Exclusion in the Early Modern Reformed Tradition*. Brill's Series in Church History 40. Leiden: Brill, 2010.

Meylan, Henri. "En marge de la correspondance de Théodore de Bèze: Un hérétique oublié." *Revue de Théologie et de Philosophie* ser. 3, 9 (1959): 177–81.

Meylan, Henri. "L'affaire des quatre pasteurs du Chablais, champions et victimes de la prédestination (1558)." *Revue Historique Vaudoise* 80 (1972): 15–31.

Monter, E. William. *Calvin's Geneva.* New Dimensions in History: Historical Cities. New York: John Wiley and Sons, 1967.

Mosheim, Johann Lorenz von. *Anderweitiger Versuch einer vollständigen und unpartheyischen Ketzergeschichte.* Helmgeaede: Christian Friederich Weygand, 1748.

Muller, Richard. *The Unaccommodated Calvin: Studies in the Foundation of a Theological Tradition.* Oxford Studies in Historical Theology. New York: Oxford University Press, 2000.

Muller, Richard. "De Zurich ou Bâle à Strasbourg? Étude sur les prémices de la pensée eucharistique de Calvin." *BSHPF* 155 (2009): 41–53.

Muller, Richard. *Calvin and the Reformed Tradition: On the Work of Christ and the Order of Salvation.* Grand Rapids, MI: Baker Academic, 2012.

Mützenberg, Gabriel. "Christophe Fabri et les débuts de la Réforme dans le Chablais." In *La Dispute de Lausanne (1536): La théologie Réformée après Zwingli et avant Calvin*, edited by Eric Junod, 189–99. Bibliothèque historique vaudoise 90. Lausanne: Bibliothèque historique vaudoise, 1988.

Naphy, William. *Calvin and the Consolidation of the Genevan Reformation: 1541-1557.* Manchester, UK: Manchester University Press, 1994.

Neuser, Wilhelm. "Stations: France and Basel." In *The Calvin Handbook*, edited by Herman J. Selderhuis, 23–30. Grand Rapids, MI: Eerdmans, 2009.

Nugent, Christopher. *Ecumenism in the Age of the Reformation: The Colloquy of Poissy.* Harvard Historical Studies 89. Cambridge, MA: Harvard University Press, 1974.

Ong, Walter J. *Ramus, Method, and the Decay of Dialogue: From the Art of Discourse to the Art of Reason.* Cambridge, MA: Harvard University Press, 1958.

Ott, Michael. "Commendatory Abbot." *The Catholic Encyclopedia*, vol. 4. New York: Robert Appleton Company, 1908. Available at http://www.newadvent.org/cathen/04155b.htm.

Panksepp, Jaak. *Affective Neuroscience: The Foundations of Human and Animal Emotions.* New York: Oxford University Press, 1998.

Panksepp, Jaak, and Kenneth L. Davis. *The Emotional Foundations of Personality: A Neurobiological and Evolutionary Approach.* New York: W. W. Norton, 2018.

Parker, T. H. L. *Calvin's Old Testament Commentaries.* Louisville, KY: Westminster/John Knox, 1986.

Peter, Rodolphe. "Strasbourg et la Réforme française vers 1525." In *Strasbourg au coeur religieux du XVIᵉ siècle, Hommage à Lucien Febvre, Actes du Colloque international de Strasbourg (25-29 mai 1975)*, edited by Georges Livet and Francis Rapp, 269–83. Société savante d'Alsace et des régions de l'Est, Collection "Grandes publications" 12. Strasbourg: Librairie Istra, 1977.

Pétremand, J. "Etudes sur les origines de l'Église Réformée neuchâteloise: Les premiers essais d'organisation de la Classe, serment et discipline du clergé, les Articles calvinistes de 1541 et les Ordonnances de 1542." *Revue d'histoire suisse* 8 (1928): 321–70.

Petrin, Sylvie Moret. "Ces Lausannois qui 'pappistent': Ce que nous apprennent les registres consistoriaux lausannois (1538-1540)." *Revue historique vaudoise* 119 (2011): 139–51.

Pfeilschifter, Frank. *Das Calvinbild bei Bolsec und sein Fortwirken im Französischen Katholizismus bis ins 20. Jahrhundert.* Augsburg: FDL-Verlag, 1983.

Picot, Emile. *Notice sur Jehan Chaponneau, Docteur de l'Eglise réformée, metteur en scène du Mistère des Actes des Apostres, joué à Bourges en 1536*. Paris: Damascene Morgand and Charles Fatout, 1879.

Plath, Uwe. *Calvin und Basel in den Jahren 1552-1556*. Basler Beiträge zur Geschichtswissenschaft 133. Basel: Helbing & Lichtenhahn, 1974.

Reid, Jonathan. "French Evangelical Networks before 1555: Proto-churches?" In *La Réforme en France et en Italie: Contacts, comparaisons et contrastes*, edited by Philip Benedict, Silvana Seidel Menchi, and Alain Tallon, 105-24. Collection de l'École française de Rome 384. Rome: École française de Rome, 2007.

Reid, Jonathan. *King's Sister—Queen of Dissent: Marguerite of Navarre (1492-1549) and Her Evangelical Network*. SMRT 139. Leiden: Brill, 2009.

Reynaud, Hector. *Jean de Monluc, Évêque de Valence et de Die: Essai d'histoire littéraire*. Geneva: Slatkine Reprints, 1971 [Paris, 1893].

Roget, Amédée. *Histoire du peuple de Genève depuis la Réforme jusqu'à l'Escalade*. 7 vols. Geneva, 1870-1883.

Roldan-Figueroa, Rady. "Antonio del Corro and Paul as the Apostle of the Gospel of Universal Redemption." In *A Companion to Paul in the Reformation*, edited by R. Ward Holder, 389-426. Leiden: Brill, 2009.

Rott, Jean. "Bucer et les débuts de la querelle sacramentaire." *Revue d'histoire et de philosophie religieuses* 34 (1954): 234-54.

Rott, Jean. "Un réfugié français en Suisse romande en 1550: Deux lettres inédites de Jean Morély à Guillaume Farel." In Jean Rott, *Investigationes Historicae, Églises et société au XVIe siècle, Gesammelte Aufsätze zur Kirchen- und Sozialgeschichte*, 2 vols., edited by Marijn de Kroon and Marc Lienhard, 2:83-92. Société savante d'Alsace et des regions de l'Est, Collection "Grandes Publications" 32. Strasbourg: Oberlin, 1986.

Roussel, Bernard. "Jean de l'Espine (c. 1505-97): écrire dans un temps de troubles." In *The Sixteenth-Century French Religious Book*, edited by Andrew Pettegree et al., 138-56. St. Andrews Studies in Reformation History. Aldershot, UK: Ashgate, 2001.

Royannez, Marcel. "L'eucharistie chez les évangéliques et les premiers réformés français (1522-1546)." *BSHPF* 125 (1979): 548-76.

Ruchat, Abraham. *Histoire de la Réformation de la Suisse: Édition avec appendices et une notice sur la vie et les ouvrages de Ruchat*. 7 vols. Edited by L. Vulliemin. Nyon: M. Giral-Prelaz, 1835-1838.

Russell, Alexander. "The Colloquy of Poissy, François Baudouin and English Protestant Identity, 1561-1563." *Journal of Ecclesiastical History* 65 (2014): 551-79.

Ruutz-Rees, Caroline. *Charles de Sainte-Marthe (1512-1555)*. Studies in Romance Philology and Literature. New York: Columbia University Press, 1910.

Ryrie, Alec. *Unbelievers: An Emotional History of Doubt*. Cambridge, MA: Harvard University Press, 2019.

Schepper, Hugo de. "Frederick Perrenot van Champagney (1536-1602), het 'enfant terrible' van de Familie Granvelle." In *Les Granvelle et les anciens Pays-Bas*, edited by Krista De Jonge and Gustaaf Janssens, 233-44. Leuven: Leuven University Press, 2000.

Schillings, A. *Matricule de l'Université de Louvain*. Brussels: Palais des Académies, 1903-.

Schmidt, Charles. *Gérard Roussel, Prédicateur de la Reine Marguerite de Navarre: Mémoire servant à l'histoire des premières tentatives faites pour introduire la Réformation en France*. Strasbourg: Schmidt & Grucker, 1845.

Scott, Tom. *The Swiss and Their Neighbors, 1450-1560: Between Accommodation and Aggression*. Oxford: Oxford University Press, 2017.

Scribner, Robert W. *For the Sake of Simple Folk: Popular Propaganda for the German Reformation.* New York: Oxford University Press, 1994.

Selderhuis, Herman J. *John Calvin: A Pilgrim's Life.* Translated by Albert Gootjes. Downers Grove, IL: Intervarsity Press, 2009.

Selderhuis, Herman J., ed. *The Calvin Handbook.* Grand Rapids, MI: Eerdmans, 2009.

Skalnik, James. *Ramus and Reform: University and Church at the End of the Renaissance.* Sixteenth Century Essays and Studies 60. Kirksville, MO: Truman State University Press, 2002.

Spierling, Karen. *Infant Baptism in Reformation Geneva: The Shaping of a Community, 1536–1564.* Louisville, KY: Westminster John Knox, 2005.

Spierling, Karen E., Erik A. de Boer, and R. Ward Holder, eds. *Emancipating Calvin: Culture and Confessional Identity in Francophone Reformed Communities.* Leiden: Brill, 2018.

Sprenger, Paul. *Das Rätsel um die Bekehrung Calvins.* Beiträge zur Geschichte und Lehre der Reformierten Kirche 11. Neukirchen: Kreis-Moers, 1960.

Springer, Michael S. *Restoring Christ's Church: John a Lasco and the Forma ac Ratio.* St. Andrews Studies in Reformation History. Aldershot, UK: Ashgate, 2007.

Spruyt, Bart Jan. *Cornelis Henrici Hoen (Honius) and His Epistle on the Eucharist (1525): Medieval Heresy, Erasmian Humanism, and Reform in the Early Sixteenth-Century Low Countries.* SMRT 119. Leiden: Brill 2006.

Sunshine, Glenn. *Reforming French Protestantism: The Development of Huguenot Ecclesiastical Institutions, 1557–1572.* Sixteenth Century Essays and Studies. Kirksville, MO: Truman State University Press, 2003.

Szczech, Nathalie. *Calvin en polémique: Une maïeutique du verbe.* Bibliothèque d'histoire de la Renaissance 10. Paris: Classiques Garnier, 2016.

Tallon, Alain. "Gallicanism and Religious Pluralism in France in the Sixteenth Century." In *The Adventure of Religious Pluralism in Early Modern France: Papers from the Exeter Conference, April 1999*, edited by Keith Cameron, Mark Greengrass, and Penny Roberts, 15–30. Oxford: Peter Lang, 2000.

Tallon, Allain, ed. *Un autre catholicisme au temps des Réformes? Claude d'Espence et la théologie humaniste à Paris au XVIe siècle*, Nugae humanisticae 12. Turnhout: Brepols, 2010.

Tamizey de Larroque, Philippe. *Notes et documents inédits pour servir à la biographie de Jean de Monluc, évêque de Valence.* Paris: Auguste Aubry, 1868.

Taplin, Mark. *The Italian Reformers and the Zurich Church, c.1540–1620.* St. Andrews Studies in Reformation History. Aldershot, UK: Ashgate, 2003.

Tazbir, Janusz. "Les échos de la persécution des hérétiques occidentaux dans les polémiques religieuses en Pologne." *BHR* 34 (1972): 125–36.

Thireau, Jean-Louis. *Charles Du Moulin (1500–1566): Etude sur les sources, la méthode, les idées politiques et économiques d'un juriste de la Renaissance.* THR 176. Geneva: Droz, 1980.

Tillich, Paul. *The Protestant Era.* Abridged edition. Translated by James Luther Adams. Chicago: University of Chicago Press, 1957.

Trocmé, Etienne. "Une révolution mal conduite: À propos d'un centenaire et d'un livre." *Revue d'histoire et de philosophie religieuses* 39 (1959): 160–68.

Turchetti, Mario. *Concordia o tolleranza? François Bauduin e i "Moyenneurs."* THR 200. Geneva: Droz, 1984.

Turchetti, Mario. "Concorde ou tolérance? Les Moyenneurs à la veille des guerres de religion en France." *Revue de théologie et de philosophie* 118 (1986): 255–67.

Turchetti, Mario. "Religious Concord and Political Tolerance in Sixteenth- and Seventeenth-Century France." *SCJ* 22 (1991): 15–25.

Van Raalte, Theodore G. *Antoine de Chandieu: The Silver Horn of Geneva's Reformed Triumvirate*. Oxford Studies in Historical Theology. New York: Oxford University Press, 2018.

Van Stam, Frans Pieter. "Le livre de Pierre Caroli de 1545 et son conflit avec Calvin." In *Calvin et ses contemporains, Actes du colloque de Paris 1995*, edited by Olivier Millet, 21–41. Cahiers d'Humanisme et Renaissance 53. Geneva: Droz, 1998.

Van Stam, Frans Pieter. "The Group of Meaux as the First Target of Farel and Calvin's Anti-Nicodemism." *BHR* 68 (2006): 253–75.

Van Veen, Mirjam. "'In excelso honoris gradu': Johannes Calvin und Jacques de Falais." *Zwingliana* 32 (2005): 5–22.

Van Veen, Mirjam. "'Contaminated with David Joris's Blasphemies': David Joris's Contribution to Castellio's *De Haereticis an sint Persequendi*." *BHR* 69 (2007): 313–26.

Van Veen, Mirjam. "'. . . Stoica Paradoxa . . .': Sebastian Castellio's Polemic against Calvin's Doctrine of Predestination." *BHR* 77 (2015): 325–50.

Veissière, Michel. *L'évêque Guillaume Briçonnet (1470–1534): Contribution à la connaissance de la Réforme catholique à la veille du Concile de Trente*. Provins: Société d'histoire et d'archéologie, 1986.

Viénot, John. *Histoire de la Réforme dans le Pays de Montbéliard depuis les origines jusqu'à la mort de P. Toussain, 1524–1573*. 2 vols. Paris: Fischbacher, 1900.

Viénot, John. "Un Apologiste de la Saint-Barthélemy: Pierre Charpentier." In *Séance de rentrée des cours de la Faculté libre de théologie protestante de Paris le lundi 3 novembre 1902*, 19–42. Paris: Fischbacher, 1902.

Voogt, Gerrit. *Constraint on Trial: Dirck Volckertsz Coornhert and Religious Freedom*. Sixteenth Century Essays and Studies 52. Kirksville, MO: Truman State University Press, 2000.

Vuilleumier, Henri. *Histoire de l'Église Réformée du Pays de Vaud sous le régime bernois*. 4 vols. Lausanne: La Concorde, 1927–1933.

Waardt, Hans de. "Justus Velsius Haganus: An Erudite but Rambling Prophet." In *Exile and Religious Identity, 1500–1800*, edited by Jesse Spohnholz and Gary K. Waite, 97–109. London: Pickering and Chatto, 2014.

Waddington, Charles. *Ramus (Pierre de La Ramée): Sa vie, ses écrits et ses opinions*. Paris: Meyrueis, 1855.

Waite, Gary K. *David Joris and Dutch Anabaptism, 1524–1543*. Waterloo, ON: Wilfrid Laurier University Press, 1990.

Walton, Robert C. *Zwingli's Theocracy*. Toronto: University of Toronto Press, 1967.

Wanegffelen, Thierry. *Ni Rome ni Genève: Des fidèles entre deux chaires en France au XVIe siècle*. Bibliothèque littéraire de la Renaissance, ser. 3, 36. Paris: Honoré Champion, 1997.

Weber, Bernerd. "The Council of Fontainebleau (1560)." *ARG* 45 (1954): 43–62.

Welti, Manfred. "La contribution de Giovanni Bernardino Bonifacio, marquis d'Oria, à l'édition princeps du 'De Haereticis an sint persequendi.'" *Bolletino della Società di Studi Valdesi* 90, no. 125 (1969): 45–49.

Wendel, François. *Calvin: Origins and Development of His Religious Thought*. Translated by Philip Mairet. Grand Rapids, MI: Baker Books, 1963 [Paris, 1950].

Wilbur, Earl Morse. *A History of Unitarianism*. 2 vols. Boston: Beacon Press, 1945.

Woo, Kenneth J. *Nicodemism and the English Calvin, 1544–1584.* Brill's Series in Church History and Religious Culture 78. Leiden: Brill, 2019.

Wright, David F. "Why was Calvin so Severe a Critic of Nicodemism?" In *Calvinus Evangelii Propugnator: Calvin, Champion of the Gospel,* edited by David F. Wright et al., 66–90. Grand Rapids, MI: Calvin Studies Society, 2006.

Zijlstra, S. *Nicolaas Meyndertsz. van Blesdijk: Een Bijdrage tot de Geschiedenis van het Davidjorisme.* Van Gorcum's Historische Bibliotheek 99. Assen: Van Gorcum, 1983.

Zuidema, Jason, and Theodore Van Raalte. *Early French Reform: The Theology and Spirituality of Guillaume Farel.* St. Andrews Studies in Reformation History. Burlington, VT: Ashgate, 2011.

Zweig, Stefan. *The Right to Heresy: Castellio against Calvin.* Translated by Eden and Cedar Paul. New York: Viking Press, 1936.

Index

For the benefit of digital users, indexed terms that span two pages (e.g., 52–53) may, on occasion, appear on only one of those pages.

Figures are indicated by *f* following the page number

Aachen. *See* Aix-la-Chapelle
Aconcio, Giacopo, 190–91, 290–91
   Satan's Strategems (1565),
      190–91, 290–91
Affair of the Placards (1534), 10, 28–29,
      30, 34–35, 48–50, 56–57, 68–69,
      75, 104–5, 141
Agrippa, Heinrich Cornelius, 57
Aigle (Switzerland), 45–47, 53, 182,
      260n.13
Aix (France), 211n.1
Aix-la-Chapelle (Empire), 281–82
Alamanni, Ludovico, 284n.135
Albret, d' (royal family of Navarre)
   Henri (King of Navarre, second
      husband of Marguerite), 24n.54, 25
   Jeanne (Queen of Navarre), 29–30, 194–
      95, 243–45, 246, 252–53, 278n.95,
      287–88, 300
   Louis (Bishop of Lescar), 211n.1
Alençon (France), 10–11, 12, 68–69
Allanjoie (Montbéliard), 185n.25
Almenêches (France), 12, 68–69
Amboise (France), 28–29
   Conspiracy of (1560), 270–71, 272–73
Ambrose, 235
Amerbach (elite family in Basel), 145–46
   Boniface, 240n.114, 242–43
Amiens (France), 21–22, 77n.48, 196
Anabaptists and Anabaptism, 148–50,
      158, 188–89, 194–95, 196, 208–9
Andelot. *See* Coligny
Andernach, Günther von, 26–27
Angoulême (France), 56–57
Antiauthoritarianism, 6–7, 140, 302, 310

Antichrist, 9–10, 83n.77, 236,
      241–42, 278–79
antitrinitarianism, 131–32, 148–49,
      188, 190–92
Antoine of Navarre. *See* Bourbon
Antoine de Croÿ. *See* Porcien
Antwerp (Low Countries), 188–89, 196
Arande, Michel d', 17, 19–20, 21–22, 24,
      25–27, 29–30, 51, 211–12
Aristotle, 15, 290–91
Arius and Arianism, 65, 72–73
Arminianism, 198, 280–81
Arras (Low Countries), 219–21
Articulants (Geneva faction), 81–82, 84
Artus, Humbert, 185n.25
Athanasius and Athanasian Creed, 72–73
atheists, 208–9
Aubonne (Switzerland), 66n.2, 130–31
Augsburg Confession (1530), 237–38, 241,
      247, 251–52, 253–54, 281–82
Augsburger, Michael, 79n.58
Augustine, 235
Augustinians (monastic order),
      74n.38, 97
authority, religious, 1, 6–7, 33–34, 140,
      299, 302, 303, 307, 310
Autun (France), 12
Auvergne, Annibal d'. *See* Malescot

Bailliages communs. See common
      lordships
Baptism, 33–34, 89–91, 116–17, 119n.71,
      173–74, 177–78
Barbançon, Louis de, 281n.114
Baron, Pierre (*or* Baro, Peter), 280–81

Basel (Switzerland), 36, 38–41, 56–57,
    59, 61, 71, 73–74, 101, 111–12,
    125n.95, 131–32, 145–46, 149–52,
    154, 157, 180, 183–84, 186–87,
    188–91, 194–95, 199, 201n.108,
    201n.111, 202–3, 205–6, 209–10,
    239–41, 303, 304–6
    University, 182, 190, 196n.83
Bauduin, François, 135–36, 183–84, 187–
    88, 213–14, 218–39, 248–49n.154,
    250–51, 252–54, 278–79, 280–81,
    286–87, 295–96, 299–303, 304–5,
    306–8, 309
    Transformation of the Church (charge
        against Calvinists), 228, 230–31,
        235, 250
    Commentary on the Laws about
        Defamatory Books (1562), 231–33
    Discourse on Reforming the Church
        (1564), 234–35, 236–37
    On the Edicts of the Ancient Emperors
        (1557), 222, 303
    Prefaces on Civil Law (1545), 220–21
    Responsio altera ad Ioan. Calvinum
        (1562), 229–33
Bauhin, Jean (père), 196–97, 203n.120
Bauhin, Jean (fils), 196–97
Bavans (Montbéliard), 186
Béarn (principality), 29–30, 38n.1, 289–90
Beaugency (France), 187–88
Beauvoisin (France), 293
Beda, Noël, 16, 27–28, 34–35, 49–50, 67–68
    Confession et raison de foy de maistre
        Noel Beda (pseudonymous
        Protestant text, 1533), 49–50
Beldon, Louise de (first wife of Du
    Moulin), 239, 242–43
Belgium. See Low Countries
Bellius, Martin (pseudonym of Castellio),
    153, 161–62n.91, 185–86, 187
Bergerac (France), 194–95
Bergeron, Laurent, 292n.166
Bergeron, Nicolas, 292–93
Bern (Switzerland), 36, 45–48, 53–54, 61,
    65, 66–67, 80–82, 84–85, 86, 89–
    91, 92–94, 95–96, 101, 102, 110–
    11, 112–13, 114, 116, 119–22, 124,
    125–28, 132–38, 182, 201n.108,
    251n.158, 305–6

bailiffs, 94, 101–2, 133–35
city council, 28n.72, 60–61, 66–67, 72,
    75–76, 86–87, 88, 93–94, 101–2,
    119–22, 132–36, 137, 161–62,
    168–69, 239–40, 253–54, 266–67,
    269–70, 304–5, 306–7
conquest of Vaud (1536), 53–55
Disputation (1528), 114
Edicts of Reformation (1536), 53–54
La Maniere, Ordre et Fasson
    (1537), 76n.45
pastors, 114–15, 119–21,
    129–30, 133–35
synod of (see synods)
Béroald, Matthieu, 287–88
Berquin, Louis de, 20, 26
Berry (French duchy), 12, 26–27
Bertaud, François, 29n.76
Berthelier, Philibert, 128–29
Beza, Theodore, 2–3, 4–5, 26–27, 37,
    61–63, 64, 67–68, 86–87, 124,
    132n.132, 133n.137, 137, 138, 182,
    190, 191–92, 194–96, 202n.114,
    212–13, 224–25, 237, 248–
    49n.154, 253–54, 257, 289–91,
    294–98, 302, 305–8
    and Bauduin, 228, 236–37
    and Castellio, 143n.14, 146–47, 156–57,
        159–64, 166, 173–74, 177
    and Morély, 270–71, 272–73, 274–79,
        282–84, 285–86, 287–88, 292–93
    the "Cause," 257, 294–98
    Anti-Bellius (1554), 156–57, 162–63
    Apology for Lausanne pastors and
        professors (ca. 1559), 86–87
    Ecclesiastical History (1580), 3, 5,
        9n.1, 187–88, 204–5, 208–9, 213,
        308Latin New Testament (1565),
        236–37, 253–54
    Life of Calvin (1564), 3, 122–23,
        144n.22, 308
Bible. See Scripture
Bière (Switzerland), 130–31
Blamont (Montbéliard), 185n.25
Blarer, Ambrosius, 185–86
Blauner, Adrian, 138n.162
Blesdijk, Nicolaas, 186, 188–89, 203n.120
Blois (France), 25, 28–29, 48,
    66n.2, 281–82

Bodenstein, Adam, 189–90
Bois-Le-Duc. *See* 's-Hertogenbosch
Bologna. *See* Concordat
Bolsec, Jerome, 101, 103n.3, 122–35, 137, 138, 139–40, 148–49, 155–56, 160, 168–69, 170–71, 186, 193–94, 205–7, 209–10, 251n.158, 253–54, 272, 287–88, 300–2, 303
Bonifacio, Giovanni Bernardino, 190–92
Bonna, Jean Philibert, 128–29
Bonneau, Jean, 187–88, 303
Boquin, Pierre, 221n.41
Bordeaux (France), 102–3, 104–6, 107, 113, 271–72, 300
Bornard, Denise, 196–97
Borrhaus, Martin, 170n.128, 205–6
Bouillon, M. de, 194n.75
Bourbon, French noble family
   Antoine de, king of Navarre, 194–95, 218–19, 223–27, 231–32, 233–34, 236, 243, 252–53, 300, 304–5
   Louis de, Prince de Condé, 233–35, 236–37, 252–53, 281–82, 285
Bourges (France), 26–27, 55–56, 74n.38, 97, 213–14, 221, 280–82, 300
   Pragmatic Sanction of Bourges (1438), 9
   University, 26–27, 55–56, 221, 280–81
Bourgogne, Jacques de. *See* Falais
Brabant (Low Countries province), 104, 131–32n.127
Brandmüller, Johannes, 196n.83
Brederode. *See* Falais
Briçonnet, Guillaume (Bishop of Meaux), 9, 10–11, 12–16, 17–18, 19–20, 21–23, 24–25, 30, 34–35, 38–39, 65, 66n.1, 68–69, 213–14, 268–69
Briçonnet, Guillaume (Cardinal-bishop, father of the Bishop of Meaux), 13–15
Briçonnet, Jean (grandfather of the Bishop of Meaux), 13
Brie (French province), 289–90
Britannus, Robert, 104–5, 107
Brully, Pierre, 220n.31
Bucer, Martin, 2, 24–25, 40–41, 46, 54–55, 108–10, 113, 130–31, 251n.158
   Retractions (1536), 108–9
Budé, Guillaume, 26–27
Budin, Claude, 104–5

Bugenhagen, Johannes, 40–41
   Open Letter against the New Error on the Sacrament (1525), 40–41
Bullinger, Heinrich, 2, 54–55, 61, 73–74, 97–99, 107n.25, 120–21, 125n.93, 127–28, 133n.138, 149–50, 182, 196–97, 240–41, 242–43, 251–52, 290–91, 295–96
Burgundian Wars (1474–1477), 46–47
Bursins (Switzerland), 127, 130–31, 251n.158
Byse, Pierre, 130–31

Cabrières (France), 244–45
Calvin, John, 1–8, 9–11, 17–18, 26–27, 30, 33–35, 36–38, 46, 48, 50, 53–64, 65–68, 75–76, 86–87, 89–92, 93, 95–100, 101–3, 104, 113–14, 117, 122–37, 139, 146, 155–56, 158–59, 168–69, 171, 174, 176, 178–79, 180–83, 185–86, 187, 192–95, 197–99, 202, 211–12, 218, 224–25, 233–34, 250–51, 253–54, 257–58, 270, 272n.62, 280–82, 297–98, 299–310
   and Antoine of Navarre, 224–26, 236
   and Bauduin, 213, 220–22, 225–26, 227–33, 236, 278–79
   and Bolsec, 122–26
   and Caroli, 72–74
   and Castellio, 111–12, 113, 139–45, 146–47, 153, 155–57, 161–62, 163–64, 166
   and Chaponneau, 74
   and Cop, 27–28, 56–57
   and Lavau, 204–10
   and Marcourt and Morand, 77–87
   and Morély, 270–71, 272
   and Roussel, 30, 211
   and Servetus, 148–52, 157, 222
   and Zébédée, 103, 106–7, 108–10, 113, 130–36
   as "pope of Geneva" (*see also* Slipper), 123–24, 126–27, 157, 206–7, 229–30, 231–32, 278–79, 297–98, 299, 302, 303, 309
   Strasbourg exile (1538-1541), 24, 36–37, 54–55, 81–82, 87–88, 89–91, 108–9, 141–42, 272

Calvin, John (*cont.*)
  works
    Apology for Falais (1548), 219–21
    Catechism, 101–2, 130–31,
      133–35, 304–5
    Contra la secte des Libertins (1545),
      57, 208n.143
    *Defense of the Orthodox Faith against
      Servetus* (1554), 152–53, 159
    De scandalis (1550), 57
    Duae epistolae (1537), 30, 35, 57
    Institutes, 37, 58, 103n.3, 128–29,
      133–35, 192–93, 304–6
    Instruction et confession (1536), 58, 64
    Quatre Sermons (1552), 207n.141
    Reply to Sadoleto (1540), 83–84
    Response à certaines calomnies
      (1562), 202
    Response à un certain holandois
      (1562), 198n.94
    Response to a "Moyenneur"
      (1561), 227–29
Cambridge (England), 280–81
Candeley, Charles de, 104–5
Capel, Louis(?), 295–96
Capito, Wolfgang, 23, 24–25, 40, 46
Caracciolo, Antonio (Bishop of
    Troyes), 211n.1
Carmel, Gaspard, 79
Carmelites, 96–97, 122, 124
Caroli, Pierre, 17, 20, 22–23, 28–29, 65–66,
    67–75, 82–83, 87–89, 94–95, 98–
    99, 102–3, 106–7, 113, 121, 122–
    23, 139–40, 300, 305–6, 307–8
Carpentras (France), 83–84
Caselius, Gregor, 40–41
Cassander, George, 189, 221–22, 223,
    225–26, 227–28, 229, 235, 236–37,
    250, 300
    De officio (1561), 221–22, 225, 226,
      227–29, 232–33
Cassinis, François de, 127n.103
Castellio, Sebastian, 5–6, 7, 8, 111–12,
    123–24, 126–27, 128–29, 131–32,
    137–38, 139–79, 180–210, 220–23,
    231, 253–54, 273–74, 281–82,
    290–91, 297–98, 299–303, 304–5,
    306–8, 310

On the Song of Songs, 111–12,
    143–45, 155–56
Annotations on Romans 9 (1554),
    168–71, 198
Art of Doubting (1563), 162–69
Concerning Heretics (1554), 144, 153–57
    Sacred Dialogues (1543), 141–42,
    146, 179
Conseil à la France désolée (1562), 201–2
Contra libellum Calvini (1554), 151–
    52n.53, 153n.60, 156–61, 163–64,
    192–93, 198
Defense of His Own Bible Translation
    (1562), 192–93
Four Dialogues (1558), 171–73,
    192–93, 198
French Bible (1555), 131–32, 199
German Theology (1557), 176–77,
    198–200
Imitation of Christ (1563), 176–77,
    198n.94
Latin Bible (1551), 147, 192–93
Latin Moses (1546), 146–47, 163–64
    184, 185–186, 188–89, 190–192,
    202, 209–10
On Not Punishing Heretics (1555), 156–
    57, 160–61, 181–82, 186
Castellionists, 155–56, 180–210, 274–75
catechisms, 1–2, 101–2, 130–31, 133–35,
    247–48, 281–82, 304–6
Catherine de Medici, 28, 216, 217–19,
    224n.52, 226–27, 304–5
Catholics and Catholicism, 6–8, 9, 20, 22–23,
    34, 43, 46–47, 49–50, 51, 53–54, 55–
    56, 57, 65, 66–68, 70–71, 75, 83–84,
    86–87, 88, 94–95, 110–11, 139, 158–
    60, 167–68, 179, 187, 206–7, 216–18,
    223, 226–27, 228, 230, 232–33, 235,
    236, 237–38, 240–42, 243–45, 252–
    53, 293–94, 297–98, 307–8, 309–10
cause, the. *See* Beza
Caviot, Hughes, 181–83
Celsi, Mino, 190–91
ceremonies, religious, 33–35, 75–76, 89–
    91, 133–35, 166
Chablais (Bernese territory), 281n.109
Challudre, Simon (pseudonym of Du
    Moulin), 248–49n.154

Champagney. *See* Granvelle

Chandieu, Antoine, 204–5, 208–9, 274–76, 281–82, 283–84, 285–86, 291, 292–93

Confirmation of the Discipline (1566), 276–78, 283–84, 285–86, 291, 292–93

Chantonnay. *See* Granvelle

Chaponneau, Jean, 26–27, 73n.31, 74, 97–100

Chapuis, Philippe, 201n.111

Charlemagne, 218, 244–45

Charles of Alençon (first husband of Marguerite), 12, 22–23, 25

Charles of Angoulême (father of Francis I and Marguerite), 11–12

Charles V (Holy Roman Emperor), 20, 22–23, 24n.54, 28, 120–21, 123–24, 218n.24

Charles V (King of France), 11–12

Charles VII (King of France), 13

Charles IX (King of France), 218–19, 224n.52, 237, 246

Charpentier, Pierre, 257, 294–98, 306

Letter of Pierre Charpentier (1572), 294–98

Chartres (France), 211n.1

Chastillon, Castellio's family

Huguine (Castellio's sister), 182n.13

Jeanne (Castellio's sister), 200n.106

Michel (Castellio's brother), 202

Michel (Castellio's nephew), 182–83

Châtillon, Seigneurs de. *See* Coligny

Châtillon-sur-Loing (France), 283–84, 285–86

Chaumont, Jean du (Archbishop of Aix), 211n.1

Chauny (France), 281–82

Chiccand, Guillaume, 151n.48

Chillingworth, William, 191n.56

Christophe of Württemberg. *See* Württemberg

Chrysostom, 235

Church fathers, 70–71, 97, 235–36. *See also* early Christian church

church–state relations. *See* ecclesiology

Ciret, Jehan de, 104–5

Clement VII (Pope), 28

Clichtove, Josse, 16

Coct, Anémond de, 21, 37

Coligny, French noble family

François d'Andelot de, 243

Gaspard de, 243, 283–88, 295–96, 300

Odet de, Cardinal de Châtillon, 243, 252–53, 276–78, 283–88, 292, 300

Colinet, Jean, 127, 131–32, 138, 150–51, 181–83

Collonges. *See* Morel

Cologne (Empire), 123–24

combourgeoisie treaties, 47–48

common lordships (Switzerland), 47–48, 53

Comte, Béat, 77n.49, 121, 138, 141–42n.11, 182

concord, religious, 163, 223, 226–27, 230

Concordat of Bologna (1516), 13–14, 16–17

Condé. *See* Bourbon

congregationalism, 256, 262–63, 265–66, 268

consistory, 2, 5–6, 37, 55, 64, 89–92, 99, 129n.114, 182–83n.14, 186–87, 196–97, 200n.103, 200–2, 208–9, 211–12, 237–38, 247–51, 253–54, 258–60, 261, 264, 265–66, 274, 275–76, 278–79, 282–83, 285–86, 289–90, 291, 299–300, 309–10. *See also* discipline *and* excommunication

Conspiracy. *See* Amboise

Constantin, Guillaume, 202–3

Coornhert, Dirck Volkertszoon, 198

Cop, Nicolas, 27–28, 56–57

Coraud, Elie, 82n.72

Corbeil, Louis, 121

Cordeliers, 199

Cordier, Mathurin, 28–29, 48, 61–63, 66n.1, 79–80, 104–5, 107, 113, 141–42, 305–6

Corro. *See* Del Corro

Cortaillod (Neuchâtel), 183–84

Coste. *See* La Coste

Counter-Remonstrants. *See* Remonstrants and Counter-Remonstrants

Couraud, Jean, 29n.76

Courtois, Jean, 74, 97–98

Crespin, Jean, 219–21, 221n.38, 239
Crete, 294n.177
Croquet, Nicolas, 292n.166
Croÿ. See Porcien
Cully (Switzerland), 77–78
Curione, Celio Secondo, 112–13, 190,
    205–6, 209–10
Cyro, Peter, 49n.34

D'Albret. See Albret
D'Arande. See Arande
Dauphiné (French province), 184,
    205n.133, 253n.167
Davion, Jean, 137, 272, 300
Dax (France), 211n.1
deaconesses, 266
deacons, 91–92, 182, 186, 266, 274
De Ecclesia, Philippe, 127–30
Delamare, Marin, 248–49n.154
Del Corro, Antonio, 281–82
De L'Hôpital. See L'Hôpital
descent into hell, Christ's, 143–44
Désandans (Montbéliard), 185n.25
Des Gallars, Nicolas, Seigneur de Saules,
    282n.123, 286n.142, 287n.147
Des Roches, Jean Papillon, 284n.136
Die (France), 214–15
diocesan reform, 9, 10–11, 14–15, 16,
    17–18, 29–30, 31–33, 34–35, 65,
    268–69, 270
discipline, moral, 5–6, 58–61, 89–91, 93,
    99–100, 137, 185–88, 198–203,
    261, 263–64, 268, 269–70, 273–74,
    276, 281–83, 285, 286–87, 290–91,
    299–300, 302–3, 304–5. See also
    consistory and excommunication
Discipline (1559). See French Reformed
    Churches
Dole (Empire), 243
Dolet, Etienne, 57, 141
Dominicans, 66n.2, 69, 70
Donatists, 228, 230–31, 236, 250
Dort. See synods
doubt, 6n.11, 145, 155–56, 161–63
Du Bellay, Jean (Bishop of Paris),
    26–28, 29–30
Du Bois, Michel, 83–84
Du Bois, Simon, 29n.76, 69n.14

Duchemin, Nicolas, 57
Duchesne, Guillaume, 68–69
Du Mesnil, Baptiste, 285, 286–87, 292
Du Moulin, Charles, 7, 135–36, 200n.103,
    206–7, 213, 219, 221, 237–55, 276,
    278–79, 281–82, 287–88, 292, 299–
    303, 304–7, 309, 310
    Advice on the Council of Trent
        (1564), 245–46
    Against the Calumnies of the Calvinists
        (1566), 135–36, 248–51
    Apology against La deffense civile et
        militaire (1563), 247–48, 253n.167
    Catechism (1563), 247–48
    Commentary on Henry II's Edict on
        Petites Dates (1552), 239
    Commentary on Paris Customary Law
        (1539), 239
    Treatise on the Origin of the Kingdom of
        France (1561), 244–45
    Union and Harmony of the Four
        Evangelists (1565), 246–48

early Christian church, 211–12, 221–22,
    224, 230–31, 250. See also Church
    Fathers
Ecclesia, Philippe de. See De Ecclesia
ecclesiastical goods, 55, 66–67, 75, 86–87,
    89, 93, 95–96
ecclesiology, 5–6, 55, 60–61, 66–67, 75,
    86–89, 93, 139, 155–56, 177–78,
    184, 237–38, 250, 251–52, 254–55,
    256, 257, 258–71, 273–74, 275–76,
    280–81, 282–83, 286–87, 290–91,
    302–3, 304–5, 307–8
Echallens (Switzerland), 47–48, 53
Edict of January (1562), 226–27
Edward VI (King of England), 147,
    153, 154
elders, 91–92, 261–62, 264–66, 273–74,
    289–90. See also consistory
election. See predestination
elections of pastors. See pastoral elections
Elizabeth I (Queen of England), 232–33,
    237, 304–5
England, 147, 192–93, 280–81,
    282–83, 293–94
Enlightenment, 139–40, 193

Epicureans, 208–9
Erasmus of Rotterdam, 25n.55, 71, 88,
    107–8, 145–46, 190–91, 198n.94,
    219–21, 251–52
Erastus, Thomas, 263
Erb, Mathias, 184–85
Esch, Nicolas d', 24
Espence, Claude d', 248–49n.154, 252–53
Etaples. See Lefèvre
Eucharist, 1, 5–6, 7, 22, 33–35, 37, 38–40, 41–
    42, 44–45, 55, 59–61, 63, 64, 77–78,
    79–81, 89–92, 93, 95–96, 99–100, 101,
    108–10, 112–13, 114, 117–19, 120–
    21, 133–35, 137–38, 139, 167–68,
    177–78, 185–86, 187–88, 200–1, 211–
    12, 215, 226, 236–38, 240–41, 242,
    244–45, 246–47, 250, 251–52, 283–
    84, 295–96, 299–300, 302–3, 304–5
  Consensus Tigurinus (1549), 120–21
  debates between Lutherans and
    Reformed, 22, 25n.55, 37–38,
    40–41, 45–46
  ubiquity doctrine, 128, 240–41, 247
Eusebius of Caesarea, 5
excommunication, 37, 55, 58–61, 64, 89–
    92, 93, 101, 137–38, 201–2, 208–9,
    254–55, 263–64, 267, 274–76, 282–
    83, 291, 299–300
exile. See refugees
Eyssautier, Mathieu, 200–2, 206–7

Fabri, Christophe, 75–76, 94
faculty of theology. See Paris
Falais, Jacques de Bourgogne, Seigneur
    de, 101, 123–24, 125–32, 138, 139,
    140, 150–51, 181–83, 196, 205–6,
    209–10, 219–21, 251n.158, 253–
    54, 300, 302–3, 310
Falais, Yolande de Brederode, Madame de,
    123–24, 126–27
Farel, Guillaume, 10, 17, 20, 21–22, 24–25,
    26n.63, 28n.72, 28–29, 34–35, 36–55,
    57, 58, 59, 60–64, 65–71, 72–74, 75–
    78, 79–80, 82–84, 85, 87–88, 89–92,
    94–100, 103, 106–7, 109–10, 111–12,
    141–42, 149–50, 183–86, 202n.114,
    211, 253, 272, 299, 302, 305–6, 307–8
  Basel Theses (1524), 38–39, 41

Articles Concerning the Reformation
    of the Church of Neuchâtel
    (1541), 91–92
Articles Drafted by the Ministers of
    Neuchâtel (1542), 92
Confession de la foy (1537), 58n.66
Maniere et Fasson (1533), 46–47, 54–55
Summaire (1529), 41–44, 46–47, 54–55,
    58, 59, 63–64
fasting, 27–28
Faucheux, Louis, 185n.25
Favre, Caspar, 149n.41
Ferrara (Italy), 124
Ferté-sous-Jouarre (France), 194–95,
    275–76, 289–90
figures
  network analysis of Calvin, Farel, and
    Viret's correspondence, 62f
  overlapping networks of individuals
    treated in this book, 301f
Foncelet, Sebastian, 131–32,
    194–95, 206–7
Fontainebleau, Council of (1561), 216–19
Four Mandated Territories (Quatre
    Mandements, Switzerland),
    46–48, 53
France, 3, 5–7, 9–35, 36, 44–46, 48, 49–
    50, 53, 56–57, 69, 71, 75–76, 88–
    89, 102, 106–7, 113, 124, 158–59,
    177, 180, 181–82, 194–95, 199,
    200–1, 202, 203, 206–10, 211–
    55, 256–98, 300, 302–3, 304–5,
    306, 307–8
Francis I (King of France), 10–12, 13–14,
    16–18, 20, 22–23, 24–29, 34–35,
    103n.3, 244–45
Francis II (King of France), 217–19,
    272n.62
Franciscans, 14–15
Francophone Switzerland, 5–6, 36, 44, 46–
    55, 58–64, 65–100, 101–2, 106–38,
    143–45, 180–84, 190, 203, 239–40,
    270–71, 272, 299–300, 305–7
Frankfurt (Empire), 118n.65, 194, 198–
    200, 274, 281–83
fraternal censures, 91–92, 97–99
freedom of conscience, 145
freedom of religion, 223, 303

free inquiry, 140, 155, 157, 160, 167–68, 192, 251–52, 309–10
free will and free choice, 38–39, 154, 170–71, 194
Freinsheim (Empire), 188–89
French Church, 6–7, 9, 13–14, 30, 141, 211–12, 218, 224, 230, 250, 251–52, 299–300, 304–5, 309. *See also* Gallicanism
French Reformed Churches, 3, 4–6, 64, 122, 180, 187–88, 204, 208–9, 211–12, 213, 247–49, 252–55, 256–57, 262, 264, 266–67, 268, 270–71, 275–76, 278–79, 288–90, 295–96, 308. *See also* synods
  Confession of Faith (1559), 88n.106, 208–9, 276, 289–90, 306
  Discipline (1559), 208–9, 258, 260, 276–78, 282–83, 289–90, 292–93, 306, 307–8
Fribourg (Switzerland), 47–48, 110–11
Froben, Hieronymus, 145–46
Froben, Johannes, 145–46
Froment, Antoine, 48
Furbity, Guy, 69

Gallars. *See* Des Gallars
Gallican evangelicals, 9–10, 211–55, 286–87, 292, 304–5
Gallicanism, 7, 9–10, 14n.16, 17–18, 213, 218, 224, 237–39, 244–45, 251–53, 286–87, 292, 299–300. *See also* French Church
Gallus, Nicolaus, 183n.19
Gansfort, Wessel, 40
Gap (France), 28n.72
Garnier, Jean, 274
Garonne River, 105–6
Geneva, 1–2, 3–5, 6–7, 36–37, 46, 47–48, 53, 55, 58–61, 65–70, 73, 74, 75–86, 87–88, 89–, 94, 96–97, 99–100, 101–2, 104–5, 106–7, 111–12, 113, 123–36, 139, 140, 141–45, 146, 150–51, 157, 158–59, 168–69, 178, 180–83, 186–87, 190–91, 196–97, 200–2, 204, 205, 206–7, 209–10, 211–12, 216–17, 218, 220–21, 233–34, 236–38, 239–41, 251n.158,

253–55, 256–57, 258–59, 264, 268–71, 272–74, 275, 276–84, 285–91, 292, 294–96, 299–300, 302–3, 304–7, 308, 310
  Academy, 37, 61–63, 257, 290–91, 294, 305–6
  city council, 36–37, 59–60, 66–67, 70, 77–78, 79–82, 83–85, 125–26, 128–29, 143–44, 150–51, 272–73, 275
  Excerpt of the Procedures against Jean Morély (1563), 275
  Collège de Rive, 79, 141–42, 143–44
  Company of Pastors, 95–96, 98, 125n.95, 128, 132–33, 143–45, 256, 272–73
  congrégations, 114–15, 124–25, 126–27, 144
  consistory, 200–2, 251n.158, 251, 275–76
  Ecclesiastical Ordinances (1541), 91–92, 258–59
  Rive Disputation (1534), 70–71
  Servetus Affair, 148–52, 180–81, 190–91, 222
  terres de St. Victor et chapitre, 84n.82, 95–96, 201n.108
George, David. *See* Joris
Geranius, Cephas (pseudonym), 49n.34, 50, 51
Gering, Beat, 119–21
Germany, 21–22, 25, 28–29, 71, 88, 120–21, 139–40, 158n.78, 237–38, 287–88, 290–91
Gessner, Conrad, 196n.85
Gète, Jacques, 186
Gex, Pays de (Bernese territory), 67, 73–74, 82n.71, 89, 95–96, 98–100
Glant, Claude de, 94–95, 98–99, 110
Gobat (schoolmaster of Yverdon), 130–31
Goodrich, Thomas, 281n.114
goods. *See* ecclesiastical goods
Gospel, 7–8, 9, 10, 17–18, 21, 24–25, 31, 32, 33–35, 45–46, 49–50, 69, 84, 93, 95–96, 140, 159, 181–82, 196–97, 198–99, 229, 241–42, 251, 260, 268–69
Gouveia, André de, 104–5, 107
Gouveia, Antonio de, 104–5, 107

Grandson (Switzerland), 47–48, 53, 66n.1,
    73n.31, 137
Granvelle, imperial noble family
    Antonio de, 218n.24, 297
    Frédéric Perrenot de, Sieur de
        Champagney, 297–98
    Thomas Perrenot de, Sieur de
        Chantonnay, 218–19
Grataroli, Guglielmo, 182n.9
Gribaldi, Matteo, 160, 190–91
Grymoult, Léger, 150–51, 186
Grynaeus, Simon, 61
Gryphius, Sebastian, 220–21
Guillart, Charles (Bishop of
        Chartres), 211n.1
Guillemin, Gérard, 186
Guillermins, 79–80, 81, 96–97
Guise (French noble family), 272n.62
    Charles de, Cardinal of Lorraine, 214–
        15n.10, 226–27, 252–53, 304–5
    Claude de Lorraine, Duke of Guise, 22
    Mary of (Mary, Queen of Scots), 217–19
Guyenne (France)
    collège, 102–3, 104–6, 107n.24, 271–72
    parlement, 104–6
Guyot, Claude, 110–11
Gwalther, Cornelius, 189n.44
Gwalther, Rudolf, 104n.4, 107n.25,
    150–51, 196–97

Haemstede. See Van Haemstede
Haganus. See Velsius
Hague, The (Low Countries), 194
Hainaut, Quintin de, 57
Haller, Johannes, 120–21, 126–27,
    130n.121, 131n.124, 132–33
Heidelberg (Empire), 118n.65,
    221–22, 263
Helvetic Confession, Second (1566),
    88n.106
Henri II (King of France), 24n.54,
    28, 131n.126, 239, 242–43,
    244–45n.137
Henri IV (King of France), 287–88
Henry VIII (King of England), 158
heresy, 17, 20, 22–23, 26, 28–29, 69, 72–73,
    74, 77n.48, 132–35, 154, 156, 158–
    59, 173–74, 187–88, 201–2, 207–9,

    218–19, 231, 245, 251n.158, 251,
    267, 297–98, 302–3, 306, 310. See
    also persecution and toleration
    executions for, 26, 28–29, 131–32,
        140–41, 147–52, 154, 158–60, 161,
        167n.115, 184–85, 222, 231, 302–3
Hermance (Chablais), 137
Heshusius, Tilemann, 183n.19
Hoen, Cornelis, 40
Hôpital. See L'Hôpital
Hotman, François, 61–63, 219, 239–40
Houbraque, Guillaume, 118–19, 200, 281–
    83, 287–88, 295–96
    Traité monstrant comme il faut proceder
        (1567), 282–83
Huguenot nobility, 213, 218–19, 236–37,
    243, 252–55, 256, 268–69, 278,
    285–88, 299–300, 304–5, 306–7
Huguenots, 211, 213, 226–27, 236–38,
    247–48, 256–57, 294, 297. See also
    French Reformed Churches
humanists and humanism, 1–2, 5–6, 7,
    9n.1, 10–11, 13, 15–17, 26–27, 57,
    103n.3, 104–5, 107, 113, 126–27,
    141, 145–46, 147, 156, 175, 179,
    187–88, 211–12, 216–17, 219–21,
    270–71, 299–300, 304–5
Hungary, 191–92
Hyperius, Andreas, 138n.162
Hyperphragmus. See Zuttere

iconoclasm, 26. See also images
idolatry, 51–52, 57, 221, 241–42, 251
Ignatius of Loyola, 167–68
Île de France (French region), 275–76,
    283–84, 291, 292–93, 306
images, 23, 51–52, 244–45. See also
    iconoclasm and idolatry
indulgences, 1, 244–45
Inquisition, 148, 188, 189–90, 211, 213,
    281–82, 304–5
Italy, 14–15, 38, 188, 189–92

Jacques de Bourgogne. See Falais
Jamet, Lyon, 29n.76
Jeanne de Hochberg, 47–48
Jews and "Judaizing," 158, 163–64, 179,
    235–36, 244–45, 295

Joris, David, 149–50, 153n.62, 167n.115, 188–89, 196
Joris, Susanna, 188–89n.40
Jud, Leo, 58n.65
Julius II (Pope), 13
Jupiter (*or* Jove), 124–25, 147n.32, 278–79
Jussie, Jeanne de, 69
justification, 1, 5–6, 7, 19–20, 27–28, 32, 33–34, 139, 156, 173–78, 211–12, 215, 246–47, 250, 302–3
   Sola fide, 19–20, 27–28, 33–34, 38–39, 156, 174, 299–300

Kappel War, First (1529), 48–49
Karlstadt, Andreas Bodenstein von, 40–41, 189–90
keys, power of the, 59, 101, 112–13, 114–17, 291, 302–3, 304–5
Kilchmeyer, Jodocus, 119–20
Kleinberg, George (pseudonym of Castellio or Joris), 153, 154n.66, 167n.115, 188–89
Knechtenhofer, Hans, 138n.162
Kunz, Peter, 73–74n.35, 77n.49, 82

La Coste, Benoît de, 272, 287–88, 300
Lafarge, Thomas, 202
La Gaucherie (teacher of Henri of Navarre), 287n.148
La Haye, Hermès de, 281–82, 283–86, 295–96
Lake Geneva, 46–47, 94n.120, 124, 127, 131–32, 300
Lalande, M. de, 194n.75
Lambert, François, 21, 24, 37
Lancy (Geneva), 201–2
La Neuveville (Switzerland), 106–7
Lange, Jean, 127, 130–31, 132–36, 251n.158, 253–54
Languedoc (French province), 289–90
L'Anglois, Jacques, 209–10
L'Archer, Jean, 183–84
   Canons of All the Councils (1553), 183–84
La Rochelle (France), 289–91, 295–96
Łaski, Jan (*or* John a Lasco), 273–74
   Forma ac ratio (1555), 273–74
Laurent, Georges, 185n.25

Lausanne (Switzerland), 47–48, 53, 61–63, 65, 67, 72–73, 77–78, 82, 86–87, 88–89, 93–94, 99–100, 101, 102, 107n.24, 110, 114, 121–22, 124, 130–31, 138, 180–82, 239–41, 260n.13, 264–65, 268–70, 272, 305–7
   Academy, 37, 48, 54–55, 61–63, 101–2, 103, 112–22, 133–35, 136, 138, 141–42n.11, 143–44, 180–81, 182, 184, 190, 239–40, 258–59, 260, 272, 304–7
   Bishop of, 46–47, 53
   chapter (*classe*), 82n.71, 86–87, 93, 129–30, 138, 258–60
   colloquies, 114–17, 161–62
   Disputation (1536), 51–52, 53–54, 94–95
   pastors and professors, 114–15, 119–21, 129–30, 138
   synod of (*see* synods)
   Theses on the ministry and Eucharist (1547–1548), 114–20
Lavau, François de, 205n.133
Lavau, Jean Saint-Vertunien de, 187–88, 203–10, 303, 306
Lecomte, Jean, 48, 65–66, 67, 71–73, 74, 75–78, 82–84, 89, 94–95, 98–100, 106–7, 110, 300, 305–6
   Journal, 66n.1
Le Comte, Paul, 137
Le Coq, Jacques, 67, 75–76, 96–97, 98–99
Lefèvre, Jacques, d'Etaples, 9, 10–11, 14–16, 17–20, 21–26, 34, 38, 38–39n.2, 44–45, 48, 50, 51, 55–56, 66n.1, 68–69, 156, 213–14, 309
   Epistres et Evangiles (1525), 19, 20n.41
   Quincuplex Psalterium (1509), 16
   S. Pauli Epistolae ... cum commentariis (1512), 16
   See also Scripture: Vernacular translations
Léman. *See* Lake Geneva
Le Mans (France), 274
Le Maçon, Sieur de la Fontaine, 283–84
Leo X (Pope), 13–14
Lescar (Béarn), 211n.1
L'Espine, Jean de, 233–34, 282n.123, 287–88, 295–96

Lestre, Jean de, 291–92n.165
L'Hôpital, Michel de, 216, 252–53, 285, 286–87, 292, 304–5
liberal Protestantism, 139–43, 178–79, 310
libertines, 208–9, 307–8
liturgy, 46–47, 54–55, 72–73, 76n.45, 89–91, 215
Locke, John, 192–93
Lodève (France), 13
Loisel, Antoine, 292n.167
London (England), 189, 190–91, 199, 273–74, 281–82
    Stranger Church, 189, 199, 273–74
Longa, Guillaume de, 104–5
Lord's Supper. See Eucharist
Louis XII (King of France), 11–12, 13, 47n.31, 244–45n.137
Louis d'Orléans-Longueville, 47n.31
Louise of Savoy (Mother of Francis I and Marguerite), 11–12, 17–18, 22–23
Lourmarin (France), 200–1
Louvain, University of, 74n.38, 97, 104, 219
Low Countries, 104, 123–24, 150–51, 180, 188–89, 193–94, 198, 203, 219–21, 237, 304–5
Loyola. See Ignatius
Lumigny-en-Brie (France), 291–93
Lutherans and Lutheranism, 1–2, 22, 28, 32, 37, 40–41, 106–7, 128, 130–31, 153, 158, 167, 184, 237–38, 240–41, 242, 247, 307–8
Luther, Martin, 1, 17–18, 19–20, 21, 22, 37–38, 40–41, 88, 161–62n.91, 167–68, 174, 302
    Freedom of a Christian (1521), 31
    On the Bondage of the Will (1525), 25n.55
    To the Christian Nobility (1521), 302
Lyon (France), 75n.42, 96–97, 106–7, 141, 148, 180, 196–97, 202–3, 220–21, 247–48, 272n.62, 274–75, 283–84, 305–6
    Castellionist community, 202–3
    Collège de la Trinité, 141
    pastors, 196–97, 247–48

Malescot, Étienne de, 248n.152
    Censure des erreurs de Charles Du Moulin (1566), 248n.152

Maligny Affair (1560), 272n.62
Malingre, Thomas (alias Mathieu), 48, 65–66, 67, 71–73, 74, 82–84, 89, 94–95, 98–100, 106–7, 110–12, 130–31, 305–6
Mallot, Jean, 281–82, 283–85
maps
    francophone Europe, 4f
    Pays de Vaud, Neuchâtel, and the Comté of Montbéliard, 90f
Marandé (pastor), 245n.138
Marck, de la (French noble family), 26n.63, 46–47
    Robert, Prince of Sédan, Duke of Bouillon, 44–45
Marcourt, Antoine, 28–29, 48–50, 65–67, 71–72, 74–88, 89, 93, 95–96, 98–100, 106–7, 113, 141–42, 155–56, 258–59, 272, 297–98, 300, 305–6.
    See also Affair of the Placards
    Declaration de la Messe (1534), 50–51, 75
    Livre des marchans (1533), 75
    Petit traicté de la saincte eucharistie (1534), 28–29, 49–50, 75
Marguerite of Navarre, 1–2, 9, 10–13, 15, 16, 17–18, 19–20, 21–23, 24–28–, 34–35, 36–37, 44–46, 49–50, 53, 54–57, 61, 66n.1, 68–69, 74n.38, 104–5, 113, 141, 196, 208n.143, 213–15, 216–17, 221, 223–24, 231–32, 253, 299–300, 304–5
Marlorat, Augustin, 26–27, 124
Marot, Clément, 28–29
Marthoret, François, 75–76
Mary I (Queen of England), 199
Mass, Catholic, 23, 28–29, 34–35, 36–37, 38–39, 41–44, 45–47, 48–49, 50, 51–52, 53–55, 58, 65, 70–71, 110–11, 133–35, 184–85, 215
Masson, Papire, 234–35
Mazurier, Martial, 22–23
Meaux (France) and the Meaux Group, 3, 9–13, 14–15, 17–23, 24–25, 27–28, 29–31, 33, 37, 38–40, 48, 51, 65–66, 68–69, 71–72, 113, 213–14, 216–17, 223, 237, 238, 253, 289–90, 300, 304–5

Medici. *See* Catherine
Melanchthon, Philip, 63n.76, 138n.162,
    181n.3, 183n.19, 194, 196–97,
    251n.158, 251–52
Melchiorites, 188n.38
Melet, Pierre, 284n.136
Mennonites, 188–89n.40
Mercure, Sieur de, 283–84, 295–96
Mérindol (France), 244–45
Merlin, Jean Reymond, 260n.13
Metz (Empire), 24, 96–97, 98–99
Miremont (pastor), 247–48n.148
missionaries, 3, 40, 47–48, 65, 102, 180,
    184–85, 204, 209–10, 216–17, 303
monasteries, 12
    Almenêches, 12
    Essai, 12
    Notre-Dame de Francheville (Morée),
        254n.171
    St.-Andoche (Autun), 12
    St.-Ambroise (Bourges), 97
    St.-Germain-des-Prés (Paris), 13, 14–
        15, 16, 21–22, 38
    St.-Jean (Autun), 12
    Yerres, 12
Monluc, Jean de (Bishop of Valence),
    211n.1, 213–19, 225, 226, 233–34,
    238, 242–43, 247–48, 250–51,
    252–53, 268–69, 290–91, 295–96,
    299–300, 304–5, 309
    Christian Instructions (1561), 215
    Sermons on the Lord's Prayer (1561), 215
Montaigne, Michel de, 1, 104–5
Montargis (France), 281–82
Montbéliard (city and *comté*, Empire), 40,
    61, 102, 106–7, 135–37, 149–50,
    153, 180–81, 183–87, 194, 200,
    203, 209–10, 240–41, 242–43,
    251, 253–54, 268–69, 300, 303,
    304–5, 308
Montfort, Basil (pseudonym of Castellio),
    153, 155, 190
Montméja, Bernard, 281–82, 285
Montpellier (France), 137–38n.160
Morand, Jean, 48, 66–67, 77–78, 79, 82,
    83–85, 87–88, 89, 96–97, 98–100,
    106–7, 141–42, 258–59, 272, 300
Morat. *See* Murten

Morée (France), 254n.171
Morel, François, Sieur de
    Collonges, 281–82
Morelet du Museau, Antoine, 76n.45
Morély, Jean, 5–6, 99, 199, 202–3, 206–7,
    254–55, 256–98, 299–303, 304–5,
    306–8, 310
    De ecclesiae ordine (ca. 1577),
        271n.54
    *Treatise on Christian Discipline and
        Polity* (1562), 202–3, 258, 260–71,
        274–75, 276–78, 283–84
Morély, Jean (*père*), 271–72
Morges (Switzerland), 67, 75–76, 82, 83–
    84, 89, 96–97, 98–100, 107n.24,
    127, 130–31, 181n.3
Moulin. *See* Du Moulin
Moulins (France), 283–84
Moyenneurs (*see also* Gallican
    evangelicals) 7, 9–10, 211–13, 228–
    29, 236–37, 252–53, 307–8
Mudée, Gabriel, 219
Münster (Empire), 158n.78, 188n.38
Münster, Sebastian, 71
Murten (Switzerland), 47–48, 53, 75n.42
Mussard, Pierre, 137
Myconius, Oswald, 61, 73–74n.35,
    125n.93, 125n.95

Navarre
    Antoine of (*see* Bourbon)
    Henri of (Marguerite's husband) (*see*
        Albret)
    Henri of (*see* Henri IV)
    Marguerite of (*see* Marguerite)
Nérac (France), 56–57, 214–15
Netherlands. *See* Low Countries
Neuchâtel (city and *comté*), 44, 47–48, 49–
    50, 53, 66n.2, 67, 71–72, 74, 75–76,
    78n.52, 82–83, 89, 91, 94, 97–98,
    99–100, 102, 106–7, 110, 180–81,
    183–84, 186–87, 239–41, 268–69,
    280–81, 305–6, 307–8
    city council, 78n.52, 91–92, 93
    Constitutions and Ordinances
        (1542), 91–92
    Ordonnances pour la ville (1542), 92
    pastors, 92, 97–98, 125–26

Nicodemism and Nicodemites, 7, 9–10, 28–
29, 30, 50–53, 54–57, 155–56, 199,
206, 211–12, 219–21, 228–29, 233–
34, 239, 242–43, 253, 302–3, 307–8
Noailles, François de (Bishop of
Dax), 211n.1
Noël, Etienne, 185n.25
Normandy (French province), 66n.2
Noyon (France), 56–57, 281–82
Nyon (Switzerland), 96–97, 130–32,
251n.158

Ochino, Bernardino, 189–90
Thirty Dialogues, Castellio's translation
(1563), 189–90
Oecolampadius, Johannes, 2, 21, 40–41,
46, 49–50, 54–55, 59, 107–8
Olivétan, Pierre, 66n.2
Olivier, Matthieu d', 281–82
Oloron (Béarn), 10, 29–30, 35, 52–53,
211n.1, 213–14
Oporinus, Johannes, 145–46, 183–84,
191n.56, 222
Orbe (Switzerland), 47–48, 53, 69n.16,
102–3, 106–7, 110–12–, 145
Orléans (France), 28–29, 56–57, 188n.36,
239, 247–48, 254n.169, 258, 274–
75, 278–79, 280–81, 285–86, 287–
88, 289–90, 306

Palatinate (Empire), 188–89
Papillon. See Des Roches
papist (as derogatory term) 7, 34, 65, 70,
80–81, 95–96, 106–7, 126–27,
158–59, 198n.94, 200, 212–13, 223,
228–29, 237–38, 240, 241–42, 244–
45, 251, 303–4, 309
Paquelon, Jacques, 182–83
Paris, 13, 20, 21–22, 26–30, 34–35, 38,
49–50, 56–57, 69n.16, 75, 113,
118n.65, 124, 196, 199, 217–18,
220–21, 239, 243, 247, 254–55,
262, 268–69, 271–72, 280–81, 289–
90, 295–96, 305–6
Paris Faculty of Theology, 9, 16–17,
19–23, 26, 27–28, 44–45, 49–50,
51–52, 65, 67–69, 77n.48, 126–27,
199, 215, 239

Paris Parlement, 13–14, 21–23, 26, 28–
29, 77n.48, 226–27, 239, 243n.130
Reformed church, 205n.129, 285–87
University of Paris, 10–11, 13–14, 66–
67, 77–78, 79, 104, 219, 239
Collège du Cardinal Lemoine, 15, 38
Collège de la Marche, 48, 66n.1
Collège Ste.-Barbe, 104–5
Parthenay. See Soubise
pastoral elections, 66–67, 77–78, 91–92,
258–60, 261, 264–66, 268, 269–70,
273–74, 276, 289–91, 302–3
pastoral power. See keys
Pavia, Battle of (1525), 22–23
Payerne (Switzerland), 47–48, 82n.71
Peace of Madrid (1526), 24n.54
Peasants' War (1525), 22, 158n.78
Pelagius and semi-pelagianism, 7,
176, 182
Penance (sacrament), 27–28, 215
Pérez, Juan (or Pierins), 281–82, 285
Catechism (1556), 281–82
Inquisitionis Hispanicae Artes (1567),
282n.119
Spanish New Testament (1556), 281–82
Perna, Pietro, 145–46
Perrenot. See Granvelle
Perrin, Ami, 128–29, 136, 206–7
Perrin, Jean, 182
Perrussel, François, 199, 233–34,
253–54, 273–74, 281–83, 285,
295–96, 300–2
persecution, religious, 46–47, 106, 123–24,
144, 147–48, 151–61, 178, 186–93,
196, 199–200, 206–7, 209–10,
285–86, 303
Petit, Guillaume, 19–20
Pfister, Nikolaus, 119–20
Philip the Good, Duke of
Burgundy, 123–24
Philippi, François, 281–82
Defense des eglises estrangiers de
Francfort (1562), 281n.114
Translation of Book of Common Prayer
(1553), 281n.114
Picardy (province, France), 66n.1, 75n.42,
77n.48, 281n.114
Pichon, Eynard, 79

piety, 10–11, 23, 50, 57, 172–73, 176–77, 179, 186–87, 198–203, 206, 207–8, 246, 299–300, 307–8, 310
Pisa, Conciliabulum of (1511), 13
plus (vote to abolish the Mass), 48–49, 53
Poissy, Colloquy of (1561), 212–13, 221–22, 224, 225–28, 230, 235, 236, 286–87, 304–5
Poitiers (France), 187–88, 203–6, 208–10, 239, 306
Poland, 180, 190–92
pope and papacy, 1, 3–4, 6–7, 22, 34, 51–52, 157, 158, 217–18, 237–38, 241–42, 245, 251, 278–79, 299, 302, 307, 309–10
Poquet, Antoine, 57
Porcien, Antoine III de Croÿ, Prince de, 194–95, 243
Porret, Michel, 127
Portus, François, 294
Poullain, Valérand, 274, 281–82
Pragmatic Sanction. *See* Bourges
prayers for the dead, 65, 72–73, 215
predestination and election, 5–6, 34–35, 37, 55, 63–64, 99–100, 101–2, 123–25, 127–35, 136, 137, 140, 154, 156, 168–74, 178, 180, 186–87, 193–98, 202, 272–73, 280–81, 282–83, 287–88, 299–300, 302–3, 310
primitive church. *See* early Christian church *and* Church fathers
printing press and printers, 21, 145–46, 202–3, 220–21, 304, 305–6, 307–8
processions, 26, 56n.57, 106n.18
prophecy, 140, 231–32, 238, 307, 309–10
proto-orthodox Christianity, 5, 8
Provence (French region), 200–1, 295–96
purgatory, 1, 43, 70–71, 215, 244–45

Quatre Mandements. See Four Mandated Territories
Quintin de Hainaut. *See* Hainaut

Rabelais, François, 57, 104–5, 141
Ramus, Petrus, 290–94, 295–96
rationalism, 139, 156, 166–68, 178–79
refugees and exile, 3, 5–6, 46, 47–48, 54–55, 66–67, 136, 138, 188, 189–90, 194, 203–4, 206–7, 304–5

Régin, Claude (Bishop of Oloron), 211n.1
Regnaudot, Nicole, 132n.130
Reims (France), 21–22
Reina, Casiodor de, 282n.119
Remonstrants and Counter-Remonstrants, 180, 192–94, 198
Renée de France, 124, 246, 252–53, 281–82, 285, 300
Retif, Jehan, 29n.76
Reuchlin, Johannes, 107–8
Rhellican, Johannes, 76n.45
Rhineland, 3, 194, 308
Rhône River, 106n.19, 253n.167
Ribit, Jean, 114–15, 117, 119
Rive. *See* Geneva
Robert, Simon, 24
Rode, Hinne, 40–41
Roma, Jean de, 38–39n.2
Romandie. *See* Francophone Switzerland
Rome, 3–4, 5–7, 13–14, 34, 200–2, 206–7, 237–39, 241–42, 244–45, 278–79, 292, 302, 307, 309
Rosier. *See* Sureau
Rouen (France), 28–29
Roussel, Gérard, 10, 17, 19, 21–25, 27–35, 38, 44–46, 50, 51–53, 55–56, 57, 65, 66n.1, 211–12, 213–15, 218, 268–69, 309
Familiere exposition, 30, 33–34
Forme de visite de diocese, 30, 31–33, 214–15
Roybet, Marie Françoise, 202
Rozay-en-Brie (France), 68–69
Rümlang, Eberhard von, 119–20

's-Hertogenbosch (Low Countries), 104n.4
Sacconex (Gex), 200–1
Sadoleto, Jacopo, 83–84
Sagittarius. *See* L'Archer
Sainte-Marthe, Charles de, 104–5, 107
Saint Bartholomew's Day Massacre (1572), 237, 257, 280–81, 293–94
Saint-Gelais, Jean de (Bishop of Uzès), 211n.1
Saint-Germain-des-Prés. *See* monasteries
Saint-Julien (Montbéliard), 185n.25
Saint-Malo (France), 13
Saint-Martin-du-Fresne (Savoy), 141

Saint-Paul, François de, 124, 127, 129–30,
    132–33, 168–69, 194, 272
Saint-Paul-Trois-Châteaux (France), 26–
    27, 29–30, 51
Saint-Romain. See Chaumont
Saint-Vertunien, Jean. See Lavau
saints, veneration and intercession, 19–20,
    23, 27–28, 32–33, 70–71, 215,
    218–19, 244–45
Salignac, Jean de, 253–54, 287–88
Saules. See Des Gallars
Saunier, Antoine, 48, 79–80, 82, 112n.47
Savoy (duchy), 46–47, 84, 295
Scaliger, Joseph, 205n.133
Schmalkaldic League, 120–21
Schmid, Konrad, 119–21
scholasticism, 15, 16, 126–27
Schore, Antoine van, 131n.123
Scripture
    commentaries, 16, 161–62,
        246–47, 305–6
    exegesis and hermeneutics, 1, 5–16,
        19–20, 23, 80–81, 92, 131–32, 139,
        140–41, 143–45, 147, 156, 161–70,
        178–79, 217–18, 229, 250, 267,
        302–4, 307
    sola scriptura, 1, 7, 27–28, 33–34, 97,
        211–12, 245, 250, 302
    vernacular translations, 17–20, 23, 26,
        31, 145, 199, 217–19
    Vulgate, 16
Sébiville, Pierre de, 21, 37
semi-pelagianism. See Pelagius
Sept, Jean-Baltasar, 149n.41
Servetus, Michael, 1–2, 5–6, 46, 131–32,
    138, 140–41, 148–52, 156–57, 160,
    180–81, 182, 183–86, 188–89, 190–
    92, 202n.114, 205–6, 208–10, 222,
    299–300, 302–3
Seville (Spain), 281–82
Sleidanus, Johannes, 244–45n.137
slipper (papal), 1, 3–4, 126–27, 131–32,
    200–1, 206–7, 302, 309, 310
Socinians and Socianism, 180, 191–92
Sola fide and sola gratia. See justification
Sola scriptura. See Scripture
Sorbonne. See Paris, Faculty of Theology
Soubise, Jean de Parthenay, Seigneur
    de, 247–48

Sozzini, Fausto, 191–92
Sozzini, Lelio, 182, 190n.52, 191–92
    Brief Explanation of John 1
        (1552), 191–92
Spain, 105–6, 281–82
Spiez (Switzerland), 138n.162
Spiritualism, 126–27, 139, 155–56,
    188n.38, 208n.143
Strasbourg (Empire), 10, 21–22, 23–25,
    36, 40–41, 44–45, 54–55, 108–9,
    118n.65, 141–42, 163–64, 194,
    221–22, 274
Sturm, Johannes (Jean), 26–27
Suisse romande. See Francophone
    Switzerland
Sulzer, Simon, 61, 95–96, 119–21, 125n.95,
    148, 149–50
superstition, 32–33, 95–96, 176, 198n.94,
    211–12, 217–18, 244–45, 251
Sureau du Rosier, Hughes, 278–79, 280–
    81, 285, 287–88, 292–94, 295–96
Switzerland, 10, 21, 28–29, 37, 38, 46, 49–
    50, 54–55, 61, 72–73, 77–78, 80–
    81, 82–83, 87–89, 102–3, 106–7,
    108, 113, 135–36, 189–90, 237–38,
    242, 264, 290–91
synods, 5–6, 261, 267–70, 274–75, 278,
    287–88, 304, 309–10
    National Synods of the French
        Reformed Churches, 3, 64, 211–12,
        297–98, 306
    Poitiers (1557), 204, 208–9, 306
    Paris (1559), 204–5, 208–9, 258, 260,
        274, 306
    Orléans (1562), 258, 274–75
    Paris (1565), 247–48, 250, 276–78,
        281–82, 283–84, 285–86, 289–90
    La Rochelle (1571), 289–91,
        295–96, 306
    Nîmes (1572), 292–94, 306
    Provincial Synods, 266–67, 268–70,
        275–78, 285–86
    Synod of Bern (1537), 73–74
    Synod of Dort/Dordrecht (1619), 198
    Synod of Ferté-sous-Jouarre (1565),
        194–95, 275–76, 289–90
    Synod of Lausanne (1537), 73–74
    Synod of Lausanne (1538), 89–91
    Synod of Lourmarin (1562), 200–1

synods (*cont.*)
    Synod of Lumigny-en-Brie
        (1572), 291–93
    Synod of Meaux (1519), 14–15
    Synod of Neuchâtel (1542), 92
    Synod of Orléans (1566), 285–86
    Synod of Yverdon (1536), 94–95

Theodosius (Roman emperor), 222
Thiery, Quintin, 208n.143
Thonon (Chablais), 82n.71, 94, 137, 138
Tillich, Paul, 309–10
toleration, 139–40, 147–48, 150–51, 156–
    61, 186–93, 206, 207–8, 222–23,
    299–300, 303
Tournes, Jean de, 202–3, 274–75, 300
Tours (France), 28–29
Toussain, Pierre, 25, 45–46, 49–50, 61,
    149–50, 184–86, 194, 302–3, 304–5
transubstantiation, 38–39, 41–42, 176
Transylvania, 191–92
Trehet, Robert, 248n.152
Trent (Empire), 190–91, 218
    Council of, 34, 218, 231n.77, 245
trinity and trinitarian doctrine, 72–74, 97–
    98, 152, 154, 189–90, 192. *See also*
    Antitrinitarianism
Trolliet, Jean, 128–30
Troyes (France), 211n.1
Tübingen (Empire), 196n.83, 240–43, 247,
    252n.162

Unitarians, 191–92
University of Paris and its colleges.
    See Paris
Uzès (France), 211n.1

Val de Liepvre (Empire), 194
Valence (France), 211n.1, 213–15,
    253n.167
Valentigney (Montbéliard), 185n.25
Valier, Jacques, 133n.137
Vallée, Briand de, 104–5
Valois (French royal family)
    Charles (son of Francis I), 25
    François (son of Francis I), 24n.54
    Madeleine (daughter of Francis I), 25
Van Haemstede, Adrian, 189, 190–91

Van Limborch, Philippus,
    192–93–193nn.67–68
Vaquerie (France), 21–22
Varesnes-le-Noyon (France), 281n.114
Vaud, Pays de (Switzerland), 3, 45–47, 48,
    53–54, 61–63, 65, 66–67, 72, 75–76,
    82, 85, 86, 91, 101, 102, 103, 104n.4,
    107n.24, 114, 117, 121, 124, 127–28,
    129–30, 132–33, 136–38, 140, 145,
    155–56, 168–69, 181–83, 184, 186–
    87, 194–95, 205–7, 209–10, 250–51,
    263, 266–67, 269–70, 272, 300, 303,
    304–5, 306–7, 308
Vauville, Richard, 273–74
Védaste, Jean, 24
Veigy (Chablais), 101, 123–24, 126–28,
    129–32, 150–51, 209–10
Velsius Haganus, Justus, 194
Venice (Italy), 25
Vergerio, Pier Paolo, 149–50
Vermigli, Peter Martyr, 2, 221
Versoix (Switzerland), 95–96
Vervins (France), 77n.48
Vevey (Switzerland), 124, 127, 129–30,
    260n.13, 272
via media religious solution, 232–34,
    237, 304–5
Vienne (France), 205n.133
Villeroche, Pierre, 194–96
Villiers. *See* Morély
Vingle, Pierre de, 44, 48–49, 66n.2, 280–81
Viret, Pierre, 8, 36, 37, 48, 53–55, 61–63, 66–68,
    69–70, 72–74, 86–87, 89, 91, 93–97,
    99–100, 101, 102–4, 106–7, 110, 111–
    22, 123–24, 129–30, 137–38, 141–
    42n.11, 143n.14, 180–81, 182, 183–84,
    196–97, 258, 260n.13, 269–71, 272,
    274–75, 288, 302, 304–7, 307n.3
    De la vertu et usage (1548), 117
Vivès, Juan Luis, 219
Vivier, Jeanne du (second wife of Du
    Moulin), 243, 247–48
Vuarrens (Switzerland), 66n.2

Wäber, Johannes, 119–20
Waldensians, 106–7, 111–12, 244–45
    Confession of Faith (1544), 244–45
War of Kappel. *See* Kappel

Wars of Religion, 3, 9, 158–59, 213, 226–27, 228, 233–34, 237, 247–48, 252–53, 281–82, 286–87, 307–8

Wassy, Massacre of (1562), 226–27

Wesel (Empire), 199

Westphal, Joachim, 307–8

Wittenberg (Empire), 37, 40–41, 272

Wittenberg Concord (1536), 108–9

Wolmar, Melchior, 26–27, 55–56

Württemberg (Imperial duchy), 240n.119, 304–5
    Christophe of (Duke), 153, 184, 242–43
    Georg of (Count of Montbéliard), 185–86, 242–43
    Ulrich of (Duke), 153

Yverdon (Switzerland), 66n.2, 67, 71–72, 82n.71, 89, 94–95, 98–100, 110–13, 122, 130–31, 135–36, 145, 287–88

Zanchi, Girolamo, 138n.162

Zébédée, André, 48, 94n.122, 101–22, 123–24, 126–28, 130–36, 138, 140, 141n.9, 145, 150–51, 155–56, 168–69, 181–83, 194–95, 205–6, 209–10, 233, 251n.158, 253–54, 271–72, 297–98, 300–3, 305–7

Zurich (Switzerland), 37, 40, 61, 73–74, 88–89, 98–99, 101, 114–15, 116, 117, 120–21, 125n.95, 127–28, 136, 150–51, 189–90, 196–97, 272, 295–96

Zurkinden, Niklaus, 183n.15, 306–7

Zuttere, Pieter Anastasius de, 150–51

Zwingli, Ulrich, 1–2, 5–6, 21, 36–37, 40–41, 46, 49–50, 54–55, 63, 87–89, 107–9, 113, 114, 119–20, 161–62n.91, 167–68, 299–300

Zwinglians and Zwinglian theology, 41–42, 60–61, 66–67, 75–76, 81, 87–88, 89, 92, 98–99, 103, 107–10, 116–21, 123–24, 127–28, 139, 158, 167–68, 184, 237–38, 251–52, 263, 300–2, 304–5, 306–7